DOWN AT THE END OF LONELY STREET

DOWN AT THE END OF LONELY STREET

THE LIFE AND DEATH OF ELVIS PRESLEY

Peter Harry Brown and Pat H. Broeske

A DUTTON BOOK

DUTTON
Published by the Penguin Group
Penguin Putnam Inc., 375 Hudson Street, New York, New York 10014, U.S.A.
Penguin Books Ltd, 27 Wrights Lane, London W8 5TZ, England
Penguin Books Australia Ltd, Ringwood, Victoria, Australia
Penguin Books Canada Ltd, 10 Alcorn Avenue, Toronto, Ontario, Canada M4V 3B2
Penguin Books (N.Z.) Ltd, 182-190 Wairau Road, Auckland 10, New Zealand

Penguin Books Ltd, Registered Offices:
Harmondsworth, Middlesex, England

First published by Dutton, an imprint of Dutton Signet,
a member of Penguin Putnam Inc.

First Printing, August, 1997
1 3 5 9 10 8 6 4 2

 REGISTERED TRADEMARK—MARCA REGISTRADA

Library of Congress Cataloging-in-Publication Data is available

Printed in the United States of America
Set in Transitional 521
Designed by Jesse Cohen

This book is printed on acid-free paper. ∞

For Irv Letofsky,
who first sent me to Memphis
　　　—PAT H. BROESKE

For Gina Lubrano,
with love
And Angie Lubrano,
in loving memory
　　　—PETER HARRY BROWN

Contents

Authors' Note

We never thought it would be easy. But neither did we think it would be quite so hard. There we were, midsummer in Memphis, on our way to talk to a key source about the hows and whys of Elvis Presley's death. Suddenly our Drug Enforcement Agency (DEA) contact motioned for us to pull our car over. We did, and he pulled alongside us and climbed into the backseat. "Y'all seem like honest, straight-up journalists," he began, going on to explain that he'd just learned that he could no longer take us to the interview that had been arranged. The reason: "somebody high up" had decided that interviews had to be called off, and certain documents embargoed.

Who had the power to do such a thing? Our DEA contact didn't answer. But in Memphis, it's well-known that Graceland—which is run by Elvis Presley Enterprises (EPE), headed by Presley's ex-wife, Priscilla Presley—wields considerable civic and political power. Moreover, Graceland is not in the truth-telling business but rather the myth-making industry. And the myth is growing more golden with every year.

When we sought information about Presley through EPE, we were told that the company prefers to work with "authorized" projects. Some of those projects rely on the anecdotes and insights of major Presley sources—some of whom we would have liked to talk with, had they not been leery of incurring the wrath of Graceland, and thereby harming their moneymaking potential.

Adding to our challenge: some sources who are not in the good graces of the folks at EPE would speak only on the condition that they were financially reimbursed. "We're willing to entertain offers," we were told by the wife of one of the Memphis Mafia members. Then there was the performer—who'd had a single successful record in the early fifties—who would speak "only if it's going to do something for my career." Alas, we could not dispense money or miracles.

Because Presley spawned a cottage publishing industry, some associates—and relatives—have literally specialized in telling-all since his death in 1977. Some change their stories and anecdotes from project to project. One family member topped previous sordid accounts with unfounded allegations about Presley's having had sexual relations with his own mother. Among many who knew Elvis, there is a sense of one-upmanship.

All this is a way of saying that it's not always easy knowing whom to trust in regard to Elvis Presley.

Presley himself contributed to some of the confusion. During his lifetime he forbade his close circle of friends—including the women in his life—to speak to the media. Far smarter than he has ever been depicted, he knew that some of his proclivities were at odds with his public image. Indeed, under the tutelage of his shrewd and brilliant manager, Colonel Tom Parker, Presley was party to the creation of his own myth.

We have sought to break through that myth, to deliver a flesh-and-blood portrait of a man who has, for too long, been misunderstood and misportrayed.

At first our friends thought we were crazy. Our mothers worried about us. Colleagues raised their eyebrows. Repeatedly, we were asked, "Why would anyone want to do another book on Elvis?" A sentiment echoed rather audaciously by past "Elvis authors" was "What more is there to say?"

We understood the collective concern. At least three hundred books, give or take a few dozen, have been written about the late Elvis Presley, making him perhaps the most scrutinized of all American icons. Yet for all that has been in print, it's been hard to determine what's real and what isn't.

Numerous fawning titles have all but anointed him. Then there have been the lurid tell-alls, which concentrate on the darker side.

In truth, Elvis Presley was somewhere in the middle. He was not perfect, but neither was he a monster. Considering that the kind of fame he experienced was unprecedented, and that he was a baby—just twenty-one years old—when he became a symbol for changing times in music and popular culture, he probably handled it as well as anyone could.

More than three hundred people helped us to tell his story. We also pored through mountainous stacks of materials—which we've been amassing for a decade. Documents regarding his death, the ensuing investigation, and various (and revealing) lawsuits were particularly insightful. We also scrutinized the sealed autopsy and its follow-up documents, which we obtained through non-Memphis sources. We were also privy to documents detailing his medical history during the sixties and seventies. Sadly, he was involved with drugs longer than anyone previously realized.

As fans of Elvis Presley, we were sometimes disappointed in what we uncovered. As biographers, we could not ignore it.

We like to think that by humanizing Elvis Presley—faults and all— we have elevated him. After all, his is a story of dizzy success, lonely despair, and incredible determination. That he kept on singing to the end is a tribute not only to his spirit, but to his status as one of the greatest of all American originals. It was a privilege for us to get to tell his story.

Acknowledgments

From the onset, we must thank our editor, Michaela Hamilton, for her support, her guidance. Considering that there had been more than two hundred English-language books on Elvis Presley, it took an editor with her sharp eye to realize that the essence of the man's extraordinary life had yet to be captured, and that no one had ever attempted a traditional birth-to-death biography of the star. Her guidance along the way was exceptional, and her unstinting help in shaping the final book proved invaluable. It's our belief this book would not exist without her foresight.

As usual, Dutton's associate publisher Arnold Dolin's understanding of the literary market and his grasp of our objectives in joining the vast parade of Elvis authors made this dream of ours come true.

Of course, our agents, Mitch Douglas of International Creative Management and Alice Martell of the Martell Agency, played integral roles. Brown's agent, Douglas, not only plunged headlong into literary resistance to yet another Presley bio, but also offered guidance on how to deliver a book this ambitious within its constricted time frame. Nor was Broeske's representative, Martell, ever intimidated by the notion of another Presley book. Moreover, her enthusiasm and upbeat personality assuaged worries about daunting due dates.

Writing a book of this nature is a "team" effort, and we count ourselves lucky that our spouses, Pamela Brown and James Broeske, aided us with their time and support. They not only had to live with us during an arduous period, but they were also ever ready to assist us. Pamela was especially helpful in making sense of the complicated medical scenario involving Presley's dependence on drugs, and his death. Jim was our bookkeeper and oversaw much of our photo research.

Author and great friend Lucy Chase Williams was also intimately involved. Not only did she read the bulk of our original manuscript and provide astute editing suggestions, but she also ushered us into the new age—so we could use the Internet and correspond by E-mail. We are ever grateful for her efforts, her support, and her friendship.

Dozens of our interviews with Presley's Hollywood associates were conducted by author Tom Weaver, whose inside knowledge (and photographic memory) of movies proved as helpful as his interviewing skills. Providing insight as well as great transcriptions of our myriad interview tapes was Brian Zoccola, who likewise looked through myriad newsreels and videotapes of Presley. Sandy Hague organized and filed our thousands of articles, did transcriptions, handled mailings, and also served as our computer adviser, as did her friend Ron Young—who patiently helped us overcome several technological crises, including a computer virus. We were greatly assisted by the editing suggestions of Sigman Byrd IV. We also extend our thanks to Memphis's Shannon Magness and Kimberly Von Magness, for their assistance with interviews; to Stephanie Garside for her help with our mountainous photocopying; and, to Deborah Mather for assisting with our initial photo selection. And we remain in awe of Carole Huntington's lightning-fast copy transcription.

Also, thanks to two fine journalists and editors, Al Jacoby, former managing editor of the *San Diego Union,* and Gina Lubrano, reader's representative of the *San Diego Union and Tribune,* for lending their experience in the book's organization and content. Jacoby was insightful in piercing through the mass of data about the singer's life. Also, the suggestions of his wife, Pat Jacoby, over a memorable brunch, added qualitatively.

Irv Letofsky, our former Sunday Calendar editor at the *Los Angeles Times,* was and remains a source of support and guidance. We're gratified that we can (and do!) frequently call on him.

Our book had its beginnings more than a decade ago, with trips to Memphis and ensuing stories about Presley's death—its effect on Memphis, the media, and those closest to him—as well as pieces about Presley-themed projects and the merchandising of his image. During that period we spoke with numerous Presley associates, among them Sun Records pioneer Sam Phillips; Memphis Mafia members Joe Esposito, Charlie Hodge, George Klein, Marty Lacker, Jerry Schilling, and Red West; as well as Vernon Presley, Vester Presley, and easily the most colorful figure in a life dominated by colorful figures, Colonel Thomas Andrew Parker. The information they provided then greatly helped us in the research of this book.

Because Presley was a son of the South, this book took us on travels throughout Mississippi and Tennessee, and even across Arkansas's Ozarks (as our "mascot," Skeeter Joe, entertained us with constant meowing). Once again, as with our book on Howard Hughes—which took us to Texas—we encountered the famous "Southern hospitality." It is no mere cliché; in fact, it was one of the many pleasures of doing this book.

In Tupelo, Mississippi—Elvis's birthplace—we were welcomed and assisted by genealogist and local historian Roy Turner, who gave us a tour of young Elvis's haunts and a sense of what his life was like in the thirties. Through Roy we met Becky Martin, a Presley friend since childhood, who in turn paved our way to meeting Elvis's kin Annie Presley.

Memphis's Bill Donati—himself an author and Hollywood authority—also assisted us by keeping us abreast of the latest Elvis news as it broke in the various Memphis media. It was also our good fortune to be able to call on Elvis archivists Bill E. Burk, and his wife, Connie Lauridsen Burk, for their expertise and suggestions. During his years at the *Memphis Press-Scimitar,* and in his current life as the publisher of *Elvis World*—one of the most authoritative publications about the King—Burk has written literally hundreds of articles about Presley.

Another writer who proved enormously generous with his time and his materials is rock journalist Jerry Hopkins—author of the first biography of Elvis Presley in 1971—who reflected on his writings about Presley, and whose research materials were made available to us through Memphis State University, where they are a part of the Mississippi Valley Collection. A special thanks to the university's Ed Frank and his staff for assisting us in our search through Jerry's files.

Lee Cotten, author of several books on Elvis—including one that traces Presley's daily whereabouts from 1954 to 1977(!)—looked through his exhaustive files to help us clarify certain periods in Elvis's life. Author Howard De Witt, who chronicled Elvis's Sun Records career, was equally generous with his information. We were also aided by the collection of Gladys Presley's biographer Elaine Dundy, which we found at the Lee County Library in Tupelo, Mississippi.

We are also grateful to the following authors-journalists who reflected on their writings and knowledge of Presley: Nancy Anderson (who, as a Tennessean and the West Coast editor of *Photoplay* in the sixties, may have known Presley better than any other writer), Louis Cantor (a Beale Street authority), Vernon Chadwick (founder and director of the University of Mississippi's International Conference on Elvis), Neal Gregory (who, with his wife, Janice, chronicled the media's handling of the death of Elvis), Patsy Guy Hammontree (whose nine years of work led to an enormously helpful "bio-bibliography" of the singer), Sandra Harmon (Priscilla Presley's coauthor), Charlies Raiteri (a Dewey Phillips expert), Charles C. Thompson II (who, with James P. Cole, authored a landmark study about Presley's death), and Dr. Peter Whitmer (author of Presley's "psychological biography").

Also, we must extend thanks to our personal colleagues Lee Grant, arts editor of the *San Diego Union and Tribune;* Nancy Ray, formerly with the *Los Angeles Times;* John Philip Sousa; film-industry reporter Judy Brennan; investigative journalist Dennis McDougal; and Beverly Beyette, "Around Town" columnist for the *Los Angeles Times.* They provided friendship, suggestions and support. We are also grateful to the friends who joined in the spirit of our quest by actually journeying with us to Memphis and Graceland. Dan and Sylvia Wybrant were with us during our earliest resource-gathering mission. Still later we were joined by Barbara Peterson, who underwent a conversion during the Graceland tour, and wound up an Elvis fanatic!

It's unusual in a biography of this breadth and scope to single out a single source as summing up its heart and soul, but in this case, Memphis's General Sessions Court judge Sam Thompson's impassioned, three-hour soliloquy on his friend Elvis captured the person we'd hoped to portray. His guidance in our future interviews was just as valuable. He is a source in a million who opened dozens of doors for us. Thanks are not enough.

We are also very grateful for the time and recollections of Dr. George Nichopoulos, one of the most misrepresented names in the Presley saga. He was a patient repeat-interview subject (who also took our myriad follow-up calls). In the sixties, when he was asked to treat Elvis at his ranch in Mississippi, "Dr. Nick" could not have known the depths of his famous patient's problems—or that he would ultimately be wrongly singled out as the cause of these problems.

Sam Phillips remains one of the true legends of the music industry; it is always an experience and a pleasure to talk with him. We also found the comments of Presley intimates Richard Davis, Joe Esposito, and George Klein especially helpful, and we are equally grateful for the time and recollections of Dick Grob, Mike McGregor, Kathy Westmoreland, and Becky Yancey, all of whom worked closely with Presley in Memphis and on the road. And a special thank-you to Ginger Alden, and her family—sister Rosemary Alden, and mother Jo Alden—for helping us to better understand Presley during his final months.

Helping us to catalog Presley's complicated medical scenario were Maurice Elliott, former administrator of Baptist Hospital, and Dr. Forest Tennant. Because of the groundbreaking work of Dr. Tennant, toxicologist and physician, formerly of UCLA and now director-founder of Community Health Projects Medical Group, we were able to fully understand Presley's drug use and his eventual addiction. Others who aided in our investigation of Elvis's medical problems and death include Dr. Pierre Brissette, Dr. Dan Brookoff, Ulysses Jones, Tish Henley, Dr. Lester Hoffman, Dave McGriff, Dr. Kevin S. Merigian, Dr. Thomas Noguchi, Jim Orwood, Dr. Dwight Reed, Dan Warlick, and Dr. Ronald Wright. And a special thanks to Dr. Stanley A. Terman, medical director, Institute for Strategic Change, and to leading pathologist Dr. Joseph Davis. As the former physician of Gladys Presley, Dr. Charles Clarke also helped us to better understand Presley's relationship with his mother, and her own health woes.

Don Wilson—aka "The Great Don-El"—was just ten years old, suffering the traumatic accidental deaths of his parents and sister, when he met Elvis backstage at a Houston concert. For the next six years he found solace in the cards and records that Elvis sent. Don, who went on to become a Graceland visitor, and an Elvis authority (as well as disc jockey and impersonator), provided insight and anecdotes and shared with us rare audio and video recordings. Throughout his assistance he constantly stressed the generous, caring side to the King.

Also, we cannot overemphasize our gratitude to Diana Magrann, an artist who is also one of the most astute Elvis authorities we have ever encountered. She was generous with both her time and her information.

Among Presley's Hollywood colleagues, a special thanks to Mary Ann Mobley and Kitty Jones, for assistance above and beyond. Of the many others who helped us to better understand Presley's Hollywood years, we are especially indebted to Steve Binder, Stanley Brossette, William Campbell, Gail Ganley, Anne Helm, Will Hutchins, Lance Le Gault, Gary Lockwood, Marlyn Mason, Nancy Sinatra, and Deborah Walley.

As we noted earlier, the Elvis World is populated by colorful characters. Among the most memorable was Jimmy Denson, who knew Presley while at Lauderdale Courts. Though we do not share some of Jimmy's beliefs about Presley, we appreciate his sharing his information with us. We will likewise always remember the day we spent with Paul and Elvis McLeod, who operate the mind-boggling Presley homage Graceland Too, in Holly Springs, Mississippi. They are truly foremost among the keepers of the flame.

For their support/assistance in helping us to put together Presley's extraordinary story, we also thank the following: Jeff Abraham, Valerie Allen, Merry Anders, Tony Angellotti, Michael Ansara, Larry Anthony, Louis Balint Jr., Gregg Barrios, Ned Bernds, Alan Betrock, Eddie Bond, Milton Bowers, John Bramlett, Bob Cawthorn, Jimmy and Bessie Chachas, Tina Chase, Karen Conrad, Margaret Cranfill, Tony Curtis, H. W. "Bud" Daily Jr., Phyllis Davis, Joan Deary, Fred De Cordova, Bill Denny, Paul Dougher, Ruby Dougher, James Drury, Steve Easley, June Ellis, Anthony Eisley, Billy Emerson, Mrs. Eddie Fadal, Johnna Danovi Fenrick (and her extraordinary family), Mike Fenton, Evan "Buzzy" Forbess, Diana Fortin, Bill Gallagher, Arthur Gardner, Patsy Presley Geranen, Anne Rowe Goldman, Tom Gray, Shecky Greene, Cathy Griffen, Paul Grubb, Sydney Guilaroff, Billy Harbach, Dorothy "Dottie" Harmony, Susan Hart, Milo High, Leonard Hirshan, Virginia Hornbuckle, Peter Hopkirk, Larry Hutchinson, Margaret Jamison, Peggy Jemison, Carolyn Jones, Ira Jones, June Juanico, Bob Kendall, Millie Kirkham, Stanley Kramer, Steve Kroh, Barbara Leigh, Genevieve Lewis, Minabess Lewis, Pat Lightell, Joanne Lyman, Frank Magrin, Bob

Marcucci, Becky Martin, Walter Matthau, Sandi Miller, Bob Moreland, Ben Morton, Dan Moulthrop, Donna Presley Nash, Michael Norwood, Mr. and Mrs. William Norwood, Gloria Pall, Dolly Parton, Brenda Patterson, Minnie Pearl, Gil Perkins, Dorothy Phillips, Jim Pinkston, Bill Powers, Annie Presley, Terry Press, Cheryl Pruett, Sherry Adler Riggins, Harold Robbins, Alex Romero, Nancy Rooks, William Schallert, Don Siegel, Colonel Fred Sitler, Jeremy Slate, Ronald Smith, Jack Soden, Andrew Solt, David Sorensen (and family), Donald A. Stanwood, Stella Stevens, Gordon Stoker, Corinne Richards Tate, Norman Taurog, William J. Taylor Jr., William Thomas, Isaac Tigrett, Patricia Towle, Dorothy Treloar, Justin Tubb, Laura Turley, Mamie Van Doren, Jere Walker, Martha Nell Payne Wallace, Dorothy Fellows Weems, George Weiss, Jo Weld, Diana Von Welentz Wentworth, Clarence Wilson, John M. Wilson, Walter "Buddy" Winsett, and Randy Wood.

We are grateful to a myriad of agencies, libraries, historical societies, and other organizations and their representatives, including the following in Tennessee and Mississippi: Memphis Courthouse; Sun Records; Jerry Strobel and the Grand Ole Opry; National Academy of Recording Arts and Sciences, Memphis and Nashville offices; Trish McGee and Ryman Auditorium; Memphis-Shelby County Library; principal Marion Brewer and Humes Junior High School; Tupelo Hardware; Lee County Library of Tupelo; Elvis Presley Birthplace, Tupelo.

Our thanks, too, to the staff of the Freedom of Information at the FBI, especially J. Kevin O'Brien; Linda Meher and her staff at the Margaret Herrick Library, the Academy of Motion Picture Arts and Sciences (Los Angeles), including Sam Gill and Faye Thompson, of the Academy's Special Collections, who made possible our examination of the mammoth Hal Wallis Collection; the Louis B. Mayer Library, American Film Institute (Los Angeles); the Film and Television Library, UCLA; the Santa Ana (California) Public Library; the Long Beach Public Library; St. Joseph's Hospital in Orange (California).

Thanks, too, to Carolyn Kozo Cole, manager of photo collections at the Los Angeles Public Library; Steve Hanson and Ned Comstock, University of Southern California Cinema-Television Library; Dace Taube, curator, Regional History Center, University of Southern California; Frank Wright, Nevada State Museum and Historical Society; the Las Vegas News Bureau; the library at the University of Nevada, Las Vegas; the Clark County Library in Las Vegas; and the New York Public Library.

And last though far from least, we must acknowledge our families, especially our parents, Frances Saunders Brown, Helen Holgate Twedell, Claude and Hazel Hague, and Don and Ruth Broeske. Thanks for your patience. And to Sharon Coles, our gratitude for the "care packages" (great peanut brittle!) during our Memphis stay.

*There are no villains in this story;
no evildoers. Only ordinary
men and women, whose lives
became entangled with that of an
extraordinary man . . .*

—Judge Sam Thompson*
Juvenile Superior Court
Memphis, Tennessee
May 1996

*a former bodyguard and roadie for Elvis Presley

1

Omens

The doctor peered through the windshield of his Model T Ford into desolate blackness. He was looking for the muddy banks of a rushing gully that separated Tupelo from its unwelcome suburb. East Tupelo was the home of the working poor and host to a piddling redlight district known as Goosehollow. Among the white-washed shacks, the homes of men and women who were pulling themselves out of the Great Depression were also the homes of grifters and moonshiners.

Dr. William Robert Hunt was determined to get to the Presleys' to deliver a baby. Since he was a "welfare obstetrician," he rarely saw the patient until she was just minutes from birth. Doc Hunt's patient, in this case, was ethereal, dark-eyed Gladys Presley. She had the voice of an angel when she sang, but also possessed the toughness of her great-great-grandmother, a full-blooded Cherokee named Morning Dove who had deserted her tribe and married a white man.

Since sleet was pelting much of the northeastern corner of Missis-sippi that early morning, Doc finally leaned his head out of the window to guide the old car through the gully and over two sets of railroad tracks that marked the eastern border of respectable society. Looking up the hill toward Old Saltillo Road, he caught sight of a frantically motioning young man. At nineteen, Vernon Presley was a handsome rogue who had borrowed $180 to build his family a "shotgun shack" that was boosted up on a stone-pile foundation.

After a hasty greeting Vernon ushered the doctor inside, shut the door against the early-morning chill, and motioned to the woman in the bed that dominated the tiny room. Gladys was delirious, her raven hair damp with perspiration, as she clutched the hand of midwife Edna Robinson and that of Vernon's mother, Minnie Mae Presley.

Gladys was in her tenth hour of labor. "And I don't like it," said the midwife. Oil lamps sent shadows flickering onto the walls, creating a tableau of prebirth apprehension—the sharp silhouette of the midwife and Minnie Mae's hands gripping Gladys's shoulders. Outside the home, Vernon paced back and forth. His father, Jessie, sat nearby in a drunken stupor.

Inside, Doc Hunt ordered the lamps to be placed around the bed and warned, "Stand back, so we can do our work."

For an agonizing hour, twenty-two-year-old Gladys Presley labored under Doc Hunt's guidance to give birth to Vernon's child, a child she hoped would put life back into her already troubled two-year marriage. Since learning of her pregnancy, she had been on her knees every afternoon, asking God for a beautiful and perfect son—her gift to a husband she suspected of straying.

At four o'clock, Gladys let out a piercing cry. Vernon was summoned to her bedside. Alongside her lay a motionless child. Vernon glanced sadly at Doc Hunt, who shook his head.

The room grew so quiet that the sleet pelting the roof seemed deafening.

Too drunk to notice the tragedy at hand, Jessie Presley began running his finger along the baby's stomach. "Gitchy goo, gitchy goo!" he babbled. "Gitchy, gitchy goo."

Vernon turned angrily. "Goddamn, Daddy! This baby is dead!" Tears ran down his face. "My son is dead."

As Vernon Presley recounted decades later, it was his father who placed his hands on Gladys's stomach and announced, "But, Vernon, there's another baby in here."

The doctor rushed to Gladys's side. "He's right! There's a twin."

On January 8, 1935, at 4:35 A.M. Elvis Aaron Presley was officially logged in. At almost the same moment, the storm clouds drifted off, and a tiny blue edge of sky appeared atop the Tupelo hills. Vernon glimpsed the harbinger of dawn as he collected his bundled stillborn son and placed him in a shoebox. Decades later, when the media was intent upon mythologizing Elvis Presley, Vernon spoke wondrously of a dazzling blue light that he claimed had appeared when Elvis was born. And among his friends, he claimed to have "blacked out" at the moment of his son's conception.

Gladys believed in another sort of portent. "I knew all along that I was carrying twins. When you can actually feel four tiny feet kicking inside you, it's gotta be twins. Besides, you can feel both little souls." She believed that "the twin who lives inherits the strength of the baby that died"—the superstition of a woman raised in the hills. Some say that Gladys instilled in her living son the belief that he had a responsibility to live for two—himself and his dead twin, Jesse Garon.

Doc Hunt—whose fifteen-dollar fee was later paid by welfare (and who did not circumcise the infant Elvis, because that would have resulted in a higher fee)—wanted Gladys hospitalized after the birth, but she steadfastly refused. She would not go until her baby received a proper burial.

The next morning, Jesse Garon was dressed in a blue baby suit and placed in a tiny coffin, set atop the kitchen table. By midday, members of the Smith and Presley families had gathered for a protracted memorial, which ended with mournful hillbilly "songs of the dead," a sign of respect for the lost soul. Each of the kinfolk talked softly to the dead Jesse Garon. Then the small casket was carried out into the winter afternoon so that he could be buried before sunset.

He was laid to rest at the Priceville Baptist Cemetery in an unmarked grave. Vernon and Gladys could not afford the additional $3.50 cost for the headstone. There were no flowers. The distinctive hillbilly wails of farewell were the twin's only send-off.

Back at the Presley home, Gladys was semiconscious from the constant hemorrhaging inside her uterus. "We've got to get her to the hospital!" said Doc Hunt, who feared his patient was dying.

Because she was nursing her baby, Elvis went with her to the Tupelo hospital charity ward, where they remained for nearly two weeks—the first of many protracted bonding periods between mother and son. Vernon and his family haunted the hospital corridors, praying that Gladys's insides had not been irreparably damaged by childbirth.

Relatives on both sides of the family hoped that the crisis, and the responsibilities of raising little Elvis, would bring maturity into the lives of these two stubborn free spirits. Their union had had its beginnings at a country store and in an inelegant elopement just weeks later. Neither family was too surprised.

Gladys's family tree was trouble plagued. Four of her cousins suffered from depression. Her mother, Doll Smith, spent a dozen years in bed, "too morose to get up." In her teenage years Gladys suffered so-called "nervous spells" and "attacks of the vapors." With her blow-away black hair, luminous dark eyes, and slender figure, she also became one of Tupelo's better-known party girls.

Despite her twelve-hour daily shifts at the Tupelo Garment Plant, she was notorious at the town's dance halls for her wild abandon. She was said to be so spirited on the dance floor that crowds would form and her partner would politely back off, so she could solo across the slickly waxed surface.

She needed room—since she more often than not indulged in "buck dancing," considered so scandalous it was banned at country clubs and even the more common Tupelo Dance Pavilion. It was an animalistic mating dance that Gladys gave herself up to—one in which she swiveled her hips and gyrated her lower limbs. Decades later, by an uncanny coincidence, her singer son performed similar moves in his bid for stardom.

Gladys came from a sharecropping family that could trace its heritage to Scotch-Irish ancestors who arrived before the American Revolution. Vernon's lineage was similar. Both were born and raised in Mississippi, both came from poor but proud large families; in both families' backgrounds was a tradition of selling moonshine and illegal whiskey.

Gladys Love Smith was twenty-one when she caught sight of Vernon Presley one afternoon in 1933 as he entered Roy Martin's grocery store. Though he had just turned seventeen, she was struck by his height, blond hair, blue eyes, and finely chiseled face. Along with his looks he had developed a suave and knowing way with women, much like his philandering father, Jessie.

In a sense it was a case of opposites attracting. She was brash, determined, hardworking, as well as the moving force behind her mother and seven siblings. He was easygoing and, whenever possible, eschewed making decisions—as well as hard labor.

They became a familiar twosome at the First Assembly of God services, where Gladys's uncle delivered the sermon, and at the roller rink, where they skated hand in hand. Vernon proposed to Gladys over cherry Cokes on the morning of June 17, 1933. Between sips of soda, she accepted. Presley, broke as always, borrowed three dollars from a friend and drove off with his fiancée of one hour to the tiny hamlet of Verona. There circuit court clerk J. M. Gates handed them a license and they were married ninety minutes later. They lied about their ages. He said he was twenty-two; she vainly claimed to be younger—just nineteen. The couple celebrated with a postnuptial dinner at a roadside barbecue. They didn't want to tell their families what they had done, so they spent their first night with Vernon's cousin, Marshall Brown.

The next morning at six o'clock both routinely returned to their jobs—she to the Garment Plant, he to the farm of his landlord, Orville Bean—as if nothing out of the ordinary had happened.

Though Vernon's father was initially furious, he calmed down at the notion that marriage—and Gladys—might make a man of the son he already considered a wastrel. According to friends of the couple's, they spent their first year of marriage enjoying socials with friends and family. "We used to sit on the front porch and sing spirituals," recalled Annie Presley, who was married to Vernon's cousin.

No longer a party girl, Gladys was said to be deliriously happy when she discovered she was pregnant. In her newfound fervor, she became extremely religious and vowed to give up moonshine. Though her body became so swollen she had to wrap her legs with rags to survive the twelve-hour workdays, she had a reputation for cheerfulness at the factory.

The expectant young father directed his energies toward building their two-room house, situated on a lot next door to Jessie and Minnie Mae's house. Called a shotgun shack because its doors were perfectly aligned—allowing a straight shot through the house—it was just 450 square feet. Smaller than many contemporary living rooms, the house comprised a bedroom and a kitchen in the back. Vernon built the house with his father and brother Vester, although according to Vester, Vernon mainly supervised, while Jessie and Vester provided the manpower.

Because of Elvis's survival, which Doc Hunt called "miraculous," Gladys fervently held to folk beliefs, of rings around the moon the morning of her son's birth, and of what she felt was God's magnificent plan for Elvis. She constantly looked for omens to guide her. Another soon reinforced her certainty.

On April 5, 1936, a tornado roared through Tupelo, destroying forty-eight city blocks and killing 263 people. Amazingly, the Presleys' small house remained standing, though catastrophe surrounded it. A church across the street and four nearby residences were completely leveled.

Holding Elvis's tiny hand in hers, Gladys looked out at the swath of destruction cut through the town and explained to him that this was but one more sign that he was on earth to do something special.

"You was saved," she told him.

2

The Song in His Heart

In the middle of a Mississippi cotton field, Gladys Presley prepared for a day of picking. Even though it was cold this late-November morning, she was wearing only her old housedress and loosely knit sweater. She knew the vermilion ridge on the eastern skyline signaled the rise of the sun that would be blistering hot.

Slowly she wrapped her arms with layers of bandage gauze. She tied some more around her throat and adjusted a huge straw hat. Even with a weak sun, Gladys's skin was so fair that it broke out in red splotches from minimal exposure.

But her delicate hands received no protection. Even the thinnest gloves made it impossible to pluck the full cotton bolls out of their prickly, thistlelike leaves. Ready for "old red," she stooped over and grabbed the neck of her six-foot gunnysack, pulling it along the furrow between the rows. She wanted to keep one-year-old Elvis asleep as long as possible. He spent much of the day slumbering as she pulled him through the fields on the soft sack.

Working at a slow, steady pace was the only way to make money picking cotton, which earned Gladys a dollar and fifty cents for every hundred pounds she poured out onto the scales. As they worked alongside her, the Negroes would hum and sing songs that were as old as the

South. When the songs and chants—part gospel, part African, part blues—drifted over the fields, Elvis smiled, wide-eyed. Life, said his aunt Delta, "was a symphony for Elvis Presley."

His interest in what he would later call "the wonderful music of Tupelo" began at a precocious age. When he was still a toddler, he actually followed the music's notes. One Sunday morning just before his third birthday, he surprised his mother and the local church congregation when he slid off Gladys's lap, ran down the aisle, and stood directly before the choir, copying the motion of the lips and squeaking out an ear-shattering imitation of their hymns.

At four he had his first guitar, crudely fashioned from a broom handle, a cigar box, and a couple of loose strings. It was frightful to hear, as was his fledgling voice. Not long afterward, Vernon bought him a Sears and Roebuck Victrola and a small collection of records. Elvis would sit on a chair and listen to them for hours on end.

Sometimes Gladys would take her son "church hopping" to sample the music of the region's churches—especially those of the holy-rolling Assembly of God. They had services in the morning as well as an evening sermon. "If you got home by midnight, you were doing good," recalled Annie Presley.

Tragedy descended on the family in late 1937, when Elvis was nearly three. Sometime in the early winter of that year, Vernon, his brother-in-law Travis Smith, and friend Lether Gable sold a calf to Vernon's boss, Orville Bean. Because Bean was the sole buyer of livestock in East Tupelo, he didn't feel bound by the animal's fair market value of twenty-five dollars. He paid them four dollars. Furious and embarrassed, the three men sat in the woods drinking moonshine. In the whiskey haze, Travis suggested that they add a zero to the check, which they cashed the next morning.

Bean had all three men arrested. When the police came to take Vernon away, Gladys collapsed in tears and cried out, "He only did it because we were hungry!" The law officers turned their backs on her and marched Vernon off to county jail.

Vernon's father bailed out Travis, a man he barely knew. But Jessie Presley left his own son to languish in jail for six months.

Almost daily Gladys prepared a boxed lunch and dinner and walked across town, usually with Elvis in tow, so that Vernon wouldn't have to eat the meager jailhouse food. "She stuck by him one hundred percent. The times were hard. We all understood what made Vernon do it," says Annie Presley.

On May 25, 1938, Tupelo Superior Court judge Thomas J. Johnston, known as "the hangin' judge," sentenced Vernon Presley to three years in Mississippi's brutal penitentiary, Parchman Farm. The charge was forgery.

Following his stiff sentencing, Vernon was herded onto a prison bus for the two-hour ride. Gladys took Elvis down to kiss his father good-bye, and the two watched the bus disappear down the road into the night.

The next afternoon, a county marshal knocked on the door of the Presleys' house. He had an order of repossession. Bean, who had loaned Vernon the money to build the house, wanted Elvis and Gladys out. Members of Gladys's family tried to intervene, but Bean wanted the house, not the $120 remaining on the note, since by then the shotgun shack was valued at $500.

He gave Gladys twenty-four hours to move her few possessions, so she had little choice but to move in next door with Vernon's parents, Jessie and Minnie Mae. Not surprisingly, she hated moving in with a father who had turned his back on his son. One night she courageously asked Jessie why he hadn't come to his boy's aid. "Because he is a shiftless, lazy no-account," bellowed Jessie. "And this oughta damn well teach him a lesson."

The next day Gladys moved into a small extra room at the home of Frank and Leona Richards. Frank was her first cousin. In exchange for room and board, Gladys was expected to work as a housekeeper and to baby-sit the Richardses' youngsters.

This humiliation was yet another blow for young Gladys, who had in fact never recovered from the trauma of childbirth three years earlier. "Gladys was never the same after her twins were born," recalled second cousin Christine Roberts Presley. "Her nerves were shot. She confided that she came home from the hospital and said she was 'quaking with anxiety I can do nothing about.'" Christine particularly remembered one afternoon when her son threw a rock at their cellar door. The resulting pop was so loud that both Christine and Gladys thought a gun had gone off. "I thought Bobby and Elvis had slipped the shotgun out of the house and were target practicing," Christine said.

She looked over at Gladys. "Her face was frozen with fear, but the muscles in her back and legs were just a-twitchin'."

In hindsight, it is easy to see that Gladys never got over her deep grief over the loss of the first of her twins. "With the dead twin, and

Vernon's imprisonment, her emotions were never the same," said Vernon's mother, Minnie Mae.

Not that Gladys discussed her heartache. "She kept it bottled up," recalls Annie Presley. Gladys did admit that she did not want to become pregnant again. "She was afraid to have another child," adds Annie. Obviously, Gladys talked about the twin to Elvis because, according to his childhood friend Jim Ausborn, he used to go to visit the unmarked grave of Jesse, where he conversed with his brother.

During Vernon's term in prison Gladys went to work at a laundry. Every other weekend she and Elvis took the bus to Parchman for a day-long visit. Too young to comprehend what had happened to his father, little Elvis used to sit by the window and look out at the countryside, growing excited over the prospect of the picnic lunch they would share with Vernon.

Although most prisoners at Parchman worked punishing hours in the fields, Vernon was not one of them. He was quickly made a "special trustee" to the warden, who gave him a relatively easy prison stay, including the right to "conjugal visits." The warden even allowed the Presleys to visit in his guest bedroom, while Elvis played in the living room.

In the meantime, Gladys raged over the injustice her husband was suffering and began a petition campaign. Soon townsfolk became used to seeing mother and son going from store to store, and house to house, collecting signatures. Towheaded Elvis would look people in the eye and tearfully plead, "If you sign this, my daddy can come home."

After Gladys submitted her signed petition, the governor reacted favorably. Vernon was released after nine months.

But in his absence—sixteen months in all—Gladys and Elvis had formed a new family of two. Elvis came to understand that he was the most important person in the world to Gladys, and he repaid that attention by becoming—as best he could—the little man of the house. Relatives remember that he constantly fetched his mother water or her knitting needles. He used to pat her on the head and declare in his baby voice, "It's gonna be all right, little baby. It's gonna be okay, baby one."

He and his mother developed their own secret language—which would last throughout their lives. Water was called "butch," for example, and feet were "itsy-bitsy sooties." When Gladys returned home from working at the laundry, Elvis would be waiting to "rub her little sooties" and to bring her tea.

Elvis's pet names were Ageless (first applied to him by a little cousin who couldn't pronounce Elvis), Naughty (as in "naughty boy"), and Baby. The most special word of all was Satnin, which Elvis fashioned for Gladys when he was just a tyke. Satnin was a brand name for a lard product that came in a canned brick. In Presley-speak, Satnin meant that Elvis's mama was chubby, round, and comfortable.

Lamar Fike, later a member of Elvis's entourage, said that even when Elvis was an adult, it was possible to be in a room with him and Gladys "and not understand a word they were saying."

Along with their own language, mother and son communicated with food. From the time he was a toddler Elvis had obsessions for certain foods. Gladys did whatever she could to cater to them. Potato salad was such a favorite that Gladys would serve it as a main dish. His uncle Vester was just kidding when he threatened to take away Elvis's beloved peanut butter and crackers, but the child was dead serious. Whenever he spied Vester walking up to the porch, he would yell to his mother, "Hide them!" If she didn't respond, he would boost himself up on a chair and tuck the peanut butter jar into a cupboard.

He once talked his mother and aunt into walking him downtown so that they could buy some bananas—another favorite. "Only if you will carry them back," said Gladys. And Elvis did, for a while. When the bananas became too heavy, he cleverly talked his mother and aunt into taking turns carrying him as he clutched the bananas. The two women laughed all the way home.

He wasn't just particular about what he ate, but was also fanatical about what he ate it with. He had his own plate, cup, glass, and utensils. And when he went to school, his knife and fork went with him— tucked into his back pocket. "It was a habit he did not break until he was in the army," said his cousin Billy Smith.

Early on, Elvis's protectiveness of his mother awed family and friends. One infrequent visitor to the Presley home recalled how five-year-old Elvis dropped a truck he was playing with to rush onto the porch and climb into his mother's lap. As Alice Robinson and Gladys Presley sat across from one another in front-porch swings, Elvis placed a comforting hand on his mother's. He then sat silently "watching every move I made and concentrating on each word I uttered," recalled Robinson. At one point Elvis asked his mother, "Can I get you anything, my little baby? Do you want a glass of water?" Robinson remembered it as "the dearest thing I had ever seen."

But the dear child could also display a devilish streak. When he was just five years old, he had a tantrum in which he picked up a baseball and threw it at his grandma Minnie Mae—who evaded it so adroitly that she was nicknamed Dodger. (Minnie Mae was a constant in Elvis's life. He adored her and, as an adult, cared for her.)

When Elvis began attending East Tupelo Consolidated elementary school, Gladys used to awaken before dawn, prepare to go to work, then attend to Elvis. By seven o'clock in the morning she got him out of bed, scrubbed his face, neck, and ears with homemade soap, put him in clean overalls, and walked him to the highway where she saw him safely across. This initiated a ten-year ritual that Elvis would later find embarrassing.

One morning he turned around and declared, "Mama, once in a while you can hide in a tree or something."

When Vernon was released from Parchman, he joined his wife and son at the Richardses' home. Gladys was overjoyed to have him back, yet leery as well. During his first weeks of freedom Vernon made several clandestine runs—delivering jugs of moonshine and bringing back a carload of sugar, which was a necessity for the making of "white lightning." Gladys feared that he would be caught again on a minor offense and sent back to do "harder time."

She held her tongue, though. As an ex-convict, Vernon had difficulty finding legitimate work. Thanks to the connections of his uncle Noah, who was mayor of East Tupelo, Vernon found a string of odd jobs. Between 1940 and 1948 he would hold at least eight different jobs. He worked in the shipyards on the Gulf Coast, for the Works Progress Administration building a prisoner-of-war camp for Germans, cooked hot dogs and bologna for the Tupelo Meat Packing Company, and prior to the outbreak of World War II, worked on the assembly line at a munitions plant in Memphis.

The longest of these stints was at the L. P. McCarty Wholesale House, where he worked for three years, from 1945 to 1948. "Old Man McCarty," as the town called him, took a liking to Vernon and was so impressed by his "transformation" that he loaned him a new, high-powered Ford truck for weekend use. Vernon put the vehicle to use, all right—to expand his moonshine transport.

All the while, Elvis was growing up largely unmindful of his father's woes. Like Gladys, Vernon indulged the child. "I only wanted Elvis to do what made him happy. . . . I didn't try to persuade him to go against his feelings," said Vernon. And so, unlike other fathers and sons in Tupelo, he and little Elvis didn't go hunting. As Vernon once fondly related, when he asked the boy about a hunting trip Elvis told him, "Daddy, I don't want to kill birds."

As an adult, Elvis liked to remind his father of the times they slipped off to the movies, though the First Assembly of God forbade going to the pictures. Father and son would hunker down in their seats, lest someone they knew see them. At the Lyric movie house, young Elvis immersed himself in the cinematic adventures of Tarzan and Roy Rogers. At the Strand, which was a rerun house, he would sit in the moth-eaten seats and, ignoring the occasional rat that scurried along the floor, lose himself in the musicals of Bing Crosby and Ginger Rogers and Fred Astaire. When the credits flickered across the screen, he would look over at his father and beg to sit through the picture a second time.

But most of all, while growing up, Elvis was transfixed by music. From age eight on, he would wander through town, seeking anyone who could help him learn to pick out a tune on his second guitar, a pasteboard creation that emitted chords that were, said his uncle Vester, "out of this world."

He sat on porches of willing and semi-willing neighbors—even his reverend—and plucked out a makeshift accompaniment for the song he knew best, the lament about a boy and his dog called "Old Shep." "Oh, honey, it could set your teeth to hurtin' at first. Course, as the whole world knew, he did get better," said Vester Presley.

Along with remembering him for his collection of comic books, which he kept in pristine condition, his former classmates can recount his enthusiasm for performing in "chapel," which was held each morning before classes began. "Even then, he would sing with such meaning. Some of us actually swelled up with tears," said Becky Martin, who attended Lawhon Elementary with Elvis.

At age twelve, his family moved to a house near Shake Rag, the town's colored community. Elvis would sometimes sneak into its honky-tonks during the day to listen to the black musicians rehearse. As ever, he toted his guitar and asked for help with his chords.

He sang the dog-eared "Old Shep" to his playmates so often that one childhood critic moaned, "Oh, no, Elvis. Not another chorus of 'Old Shep'!" He performed it before his classmates during chapel at East Tupelo Consolidated. When he was in the fifth grade, he performed it before a crowd of two hundred at the Tupelo fairgrounds, during the Mississippi-Alabama Fair and Dairy Show. He also performed it at Milam school, where he attended sixth and seventh grades.

No matter what he sang, his greatest fan and most optimistic critic was, of course, Gladys. Her blessing was all he wanted.

Even early on Elvis had stars in his eyes. At age nine he began building a repertoire of local "countrybilly" songs in preparation for an audition with Tupelo's king of country, and young Elvis's musical icon, Mississippi Slim. Also known as Carvel Lee Ausborn, "Slim" did a daily hour-long afternoon broadcast, sponsored by the Tupelo Black and White Store, on radio station WELO. Perhaps not so coincidentally, one of Elvis's closest friends was Slim's little brother, Jimmy Ausborn.

Elvis used to sit on the curb outside WELO listening to the show—which featured a roster of country musicians—and sometimes sing along, as bemused downtowners looked on. But Elvis didn't want to meet Slim in person—not until he owned a "real" guitar. He didn't think his pasteboard model was good enough for Slim.

Over the decades there has been much conjecture over who actually sold Elvis his first real guitar. His parents told varying accounts to fan magazines. Elvis himself changed the story to fit his mood. Whatever the "truth," the honor is generally bestowed upon Tupelo Hardware.* As the myth goes, Elvis wanted a bicycle for his eleventh birthday, but his parents could not afford one. He instead chose a guitar that he had spotted in a glass case next to the cash register. Cost of the guitar: $7.95.

Armed at last with a respectable instrument, Elvis was ready to meet Slim.

On April 10, 1944, Elvis tentatively made his way inside the WELO studios, where he found his idol taking a coffee break before heading for a concert in Biloxi, Mississippi. Slim could barely get out a "howdy" before Elvis precociously took a seat on the desk and began singing, of course, "Old Shep" and several country hits of the day. Listening attentively, Slim slapped Elvis on the back. "You are very, very good for your age, Elvis. Just keep practicing and learning new songs. . . . You'll make it."

On May 15 Slim further encouraged his protégé by booking him to perform two songs on the *Black and White Jamboree*. Naturally one of Elvis's selections was "Old Shep," which he sang with special intensity. The pint-size singer was booked three more times on Slim's show—and each time was presented with a special ribbon, which he proudly took home and gave to his mother.

---

*For serious Elvis fans, Tupelo Hardware, and its well-worn glass case, is a shrine.

Presley's tutelage at the hands of Slim lasted until 1948. In November of that year, however, Elvis and his parents left town so suddenly they barely had time to say good-bye to relatives. They fled in the middle of the night in their 1939 Plymouth. In all probability, Vernon's problems with the law led to their hasty departure. Years later, Elvis confessed, "We were broke, man, broke."

Memphis, hardened and blighted by the end of wartime, lay ahead.

In Tupelo, Elvis had never quite realized he was poor. But in Memphis, class difference was a way of life.

Elvis was soon to endure the label "poor white trash."

In the Ghetto

t was September in Memphis and the small room was sweltering. But Elvis was oblivious to the heat as his eyes greedily surveyed the apartment's living room. If he noticed the peeling paint on the walls and ceilings, he showed no signs of it. Nodding at his mother, he walked quickly down the hall to see his cell-sized room in the rear, just large enough for a small bed, chair, and table. His heart jumped when he saw a corner just made to hold his prized collection of comic books.

After nearly eleven months in Memphis, the Presleys had moved up—with the help of welfare. They were now living at Lauderdale Courts.

At first, home had been a cockroach-infested boardinghouse on Poplar Avenue where Vernon, Gladys, and Elvis shared a single, shabby room. The rent was at first paid by Gladys's salary. She found work, first, as a seamstress making curtains. Then Vernon managed to get hired by a munitions manufacturer.

They didn't have the money to move, so the home service adviser for the Memphis Housing Authority, Jane Richardson, visited the family there to determine eligibility for public assistance.

Elvis never forgot the meeting that led to the family's liberation from that one-room hellhole. Pencil in hand, Richardson politely but officiously took note of the deficiencies and summed things up as "substandard." The heating was inadequate, and all of the family's water came from the bathroom—which was being shared with eight other people. There were no kitchen facilities, either; Gladys had to cook the family's meals on a hot plate.

Taking a chair opposite a nervous Mrs. Presley, Richardson moved quickly down a checklist. Where was her husband now working? For how long? How much was he making? Who was the nearest living relative? How old was their son?

"I'm fourteen, ma'am," Elvis piped up.

Mrs. Richardson turned around to get a good look at the rangy young man before her. A "nice boy" was how she described him in her official report. She was equally impressed when Elvis walked up behind his apprehensive mother and laid a comforting hand on her shoulder.

That meeting resulted in the Presleys' moving into Apartment 328 on the first floor at 185 Winchester, part of the sprawling red-brick complex called Lauderdale Courts. It was considered a model of public housing in the mid-South. "From slums to public housing to private ownership" was the motto of the Memphis Housing Authority.

The buildings were austere and institutional, and the apartments showed gritty signs of wear and tear. In the Presleys' unit the wall around the bathtub had mildew, and the sink was clogged. The light in the front hall flickered constantly. The window shade in the bedroom wouldn't retract—it just hung there. But nonetheless it was a move "uptown."

Since Vernon had obtained a steady job at the nearby United Paint Company, stacking cans for eighty-three cents an hour, the family was considered upwardly mobile and, as Mrs. Richardson described it, "deserving."

An annual paycheck of $3,000 or more would have disqualified the family, but Vernon earned just under $2,000.

When the lease was signed, Elvis and Gladys were elated. Her eyes filled with tears as her son hugged her and proclaimed, "It's gonna get better, Mama. I promise." She immediately went to work stripping away the old floor wax with soap she made herself. Then she buffed the oak floors to a high gloss. She scrubbed the basins, too, and rubbed the linoleum until it sparkled.

As his mother cleaned, Elvis wandered outside, where he met thirteen-year-old Paul Dougher, who lived with his mother in a third-floor Courts apartment. "We just said hi to each other and talked for a while. Then he said he had to go in the house," recalled Dougher, who saw his new neighbor the very next day. "And I started telling him about the people in the Courts—there were a lot of kids. And he was very excited about meeting other people, and as we were talking, some girls walked by who lived at the Courts. And right away, he wanted to know who they were."

Elvis proudly showed off his bedroom to Dougher, "even though my room was the exact same size, because the apartment floor plans were the same." Elvis had constructed a wire holder for his comic books and had arranged all of his possessions, including an old windup train, with military precision. He kept his guitar next to his bed, where he could easily grab it. The residents of Lauderdale Courts would soon become familiar with his twangs, as well as the lyrics of the soulful, somber "Old Shep."

They would also become familiar with Gladys's protectiveness toward her son.

"She would not let him take off by himself. She wanted him to be with somebody she knew," said Dougher. As Annie Presley noted, "Memphis was awfully big. Gladys used to worry all the time about what could happen to her boy there."

One day when Elvis hadn't come home from school by three o'clock, Gladys became so distraught that she sent her husband in search of him. After asking around, Vernon finally found Elvis at the home of classmate Bonnie Jean Dixon, "just fixin' to sit down to have supper." Elvis got to finish his meal, and to take Bonnie to a movie that night. But he also apologized to his mother.

Elvis sometimes balked at his mother's obsession with his whereabouts. "I used to get very angry at her when I was growing up," he admitted.

He sometimes went to lengths to fit in with friends who enjoyed more freedom. One incident occurred at the public swimming pool. Because he didn't swim, he had to be content to splash in the shallow section, watching his friends carouse in the deep end. When they started taking turns jumping off the diving board, Elvis decided to join in. Taking a deep breath, he jumped—without realizing how deep the water was. He came up gagging and coughing and flailing to stay afloat—then went down again. "We drug him out," remembers Dougher. As his friends guided him to the side of the pool and boosted him up onto the concrete decking, Elvis fought back tears.

"They treated him like he was two years old," said Ruby Black, a neighbor and the mother of Bill Black (who would go on to become Elvis's bassist). She added, "Mrs. Presley talked about her twin babies, and she just lived for Elvis."

When the school year began, Elvis became one of sixteen hundred students at L. C. Humes High—which filled an entire city block. To Gladys, the school was as daunting as the city itself. For her son's first three years at school she often accompanied him during the ten-block walk, especially if Elvis complained about bullies picking on him. "And a lot of times, she would hide behind a bush and follow him home without him seeing her," recalled cousin Billy Smith.

Billy and his parents had accompanied the Presleys on their trip to Memphis—and were soon followed by other Smith and Presley kin, including Grandma Minnie Mae, who eventually moved into the Lauderdale apartment. Throughout his life, Elvis took family ties—and obligations—seriously. But as Gladys liked to remind her son, "None of my kin finished high school, and none of your daddy's kin, and we've suffered plenty for it. That won't happen with you." By walking him to school, she was assured that he got there.

In the beginning, Elvis didn't try to impress anyone at Humes High. He was content just to get by. "His English was atrocious," recalled one instructor. Still another chided him for speaking too quickly, and for slurring his words in an accent thick with Mississippi mud. His slight stutter didn't help.

During his freshman and sophomore years, Elvis drifted in anonymity. He worked as a volunteer in the library, where he quietly stacked books. He didn't join clubs, didn't play sports, shied away from crowds. In class, he sat in the back row and seldom raised his hand. During lunch, he often wolfed down a sandwich at a deserted table in the cafeteria or sat by himself in the school's auditorium. At first his classmates were unaware that he had a special interest. But, as in Tupelo, he had music on his mind.

The Courts were built on what had once been rich farmland. On warm summer nights, the residents would bring out chairs and quilts and sit on the well-tended lawns beneath the shade trees. A discordant symphony of radios would mix with the night air. The strains of Mahler's Fifth, Hank Williams, and Rosemary Clooney sometimes intertwined. In time, with coaxing, Elvis would come outside and sit on the steps and play along with whatever was on or sing his Tupelo standards. When he had worn out "Old Shep," he went in search of new material.

For a budding young musician, he couldn't have moved to a better city. Memphis was a mecca of musical influences.

Just a half mile to the south was Beale Street, that brightly lit, tanked-up home of the blues. Among those who had performed there were Louis Armstrong, Big Mama Thornton, and Dinah Shore. Even Broadway's Ethel Merman stayed a week, gorging on barbecue and soaking up the backwoods tempo she would need for her new show, *Annie Get Your Gun.*

Meanwhile, the sounds of gospel echoed throughout the city's countless churches and meeting halls and spilled out onto the streets. Roadhouses hosted hillbilly bands from the Ozarks and cowboy singers from Nashville.

Ever since 1909, when black band musician W. C. Handy, famed for his "St. Louis Blues," had made Memphis his home, the city had been on the cutting edge of musical inspiration. By the 1950s it was also in the forefront of racial change. Blacks and whites had begun playing alongside each other in the clubs. "Race" radio stations such as WDIA, home to Nat D. Williams's *Tan Town Jamboree* and the B. B. King-hosted *Sepia Swing Club*, found themselves playing to whites as well as blacks.

Elvis used to lie on his bed and turn his radio dial from station to station. From a country lament by Hank Snow, he could jump to the heavenly glory of Sister Rosetta Tharp. And like every other young person in town, he would tune to Dewey Phillips—aka "Daddy-O" Dewey.

A white man with diverse musical tastes—ranging from Dean Martin to Patti Page to Nat King Cole to B. B. King—Phillips was a motormouth who was also Memphis's most talked-about disc jockey. He was on the air five nights a week, from nine to midnight, with more than one hundred thousand listeners.

Dewey's *Red, White & Blue* show, broadcast on WHBQ, initially catered to black listeners. However, it soon became required listening for *all* the city's youth for the simple reason that Dewey pushed at boundaries. Teenagers felt imprisoned by the era's conservative mores and were tired of mom and dad's mainstream music, then dominated by "safe" and syrupy pop ballads. Free of any restraints, Phillips got down and dirty. In the days before Top 40, before radio was taken over by "formula" shows and approved playlists, listeners never knew what

Dewey might do, might say, might play. For kids whose parents refused to sanction rhythm and blues, then called "race" music, Dewey made sure they got their fill of it.

He provided laughs, too. If his listeners didn't want to drink Falstaff beer, a major WHBQ sponsor, he advised them to "open up a rib and pour it in." If he touted a product with a payment plan, he yelled, "Pay for it while you're wearin' it out!" If he disliked a record, he'd snatch it off the turntable—in a cacophony of destructive sound.*

Elvis was also awed by another man shaking up the status quo. Over at Sun Records on Union Avenue, a man named Sam Phillips, no relation to Dewey, was specializing in recording music other companies were ignoring. As Phillips once explained, he saw "a great wealth of music that was not being exposed . . . and a large part of it was coming from the colored man." In defiance of the era's racial barriers, the Sun motto was "We Record Anyone-Anywhere-Anytime."

Elvis's tastes were equally eclectic. When all-night gospel sings became the rage—with crowds of fifteen hundred filling downtown's Ellis Auditorium—Elvis was there. He spent hours flipping through the bins of 78s and 45s at record shops on Poplar and Main and gloried in the gospel sings sponsored by Memphis's First Assembly of God church. Yet he also turned his radio dial to Nashville's illustrious *Grand Ole Opry*. On rare occasions, he snuck into black clubs on Beale.

His education on the guitar continued to flourish.

At Lauderdale, as he played on the steps, Jesse Lee Denson would sit patiently alongside him, going over his chords. Denson was the son of the Reverend Jesse James and Mattie Denson, who ran a nearby Pentecostal gospel mission where Gladys and Elvis sometimes attended the prayer meetings. Jesse Lee was one of a number of young musicians in the area who jammed on the grassy area in the midst of the housing complex. Sometimes, the boys took over the Courts' laundry room—their sounds booming through the complex.** According to Jesse's brother, Elvis was usually too shy to join in. "He felt inadequate. He could barely learn his chords," says Jimmy Denson.

However, that wasn't the case when Elvis was with his friends. They would set up a portable Sears record player in the Courts' basement—

---

*Crazy Dewey's on-the-air antics were equaled by the excesses of his private life—the result of his rampant pill-popping that began after a crippling 1951 car accident.
**Jesse Lee went on to record under the names Jesse James and Lee Denson and to become a prolific songwriter. In 1971, Elvis recorded Jesse Lee's religious song "Miracle of the Rosary."

or throw parties in the Presley apartment, with Vernon and Gladys chaperoning. "If Elvis knew everyone, he would get up and sing and play. But he could be shy about performing," says Evan "Buzzy" Forbess, a close friend who lived by the Courts. Forbess figures he sat in the Presleys' apartment every day for a week as Elvis rehearsed for a performance he was supposed to give at his biology-class Christmas party. "On the day of the party, he forgot his guitar," recalls Forbess. "Obviously, he chickened out."

It wasn't for lack of support from his parents. Gladys, especially, fostered her son's interest in music. She also worked extra jobs, as a waitress, and later as a nurse's aide, to indulge his interests.

She even participated in his efforts to reshape himself, an infatuation that manifested between his sophomore and junior years at school. For a while, he came to school with his blond hair slicked back and darkened by rose oil. When other boys had GI crew cuts, he let his hair grow longish—with sideburns. He even had the audacity to try what one Lauderdale friend later described as a Mohawk-type cut and the patience (and the nerve) to sit for hours in the kitchen while his mother carefully applied a Toni home permanent. "You couldn't help but notice it. His hair was naturally straight as a board, and suddenly he had all these curls," says Buzzy Forbess.

He experimented just as daringly with clothes. At a time when most boys his age wanted a tough image, Elvis wore pink. As opposed to Levi's jeans, he opted for gabardine slacks in black, with a pink stripe down the sides. While the other boys wore plaid shirts, he went for a garish "pimp" look in, again, black and pink. In his shop class—where Elvis made his mother a salad bowl—the other students certainly noticed. "For someone as shy as he was, he certainly started to stand out," notes Louis Cantor, a Humes classmate.

Elvis had what some classmates called a "greasy" look, with his strange clothes and goopy hair. He also developed a bad case of acne. "Don't buy that story about him being cool in high school," says Pat Lightell. She and her girlfriends would hurry down the hall rather than stop to talk to Elvis. Other classmates turned away when he approached.

Though he wore pink, he was no sissy. Paul Dougher saw Elvis's temper in action the day a group of boys had gathered and one of them said something that riled Elvis. "There was a quick flash in his eyes. It was as if he just snapped all at once," remembers Dougher. Within seconds Elvis had grabbed the boy, pushed him to the ground, and was on top. "That was the first time I'd seen that aggressiveness in him," adds Dougher.

He saw more signs of aggressiveness during Elvis's junior year, when Presley—who had shot to six feet yet still weighed only 150 pounds—tried out for the football team. "He was fast. He had good hands and he liked to hit. . . . I thought he was going to be good," Dougher recalled. But Elvis balked at having to wear the helmet over his slicked-back hair. Coach Malcolm Phillips, who started Elvis as a lineman, remembered having to yell at him, across the field, to put it back on. "And he didn't have any real skills as a lineman."

His distinct look led to new friendships. He met Robert "Red" Gene West as the result of a fight in the boys' bathroom. As the story goes, Elvis was being roughed up—by classmates who didn't appreciate his look and mannerisms—when West came to his aid. A superb athlete who was an all-Memphis football player, West went on to become one of Elvis's closest friends—and a member of his so-called Memphis Mafia.

George Klein, a Humes High overachiever—he was student body president and editor of both the school newspaper and the annual—also befriended Elvis during their senior year. Because of his status on campus, Klein initially considered Elvis "totally uncool." Klein says, laughing, "Today we all know the truth."

Remembering the first time he noticed Elvis, Klein says, "Here was this classroom full of guys in jeans and T-shirts, penny loafers and an occasional sports shirt, and in the middle sat a dark-haired, dark-eyed boy in a pink sports coat, pink and black pants with regimental stripes down each side. He spilled out of his chair, legs spread forward and his arms hanging purposely over the back of the chair. He had a look of disdain."

Elvis's demeanor may have seemed uncool, but Klein found himself thinking, "This guy's got balls."

After the two started becoming friends, Klein told Elvis, "You know, those clothes and that guitar set you apart from everybody."

"Sure does," Elvis answered. "That's what I'm after."

During those days, reflects Klein, "there were only three ways to achieve high school status—by becoming a sports hero, a student leader, or a cheerleader. Elvis found another way, by transforming himself into a rebel."

In retrospect, Klein calls Elvis Memphis's first greaser.

*   *   *

Always an avid moviegoer, Elvis regularly plunked down fifteen cents for admission to downtown's Suzore No. 2 theater, where he would endure a leaky roof and a rattling fan to see a double feature and serials. He came to watch favorite stars—he loved westerns and comedies. But as he came of age, he was increasingly attracted to the new hero of the screen: the rebellious teen.

Both he and his mother followed the new pretty-boy movie star Tony Curtis, who was making a name for himself playing juvenile-delinquent types, in such pictures as *City Across the River* and *Johnny Stool Pigeon*. But it wasn't so much the movies Elvis and his mother liked as Tony's photogenic looks. Both shrewdly noticed that Curtis's jet-black, curly hair helped to make him a more dynamic presence. Especially with his steely blue eyes—the same color as Elvis's.

Elvis was fifteen when he began working as an usher at the Loew's State Theater on Main Street. "Careful, folks," he would say as he brandished a flashlight and guided young couples to their seats inside the darkened auditorium.

Elvis loved the job. Not only did he see movies for free, he got to wear a uniform—a brown jacket with shoulder pads and tan pants with a brown stripe down the sides. And when work was over and the lights of the marquee were dimming, he had time to visit with his musician friends.

He would walk briskly down the late-night streets—trying to avoid any confrontations with the rowdy sailors who stumbled out of the local bars—and head toward the Grit-Iron, an all-night eatery. There he would take a place at the counter alongside Ronald Smith, a guitarist and student at South Side High who also worked as an usher (at the Warner Bros. Theater).

"We'd talk about music. The latest things we'd heard, ideas we had," remembers Smith. "Then we'd hit up on the waitresses and raid the pie rack."

When Elvis's parents found out he was dozing in class, they made him quit his job, and again Gladys returned to work as a nurse's aide at nearby St. Joseph's Hospital. The family needed the extra money because a bad back was affecting Vernon's ability to work. A "bad back" was also, of course, the easiest way to collect disability. Vernon, said one welfare officer, was the "crown prince of lower-back pain."

"Are you bored? Man, I am," said Elvis. He and Paul Dougher were in the balcony of the Loew's State, where they were working as ushers.

It was summer, 1951—Elvis had returned to his old job. "It was a way to make fifteen dollars a week," said Dougher.

When the theater wasn't full, Elvis and Dougher would watch the movie or just goof off. They got so bored one night that Elvis decided to stir up some excitement. Dougher stood guard in the lobby as Elvis ran down the aisles yelling, "Fire!" Dougher helped usher the panicked patrons out onto the street, where Elvis later consoled them. "Folks," he said, "it was a false alarm." He added, "It was just a small one. It went out by itself."

Another time, when Elvis and Dougher had to distribute flyers advertising an upcoming movie, they eventually tired of the task. After what seemed a respectable period of tucking *King Solomon's Mines* bills into doorways, they found a drainage ditch and dumped the rest.

Elvis was eventually fired from the job when it was discovered that he was coaxing the candy-counter girl into giving him free samples. "Elvis was loafing and sitting around when he should have been working," explained manager Arthur Groom. The incident led to one of Elvis's early displays of fury. When Elvis found out that another employee had snitched on him, he decked the boy.

His next job, with after-midnight hours, was as a sweeper at a metal-products company. One day in history class the bell rang and Elvis, "like a little boy, raised his head, got to his feet, and wandered out like a sleepwalker." Teacher Mildred Scrivener notified the Presleys, and once again they made him quit. But Presley vowed to find another job. "He liked what money could buy," recalled Paul Dougher.

He also liked that working got him out of the house.

On the surface, life appeared almost idyllic at the Presleys' Lauderdale unit. The boy was so indulged by his parents that he was one of the few students at Humes to have a car. Never mind that it often gave out ("We pushed that thing all over Memphis," says Ronald Smith, laughing) or that the window on the driver's side wouldn't roll up (Elvis dropped in a piece of cardboard) or that it spewed fumes. The 1941 Lincoln Zephyr was a symbol of prestige at a time when few young people had their own car.

There is no doubt that to Gladys and Vernon, Elvis was their life. But his parents also had secrets—which sources have only recently begun talking about.

For years, both Gladys and Vernon were closet alcoholics. As the children of moonshiners, both had had access to alcohol while growing up. That access increased during Vernon's moonshiner days, and once they had moved to Memphis, the steady drinking continued.

Elvis's friends occasionally glimpsed the family's shame. "There was a lot of drinking," said Paul Dougher, who remembered Vernon sitting in the kitchen, imbibing throughout the evening. Dougher and Elvis didn't talk about it. "We just went in his bedroom and Elvis closed the door." Other friends saw Gladys hiding her beer in the corners of a cupboard.

The drinking led to fighting. "When their window was open, you could hear them arguing. You couldn't help but hear it," says Margaret Cranfill, who was a young mother when she was at the Courts. Sometimes, these arguments would escalate to physical abuse. "I understand she called him every name in the book as his hand stung her face, again and again," recalls Marty Lacker, who met Elvis in high school. "She was such a sweet little thing, you couldn't imagine anyone doing that to her."

Elvis learned about the abuse just months after the family arrived in Memphis, when he found his mother powdering away at blue bruises on her neck.

"Daddy do this?" Elvis asked.

Tears were Gladys's only answer.

When Vernon got home at two in the morning, Elvis was waiting. He sprang off the sofa and slammed his father against the wall. "Daddy, if this happens again to my mama, I swear, I'll kill you!"

According to what Presley told Lacker, the violence tapered off for a while, only to resume when Elvis was away from home at night. Eventually, Gladys decided to fight back with a marble rolling pin. The next time Vernon came lurching into the house with battery on his mind, Gladys crept through the dark and knocked him out cold. Neither Elvis nor Lacker ever saw another bruise on Mrs. Presley.

The drinking, however, accelerated. Gladys's elder sister, Lillian, remembered her sister stumbling around the Lauderdale living room, attempting to pour some tea.

Gladys was ashamed: "I don't want my son to ever see me this way."

Taking her hand, Lillian replied, "Just stop. It don't do you no good. I can tell you from experience."

Early in 1953, during Elvis's senior year, the Presleys were turned out of Lauderdale Courts by the Memphis Housing Authority with little warning. As poor as they were, their combined incomes rendered them ineligible for public assistance. So they briefly relocated to a two-room apartment in a run-down rooming house several blocks from Humes. "Don't bother to come by," a humiliated Elvis told his friends. He was relieved when the family was able to move to a better apartment—in a roomy Victorian near the old neighborhood.

Another change was coming in his life as well. He would soon graduate. To his high school prom he took fourteen-year-old Regis Vaughan, whom he had met while she lived at Lauderdale. Ironically, in light of his later flamboyance, they never once danced. "I don't know how," Elvis confessed to his date.

On June 3, Elvis went to a job-placement office and was sent on to M. B. Parker Machinists, where he was interviewed and hired for a job.

That same night he was among the Humes High seniors who gathered in the South Hall of Ellis Auditorium for commencement exercises. Students were cited for having completed the required course of study and for "having sustained a correct moral deportment." As for Elvis's academic achievements, teacher Mildred Scrivener noted, "I can't say he was at the top of his class, but at least he made it without worrying me."

One by one, to the strains of "Pomp and Circumstance," the graduates marched up onstage. Elvis looked relieved as he exited, diploma in hand. Waving to a classmate, he proclaimed, "I done got it."

The Memphis
Flash

His guitar slung over his shoulder, Elvis paced back and forth before the nondescript brick building. It was a lunch hour in July 1953—just six weeks since his graduation—and the Memphis air was heavy with humidity. But the perspiration that dampened his shirt wasn't due to the weather. There were squirrels in his stomach as he took a deep breath and opened the front door.

"I thought he was a drifter looking for a handout," recalled Marion Keisker, the manager for Memphis Recording Service.

Elvis himself would later claim that he didn't know it was a record company: "I thought it was just one of those stores you can make a record in." After he became a household name, the publicity machinery would trumpet his entry into these doors as some accident of fate.

But it was no accident when Elvis made his way into 706 Union Avenue—home of the Sun Records label. He was very familiar with the Sun label and knew just what he was doing. He was a big fan of "Mystery Train," recorded in the studio earlier that year by Little Junior Parker. From the booths of Taylor's Café, located right next door, he had heard stories about the company and its gutsy founder, Sam Phillips.

In fact, Phillips and Sun had recently been the subject of a story in the local newspaper. Sun had recorded a quintet from the Tennessee State Penitentiary. Under heavy guard, the convicts had journeyed to the studio to record "Just Walkin' in the Rain." It was not by coincidence that the Prisonaires, as they were named, were black. Sam Phillips, a native of Alabama who had grown up in the cotton fields and later worked as a disc jockey in Decatur, Nashville, and finally Memphis, had a reputation for recording colored talent, particularly when they sang the blues.

By the time Elvis nervously ventured inside its doors, the company's bright yellow label—depicting a rooster perched beneath the sun's rays—was familiar at radio stations throughout the South. Phillips had already recorded such artists as B. B. King, Bobby Blue Bland, Howlin' Wolf, Big Walter Horton, Big Ma Rainey, and Rufus Thomas. He would go on to record such legendary talents as Johnny Cash, Roy Orbison, Charlie Rich, and Carl Perkins. Little wonder that in years to come, Sun would be nostalgically regarded as a rock-'n'-roll Shangri-la. Writing in his 1975 book about American rock 'n' roll, *Mystery Train*, critic Greil Marcus waxed, "Sun was a space of freedom, a place to take chances." Its music was "as authentically new as any music can be."

That music emanated from a former radiator shop on what was once called Automobile Row. Phillips leased the downtown building in 1950; he and Marion Keisker personally transformed the interior, putting in the white acoustic tiles that covered the ceiling and walls. Rockabilly star Carl Perkins would call the place the "polky-dot studio."

Now Elvis stood in its tiny reception area, as a paying customer. He knew all about vanity recordings from his talks with the veteran musicians whom he incessantly sought out. With the necessary four dollars in his pocket, Elvis was ready to record his voice for the first time.

As was always the case with Elvis and his music, however, he had a game plan. Before paying for the ten-inch acetate, he told Keisker, "If you need a singer, I'd be very interested."

Keisker surveyed his sweat-stained khaki clothes, greased-back hair, and sideburns. "So what kind of singer are you?" she asked.

"Ma'am?"

"What kind of singer are you?"

"I sing all kinds."

"Who do you sound like?"

"I don't sound like nobody."

Once in front of the microphone, it took less than fifteen minutes for Elvis to sing "My Happiness," a ballad that had been a hit for performers including the Pied Pipers and Ella Fitzgerald, and "That's When Your Heartaches Begin," which had been popularized by one of Vernon's favorite groups, the Ink Spots. "I was terrible," Elvis later confessed. "My guitar sounded like someone beatin' on a bucket lid or something."

Keisker thought otherwise. Before Elvis left to return to work, she took his name and number and alongside it wrote down the words, *Good ballad singer. Hold.*

Another critique was offered by an anonymous woman who was in the building with her son. After inquiring about the identity of the young man who was singing, she told Keisker, "He gives me goose pimples."

Elvis told friends, and it became a part of his lore, that he recorded "My Happiness" as a birthday present for his mother. Within days he was playing "Gladys's record" for anyone who would listen. Word raced through his old Humes High crowd that the song wasn't half-bad. But talk of its being a "birthday gift" resulted in laughter.

When George Klein and Elvis rendezvoused one night, George cocked his finger at him and said, "Elvis, your mom's birthday is months away. You're trying to impress Sam Phillips, right?"

Elvis nodded bashfully. "How else could I have gotten inside Sun Records?"

"He was planning his course from the first," recalls Klein. "The clothes, the guitar, and the 'amateur records' were all part of the plan."

When Elvis made that first recording for four dollars, said Klein, "he was auditioning."

By summer's end, Elvis was working at Crown Electric Company, where he made deliveries in the company truck. Gladys Tipler, wife of Crown owner James R. Tipler, once recalled being asked by a representative from the State Employment Office not to judge Presley on his appearance. Said Tipler, "With that wild hair and those shaggy sideburns, he looked like the original goon boy."

Shortly after finding fame, Elvis confessed that he used to envy a driver's life. "I used to see them drivers with their shirts off, handkerchiefs around their neck, a little cap on their head. They looked darin' to me. I always dreamed of being a real wild truck driver."

His own truck-driving days were far from wild. To help keep him company, a neighbor lady in her seventies named Viola "Mommy"

Massengill sometimes rode along on his deliveries. "He would pick her up two or three times a week," remembered her grandson, Walter "Buddy" Winsett. "Over dinner, she would tell us, 'I went riding with Elvis again today.' She said he needed someone to talk to. She enjoyed driving around Memphis with him."

He told some of his friends that he was studying nights to become an electrician. But in fact he was prowling the area's bars and road-houses, trying to get onstage. At Doc's, a beer bar in nearby Frayser, he sang wearing a cowboy hat, Western shirt, and string tie. During breaks he sipped Cokes and listened to the locals discuss his performance. B. B. King once spotted him looking in on the musicians on Beale Street.

From time to time he also stopped by the offices at Sun, hoping to catch Sam Phillips's attention.

By this time Elvis was a familiar presence at Ellis Auditorium's "all-night" gospel sings. In fact, he caused heads to turn in the auditorium as he sang along with the performers. Some nights, long after the rest of the audience had exited, he sat by himself in the darkened hall.

With Ronald Smith, he performed at the talent show at South Side High, and they had gigs at the local Odd Fellows lodge, and for patients at local hospitals including the Home for the Incurables.

Back in April, Elvis's classmates had been startled when he got up the nerve to appear in Humes's "Annual Minstrel Show." Wearing a red flannel shirt he borrowed from Buzzy Forbess, Elvis bounded out onstage—and initially froze in fear. Then he took a deep breath and began playing and singing the Teresa Brewer hit "Till I Waltz Again With You." Remembered Forbess, "The teachers started to cry . . . they just started boo-hooing." So many student acts were in the show that there was time for only one encore—for the performer who had garnered the most applause.

That performer turned out to be Elvis, who sauntered back onstage and began performing his signature song, "Old Shep."

Red West, who had played the trumpet in the show, watched Elvis with surprise. "I never even knew he sang."

More ambitious than anyone had ever realized, Elvis made a second vanity record at Memphis Recording Service in January 1954, per-forming the Joni James hit "I'll Never Stand in Your Way (Little Darlin')." This time he got Sam Phillips to listen and even to take down his name.

After hours, he continued to indulge his obsession with music. He sat in with the musicians at local clubs such as the Hi-Hat and the Bel Air. He performed at beer joints near the Lauderdale Courts. And he frequented the clubs on Beale Street, where he also browsed through the racks of hip threads at Nate Epstein's pawnshop.

His musical efforts weren't always successful. One night in the summer of 1954 he talked Roy Hall, a boogie-woogie piano man and hillbilly singer, into letting him perform at his club in Nashville. The Music Box boasted blackjack tables and roulette wheels and a clientele that included Grand Ole Opry performers. He was not asked back. Hall remembered, "I was drunk that night, didn't feel like playin' piano, so I told 'im to git up there an' start doin' whatever in hell it was that he did." Added Hall, "I fired 'im after just that one night. He weren't no damn good."

In late June 1954—nearly a year after Elvis had first gotten up the nerve to walk through Sun's doors—Sam Phillips returned from Nashville with a demonstration record of a ballad entitled "Without You." What he needed was a vocalist who could sing ballads—a rarity in the blues city.

"Call that kid with the sideburns," Keisker said.

She telephoned Elvis: "Can you get over here in three hours?"

A panting Elvis got there in less than a half hour. She kidded him, "What did you do? Run all the way?"

After all that time spent attempting to get Sam Phillips's attention, though, Elvis couldn't deliver what he wanted. On the ninth take, Phillips stood up: "This isn't working. Let's take a break."

Presley pretended he didn't hear him and broke out into an improvisational repertoire. "I sang everything I knew," Presley recalled, "pop stuff, spirituals, just a few words of something I remembered." That included what seemed like an entire catalog of Dean Martin hits. When Elvis tore into "That's Amore," Phillips cried, "Dammit! I'm not looking for a crooner."

Phillips wanted "a white man who can sing like a Negro." He had been thinking that Elvis might be the one he was looking for, but he recognized that the boy had to be handled carefully. "He was probably innately the most introverted person that had ever come into Sun," Phillips said. Moreover, Elvis's guitar playing was strictly rudimentary. What Elvis needed, Phillips decided, "was somebody pretty damn good on the guitar, with a lot of patience."

So Phillips teamed Elvis with master guitarist Scotty Moore, a Navy veteran who had a reputation for precision. For bass, Phillips chose Bill Black, who was known for his gregarious sense of humor and his high-energy performances.

Elvis was not completely unknown to Moore and Black. Both men were members of Doug Poindexter and His Starlite Wranglers, a hill-billy band Elvis had seen perform (and Phillips had recorded). More-over, Black's younger brother Johnny had grown up near Lauderdale and had jammed with Elvis. Ruby Black, their mother, was a friend of Elvis and Gladys's.

Like Presley, both Moore and Black had day jobs. (Moore was a hatter; Black sold tires.) Black was twenty-seven and Moore, twenty-two—both young enough to relate to Elvis. Or so it seemed.

On the night of their informal rehearsal, Elvis showed up at Moore's house in a pink shirt and matching slacks with a white stripe down the side. He sported Imperial curls, courtesy of a home permanent.

"He looked about twelve," remembered Moore. Black considered him "a snotty-nosed kid."

Yet after their session when Elvis had driven off in his sputtering Lincoln, Moore called Phillips: "With work, he might amount to something."

Moore's analysis was not only prophetic, but astute. Despite popular legend, Presley was hardly a golden-voiced instant success. His early vocal style veered between the smooth and the amateurish. It would take time—and literally hundreds upon hundreds of nights on the road—for him to perfect his delivery.

Still, Elvis intuitively knew something important had happened during his encounter with Moore and Black. "[He] talked to me like he had finally found a winning combination," recalled cousin Gene Smith.

What Elvis sensed was chemistry.

The next night, Elvis, Moore, and Black met Phillips at Sun. Although the city was suffering from a heat wave, nothing sizzled in the studio that night. Sitting in the control booth, Phillips endured five unimpressive cuts of "Harbor Lights" and a version of Elvis's favorite love song, Eddie Fisher's "I Love You Because." Moore recalled, "None of us were really happy with any of them, so we stopped and sat there in the studio, just drinking Coke and shooting the bull."

Finally, Phillips burst out of the control room and challenged the kid: "Elvis, ain't there something you know that you can sing?"

Elvis grabbed his guitar and began fooling with a sped-up version of

Arthur "Big Boy" Crudup's "That's All Right (Mama)." Moore kicked in with a pounding guitar riff, and Black slapped his bass, almost angrily. At first Phillips was stunned. "It was just amazing to me that he even knew a Big Boy Crudup song. So that just knocked me out." As the three musicians charged into the chorus, Phillips finally yelled from the control booth, "What are y'all doing?"

"We don't know," hollered Moore.

Later, Moore reflected, "We were just trying to make as much noise as we could . . . But when we heard a playback, we knew we had some kind of rhythm, a little different rhythm, but none of us knew what to call it, so we didn't call it anything at that time."

The trio performed take after take—at least nine. Listening to the playbacks, they knew they had something unique. Elvis's voice was mesmerizing, a mix of gospel, the low, gravelly growls of country, and a startling "black" sound. "Good God!" said Moore. "They'll run us out of town when they hear this!"

For the first time Elvis had found his voice. Now, the song needed exposure.

Enter disc jockey Dewey Phillips.

Memphis's most popular disc jockey seldom played a record unless he liked it. As it turned out, he loved "That's All Right," which Sam Phillips slipped to him as a demonstration disc. He first played the song at approximately 9:30 P.M. on July 10, announcing, "That'll flat git it." And it did.

With its odd synthesis of blues and country, and Presley's unique vocal inflection, "That's All Right" generated immediate listener response. Calls poured in to the station. The frenetic Dewey Phillips was more energized than ever. "He was so excited about the record being different—about it having a different sound—that he called me to say he had a hit," remembered his widow, Dorothy Phillips.

Dewey also called the Presleys, seeking an interview with the young singer, but he had gone to the movies. "I guess he was too nervous to listen," Gladys explained.

"Well, go find him and bring him down to the station."

So Gladys and Vernon rushed to the Suzore No. 2 and into the darkened auditorium. As the image of Gene Autry flickered on the screen, Gladys combed one aisle while Vernon went down another. Elvis, who was seated in the center, jumped when his mother tapped him on the shoulder.

"What's happened?" he asked. His face was white.

"Plenty," said his mother. "All of it good."

Elvis looked dazed as he made his way into the WHBQ studios, located on the mezzanine level of Memphis's Chisca Hotel. Phillips had Elvis take a seat across from him. Elvis protested, "I don't know nothing about being interviewed."

"Just don't say nothin' dirty," advised Phillips.

Then the deejay started up a casual conversation, drawing out his young subject. "Elvis didn't know he was in front of an open mike," recalled Dorothy Phillips. When Dewey wrapped up the conversation, Elvis whispered, "Mr. Phillips, I thought you was gonna interview me."

Phillips smiled and declared, "I just did."

Indeed, during his talk with Presley, Phillips had cleverly dealt with the race issue without ever mentioning color. When he asked Elvis which high school he had attended, Elvis responded, "Humes High, sir." Listeners realized that no matter how black he sounded, the singer was a white boy, since Humes was an all-white school.

By eleven o'clock that night, WHBQ had received more than a dozen telegrams and nearly fifty phone calls about the song and its singer. "The next day, it was the talk of Memphis," recalled Elvis's friend Paul Dougher. Humes High graduates especially were buzzing. It seemed that strange classmate of theirs had made good.

Over the decades, myths have grown about that hot July night. The playing of "That's All Right" has been credited with bringing Elvis overnight success. In reality, the scenario did make Elvis a *local* celebrity. National fame, however, was three more grueling years down the road.

Sam Phillips brought back Elvis, Moore, and Black to cut a flip side for "That's All Right." They wound up doing an up-tempo version of the revered waltz "Blue Moon of Kentucky," written by Bill Monroe, the father of bluegrass. Without a fiddle or steel guitar, a rockabilly sound emerged. Or, as Phillips deemed it, "a pop song, nearly 'bout!"

Copies of Elvis's first record went to all the town's disc jockeys, and both "That's All Right" and "Blue Moon of Kentucky" quickly became local anthems. Within days, Sam Phillips's Sun Records received six thousand orders. During his lunch breaks at Crown Electric, the young singer used to wander into Poplar Tunes on Main Street and hide behind the Coke machine. "After everyone left, he'd ask me if anyone had bought his record," recalled employee Mary Ann Linder.

Elvis made the papers as well. On July 27, Marion Keisker brought him to the offices of the *Memphis Press-Scimitar*. According to newspaper columnist Edwin Howard, Elvis looked decidedly uncomfortable. He was skinny, with a "plastered-down, growing-out flattop" and lots of pimples. Wearing a buttoned-to-the-top plaid shirt and a bow tie, Elvis was so flustered that he merely answered yes or no to Howard's questions. He wasn't even quoted in the story that finally ran.

Keisker supplied the talk. She told Howard, "This boy has something that seems to appeal to everyone."

Presley's shyness was not only public. "He was over to our place quite a bit after Dewey played that record," said Dorothy Phillips. "He was a kid, and he was scared, you know. In fact, I always thought he was a little bit nervous. Anyway, the attention frightened him and excited him at the same time."

In late July the glare of the spotlight turned hotter. At the Bon Air Club, located out on Highway 70, he joined Scotty and Bill and the rest of the Starlite Wranglers onstage. His confidence building, Elvis occasionally exhibited some fancy footwork.

But it was at an outdoor "hillbilly hoedown," held at the city's Overton Park Shell, that he first cut loose. Slim Whitman, then famed for his "Indian Love Call," was the headliner. But all eyes were on the newcomer, whose name was misspelled (as Ellis Presley) in one of the newspaper ads for the event.

Elvis was so scared he paced back and forth backstage. Once onstage with Scotty and Bill, he couldn't stand still, either. "Instead of just standing flat-footed and tapping his foot, well, he was kind of jiggling," recalled Moore. With a nod to the loose "britches" they all wore that night, Moore mused, "You shook your leg, and it made it look like all hell was going on under there." Elvis's delivery more than lived up to the expectations of the audience, which included screaming girls.

Whitman had the unfortunate task of having to wrap up the show after the newcomer. "I felt sorry for Slim, because when he came out, those people just wanted to see more Elvis," Sam Phillips said.

The exposure raised him to a new level. The Eagle's Nest made him a semiregular. Hailed by *Billboard* as a "strong new talent," Elvis and the boys began a series of nighttime and weekend playdates.

When a new shopping center opened, Elvis was the novelty attraction. For the opening of the Lamar-Airways center, a crowd of three hundred gathered when he performed out behind Katz Drug Store from the back of a flatbed truck. "The shopping center was full of boys and girls when we got there," remembered Becky Yancey, who was a teenager when she talked her parents into taking her to the performance.

By coincidence she and Elvis were color coordinated. He wore a pink shirt and black pants, his hair greased back into a ducktail. She wore a pink sweater and tight black skirt. When she approached him and asked him for his autograph, he surveyed the stunning blonde before him and coolly quipped, "Sure. But who do I sign this for? Marilyn Monroe?" Years later, Yancey would become reacquainted with Presley, and he would make her his secretary.

Elvis's performances weren't confined to the city limits, however. After feverish campaigning by Sam Phillips, he was invited to be a participant in country music's great shrine. Elvis Presley was going to play the Grand Ole Opry.

5

Road Trip

lvis Presley bent down and ran his hands across a battered oak pew. He raised his head and took in the vibrant colors of the stained-glass windows above. Ryman Auditorium, the home of the Grand Ole Opry, had been built in 1891 for a hellfire-and-brimstone evangelist. For the nineteen-year-old Presley, this performance here would be the first of his many baptisms by fire.

According to Scotty Moore, when he and Bill Black and Elvis made their way into the 3,500-seat, red-brick, barn-shaped hall, they were initially disappointed. Their collective response to what was known as "the Mother Church of Country Music" was, "This is it?" The paint on the walls was peeling, and except for the stained glass, and the red-trimmed curtain across the stage with its depiction of a barn, the hall was devoid of adornment—and air-conditioning. Patrons fanned themselves with programs. Backstage, the entertainers' quarters were so cramped that crowds of musicians spread out the stage door into the alley beyond. Men had to wait their turn to use three small dressing rooms; women had only one.

The Opry, though, was country music's most revered venue—and the most popular live radio show of all. As a boy growing up in Tupelo, Elvis and his family had spent countless Saturday nights sitting around the radio, listening to the antics of Opry comics such as Minnie Pearl or Cowboy Copas, or Roy Acuff's frenetic fiddling or Eddy Arnold's vocals. And now, on October 2, 1954, Elvis Presley was to be a part of the revue himself.

A newcomer amid a "family" of performers frequently billed together, at the Opry and at traveling shows, Elvis was so nervous that he was shaking visibly as he stood backstage. Spying the shell-shocked novice, musician Buddy Killen ambled over and extended a hand. "Who are you? And what's the matter with you?"

"I'm Elvis Presley and, man, I'm scared to death. They are going to hate me!" he predicted.

Because the Opry's performers tended to stick with country music standards, he was to sing his version of the classic "Blue Moon of Kentucky," a country-chart hit for him at the time. His nervousness intensified when he spied Bill Monroe—an Opry member since 1939, and the man who had written "Blue Moon." "I hope I haven't upset you, sir," Elvis said, referring to the rhythmic liberties he had taken with Monroe's sacred bluegrass tune. Monroe not only gave Elvis's rendition his blessing, but he also confessed that he himself had just cut a more up-tempo version.

As Elvis walked away in relief, Monroe wondered about the boy's red satin pants, ornate cowboy shirt, and all that hair. Still another Opry veteran, guitarist Chet Atkins, would wryly note that Elvis was wearing eye shadow. "I was astonished. . . . I'd never seen that on a man before," Atkins recalled.

Performed in thirty-minute segments, each with a different sponsor and headliner, the Opry aired from six-thirty to midnight. That night Elvis went on at ten-fifteen in a segment headlined by the venerable Hank Snow and sponsored by Royal Crown Cola.

He didn't bomb, but he didn't particularly impress the country fans, either. "He got nice applause—the audience was polite," said Bill Denny, son of the late Opry manager Jim Denny. "Country people weren't acquainted with what he was doing, and they weren't that much into rock and roll," explained Opry singer Marty Robbins, who admitted that "up until just before [Elvis's Opry show], I thought he was black."

"He did not really go over that well. . . . He didn't tear the house down. But remember, they were mostly older people who went to the Opry in those days," recalled Justin Tubb, who gauged audience reaction from backstage. Just seven months younger than Elvis, and the son of Opry legend Ernest Tubb, Justin was then a disc jockey with a country music station in nearby Gallatin, Tennessee. Elvis's "Blue Moon" was number one on his listener-request list.

"Everybody was talking about this kid from Memphis," said Justin, who also saw Elvis perform at the *Midnight Jamboree*, the radio show that was broadcast from Ernest Tubb's Record Store after the Opry wrapped. "Elvis seemed kind of bewildered by what had happened at the Opry," recalled Justin. "I'm sure there were some people who smarted off to him. Because there was a lot of ill will about him at that time. . . . A lot of country people objected to him because they didn't really think he was country." In a measure of the country music world's indifference, his performance wasn't even reviewed at the time.

Over the years there have been conflicting accounts regarding Elvis's Opry show. According to one report, after he left the Opry's stage, Jim Denny cruelly advised him to keep on driving a truck. Bill Denny denies his father ever said that. "Would I have gone on to work for the Colonel, during Elvis's later shows, if my father had made that remark?"

In any case, Elvis was never invited back.

Even though the Opry had proven to be the wrong venue, Elvis, Scotty, and Bill were still the hot act in and around Memphis. "We just kept spreading out, and the farther we went, the bigger the price. I mean, fifty or sixty dollars. And we were glad to get it, so we could buy gas to get home," remembered Scotty Moore, who initially acted as Elvis's manager. A second Sun record—"Good Rockin' Tonight" and "I Don't Care If the Sun Don't Shine"—was released in Memphis, leading to bookings at high school auditoriums, civic halls, and at their regular venue, the Eagle's Nest.

By now known as Memphis's "homegrown hillbilly singer," Elvis got a second shot at a major audience when Sam Phillips set up a performance in Shreveport on the *Louisiana Hayride*. Though it was just in its sixth year, the *Hayride* was second in popularity only to the Opry, reaching listeners in thirteen states over two hundred stations. It was also more open-minded about using new talent.

The *Hayride* was broadcast on Saturday nights from an old red-brick municipal auditorium that seated 3,800—and, unofficially, a smattering of sparrows that clustered on the ceiling beams. The show's headliners got private dressing rooms, but Elvis was shown to a common dressing room on the second floor. He donned white pants, black shirt, and a pink jacket—accessorized by a bright, clip-on bow tie. Then he ritualistically oiled, greased, and combed his hair, though to hear some of the *Hayride* musicians tell it, he might have been better off washing it. "It was dirty. And so was his neck," recalled one performer.

What caught the attention of Hayride manager Pappy Covington, however, was Elvis's energy—and undeniable charisma. Flanked by a backdrop for Lucky Strike cigarettes, with Scotty and Bill in Western wear, Elvis said in his halting stutter, "We-we-we're gone do a so-so-song for you we got on the Sun Record label. It goes somethin' like this . . ." The band launched into "That's All Right." And, unlike the Opry, the crowd was with him throughout every beat.

Elvis was so strikingly unique that some members of the audience wound up sitting through the subsequent show—during which time they applauded even before he began to play.

Victorious, Elvis drove back to Memphis the next day with his buddy Red West. They had a traveling companion: a Houston schoolgirl who had met and talked with Elvis at the *Hayride*. Kitty Jones was a resourceful fourteen-year-old who had convinced neighbors to give her a ride to the show after fabricating a story about intending to meet a girlfriend and her family there. In fact, Jones had come hoping to talk with Tommy Sands, a young singer who was doing the warm-up show. She wound up spending her time with Elvis instead. "But there was no romance," said Jones, who stayed a few days with the Presleys and then took a bus back home.

A bubbly, blue-eyed blonde, who was often told that she resembled Kim Novak, Kitty was warmly welcomed by Gladys Presley, who made her up a bed in the living room. Vernon Presley was also friendly to his son's young friend. Recalled Jones, "Whenever Gladys and Elvis weren't in the room, he'd hit up on me." But she never told Elvis.

Kitty Jones would go on to become a close friend of Presley's, and a confidante during his wild Hollywood years.

Initially, Vernon balked when his son wanted to quit his job at Crown Electric. Elvis, who had been promoted to the front office, where he answered the phones, wanted to accept a one-year contract with the *Hayride* and concentrate full-time on a music career. "I never saw a guitar player that was worth a damn," complained the chronically unemployed Vernon.

Elvis quit anyway. He took his parents with him to Shreveport—

putting them up in the swank Captain Shreve Hotel—the weekend that he signed his *Hayride* contract. He would earn eighteen dollars a show; Scotty and Bill would each get twelve. They were, Elvis sensed, on their way.

Known as the "cradle of the stars," the *Hayride* had helped to make Hank Williams a legend and bolstered the careers of Slim Whitman, Jim Reeves, and Faron Young. It would prove just as pivotal a launchpad for Elvis Presley, propelling him not only across the airwaves, but also across parts of the country he might otherwise not have played. With Scotty and Bill, Elvis began to cut a swath through east and west Texas, Louisiana, and Arkansas.

Touring became dominant during this phase of his career. From the time that Elvis signed with the *Hayride* in late October 1954, the trio's lives became an extended road trip. On Saturday nights they took the stage in Shreveport, where Elvis sang his Sun tunes and even performed a commercial for "pipin' hot" Southern Donuts. Once the curtain dropped on their set, the boys strapped Bill Black's bass atop Scotty Moore's battered Chevy and climbed in. As Moore recounted, "It was drive all night, sleep all day. . . . All we knew was drive, drive, drive." During one three-month period, from late 1954 to spring of 1955, they logged more than twenty-five thousand miles. At times they performed with the *Hayride*'s touring packages, but just as often they were on their own, playing for either a set fee of between fifty to seventy-five dollars a night or a percentage of the house.

With veteran country-music disc jockey Bob Neal now managing them—and sometimes coming along to do radio promotions—they played outdoor stages at fairs and livestock shows, high school and civic auditoriums, and smoky honky-tonks and roadhouses located on otherwise lonely roads in backwater towns.

Across from the port of Houston, at what was then called Buffalo Bayou, they performed Sunday-afternoon hoedowns on the shedlike wooden stage at the outdoor Magnolia Gardens. In downtown Houston, they played the Fraternal Order of Eagles building. In Gladewater, Texas, Elvis sang from a flatbed truck parked at second base in a baseball stadium. Near Hawkins, Texas, they played a gig at a recreation hall in the midst of the Humble Oil Camp. For the show in the Helena, Arkansas, Catholic Club, tickets could be purchased in advance for seventy-five cents at the local pharmacy.

One night in Sikeston, Missouri, as two National Guardsmen arranged folding chairs in the armory, Elvis raced past them, in a hurry to use the bathroom. Later, the men asked if he knew if the night's headline singer, "the Presley boy," was white or black. "He's a white boy who just sounds black," said an authoritative Elvis, who went on to confess, "I am the Presley boy." He then rushed outside to the car and came back with a sack from the Piggly Wiggly store. As the Guardsmen looked on, he tipped the bag and out tumbled his pink silk suit.

In the beginning, everyone had difficulty getting his name straight. Newspaper ads for the shows touted "Alvis" Presley, "Alvin" Presley, Elvis "Prestly," Elvis "Pressley." Categorizing his music proved equally confounding. How did he come up with his particular style? "To be honest, we just stumbled upon it," admitted the shy young singer. And what did he call his sound? "I never have given [my music] a name," Elvis told a radio interviewer. That was left to the disc jockeys and promoters, who alternately branded him "the bopping hillbilly," "the hillbilly cat," a "bebop Western star," the "Memphis flash," "king of Western bop," and even a "folk music talent." The magazine *Country Song Roundup* declared, "This youngster is a real 'folk music fireball.' "

Of one thing there was no question: no one had ever seen or heard anyone quite like him.

He had not yet perfected the gyrating body movements that would become a Presley trademark, but his look and demeanor were still distinct enough to warrant gasps from unsuspecting audiences. When he performed at a high school auditorium in Breckenridge, Texas, wearing black pants and jacket with apricot-orange piping to match his shirt, many of the teenage girls in attendance "swooned." The reviewer for the *Breckenridge American* noted that, in turn, their boyfriends heckled the pimple-faced singer and bragged loudly about how they'd like to beat him up "behind the barn."

In Kilgore, Texas, Elvis wore red pants, a green coat, and pink shirt and socks. While tuning up his guitar, he snapped a string. Then he stood silently "for what seemed like five minutes" in front of the microphone, looking out over the crowd through his slumberous eyes, and broke into a slight sneer. The high school girls started screaming. When he at last moved, "it was like he had a thing for his guitar," recalled country-music singer Bob Luman, who added, "He made chills run up my back, man, like when your hair starts grabbing at your collar."

His onstage electricity caught the eye of music scout Oscar Davis, who caught Elvis's act at the Eagle's Nest during a trip back home to Memphis. Davis put in a call to an already legendary music man:

"There's a boy out here you might want to take a look at." On the other end of the phone was Colonel Tom Parker.

In the Southern entertainment world of the 1950s he was known simply as "the Colonel." The title had been bestowed upon him in the forties by Louisiana governor Jimmy Davis, a former hillbilly singer. "He don't forget old friends," remarked Thomas Andrew Parker on the occasion of his honorary commission.

Colonel Tom Parker had come out of the U.S. Army, after serving with the Sixty-fourth Coast Artillery from 1929 to 1932, and onto the carnival circuit, where he ran penny arcades and worked as a press agent. (Word was he'd invented the foot-long hot dog.) In Tampa, Florida, he operated a trained-pony ring and served as the dogcatcher. He went on to manage cowboy star Gene Autry and country singer Eddy Arnold, to handle promotions for the Grand Ole Opry, and to form a successful booking company. He was managing the career of Grand Ole Opry headliner Hank Snow when he agreed to meet with Bob Neal, Sam Phillips, and Elvis at a Memphis coffee shop in early February 1955.

The historic meeting took place at Palumbo's, in between Elvis's two sold-out homecoming concerts at Ellis Auditorium. As Elvis drank a Coke and the others had their coffee, the Colonel looked the young man in the eye. "You know, son, get out of those Monday-night school-house dates and up where the money is."

"Yes, sir!" said Elvis.

"And you know somethin' else, boy? Sun Records isn't the right company for you."

Elvis looked stricken and glanced nervously at Sam Phillips.

"You need a big company. Better possibilities for a guy like you, on a big label," said Parker as he lumbered out the door.

Bob Neal remembered thinking the meeting was a bust, that the Colonel "didn't think there was anything sensational here." Elvis was crushed; he thought Parker had given him the brush-off. Actually, Parker had just baited the hook. The cagey Colonel had secretly been tracking Elvis on the concert trail for months.

Hank Snow proved to be a pawn in Parker's quest to sign the young singer and build him into a star. Just days after Parker and Snow formed Jamboree Productions, the Colonel hired Elvis as the tour's newest "guest star" on a bill that also included one of Gladys's favorite entertainers, the cornpone comedian known as the Duke of Paducah. The troupe made its way through Texas, New Mexico, and Louisiana, with Elvis in the coveted spot of performing just before Snow. Special lighting was added to fire up Presley's increasingly sensual body movements.

The Colonel also provided Elvis with a roommate on some of Hank's tours—Hank's son, Jimmy Rodgers Snow, who submitted rave "reviews" to Parker, including this excerpt: "Hips grinding and shaking, legs jerking and snapping, and flailing the guitar to a fast drumbeat, he drove the women into hysterics."

During the Colonel's quest to woo Presley, talent booker Arnold Shaw dropped by his office—a shack, actually, out behind his house in Madison, just outside of Nashville. Shaw spied a stack of 45s with labels printed in yellow and orange—Sun records. "Listen to this boy," said the Colonel, spinning a platter. Shaw remembered being surprised to learn that the singer, who had "a distinctly Negroid quality," was actually a white boy.

The Colonel looked up. "No one's heard of him north of the Mason-Dixon line. But I'm not snowin' you when I tell you that he's the biggest thing to hit the South in years." As the Colonel lit one of his trademark cigars, he added, "The girls would tear his corduroys off if they could."

As the "Hank Snow Jamboree" toured, the Colonel launched a separate publicity campaign for Presley, putting his picture on flyers and salting the local radio stations with the Presley Sun releases. To an exasperated Hank Snow he said, "I got to get the young folks in." He added, "He has an entirely different audience than you."

Snow was understandably sore when he went onstage, in his rhinestone cowboy getup—with matching alligator boots—and faced an audience that was increasingly filled with young Southern girls who had dragged along their frowning boyfriends just to see Elvis. "It was just incredible," recalled RCA producer Felton Jarvis. "I mean, Elvis just wiped them out. They were hollerin' and stompin' and they wouldn't let him off the stage. And when Hank Snow came on, they booed him." Because he was preceded by the "kid with the guitar," Snow's opening songs were sometimes punctuated by the sound of a mass retreat; the jingle-jangle of charm bracelets and teenage chatter sounded as Elvis fans vacated the auditorium. "Poor Hank Snow. The headliner never had a chance," is how *Memphis Press-Scimitar* writer Ken Jones summed it up more than two decades later.

Snow inevitably came to the decision to let Elvis close the show. "It was the only solution," he remembers. "It took the pressure off."

Although Elvis was making hearts throb in the South and Southwest, he had yet to crack other parts of the country. When he played a "Hillbilly Jamboree" at the Circle Theatre in Cleveland, the audience did not respond. They were unfamiliar with his songs because Sam Phillips had yet to find local distribution. They also had difficulty deciphering the Mississippi native's thickly accented banter between songs. It was his good fortune to find an ally in Cleveland's Bill Randle, recently singled out by *Time* as "the United States' top disc jockey" on station WERE.

Following the Cleveland performance, Bob Neal took Elvis and the boys to New York. The trip resulted in an even bigger blow than the cool reception they'd gotten at the Opry. Though Neal thought Elvis was a natural for CBS-TV's popular *Arthur Godfrey's Talent Scouts*—where an "applause meter" determined each show's winner—the audition proved a bust. Neal later heard that Elvis's acne was a turn-off to the talent scouts, looking for close-ups on camera, who also found him too nervous and frightened. Recalled Neal, "Their reaction was, 'Don't call us, we'll call you.' And of course, they never called."

However, Elvis was flourishing as Memphis's homegrown celebrity.

Only six months after Dewey Phillips had slapped "That's All Right" on the turntable, Elvis was able to move his parents to a four-room apartment.

He was also able to indulge his childhood dreams of sleek, shiny automobiles. "I told myself if I ever got any money, I was going to get my fill of cars," Elvis once explained. Vernon and Gladys junked their battered green coupe for a pink-and-white Crown Victoria, which Elvis sometimes took on tour. Elvis bought himself a 1951 Cosmopolitan Lincoln and promptly had the words *Elvis Presley—Sun Records* painted on the side.

He splurged on a new guitar, too, spending a pricey $175 for a 1942 Martin. He also became the favorite customer of Lansky's on Beale Street, where he carted out armloads of peculiarly tailored and excessively colored pants and sports coats, which would soon spawn a national fashion craze.

Audaciously, he opened his own office. Located at 160 Union Avenue, just a few blocks from Sam Phillips's Sun Records, Elvis Presley Enterprises had a pink-and-black motif, complete with black wrought-iron furniture, pink metallic drapes, and pink telephone. Black metal baskets on the desk were piled with fan mail; by spring of 1955,

Elvis was receiving sixty to seventy-five letters a day, many requesting photos.

At first Elvis sent off photographs at no charge, but when the requests multiplied, he requested twenty-five cents for each picture, or eight cents apiece for mass orders. One of the pictures he sent out was a dreamy-eyed head shot—the result of Elvis's first professional photo session. "He came off like dynamite," recalled Bill Speer, whose lens captured Presley in late 1954. "As soon as I sat him in front of a camera, I knew he had it." Speer's wife, Vacil, was certainly impressed the evening Bob Neal brought Elvis to the studio. "Oh, I opened that door, and his animal charm, his animal magnetism!"

When Bill had finished taking the requisite portraits of Elvis in sports coat and shirt, the photographer said, "Well, if that's all the clothes you brought, I guess we're done."

"No, honey," Vacil protested. "Get him to take his shirt off!" Though the young singer at first protested, he at last shyly unbuttoned his shirt and slipped it off. When he was later sent copies of the shirtless shots, Elvis scrutinized one of them and scribbled on the back of it, "This has got to go! Ha ha ha!"

Less than a year later, a far more self-assured Elvis faced the camera of Lloyd Shearer of *Parade* magazine. Shearer wanted to snap him with one of the teddy bears that were piled high in a corner of his bedroom. But Elvis shook his head: "I don't imagine you could ever get Gary Cooper or Marlon Brando to do a thing like that."

The country boy was savvier than anyone might have imagined. When he met with Shearer in the sixth-floor suite of Memphis's posh Peabody Hotel, Elvis didn't want to be photographed smiling, "even if I'm just grinnin'." As Elvis explained, "I've made a study of Marlon Brando. I've made a study of poor Jimmy Dean [who had recently died]. I've made a study of myself. And I know why girls, at least the young'uns, go for us. We're sullen, we're broodin', we're somethin' of a menace."

Claiming to know nothing about Hollywood—though he read stacks of movie fan magazines every week—Elvis said, "I know that you can't be sexy if you smile. You can't be a rebel if you grin. If you don't mind, just let me pose myself."

With commanding aplomb, he stripped off his shirt, dropped to the floor, and moved up against the bed. Putting his head against the mattress, he looked upward with a soulful stare.

*   *   *

Gladys Presley was left behind as her son roamed farther and farther from home. When Elvis took off for concerts, Sam Phillips frequently stopped off at the Presleys' to comfort the concerned Gladys. "She was a strong woman—one of the strongest women I have ever known. But she knew, I think, that what was happening to Elvis was something she could not control," Phillips observed.

When Elvis was on the road, she would sit in her easy chair, racked with fear that something was going to happen to her son. On those occasions when he had to fly, she agonized over the possibilities. Gladys feared flying, and after an early touring experience, so did Elvis. He and his musicians were on board a twin-engine aircraft leaving Amarillo at midnight, headed for a Nashville recording session, when a fuel problem suddenly caused the small plane to lose altitude. As Elvis and his boys felt themselves plunging from the sky, they dug into their seats with clenched fists and exchanged silent, frantic looks. "It's okay. We'll bring this baby down and take care of the fuel problem," said the pilot, who did just that on an emergency landing strip in a backwater town in Arkansas. Then they were off, but in trouble again when the fuel gauge acted up. "Here, hold the wheel," said the pilot to Scotty Moore. "What!" exclaimed the terrified Moore. After tampering with the instrument the pilot made yet another emergency landing, this time in Memphis. As Elvis and his friends stood about the field and muttered under their breath, the pilot tinkered around, and after he reassured them, they climbed in for the third and final leg of their journey, which at last deposited the harried musicians in Nashville. As they walked across the field on shaky legs, Elvis kept declaring, "We are never, ever, getting in a plane with that guy again!"

Nor would he readily climb into any airplane, in the immediate future, unless there was no other recourse. "I promise," he solemnly told Gladys.

No matter how he traveled, whenever he returned home from his trips, she would appear out of the darkness to wrap her arms around him. "Thank God you're back!" she would cry, sometimes digging her nails into his arms with such force that he recoiled in pain.

She used to fantasize that the fans, in their growing hysteria, would harm him. Or worse, that their boyfriends would beat him to a pulp. "The guys wanted to knock the shit out of this pretty boy," said June Juanico, who became an Elvis steady in 1956. "They wanted to change his face. They wanted a piece of Elvis's ass." Aware of their anger, Gladys kept fistfuls of mail from angry young men. "Just read these," she pleaded to her son. "Read what they're sayin'. These boys want to rip you up."

Gladys sat in her shapeless housedresses and increasingly nursed two potent addictions: alcohol and diet pills. The pills were Dexedrine, which doctors prescribed for her by the hundreds. But her dependency on alcohol was what her sister, Lillian, called her "hidden shame": Gladys sipped beer throughout the day, hiding telltale cans behind the couch or her favorite chair. At night she would sneak empties into the garbage can.

If Gladys had her way, Elvis would have remained a local, home-bound star who came back to their apartment for dinner and spent the weekends with his mother. "The only models she had to go by were Mississippi Slim and Whitey Ford [the Opry comic, the Duke of Paducah]," men who fielded country music careers but still came home for Sunday supper, recalled Lillian.

Elvis's appeal, though, was not confined to country music audiences; his growing chorus of fans was giving him a hunger for stardom on a bigger level. "He was impatient," said Bob Neal, who remembered the singer's persistent urgings: "We got to figure out how to do this. We got to get ahead."

Gladys fought back the only way she could—by treating Elvis as a child. As her son dashed out the door one evening, guitar in hand, she stopped him. "Just when are you going to be home? You know you don't have to be out so late!"

Elvis wrapped his arm around her. "Mama, don't you worry none," he teased. "I'll be with five hundred people."

To placate his mother, Elvis had her attend some of the more sedate concerts—high school dances and carnival jamborees. "At first she was very proud of his performances," said Gladys's sister. "She said to me, 'Lillian, you should hear how much better he sings.'" For several months Gladys and Vernon—she in her Sunday best, he in a new sports coat—went to see their son perform. From the stage, Elvis would watch his mother intently. What he saw was a middle-aged country woman lost in the throng of young girls in cashmere sweaters and billowy skirts. According to her biographer, Elaine Dundy, Gladys was initially thrilled to see her son growing with each performance. "However, she saw how much it was taking out of him, so it began to take a lot out of her as well."

One balmy spring evening in Mississippi, a gymnasium full of girls tore away from their boyfriends. Shrieking, clawing their way up onto the stage, they flung themselves on top of Elvis, groping at his pink jacket and black pants. Swinging her purse as a weapon, Gladys bounded from her seat and elbowed her way through the hysterical teenage horde. At her son's side, she seized the closest girl, pulling her off Elvis. "What are you trying to do? Kill my boy?"

"No," said the teary teenage girl. "I just want to touch him . . . just once."

"Get away!" Gladys bellowed. With a shake of her head she admonished, "This ain't no way to act."

She and Vernon helped Elvis make his way through the fans and out to the car. Only then did Gladys break down. "They're gonna kill you, Son," she sobbed. "One of these days they're gonna kill you." They drove home in silence.

The next morning, with Vernon at her side, Gladys confronted her son. Despite the fact that the family's sole income was the money Elvis brought home, Gladys demanded an end to it. "It's time you got a presentable job."

"But, Mama, this is my job," Elvis protested. "You and Daddy better git use to it. This is gonna keep right on happening. This is what I do."

Family friend Mack Gurley, who witnessed this family schism, recalled, "Gladys never realized that what he was doing really was a career. She wanted him to go out and get a 'real' job, marry a nice Memphis girl, and settle down in Memphis."

Biographer Elaine Dundy views this as "Elvis's long-deferred Declaration of Independence. Take it or leave it, Elvis was saying. From here on in, fame is my first home. He had a job to do, and he had to go out into the world to do it."

Elvis used to tell Gladys, "I'm doing this for you, Mama." And once again, as he had done in childhood, he called her "little baby." "There, there, little baby," he would say soothingly, every time he went out the door. "It's gonna be okay."

But for Gladys, things would never again be okay. Her son was drifting further into the chasm of fame and, with it, an increasingly unbridled private life.

Red West, who was often along during Elvis's 1955 tours, saw the change. "He was still pretty shy, but gradually the waves of applause and craziness around him started to loosen him up a bit."

Marion Keisker was working in the Sun office the day Elvis pulled up "with four or five real good-looking girls" in the backseat of his car and asked her if she wanted to go for a ride, too. They'd gone just a few blocks when Elvis turned to her, grinning, and said, "Marion, I'd like to introduce you, but, I don't know their names yet!"

The boy who had always felt more comfortable in the presence of women began to slowly undergo a metamorphosis into a man who would forever rely upon them—often as playmates, occasionally as soul mates, and always as friends. More than his male companions, women were his link to life—his sounding boards, his confidantes.

In the seventies, when Elvis looked back on his stardom, he claimed he had "screwed everything in sight." That phase, however, did not come until later, after he had entered the Army. During his early years he was constricted not only by the strictures of the Bible Belt—but by the era itself, an era he himself would ultimately help to explode.

According to a latter-day Presley girlfriend, he once revealed that he didn't lose his virginity until around the time of his high school graduation. In fact, his relationships with Memphis girlfriends were chaste, complete with vows of purity and earnest talks with preachers about not "straying."

He was nineteen when he caught the eye of pretty Dixie Locke, a fifteen-year-old from the Assembly of God Church. "I knew the first time I met him that he was not like other people," Dixie said. He certainly wasn't anything like the other young men who made up the Bible study group known as the Christ Ambassadors. It wasn't just his appearance—the trademark long, greasy hair and his outlandish clothes in pink and black—but also his intensity as he pored over his Bible and joined his brethren in intense, spoken-aloud prayers to the Almighty. From what she could tell, the Lord was as important to him as his looks.

He presented a startling picture when she saw him one weekend at the local roller rink. All alone, he was dressed in tight-fitting black pants with a pink stripe running down the sides, a ruffled shirt, and a short bolero jacket. He wore skates, too, but he didn't use them that night. After Dixie glided up, wearing a flouncy skating skirt with white tights, he rapidly became uninterested in skating.

The two unlaced and stowed their skates and went off for Cokes. Still later that night they had burgers and milk shakes. They also exchanged a kiss in the front seat of his Lincoln. And the very next day, Elvis came calling.

The romance that followed was decidedly homespun. They spent evenings with their families, baby-sat cousins, watched television, and held hands during double features. She liked him for his distinctiveness—and for his sensitivity. He sometimes bared his soul about his family life. He liked her for her petite brunette beauty, and for her sense of optimism. He said she had "the biggest smile that I've ever seen anywhere."

The two vowed to remain pure until they were married. At one point the would-be young lovers talked about running off to see a justice of the peace in nearby Hernando, Mississippi. But both decided against it. Dixie, after all, had two more years of high school. Besides, Elvis had other romantic interests.

According to his guitarist friend Ronald Smith, at the same time Elvis was dating Locke, he was also seeing a particularly shapely fifteen-year-old. After dropping Locke off at her front porch, Elvis would swing by the other girl's house and sometimes sit with her on her porch until one in the morning. "He couldn't stay much later. Her daddy would have run him off," says Smith. "You know how some girls look eighteen by the time they're twelve? That was what this girl was like. I don't mean that derogatory."

Elvis, adds Smith, had "a roving eye that wouldn't quit."

With women he would reveal things about himself that he did not communicate to his male friends. With Dixie Locke, he discussed problems at home. To his prom date, Regis Vaughan, he vowed, "All I wanna do is buy my mama a house." With Billie Wardlow, a Lauderdale neighbor who became one of his first girlfriends, he openly wept after finding a photo of another beau in her wallet, and jealously tearing it up. As Wardlow later admitted, "Until that night I had never seen a man, or a boy, cry."

During his first days on the road, he was content to look—and to flirt. At Shreveport's Murrell's Café, located near the *Hayride* offices, he would eat a plate of extra-well-done cheeseburgers ("I ain't orderin' a pet," he liked to say) and slurp three or four milk shakes in a row, all the while girl-watching. In concert, he frequently picked out the prettiest girls in the front row, teasing and tempting from the stage. At the show's end, he would zero in on a willing participant for gropings and fondlings in the backseat.

The concert dates continued to pile up, though, and the farther he got from home, and his mother's watchful eye, the less he remembered vows of purity. Within a few months Elvis fell into the habit of taking several women at a time to his motel room.

"He just loved women, and I think they knew that," said Jimmy Rodgers Snow, who sometimes found himself locked out of the room he shared with Elvis on tour. Justin Tubb, who also toured with Elvis, noted, "He didn't smoke and he didn't drink. But he had a vice—girls."

According to deejay Bill Randle, some of the "very well developed young women" who congregated backstage at Elvis's shows later cuddled with him inside his parked car. "There was a lot of activity in that car," recalled Randle, adding, "Elvis was a highly sexed young guy—a randy rooster."

In the beginning he was sexually naïve. Sam Phillips likes to tell about the time a flustered twenty-one-year-old Elvis showed up at his home to anxiously confess, "Mr. Phillips, ahhh, Mr. Phillips, I got somethin' I'm just worried to death about." With that, Elvis dropped his pants to reveal a festering sore just above his pubic hair. "He thought he had syphilis," said Phillips, who went on to diagnose Elvis's "risin' " as a "carbuncle boil" (later lanced by a physician).

Just as he used clothes and his sneering pout to get attention, he began to play around with his body movements. Musician David Houston, who was on the road with Elvis during this period, has claimed that the singer even fashioned a prosthesis of sorts—to rock and roll inside his baggy pants. Said Houston, "He would take the cardboard cylinder out of a roll of toilet paper and put a string in one end of it. Then he'd tie that string around his waist. The other end, with the cardboard roller, would hang down outside his drawers." Once onstage, as Elvis pulled his body backward as he began strumming his guitar, he would also yank at the string.

To the Eisenhower-era girls seated in the front row, Elvis Presley didn't just represent a new type of music; he represented sexual liberation.

Gladys Presley sternly warned her son about the distinction between "good" girls and "bad" girls, and about the teachings of the Lord. Given her own rowdy Tupelo past, she had long worried about what would happen when her son came of age.

Back when Elvis was just a tyke, he had witnessed his mother and her sister-in-law as they broke into an impromptu dance. As they moved, they lifted their skirts. Elvis glimpsed their white panties beneath their print dresses and rushed toward his aunt, grabbing her leg and hollering, "Oh, my peter!" Gladys's sister-in-law burst into fits of giggles. But not Gladys. "Quit that damn dancing! Look what you're doing to him!" she said, snatching up her little son.

Now Gladys was unable to protect her son from sin—and sex.

To keep her boy in check, she sought to make comrades of Elvis's traveling companions. "Now, Red, look after my boy. Just look after my boy," she implored. Cousin Gene Smith was also enlisted to keep a watchful eye. But more often than not, Elvis's buddies joined him.

During one trip home to Memphis, Elvis and Red were cruising in the Crown Victoria when they came upon two young women— "pickups," according to West. West was still living with his mother in one of Memphis's housing projects. But Mrs. West wasn't home the day her son and Elvis brought the girls over. Red took his date into his bedroom and closed the door. Elvis took his girl into Mrs. West's bedroom, not realizing that the sagging mattress on her bed was atop a slab of plywood.

When Red heard screams coming from his mother's room, he pulled on his pants and went running. His first thought was that Elvis's date had changed her mind "and Elvis was trying to force the issue." But when he burst into the room, he instead found Elvis and his date "half-assed dressed and giggling like schoolkids." In the midst of their energetic lovemaking, the earth had moved: they had crashed through the sheet of wood.

In Jacksonville, Florida, an audience erupted into the first full-fledged riot of Elvis Presley's career. It happened at what is now called the Gator Bowl, when fourteen thousand people turned out for the "Hank Snow Jamboree." At that time the Snow tour was touting both veteran performers—Snow, Slim Whitman, the Carter Sisters with Mother Maybelle—as well as a slate of newcomers such as the Davis Sisters (including Skeeter Davis) and Elvis.

Elvis's records weren't yet familiar to Florida audiences, but the young people there had been hearing about the heavy-lidded twenty-year-old. On the night of May 13, 1955, he lived up to their expectations with a concert that left little to the imaginations of teenage girls. When his act came to an end, a sweaty, heavy-breathing Elvis drawled into the mike, with a taunting sneer, "Girls, I'll see y'all backstage."

They took him at his word. Before Elvis could safely make his way to his dressing room beneath the dugout locker room, hundreds of hysterical girls were off and running. "I thought Elvis was going to be killed right then. The crowd was as out of hand as a lynch mob," recalled

Vernon Presley, who was never more frightened for his son's safety. Mae Boren Axton, a publicist for the show, was in the dressing room area when she heard "feet like a thundering herd" and Elvis's frightened yelps. A horrified Skeeter Davis watched as police tried to make their way into the dressing room where Elvis frantically tried to take cover.

When order had at last been restored, Elvis climbed down from the top of one of the shower stalls. He had been stripped to the waist—his pink lace shirt torn and shredded into dozens of souvenirs. His jacket was torn. His shoes and socks had been yanked from his feet. Bruises were beginning to show on his arms and chest, and his face was smudged with lipstick, his own mementos of earnest fans.

Out in the parking lot, his beloved Cadillac looked ready to be junked: upholstery had been torn by souvenir hunters; dozens of phone numbers had been scratched into the sides; the windows were a mass of lipstick markings.

The trade publications *Billboard* and *Cashbox* breathlessly reported the riot. No one needed to tell Colonel Tom Parker what had happened, though. He had witnessed everything, along with a colleague who represented powerful RCA Victor. With one event, the die was cast.

From the moment Elvis went home for a much needed vacation, he began to sing the praises of the man who could get him a contract with "Victor" (RCA), the man who could get him into the movies, the man who could make him a millionaire.

Gladys was unnerved. Like Vernon, she had witnessed the riot and it had terrified her. Now her son appeared gaunt and exhausted, and desperately in need of a bath. Purple circles underscored his eyes. His suit hung loosely on his body. Lack of bathing had led to a patchwork of acne on his face, neck, and back. "Baby, you're half-dead," Gladys said, guiding Elvis to his bedroom. "You get some sleep. I'll get dinner ready."

In the months since Elvis had been touring, his income had slowly risen. The family was now living in a rented two-bedroom brick house, their first house since leaving Tupelo. Elvis also had money for his cars—he had a new pink-and-black Cadillac—and his flashy wardrobe. Yet there was little extra.

Though Elvis was earning from $75 to $250 a night, he had to pay out almost forty-five percent of that in salaries as well as travel costs. His third Sun single, "Baby, Let's Play House" (with "I'm Left, You're

Right, She's Gone" on the flip side) had recently been released, but its distribution was limited. When he arrived home, a royalty check for a paltry $178 awaited him on the kitchen table.

Once recovered and rested, Elvis settled in at home. He sat out on the screened-in front porch with his grandma Minnie Mae. He tinkered on cars with his father and his uncle Vester. He met the new neighbors, who were in awe of the young celebrity. He took Dixie to her junior prom, though by now it was apparent that wedding bells were not in their future.

What he wanted, he told his parents, was for them to permit him to sign a contract with Colonel Tom Parker. But the Presleys balked at giving over the underage boy to the man who had publicized the notorious Jacksonville concert, which had left their son half-naked, and his Cadillac trashed.

"Mama, you don't understand," Elvis mumbled.

"There's one thing I do understand," Gladys declared, "and that's that your daddy and I want you to come home, regular. You're travelin' too much, playin' too many towns." According to Bob Neal, Gladys fervently believed that her son could make a good living by performing close to Memphis.

Said Sam Phillips, "I don't think she understood the ramification of what was taking place—the magnitude of it all. None of us did. Remember, there had never been a stardom like this."

In his chronicle of Elvis's early career, biographer Peter Guralnick noted: "Elvis wanted to sign with the Colonel more than he had wanted to do anything in his life. But Gladys said, 'Not another word.'" As Vernon once recalled, "Gladys and I warned him that we really didn't know anything about this man."

Like the Colonel, Gladys, too, had an agenda: she wanted her son to work less, not more. She wanted him to sing gospel and country, not rockabilly. She wanted him to concentrate on having a family, not a career. Because of her close friendship with Bob Neal, and his wife, Helen, she had a measure of control over Elvis's career. She knew she would lose that if the Colonel took over.

When Elvis rejoined the "Hank Snow Jamboree," he felt he had little prospect of living out the Colonel's goals. Still, when the troupe stopped at Little Rock, Arkansas, the Presleys drove down for a meeting with the Colonel.

"He seemed like a smart man, but we still didn't know too much about him, so we didn't sign," Vernon remembered. Gladys Presley was deeply suspicious. When the Colonel tried to pass himself off to the Bible-toting Gladys as a regular churchgoer, she shot back, "Which church?" The Colonel had no answer.

Tom Parker was no quitter. Six weeks later, on the evening of August 15, he hosted a swank dinner at Memphis's Peabody Hotel, for Elvis, his parents, Sam Phillips, and the Neals. Also on hand: Hank Snow, a personal favorite of Gladys's.

The Colonel had asked Snow to attend in case his carny-honed powers of persuasion failed to convince "the old lioness," as he now privately called Gladys. A charted plane in Nashville whisked Snow to Memphis, following a call from the Colonel, who said, "Gladys wants to talk with you, not me." He added, "We're not gonna get the boy without you."

What the country star didn't realize was that Parker had strongly hinted to Gladys that Snow's guiding hand would be behind every move that Parker's agency made. She couldn't help but be impressed. Hank Snow was one of the most successful of country stars; he banked $800,000 a year from his RCA record sales alone. More important to Gladys, his songs were Christian-based and cautionary. In his famous baritone wail, he warned of the dangers of drink, loose women, and honky-tonks.

Snow arrived at the Peabody to face a stubborn and sullen Gladys. Elvis, wearing an oversize scarlet suit, was clearly agitated. The Colonel was unctuously flattering everyone at the table. Aware of what was expected of him, Snow said, "Colonel, mind if I take Mr. and Mrs. Presley into that corner nook so we can chat for a while?"

Recalled Snow, "I realized instantly that Gladys had all the power, made all the decisions. So I carefully explained to her that, as partners, Parker and I would move Elvis up into the world of bigger concerts, get him on national television. And I promised to do all I could to convince RCA to sign him up."

Gladys was at first unimpressed. Then she leaned over and lamented, "Mr. Snow, they're just workin' him to death. He don't never come home."

Snow was reassuring: "All this will change." After all, bigger concerts and a record deal would lead to plenty of free time, "plenty of time to settle down and raise a family."

In tears, and tired of fighting both her son and her husband, Gladys Presley at last agreed to a contract that she knew would take Elvis away to other worlds she could only imagine. She was sure of only one thing: she would be left behind.

As flashbulbs popped and champagne was poured, she and Vernon summoned up false smiles and signed their names.

Only the uninitiated and ill-advised would have agreed to this financially ruinous document. Elvis was in debt to Parker, his "special adviser," the moment he signed the pact—which required Elvis to pay Parker $2,500 in five installments. In addition, he committed to playing one hundred concerts at $200 apiece, including the cost of musicians. Since Parker planned to raise Elvis's price to $500 a concert, he would earn more than his client.

Later that night Parker bragged to Snow that he had "suckered the Presleys." As the two drove back to Nashville, the Colonel patted his left coat pocket and said, "I had a second contract tucked right in here. It's far more realistic. If they signed the first one, I knew Elvis Presley would support me for the rest of his life."

Snow was elated. "Colonel, I think he's going to be big! We'll both do all right."

Parker stared blankly ahead. "You're wrong, Hank. I signed Elvis to myself exclusively. You aren't in it at all."

"But we're partners," said an astounded Snow. "Can you do that?"

"Check your contract, Hank."

Snow was not only angry with the Colonel, but felt sorry for Elvis. "It was a mess. I could have sued," he said decades later. "But it was too much trouble. I don't know why I was surprised. Parker was the most egotistical, obnoxious human being I ever met."

To this man the Presleys had just mortgaged their son's future.

6

Sing, Boy, Sing

On January 10, 1956, Elvis Presley—who had just turned twenty-one—stood ramrod straight in the Nashville recording studio of RCA Victor, two cold and barren rooms that were almost five times bigger than the Sun studio, which had been his artistic home for nearly two years. Surrounding him were worried-looking RCA executives in pinstripe suits, and recording engineers who had worked with country giants such as Hank Snow and Eddy Arnold. A single microphone, enormous and intimidating, hung just above Elvis's head.

"We wanted the impossible," remembered producer Steve Sholes, who compared his task to "catching fireflies in a bottle." Explained Sholes, "[Elvis's] voice was quicksilver, which slips through your fingers as you try to capture it."

Elvis was instructed to stand on a crudely painted X in the middle of the cavernous chamber. "Whatever you do, don't move," warned Sholes, a hulking bear of a man who treated all of his artists gently. Presley responded easily to Sholes's nurturing manner and slowly began to bond with the man who would be involved with his career for the next two decades.

Sholes realized the intricacies of capturing Presley's elusive, haunting vocal quality the moment Elvis sang the first chorus of "I Got a Woman." Sensing something was amiss, Sholes realized that the RCA master recorder was picking up only random lyrics, and random licks of the singer's guitar. Glancing worriedly at his new star, Sholes immediately saw what was wrong. As was his style, Elvis was moving—slipping and sliding—along with the music. He also occasionally reared his head back, in the hillbilly wail that made his sound so distinctive.

Since early in the century, when Enrico Caruso's tracks were laid down, RCA's performers had stood still as they recorded. In those primitive days if Caruso so much as moved his head from side to side, the enormous mike picked up only fragments of sound.

By performing in his signature fashion, Presley was moving in and out of the range of the enormous single mike. Thus, the sporadic audio.

"Kill it. Everybody take a break," Sholes instructed.

He slung his arms around Elvis's shoulders. "Look, I know you're used to doing the full routine onstage, but can't you do these songs while you are standing still?"

"No, sir," Elvis answered. "No, sir. I've gotta jump around to sing it right. It's something that just happens—just a part of the way I sing."

Sholes thought about this a minute, then confidently said, "I can fix that." After giving Elvis and the musicians a break, Sholes called in a crew of engineers, who totally remiked the Nashville studio to capture Presley's voice no matter where he was. Unwittingly, they partially re-created the echo effect that had been so integral to his Sun Records releases.

For all of its electronic wizardry, however, Elvis doubted that Victor could duplicate what his mentor, Sam Phillips, had achieved for him. Phillips had understood his concerns. He had sometimes worked day and night until the singer was satisfied with the results. Could this possibly happen in the fifty-year-old corporate world of RCA Victor?

Scotty Moore, who was playing guitar for the session, watched Elvis stand on his RCA X. "Even I felt like a piece of fresh meat—to be cut, diced, sliced any way that struck RCA's fancy. How must Presley have felt?"

Eight weeks earlier, Colonel Parker and Phillips had sold Elvis to RCA for $40,000—$35,000 of which went to Phillips and $5,000 to Elvis, to cover the royalties Sam owed him—after silently shopping the singer to labels including Dot, Atlantic and Columbia. The sale of the Presley contract made headlines because it was the highest amount ever paid for a pop vocalist.

Over the decades Phillips has been pressed about why he decided to sell Presley's contract. The reason is simple: he needed the money. As for Elvis, he initially worried about his future at a major label. Said Phillips, "He didn't know how comfortable he'd be in their studio and control room after having worked at Sun. I told him, 'Look, just be sure you're in charge of your sessions. You keep the creative control.'"

Once the RCA deal was agreed upon, two recording schedules were set: the Nashville session and another in New York on January 30.

According to the recording industry's powerful publication, *Billboard*, "The prevailing attitude is that anyone who buys Elvis Presley will get stuck!"

"RCA was convinced, despite his popularity, that he was good for only a handful of hit singles and an album or two before the public grew tired of this new 'fad,' rock 'n' roll," said Joan Deary, Sholes's assistant. "They all thought he was a flash in the pan. They even rushed up the recording sessions to get the product out there and sold before the novelty wore off."

When RCA publicist Anne Fulchino hired freelance photographer Alfred Wertheimer to follow Presley over a four-month period, she instructed, "Don't waste any color film on him. Use black-and-white. He may not last longer than six months."*

Gordon Stoker and the Jordanaires, Elvis's Nashville-based backup group, were warned again and again to get their money—fast. "We were told, 'Get it while you can because he won't be around for long,'" remembered Stoker. "All the record executives and heads of the Nashville publishing companies said that."

Still, by the first afternoon, Presley had completed recordings of "I Got a Woman," "Money Honey," "I Was the One," and a song no one liked but Elvis, a throbbing lament about the dark side of love. It was called "Heartbreak Hotel."

Elvis had first heard the song in the fall of 1955 when he was in Nashville and chanced to run into publicist Mae Boren Axton. She had closely followed Presley's career since the riot in Jacksonville. "What you need is a hit, honey," Axton told Elvis. Then she invited him to listen to a demo of a song she had written with Tommy Durden. The song had its origins in a newspaper article: a suicide victim had left a

---

*Ironically, forty years later, Wertheimer's photographs are some of the most sought-after images of Presley. Many of the photos command art gallery fees of $1,000 to $2,000 each.

note that read, "I walk a lonely street." In about twenty minutes Durden and Axton wrote the mournful dirge about ill-fated love and a hotel located "down at the end of Lonely Street."

In recording "Heartbreak Hotel," Elvis thought that even Sholes's ingenious remiking wasn't enough. So, in a brilliant stroke, Presley performed the song in a stairwell—resulting in the eerie echoes that characterized the soon-to-be monster hit, one of rock 'n' roll's anthems.

Elvis's raw rendition of the song rolled smoothly onto the tape. Though his version was copied almost note by note from the demo, the lonely howls were Presley's alone. "I never realized how haunted he was until I heard the playback. It was spine-chilling," said Deary.

When the session's rough tapes were flown to New York and played for the executive corps, they responded with dead silence. Internal RCA memos show that another executive meeting was convened after Sholes was ordered back to Nashville. Every one of the five men at the conference table hated "Heartbreak Hotel," particularly someone identified in the memos as "D.J.," who sternly commented, "We certainly can't release that one." Another executive, a marketing representative, noted that the marketing and distribution departments were in agreement: " 'Heartbreak Hotel' is a bomb."

"I don't get it," said the executive identified as D.J. "These songs don't sound like anything this kid has ever done. What's up?"

The January 30 recording session in New York boded no better. It started with Elvis's penchant for practical jokes: when he met the RCA executives, he greeted them with a jolting handshake—thanks to a handshake buzzer. Presley burst out laughing. The record company representatives were expressionless. Then, the Colonel alerted the press to Elvis's presence, who in turn broadcast the news to the teenage audience. "Great crowds of girls swarmed at the front entrance," said Deary. "It took our security force and the New York Police Department to keep them at bay. And later in the day we had to hire extra security guards. It was a nightmare."

Because word had leaked back to Elvis that the RCA brass hated his work, he was apprehensive during the New York session, working at a slow, determined pace doing rocked-up versions of songs such as "Blue Suede Shoes" and "My Baby Left Me."

Sholes by now realized that this singer's virtuosity had been unappreciated, obscured by his "aw-shucks" country-boy demeanor. This was not the country-pop artist they had signed. Elvis was trying to break new ground.

Sholes called Sam Phillips, who told him, "The worst thing you can do with Elvis is to mold him into some damned country-pop singer. . . . Just give him all the latitude he wants. That is primary, Steve."

The steady parade of executives who marched through the Manhattan control booth were not so foresighted. They watched glumly, occasionally shaking their heads. According to RCA's Deary, company insiders were saying they'd hired a freak—a musical curiosity with no staying power. "They demanded immediate completion of the first album so they could cash in," she recalled.

What RCA didn't know was that Sholes already had enough cuts for Elvis's first album by combining RCA songs with the best of the Sun Records sessions. And he was ecstatic.

As he watched Elvis from the booth, Sholes said sarcastically, "Gee, those sideburns bother me. I wonder if I should get him to a barber?" Turning to Deary, he smiled and added, "But, hell, you can't argue with this sort of success."

Actually, the late January release of "Heartbreak Hotel" was not the event that RCA had hoped for. "Oh, honey, that record came out and just laid there. And Steve Sholes called and asked, 'Did I buy the wrong man?' " recalled Phillips, who went on to reassure Sholes "to just be patient." Presley, meanwhile, never lost his faith in the song, which he performed in early, headline-making TV appearances and in concert. Slowly, teenagers across the country came to share in his passion for the downbeat requiem to lost love. By mid-April, it was number one on *Billboard*'s Top 40 pop charts. It also topped the country charts and the rhythm-and-blues countdown, making it the first record in history to top all three charts. This one single accounted for a fifth of RCA's sales that year.

Even so, the company's executives were not impressed. They wanted to mold Elvis into a "gentleman country singer." Among a series of secret internal RCA memos on the hit are documents proving that RCA had been monitoring Elvis since 1954. They had sent a scout incognito to gauge the results of Presley's final recording session at Sun. The prediction: "Sun Records has a hot new singer." The scout further surmised that "the Presley boy" had about a year's worth of "shelf life."

Yet by the end of 1956 Elvis had sold 10 million albums for RCA, accounting for one-half of the label's sales that year. He became the top-selling artist at the aging record company, eclipsing stalwarts Mario Lanza and Glenn Miller.

During his concerts, the instant he broke into "Heartbreak Hotel," audiences erupted into screams and applause unheard of on the circuit. But Elvis's fellow musicians weren't all cheering. "There was a lot of jealousy and resentment. I don't think there's any question about that," remembered Justin Tubb. At the *Louisiana Hayride*, where he now received $200 a show, Elvis sometimes got the cold shoulder. The simmering undercurrent of resentment eventually boiled over during a tour with Opry performers, including the Carter Sisters and Mother Maybelle and Charlie and Ira Louvin, who happened to be favorites of Gladys's.

Prior to a show, the Louvins were backstage, singing gospel hymns, when Elvis joined in. Afterward he declared, "Boy, this is my favorite music!"

"Why, you white nigger, if that's your favorite music, why don't you do that out yonder?" snapped Ira Louvin, pointing at the stage. He went on to badger Elvis about the music he performed as opposed to what he really wanted to sing.

As a red-faced Elvis told him—and as he would tell others—he performed the music he thought his audience wanted to hear.

To promote the record, Elvis had to drastically increase his tour schedule. But now, instead of strapping instruments atop a battered car, Red West packed them up in a spiffy new pink-and-gray trailer, emblazoned with Elvis's name and pulled by his Cadillac. "People don't realize that it was a lot of hard work, tears, and sleepless nights," Elvis once related. He began suffering a series of nightmares in which he was "fighting for his life" or "about to be in a car wreck" or was "breaking things."

On February 23, Elvis collapsed in the parking lot of the Gator Bowl in Jacksonville. "He just fell out cold," said Bill Black, who was loading instruments. When Elvis awakened at a local hospital, he was surrounded by attentive nurses and a doctor who sternly advised, "Slow down, or you won't be doing any concerts at all for the next couple of years." Elvis checked himself out, and the very next night he was back on the stage at the Gator Bowl.

He now put so much passion into his performances that he was soaking wet when he emerged from his sets, which now included the staccato drums of D. J. Fontana along with Scotty's guitar and Bill's bass. Elvis's gyrations had intensified and were now so suggestive that one night a booking agent standing in the wings looked out over a performance and gasped to the Colonel, "Goddamn! He's fucking! Right up there onstage. . . . Hell, he's screwing every woman in the audience."

Parker calmly replied, "Sex *is* a best-seller."

According to Gabe Tucker, who worked as a publicist for the Colonel, Parker himself was the one who suggested that Elvis crank up the bumps and grinds. In his memoirs, *Up and Down with Elvis Presley*, Tucker quoted the Colonel as telling Elvis, "I want you to shake your butt. It'll excite the girls. It's simply a turnabout of what a striptease artist does in her act to excite men."

Elvis later admitted that the "wild thing" persona was carefully constructed. "The Colonel made me controversial to get me going, but we haven't done anything bad. I trust him. He really is like a daddy to me when I'm away from home."

The show was not confined to the stage. Girls surrounded his motels and gathered in groups outside his house. When they stood on the streets outside his hotel, screaming, "Come to the window! Let us see you!" Elvis would peel off his shirt and thrust back his shoulders before walking back and forth. Sometimes he leaned out the window with a sultry look on his face, slowly caressing his chest, moving on to his neck, then running his fingers upward to his hair—eyes closed, mouth passionately open.

Along with shows came a rising obsession with his appearance. Again and again when Sun Records had negotiated to sell his contract, the competing record executives had stated that what made this boy truly different were his matinee idol qualities. So Elvis began using cosmetics.

Today, some male rock stars wear more makeup than models on runways. In the fifties, though, it was almost unheard of for men. During his tours Elvis relied on heavy Pan-Cake makeup to hide pimples, and both mascara and eye shadow to dramatize his already hypnotic eyes. Unfortunately, performing on the humid concert stages in the Deep South often caused his eye makeup to run. He would dab it off with a handkerchief, hoping no one would notice. Eagle-eyed and hostile reporters loved to mention his running mascara.

Because he represented a music form that was being targeted from all sides, and because the Colonel had long-range plans for him, Elvis had to be careful about what he did and whom he did it with. But so did his fifties-era dates. The women who became known as his girl-friends during this period all say that although they were tempted to have intercourse with him, they never did. After all, Elvis was a young man on the move and they had their "reputations" to consider.

Parker wanted the sexiness to be only for the show, not for real. So he had Elvis under surveillance—often by Presley's own friends, who were on the singer's payroll on these tours. "Be careful, Elvis. We don't want no problems," the Colonel repeatedly warned.

Elvis was bolder when he was with girls who were, to use an expression of the decade, "good sports" or "in the know." At one party Elvis sidled up to a platinum blond photographer's model and whispered, "I'll bet you aren't wearing any panties under that dress, are you?"

Though "groupies" had yet to come onto the music scene, young, knowing women showed up at Elvis's various hotels as he toured. When Elvis played Lexington, North Carolina, in late March 1956, girls gathered in the lobby of the New Lexington Hotel, where he was staying. According to a policeman who stood guard at the hotel, when Elvis came in at two-thirty in the morning and made his way up the stairs, one girl wanted to go with him. Instead, Elvis made arrangements for another young woman he had spotted. Said the policeman, "That's the one Elvis asked for and that's the one he got."

Some of these one-night stands had repercussions. One morning in South Carolina, Red West stood outside the door of Elvis's motel room and hollered, "Come on, man!" He beat on the door. "We got to hit the road!" As he looked at his watch, West wondered if they could make it in time to the next show.

Elvis was in no hurry. "Whatever that gal was doing, Elvis sure liked her act because he wouldn't get out of the sack," remembered West. Finally Elvis appeared, toting his guitar and gear and looking, said his friend, "like he had been mixed up with an eggbeater. She really gave him a going over."

After a frantic drive through rain, sleet, and winding roads, Red got the singer to an auditorium in Virginia. "Where in hell you been?" bellowed the Colonel, giving West a look "as if he was going to rip a yard from my ass." As Elvis raced to get ready, the Colonel read the riot act to West. "I was scared to go near [him] all night."

When another motel fling led to threats of rape charges, Elvis talked his way out of trouble by meeting with the girl's mother. He later bragged to musician David Houston that had he wanted, he probably "could have had the mother, too."

That crude attitude about women went public during an interview in San Antonio when Elvis was asked, "When do you think you'll get married?" "Why buy a cow," he quipped, "when you can get milk through the fence?" The remark infuriated the Colonel. In future interviews Elvis tried to politely duck the issue of matrimony.

Yet the shy boy in Elvis had not disappeared altogether.

According to Alan Fortas, an all-Memphis football halfback who became a bodyguard and part of the Presley entourage, "Elvis needed someone to baby more than he needed a sex partner. He craved the attention of someone who adored him without the threat of sexual pressure, much as a mother would."

Following the Presleys' move to a ranch-style house in an upper-middle-class Memphis neighborhood, Elvis befriended some of the young girls who used to cluster adoringly in his driveway, or outside the fence that was eventually erected. Some of the girls were as young as fourteen. Fortas said they were frequent houseguests who attended his concerts as part of "Elvis's personal traveling show."

Out in the backyard, they romped with Elvis in the Doughboy pool and challenged him to watermelon-seed spitting contests. They also slipped into his bedroom—which Gladys had decorated in flouncy pink-and-white floral wallpaper with matching bedspread—for rambunctious pillow fights. Sometimes they would all sit cross-legged with him on the bed, flipping through his fan magazines or admiring his stuffed-animal collection. Often they would all lie down together and cuddle. But what went on was horseplay, not foreplay. Amidst the giggling and silliness, and innocent hugs, Elvis assured them that he would never make any fast moves. "I'll never break a virgin," he said solemnly. "There's too many prostitutes walking around."

As Fortas once marveled, "Elvis, who could have had his pick of some of the world's most desirable women, spent a considerable amount of time with these fourteen-year-olds." As always, Elvis preferred to be in the company of girls and women, for Elvis himself had a strong feminine side. "He wasn't homosexual. In fact, he was fairly homophobic," said Sandra Harmon, who spent five years studying Presley's life as the co-author of *Elvis and Me*, the memoirs of Priscilla Beaulieu Presley. Nor was the singer bisexual. He was simply extremely sensitive at a time when such a quality wasn't considered masculine. For instance, when he was on tour with petite country singer Skeeter Davis, he confessed how shaken he had been by the news of her performing partner's death several years earlier. He had been driving a Crown Electric truck when he learned of the fatality. "It hurt me so bad that I had to pull over to the side of the road, where I wept and reached out to God." After the confession he proclaimed, "I'm telling you the truth, Skeeter!" He teared up as he added, "Do you think I'm weak? A man ain't supposed to cry."

With women he shared the latest revelations from the movie fan magazines he so loved, and he sometimes offered big-brotherly advice. He also freely dispensed hair-care and makeup techniques. In later years, Elvis would supervise "makeovers" of girlfriends, right down to the color of their hair.

When Elvis suggested to some of his Memphis Mafia buddies that they, too, might enjoy wearing makeup, the guys understandably balked. As a rule, though, Presley wanted the guys to see him at his most masculine. In fact, Elvis and his friends became known for their rough-and-tumble football games, and for bruised and bloodied skating sessions on the roller rink.

In front of them, Elvis played the guitar—though, ironically, he never, ever mastered it. "I mainly bang on it," he said truthfully. But in his quieter moments Elvis found solace at the keyboard; he was a self-taught pianist who played eloquently, without reservation, in front of women.

As long as her son "behaved," Gladys welcomed Elvis's female company, whatever their ages. After all, she enjoyed the companionship. She liked to ply the girls with Coca-Colas and huge slices of her famous coconut-frosted cake, which she baked for Elvis daily. She once startled a reporter, who had called the house looking for Elvis, when she casually replied, "Oh, he's in his bedroom with some li'l ole blonde."

Gladys would have loved to keep him at home forever.

Network brass and top producers repeatedly informed Tom Parker that he had no chance of getting his controversial boy on television. "Not photogenic enough," ruled Arthur Godfrey. "Offensive," declared the CBS censors. Ed Sullivan, who hosted the country's leading variety revue, initially said with a scowl he "wouldn't touch him with a ten-foot pole."

Parker refused to accept such shortsightedness. So one day in the fall of 1955 he mailed a brooding eight-by-ten glossy off to Jackie Gleason, who was a household name as the producer and star of CBS's hit comedy series *The Honeymooners*. But Gleason also produced a new variety program, *Stage Show*, starring bandleaders Tommy and Jimmy Dorsey. It was the lead-in program to *The Honeymooners*.

On the back of the photograph the Colonel scrawled, *JG: This is Elvis Presley. About to be Real Big. . . . Colonel.* The informal tone was a testament to Parker's long-time friendship with Gleason, who carried the picture into a key producers meeting and told his staff, "If this guy can make any kind of noise at all, let's sign him up."

"But he's an unknown," complained one of the bookers.

Gleason was renowned at the time for being one of the savviest men on TV. He knew a good thing when he saw it, and when he saw the photo of Elvis, he was intrigued. "Look, this guy is Brando with a guitar," Gleason insisted. "He has that same sensuous, sweaty animal magnetism that made Brando a star." Ever practical, Gleason paused before adding, "But first, let's find out if he can sing." After listening intently to Elvis's latest release, Gleason bellowed, "Sign him up!"

And so Elvis, backed by Scotty and Bill, was finally scheduled to sing "Shake, Rattle and Roll" on national television. Gleason gave the young sex symbol carte blanche when it came to the use of his hips and legs, snapping at a pesky CBS executive, "To hell with the censors!"

Back in Memphis, in anticipation of his national television debut—for which he would earn $1,250—Elvis choreographed the sexiest routine possible in front of a full-length mirror he installed for that specific purpose. Despite his own protestations of his onstage innocence ("I cain't help it, guys, my legs move along with the music. I'm not even conscious of it"), every sexual nuance was practiced hundreds of times before Presley at last walked out onstage on January 28, 1956.

The Dorsey show was Elvis Presley's first exposure to a national audience, and the young man gave it his all. He made certain that night's "Shake, Rattle and Roll" was the most overtly sexy version to date. When he climaxed it by segueing into the ending of "Flip, Flop and Fly," Gleason, who was watching from the control room, could only exclaim in an understatement, "Wow!" Clutching an oversize coffee mug, which actually contained Scotch, he instructed an assistant, "Run down there and have him sing another song."

When asked "Which song?" Gleason paused. "I dunno. Ah, that thing about I got a woman way downtown. Or uptown. Or wherever. He'll know what I mean."

Elvis broke into "I Got a Woman" with primitive intensity, and in the exuberance of the moment, Gleason booked the singer for five more appearances through the spring.

However, since the Dorsey show was a big-band revue, its biggest audience was older viewers, who tuned in to watch the weekly routines by the June Taylor Dancers and evolving variety acts, such as fifty bathing beauties playing the xylophone in tandem. During the three months of his *Stage Show* tenure, Elvis shared billings with jazz great Ella Fitzgerald and comedian Joe E. Brown, along with acrobats, the performing chimps Tippy and Cobina, a ventriloquist and his dummy, and an eleven-year-old organist. It was little wonder that in terms of ratings, Elvis made almost no impression on the show.

Realizing that he couldn't break Elvis nationally without a block-buster weekly show, Parker sent some tape from *Stage Show* and a stack of records to NBC's Milton Berle. Berle was one of the grand old men of early television, and at the time his influence was enormous. He earned the appellation Mr. Television because of his staggering popularity, especially among working-class viewers.

The Milton Berle Show booked Presley for the biggest show of the season, to be broadcast from the flight deck of the USS *Hancock*. Docked in San Diego Bay, it was manned by hundreds of young sailors—Presley's generation—who would serve as a live audience for Presley's three-song set and a goofy skit with Berle, who played his twin brother "Melvin Presley."

More than 40 million viewers—one out of every four Americans—tuned in to the show on April 3, 1956. Most of them were seeing the musical phenomenon for the first time.

But not everyone was appreciative of his talents. During the show's taping, when Elvis broke into "Blue Suede Shoes," drummer Buddy Rich, who was there performing with the Harry James Orchestra, rolled his eyes and declared to James, "This is the worst."

Berle went on to book Elvis for a second show on June 5. For this one Elvis spent weeks debating just how sexually charged his performance of the song "Hound Dog" was going to be. Written by Jerry Leiber and Mike Stoller for blues empress Big Mama Thornton, who turned it into a down-and-dirty hit, the song was ostensibly about a philandering gigolo. Elvis happened upon it in Las Vegas, where it was being performed in comedic style by Freddie Bell and the Bellboys. He later scoured the record shops of Memphis, searching for Thornton's 1953 version to use as a basis for his own jived-up redo.

Back in front of his private rehearsal mirror, with Big Mama blasting on the hi-fi, Elvis choreographed his rawest routine yet, doing a modified bump and grind punctuated at the end of each lyric with a thrust of his pelvis. He concluded the number by slowing down the tempo, bending backward as far as possible while rearing up on his toes. By lowering his eyes with each twist, he knew he would be sending a secret sexual message to his target audience, America's teenagers.

"This is dangerous stuff," he proudly told Gordon Stoker, who joined him on the show.

During the broadcast Elvis met Debra Paget, a stunning raven-haired, twenty-two-year-old starlet who was typecast in exotic roles, such as island princesses and Indian maidens. Within the year Paget would actually costar with Elvis in his first feature film. On this evening it was her "assignment" to mime Elvis's teenage fans by bursting into shrieks, grabbing him, and planting a big kiss on his lips.

She didn't need much prompting. Elvis's routine was as hot as he'd planned it. His rendition of "Hound Dog" stole the show and thereby ignited the wrath of ministers, newspaper columnists, community leaders, and especially, parents across the country.

The New York Times' powerful television critic, Jack Gould, sounded the clarion call when he accused Elvis of having a "tin ear" and of dressing abominably. "Mr. Presley has no discernible singing ability, but he is a rock and roll variation on one of the most standard acts in show business: the virtuoso of the hootchy-kootchy ... a gyration which never had anything to do with the world of popular music and still doesn't."

Scores of other newspapers followed Gould's lead, with coverage that included liberal uses of the words "obscene" and "suggestive." A photo that often accompanied the stories captured Presley in full grind, up on his toes, his torso thrown forward and his head tossed back, lost in the passion of the music.

Called upon for a response to the media assault, Presley continually played the wide-eyed innocent: "My arms and legs just follow the music." In an interview with the Charlotte Observer, he said, "Debra Paget had on a tight dress and wiggled more than I did. She bumped-pooshed all over the place ... talk about sex! But who do they say is obscene? Me!"

Steve Allen, the most erudite of television variety-show hosts, could always be counted on to voice his opinion. His prediction for young Presley was "Elvis is a flash in the pan. He won't last a year."

However, Allen quietly set out to hire Presley to headline his new NBC variety show, which ran opposite CBS's warhorse, The Ed Sullivan Show. Though Presley had been deemed "dangerous" by the NBC censors, Allen's executive producer, Billy Harbach, didn't care. "After all," he explained simply, "we were out to beat Ed Sullivan." But the censors warned, "Be ready to cut this guy off at the waist, any second."

Allen's plan was more calculating. First, he decreed that the hepcat be imprisoned in black tie and tails, tailored so excruciatingly tight that the mere bending of a knee would burst the inseam of the pants. The lines of the coat would cut deeply up into the armpits. The entire effect was castration by costume.

Even more belittling, Allen accessorized the act with a trained hound dog—wearing a little top hat and tuxedo collar—which Presley was to serenade with "Hound Dog." Backstage, when Allen described the sequence to Elvis, the young singer glumly looked down at his feet, then up at the Colonel, obviously hoping for rescue. When his manager failed to meet his eyes, Elvis again looked downcast.

"Parker was always there in the background but not making any demands," recalled Harbach. "And Elvis was in a haze, acting very naive, almost as if network television was too much for him."

Prior to airtime, though, in the dressing room with the Jordanaires, Elvis angrily paced back and forth, unable to sit down, incapable of asserting his rights. Gordon Stoker grabbed his shoulder: "Look, man, if you don't want to do this, just tell them that you're the boss. Tell Allen you're going to do this song as you always do."

Elvis's eyes flashed briefly. Then he looked at the floor and muttered, "Oh, hell, man, let them have their way. I'm not going to argue with them."

"I could tell he was always running scared when it came to Colonel Parker," said Stoker. "Elvis was afraid if he gave him any back talk or any trouble that all the success would vanish. Since he was resigned to play that hound dog skit, we gave him as much support as possible."

That night Elvis made the best of a bad situation. After all, it was *The Steve Allen Show*. Not only did he caress the chin of the sad-eyed dog, he even gave it a quick kiss at the end of the song.

As if performing with the hound dog wasn't enough, Elvis also appeared in a hillbilly skit in which he had to spout illiterate dialogue and wear a six-gun alongside costars Imogene Coca and Andy Griffith. "Elvis despised that show," said Stoker. "He never wanted it mentioned again, and he never, ever watched the tape they sent him. He was hurt deeply by the slurs on his background; he knew they were laughing at him, and it hurt bad."

For Steve Allen, Elvis's appearance paid off big time. The show trounced *The Ed Sullivan Show*. That night *The Steve Allen Show* was watched by 55.3 percent of the television audience, compared to Sullivan's 39 percent.

The next day, Ed called the Colonel, agreeing to meet the asking price of $50,000 for three appearances. What followed marked a turning point in the career of Elvis Presley.

The Ed Sullivan Show wasn't just TV's top variety series, it was *the* variety series. Its stone-faced host, who also wrote a Broadway newspaper column, was just as famous as the stars of the day—many of whom had made their TV debuts on his series. Dean Martin and Jerry Lewis first appeared on *Sullivan*; so did legends Bob Hope and Jackie Gleason, back when the show was called *Toast of the Town*. So powerful was the *Sullivan Show* that it turned a rodent into a household name: little Italian mouse puppet Topo Gigio was one of Ed's favorite guests.

Decades later, *Washington Post* television critic Tom Shales explained the conditions that made Sullivan cave in: "Elvis came on and 'wiggled hip deep' in the American mainstream when he sang 'Hound Dog,' 'Blue Suede Shoes' and 'Heartbreak Hotel.' In cultural terms it was like splitting the atom or inventing the lightbulb. All hell broke loose."

While he was still seething over the *Allen* skit, Elvis agreed to speak with Hy Gardner, the host of New York's most popular late-night television show, *Hy Gardner Calling*. The program had a split-screen format, showing Gardner speaking from the TV station on one side and his guest on the other. Elvis spoke by phone from his room at the Warwick Hotel.

After opening pleasantries Gardner quickly honed in on Elvis's critics. "Your style of gyration has been bitterly criticized. Do you bear any animosity to these critics?"

"Well, not really. Those people have a job to do, and they do it."

"And do you think you have learned anything from the criticism leveled at you?" Gardner wondered, sounding like a father admonishing his child.

Elvis was adamant: "No, I do not."

Gardner actually pursed his lips when he said, "You have not, eh?"

"No, because I don't feel I've done anything wrong," the young man proudly insisted. "I don't see that any type of music would have a bad influence on people. It's only music. I can't figure it out. I mean, in a

lot of papers they say rock 'n' roll is a big influence on juvenile delinquency. I don't think it is."

Whatever Elvis thought, rock 'n' roll had unleashed a hurricane of
controversy. And the twenty-one-year-old from Memphis was caught in
the eye of the storm.

Wild in the Country

lvis Presley was by no means the first rock 'n' roller. As its most prominent representative during the fifties, though, he was a magnet for the fiery criticism directed toward the music. In his panoramic study *The Fifties*, Pulitzer Prize–winning journalist David Halberstam proclaimed, "In cultural terms, [Elvis's] coming was nothing less than the start of a revolution."

When Elvis came onto the scene, the established hitmakers were artists such as Frank Sinatra, Rosemary Clooney, Joni James, Perry Como, Doris Day, Eddie Fisher, and the Ames Brothers. Yet at the same time a wholly unprecedented phenomenon was taking place. Starting early in the decade, the growing popularity of "race" artists such as Fats Domino, Little Richard, and Chuck Berry was changing the face of music. They had a startling new sound—a raw mix of gospel and rhythm and blues, which Cleveland disc jockey Alan Freed christened "rock 'n' roll."

Not until rock 'n' roll was performed by *white* artists, however, would the music become accessible. With their one-two punch of "Shake, Rattle and Roll" and "Rock Around the Clock," Bill Haley and his Comets were foremost among the pioneers. The "black sound" of Elvis Presley's voice would provide a vital transition, and Elvis's

willingness to defy the status quo paved the way for an entire generation of young people. Writing in the *New York Times* magazine, Robert
Blair Kaiser noted, "Little white girls in middle America had a hard
time getting any kind of fantasy going with a black man. It was easy,
though, with Elvis."

When Elvis blew into the arena, it didn't matter that he had acne,
or that his blond hair hung in greasy clumps. Or that initially he spoke
with an accent thick as grits. Teenagers realized that he was the musical
equivalent of cinema rebels such as James Dean and Marlon Brando.
His music brought fear to their parents and teachers. As did his sexual
posturing.

From coast to coast, extreme measures were taken. In San Antonio,
Texas, rock 'n' roll was banned from jukeboxes near the public swimming pools, to keep "undesirable elements" from dancing together in
their bathing suits. In Asbury Park, New Jersey, the music could not be
played in city dance halls; in San Jose, California, it was prohibited in
civic buildings. Boston went a step further: it labeled disc jockeys
"social pariahs," responsible for "increased juvenile delinquency." As
such, the deejays were forbidden to participate in record dances.

The media stampeded to analyze the phenomenon—and the young
singer who had come to be its prophet. Elvis was often humiliated in
print. The leading Catholic magazine, *America*, warned parents that
Elvis delivered "a striptease with clothes on."

Aline Mosby of United Press grilled him about the findings of a psychiatrist who said that bobby-soxers were reacting to the sexual over-
tones of his movements. Elvis disputed the theory, claiming he wasn't
trying to be sexy. Along with reporting his comments, Mosby dryly
noted that during the interview Elvis wore a brightly colored sport shirt
unbuttoned almost to the waist.

Asked by *Cosmopolitan* to assess the young performer's impact, jazz
musician Eddie Condon said Presley's singing sounded like something
out of the dog pound and surmised that like "mah-jongg . . . [and] John
Dillinger," the Elvis infatuation would pass. He went on to quote his
pal Jackie Gleason as saying, "He can't last."

After asking Elvis what his mother thought of the furor, Associated
Press quoted him, demeaningly printing its version of his accent:
" 'Momma,' ah said, 'Momma, you think ahm vulgah on the stage?' " As
Elvis went on to explain, "Ah can't help it. Ah just have to jump arown'
when ah sing." As if that wasn't cruel enough, the Associated Press
article made mention of his "décolletage" and his pompadoured hair.

In Britain, the *Evening News* likened Elvis to "a shouting, screaming dervish" and said that a "top psychiatrist" had determined that rock 'n' roll was both "cannibalistic and tribalistic."

Even the scandal magazines joined in, with *Whisper* asking, "Is the Elvis Presley Craze Crippling America's Youth?" The publication went on to warn parents of the purported physical ailment "rock 'n' roll shoulder."

As moral indignation grew, Elvis's concerts became increasingly controversial. When he returned to Jacksonville, Florida, in August 1956, authorities didn't want a repeat of the riot he had generated there in 1955. "Keep it clean," ordered local juvenile court judge Marion Gooding, who prohibited any bumps and grinds. Elvis did the concert practically standing still.

To offset Elvis's influence on Jacksonville's young people, a local church held a social, complete with "respectable" dance. It was preceded by a sermon entitled "Hotrods, Reefers and Rock 'n' Roll."

The hostile reaction caused Elvis to lament, "I can't figure out what I'm doing wrong. I know my mother approves of what I'm doing . . . If I had a teenage sister, I certainly would not object to her coming to watch a show like this."

Only on rare occasions did Elvis snap at his critics.

During one radio interview a disc jockey surprised Elvis by reading aloud an attack by Herb Rau of the *Miami News*. Rau had called Elvis a "no-talent performer" and "the biggest freak show in history." The young singer countered, "He ain't nothin' but an idiot, or he wouldn't sit up and write all that stuff. He just hates to admit that he's too old to have any more fun." As for Rau likening him to a strip artist, Elvis shot back, "Well, he should know. I guess that's where he hangs out."

Another time, when told that a station in Nova Scotia had tossed out all of his records, Elvis deadpanned, "I didn't know there were any radio stations in Nova Scotia."

Though his response was muted, privately he was hurt by the barbs aimed at his Southern roots. When both *Life* and *Newsweek* branded him a "hillbilly," Elvis realized what they really meant was "redneck." He also bristled at the media's use of the word *rockabilly*. "Elvis felt the term was a put-down, like *poor white*, or *white trash*," said his cousin Gene Smith.

Ironically, the media never took cheap shots at Pat Boone, one of Elvis's leading competitors and a fellow Southerner. As it happened, Boone was also the antithesis of Presley. At twenty-two, Boone—a direct descendant of Daniel Boone—was married, the father of three, and a student at Columbia University, where he maintained a straight-A average. While Elvis had been deemed too "greasy" for the Arthur Godfrey television show, the clean-cut Boone—known for his pastel cardigans and white buck shoes—was a repeat guest. Pat's song "I Almost Lost My Mind" was a top seller when some of Elvis's songs were lingering lower on the list. Naturally, the media concocted a "feud" between the two entertainers (who, odd as it might seem, actually liked and respected each other).

But for all the opposition, Presleymania was in full swing. When a disc jockey in Boston claimed to have seven strands of Presley's hair—the removal of which was allegedly witnessed by a notary public—five thousand listeners wrote in requesting the hairs as souvenirs.

As the result of a deal arranged by the Colonel with Hank Saperstein—who was responsible for Disney's Davy Crockett merchandise line—there would soon be an array of products bearing Elvis's likeness. From bookends to bracelets, from lipstick to denim jeans, the campaign was, reported *Daily Variety*, "unprecedented" as the first merchandising drive aimed at teenagers with their own money to spend.

Life, famous for its photographic essays, showed teenage boys lined up for ducktails at barbershops. A sixteen-year-old in Romeo, Michigan, made news when he was expelled from school because of his "Elvis Presley haircut." The circuit judge who upheld the school's expulsion noted, "The court does not quarrel with the right of the individual to be as ridiculous as he chooses to be. However, the school board has the responsibility to maintain discipline."

These attempts were merely swimming against the tide. In Tennessee, a fifty-member Anti-Elvis Presley Club sent petitions to deejays, asking them to "stop spinning Elvis's platters." But the campaign lasted only two weeks, after protests from Elvis fans.

Unlike many stars, Elvis did not endure his army of fans; he loved them. Whenever possible, he took the time to talk with fans, pose for snapshots, and to sign autographs. As he often said, "If it weren't for the fans, I wouldn't even be here."

Up to four thousand letters a day were arriving at the national office of the Elvis Fan Club, which oversaw clubs across the country. One such club, based in rural Victoria, Texas, was run by fourteen-year-old Gregg Barrios, who traveled 240 miles round trip by bus with his club members to see Elvis in concert in San Antonio. Once there, they presented their membership cards and were ushered backstage, where

Elvis hugged the female members and shook hands with Barrios, who was relieved to discover that his idol had a poor complexion—that "he wasn't perfect looking." Barrios's club later participated in a March of Dimes program promoting the Salk polio vaccination. The entire fan club was vaccinated and, in turn, received an autographed photo of Elvis receiving his shots.

After several girls ran away from home and hitchhiked to Memphis in hopes of meeting their idol, Gladys Presley sent a letter to the clubs, warning fans that they shouldn't journey to Memphis without their parents' permission. Anyone who did, said Gladys, would not get to meet her son.

There was even an Elvis Presley Midget Fan Club, though this was just a publicity stunt. Colonel Parker came up with the idea for recruiting members from the carnival circuit and Hollywood, including some of the original Munchkins from the classic film *The Wizard of Oz*. Elvis laughed when he heard about that one.

With the growing fan worship came explosive consequences.

In San Diego, where Elvis's opening acts consisted of a female vocalist, an acrobatic dance team, a comedian, and a xylophone player, the audience was so unruly during his performance that he had to repeatedly tell them to sit down "or the show ends!" The performance that ensued so infuriated police chief A. E. Jansen that he put Presley on notice: if he ever returned to town and delivered a similar show, he would be jailed for disorderly conduct.

At Houston's city auditorium, where he wore a heavily padded purple sports coat with black slacks, he pleaded with the packed house of four thousand to quiet down enough to listen to him. They wouldn't. But at the show's climax they did hear his goofy closing line: "It's been a wonderful show, folks. Just remember this. Don't go milkin' the cow on a rainy day. If there's lightning, you may be left holding the bag." The arena thundered with female screams.

In Amarillo, girls kicked out the plate-glass window of the arena to rush Elvis—and request that he autograph their arms and their underwear. By now girls were opening their blouses for him, so he could sign their bras. In the riot that followed, Elvis lost his own shirt and was scratched and bruised.

Only swank Las Vegas was left untouched. From the time Elvis and his cousin Gene Smith pulled up in front of the entrance to the New Frontier Hotel on April 23, Presley felt as if he had been transported to another universe. The otherworldly feel intensified when he encountered a twenty-foot likeness of himself—"The Atomic-Powered Singer"—that stood guard over the casino entrance.

Once inside the New Frontier, Elvis was awestruck. There were lilac carpeting and lilac and magenta walls and chandeliers in the shape of flying saucers. The Cloud 9 Cocktail Bar had wall reliefs of planets and spacecraft, and in the Venus Room, where Elvis was to open for bandleader Freddy Martin and comedian Shecky Greene, the stage revolved—like the solar system. For all its space-age decor, however, the Venus Room—like all Las Vegas entertainment venues—was not pioneering in its choice of performers. The gambling capital lured high rollers with "respected" names such as Marlene Dietrich, Noël Coward, Lena Horne, the McGuire Sisters, and Sophie Tucker. Typical of the hot "new" talent was the pop vocal quartet The Four Lads—whose members were former choir boys. They were playing the Thunderbird when Elvis came into town.

The rock 'n' roll star may have been a gamble, but the Colonel saw to it that he was well paid for his two-week engagement. Elvis received $7,500 a week—a hefty fee for a newcomer. (By contrast, at the Riviera, veteran headliner Liberace was making $50,000 weekly and Marlene Dietrich $100,000.) The money was also reportedly paid in cash. After all, said the Colonel, "they got an atom-bomb testing place out there in the desert. What if some feller pressed the wrong button?"

On opening night, the moment Elvis nervously introduced his hit tune "Heartbreak Motel," he knew he was in trouble. He was performing before a dinner crowd, amid the clanking of dishes and the clattering of silverware, and he was greeted by blank expressions. The reaction didn't improve during his low-down rendition of "Blue Suede Shoes." In fact, the adult audience only warmed up when Freddy Martin appeared onstage to begin his lavish $40,000 floor show, which included sumptuous Tchaikovsky selections. Then came Shecky Greene, with his popular routine about Mademoiselle Gouletush.

Today one of Las Vegas's most venerable names, Greene acknowledges that, in retrospect, "the booking was pretty mish-mash. The whole idea of having Elvis lead into Freddy Martin was ridiculous." Adds Greene, "I don't know what the management expected of the kid. He wasn't prepared for doing a Las Vegas show. The songs weren't right for the crowd, his clothes weren't right, he had no production."

Critics who had been gunning for Presley had a field day. Typical of the jabs was *Newsweek*'s wry comment that he was "like a jug of corn liquor at a champagne party." Even other Vegas acts poked fun. In the

Casbah Room of the Sahara, Frank Ross, of the Mary Kaye Trio, wore tattered blue jeans and a torn shirt in a takeoff of a hillbilly singer. He didn't know it, but Elvis was seated among the audience. Presley laughed along with everyone else, but inside he was seething. He later defended his Las Vegas stint, noting, "The hotel kept me two weeks, didn't they? They don't keep flops two weeks."

In fact, the Las Vegas stay wasn't a total disappointment. Elvis sold out a special show for the town's teenagers, who later chased him to his hotel suite, broke down the door, and stripped him of his shirt. When he wasn't performing, he also took advantage of the town's amenities, including its twenty-four-hour restaurants and round-the-clock menus. One morning he had two orders of cantaloupe and ice cream before ordering a full breakfast, with a large side dish of bacon. He also got an autograph from Liberace, which he promptly presented to his mother when he returned home to Memphis.

His family had just moved into a $40,000, seven-room ranch-style house on Audubon Drive. Elvis bought them the home, which became a tourist attraction. But it wasn't just young women who were rushing to see Elvis.

As his uncle Vester noted, "He had the looks and he had the personality. The looks got the women, the personality got the men." In disciple-like fashion, his inner circle grew to slowly extend beyond kinfolk and high school buddies. Lamar Fike used to hang around the gates outside Audubon until he was invited in. Cliff Gleaves, a raucous disc jockey and sometimes rockabilly singer, met Presley in downtown Memphis. Days later Presley summoned him to New York. And Gleaves, known for his fast, furious jokes (and the drawn-out disclaimer, "Good God, mister! Good God!"), later accompanied him to Hollywood, joining what he called Presley's "good ole boy network." Elvis loved people for their entertainment value. As his (colorful) friend Lance Le Gault once surmised, "He had this attitude that life is short enough already. Enjoy it by being around people you like."

Sadly, the person he loved most turned to reclusiveness and martyrdom. For Gladys's only interest was Elvis.

On those occasions when Elvis brought home girlfriends, Gladys clung to them—believing the right girl could fulfill her ultimate fantasy of having Elvis living next door, with a doting wife and a passel of grandchildren.

In June Juanico, Gladys thought she had found the one. A brunette with bewitching eyes—eyes that reminded Gladys of her son's—June was just seventeen when she caught Elvis's attention in 1955 in a Biloxi, Mississippi, nightspot. Elvis had just performed in a show with Marty Robbins and Sonny James and was en route to his next gig at Keesler Air Force Base.

Though Presley was immediately taken by her striking appearance, and her gutsy demeanor, he didn't see June again until the summer of 1956 when she happened to be in Memphis, visiting friends. On a whim she went to the house at Audubon, where she stood among the crowd of fans. Elvis spied June as he pulled his Cadillac into the driveway. He was returning from a grueling tour: as with many of his romances, timing was crucial.

Though he still occasionally saw Dixie Locke and had a new, sophisticated Memphis girlfriend named Barbara Hearn, Presley embarked on a madcap summer romance with June, of which Gladys approved. But, in a whisper, she warned her son, "You just better not let Colonel Parker know how serious you are about June. You know how he feels, especially about marriage."

The advice was part of Gladys's tragic attempt to regain control of her son. She and Parker were locked in a vigorous struggle over control of the boy. Gladys was determined to get him married and settled near her. The Colonel was equally determined that Elvis maintain his image of a rock 'n' roller who was "available" to the legions of girls filling the concert stands. The Colonel wouldn't even sanction a steady girlfriend.

But in June Juanico, Gladys sensed someone with enough strength to be able to stand up to the Colonel.

While June was in Memphis, Elvis shared his childhood haunts with her, taking her to Lauderdale Courts, where he pointed out the old family unit, then on to Humes High, where he laughed about his efforts in shop class. To impress her further, he proudly showed her off to Dewey Phillips, a man the young singer still regarded as a close friend and confidant. Elvis and June also held hands as they strolled through the tiny recording studio where his fame originated. Throughout, Elvis showed June a sweet and unaffected nature—the opposite of his onstage persona.

When they went to Mississippi's Occan Springs resort for a July vacation, he told her a story he had believed in since childhood. While sitting on a pier, looking at the nighttime sky, he said that if she let her mind and body relax and closed her eyes, she could float right into space and nestle between the stars and the moon.

Celestial bodies weren't all Elvis was interested in. He desperately wanted to have sex with June, who adamantly refused. He had already told her he couldn't get married *for years*—because his career came first, and because the Colonel felt it was important that he remain single.

"I've gone out with a lot of guys and never really done anything," she told him.

He teased, "Does that mean you're still a cherry?"

June proudly shot back, "I'm not only a cherry, George. I'm the whole pie."

As Juanico noted five decades later, "It was another time, another sensibility. There were a lot of virgins running around—including me." She had her suspicions about Elvis, as well. "I had the feeling he really hadn't been around all that much, because he was so gentle." They were both apprehensive. The big fear then, reminded June, was pregnancy. "And if you got pregnant, you got married."

She did allow him to kiss her passionately. And they engaged in serious and creative foreplay. When Elvis's parents came down to Ocean Springs after their son told them about the boating and the deep-sea fishing, Gladys Presley became enamored of her son's latest girlfriend. But when things became too quiet in the bedroom of Elvis's rented house, Gladys would tap at the door.

June and Elvis were snuggling in the bed one morning, both practically naked, when they heard Gladys's voice from outside: "Elvis . . . we don't want no babies."

During this vacation Elvis went deep-sea fishing one day with June, her mother, his parents, and Eddie Bellman, a friend of June's. The weather was idyllic as they sped through the Gulf, twenty miles off the coast, on the *Aunt Jenny,* a converted shrimp boat. Sauntering about, stripped to the waist, Elvis and Eddie worked to land a shimmering bonito. June, her hair in bobby pins beneath a scarf, urged them on. So did Elvis's mother, who hollered, "You can do it, baby!"

His mother wore a pink shirtwaist dress with pearls; Vernon was in a shirt and slacks. Elvis had called them at the last minute, urging them to join him on the coast. They did not bring their "resort" clothes with them.

Eddie Bellman's 8-mm movie footage of that day shows a relaxed Elvis cavorting with June on the deck, moving in for kisses as they rolled on the stern. As Juanico later recalled, Elvis liked to be near the water—because he liked his hair to be wet. "He liked his hair dark." When it was wet, the blond turned to brown.

According to Juanico, during his Mississippi stay Elvis proposed one hot, sticky night. But the offer came with a disclaimer: "Will you wait for me?" he asked. "I can't get married for the next three years."

Whatever the truth of that statement is, Colonel Parker put an end to Elvis's romantic dreams. "He was dead set against me," Juanico said. "Colonel Parker just wanted me out of the picture completely." After all, she added, "I was a threat to Elvis's career, his future."

Indeed, when a local radio station reported that June had said the two were engaged, Elvis dropped in on the station to put such talk to rest, stressing, "I have no plans for marriage."

He moved on to Florida, for three weeks of manic concerts. Anne Goldman—then a twenty-year-old "girl reporter" for the *St. Petersburg Times*—didn't think anything of it when she was assigned to cover his show at Tampa's Fort Homer Hesterly Armory ("where they also held the wrestling matches"). Like many journalists of the day, she was assigned to cover a phenomenon as opposed to a star. As Goldman pointed out, "You have to remember, nobody really knew that Elvis was going to become what Elvis became." Still, she was overwhelmed when she came upon the lines of anxious teenage girls awaiting Presley's arrival at the armory. She was also charmingly disarmed by the singer— who playfully nuzzled her, to the delight of the paper's photographer.

As summer came to an end, Presley readied for his first starring role in the movies. Hollywood would put added distance between mother and son, as well as between Presley and girlfriends such as June Juanico. The women in Elvis's life would increasingly come from the world of show business.

One of them was Dottie Harmony. She was working as a dancer at the Sahara when Elvis chanced to be in town, on a brief vacation.

But it wasn't Presley who approached the petite blonde as she sat at a table in a casino. It was a young stranger with a heavy Southern accent who said, "Ma'am, Elvis would like to have a drink with you."

"Get lost," said Harmony, who thought the man was joking.

The stranger reappeared a few minutes later, repeating the request. This time Harmony realized he was serious but demanded, "Look, if Elvis wants to have a drink with me, he'll have to ask me." The emissary turned and walked away, "and I thought that was the end of that."

Soon afterward she realized someone was nearby. She turned to see Elvis at her side, kneeling, looking into her eyes. "Ma'am," he gallantly offered, "you're the most beautiful woman in the world. Would you have a drink with me?" So began his courtship of this brash blond beauty.

The two wound up sharing a restaurant booth where they sipped Cokes and made plans for a date. "Could you find someone for my cousin Gene and we'll double?" asked Elvis. Dottie lined up a girlfriend, and she and Elvis and Gene Smith later met at the Sahara, where fans kept encircling Elvis, who interminably signed autographs. "Look, did you ask me out so you could sign autographs? Or did you ask me out?" Harmony snapped. Elvis was so thrown by her audacity that he grabbed the hand of her girlfriend—leaving Dottie with Gene.

Once outside, Elvis and his impromptu partner climbed into the front seat of his Cadillac, consigning Dottie to the back with Gene. Presley silently drove down the city's so-called Miracle Mile of neon-adorned hotels, passing the elegant new Sands, the wood-and-stone-arched entrance of Wilbur Clarke's Desert Inn, the champagne towers of the Flamingo, and the Dunes with its enormous fiberglass sultan standing guard atop the entrance. As they headed farther out the highway that led to the desert, Elvis said little. But to Dottie's bemusement, he studied her from the rearview mirror.

"He was pissed," she said, laughing.

Eventually, the foursome wound up at the distant Hacienda Hotel, which stood fortresslike on a solitary stretch of the Las Vegas Strip. Billy Wood, an old friend of Elvis's, was performing there, along with the Dominos. "You guys wanna go on in and see the show?" mumbled Elvis as he guided the group through the casino.

Later, in the Hacienda lounge, Dottie caught Elvis eyeing several beautiful women who were seated in one of the booths. So she started looking around, too. Elvis reacted angrily, kicking the table and flinging aside several chairs. "C'mere!" he said, taking her by the hand. "What are you doin'—cuttin' your eyes for those other guys?"

Harmony was recalcitrant, declaring, "If you can do it, so can I."

For the remainder of his Las Vegas stay, Elvis tried to be as attentive as possible. They saw shows. They went to McCarran Airport and watched the planes landing and taking off— "Elvis just loved that," recalled Harmony. They took drives through the desert at dawn. During one of the drives they came upon an old man with a "beat-up old truck," which had a flat tire. Elvis matter-of-factly pulled his Cadillac over, got out, and changed the tire. "And he didn't think another thing about it," said Harmony.

At his suite at the New Frontier they sometimes curled up to watch old movies on television. They saw *Wuthering Heights* and discussed how sad they felt for the ill-fated lovers, Cathy and Heathcliff. And they applauded Bette Davis's brassy performance as the society climber of *Mr. Skeffington*. "Elvis was a big Bette Davis fan," said Harmony.

She was introduced to Gladys during one of Elvis's daily phone conversations with his mother. "When he was through talking with her, he put me on," said Harmony. During one of their talks, Gladys exclaimed, "Darty [Elvis's pet name for Dottie], you will not believe the tomatoes I've grown! As big as your two fists!"

Harmony had claimed to be twenty-one when she arrived in Las Vegas, but she had lied. She was actually eighteen, although wise beyond her years. As much as she liked Elvis, she saw that he was enormously spoiled and possessive, and she didn't like to be owned by anyone—not even a famous singer. So the two never progressed to a sexual relationship— "Remember, this was during the fifties," said Harmony—but they developed a closeness and enjoyed playing off each other's contrasting traits.

To Elvis, the Brooklyn-born Harmony was tougher than the Southern belles he had courted. Unlike the Memphis girls, she was savvy about show business—she had worked in both Hollywood and Las Vegas. And unlike some of the other women who acquiesced to his every demand, she wouldn't. The challenge excited him.

He pestered her about her smoking. "I'll give up cigarettes if you quit biting your nails," she told him. Then he tried to talk her into eating more. "You're such an itty-bitty thing," he would say of her five-foot-four, ninety-eight-pound frame, which he thought was too frail. She tried to placate him by drinking more milk shakes. But instead of gaining weight, she lost. Elvis was perplexed. Already he had the tendency to get fleshy, thanks to an insatiable appetite that was already becoming legendary. During one single sitting he put away eight deluxe cheeseburgers, two bacon, lettuce, and tomato sandwiches, and three chocolate milk shakes—a feat that made the newspapers.

His dates with Dottie also garnered press. As a result, when she showed up in Memphis to spend the Christmas holidays with the Presleys, the girls in town had been forewarned.

Harmony was exhausted from lack of sleep when her plane at last touched down on the runway. She had endured two days of travel woes trying to get to Tennessee. But once inside the airport she realized no one was there to meet her—save for a group of girls who carried a banner that read, "Go home, Dottie Harmony!" Confident that eventually someone from Presley's retinue would be coming for her, she took a seat next to a radiator and was lulled asleep by its warmth.

She was awakened, finally, by Elvis—who gently shook her shoulder.

"I'm here at last!" Dottie squealed slightly as Elvis swooped her into his arms and carried her out to his waiting car. Inside the Cadillac, Dottie snuggled back into the leather upholstery and wondered what his family would be like.

The moment the door swung open at the Audubon house, she felt enormous warmth for Gladys, whom she heartily embraced. "But I didn't hug Vernon," recalled Harmony. "Somehow, it didn't seem that I should."

After her ordeal to get to Memphis, what Dottie wanted was sleep. But Gladys had other plans.

"Y'all have got some Christmas shopping to do," she said, plopping a list for girls in Dottie's hand and one for boys in Elvis's.

And so, Dorothy "Dottie" Harmony spent her first Memphis date with Elvis on a shopping spree in a major downtown department store. "He shopped in the men's section, I was in the women's." When crowds spied the singer, there was a stampede through the aisles—and Elvis made an escape in a car waiting outside. Now Dottie was both dead tired and stranded. Eventually someone came to rescue her and take her back to the Presley home, where she was given Elvis's pink-and-white bedroom. He slept in the playroom.

During her visit with the Presleys, Dottie witnessed the undivided attention Gladys lavished on her son. "She made him a coconut cake every single day. And she would mash bananas and mix them up with peanut butter for him. She just loved to feed him."

Dottie was amazed to find that nothing he did seemed to upset his mother, no matter how outrageous. One afternoon he spied a monkey in a pet store and impulsively purchased it and brought it home. Gladys didn't say a thing. "She wanted Elvis to be happy," said Dottie, who had to hold the rambunctious monkey on the drive from the pet store to Audubon. She was wearing a white dress, with a red leather coat with white satin lining, and of course Jimbo, the little monkey, had to have a bowel movement in the car.

Elvis pulled his car into a gas station, sending Dottie and the monkey into the ladies' room to clean up, while he cleaned out his white interior. "But the monkey got loose in the rest room and was running around in there, and I couldn't catch it," recalled Harmony.

When Jimbo was at last cornered and snatched up, she returned to the car, throwing Elvis an angry look. He salvaged her coat by sending it to the dry cleaner's, where the lining was replaced.

During meals at the Presleys', Elvis sometimes fed Jimbo from his own plate. When supper had ended, he and Dottie would walk to the gate of the yard to talk with fans. "And some of them even asked *me* for autographs," said Harmony, smiling.

He bought matching black leather outfits, and they rode through the streets of Memphis on his motorcycle. When they returned home, he would sometimes pull out his dog-eared Bible and begin reading. "I'm not kidding. We read the Bible aloud together," said Harmony. "He also looked over scripts he was getting from Hollywood. And we talked about what sort of career he would have in the movies."

On Christmas morning, Dottie found herself deluged with presents—a wristwatch, a little turquoise portable radio, piles of stuffed animals. In turn, she bought Elvis a St. Christopher medallion to protect him in his travels, and to soothe his fear of flying. Sensing a photo opportunity, the Colonel arranged for a photographer to take holiday photos of the Presleys and Elvis and Dottie. The wire services carried the shots of Elvis and his "showgirl."

Whenever Elvis was out of the house, Dottie and Gladys engaged in "girl talk." Dottie would watch Gladys pop one of her secret beers and pour it over ice. "She had to hide them in the corners of the cupboards because Elvis didn't like to see her drinking." Harmony never saw Elvis take a drink. But she did see him take what he said was his very first sleeping pill. "I gave it to him," said Harmony, who didn't think anything of it at the time.

After Dottie left Memphis, Gladys was left alone again. She would often settle into a kitchen chair or on the living room sofa and flip through the scrapbooks she kept on her son. Worry, amphetamines, and beer now dominated her life and nursed her through the long days when Vernon was at the neighborhood bar and Elvis was on the road. Though the neighbors were at first friendly and curious about the celebrity and his family, Gladys increasingly pined "for the happy days back in Tupelo."

By the end of the year Elvis would buy her a new pink Cadillac, but as he was to later admit, though he showered his mother with gifts—clothes, a fur coat, household appliances—"she never really wanted anything." He sighed, "She just stayed the same all the way through the whole thing."

In fact, she was still hanging her wash out on a clothesline—to the irritation of the other residents on Audubon Drive. And instead of driving away the fans, Gladys frequently invited them inside. "Greyhound buses drove by. On Sundays we needed five policemen to move the traffic along. The fans were a pain," said former next-door neighbor Peggy Jemison, who recalled clusters of girls attempting to climb into Elvis's bedroom window, pressing their noses against the picture windows, and gathering on the Presley driveway.

On one occasion the Jemisons received a phone call from an out-of-state fan who had used a city directory to locate the Presley's immediate neighbors. The caller pleaded, "I am desperate for some grass from Elvis's front lawn." So the Jemisons sent their son over to the Presley lawn to pull some grass. "But first, he asked us, 'Why can't I just pick it from our yard? What's the difference?' " No, he was told. The fan was promised grass from Elvis's yard, and that's what she would receive.

The grass was tucked into an envelope and mailed off. Later, the Jemisons heard from the grateful fan, who said, "The grass changed my life."

Eventually, a wrought-iron gate decorated in music notes was built around the Presley property. But their hopes for a guitar-shaped swimming pool were quashed by neighbors' protests and the claim that the property lots weren't big enough to accommodate such pools.

In truth, the Presleys were not wanted on Audubon, where the residents were mostly professional. "They were good people, but they were clearly out of place. They had been transplanted out of their world," said Jemison.

Ironically, though they never felt truly at home on Audubon, Gladys and Vernon found themselves becoming prisoners of the house. Whenever the two went out to the grocery store or to a nearby café, crowds followed them. Nestled in a booth in the Audubon Café, Vernon could feel eyes on him as he ate a piece of pie. Gladys was scrutinized as she sipped her beer. They, too, had become prisoners of fame. Yet the only face she wanted to see was seldom around.

According to psychologist Peter Whitmer, who analyzed her decline, "all of Gladys's fears of abandonment were brought to the surface.

"Elvis had always been Gladys's caretaker," wrote Whitmer. "Therefore she dreaded his being on the road both for his safety and hers. His absence forced her to interact more with Vernon, something she had not done for over twenty years, and this was not comfortable."

"I wish my boy would stop right now, buy a furniture store, and get married," was one of Gladys's often repeated refrains. Her petulant complaints multiplied whenever Elvis returned home, but in time this caused him to abandon Audubon as a refuge from the road. It was easier to extend his concert schedule than to face his mother. During 1956 he returned home for only a half dozen visits. During these he often slept all day and pursued a nocturnal life. After one of his nights out he slipped quietly through the front door and found his mother at the breakfast table. Their eyes locked as Gladys softly said, "I don't believe it." He lowered his eyes and responded, "I don't either."

Elvis, who later recounted the incident, explained, "We were caught up in something neither of us could do anything about."

Gladys was also crippled by shame. Though Elvis never knew it, his deeply religious mother was wounded by the attacks emerging from the pulpits across the country. After a particularly incendiary attack on Elvis's "lewdness" she led a neighbor into her house and showed off Elvis's closet full of clothes. "He don't deserve all that stuff that's being said about him," said Gladys, gripping the woman's arm. "He's not vulgar. He just puts his whole self into what he does."

As the date for his performance on *The Ed Sullivan Show* approached, Elvis immersed himself into coming up with just the right "look." One morning in late August, he dashed through the doors of Lansky's on Beale Street and announced, "Mr. Lansky, I'm gonna be on *Sullivan*, and I need some new clothes."

"We can handle that," said Bernard Lansky. He reveled in Presley's newfound ability to "buy anything he wanted—quite a change from the shy young man who'd pressed his nose to the window, admiring the latest coats."

Lansky bustled through his emporium, grabbing armfuls of rainbow jackets, slacks, and vests, and a wild array of shirts, including one of velvet in midnight blue. Elvis bought the shirt, with a gold-lamé vest and belt to match. He was also intrigued by an oversize kelly green sports coat with black flecks woven into it, and a dizzy checked coat with a matching shirt of contrasting checks. Elvis also grabbed three pairs of black trousers, some with a black-on-black stripe down the side, and two pairs of two-toned black-and-white shoes.

"Why, Son, you bought out the store," exclaimed Gladys when her son returned home and laid out his finds.

"But Mama, this is *Sullivan!*"

The mood was more somber at Sullivan's executive offices in New York. Ed, always suspicious and temperamental, had received a confidential call from an RCA publicist: "I shouldn't be saying this, but you had better watch Elvis closely."

"What does he do," said Sullivan, "unzip his pants during the show?"

"Everything but," the tipster warned.

The television impresario immediately watched clips of the *Steve Allen* and *Milton Berle* shows. After viewing the segments twice he pointed to Presley's crotch. "Look at that," he told producer Marlo Lewis. "He's got some kind of device hanging down below the crotch of his pants—so when he moves his legs back and forth you can see the outline of his cock." He shook his head, then added, "I think it's a Coke bottle."

He was troubled. "We just can't have this on a Sunday night. This is a family show!" He turned to Lewis and ordered, "Do what you have to do in order to fix this."

Sullivan wasn't the only one on edge. The *New York Times'* Jack Gould issued another warning, targeting CBS: "When Presley executes his bumps and grinds, it must be remembered by the Columbia Broadcasting System that even a twelve-year-old's curiosity may be overstimulated. Over the long run, however, maybe Presley is doing everybody a great favor by pointing up the need for early sex education."

Elvis's segments for the September 9 show were going to be fed live from CBS's studios in Hollywood. Because Sullivan didn't trust his second unit on the West Coast, he dispatched Marlo Lewis to Hollywood with orders to "keep that boy's lewdness off the screen."

Presley opened with "Don't Be Cruel"—his personal favorite—and true to form, his repertoire of bumps and grinds emerged. A panicked Marlo Lewis raced over to the primary cameraman and personally pushed his huge rig to the side so that Elvis's gyrations were masked. According to documentary filmmaker Andrew Solt, who has spent almost a decade directing special programs based on the *Sullivan* tapes, "They relied on side or long shots to blunt the sexuality."

Because Sullivan was recuperating from a car accident, the distinguished British actor Charles Laughton hosted the show. Since the thirties, the Academy Award–winning Laughton had been known for his range in the movies. He also delivered readings on tour: his "act" on the Sullivan show was a Shakespeare recitation. But nothing had quite prepared him for the furor over Presley. "It was excruciating," he later said. He was also left "wondering if the show would squeak past the censors."

It not only passed, it pulled in eighty percent of the audience—topping Elvis's appearance on Steve Allen's show. Elvis's follow-up performance in October was equally triumphant, with eighty-five percent of viewers watching. The Sullivan publicity machinery began touting its January 6 show, a spectacular that would feature seven Presley songs.

It seemed the whole world was looking on when Elvis returned to Tupelo for a homecoming concert at the Mississippi-Alabama Fair and Dairy Show—where he had performed "Old Shep" as a youngster. This time Elvis would be the headliner for an afternoon and an evening show. In an editorial, the local newspaper advised its readers to be on good behavior. After all, the *London Sunday Express* had sent a correspondent, and Fox and Movietone News had dispatched camera crews.

In the downtown, near the very building where Elvis made his radio debut with Mississippi Slim, "Welcome" banners spanned the streets. A celebratory menu at the popular Rex Plaza Cafe featured Love Me Tender Steak, "Hound Dogs" with Sauerkraut, and Rock 'n' Roll Stew.

At the fairgrounds, as at all county fairs, housewives showed off their canning and cooking. They competed for prizes in the "sew with cotton bags" competition. At the flower display, sweepstakes honors went to a bowl of spider lilies and coleus. More than two hundred dairy animals were on display, and for the first time swine were exhibited in the new swine barn.

All eyes, however, were on the hometown boy who had made good on the *Sullivan* show. Crowds gathered in the stands awaiting his arrival. The mayor rehearsed the presentation to the singer of a guitar-shaped "key to the city."

Before going onstage for the nighttime show, Elvis huddled in a tent with members of the press, a quartet of armed state troopers, the governor of Mississippi, and from time to time, teenage girls who managed to get through the protective cordon formed by the National Guard, the city police, and the state highway patrol.

Strutting in a blue velvet shirt—worn open to reveal his chest—black speckled pants, and white shoes, and two gold rings on his left hand, Elvis stood still as one female fan reached out to rub her fingers along his three-inch sideburns. She exited the tent, screaming, "I touched him!" Another girl, wearing a sundress, asked Elvis to sign her bare back; he obliged, using her tube of lipstick.

By now a pro at fielding questions about his stage movements, he said to the *London Sunday Express*'s Peter Dacre, "People tell me, 'You've gotta stop squirming like a tadpole.' But I'd sooner cut my throat than be vulgar." He later told the governor, "If I ever leave this business, I'll go into politics." Asked what he would run for, Elvis grinned and replied, "The city limits."

Finally, under guard, he left for the arena, making his entrance in a white Lincoln Continental bathed in spotlights. A roar went up from the outdoor stands. Among those breaking out into applause were Gladys and Vernon, who had accompanied their son back to Tupelo.

Before he climbed on the stage and delivered a frenzied, emotionally wrought performance, an announcement blared out from the intercom: "We've got five hundred National Guard and police here, so let's have no trouble. And please keep away from the stage. The last show some of them got burned, some of them were crushed, but none of them got Elvis."

Nor did they that night, but after Tupelo, Elvis went back on the road for a series of concerts that grew increasingly out of control. More than a hundred Dallas policemen had to patrol the Cotton Bowl when he appeared, and medics and nurses were hired to treat the girls who fainted or were battered as they rushed the eight-foot restraining fence that encircled the performing area.

Elvis himself was visibly groggy when he arrived for the show. Because of increasing insomnia, he'd had only four hours' sleep over two days. He climbed into a waiting convertible that transported him inside the stadium, in the glare of a spotlight, right to a platform on the fifty-yard line. He cut a weirdly mesmerizing figure: kelly green sports coat, a raw-silk pleated shirt, charcoal pants, white buckskin, high-topped shoes with red heels—accessorized by an electric blue tie.

He was awake by now. Grabbing the hefty, standing mike, he began to belt out the opening lines of "Heartbreak Hotel," doing what a *Dallas News* reporter called "a staggering, shuffle-footed dance." It seemed, mused the reviewer, that Elvis was throwing his famed pelvis "from the 50-yard line to the 35." The theatrics paid off: all 26,500 spectators in the arena erupted into screams—which continued right through the singer's bizarre "Hound Dog" finale, in which he came down off the platform and got down on all fours, twisting and writhing and seeming to gnaw at the stadium turf. "Sheer voodoo acrobatics," wrote the stunned reviewer.

All the while, Colonel Parker milled about outside the bowl— selling autographed pictures of his boy for ten cents.

As Elvis moved on to shows in Waco, Houston, and Corpus Christi, the wages of touring began to take a toll. During interviews, which he gave backstage before the concerts, his nervousness increased. He sometimes reached up to rub or feel his teeth. He moved his right leg incessantly. His hands constantly twitched. He rubbed his blood-shot eyes.

Along with stardom was the price of fame. In the latter part of the year he was involved in two highly publicized fistfights, one at a Memphis gas station, the other in a hotel in Toledo. In both cases he was a marked man before a single punch was thrown.

The Memphis encounter began innocently enough. Elvis pulled his Lincoln Continental into a gas station and asked the attendant to take a look at the air-conditioning unit. When passersby spotted the singer, they surrounded him. Presley was signing autographs when attendant Edd Hopper asked him to move. "Okay, man, just gimme a minute," said Elvis, who continued scrawling his signature for fans.

Becoming enraged, Hopper slapped Presley across the face. "I said, move on!" Elvis jumped forward and clobbered Hopper, who was reportedly thrown back ten feet. When another attendant came to Hopper's aid, Elvis threw a punch at him, too. "He just barely hit me," said Aubrey Brown. Hopper, however, suffered a shiner and a cut above his left eye.

All three men were booked on charges of assault and battery and disorderly conduct. When the arresting officer asked his name, Elvis drawled, "Well, maybe you'd better put down Carl Perkins." United Press dubbed him "Kid Presley" in a story accompanied by a photograph of the "champ" holding his tiny dog, Sweet Pea.

More than forty female fans called the police department and offered to pay Elvis's bail. His lawyer beat them to it.

The next day, Elvis appeared in court, accompanied by his father. Hopper and Brown wound up being fined, but the judge dismissed the charges against Presley. When the packed courthouse broke out in cheers, the judge was furious. "Stop this applause! This is a courtroom, not a show!"

A second brawl occurred in late November in the swank Shalimar room of Toledo's Commodore Perry Hotel. Nineteen-year-old Louis

Balint Jr. was a rough-and-tumble construction worker who was trying to impress a woman he had met at a bar. "Obviously I had been drinking," admitted Balint more than four decades later.

He entered the lounge and found Elvis seated at the head of a long table, with his musicians around him. "Are you Elvis Presley?" asked Balint.

Elvis stood and reached out his hand, to shake. But Balint responded with what he called "a Cagney slap," right across Elvis's face. The singer was momentarily stunned, but not his musicians. Scotty Moore jumped up and rushed Balint, who pushed Moore over a banister. He also pushed away two other Presley pals.

Elvis walked across the room and took a seat at the corner of the bar. "I don't know what this is about, man," he told Balint.

Suddenly, two police officers moved in from behind, grabbing Balint. Elvis reared up off the barstool and moved forward. He launched a punch and Balint ducked and Elvis hit a Toledo cop instead. But it was Balint who was taken to the police station—after being beaten with billy clubs—and was sentenced to twenty-one days in jail. "My father bailed me out," remembered Balint.

Because of all the publicity, Balint didn't want it to look as if he'd been "kicked in the butt" by a singer. So he called reporters, claiming the fight had been staged—a claim that Colonel Tom Parker hotly denied.

In an odd turn of events, Balint—who went on to become active in the martial arts community—went to work for Presley as a bodyguard in 1970.

The notoriety had its good sides as well, though. One afternoon, Elvis slipped into the Sun studio with Las Vegas showgirl Marilyn Evans clinging to his arm. His once sandy-colored hair was jet-black; his complexion was smooth—even the acne on his neck was gone.

Rocker Carl Perkins, there recording with his band, was startled by the makeover. "Man, he looked sharp and great," recalled Perkins. As Carl conversed with Elvis's female friend, Presley slid onto the piano stool and began toying with the keyboard. That's when the young man who was playing piano for Carl strolled over and introduced himself.

"So you're Elvis Presley, huh?"

"I ain't nobody but," Elvis said to the redheaded stranger, who went on to introduce himself.

"Well, I'm Jerry Lee Lewis."

When up-and-comer Johnny Cash wandered in the door, Sam

Phillips sensed that something magical was going to happen. It did: Elvis Presley, Carl Perkins, Jerry Lee Lewis, and Johnny Cash spent the entire afternoon jamming—singing gospel, playing around with jukebox hits, rocking and rolling.

Phillips was so excited by what he has called "probably the highlight of my life" that he put in a call to the *Press-Scimitar*. A photographer raced to the studio and found Elvis playing piano, Carl hovering behind him on acoustic guitar, and both Jerry Lee and Johnny looking on. The photo identified the foursome as "The Million Dollar Quartet."

Over the years the story of the four men—all musical geniuses in their own right—and their impromptu session has come to be regarded as one of rock 'n' roll's most momentous occasions. That it happened at Sun, the little recording studio that discovered Presley, adds to the lore. Sam Phillips has likened what happened that day to a "spiritual awakening." For Elvis, it was a golden moment in a career that was about to make a momentous leap.

Anticipation was mounting as his third and final *Ed Sullivan* appearance neared. Even the Colonel was anxious. He understood the tremendous power that emanated from TV. Elvis felt the pressure full bore, as was evident then on the late afternoon of January 6, 1957, at the CBS Theater in Manhattan. Elvis was rehearsing seven numbers for the show—an honor not duplicated before or after—but the rehearsals were lifeless. Because of a series of recent slams directed at him in print and on interview shows, and some sharp words from Sullivan himself, the singer was distinctly ill at ease.

Shortly before curtain time, Elvis cornered Gordon Stoker. "I can't dance; I can't sing; I'm not really a good musician. So, what do they want me for?"

"Look, Elvis," said the backup singer, "that's just a foolish notion. You've got a top spot on the top show in America and a whole list of hit songs."

What Elvis really needed, thought Stoker, was encouragement from the Colonel. "Elvis wanted someone to love him, but the Colonel was not that type of man. He was very hard-nosed, rude and crude," said Stoker. "So he was no help backstage on the important night."

In the end, Elvis did what he had always done: he came through for himself. His hair was brilliantined when he strode out on the stage wearing a gold-lamé vest with the blue velvet shirt he had worn for the Tupelo homecoming. His face was even more handsome than usual. Not only was he clear-complected, but his nose was slightly different—

as the result of minor plastic surgery. When he smiled, his teeth were absolutely perfect—newly capped.

Looking tanned and confident, he did a medley of hits that included a mesmerizing "Don't Be Cruel." He ended the song by giving the live audience a toned-down version of the Presley gyrations—first warning the Jordanaires, "Here we go, boys." Though he was filmed waist-up for TV, viewers at home got the message.

The commanding performance brought down the house, causing Sullivan to step out of the wings and motion to the live audience to be quiet.

With his hand on Presley's shoulders, Sullivan told Elvis "and the country" that "this is a real decent, fine boy, and we want to say we have never had a more pleasant experience on our show with a big name than we have had with you."

The audience, which included many parents, applauded heartily. Elvis looked as if he were going to burst with pride—and victory. He took a quick, gracious bow, and then he and the Jordanaires closed the show with the reverent gospel song "Peace in the Valley."

"That speech came directly from Ed's heart," said producer Andrew Solt. "It was not rehearsed. He had been surprised, in the end, that he had such tremendous liking for this young man."

Recalled Stoker, "Sullivan provided what Elvis needed, at that particular point in his life, to push him forward and make him a truly great star."

Back in Memphis, Gladys wept with joy as she watched her son's triumphant performance. But she also wept at what she knew would be her loss.

The Moving Image

I t was inevitable that Elvis Presley would go to Hollywood. Since the advent of the talkies, any good-looking male singer with a hit song got at least one shot at film stardom. Some of the biggest stars in Hollywood had leapt right off the hit parade and onto the big screen. Elvis's favorite crooner, Dean Martin, had done it. Bing Crosby and Frank Sinatra had even won Academy Awards for their film performances—Crosby for his role as the singing priest in *Going My Way* (1944) and Sinatra for his straight dramatic turn as the scrappy, ill-fated soldier of *From Here to Eternity* (1953). From Vic Damone to Dick Powell, from Frankie Avalon to Kris Kristofferson, the movies have always courted attractive singers.

They haven't always succeeded. Johnnie Ray, the heartthrob singer of the early fifties, whose emotional, shrieking style—and hit tunes such as "Cry"—led to his nickname, the Prince of Wails, had a shot at film stardom that fizzled. Still, going to Hollywood was the obvious next step in Presley's aggressive career.

It was also the fulfillment of his most secret dream.

As a child in Tupelo, Elvis had immersed himself into the fantasy world of his favorite heroes at the Strand and Lyric movie houses. As a teenager in Memphis, when he worked as an usher at the Loew's State

Theatre, he had stood at the back of the theater, flashlight at his side, mouthing the lines of dialogue as the movies unspooled over and over.

While touring the South with Scotty and Bill, and Bob Neal and his wife, he would chatter endlessly about what to the others seemed lofty goals. At a point when they were barely filling high school auditoriums and Future Farmers of America halls, recalled Neal, "his ambition was to be in big movies."

Elvis's undeniable relationship with the camera had already been proven in his first television appearances. The Colonel's role in mining this talent was also integral. A longtime friend, Abe Lastfogel, had been the William Morris agent who engineered Eddy Arnold's cowboy movie deals back when Parker was handling him. By 1956, Lastfogel was not only in command of the prestigious Morris talent agency, but also had a client list that included Marilyn Monroe, Sinatra, Academy Award winners Vivien Leigh and Katharine Hepburn, and the luminous Lana Turner. Elvis Presley would be in good company.

The rock-'n'-roll star definitely turned heads the day he arrived at the Morris offices for his introductory meeting. Wearing jeans, a ripped T-shirt, and eye makeup, he also had an air about him—body odor so powerful that the secretaries had to press their handkerchiefs to their nose as he sauntered by their desks.

In all probability Elvis thought he was "auditioning" to become the next James Dean, the iconoclastic rebel actor he so admired and who had died six months earlier in a car accident. Like most young people of the era, Elvis had been greatly affected by Dean's haunted performances. Presley knew every line of Dean's *Rebel Without a Cause* and was just as familiar with the films of that other fifties firebrand, Marlon Brando, who roared onto the scene as the scowling biker heel of *The Wild One*.

When Presley first arrived in Hollywood, he spoke hopefully about the artistic movies he hoped to make, and the accomplished actor *he* hoped to become.

Valerie Allen was a contract actress at Paramount Pictures when she saw a screen test, which was directed by her drama coach, Charlotte Clary. The scene was from the William Inge play *The Girls of Summer*. In it a young man speaks earnestly to a girl as she leans against a window in New Orleans. He is obviously in love with her, but she is pining for the musician who lives upstairs. As he speaks desperately to her, she directs her attention out the window, where the sound of a trumpet can be heard.

Elvis played the young would-be lover with such affecting intensity that, as the scene came to a close, Charlotte Clary turned to her class of young Paramount Pictures players and enthused, "Now, *that* is a natural-born actor."

In another screen test, Presley is a young man at odds with his father (played by veteran character actor Frank Faylen) in a scene from the hit play *The Rainmaker*. The formidable producer Hal Wallis was planning a screen adaptation to star Burt Lancaster as a charming con man (who promises rain during a drought) and Katharine Hepburn as a spinster who falls in love with him. Initially, Wallis envisioned Presley as Hepburn's suspicious brother (eventually portrayed by Earl Holliman). Elvis went on to tell several reporters excitedly that he was going to star opposite Lancaster. Asked who would play "the girl," Presley replied, "Katharine Hepburn," and innocently added, "if you could call her a girl."

No one was more surprised than Hal Wallis the day Elvis tentatively entered his Paramount office. "I expected him to be as aggressive and dynamic in person as he was onstage," recalled Wallis. "But he was slender, pale, extremely reserved, and rather nervous."

After reviewing Elvis's screen tests, though, Wallis knew he had a star. "The camera caressed him," said Wallis, who likened the newcomer to Errol Flynn, the rakish, athletic star of swashbucklers and costume adventures. According to Wallis, Elvis evoked "the same power, virility, and sexual drive."

Wallis, who was one of the town's leading independent producers, signed the young man to a seven-year, nonexclusive contract. Elvis—who was to receive $100,000 for his very first movie—was in awe as he shook Wallis's hand, with the Colonel looking on. After all, Wallis was the former Warner Bros. production chief who was famed for such classic titles as *Little Caesar*, *Casablanca*, and *The Maltese Falcon*. More recently he had filmed the great Tennessee Williams play *The Rose Tattoo*, about the unlikely relationship between an Italian war bride (Anna Magnani) and a rowdy truck driver (Burt Lancaster).

Though Wallis promised Elvis he would try to find him dramatic roles, he nonetheless also had a test made—in wide screen and high fidelity—of Presley "performing" his hit "Blue Suede Shoes." Flanked by a backdrop of rich draperies, and wearing an Edith Head–designed coat and jacket, Elvis pretends to play his guitar—which has no strings—and lip-synchs to the lyrics. The number was done in two takes, and as lights were adjusted, Elvis stood without complaining, bathed in sweat. "There was no stand-in," said screenwriter Allan Weiss, who recalled how the young novice apologized several times during the test. "I'm not as dead-on as I can be," he explained.

Shot with three cameras, the test's emphasis is on Presley's rhythmic moves and on close-ups as he comes to key emotional points in the song. Wallis and Paramount may have talked with Elvis about dramatic roles, but the test shows clearly that they were most interested in him for his musical abilities. In the end, after all the accolades about the promising young performer, Elvis was just another commodity.

Ironically, after signing Presley the producer claimed he couldn't find a suitable vehicle for him. For a while Wallis mulled over the idea of Presley starring in *The Rat Race*, about a struggling musician trying to make it in Manhattan. But the male character was described as a "naive, innocent boy." As one studio executive put it, "Elvis Presley just doesn't look like that." (The movie eventually starred Elvis's own teen idol, Tony Curtis.)

Because Jerry Lewis and Dean Martin had just split up—after a partnership that had spanned seventeen movies—Wallis also briefly, and incredibly, considered pairing Presley opposite Lewis. In addition, a Broadway contingent approached the Colonel about having Elvis star in *Li'l Abner*, the musical based on satirist Al Capp's comic strip about the hillbilly denizens of the fictional community of Dogpatch. Try as he might, Elvis could not shake his "hillbilly" image.

Finally, Wallis allowed him to be "loaned out" to Twentieth Century-Fox to star in *The Reno Brothers*. Elvis was cast as Clint, the youngest member of a Confederate family, who marries the fiancée (Debra Paget) of a brother thought to have died in battle. When Vance Reno (Richard Egan) unexpectedly returns, there's formulaic trouble—and a love triangle.

When Elvis was driven onto the Fox lot for the first day of filming, fans—including many daughters of studio employees—clustered along the studio thoroughfares holding "Presley for Prexy" signs that had hastily been made up by the art department. The Colonel was delighted. Newsreel crews, radio disc jockeys, and some of the town's leading reporters also descended on the new star, among them Army Archerd, who covered the momentous day for *Photoplay*. Enthused Archerd, "There hadn't been this much excitement on the lot since Tyrone Power was the big new threat."

On the surface Elvis seemed cool, collected. He graciously signed autographs for fans, who had waited hours for his arrival. He flirted with the studio secretaries, who seemed to have abandoned their respective offices en masse. But his nails were bitten to the quick. He continually ran his fingers through his sandy hair. And though his stutter had been dissipating, it resurfaced with the bombardment of questions.

His unassuming nature surprised reporters. He seemed genuinely concerned when a female interviewer lit a cigarette. "Should you be doing that, ma'am?" To her quizzical look, he intently added, "That might kill you one day."

Anxious to impress his costars and the film crew, he showed up with the entire script memorized. He was unaware that already other actors were balking about working with him. Just two days earlier, Cameron Mitchell had angrily pulled out of the film after he realized it was actually a—God forbid—vehicle for a rock-'n'-roll singer. Richard Egan, then a prominent leading man, was threatening not to show up for work if the "new kid" was billed above him in the credits. Memos flew back and forth, and Egan was assured that he would get star billing—along with Paget. In fact, Elvis's name would bring up the rear, for the picture was "introducing Elvis Presley."

Egan also griped about the movie's publicity, which naturally centered around its young newcomer. Costars William Campbell and Neville Brand used to drop by Egan's dressing room for a drink, where Egan would complain about the upstart actor. "Jesus Christ! I'm the damn star of this picture," yelled Egan one evening. "And I haven't gotten a bit of publicity!" After having another drink, he put in a call to the movie's publicist, who rushed over and told Egan, "Sir, if you've got a kick about that, you'd better talk to somebody bigger than me. I've been ordered to take pictures continually of Elvis Presley."

Egan eventually cooled off, and occasionally—over the seven weeks of filming—acted chummy with the first-time actor. After all, sitting next to Presley meant that Egan was photographed, too.

With Elvis's first movie would also come his first Hollywood infatuation. Prior to the start of filming, Elvis sat in a darkened projection room at Fox and watched screen-test footage of the green-eyed, flame-haired Debra Paget as if seeing her for the first time. "Gosh, ain't she *purdy?*" he said loudly. The Colonel nodded his head.

"Am I gonna have to kiss her in the picture?" Elvis asked hopefully. The Colonel just laughed.

Actually, Elvis would have to wait until his second movie to enjoy a screen kiss, but he made no secret of his off-camera interest in Paget, whom he first met during the taping of *The Milton Berle Show*, when Paget had pretended to get hysterical over the singer. He even told several radio interviewers about his California girlfriend "Debbie."

For perhaps the first time in his career, however, the attraction was not mutual. He was flabbergasted when the twenty-three-year-old actress told him she wasn't allowed to date. Not coincidentally, Paget had one of the industry's most prominent stage mothers. Marguerite Gibson was a former burlesque queen who had been shrewdly supervising her daughter's career since Debra was fourteen and measured 36-21-35. On film sets Gibson was omnipresent, pulling up in her gem-encrusted white Cadillac and seeking out her daughter, whom she hovered over protectively.

Though Elvis would eventually be invited to the family's sprawling twenty-six-room home in Beverly Hills, he was not made to feel comfortable there. In the hallway, he playfully rubbed a rhinestone brassiere that hung modestly over a massive painting of mermaids. "That's not funny, young man," said Debra's mother. She later caught Elvis nestling against Debra's shoulder as he played the piano. "Go ahead and play, young man," snapped Marguerite. "But play the piano."

When the two young people decided to go swimming, Debra bounded upstairs to change. Elvis was following her until Marguerite hollered, "Young man, downstairs! You will dress in the cellar."

To Elvis's exasperation, Debra's mother even told her when it was time to go to bed. One evening it was still light outside when Marguerite said, "You'd better head for home, Elvis. Debra has to go to bed early. She's due on the lot early tomorrow."

What went unspoken was that Debra had another suitor—a man so powerful he ran his own film studio and aviation empire. Elvis made that discovery the evening he rode his motorcycle out of Debra's driveway and hid in the shadows of bushes near the house. As he suspected, a dark sedan appeared. Elvis scribbled down the license plate number and had it traced.

His vestal virgin was being courted by none other than Howard Hughes, the renowned ladies' man whose romantic modus operandi included ingratiating himself with the mothers of the young women he pursued.

Elvis was clearly out of his league, but he would not give up. When filming wrapped, he telephoned Debra long-distance and proposed marriage. "My family didn't go for the idea," said Paget with considerable understatement.

Presley would never overcome his obsession with Debbie Paget. Indeed, he would go on to marry a young woman who looked so much like her that they could have been twins.

This is not to say that Elvis was pining away in Tinseltown. At the Hollywood Knickerbocker Hotel, where he shared the eleventh-floor penthouse suite with his cousins Gene and Junior Smith, there was no lack of female company. The switchboard logged 237 calls the first day Elvis was there.

Fans clogged the lobby and congregated outside the Ivar Avenue entrance, just down from Hollywood Boulevard. The more industrious ones daringly climbed the fire escape—and beat at the window trying to get Elvis's attention. One evening he pulled two giggling girls in and scolded them. "What would your mamas say!" Stressing how dangerous their stunt had been, he said sincerely, "Why, I never would have forgiven myself if you'd been hurt on my account." After lecturing them, he gave them friendly hugs and sent them off with stuffed hound dogs.

He was sometimes dateless as he prowled Long Beach's Nu-Pike amusement park, with its colorful midway—complete with a flea circus and rows and rows of games. He proved especially adept at knocking down milk bottles with baseballs. One night he won seven stuffed teddy bears, which he promptly gave to girls who recognized him. Other nights he ducked into the structure that housed the Plunge, the park's giant indoor saltwater pool. As he wandered the ride concourse and ate cotton candy, Elvis looked up at the brightly lit double Ferris wheel and the towering Hi-Ride, whose riders were transported upward in a spinning cage. He loved watching—and riding—the Cyclone Racer, the wooden roller coaster that jutted out over the Pacific.

He found the ocean more awesome than any ride. To him it was soothing—and pure escape. "I can't believe it's so big," Elvis used to say as he gazed out over the cresting waves. When he watched the sea, he occasionally mused about the seaside vacations he would like to give his parents.

Some evenings he and Bill Campbell would climb into Campbell's little Thunderbird and head down Olympic Boulevard to Venice Beach. "Oh, God, this is a *beautiful* beach down here!" Elvis exclaimed on his first visit. He liked to eat at a greasy spoon across from the ocean. One evening, said Campbell, Elvis told the cook—who wore a dirty apron and hat and had a dirtier hot plate—to "give me a nice big, double-greasy hamburger. The greasier the better." The man behind the counter complied, and Elvis hungrily tore into the dripping sandwich.

Campbell later tried to talk Elvis into trying a classier burger joint—the trendy Strips on the (Sunset) Strip. "I told him the meat was freshly ground . . . and that they had a beautiful apple pie," Campbell recalled.

"Bill, do I have to go there?" Elvis asked. Campbell assured him he didn't—but pointed out that they would be less likely to suffer food poisoning there than at the Venice dive, which he nicknamed Ptomaine Alley.

"But, Bill, I like that greasy hamburger," said Elvis. "And the other thing I like is that goddamned guy doesn't know who I am! If he knew who I was, then the whole thing would change." With a goofy grin Presley admitted, "I like the way he growls at me when he gives me my hamburger."

Actress Valerie Allen used to sit in the little kitchen of Elvis's suite at the Knickerbocker and watch him as he mashed bananas and mixed them with peanut butter for his sandwiches. "To think, he could have had anything. But he made his own sandwiches," said Allen, laughing. "And when he offered you 'a drink'—and he was always very polite about that—he meant a Coca-Cola or a 7-Up. That was his world."

She first saw Elvis as he and Gene Smith tossed a football on the Paramount lot, where Elvis made his screen test. Allen didn't recognize the tall, blond man in white shirt and slacks. "He was so great looking—and I can't emphasize how much better he looked in person than on the screen, or in photographs—that you would have looked at him if he'd been anyplace in the world," she said.

The young actress didn't have a serious romance with Presley ("I was involved with someone at the time"), but Allen and Elvis did engage in serious necking. "He absolutely loved women. And he had this marvelous quality—he was so manly, but he also wasn't afraid to show his sensitivity."

The pressure of stardom was still taking its nightly toll. Often, Gene Smith, asleep in the twin bed across from Elvis, awakened to see his cousin jumping up. Elvis would be having another of his nightmares.

One time Elvis described "three men with knives," and he tried to battle one of the invisible attackers. "Look out!" he warned, letting loose a kick—and accidentally hitting the bed.

The next morning, Elvis laughed when he learned of his latest nighttime drama. But his anxieties were escalating in Hollywood, where he increasingly felt like an outsider. The Colonel liked to brag about that side of him. In spite of the fame and the money, Elvis was still a country boy who was "not fixin' to change." Said the Colonel, "You can't get Elvis into fancy restaurants or nightclubs. He doesn't feel right in 'em and I don't know as he ever will."

As long as Elvis remained an unworldly bumpkin, the Colonel knew that he could keep better control over his young performer. When Elvis briefly began to run with a Hollywood crowd—the only such time in his career—Parker was understandably anxious.

Fair-haired and wiry, with a reputation as a hungry young actor, Nick Adams had talked his way into small roles in movies including *Mister Roberts*, *Picnic*, and *Rebel Without a Cause*. But he wasn't just blustery talk: his work had an edgy, intense quality that would lead to an Academy Award nomination (in 1963 for the courtroom drama *Twilight of Honor*, opposite Richard Chamberlain), and the starring role in a popular early-sixties TV series, set after the Civil War, called *The Rebel*.

When he met Elvis for the first time, Adams was, as usual, hustling. He wanted a role in Presley's movie. "Hey, man, Cameron Mitchell can't do the film. So they need someone for his role, right?" Adams said after introducing himself on the set.

Impressed by Adams's moxie, and the fact that he had appeared in *Rebel Without a Cause*, Elvis good-naturedly put in a word for the actor, but director Robert Webb wanted to cast someone older.

Adams and Presley struck up a friendship anyway, which led to Elvis's introduction to the hip Hollywood contingent that included the young Natalie Wood and angry young actors Dennis Hopper and Russ Tamblyn. Hopper was then primarily known for having been a supporting actor opposite James Dean in the pictures *Rebel* and *Giant*. Tamblyn was a former child actor who could deliver dazzling dance routines (as in *Seven Brides for Seven Brothers*) and convincing portrayals of young punks.

Elvis was flattered to be a part of the crowd.

Natalie Wood, meanwhile, was intrigued to discover that Elvis Presley was nothing like his image—that "he was never a lothario." At eighteen, Wood had virtually grown up before the cameras. An affecting child star, she was the little girl who at first refused to believe in Santa in the 1947 classic *Miracle on 34th Street*. When she met Elvis, she was moving into more grown-up roles, such as the conflicted teenager who bonds with Dean in *Rebel*.

Brown-eyed and beautiful, she was also a wild child—a chain-smoking, party-going teenager far wiser than her years. She and Presley were a study in contrasts.

"Why you wanna go smoke those things?" he asked of her perpetually brandished cigarette. When she drank at parties, he loudly ordered, "A Coca-Cola, please." He couldn't figure out why she had her own apartment. Why couldn't she just live at home with her parents, the way girls should?

Still, he was entranced. She was defiant and talented—already an Oscar nominee (for *Rebel*)—and compelling. As for Wood, she said that being with Elvis was "like having the date I never ever had in high school." She was especially taken by his devotion to religion. Until she met Elvis, the Jewish Natalie Wood had never known anyone who was so serious about God and the Bible. How could such a sultry-looking man be so sincerely pious?

"He felt he had been given this gift, this talent, by God. He didn't take it for granted. He thought it was something that he had to protect," remembered Wood, who was thunderstruck at how Elvis tried to be kind to others. If he didn't, he told her, God would take away all that he had been given.

The two dined at the Terrace Room of the Beverly Hills Hotel, took in hit movies like *Bus Stop* and *The King and I*, and roared through the Hollywood Hills in the night. Wearing jeans and a sweater, with a scarf around her dark hair, Wood would cling tightly to Elvis's waist as he confidently guided his Harley along the bends of the darkened roads.

When Elvis invited Natalie to Memphis to meet his family, she easily got her parents' approval. They, too, were bowled over by Elvis's sweetness. Nick Adams tagged along on the visit, which included on-the-air visits with Dewey Phillips. The latter was Elvis's idea. Every time he was in town, he tried to stop off at the Hotel Chisca to update Dewey, and his listeners, on his career.

As always when Elvis went home, he found his house surrounded by fans. Natalie was shocked at how casual Elvis was about living in what she saw as a virtual goldfish bowl. "A mob of people stood outside his house day and night. Someone sold hot dogs and ice cream from a wagon," she recalled. "It was like a circus come to town."

The first night they arrived at the house on Audubon, Elvis rolled down the car window and called to the fans to please let them up the driveway. "Give us a few minutes. We'll be back to visit."

Wood thought he was kidding. But after they got their bags inside and made the acquaintance of Gladys and Vernon, Elvis escorted Natalie and Nick back outside, where they stood on the lawn and chatted for more than an hour with fans.

"Elvis, could you sign this?" squealed one girl.

"Natalie, do you have any plans to marry Elvis? Or Nick?" yelled one fan.

Glad to have her son back at home, Gladys prepared a welcoming meal of all his favorites: country ham, black-cyed peas, creamed potatoes, hominy grits, corn pone, hot biscuits, fried corn, and okra. "Eat up, y'all," she said, beaming.

Wood politely took a small portion of each, but Adams looked suspiciously at the corn pone and okra and asked, "What's that?" Simultaneously, the Presleys burst into laughter.

When Elvis, Nick, and Natalie went out for a motorcycle ride, an instant "motorcade" formed behind them. "The line must have been a block long. I felt like I was leading the Rose Parade," said Wood.

When she returned home after a few days, she declined to make any public comment about her Tennessee adventure. In fact, for years she would not talk about Elvis. To this day, there are differing accounts about what went on between the two celebrities.

In the book she wrote about her famous sister, Lana Wood said that when Natalie was visiting with the Presleys, she frantically called home, saying, "Gladys has wrecked everything. I don't have a chance. Get me out of here, fast." Once back in Los Angeles, Natalie confided to Lana, "God, it was awful. He can sing, but he can't do much else."

Yet in front of his Memphis buddies, Elvis bragged about "getting laid" by Wood. It happened, he said, the night before he had to do a particularly sad movie scene. Said Elvis, mugging, "You know, guys, I'm having trouble acting sad, because last night I was in bed with Natalie Wood. How can you be unhappy after that?"

Dewey Phillips heard another variation of the Presley-Wood encounter. Dewey and Sam Phillips had once liked to watch the young Elvis recoil as they swapped stories about "eatin' pussy." According to Dewey, after dating Natalie, Elvis confessed, "You remember when y'all used to make me sick talkin' about eatin' pussy? I eat me some the other night. But, man, now I'm in trouble." Explained Elvis, "Damn if I didn't fall in love with it."

During the making of *The Reno Brothers* Elvis talked hopefully about portraying James Dean. "I think I could do it easy," he told his producer, David Weisbart. "I want to play that more than anything else."

Weisbart, who listened politely, had produced *Rebel Without a Cause* and was considering a screen biography about Dean.

Sometimes between takes, Elvis would sit cradling a mug of coffee and listen as Weisbart compared his two actors to members of the press. To Weisbart, Elvis was "a safety valve"—someone kids could get verbal over, with screaming and yelling. But when they watched Dean, they kept a lid on their feelings.

Weisbart also cited differences in their professional habits. Elvis was always on time and cooperative. But when it came to working with Dean, "there were times . . . when you were walking on jagged edges of broken glass."

There were other differences: Dean was a stage-trained performer who worked with acting coaches. No one ever suggested that Elvis might benefit from some training. Also, Dean was an active voice in the making of his movies; Elvis did what he was told.

When *The Reno Brothers* was hastily retooled—to showcase Elvis's singing—he didn't publicly balk. In fact, he liked the ballad "Love Me Tender"—which also became the movie's new title. He even performed it for girlfriend June Juanico over the telephone. But when three other songs were hastily added, he put in another call to June, this time raising "holy hell."

"Dammit! They've thrown in some garbage—some silly songs!" Elvis was further agitated that he was not allowed to perform the music with Scotty Moore and Bill Black. The studio instead made him work with the trendy but less adept Ken Darby Trio.

Then Fox mavens decided the picture also needed a new ending— one that lessened the blow of Presley's character's on-screen death. Presley reported to studios in New York for eight hours of retakes so that the movie could close with his ghostly image superimposed over the final scene, as he performed the haunting title song.

When *Love Me Tender* opened, fans did not seem to mind that their idol was rocking and rolling amid crowds of clapping Confederate veterans. Within three days at the box office, the movie had earned back its $1-million budget.

The movie's debut at the Paramount Theater in New York was as much an event as one of Elvis's live concerts. Before the theater doors opened, a forty-foot Elvis cutout—affixed to the marquee—was undraped, and the "world's largest charm bracelet" was placed around the figure's giant wrist.

Inside, the first two thousand ticket buyers received "free gifts" from Elvis—one of the Colonel's ideas, of course. In less than a half hour, the lucky ones loaded up on Elvis scarves, hats, campaign buttons, and charm bracelets. As the mob grabbed over the mementos, truant officers for the New York Board of Education paced and scanned the lobby. After all, it was a school day.

Not surprisingly, the movie critics were also lying in wait. *Time* was vicious, leading off its attack with, "Is it a sausage? It is certainly smooth and damp-looking, but who ever heard of a 172-lb. sausage 6 ft. tall? Is it a Walt Disney goldfish? It has the same sort of big, soft, beautiful eyes and long, curly lashes, but who ever heard of a goldfish with sideburns? Is it a corpse? The face just hangs there, limp and white with its little drop-seat mouth, rather like Lord Byron in the wax museum."

Writing in *The New Republic*, Janet Winn suggested that Elvis team with Marilyn Monroe in *The Brothers Karamazov*, which the actress had been quoted as saying she wanted to do. Elvis, sneered Winn, would be "just *great* as the other brother."

The *New York Times*'s Bosley Crowther credited Elvis for his enthusiasm for a B movie, but said he "goes at it as though it were *Gone With the Wind*." The reviewer for the *New York Herald-Tribune* couldn't comment on the dialogue because he couldn't hear it—due to all the screams in the auditorium.

Elvis was devastated and embarrassed. To save face he later said of his film debut, "It was pretty horrible. . . . I knew that picture was bad when it was completed. I'm my own worst critic." But he was tenacious: in January 1957 he returned to Los Angeles to begin work on his second film. This time he would play a young performer struggling with growing stardom. And, yes, he was going to sing.

He was not ready to settle down out there, however. In March he went back out on the road—where he had the control, not Hollywood. He might have bombed with the movie critics, but he knew how to dazzle a live audience.

In Detroit more than fourteen thousand fans showed up for each of

Presley's two shows at the Olympia Stadium where, said the *Free Press*, he gave off "more electricity than the Detroit Edison Co.'s combined transmitters." Little wonder: Elvis strutted into view in a $2,500 gold-lamé suit—worn with gold string tie and gold shoes with sequined laces. He carried a guitar on which his name was written in gold script.

A hundred and forty extra city policemen were on duty, as well as a dozen police commandos and ten policewomen. But they failed to quell the crowd that congregated after the second show. Elvis was still on the stage when what looked like thousands of fans rushed toward him. Snatching up his new guitar, he yelled, "Let's get out of here fast . . . they're coming after us!" The musicians and the backup singers began running. "It looked as if someone had set loose millions of bees, and they were swarming along the aisles, over seats, and onto the stage," recalled Gordon Stoker.

With Elvis leading the way, the performers raced down the stadium stairs and into a waiting car, which was surrounded by police. Once inside, said Stoker, they all congratulated themselves on "saving Elvis from certain disaster." Presley was unfazed. "Man, we were lucky that time," he told his shaken associates. "In a crowd like that I usually lose a coat and a shirt!"

Within days, Elvis had shed his suit's gold pants for black trousers—the better to show off that sparkling coat, which had its inspiration in Liberace's wardrobe. Nudie's of Hollywood, famed for its rhinestone-studded cowboy wear, had come up with Elvis's suit at the Colonel's request.

What seemed like fifteen thousand flashbulbs went off when Elvis climbed onstage at Toronto's Maple Leaf Gardens. Caught in the glare, his jacket was so bright it might have been visible from outer space. This time, he wore it with a black shirt open at the chest, and built-up, gold-spangled shoes on which he managed to balance himself on both toes—his knees forward—in gravity-defying positions.

His Canadian tour also took him to Ottawa, where a reporter for the *Evening Journal* caught him skipping "like a girl" after he disembarked from the train. Moreover, "traces of makeup and what looked like mascara failed to hide tired lines around the wobble-singer's Grecian nose."

This sneering reflected the outrage he continued to inspire. In Ottawa, too, students of the Notre Dame Convent were instructed, via the school's public address system, not to go to the Elvis Presley show. The girls had to write an oath on the blackboard promising "that I shall not take part in the reception accorded Elvis Presley and I shall not be present at the program presented by him at the Auditorium on Wednesday, April 3, 1957." Eight girls were eventually expelled.

In St. Louis, high school girls burned a life-size Elvis picture while reciting prayers as public reparation for the excesses committed by other teenagers.

In a Los Angeles case involving juvenile delinquency, a judge made headlines with the statement, "It is strange that in all these cases involving boys under age, every one has been wearing an Elvis Presley haircut." In summation he added, "I wish that Elvis Presley had never been born."

So did the Iranian government, which simultaneously launched a "Hate Elvis" campaign and banned rock 'n' roll as "a threat to civilization." As a result, Radio Tehran would no longer play Presley's records, which had come to be in demand by Iranian boys, while girls were defying Moslem custom—forbidding undignified behavior of women in public—by wearing "I Like Elvis" buttons.

On the flip side, the man and his music represented nothing less than freedom.

In a letter sent to *Harper's*, a reader in Communist Czechoslovakia wrote: "I heard about rock 'n' roll. Is it a new style of jazz, or does it belong to popular music? I would be glad to hear it. How does Elvis Presley sing? I had [sic] lent a Canadian journal, *Liberty*, issue from August 1956 and in this is a picture from [sic] Elvis Presley while singing and playing on guitar. He looks as in ecstasy. Please, be so kind as to write me something about it."

But Presley's ecstatic performances were numbered. The road trip he had begun in 1955 was headed for an end.

The Cool and the Crazy

n the spring of 1957, Elvis decided it was time for him and his parents to move from Audubon, where the neighbors were increasingly hostile about the Presley sideshow of noise and fans. What they wanted, said Gladys, was privacy and space. Elvis bought an eighteen-room house situated on thirteen acres in Whitehaven, a rural suburb of rolling meadows and ancient oaks. The Georgian colonial-style house at 3764 South Bellevue Boulevard had been built in the thirties and was named for the original owner's mother, Grace.

Elvis Presley paid $100,000 for Graceland. But its patrician decor—ivory and beige walls, with baroque ceilings—wasn't to his taste. He wanted color and panache. When he set about making costly renovations, his mother had to talk him out of purple walls with gold trim for the living and dining rooms. He instead settled on pavilion blue; but he did have his bedroom decorated in "the darkest blue there is," with a mirror covering one wall, and a specially built eight-foot-square bed. He also had a soda fountain—complete with counter stools and a Coke machine—installed in the game room.

His entrance hall emulated an effect he had seen at Grauman's Chinese Theater in Hollywood where tiny lights situated in the ceiling simulated thousands of stars, which flickered amid hand-painted clouds. Elvis was thrilled to have his own personal sky.

A limestone wall, with a gate with music notes, was built to encircle the property. Other improvements included a swimming pool and patio.

While Elvis indulged his decorating flair, Gladys added touches of backwoods Tupelo. Vernon built a hog pen so they could keep a pair of hogs—to be slaughtered for winter bacon, ham, and sausage. An old pumphouse served as a makeshift smokehouse. Gladys even got a chicken coop.

The move to the house marked a dramatic change in the lives of all the Presleys. Some of Memphis's social movers and shakers referred to Graceland as "the castle rock and roll built." To others, less kind, the mansion was termed the Hillbilly Palace. But to Elvis, it was proof that he had reached the pinnacle of success.

To Vernon, it meant that he could live in unexcelled comfort for the rest of his life without ever having to work again.

To Elvis's ever-present comrades, it was the house of games where lavish meals appeared at the snap of a finger and where beautiful girls by the score milled about.

Cliff Gleaves, who actually moved into one of the bedrooms, was with Elvis the night he arrived home from Hollywood and saw his newly refurbished home for the first time. As the two men walked between the Corinthian columns on the front portico, the front door opened. There stood Gladys, with a Cheshire grin. "Welcome home, Son!"

To Gladys, however, the house slowly became a mausoleum—complete with servants Elvis hired. "They won't let me do anything out here," she told her sister Lillian. During a visit to Tupelo, Gladys sat with Annie Presley on her front porch and lamented, "I'd give the world if I could live next door to you all again. I want to live where I can raise my chickens and do my own cookin'.'"

Said Annie Presley, "She was not used to that type of life."

What life she did have was increasingly lonely, for Elvis was seldom home. Though Gladys never said it, she believed that the house, the cars, the drivers, and the servants had been bestowed to assuage her son's guilt. When Graceland was totally redecorated, Gladys gestured toward the rooms filled with furniture and porcelain bric-a-brac and asked, "What in the world are we going to do with all of this?"

Elvis was not blind to his mother's despair. He guiltily knew that the booty he showered on her was a smoke screen.

"It was when they moved into Graceland for good that Gladys started getting really depressed," said her sister Lillian. "She was always saying she wished she was back poor again when we lived in those little bitty houses near each other."

According to psychologist Dr. Peter Whitmer, author of an exhaustive psychological study of Elvis, "The move to Graceland represented severe culture shock. To Gladys, life in Graceland was disintegrating [her] very sense of self . . . erasing, one by one the little things that gave her life meaning and enjoyment."

Turning over command of her kitchen to strangers was the greatest sacrifice. "Now, this was a family to which the giving and taking of food was a powerful act of love, and had been so since Elvis was a toddler," recalled Annie Presley. "It was the thing that held them together in the poorest of times. Gladys got food on that table no matter what . . . even if she had to work two jobs and barter with the Tupelo meat market to do it."

Elvis made token gestures to render Graceland more palatable to his mother. He installed guest quarters behind the sprawling house and moved Vernon's mother, Minnie Mae, into a suite. His money also allowed Gladys's sisters, Cletes and Lillian, to live solid middle-class lives in what Cletes called "the big, bad city." And he gladly allowed his mother to turn the backyard of Graceland into a farm and a versatile kitchen garden—much like the victory garden she had lovingly tended back in Tupelo.

When his mother demanded farm animals, Elvis dutifully provided them in a chicken-duck-and-peacock-acquiring expedition that ended in high farce. Instead of merely ordering the livestock from one of the many suppliers in Memphis, Elvis loaded Lamar Fike and Vernon into his big yellow '54 Cadillac limousine and headed out to haggle with a rural farmer in Germantown, an outlying Memphis suburb.

As specified by Graceland's mistress, they purchased eight ducks, twenty chickens, a pair of peacocks, and a fully grown turkey. Elvis asked the farmer, "Could you put them in the backseat of my car?" The farmer warily obliged: "You'll wish you had 'em delivered."

True enough, within minutes the feathered flock began fighting. Chests puffed, wings flapped, beaks lashed out, feathers filled the car. The peacocks emitted constant shrieks. "Goddammit, I can't see," Elvis said, laughing, from the front seat, where a blizzard of feathers and down were swirling.

"Lamar, you get in the backseat and hold the turkey. Keep the ducks and the chickens apart, and for God's sake, keep them still!" Elvis commanded. The hefty Lamar—who weighed nearly three hundred pounds—dutifully climbed into the backseat.

Vernon grabbed a section of newspaper and began trying to fan the feathers back toward Lamar, who then started sneezing violently. "Man, these birds are shitting all over me and the car. . . . Drive as fast as you can," Lamar pleaded. "The shit is all over me and now all these feathers are sticking to me."

Elvis glanced in the mirror and doubled over with laughter, swerving from one lane to another.

"Don't do that, son," said his father. "Every time you move this car, they shit just a little bit more."

Finally they arrived at Graceland, pulling the car up in back where they turned loose the collection of fowl—but not before Gladys wandered out to have a look. It was the first good laugh she'd had in weeks.

Though the Cadillac was later cleaned and fumigated, it was never used again. Elvis told Vernon it was time for a new car anyway. As for the assorted birds, they were soon to be joined by two pigs and four donkeys. After setting up the menagerie that afternoon, Elvis cleaned up and rode off with his buddies to the roller rink and the movie theater, to return after dawn.

Forty-eight hours later he sped off—back into the land of fame.

"The more Elvis worked and the more he became famous, the more concerned Gladys became," said Fike. "Here was a lady who grew up on the wrong side of life, a simple woman who could not deal with the onslaught of people and fans coming at her." Once when a particularly large group of fans was mobbed at the gate, she looked out: "You know, Lamar, I am afraid they might hurt him. What scares me is that there's only one of him."

She also dreaded being left alone with Vernon, who was physically abusing her again as he had done in Lauderdale Courts. And this time he wasn't so guarded. Lillian reported that Vernon even belted Gladys "while other people were in the house. There was no shame."

Now that her son's concerts were continuous, Gladys felt abandoned and alleviated her fears with alcohol and pills in greater doses. She was certain the Benzedrine would prevent the inevitable bloat from consuming that much alcohol. She also began stiffening her "tall beers" with vodka—guiltily supplied by Vernon as compensation for his increasing womanizing.

As Elvis flashed in and out of Graceland, he ignored all the signs of his mother's life-threatening addictions: her giddy, giggly greetings when he returned; her drunken renditions of his songs; her morose, tear-ridden sessions with the family scrapbooks she had assembled over twenty years. Elvis was in deep denial. "He just couldn't see it," remarked Lillian.

"You don't need to be no more important nor more rich," Gladys declared one evening. "You got plenty of time to spend here with us. You just don't want to."

Elvis answered ambiguously, "You don't know what it's like, Mama."

Finally, he declared his freedom from Gladys and Vernon in an interview that ran in dozens of newspapers. When a Vancouver reporter asked, "Well, Elvis, how do you feel about being on the road all the time? More important, how do your parents feel? I mean, doesn't it bother them that you're away all the time? Wouldn't they like to see their son once in a while?"

Elvis replied, "Well, it's my life, you know, and they don't say too much about it."

"In other words, they have to accept it?"

"Yes."

Unofficially, Elvis began to make a second home of Hollywood, where he made two movies back-to-back in 1957. Early in the year he began filming *Loving You*, which Paramount and Hal Wallis billed as "the first big modern musical built around the fiery personality of Elvis Presley." Director Hal Kanter even spent several weeks following Presley, in Memphis and in Shreveport—where Elvis finished out his *Louisiana Hayride* contract with a farewell concert.

The resulting film followed a sweet-natured (but sexy) singer named Deke Rivers, from his barnstorming days with a hillbilly band to his emergence as a star. Filled with loose parallels to Presley's own life, and tunes ranging from "Teddy Bear" (which became a signature tune to Elvis's teenage fans) to "Mean Woman Blues," the movie finds Rivers having to face persistent fans, being goaded into fistfights, and being manipulated by press agents. Through it all, as Deke Rivers's star continues to rise, he remains the same unaffected country boy.

The same could not be said for Elvis—at least physically.

When he showed up on the film set late in January 1957, he had been glamorized—with the help of one of Hollywood's leading plastic surgeons. Both he and his high school buddy turned disc jockey,

George Klein, had become patients of Dr. Maury Parks, who was known at the time as the "nose doctor." Klein's surgery has never been a secret, but Elvis insisted on it. "He wanted someone else to have the operation at the same time," said Joe Esposito, a longtime Presley confidant. According to Esposito, Elvis's nose was altered "only slightly." The acne scars disappeared and his complexion was suddenly flawless. Elvis would go on to be a repeat customer for Dr. Parks.

Other changes were made as well. Elvis's teeth had been capped. And most noticeably, after years of temporarily darkening his hair—with greases, oils, and on rare occasion, even shoe polish—he finally dyed it black. With rare exceptions he would retain that color for the rest of his life. In fact, Elvis Presley's black hair became such a part of his image that many people would never realize he was once sandy blond.

Notwithstanding these cosmetic triumphs, producers ignored his acting skills. *Loving You* was only the first of many enjoyable but undemanding roles that relied entirely on Presley's musical presence. Answering critics decades later, Hal Wallis was unapologetic: "Elvis was a great entertainer, a great personality . . . and that is what we bought when we bought him." Added Wallis, "The idea of tailoring Elvis for dramatic roles is something that we never attempted because we did not sign Elvis as a second Jimmy Dean. We signed him as a number one Elvis Presley."

For his part, the Colonel had no interest in good films. He only asked one question: "How much does it pay?"

The Motion Picture Association of America, however, had concerns. The self-censorship organization of the movie industry wanted to clamp down on Presley's sexuality. In *Loving You*, he was to refrain from giving any "lustful" or "open-mouth" kisses.

The MPAA needn't have worried. The movie was vapidly wholesome, from the young hero's earnest defense of his music before the stodgy townsfolk at a televised "trial" of rock 'n' roll to his chaste relationship with a ponytailed singer who, in fifties fashion, becomes his "true love." As costar Dolores Hart put it, when the two finally did get to kiss, "we went into the clinch in front of three hundred and fifty technicians." She was so embarrassed that she blushed right through the makeup. "The gag in the makeup department was that for the first time they had to develop a blush-proof makeup." Dolores and Elvis both burst into hysterical laughter.

The nineteen-year-old Dolores and Presley developed a close

friendship based on their shared sense of humor and deep religious beliefs. The niece of Mario Lanza, one of Elvis's favorite singers, Hart had the honey-blond patrician beauty of a teenage Grace Kelly. A devout Catholic, she was just eleven when she made the decision, on her own, to convert to Catholicism. So strong were her religious convictions that in 1963 she quietly left Hollywood to enter a Catholic convent in Bethlehem, Connecticut. During her career Hart was known for her depictions of "good girls"—who chose to wait until marriage before having sex. That romantic lead would become a stalwart of the Presley movie formula.

Jailhouse Rock also portrayed a good girl, a music promoter played by Judy Tyler. But in this movie, Elvis portrayed an outright heel.

Whereas *Loving You* looked at stardom in glorious Technicolor and VistaVision, *Jailhouse Rock* showed the flip side of fame, in gritty black-and-white CinemaScope. Because it centered on the story of a surly ex-con who doesn't care whom he hurts on his way to singing stardom, MGM initially entitled the movie *The Jailhouse Kid*. Then the Colonel intervened. At a production meeting with executives, he lit a cigar and declared, "Now listen, the people are gonna come see my boy no matter what you call the movie. But I don't like that title at *all*." Letting out a billow of smoke, he drawled, "It's got a bad connotation."

When one of the executives mumbled something about *Jailhouse Rock*, Parker enthused, "That's perfect! I pick *that!*"

In a follow-up meeting a few days later, choreographer Alex Romero also chose *Jailhouse Rock* from a variety of possible tunes for the movie's big production number—Elvis's first choreographed routine.

Romero and Presley met for the first time in a rehearsal hall that had once been used by tap-dance queen Eleanor Powell. "I don't want anybody to go and make a Hollywood boy out of me," warned Presley.

Romero was amused. "I guess he thought that I was going to give him some slick dancing steps, like they had in the MGM musicals. No, I was gonna do Elvis. I chose steps that were foreign to him, but that were also *like* him, so he could pick them up."

Initially, Elvis was terrified. "I could see it in his eyes," said Romero. "I think he was intimidated by MGM. After all, MGM is like playing the Palace of motion picture studios. He felt he was out of his league."

The home of Greta Garbo, Joan Crawford, Lana Turner, Judy Garland, Clark Gable, and Jean Harlow, it was the Rolls-Royce of studios.

MGM, however, was also in awe of Elvis Presley. "It was amazing the amount of people that decided they had business on the lot," said author Gore Vidal, then working at the studio. Sometimes as many as a hundred young women clustered outside the soundstage door. "After a while he got to doing funny things, like wearing a crazy hat for a disguise, you know?" said Romero.

The giddiness over Elvis intensified when he swallowed one of the caps on his teeth during filming and had to be rushed to nearby Cedars of Lebanon Hospital, where he found himself surrounded by pretty nurses. An X ray—later published in the newspapers—showed that the tooth had gone down into his trachea and lodged in the lung. Elvis was genuinely worried, but doctors easily extracted it with long forceps and a bronchoscope, then kept their famous patient for overnight observation.

Naturally, Elvis's "boys" joined him at the hospital—the singer said he needed to be entertained. The entourage was growing both in number and in clownish visibility, becoming as ubiquitous as Presley, who often found himself defending them. "I get lonely and these fellows spell home to me," he explained.

Two days later he was back on the set to perform the definitive musical number of his career.

The "Jailhouse Rock" dance sequence required sixteen male dancers. Aware that the performer might be leery of working with effeminate hoofers, Romero surrounded him with tough-looking professional dancers.

One of them, Frank Magrin, confessed to having "this little bit of attitude" about meeting Elvis, though Presley was trying his best to be friendly.

"I don't know what I'm doin' here. I can't dance," Elvis joked.

Magrin shot back, "Can you sing?"

Elvis smiled. "Oh, a Pat Boone fan, huh?"

After four days of rehearsal, Elvis still had trouble learning his steps for the big dance sequence. "He was like an epileptic fit put to music," said Magrin. "He had great rhythm, but he couldn't dance."

The completed sequence was a mix of Romero's steps and Presley's own unbridled moves. When it wrapped, a grinning Elvis approached Romero and said simply, "Alex, you're a good ol' boy." The choreographer proudly took that as a compliment.

If Elvis couldn't quite remember his dance steps for the camera, he remembered them one night when he was out with friends in Hollywood. They'd all just left a Doris Day movie because members of the audience recognized Elvis—and kept walking up and down the darkened aisles to get a look at him.

Elvis and his friends climbed into his Cadillac and were headed back to his suite at the Knickerbocker Hotel when Elvis turned on the radio and chanced upon "Jailhouse Rock." "Hey, guys, hear that?" He loved to listen to himself on the radio.

He turned up the sound and pulled the car over, cranking up the volume full blast. He climbed out of the car, and as his friends looked on, Elvis went through his "Jailhouse Rock" routine on a deserted Hollywood side street, in a light rain, as the headlights cast dancing shadows.

"He was so tickled, like a kid playing in a mud puddle," recalled friend and songwriter Shari Sheeley.

Sheeley, who visited with Presley at the Knickerbocker, was also with him the night the television show *Rocket to Stardom* launched its search for "the new Elvis Presley." Sitting on the sofa, Elvis laughed and applauded some of the acts. When one young man broke out with his rendition of "Hound Dog," Elvis yelled to the screen, "Watch it, boy, you're never going to make that next note, not at the rate you're goin'." The boy, in fact, did miss that follow-up note. "I told him he wouldn't hit that thing!" Elvis said.

Presley impressed Sheeley with his humility. "You can never forget who put you where you are and how many people would like to change places with you," he told her.

Elvis did not stay at the Knickerbocker for long. So many people descended on him—and also ascended, climbing all eight stories of the fire escape—that he eventually had to move to the more private Beverly Wilshire Hotel. Elvis and his Memphis cohorts took over an entire wing—four bedrooms, a living room, dining room, and den. Suite 850 became one of the town's legendary bachelor pads—and the royal headquarters for a young man who was fast becoming the screen's newest king.

Robert Mitchum, then famed for his forties-era tough-guy roles, paid homage—and even tried to talk Elvis into costarring with him in *Thunder Road*, a film about moonshiners who take on the feds and the mob. Elvis listened intently to Mitchum's plans but demurred, "Well, I can't. Not unless the Colonel says I can."

Mitchum couldn't believe his ears. "Fuck the Colonel!"

Elvis offered up a weak smile.

Natalie Wood showed up several times, once to threaten suicide. "We started calling her the Mad Nat . . . she was nuttier than a fruitcake," said Lamar Fike, who joined the entourage in 1957. He was on hand the time Wood climbed out on the window ledge and began babbling about committing suicide over Elvis.

"What do we do, boss?" asked the frightened Fike.

"Screw it!" said Elvis. "She ain't gonna jump."

After a half hour, Wood climbed sheepishly back through the window. "I told you she wasn't gonna do anything," Elvis snorted.

A veritable who's who of the town's hip names made the pilgrimage to Suite 850. Vince Edwards, then a rising young actor, was a regular. Glenn Ford showed up. Sammy Davis Jr.—one of Elvis's favorites— once gave an impromptu performance in the living room. Nick Adams and his crowd also came around. Adams was sometimes so antic that some Presley associates wondered if the young actor was taking drugs.

June Juanico, whose relationship with Elvis had ended after the filming of *Love Me Tender*, frankly wonders if Adams was the one who introduced Elvis to drugs. Juanico, who was at the Presley home during Adams's visits, said, "There is no question in my mind but that Nick was wired at the time. I mean, wired."* Though Juanico never saw Presley become similarly "wired," she speculates that his gradual descent may have been prompted by his early Hollywood associations.

Presley was certainly a live wire for pretty women. In her memoirs, flame-haired stripper Tempest Storm said she and Presley spent an eventful week in 1957 in Las Vegas, where she was headlining in Minsky's Follies. Presley was so anxious to get at her that, to her delight, he scaled an eight-foot fence outside her hotel before climbing up the back way. She was wearing a short, blue see-through nightie and was cradling her tiny toy poodle when he entered through her sliding glass door. She kidded him about his torn pants. Clothes were the last thing on his mind. Wasting no words, he grabbed her hand and headed down the hall, saying, "I'm as horny as a billy goat in a pepper patch. I'll race ya to the bed." According to Storm, he was an "impatient lover" who jokingly threatened to strangle her little dog when it kept yipping in reaction to their heated cries during "a marathon" session of lovemaking.

Actress Venetia Stevenson, whom Ed Sullivan chose as the "most photogenic girl in the world," was romantically linked to Elvis after meeting him in Hollywood and later visiting with his family in Memphis. Starlet Yvonne Lime, who starred opposite a hairy Michael

---

*Adams died in 1968 as the result of an overdose of prescription medication.

Landon in *I Was a Teen-age Werewolf*, also visited the family home and made headlines when columnists erroneously reported she and Presley were engaged.

Marriage, at least to an actress, was not in the cards. Actress Anne Neyland, a *Jailhouse Rock* costar, told the fan magazines, "Elvis is a very funny boy when he likes a girl. . . . He puts her on a pedestal, and he makes her out to be so sweet and so naive that she can't look at other boys when she's going around with him." Neyland was a good example. She was originally cast in *Jailhouse* as a glamorous movie star who had "been around." But after Elvis started dating her, he had her put in another role—a smaller part, playing a more innocent character. "I was quite shocked and upset when I discovered this. I tried to explain to him that it was my business. That I want to play all kinds of roles, and the parts I play have nothing to do with what I am like myself," said Neyland. "But he thinks if he likes a girl well enough to marry her, she wouldn't be in this business."

Fan magazines of the late fifties often offered up a roll call of Elvis's many dates in order to raise the question "Why isn't the world's most eligible bachelor married?" No one ever supplied the answer. But the fact is, as the fifties neared its end, social changes were afoot. The delineation between "good" and "bad" girls was gradually blurring. In the sixties that line would disintegrate. Elvis would soon wonder at the growing numbers of women who would openly seek sexual pleasure, and he would be downright vexed by the many women who would see nothing wrong with wanting both careers and marriage.

Elvis Presley couldn't figure it out. And he never would.

Life at the top ensured that he would continue to have critics. He was vilified for putting out an album of sacred music, including "Peace in the Valley" and "I Believe." And he took hits for his first yuletide album—which *Time* branded "the most serious menace to Christmas since 'I Saw Mommy Kissing Santa Claus.' " It seemed he was forever being asked to defend the music he had popularized, especially when the industry desperately attempted to unleash new musical crazes, led by, of all things, calypso and Hawaiian music.

By the end of the year, several of Hollywood's biggest names were taking shots at the new kid in town. Bing Crosby told *Daily Variety* that Elvis needed "more training and more diversified material," and added, "I can't see where he's advanced much in the past year." The crooner even attacked Presley's posture: "He slouches."

Frank Sinatra called rock-'n'-roll fans "cretinous goons" and Presley's music "deplorable, a rancid-smelling aphrodisiac." Writing in the magazine *Western World*, Sinatra ranted, "My only deep sorrow is the unrelenting insistence of recording and motion picture companies upon purveying the most brutal, ugly, degenerate, vicious form of expression it has been my displeasure to hear, and naturally I'm referring to the bulk of rock 'n' roll."

Although Presley was baffled, hurt, and angry, he was polite publicly. "He has a right to his own opinions," he said of Sinatra, whom he called "badly mistaken."

Loving You generated mixed opinions from the reviewers. Taking a shot at both the movie and the star's fans, *America* said, "By any sensible standard it is an unbearably bad movie . . . but sensible standards are no concern of Presley's many admirers." But *Daily Variety*—which wondered if the "rock 'n' roll craze" hadn't "passed its peak"—gave Presley high marks for showing "improvement as an actor."

Jailhouse Rock was another matter. Some theaters wouldn't even play it because of the small-scale riots that broke out during screenings of another youth picture, *Blackboard Jungle*. *Time* railed against Elvis's performance, saying he'd been "sensitively cast as a slob." Noting that Presley's screen character spouts the line "I'll grow on you," *Time* further quipped, "If he does, it will be quite a depressing job to scrape him off."

The British press all but went on a rampage, assailing the picture for a prison scene in which the bare-chested Presley is brutally whipped by a prison guard, and for his character's reprehensible treatment of women.

"Elvis, You're a Bore!" was the headline for the *Daily Mirror* review by Donald Zec, who called the movie "a muddy brew of delinquency, cheap sentiment, bad taste and violence." Opined Zec, "Elvis Presley should stay off celluloid . . . and get back in the groove where he belongs."

Elvis got his revenge, though. *Jailhouse Rock* became one of the year's most successful movies, earning back its $4-million budget in a matter of weeks. As 1957 came to a close, Elvis Presley was the fourth-ranked star at the U.S. box office (Rock Hudson was ranked number one). The whining Frank Sinatra had to be content with fifth place.

In Britain, Presley became such a sensation that fans formed an Elvis Presley fan club. As for the *Daily Mirror*'s Donald Zec, he was the recipient of so much hate mail from angry teenagers that the newspaper ran a full page of replies, illustrated with a cartoon of Zec being hanged from a tree.

In the meantime, Elvis went on tour, returning to Tupelo for the second year in a row for yet another triumphant homecoming, this time in gold lamé. He headed next for the arenas of the Pacific Northwest, then on to Los Angeles for a pair of concerts before a star-studded crowd. The shows remain legendary both for Presley's incandescent performances and the crowds' hysteria.

He was already hot at the Memorial Stadium in Spokane, Washington, where he emerged in his gold-lamé suit and, bathed in pink floodlights, began a rendition of "Hound Dog" so frenzied that the screams of 12,500 fans drowned out his singing. At show's end, many of the ticket buyers swooped out onto the field, scooping up soil as a souvenir.

In Tacoma, following an opening act of jugglers, musical quartets, and marimba players, he again emerged in his gold suit—worn with a black shirt opened to the waist. Reporters were baffled; less than an hour earlier, in a backstage interview, he had been shy, stuttery, and wearing collegiate-looking clothes—and, inexplicably, a straw hat. But then, as Elvis had warned them, "I lose myself in my singing. Maybe it's my early training singing gospel hymns. I'm limp as a rag and worn-out when a show's over."

When he played Portland's Multomah Stadium, he climaxed his act with a "Hound Dog" of such sinuous writhings—and overt sexuality—that he appeared to crawl across the stage through half the song. So desperate was the management to get the crowd out of the stadium at show's end that an announcer boomed, "Ladies and gentlemen, Elvis Presley has left the stadium!"

In Hollywood, there was no stopping him once he got onstage in the Pan Pacific Auditorium. The very epitome of Streamline Moderne architecture, he shook the hall to Richter-scale intensity. "You could hear the screams two blocks away," said Wally George, who covered the show for the *Los Angeles Times*. Before a crowd of nine thousand he delivered a fifty-minute, eighteen-song set—including his monster hit "Jailhouse Rock"—that seemed to defy gravity with his bolts, slides, leaps, and bumps. He even grabbed RCA's omnipresent three-foot-high canine symbol and rolled around with it between his legs.

Reviewers were infuriated: on top of everything else, it looked as if Elvis Presley was trying to have sex with Nipper.

The next day the press was gunning for him. The *Los Angeles*

Mirror-News's Dick Williams led the infuriated pack. The show, he declared, was a "corruption of the innocent" and "a lesson in pornography," comparable to "one of those screeching uninhibited party rallies which Nazis used to hold for Hitler."

Still other enraged reporters bandied about adjectives including "indecent," "screeching," "uninhibited." Why, according to some accounts, some irate parents—including actor Alan Ladd—had protectively dragged their innocent kids out of that auditorium in midconcert.

As he flipped through the morning papers, the Colonel had some advice for his client: "Better tone it down tonight. . . . And don't go round screwin' that dawg."

Elvis recoiled in fury, letting loose a string of epithets. "Those motherfuckers!" he raged. "I am not obscene! I have never been obscene!" Storming away from the table, he told the Colonel, "I'm sick and tired of this shit! I'm gonna do my show the way I want. And I promise, tonight's will be one helluva concert!"

It seemed everyone in town was there. Ricky Nelson (who got to meet his idol after the performance), Nick Adams, Vince Edwards, Rita Moreno, Tommy Sands, Russ Tamblyn. "All of us absolutely blown away. Because there has never been anything quite like that night," remembered Valerie Allen.

Since it was being photographed by the LAPD vice squad, the delivery was more subdued. This time Elvis didn't attempt to hump Nipper. But his defiance was patently on display. As he sang, he occasionally thrust his groin forward and tauntingly yelled toward the police movie camera, "You guys shoulda been here last night!" Gloating and grinning, he took his thumb and forefingers to form a halo over his head, taunting, "I'm an angel tonight!" At times he put his hands behind his back and feigned being put into handcuffs.

Even some of Elvis's celebrity friends were shocked by his defiant and crass behavior. One former girlfriend was spotted bursting into tears as Presley played up his bad-boy reputation to the hilt.

From L.A. he went on to Oakland, San Francisco, Hayward, and finally to Hawaii for a trio of shows. In time he would find a special peace in the Hawaiian islands. But during his first trip he was exhausted.

He was also anguishing over changes in his life. Because of his Hollywood schedule, Scotty and Bill had been languishing professionally as well as financially. They would soon quit performing with Presley. He had also broken off contact with Dewey Phillips, whose irascible personality hadn't been appreciated during trips to Hollywood—where he'd proven embarrassing to the new star. Elvis actually apologized to Yul Brynner, following Phillips's startled observation: "You're a short little mother, aren't you?"

Tired and confused, Elvis returned home to Memphis where his private, sensitive side reemerged. He was somewhat ashamed about the raunchiness of his performances, and he talked over his concerns with his minister. "Am I making too much money? Am I moving too fast? Am I doing things I shouldn't?" he asked.

With no ready answers, he reached out for someone to talk to.

A fan who stood outside the fancy ironwork gates of Graceland, after having journeyed from Colorado, got a surprise visit with her idol when the gate guard ushered her inside to meet the singer. When twenty-year-old Sadie Gonzales reemerged, she delivered a message. While she was there, Elvis had paced the floor, biting his nails, running his hands through his hair, pouring his heart out for three hours. "He told me he was very, very lonely. He said he could have anything he wanted, but he wasn't as near God as he used to be," said Gonzales. "He said sometimes it all seems like a dream."

Elvis Presley was about to get a wake-up call. The U.S. Army wanted him.

Soldier Boy

On a crisp Memphis night during the Christmas season of 1957, the secret wish of millions of teenage boys came true: Elvis Presley received his draft notice. Not a few parents heaved a sigh of relief as well. There was even a delicious rumor that he would be sent overseas to the frozen wastes near the Communist border.

The moment the Memphis Selective Service Commission announced its decision to draft the king of rock 'n' roll, mailbags full of letters began arriving at the doorstep. Angry parents, especially, congratulated the three board members for "ridding America of this menace." Had they known that Elvis, despite publicity to the contrary, was being handled with kid gloves, their satisfaction might have been diminished.

On the night of December 18, with frigid bursts of wind buffeting Memphis, Milton Bowers, head of the draft board, drove through the gates of Graceland to deliver the dreaded draft notice to its notorious recipient. He was not unexpected, for Elvis had already gone through specially arranged pre-induction exams and had been classified 1-A.

Elvis threw open the mansion's double door and stepped onto the porch. He wore a red cashmere sweater, black pants, and penny loafers with a spit shine so dazzling that even the toughest sergeant would have approved. "Hey, Mr. Bowers," said Elvis, extending his hand. "Welcome to Graceland." The singer's grip was firm and friendly.

Bowers stood silent for a few minutes, stunned both by the mansion's multitudinous Christmas lights and by Presley's striking looks. "The most astoundingly good-looking man I had ever encountered," he said later.

"Get on in here," Presley urged again. "And why didn't you drive your car right up to the door?"

The Selective Service messenger, though, stayed only a moment, refusing eggnog, before driving off into the dark. Presley dismissed him from his mind and plunged into the lavish Christmas in Graceland.

He was by now the reluctant property of the military. The last five days at Graceland had been dominated by underhanded negotiations between Parker and the Pentagon including telegrams, a respectful parade of Army and Navy brass in their uniforms, and telephone conferences with the Colonel.

Chief Petty Officer D. U. Stanley had come first, to outline a "celebrity enlistment package" that the Navy had assembled just for Elvis. Among other perks, he would be allowed to perform in Las Vegas and would be provided with sumptuous VIP quarters. "Mr. Presley, sir," said Stanley, "we would even be willing to allow you to form an 'Elvis Presley Company,' packed with boys from Memphis." There was a surprise bonus: he could enlist any friend of his choice. A leather folio with Navy enlistment papers was handed to him.

"Sir," said Elvis, "I'd like some time to think this over."

The Army was equally solicitous, promising a packet of special privileges, including first-class tours of bases all over the world. Again he answered politely, "Sir, give me some time to think this over."

Finally, the combined powers at the Pentagon offered what many American soldiers and veterans call "the celebrity wimp-out"—a place in Special Services, where Elvis would serve his country by entertaining the troops while living in priority housing and dining at the officers' mess.

To weigh these offers, the Colonel drove down and closeted himself with his client. As Parker paced the floor and Elvis sat, arms folded, on his huge bed, the men talked for hours, mainly about salvaging Elvis's career. "You gotta go in as a line soldier just like a regular guy, serve as any other recruit, and come home a hero," Parker said. "Taking any of these deals will make millions of Americans angry."

Presley agreed. He then walked down the stairs to the living room, where he told his parents, "I'm going to accept the letter from the draft when it arrives, and I'm demanding a combat unit."

Gladys began to cry, but Vernon approved. "I agree with Parker," he said. "That's the best way for you to go—like any other American guy."

Frightened, Gladys fled to her room and didn't talk to Elvis until the next day, when she warned, "You go in, you won't come back alive."

"It was my son's choice," Vernon said later. "Parker just laid everything out, and Elvis went with a combat unit. He wanted to tough it out. If he had to do this, he wanted to do it as a real soldier."

The Pentagon, however, didn't really want a field soldier named Elvis Presley. The celebrity would need extra security no matter which unit he joined. So they made an amended offer. If he joined the Army and let them "train the hell out of him," they would then send Elvis from recruiting center to recruiting center in a series of public appearances. Presley would be the Army's front man in an attempt to sign up fifty thousand new boys.

Elvis, realizing that he would be just another glorified actor, politely declined. He demanded combat training, "just like any other guy." The Pentagon, anxious to end this standoff, capitulated before the press got wind of it.

After surrendering, the Pentagon appointed a clandestine Elvis Presley Committee to monitor the "enormous cost" and the "complicated procedures" necessary to turn a rock-'n'-roll star into a frontline soldier. It was estimated that security and press liaisons alone would eventually cost $500,000. There has never been a cost breakdown for Presley's tour of duty, but a specially designated team followed quietly behind Elvis from the time he boarded the bus until he was well settled into his company. A privately authored "Presley Dossier" and a special booklet entitled *Private Elvis Aaron Presley—Protocol* have disappeared from Army files.

The day after he received "the official letter," Elvis happily agreed to photo coverage of the present he was giving Colonel Parker for Christmas, a brand-new, $1,800 BMW Isetta—one of the smallest vehicles in the world—so small that there wasn't room for conventional doors. To enter the automobile it was necessary to open the front end, a fact made possible by a rear engine.

A journalist asked, "Mr. Presley, if I bring along a pair of Army fatigues and a cap, will you wear them for the photos?"

Elvis was silent for several seconds before agreeing: "Sure, why not? I gotta get used to wearing them anyway."

They drove down to Parker's home in Madison, Tennessee, and Presley parked out of sight, near a cluster of trees. When Parker opened his front door and saw "Private Presley," he doubled over laughing. Not only were the pants and jacket excruciatingly tight, the hat was so large that it drifted down around his ears. "Can you sit down in that uniform?" asked Parker.

"Just about," said Presley, "and the girls seemed to like it when I stopped at the last gas station." He smiled, adding, "Come on outside. I brought your Christmas present."

When Parker caught sight of the Isetta and the newspaper photographer, he glowered at first. Then recognizing a publicity coup, he carefully eased his bulk down into the baby car. When Elvis squeezed in beside, the Italian automobile was wall-to-wall flesh.

"Ah, Christmas, isn't it wonderful," the Colonel said to the photographer, while fogging up the tiny car with smoke from his ever-present cigar. He added, "It is snug." "Yes," said Presley, grinning. "It is only a small, small way of showing my feelings for you."

Later that night it struck Parker that something was wrong in the draft notice. Even though it was one o'clock in the morning, he called Elvis:

"What's the date on that induction? When do you have to report?"

Elvis ran downstairs to fetch it. "I go in on January twentieth."

"Damn," said Parker. "What the hell are we going to do about *King Creole*? We've got a start date and the sets are built. We need a six-week reprieve. Paramount's got a bundle tied up in this movie. But you never mind, I'll fix it."

Parker began calling people in Washington, New York, and Hollywood, spreading the word that "his boy" needed "a special favor." As he explained to Elvis, "We don't want it to appear that you are asking for more time. That would hurt bad. You must give every appearance of a normal boy caught between big business [Paramount] and the government."

During Parker's call to Paramount studio head Y. Frank Freeman, Parker insisted that the studio itself call for the extension. "If you do it, there's absolutely no problem." Three days later, Freeman sent the Memphis draft board a certified letter asking for a sixty-day deferment for Elvis "because of financial hardship." Elsewhere in the declaration

Freeman noted that the studio had already spent between $300,000 and $350,000 in preproduction costs for the movie.

Bowers telephoned, saying he was inclined to give the extension, adding, "The only person who may apply is Elvis himself."

"Goddammit," Parker raged. "It's going to look like you want it. Be very, very careful how you word your request."

Early on Christmas Eve, Elvis sat at his upstairs desk and scrawled out the letter. "I hope you understand that I am not acting for myself but on behalf of the studio. Paramount helped start my career, and now I feel it is only fair to go along with the request, so these folks will not lose so much money on everything they have done so far."

He closed it: "Merry Christmas to everyone on the board."

As soon as the request was made public, a national scandal erupted.

"I was bombarded with angry letters and calls from all sides, even the day after Christmas," Bowers recalled. "Hundreds came from fans, but just as many were written by anti-Elvis forces who wanted to put Elvis in boot camp immediately."

One Elvis fan complained indignantly, "You didn't put Beethoven in the Army, did you?"

Bowers actually wrote back: "No, I could not . . . because Beethoven was not American, and would not have been eligible if he was one because he was deaf."

Bowers and the Memphis board were also lambasted by the national offices of the Veterans of Foreign Wars and the American Legion, all asking for the "immediate induction of Elvis Presley."

"You know what made me angry about the entire thing," said Bowers, "is that he would have automatically gotten the extension if he hadn't been Elvis Presley the superstar."

In the end, the board unanimously granted a six-week extension, and Elvis rushed off to Hollywood to begin work on *King Creole*, taking almost a dozen people with him.

The top brass in Special Services saw another opening and began throwing their weight around, hoping to force Elvis into performing while in uniform. Parker again sprang into action. He flew to Washington, D.C., to meet with the renowned World War II leader Lieutenant General William H. "Hap" Arnold, commander of the Fifth Army.

After making certain that Arnold understood that he was but an "honorary colonel" and that the two were fellow Tennesseans, the Colonel made his point. "I know you are a busy man, General, and that every moment is vital to our country. But I want you to know about something which is important to me. My boy Elvis Presley is a member of your army. He is just a plain soldier boy, and that is all he wants to be. He especially doesn't want the special treatment he would get if he were in Special Services, and he doesn't want to spend his time singing and entertaining. He wants to be a soldier, not a singer."

Lieutenant General Arnold impassively listened to each word, before finally replying, "I am very pleased you came to see me. And I was unaware of the requests of Elvis's time from Special Services. I will see what I can do."

Special Services never bothered Elvis again.

When Elvis returned to Hollywood early in 1958 for the filming of *King Creole*, Dolores Hart—once again cast opposite Elvis as the "good girl"—sensed that something was different.

The lighthearted attitude Elvis had displayed during the making of *Loving You* had vanished. Though he was still pleasant to the cast and crew, and always had a ready joke, he was clearly distracted. He no longer ate with his colleagues in the commissary; instead he took his meals in his dressing room, or in his hotel suite, as he pored over the script.

The changed demeanor was no doubt due, in part, to the looming military duty. Presley was anxious about whether his movie career would take an artistic nosedive while he was away. "I think this will be the best movie I ever made," he told anyone who would listen.

Produced by Hal Wallis and based on the best-selling Harold Robbins novel *A Stone for Danny Fisher*, *King Creole* had been adroitly tailored to Presley's talents. The book, touted as "a harsh but uncompromising novel of life in New York's toughest slum," was about the travails of a young prizefighter. The screenplay transformed Danny Fisher into a busboy-turned-nightclub-singer on New Orleans' legendary Bourbon Street. As he pulls himself up from a life of poverty and disillusionment, Danny encounters a ruthless crook named Maxie Fields, as well as Maxie's sultry mistress, and a good girl who works at a dime store.

In *Jailhouse Rock*, Elvis had proved he could effectively play a creep. With *King Creole*, he was able to explore his range—opposite an especially strong cast.

At home, Danny must rely on his sister (Jan Shepard) as an ally in his constant conflicts with his father (played by the esteemed Dean Jagger), who wants his high-school-dropout son to get a "decent" job—

not work on Bourbon Street. Meanwhile, in the gritty nightclub world, Danny collides with tough Maxie Fields, played by a then virtually unknown Walter Matthau. While Danny turns on the sexual heat with Maxie's girlfriend, played by sultry Carolyn Jones, and with Dolores Hart, he shows both sweetness and sexual swagger. (After meeting Hart, he takes her to a cheap hotel room, mistakenly thinking she "knows the score.") And on the stage of the King Creole nightclub, Presley gets to perform some of the best songs of his movie career—including "Hard Headed Woman," "Trouble," and the title song, "King Creole."

The director was Michael Curtiz, a prolific movie veteran adept at every genre and whose credits included such classics as *Casablanca*, *Mildred Pierce*, and *Yankee Doodle Dandy*.

After filming on the Paramount soundstages, cast and crew moved to New Orleans for scenes in the exotic French Quarter and the sinfully enticing Bourbon Street, which added greatly to the movie's atmosphere. The black-and-white cinematography further added to the realism of the story and setting.

Shooting on location proved to be onerous. Because of Elvis's persistent fans, just getting safely in and out of his New Orleans hotel room required special maneuvers. "He had to ride in an old sedan, lying on the floor in the back, so his fans couldn't mob him," related Jones. In fact, the crew had to rig rope ladders from rooftop to rooftop so that Elvis could enter from the adjacent building, then climb down the fire escape and through his own window.

The cast got such a kick out of Elvis's plight that one night over dinner, Jones, Hart, and Nick Adams—who was again in tow with Presley—decided to jokingly "shoot" their way up to Elvis's quarters, which were kept under guard. "We went into the hotel lobby, found a toy shop, and proceeded to purchase all the toy guns on sale," Hart remembered. Carolyn Jones* armed herself with a plastic .45. Adams chose a plastic machine gun, and Hart strapped on a pair of six-shooters.

Then the trio stormed the elevator, brandished their "weapons," and ordered the confused elevator operator: "Take us to the ninth floor—fast!" Once on Presley's floor, the threesome "overcame" Presley's guard and burst into his penthouse suite, where a trio of Elvis's aides laughingly leapt to the star's rescue and disarmed the

---

*Jones would later be known to TV viewers as Morticia of *The Addams Family*.

would-be terrorists. In the end, reported Hart, the "gang war" was won by "General Presley and his powerful three-man army."

To Hart's glee, Presley got his comeuppance the following night when, after a day's filming, he climbed into the elevator and requested to be taken to nine. The operator was leery: he wasn't supposed to take anyone up there.

"Yes, because that's Elvis Presley's floor. And I'm Elvis."

The elevator operator was not going to allow himself to be tricked a second time. He took his passenger up several floors and then made him exit. So Elvis was forced to walk up the stairs.

"What a sweet man—what a sensitive soul," is how Carolyn Jones once described her costar. She liked to joke that, on the screen, she kissed Elvis "and then he joined the Army."

Matthau found him shy. "Actually, I probably spent more time with the Colonel, shooting craps, than I did talking to Elvis. He was fairly withdrawn."

At the informal wrap party in Hollywood for the movie, Elvis sometimes seemed morose. In a few days he would become a lowly buck private. When presented with a cake decorated with a hard-sugar GI—complete with green fatigues—the singer plunged the knife in and decapitated the little figure as he cut the first piece of cake.

After he later disappeared into his dressing room, he atypically yelled at his security guards and attendants to get ready quick—they were going home to Memphis on the very next train.

For the first time he defined his retinue as sycophants, saying, "I never know when they're lying or when they are telling the truth." A journalist who watched openmouthed said later, "These boys are there for Presley's own amusement; they have no job—except to indulge in vulgar practical jokes or as partners in roughhouse games."

Even more corrosive to Elvis's life and career, the men who formed his retinue learned how to be ultimate yes-men, reassuring him again and again that his clothes were perfect, that his hair had never looked better, that his shirt was "absolutely perfect," and that his pants were just tight enough. "They became his own impenetrable 'Berlin Wall,' " said Hollywood columnist and friend May Mann. "Nobody could get through them—not even his mother."

Ignoring both the Paramount and MGM brass, who wanted to discuss "post-Army projects," Elvis herded his band of wayfarers onto the train.

Once on board he was a caged tiger, pacing back and forth in his double bedroom and gulping a few diet pills to distract him from the sense of rage and helplessness. Eventually he decided the train was too slow, so he phoned ahead to Dallas and arranged for a fleet of limos to haul the Presley court back home.

But when they glimpsed the crowds gathered at the enormous indoor station, Elvis freaked. "Never mind," said Lamar Fike. "The train slows at the next curve, and we'll just jump it." At the right second Fike tumbled off, followed by his jittery comrades, who exited running.

The distant screams and the thumping sound of penny loafers convinced Fike that they had been spotted. "Come on, guys, or we're all going to be trapped." At that precise moment Fike crashed into an old brick fence. He looked up at Presley, dazed but otherwise perfectly fine. Elvis was roaring with laughter. "Lamar," he said, fighting back tears, "we may have a use for you in the movies."

They reached the limos just in time and roared off toward Memphis. Several hours later, while Presley was in a deep sleep, he began moaning, "It's all gone. It's all gone."

One of his buddies shook him awake. "God damn, Elvis, what were you dreaming about? You sounded terrified."

"Nuthin'," Presley murmured. "Nuthin'."

Elvis later confided to Al Fortas that he'd had terrible visions of being poor again. "I dreamed that all the money was gone; the Colonel was gone; the girls at the fence had vanished just like everyone else. It was all gone—everything."

Only when the limos headed up the magnificent curving drive to Graceland did he sink back into the richly upholstered luxury and smile. Graceland would continue to provide an anchor for him for the rest of his life.

Once back home, he lived it up as time ran out. One morning he burst into the entry hall, sat with Gladys for five minutes, kissed her, and vanished as quickly as he'd come.

To release his fury over the Army he booked the Rainbow Roller-dome for seven nights in a row and gathered up a band of skaters who were strong enough and fearless enough to join him in endless games of self-invented War.

On arrival, he presented each participant with knee guards, arm protectors, and heavily padded skating suits. Then Presley divided the wary participants into two lines, each facing the other. At first the two teams silently glared at each other across the monumental rink. Then Elvis blew a shrill whistle, and the bands headed toward each other. "Remember," Elvis boomed, "anything goes."

"We would skate into the middle and have a free-for-all," recalled Will "Bardahl" McDaniel. "As we slammed into each other, the crashes echoed off the ceiling and walls." During one such "slam" Bardahl passed out on impact. When he came to, he was sitting in a chair with an ice pack on his head. Elvis's face appeared through the haze of his disorientation. "All I could do was stare back." The singer began a long apology, but Bardahl stopped him: "Hey, this is your party. Let's get back on the floor." On his third charge, Bardahl, who was only seventeen, downed Elvis—who dropped to the wooden floor, angry.

"I ran to a table and hid under it," Bardahl said. "I'm gonna die, was all I could think." But Presley's top bodyguard finally located him hiding under the tablecloth and said, "Elvis, he's over here."

Bardahl continued, "You have to remember that Elvis was considered 'all-powerful' in Memphis. There had been legendary and bloody brawls before, so you can imagine what I thought." But Elvis merely pulled Bardahl out and eyed him up and down. "Red," he said, "I like this guy. Give him the phone number to the house; he's welcome to come anytime he wants to." Bardahl had passed muster.

Opponents who took on this Memphis Flash Team marveled at the stamina of Elvis and company, but they never learned the dark secret behind their stamina. Before the games started, Elvis passed out what he termed "happy pills," which resembled candy and tasted like a triple tequila. The tablets were Percodan—a morphine derivative prescribed for the most serious forms of pain.

While the members of the Presley team each took one before they hit the floor, Presley himself gulped down as many as four at a time. But he reserved his perks for playing War.

Elvis was proud of the stoicism he displayed while he waited for his induction. But every so often his anger and sadness came to the surface. One Sunday Gladys found him still in bed at one in the afternoon. "Little baby, what's the matter?" she asked.

Presley immediately reverted to baby talk, and he and his mother spent two hours cooing and whispering in the language that was understood only by themselves. Whatever Gladys said, it worked, and he was back up by nightfall, ready for another round of wildness.

Helping him through this time was the company of his vivacious girlfriend—his most serious to date. Anita Wood, a native of Jackson, Tennessee, was hosting *Top 10 Dance Party*, a Memphis TV show for teenagers, when George Klein visited the WHBQ station where she worked in June of 1957. As ambitious as she was beautiful, Wood kiddingly told Klein, "I think you ought to introduce me to Elvis sometime. After all, he's a Memphian and I'm a Memphian now, too."

When the phone rang a few nights later, Wood instantly recognized the voice on the other end. "How about a date tonight?" asked Elvis, who had been enraptured by the platinum blonde since first seeing her on her show. A former beauty-contest winner, the five-foot-three Wood had the dazzling smile of an all-American beauty, and a voluptuous figure. But Wood, who was also making career strides as a singer, already had a date the night that Elvis rang. "But I hope you'll call me again," she said.

He did—just two nights later.

Wood, who re-created their first date for *Modern Screen*, was picked up by Elvis in a long, sleek black Cadillac. They drove down Main Street, where workmen were readying the Strand Theatre for the world premiere of *Loving You*, and then on to one of Elvis's favorite restaurants, Chenault's—just blocks from Graceland—where the private dining room had been readied and the menu selected.

Wood sat down opposite the singer, and a waiter appeared—with covered trays. While she watched in amazement, and later bemusement, she was served a juicy hamburger with fries. She thought Elvis's entrée was also a burger, but as he explained between bites, he had had it made with mounds of crisp bacon instead of ground beef.

Several nights later, Wood was Elvis's special guest at a midnight showing of *Loving You*, for which Elvis had rented the entire theater for friends and relatives, including his parents. Gladys Presley took an immediate liking to Wood and invited her to dinner at Graceland several nights later.

Wood was thrilled to be going to the family home, but she was not so happy when Elvis—in the midst of a tour— "suavely escorted me up to his bedroom" where he showed off his enormous bed.

"You take me home right this minute," said Wood, who prided herself upon being a genteel Southern lady.

"No-no-no. You got the wrong idea," Elvis stuttered. "Mama's fixin' us a special dinner downstairs, then we'll go to the show."

The banquet consisted of wieners and sauerkraut, braised potatoes,

black-eyed peas, and a platter of tomatoes. Dessert was the sumptu-
ously iced coconut cake Gladys was so famous for. Before the meal was
over, Gladys once again had a presentable bride in her sights.

According to Wood, she and Elvis frankly talked about foreplay and
sex, but she didn't sleep with him. "I had been taught there were some
things that you saved for your marriage," said Wood. "A lot of things
that people take for granted now weren't even considered back then.
To many girls, going to bed with a boy was a sin."

That was the way it was with Wood and Presley. "Still, he knew I
loved him," she said. Besides, she realized there "were pretty girls
a-plenty to give him what he wanted, and then disappear out of his
life."

One evening, after Anita told him she had other plans, Elvis called
upon one of his "available" girls. They were romping in bed when Anita
suddenly appeared at the front door.

With the help of Lamar Fike, Elvis and the girl crawled down a
creaky ladder and escaped into a waiting limo in Graceland's garage.
After a "decent amount of time," Elvis emerged from hiding, sauntered
indoors, and said offhandedly, "Oh, when did you get here? I've been
tinkering with one of the cars."

When Elvis bought her an exquisite diamond and sapphire "friendship" ring, and a 1956 Ford, Wood was besieged with queries about
"their plans." To Gladys, the gifts seemed serious enough for her to
consider Elvis and Anita "unofficially engaged." She fantasized about
the wedding she desperately wanted for her son.

Her dreams were fueled by more than wishful thinking. Gladys's
accelerated drinking had become an issue with Elvis, who used to find
empty beer cans—Schlitz "tall boys"—still wrapped in paper sacks and
tucked behind the couch and stacked behind the baking powder and
bags of sugar and flour in the pantry. Brandishing them like a detective
who has just located evidence, Elvis wailed, "It's gonna kill you, Mama,
it really is. And where would I be then?"

Gladys yelled back, "Never mind about me. You never come home
anyway until you get so tired you have to. And, speaking of danger,
you're gonna kill yourself with overwork. Either that, or the fans will do
you in."

"Mama, don't you worry too much about me. I'll be okay."

Gladys screamed in reply, "Don't you ever tell me not to worry
about you. Don't you dare after all the sleepless nights and frightened
days you've cost me."

Elvis leapt up from his chair, grabbed a plate piled high with toma-toes, and threw it against the wall. Gladys did the same with a heavy bowl of crowder peas.

Four days before Elvis's induction, Colonel Parker arrived. He and his client sat in a downstairs office and worked on a master plan to keep the Elvis empire going while the entertainer was salted away. First, a pair of recording sessions in Nashville were held. Songs including "A Fool Such as I" and "I Need Your Love Tonight" would help keep Presley on the turntables until he returned in 1960. As for the merchandise, not only would it continue, but Parker planned to add military touches to the trinkets that had been sellouts over the past year.

By this time Elvis's earnings had grown far beyond anyone's expec-tations. In 1956 alone, Presley had earned over $50 million for the com-panies he worked for, including the 11 million records sold by RCA. His phenomenal record sales continued through 1957 when he topped every artist in the history of recorded music in sales and staying power. For instance, his first album, *Elvis*, which contained the hit "Heart-break Hotel," entered the charts at number eleven then leapt to number one, where it stayed for an astounding forty-nine weeks, at one point selling seventy-five thousand copies a day. It was the biggest-selling album in RCA's long history. The single "Hound Dog," with "Don't Be Cruel" on the flip side, sold a million copies in eighteen days. By the late fall of 1957, Elvis Presley accounted for two-thirds of the record company's output.

He had also made $6 million for the film studios Paramount and Twentieth Century Fox. *Love Me Tender* grossed $1.5 million alone. As for the fledgling actor's personal earnings, he had all of Hollywood watching closely. *Love Me Tender* and *Loving You* each earned him $100,000. *Jailhouse Rock* increased his price to $250,000 plus 50 per-cent of the profits, and his *King Creole* earnings were structured the same way.

Still, merchandise was the star performer—bringing in $40 million over the first 15 months. That year fans purchased 4 million charm bracelets, 120,000 pairs of blue jeans, 240,000 T-shirts, and 7,200 pairs of "EP shoes."

After Parker explained these facts and figures and said that he had enough records in the vaults to carry the singer through his Army tenure, Presley calmed down, kissed his mother as if nothing were wrong, and then headed for the Rollerdome. He didn't return until two-thirty in the morning. At four o'clock, he was awakened by his father, who told him it was time to get dressed.

The U.S. Army was ready for Private Presley.

11

Private Presley

Ten days before induction, image-conscious Elvis Presley had slipped in the back door of a downtown Memphis barbershop, sat down in the chair, and eyed in the mirror his famous tousled hair—his most legendary trademark—as important as his choreographed moves and his notorious hips.

Barber George Aker stood alongside him, scissors in hand.

The words came painfully: "Uh, George, could you cut a couple inches off the top, an inch off the side and back?" Elvis paused before adding, "And raise the sideburns just a little bit."

He stared straight ahead as strands of black-dyed hair tumbled to the floor.

Six days later, as the countdown to conformity drew closer, the king of rock 'n' roll came through the same back door and took the chair once again. "Ax the sideburns," Elvis told Aker with a sigh. "Take another inch off the top and cut the sides and the back close to my head." As Aker later noted, Presley "didn't have the heart to cut it all off." Besides, the singer told the barber, he wanted to "leave some for the Army."

Still, he had blunted what promised to be the most anticipated haircut since Samson's—now set for the afternoon of March 25 in the no-frills barbershop in Fort Chaffee, Arkansas.

Both Presley and Colonel Parker realized that the haircut by U.S. Army barbers would be a powerful symbolic act for millions of American parents, who could hardly wait to see him in a crew cut and ill-fitting Army fatigues. Elvis Presley, the very symbol of rebelliousness, who had changed the dress, appearance, and the manners of an entire generation, was to be shorn—humiliated, some would say—before a bank of newsreel cameras and still photographers. During man-to-man meetings over the few days before induction, Parker showed Elvis how to turn this tide of ill will into a gusher of good fortune.

They could beat this, Parker explained, by having Elvis "portray" the most gung-ho, spit-and-polish draftee the U.S. Army had seen in a long time. "The whole world will be watching," Parker told Elvis and his parents. "And what they see, if we do it right, will make him a bigger star coming out of the Army than he was when he was drafted."

Parker did not have to drum up publicity this time. It had a life of its own. As the induction date approached, the Army press office received an avalanche of requests to cover the event, not just from the American press but from almost every country in Europe. Germany led the list by sending delegations that virtually filled a Lufthansa airliner. Meanwhile, the Pentagon pleaded with Parker one more time to let his client join a cushy Special Services unit.

"I'm very sorry," Parker replied. "But my boy has his mind set on being a line soldier. My hands are tied."

Actually, Elvis had little to say about it. He'd always done what Parker told him. This is shown in the misgivings he communicated to his friends: "I'm gonna be standing guard duty all night when I could have been singing two or three times a week and lolling around the rest of the time."

On the fateful morning, Elvis gathered his shaving gear, a toothbrush, and a comb and dressed in his typically loud clothes: checked sports jacket, modishly tailored gabardine pants, and a hundred-dollar pair of shoes. A weepy Gladys, an impassive Vernon, and the gorgeous Anita Wood—who had been up for an hour, dressing as carefully as if she were going to a casting call—accompanied Elvis to the center at Kennedy Veterans Hospital, twenty-five miles from downtown Memphis.

The morning was cold, foggy, and drizzly. Nevertheless the Elvis entourage was forty minutes early. But not early enough to beat the indefatigable Colonel Parker. "Why, Mr. Parker's been here thirty minutes," said an Army sergeant in dress greens, a starched shirt, and gleaming shoes. He held two enormous *King Creole* balloons that Parker had given him.

Elvis prepared himself for ordeal by flashbulbs. He hugged Gladys, who was unashamedly weeping, shook hands with his father, and kissed Anita Wood. Then he stepped inside to face the doctors, nurses, and army processors who had been awaiting his arrival.

A half hour later he was just one of a line of inductees standing and stripped to their Jockey shorts. They were instructed to follow the yellow arrows painted on the tile floors, leading from test to test in the examination center. Photographers captured him in his underwear, revealing a significant roll of fat around his middle and a relatively out-of-shape body—despite hundreds of bump-and-grind concerts. Aware of the cameras, he stared straight ahead, a defiant look on his face.

The cameramen formed a noisy, restless band as the physicians poked and thumped the singer, looking for physical defects. At one point a Twentieth Century-Fox newsreel camera followed a brilliant beam of light from the physician's intent face to Elvis, where it became a dot of light directed at the center of his eye. Several minutes later, he looked sideways at the newsreel camera and winked broadly. Only the anal exams, blessedly, were exempt "from the eyes and ears of the world."

Elvis only became uncooperative early in the afternoon when the Colonel offered the star a lengthy telegram from Tennessee governor Frank Clement. Parker dragged Elvis, still bare-chested, before the cameras and urged, "Come on, boy, read this for them. This one's a good one."

Presley whirled around, his eyes flashing, and warned, "Look, it's me that's goin' in, and what happens will be to me, not you. So I'm not going to read any damned telegram." Stunned for once, Parker slowly backed off step by step as if he were excusing himself before the emperor of China.

Finally, at the end of a long day, the recruits stood haphazardly before a colonel and swore their allegiance to the country and the U.S. Army. Before the first word was spoken, however, the Colonel bustled about, arranging the recruits into a triangle with Elvis in front. He had a *Life* magazine lensman position himself on a bench so that Presley and his commanding eyes were looking up at the officer swearing him in. Before the week was over, this photograph would grace the pages of newspapers around the world.

Bowing to the obvious, the army captain in charge named Elvis "temporary commander" as he and thirteen other inductees boarded a bus for Fort Chaffee.

Elvis took a moment to kiss his weeping mother indulgently and Anita Wood passionately. He then executed a shifty about-face, gazed at his 1958 black Cadillac, and said, "Good-bye, you long, black son of a bitch." His compatriots on the bus laughed.

Darkness descended as the bus headed toward remote Fort Chaffee. Before settling into his seat for a few minutes of sleep, Elvis walked to the back window of the bus to see if the press caravan was following. He heaved a sigh of relief; the highway was black and deserted.

The master sergeant escorting them ordered a dinner break at the Coffee Cup in West Memphis, Arkansas. Elvis was in the midst of his first army meal—spaghetti with double meatballs, salad, crackers, and two Cokes—when a passel of cars pulled into the parking lot. They had noticed the bus parked off to the side. Fans pushed their way through the doors. Struggling amid the recruits trying to break through to the bus, Elvis got tomato sauce all over himself. That wasn't all. When he was safely on the bus, he noted he had lost a fountain pen and a pencil. His shirt had practically been ripped off his back.

When the bus was back on the highway, Elvis sheepishly apologized to his fellow soldiers: "I know you guys didn't count on this, and I'm mighty sorry."

After reaching Fort Chaffee at eleven-fifteen that night, Private Presley, as the world now called him, and his fellow soldiers fell into bed—totally exhausted.

During a fitful sleep, Elvis's nightmares returned—this time with a vision of audience rejection, the loss of his voice, and a terrifying glimpse of Graceland in ruins. At five o'clock he awakened to the reality of the Fort Chaffee bunkhouse. Moving silently in the dark, Elvis made his bed, shook out his civvies, jumped into them, and was shaved, showered, and standing by the bunk when the sergeant turned on the lights.

Years later, Elvis said he enjoyed his brief period of anonymity when he was lost among thousands of soldiers. Yet the media was to get a final crack at him. After marching his band of thirteen to the mess hall, Presley dug into a substantial breakfast. He was halfway through when a melee erupted outside the mess hall doors. There was shouting, shoving, and some threats by a voice Elvis knew only too well. Colonel Tom Parker was back, this time with a greatly reduced phalanx of ten photographers, including two of his own. "If you don't think I have access, then you can call General Hap Arnold back there in Washington. He'll tell you," shouted Parker before bursting into the mess hall.

As the still and newsreel cameras went into action, Parker told the captain in charge that he was "just looking out for my boy."

The press parade continued all day, thanks to the indulgence of the base commander. Elvis, though, was getting tired of it. When Parker tried to get Elvis to wear a Western-style string tie, Elvis yelled, "Knock it off. I'm in the Army now, and I don't need you making it any worse."

One final indignity still awaited—the shearing of his hair. Prior to the momentous event the cooks at the mess hall let loose loud hound-dog barks. Elvis smiled. Parker, meanwhile, marched over the contingent of reporters and photographers, who crammed into the room and surrounded the window outside. The Colonel directed the scenario as each tousle of hair was cut away with a flourish. "Let's make it fairly slow for the newsreels," Parker demanded. "Let them each get a close-up and a distant shot," he directed barber James B. Peterson. He then asked the reelsmen to make room for the still photographers, including the two men from *Life* working with a new kind of color film that produced the same clarity as black-and-white. As the Colonel moved each group in close, he cued Peterson to shear off another strip of Presley's hair.

By the end of the session Elvis had lost his most distinctive trademark, but he had also added immensely to his personal legend.

"How does it feel, Elvis?" yelled a reporter.

"It don't feel so much different than it did before," said Presley, running his hand along the buzz cut.

"The longest hair on the top of his head was about half an inch," reported the United Press. It was enough to disorient the new soldier: Elvis wandered off without paying the barber the required sixty-five-cent fee. He had to be called back to ante up.

The GI stats were these: Private Elvis Presley, Army serial number US53310761, weighed in at 185 pounds during induction. Once his hair was military-regulation length, he stood five foot eleven. He was issued seventy five pounds of wrinkled military clothing and size-twelve boots. The million-dollar entertainer would now earn $78 a month.

The country's humorists had a field day. As the collective joke proclaimed, "It could only have happened in America."

When a weary Private Presley trudged back to his barracks that first day, he found some comfort: the press and the photographers had been booted off the base by the officer of the day. Thankfully for Elvis, they were forbidden on Fort Hood's training fields, where he was to take both his basic training and his advanced tank instruction. The aptitude test taken earlier in the day earned him a position in the Fifth Army's coveted tank corps, also known as the Hell on Wheels Battalion. He was delighted, having long ago decided that he might as well apply himself during his hitch in the Army and get into one of the tougher units. Hell on Wheels was the answer to his prayers.

At the last minute, however, the orders were almost canceled by Washington politicians. Hap Arnold telephoned Parker to inform him of forces still within the Pentagon who wanted Elvis in a Special Services unit, and that it could be done with the stroke of a pen. Parker countered by prereleasing the photos and news information on Private Presley, stressing that he had made it into the tank corps and was "reveling in it." Telegrams and letters descended upon the Fifth Army brass, who finally admitted they had been outmaneuvered by a pseudo colonel whose basic uniform was a Hawaiian print shirt, work pants, and a tattered straw hat.

Presley and a bus full of his fellow soldiers headed for Fort Hood, Texas, to begin "hell season"—the Hood's rigorous basic training. For eight weeks Presley and his squad struggled their way through combat conditions, including daily five-mile marches. For the most part, Private Presley sailed through, becoming the squad leader of his barracks and the patrol leader for the long hikes. He also shouldered the burden of being the most famous man in the world suddenly thrown into a walled city of soldiers. At first there was a mild chorus of hecklers: "Hey, Elvis, show us how you swivel your hips!" "Hey, Elvis, you lost without your sideburns?" "So, Elvis, what happened to all your girls?"

His "sheer, straight-up toughness" soon silenced the doubters. "This was a no-nonsense man trying to learn how to be a soldier," recalled Sergeant William Norwood, Presley's boot camp trainer. "I had one hundred and ninety-six guys under my supervision and none better than Presley. He did his own work and was so outstanding that he was made 'acting corporal' for a special mission and, still later, got the highest honor in the platoon—'acting sergeant.' "

Elvis bore an extra burden because of his fame. As rock journalist

Jerry Hopkins explained, "Elvis was denied the one inalienable right that soldiers hold most dear—the right to bitch. So he just took what was handed to him and kept his mouth shut."

In the weeks prior to Elvis's arrival, Norwood didn't know how to handle the rock-'n'-roll star. He'd never really listened to Elvis: "Hell, I didn't even know what he looked like." Norwood didn't meet Private Presley until his third day on the base. "First impression? I didn't like the guy! That cured me of making snap judgments. After our first conversation, I thought him arrogant . . . a star! But within hours I realized he was merely shy, perhaps the shyest man I ever met—before or since. And he was not self-concerned . . . surprising, I thought, for a man who was making a half million dollars a month."

Norwood soon noticed that at certain times of the day or on certain days of the week, Private Presley seemed racked by worry. For a while he didn't complain. Then late one afternoon Elvis trotted up to a high-ranking officer and said, "Sir, I've got a real problem. If I don't get to a phone right away, I might lose a million-dollar deal. I know there are no phone booths around." He plaintively added, "Could you help me out?"

The captain turned to Norwood. "Sergeant, don't you have a house on base?"

"Yes, sir," Norwood answered.

"Well, he can make the call from there if it's okay with you."

The sergeant nodded. "Let's go."

Presley's first phone call was regarding a Hollywood project. Then he made a second, to Gladys. Overheard were quiet sobs from Elvis and a barrage of baby talk. However, Presley's voice turned strong and serious when he asked Gladys, "Mama, how are you? You okay? You're sure?"

Although Mrs. Norwood was busy tidying up the house, she overheard parts of the conversation and noted "the deep concern" in Elvis's voice. "It was like he was expecting bad news, and he was questioning his mama carefully to see if anything was bothering her," she remembered decades later. When he at last hung up the phone, she asked him if he wanted a cup of coffee or a soft drink. "No, ma'am," he answered.

"What about a glass of milk?"

His face brightened. "Yes, ma'am, I sure would like a glass of milk."

The next morning at six o'clock, there was a knock at the Norwoods' door. The sergeant, already in uniform, answered it.

It was Elvis. "Sergeant Norwood, sir. Could I use the phone again? It's real important."

Norwood nodded.

Again, Elvis called his mother with the same question: "You okay? He treatin' you okay?" Then more of the Gladys-Elvis babble.

Lamar Fike believes Elvis called home so frequently "not to reassure Gladys that he was okay—although that was of great concern to her—but to make certain Vernon hadn't started abusing her again." Not long before, Fike had accompanied Elvis to Fort Hood, where he took a room in a nearby motel. One day Elvis came over and sat on the bed and said, "You think I call Mama all the time because I miss her? Well, that's number one. But number two, if I ever catch Daddy hurting my mama again, I'll fuckin' kill him." Elvis had confided the same concerns to Marty Lacker.

Billy Smith noted, "Vernon would not have done it, I don't think, had Gladys been sober or healthy. He picked times when she was drinking at the end of her life, when she was also very ill. At other times she was fiery enough and strong enough to deck him."

Surprisingly, none of this personal turmoil affected Elvis's performance on the drill field or in the classroom. "He pushed himself to the limit," Sergeant Norwood recalled. "He would take his field manuals into the head late at night and study—sometimes until dawn. I asked him once why he was such a perfectionist."

Elvis's answer: "Sir, those other guys, they can miss a question or two; they can march out of step once in a while; they can botch a maneuver. But I don't have that option. The world is watching."

The world was also closing in on him. Of course, Presley hadn't imported any of his entourage or his gleaming fleet of automobiles to whisk him to safety. Nevertheless a teeming mass of fans gathered outside the gates of Fort Hood. Once they realized that Hood was an open base, where civilians could wander about, Presley had to develop self-preservation tactics. Working with Norwood, he mapped out a series of escape routes, using the sprawling rows of barracks as a sort of fan-proof underground railroad.

"Whenever a group would appear," said Norwood, "Elvis would jump out of the jeep or break ranks in a marching unit and disappear through the door of the nearest barracks and then careen through one deserted barracks after another until the girls retreated. Then we would reconnoiter at a prescribed location."

When the eight weeks of boot camp concluded and Elvis moved into one of the tank battalions of Hell on Wheels, his cloistered existence also ended. From Memphis rushed in the "Elvis Machine" of lackeys, courtiers, family, and girlfriends. The party was set to begin.

That was when tragedy struck. Elvis was about to lose the one person he couldn't live without.

Broken Dreams

Elvis burst through the front door of a spic-and-span suburban house outside of Killeen, Texas, and gathered Gladys in his arms. His tailored fatigue uniform was streaked and stained with the dust and sweat from maneuvers. The soles of his boots carried clumps of mud from tank ruts. The Texas wind had blown his sun-bleached hair into ungainly clumps.

"Mama," he said, "I'm a tank gunner. I blasted the targets dead-on—third in the whole unit. Mama, they're even gonna let me teach."

Gladys Presley smiled wanly and patted her son on the shoulder. In the week since she, Vernon, and Minnie Mae had moved down to the rented house in Killeen, a small town near Fort Hood, her son's growing proficiency at advanced battle training had confused and frightened her.

She painfully eased herself onto the couch as Elvis tried to contain his excitement. In the previous three days he had blasted his way to the top of his class, placing third in tank gunnery and earning flawless scores with both his carbine rifle and handgun. He had also been designated a master marksman and a sharpshooter, prompting Sergeant Bill Norwood to yell out, "Presley, you're a born soldier! If that singing doesn't work out, come back to us." His elevation to "instructional assistant," a rare honor for a private, had also filled Elvis with pride.

But Gladys was unnerved. Not only did he look different—more lean and muscular, due to losing fifteen pounds—but he acted different. The U.S. Army had done its job. The umbilical cord was severed; Elvis had become a grown man.

Sergeant Norwood had helped to bring the young soldier face-to-face with the depth of his dependency. One evening shortly before basic training ended, Elvis sat on Norwood's couch, crying bitterly over the distance between him and his mother and about his homesickness.

The sergeant sat down next to Presley and told him that it's possible to be "too close" to parents. "Now, Presley, you can sit in here on my couch and cry all you want about your mother. You can moan all you want about wanting to go home. Be my guest, I'll even sit here and listen. But when you go out my front door, you are *Elvis Presley*. You are also a good actor and a good soldier. So, by God, I want you to act, and I want you to soldier. Leave all of that other stuff in here."

From then on Norwood noticed a degree of stoic control exercised by Presley when it came to interpersonal matters. Elvis began interacting with his fellow soldiers, even playing football with them on Sunday afternoons. Anita Wood detected a difference: "At Fort Hood, he had finally found himself. He was the way I would have loved him to be all of the time."

The changes in Elvis were not lost on Gladys. She gamely made an attempt to attend the off-duty barbecues and pool parties, but she began caving in, emotionally and physically. Her sister Lillian later stated that a woman "from the hills of Mississippi is only interested in going so far."

When Elvis rented the suburban home in Killeen, Gladys's health was deteriorating rapidly and inexplicably. Apparently, in the past months, she had graduated to taking higher doses of amphetamines and alcohol, sometimes drinking straight vodka, to assuage her unhappiness. Her sister Lillian found her "drifting through the day in the empty halls, bedrooms, and living areas of Graceland—often taking to her bed, crushed by loneliness."

Once or twice a week, she would put on one of her old housedresses, her pre-Graceland garb, and walk down the street to a small store where she sat in a chair with her beer and talked to the proprietors, who were also hillfolk and could therefore relate to her dissatisfaction with that "rich folks' castle I live in."

She expressed misgivings about joining her son in Texas and later in Germany, where the battalion was to be stationed near the Czechoslovakian border. "I can't see myself in Germany. What would I do there? I just can't even imagine going there," she told Lillian. With a shake of her head Gladys said, "It just grieves me to think about it."

In Killeen she became even more isolated than before. She suspected that her husband was out chasing women. She knew her son was enmeshed in his rigorous tank maneuvers and off-duty recreation. In response, Gladys's alcohol abuse grew worse. Often when Elvis came in, exhausted, he found his mother drunk. One afternoon he cried out, "Mama, what are you doing to yourself?" Gladys turned her head to hide the tears.

Finally, her medical condition reached a crisis. She collapsed, slipping into unconsciousness, three afternoons in a row. The alcohol, amphetamines, and a poor diet had deposited so much fat in Gladys's liver—creating scars all through the organ—that the damage may already have been irreversible. Though she'd exhibited signs of illness for years, it had gone untreated.

"You've got to remember, with poor Southern folk it is a tradition to not go to the doctor until you are *really* sick," said Sam Phillips, who wonders if Gladys's precarious health wasn't further imperiled by "nervous attacks" over her son's fame. "She was a wonderful and warm woman. But she had one flaw, if you will: Elvis was totally her life."

"By the time she sought treatment from me, too much time had gone by," said Dr. Charles Clarke, the Memphis physician who would attempt to save Gladys's life.

One afternoon a drunken Gladys and an irascible Vernon started fighting. The domestic battle ended when she hit him on the head with an iron cook pot, leaving him unconscious. Ironically, her victory revealed how ill she really was. The emotional outburst left her exhausted. Lamar Fike found Gladys collapsed on her bed after the domestic melee and saw "that her skin was beginning to have a tinge of yellow." He asked Red West to come over to validate his suspicions.

"We sat Elvis down right away," said Fike, "and we told him somethin' real, real bad was wrong with his mother, and that he ought to do something about it."

Elvis dismissed Fike's worries, maintaining, "Mama's been having these spells for years."

Red West remained concerned. "If you don't get her to a physician, she could die very soon—in weeks." Presley didn't believe him. "I need my mama here," he countered.

But Gladys's health took a turn for the worse that her son could not ignore. In early August 1958 she collapsed completely. She was unable to stand without someone else's support. Her coloring was now a vivid gray-yellow—a sign of hepatitis or cirrhosis of the liver—and she was retaining so much fluid that the pains in her right side became unbearable. Elvis had his mother driven to a doctor in Temple, Texas. Following preliminary tests, the doctor informed the private that his mother needed to return to Memphis "right this minute" so that she could enter a hospital and be cared for by her personal physician, Dr. Clarke.

Gladys and Vernon left by train on Friday, August 8, and she was admitted to Memphis Methodist Hospital on Saturday morning. At first Dr. Clarke and the specialists he called in believed that Gladys had contracted life-threatening hepatitis. More sophisticated tests were set for Sunday morning.

In the Killeen house, which was now all but deserted, Elvis spent the weekend in a rage. Denied a weekend pass to accompany his mother home, he was guilt-ridden for having allowed her to drift toward death while he blindly buried himself in the challenge of becoming a tank soldier.

Physicians drained a gallon and a half of fluid from Gladys's abdomen—liquid that her kidneys and liver could no longer process, a strong signal that she had alcohol-triggered cirrhosis of the liver. It was already being whispered in the halls of Methodist Hospital that Gladys's system had collapsed under the deadly combination of alcohol, diet pills, and a congenitally weak heart—from which her paternal relatives had also suffered.

By Monday, August 11, Gladys was drifting in and out of consciousness. When she came to, she repeatedly asked for Elvis. "Why ain't he here?" she asked Dr. Clarke, who wondered himself why the Army hadn't let him visit his mother.

The notes on her chart that morning at eleven o'clock listed her condition as "critical and deteriorating." When Elvis heard this, he went berserk. With permission from Sergeant Norwood, Elvis left the training area and ran in the wilting heat to the quarters of the officer of the day. Quietly and politely, he explained the situation and asked for a few days of emergency leave.

"How is your mother?" the captain asked.

"She's critical, sir."

"But is she dead yet?" the captain coldly asked.

"No, sir," said Presley with tears in his eyes. "But they say she might be before I get there."

The young officer was unmoved: request denied.

Elvis saluted sharply, anger showing on his face. Then he sprinted out to where Lamar was waiting. "I'm going AWOL," he said. "I'm going to get to my mama."

He ran to find Norwood. He was panting as he said, "They won't grant it, sir. And I'm bailing. I'm going to Mama."

Norwood threw his arms around Elvis and took him aside. "Look, son," he said, "if you go AWOL, it will be the most famous case of desertion in modern history. Think of your career! For that matter, think of your freedom! Now, here's what you do . . ."

Norwood sent him to his house and instructed him to call Gladys's doctor "and have him contact the base commander."

Dr. Clarke soothed the frantic Elvis by phone. "You stay right where you are," said the physician. "I'll call the commander—the Pentagon if necessary."

Less than an hour later, following a series of telephone calls, the young officer of the day was overruled (and would go on to be disciplined). Elvis received his certification of emergency leave. Within fifteen minutes he was driving to Waco to catch a plane to Memphis. He arrived on the evening of the twelfth.

At 7:45 P.M., Elvis Presley, still in his rumpled, sweat-stained fatigues, walked through the doors of Methodist Hospital and was escorted to Gladys's room by an intern. He didn't like the guarded looks he got as he walked down the hallway, and he was furious that the only verbal diagnosis he could get was that his mother had "some severe liver problems."

Vernon, who had been sitting by helplessly, brightened when he saw Elvis turn the corner. He ran up: "Son, Son, I'm so glad you're here. Wait till she sees you. You're just what she needs."

Hat in hand, Elvis slipped open the door and quietly slid into the hospital room with its array of tubes and its perpetual twilight.

Gladys rose up on the bed and smiled. "Oh, my son!"

Private Presley gathered his arms around her, careful not to press against her painful left side and abdomen. "Mama, I'm gonna stay here as long as it takes. I ain't ever leaving you again. . . . Why, we're going to Germany together. Remember?" Gladys seemed to gather strength from his very presence.

Elvis stayed at his mother's side, his hand holding hers, until the nurses shooed him away at ten o'clock. For much of their time together, mother and son conversed in their private language. He caressed her hands and kissed each finger as he repeated again and again, "I wuv your hands. Your itty-bitty hands."

Gladys answered weakly, "I love you, itty-bitty, but you've got to go back and get some rest. Why, Son, you've been awake since early this mornin'."

Elvis shook his head. "I'm staying with you."

"No." Both Gladys and Vernon were adamant on this point. Elvis needed to go home and rest.

Elvis later admitted that he wanted to remain with his mother until every ounce of his strength gave out. "Something warned him to stay— to not leave her for a second. But I think she wanted to spare her son the agony of watching her die," said Elvis's friend Alan Fortas.

As Elvis moved toward the door, he turned for a last look. He and Vernon locked eyes—it didn't seem that Gladys Presley would fight for her life. The woman who had fiercely struggled to keep her family together during hard times in Tupelo, and who had struggled to help her son achieve his dream, was giving up.

Several days earlier she had confided to her sister Lillian, "You know, Lil, I could never stand to see my boy in his coffin. And I'm scared, really scared, that he's not coming back from Germany. Seeing him die would be the worst thing I can ever imagine."

She had also "officially said good-bye" to her close friend Dotty Ayers just before Elvis arrived at the hospital. "Nonsense, honey," said Ayers. "Your boy's comin' home."

Elvis demanded to speak with three specialists before leaving the hospital, one of whom assured him, "If your mom keeps improving the way she is now, she'll be back in her own bedroom tomorrow." Buoyed by this news, Elvis took a cab home, where Billy Smith was waiting to watch over Elvis as he slept.

Once at home, the distracted Elvis pulled off his military uniform and pulled an odd combination of clothes from the darkened closet: a pair of khaki pants, a ruffled tuxedo shirt, and white silk socks. He got dressed, then fell onto the bed, burying his head in a pillow. Billy Smith looked at his watch: it was twelve minutes past midnight.

"If he has those nightmares of his, wake him and soothe him," Gladys had requested. "I don't want him alone. He's real scared if he's alone, and I don't want him to wake up alone in that huge, dark house."

As soon as he was certain Elvis was asleep, Smith lowered himself into a chair and waited in case the hospital called. It was a beautiful night at Graceland with its sprawling lawns and howling peacocks, with the scent from Gladys's night-blooming jasmine and August gardenias. The night's only other sounds came from the crickets and frogs in a small pond.

Elvis tossed and turned and mumbled endearments to his mother. At one point, he sat straight up in bed—then sighed and sank back down.

The jarring ring of the telephone broke the silence.

Elvis was half-awake as he heard vague phrases from Billy's side of the conversation. "Okay, Uncle Vernon," Billy said, nodding. "Don't worry, sir, I'll get him there." After hanging up, Billy stifled a sob and walked toward Elvis. He knelt by his cousin's bed and shook his shoulders: "Elvis, wake up. Please wake up."

Elvis opened his eyes and stared intently at Billy. He grabbed his jacket. "Tell me."

"We gotta get to the hospital," Smith said. He lowered his eyes as he added, "Elvis, your mama's dead."

"No, no, no!" Elvis wailed. "No, no! My daddy would have phoned himself."

"That was your daddy," said Smith softly. "He tells you to get down there right this minute."

Still in the formal tux shirt and khakis, Elvis threw open the mansion's doors and ran outside. Billy sprinted along behind him, jumped in the car, and drove his cousin to the scene that would forever transform his life—as well as his music.

At the hospital, Elvis raced inside and rounded the corridor leading to his mother's room. When he came face-to-face with his father, he knew the truth. Any hopes he had for resuscitation crumbled. Elvis and his father fell together into a desperate embrace. "Yep, she's gone, boy," said Vernon, weeping. "Our little Gladys is gone."

"Noooo—" Elvis cried. "No, no—" His words dissolved into unearthly wails—cries so high-pitched and haunting that even the nurses began to cry. The cries mutated into piercing, primitive singsong expressions of grief that echoed through the long hospital halls, creating an echo effect. Some nurses stopped what they were doing to lower their eyes for a moment of prayer. They recognized the hillbilly way of mourning—called keening.

It didn't matter to Elvis that those unfamiliar with his people's ways were snickering in the hallways and waiting rooms. He and his father were engrossed in their heartfelt farewell. Listening, Billy Smith later said that the cries passed through him and tugged at his heart.

When Elvis and his father left the hospital, their arms were around each other. "She was always my best girl," Elvis told the Associated Press before they headed for the lavish home that now meant so little to them.

Back at Graceland, he and his father sat on the front steps and wept openly. "My mama's going to have the finest funeral money can buy," Elvis said between tears. "I promised her that."

Over the years there have been countless interpretations of Elvis's actions in the days following his mother's death. Most have painted the portrait of a petulant child. But Elvis wasn't petulant—he was furious. He was angry with himself for abandoning his mother to seek fame, angry that she had been driven to drink and to take pills, angry at the family's early poverty, angry with his father for abusing her, and angry at fate that took her away "just as I could give her everything she wanted."

When he called Sergeant Norwood at four o'clock in the morning, the sergeant realized Elvis was filled with guilt. "His long, rambling monologue went on for hours," the sergeant said, remembering Elvis's "livid fury" over what had happened to him and his mother. "I finally eased him off the telephone by pointing out that he had to contact his superiors immediately in order to extend his leave."

Elvis's leave would be extended for two weeks. "I know this is an unusually generous death leave," announced a spokesman for the Fifth Army command. "But this is no ordinary death. It is a national tragedy and thus requires more time and, therefore, creates more duties for Private Presley."

Later that first night, Elvis, still in the curious ensemble he had worn to the hospital, paced the halls for hours, repeating, "My little Satnin is gone. She's gone and won't come back. My little Satnin is all I had in the world."

Summoned to Graceland, Dr. Clarke administered a tranquilizer shot and left a vial of pills to help Elvis sleep. The pills proved effective. Presley drifted off on his baronial bed. Aides stood guard in case Elvis tried anything desperate. "He and Gladys were so emotionally inter-twined that he must have lost his bearings—the center of his life," his cousin Billy Smith said years later.

Alan Fortas, who had had a special rapport with both Gladys and Elvis, had another viewpoint. "Repeatedly Elvis cried out, 'I lived my whole life for you.' But, of course, a good case could be made that it was precisely the other way around—and that Gladys lived her whole life *for her son*. Rarely have two people wounded each other so deeply out of love."

Elvis, tangled in the comforter on his bed, thrashed about all night, one time crying out, "All is lost. I've lost everything."

At nine o'clock the next morning, Elvis appeared at the top of the grand staircase, immaculately dressed and groomed. His nails had been cut and buffed—a ritual usually reserved for an important photo shoot. His hair had been washed and combed.

But when he tried to descend the stairs, staring ahead, his knees crumpled, and he slid down several steps. Two of his aides sprinted up to support him under each arm. At the bottom of the stairs he threw an arm around his father, in the same intimate manner he had reserved for Gladys. Wandering into baby talk, he cooed, "Oh, little baby . . . it's a gray-haired daddy . . . a Satnin' daddy. He don't know how to do any better."

When a hearse turned off the boulevard onto Graceland's tree-lined drive, everyone realized why Elvis had dressed so carefully that morning. Psychologist Dr. Peter Whitmer has noted, "When Elvis saw the hearse, he quickly regressed to a younger age and reacted as if Gladys was, in fact, returning home alive and well, as if nothing had ever happened."

He leapt to his feet, newly energized. "Daddy, look! Mama's comin' home. Mama's here. She's back." He then ran to the door and opened it to receive Gladys.

As Gladys arrived, in a blue chiffon dress that she had never worn in life, Elvis paced the porch, holding one of his mother's old nightgowns. He talked to the piece of clothing, rocking it as one would rock an infant. Finally Elvis laid the gown gently on the banister and stumbled up the stairs. "Daddy! Daddy, come quick! Mama's coming home."

Vernon, himself bereft and heavily sedated, didn't respond.

Elvis waited while attendants carried in the copper coffin and placed it inside the music room. When they moved away, he stepped forward—and threw himself over the body.

"Look at my mama," he wailed. "She's fixed up so pretty . . . so very, very pretty."

He turned to the funeral attendants and asked them to show him her feet. They hesitated.

"Please. Please do it," he sobbed.

Reluctantly, they raised the blanket and removed Gladys's satin slippers and backed away, leaving mother and son alone. Elvis cradled his mother's tiny feet in his hands, kissing them, fondling each toe. All the while he murmured in his baby talk. He also pleaded, "Wake up, Mama. Wake up, little baby, and talk to Elvis." From time to time he would look up and say, "She's only sleeping."

When Anita Wood arrived at Graceland, after flying in from New York, she found Elvis seated in a parlor chair. He was silent, as if awaiting his mother's return. She bent down, touched his shoulder, and whispered, "I'm here now, Elvis. I'm here."

He turned, as if suddenly awakened. "Oh, Little!" he said, using his pet name for her. "Thank God you're here! Come here, Little. I want you to see Mama." He sobbed, adding, "She loved you so."

As a startled Anita looked on, Elvis repeated the ritual he had performed earlier: holding his mother's feet, marveling at them. "Look here, Little. Look at her little sooties."

Later that night, as Elvis slept—with the help of a powerful injection—the funeral home attendants returned and collected the casket for the next day's service at the Memphis Funeral Home. Only close friends such as Wood and Red West understood that this was the death of a peculiar family of two. Because of the strange, unsettling bond between mother and son—one that bordered on emotional incest—Elvis believed that he had lost everything with his mother's death.

On the morning of the funeral, when he descended Graceland's staircase in an austere brown suit and tie, Elvis again nearly lost his footing—and had to be assisted by several friends. He would also need help in climbing in and out of the limousine, and at the funeral and graveside ceremony. Dixie Locke was shocked to see her former sweetheart looking so distant and detached. "He looked into my eyes, and I realized that he was now lost to us."

At the Memphis Funeral Home, the guests' names filled more than thirty guest books. The ceremony was simple. Reverend James Hamill, pastor of the First Assembly of God Church, eulogized her as "a lady of extreme modesty and simple tastes." And Elvis's favorite gospel group, the Blackwood Brothers, performed. Though the service called for four selections, Elvis kept the singers there for twelve songs, every one of them a favorite hymn of Gladys's. Among them, "Precious Memories."

At the conclusion, Vernon said, "All we have now are memories."

Elvis broke down. "Oh, Dad. Dad! No, no . . ."

Later, at the gravesite on a wooded knoll in Forest Hill Cemetery, Elvis nearly collapsed as his mother's casket was about to be lowered into the ground. J. D. Sumner, one of the Blackwoods, ached for his friend. "They had glass over his mother's coffin, and Elvis laid on that glass. I've never heard a kid scream and holler as much as Elvis did that day . . . Nor have I ever seen such strong, singular love by a boy for his mother." Flinging himself on the casket, a limp Elvis loudly cried, "Good-bye, darling. Good-bye, darling! . . . I lived my whole life for you.

"We'll keep the house, darling. Everything that you loved. We won't move a thing."

Lamar Fike finally leaned over and whispered to his friend that it was over. With tears streaming down his face, the pale and shaken Elvis was led to a waiting car.

Elvis seemed more distraught than ever during the hours following his mother's burial. The finality of her death rendered him confused and physically ill. The day after the funeral, Elvis's temperature soared to 102 degrees, and Dr. Clarke was unable to keep him warm—despite a stack of blankets on his bed. Still, Vernon and Clarke hesitated to put him in the hospital. Rather, they allowed him to hold court in his bedroom suite, beginning a custom that would continue for the remainder of his life.

Colonel Parker, who had arranged the funeral, and Elvis and his father chose not to have an autopsy performed. In all news accounts for more than thirty years, and on official documents, "heart attack" was deemed the cause of Gladys's death. Only immediate family members knew that she had died of cirrhosis of the liver. "We all knew about it. We just didn't talk about it," said Elvis's cousin Patsy Presley.

For Elvis, his mother's death overburdened him with guilt. According to Dr. Whitmer, "Given the unique bond between Elvis and Gladys, Elvis never achieved the final stage in dealing with death. The loss took with it too great a part of Elvis's personal history for him to ever become reintegrated. With Gladys, an essential part of Elvis disappeared."

The Solitary Private

lvis was almost relieved when he returned to Killeen and the numbing routine of the Army. The repetition and mindlessness of the tasks, such as polishing tanks and taking inventory of ammunition, was oddly comforting, helping to quell the ache in his chest.

In the weeks following Gladys's death, Elvis drifted emotionally. Some days were fine; others sent him into torment. Twice he blacked out. At the same time, though, Elvis also experienced an unexpected bittersweet sense of freedom.

"After his mother died, he just let loose sexually," said Lamar Fike. After reopening the rented house near downtown Killeen, Presley plunged into nonstop partying, hosting get-togethers filled with comely fans. They lasted until dawn—when Private Presley would pull on his uniform and race to meet roll call. "There was a revolving door for girls," remarked Eddie Fadal, a disc jockey friend from Elvis's early touring years. "I was always sending cars to pick up new girls at the bus station . . . all of them knockouts; all of them out for 'a piece of Presley.'"

Without question the death of his mother freed him from the guilt and the psychological frigidity imposed by Gladys, who had wanted her boy to seek chaste candidates for marriage rather than the "beautiful itty-bitty things" Elvis lusted after. Presley's close friend Eddie Fadal watched as Elvis's sexual tastes exploded in the weeks after his mother died. "He changed from a guy who liked an uncomplicated date into a sexual predator out to conquer," said Fadal. "We were running shifts of lovely girls in and out of the rented house . . . sometimes he had three girls a night. I remember some sort of whim where Elvis wanted a blonde, a redhead, and a dark brunette all in the same evening. We located the dates after considerable trouble—even in wild and woolly Texas. What we don't know is whether or not he slept with that rainbow of ladies." Recalling one session of "multiple partners," Fadal said, "I think we figured out that all he wanted to do was have foreplay with two breathtakingly beautiful ladies at one time."

Eddie would see it get weirder and wilder. "It was so sad to see him trying to shake off his heartbreak with sexual prowess—which could only provide a few moments of relief."

The Army brass, initially tolerant of Elvis's sorrow, began receiving dozens of parental complaints. Luckily for all concerned, he was ordered to Germany just in time for advanced training.

On September 19, 1958, Elvis Presley boarded a troop train bound for New York, where the USS *General Randall* waited to transport him and 1,170 other troops. With his duffel bag over his shoulder and a military hat tilted rakishly over his slightly sun-bleached hair, he waved to Anita Wood, shouted good-byes to his father and Grandma Minnie Mae, and gave a thumbs-up to the ubiquitous Lamar Fike and Red West. Then he disappeared inside, where he quickly found his sleeping compartment, replete with an old-fashioned plush couch.

As the train started up, Elvis took a seat opposite Charlie Hodge. A native of Decatur, Alabama, Hodge used to perform with the Foggy River Boys on the Red Foley TV series, *Ozark Jubilee*. Hodge and Elvis had briefly met backstage in 1956 during a taping in Memphis. During basic training at Fort Hood they had been reacquainted. But not until they shared a car on the train trip did they really get to talking.

"I got lucky," Elvis said, smiling. "Not only did I get a fellow Southerner but a musician, too."

"You may not feel so fortunate when you hear me pickin' and singin'," Hodge answered.

Presley, however, sensed a kindred spirit. After Hodge slipped off to sleep, Elvis was conscientious enough to find a blanket with which he covered Hodge. Elvis had found a new friend. By the time the train pulled into the Brooklyn Army Terminal on the morning of September 22, the two had swapped stories about mutual pals, their shared love of music.

Elvis stepped off the train into a media hailstorm—more of the Colonel's handiwork. For more than an hour, as an Army brass band played a repertoire of Presley hits, and the Navy officials looked on, Elvis posed for reporters and newsreel photographers and conducted a forty-minute press conference (which was included in an "all-talking" Elvis record, released at year's end, called *Elvis Sails*).

Because so many Elvis fans were among the young soldiers taking the same boat, Presley was stationed in the noncommissioned officers' deck. He further traded on his celebrity status when he reported to the officer in charge of room assignments and asked, "Sir, could Charlie Hodge possibly be assigned as my roommate? After all, sir, I'm the only one in that two-man suite, and it's a mighty big place."

"Consider it done," said the lieutenant. Then, as Presley saluted, the young officer said, "Sorry about your mother, Private."

Elvis's voice quavered as he replied, "Thank you, sir! The Army has been wonderful to me."

Elvis was proving to be a boon to the military as well. Back when Presley had first been declared eligible for the draft, a military officer had dryly declared, "Our studies indicate that his basic appeal is to young girls." Once the singer decided to serve his country, the Army found his appeal was far wider. Enlistment soared by twenty-five percent. Celebrity-wise, only Clark Gable's military stint in 1942 brought in more recruits.

On board the *Randall* Elvis was a spit-shine, macho soldier for all of the formations and class sessions, but he also often seemed carefree as he and Hodge roamed the ship. Hodge would play guitar and Presley occasionally sang folk songs or ballads—totally unlike the RCA star.

Nights, however, were rough. Charlie could hear Elvis tossing and turning below him—occasionally moaning, occasionally crying out, "Satnin!" Other times he heard murmured sobs, which were silenced when Elvis buried his head in the pillow. "He was grieving for his mother, but so quietly only I could hear it," Hodge remembered. "I listened to it for a couple of nights; then I couldn't stand it any longer. I climbed down and sat on the side of his bunk and told him jokes and stories until he went to sleep. For years I had been keeping an inventory of jokes . . . both good and bad."

Hodge's comforting worked. Elvis would lie back in the bed with his head in his hands and listen. Soon he would forget his troubles and fall asleep. "I made it my goal to keep Elvis laughing all the way across the ocean, just one Southern guy to another," Hodge said.

One night, as the troop carrier tossed up and down in the fog of the North Sea, Elvis looked up at Hodge and confessed, "You know, Charlie, you keep me from going crazy." Good-natured Charlie Hodge was to become one of Presley's lifelong confidants.

When the USS *General Randall* docked at Bremerhaven, West Germany, on October 1, fifteen hundred fans were waiting. Presleymania had traversed the continents. European publications, including the German teenage magazine *Bravo*, were filled with news of the new king. Anxious to get a glimpse of the young man whose music had come to symbolize the brash American spirit, some teenagers came clutching Elvis records. One young man proudly displayed his movie poster for *Gold aus heisser Kehle*—or *Gold from a Hot Throat*, the German title for *Loving You*.

In anticipation of the crowds, the Navy had strategically arranged for a troop train to be backed into the base. It was a short walk from gangplank to train for the sea of soldiers—with Private Presley in their midst. Elvis did try to oblige several autograph seekers, but he stopped when he nearly lost his balance shifting his duffel bag atop his shoulder. Shaking his head apologetically, he hurriedly boarded the train—which had temporarily been turned into a welcome wagon. Painted on the sides of one of the coaches was "Welcome to Germany, Elvis Presley."

The train carrying the world's most famous soldier journeyed south to Friedberg, twenty miles from Frankfurt and close to the border of Communist East Germany. The troops reached their destination just before dusk. But the enveloping darkness could not hide the bleak prospect before them. When Charlie Hodge exited the train, he thought he had stepped into a cold, foggy "hell of the world," surrounded on all sides by a "pitiful excuse for a forest," shrub brush and the spindly trees of the Czech foothills. Elvis, who was accustomed to the lush evergreen beauty of Tennessee, was equally taken aback. "Damn! We got better vacant lots than this!" Elvis went on to add, "Even a coon dog would laugh at it."

Private Presley arrived during a unique period of saber-rattling by the Soviet Union and its vassal states surrounding West Germany. The blustery Soviet leader Nikita Khrushchev had recently set a seven-month deadline for the surrender of large territories apportioned to the

West (and guarded by the North Atlantic Treaty Organization army) since the end of World War II.

Presley's appeal reached beyond the Iron Curtain. The large Communist daily *Freiheit*, in the East German town of Halle, declared that NATO had imported him as a propaganda weapon—to steal the hearts of Red teenagers.

Still later, when Army brass announced that Elvis's unit was headed for war games at Grafenwöhr, a large training area near the Czechoslovakian border, a new round of "Elvis-baiting" erupted. One of the most respected of the Red journals, *Neuses Deutschland*, branded Presley "the Western Pied Piper of Hamelin," out to entice the country's youth away from socialist role models Lenin and Marx.

Although Presley casually quipped, "Those commies are really squares," he didn't understand how many wanted to emulate him. In Halle, a hundred policemen were battered as they attempted to arrest three hundred members of an Elvis Presley "cult." *Freiheit* reported in its columns that the gang's leader had smuggled a large knapsack of "Presley's degenerate recordings" from the West. A leader of the secret police reported finding large "disgusting photos of Elvis—our 'villain of the year' "—on the walls of their headquarters.

Unaware of how great a stir he was causing in East Germany, Elvis collapsed into a barracks bed after diplomatically stating at a press conference that he was "ready for whatever the Army has planned for me and the other soldiers." He was, however, immediately disappointed to learn he wouldn't get to be assigned to the position he longed for—that of a turret gunner. Though Elvis had placed second at Fort Hood in tank marksmanship, the booming noise from the guns had slightly punctured his left eardrum. The Fort Hood physician had advised him to drop tank training immediately. But after conferring with Sergeant Bill Norwood, Elvis had opted to jam cotton into his ears and finish his training anyway. "Otherwise, Sarge, they're going to think I'm wimping out to avoid frontline conditions."

In Germany, however, Elvis was assigned as a driver and auxiliary scout for a wisecracking, by-the-book sergeant named Ira Jones. Noted at sniffing out hidden command posts and camouflaged tanks, Sergeant Jones was laden with honors from a handful of war games.

His first glimpse of Presley occurred the night the rock-'n'-roll star arrived with his fellow recruits. Jones headed into the barracks to "warn the new guys that we needed to be ready for an alert 'anytime' now, so be sure your gear is organized and ready to go." As Jones entered, he heard "group singing, barbershop style . . . with Presley's distinctive voice dominating." When Jones was inside, Presley leapt to his feet—along with the rest of the corps. "Just be ready for the alert, guys. And go back to your bellowing," commanded Jones.

"Private E," as some of the recruits called him, was assigned to Ray Barracks—which had once housed Hitler's SS troops. He was given bunk number 13 of Barracks 3707; he was photographed standing dutifully alongside his steel-frame bed.

In his brief time at the barracks he proved a morale booster—spinning colorful tales of glamorous Hollywood. Jones, who trained Presley as a scout, noted that only Elvis, "with his macho reputation from basic training, could have gotten away with talking about all that movie star stuff."

He lived in the barracks like an "average" soldier for just five days before moving out into civilian housing. The military sponsoring act stated that a soldier could live with his dependents if they traveled to Germany to set up housekeeping. Grandma Minnie Mae, Vernon, and the hotheaded Red West had dutifully done so. Joining them was Lamar Fike, whose devotion to Elvis was such that he had actually tried to enlist. At nearly three hundred pounds, however, Fike wasn't exactly what the military was looking for.

Noticeably absent was Colonel Tom Parker. "Sorry, son, won't be able to join you. Too much business to see to," he had told Elvis. The Colonel did oversee a shrewd publicity campaign throughout Elvis's Army stint, but was unable to join him in person. Unbeknownst to Elvis at the time, the Colonel had a secret. Thomas Andrew Parker was actually the Holland-born Andreas Cornelius van Kuijk, and he had immigrated to the United States illegally. Because he did not have the proper documentation to be in the United States, he would have difficulty returning from foreign travel.*

With his transplanted Memphis contingent, Elvis at first insisted upon occupying hotel suites—mainly to secure privacy for the one-night stands, which were now an addiction. They settled into the Hilberts Park Hotel, which was not only close to a beautiful park but was also a gathering place for comely fräuleins. But after only a few days the rowdy group was tossed out. From there they moved into a three-bedroom apartment at Hotel Grünewald, in the hamlet of Bad Hom-

---

*In his lifetime, Elvis came to suspect that the Colonel was in the country illegally. But he never knew specific details.

burg. According to Red West, the chambermaids were amenable to "doing more to the beds in the Presley suite than just making them," but the hotel management was not as well disposed. Among other things, Presley and his crew set an indoor bonfire, staged impromptu wrestling matches in the hallways, played the piano into the night, and even adopted a dog named Cherry. Ever charming, Elvis talked the hotel's kitchen help into watching the pooch while he was on the base. Not surprisingly, the Presley company was booted from Hotel Grünewald after five months.

What they needed was a house, so Red and Lamar wandered the cobblestone streets of the nearby historic spa town of Bad Nauheim, until they found a three-story, four-bedroom house at 14 Goethestrasse. Frau Pieper, the owner, agreed to rent her home for the equivalent of $800 a month—more than four times the usual fee—but she refused to move out herself. So she took an attic bedroom, becoming another member of Elvis's colorful contingent.

The bohemian household became well-known in Bad Nauheim. Red West got into beer-hall brawls. Vernon often closed down the bars and staggered home drunk. The hefty Lamar became such a familiar presence that the locals came to dub him, simply, "the fat one." Minnie Mae sneaked drinks whenever Elvis wasn't looking, and she and Frau Pieper bickered over who would get to cook in the kitchen. For her famed tenant, Frau Pieper served German versions of corn bread (which she made with a mushy consistency) and green beans (which she boiled to a pulp).

As for Elvis, he retired to his bedroom with eager German beauties—some of them as young as thirteen or fourteen. Both West and Fike were alarmed. "He was fascinated with the idea of real young teenage girls, which scared the crap out of all of us," admitted Fike. "Cops were always around because of the crowds, but never seemed to notice."

Private Presley's exploits were not confined to the boudoir, though. He was so adept at soldiering that *Stars and Stripes* became a fan. For starters, he excelled in the classroom. To succeed in the Hell on Wheels battalion required skills in map reading and minute understanding of terrain—or in Elvis's words, "knowing the place you want to get to and how to get there . . . as natural to a Mississippi boy as walkin' barefoot." According to Sergeant Ira Jones, who would become one of Elvis's closest associates in the Army, "His test scores were phenomenal."

Elvis showed the same excellence in physical training. One morning, Lieutenant Ed Hart challenged the squad to do "thirty *perfect* push-ups—with butt down and shoulders butterflied out, not an inch too high or too low.

"After thirty, the overachievers can keep on going."

The lieutenant laughed as he watched each guy stand up when he reached his limit. At sixty, Presley was still pumping while watching Hart with his left eye.

Elvis began counting: "Sixty-one, sixty-two . . ."

"Okay, okay, Presley," said Hart. "You're the Olympian here."

"Who are you trying to impress, Mr. Rock and Roll?" asked one of the squad's men.

"Nobody," said Presley. "I don't need to impress nobody. I just wanted to see if I could do it."

"Things like that were typical of Elvis," said his former commanding officer Colonel William J. Taylor Jr. (who rose from lieutenant to captain during Presley's tour of duty). "He flat-out attacked each duty, each task, as if he were storming a beachhead. This guy could soldier just as proficiently as he could sing. He was the roughest, toughest, most gung ho soldier I ever had under my command—to this day, and I mean that, despite thousands of soldiers I've been involved with. He was a born fighter." Added Taylor, "Elvis took no prisoners."

The model private had the help of his makeshift family unit, which performed with military precision. He always had double-spit-shined shoes (courtesy of Lamar), starched, hand-tailored uniforms (courtesy of Minnie Mae), and glittering brass (courtesy, usually, of Red West). Good-natured Lamar Fike was proud of the day-to-day routine they developed to help "the big guy" achieve his latest goal. "Red and I would get up to find Minnie Mae already cooking up breakfast in the kitchen. We immediately went to work laying out his uniform and giving the gleaming belt buckles and perfect creases a once-over." That job was made easier by the proper use of the hundreds of thousands of dollars that poured into Elvis's bank accounts from record and film royalties. According to Lamar, "He sent us down to purchase one hundred fatigue shirts, an equal number of pants, twenty khaki uniforms complete with hats, and everything in between. We had to smile when he won Best Dressed Soldier month after month." Added Lamar, "He even changed completely when he came home for lunch."

When Presley became an auxiliary scout—Sergeant Jones's tracker for the rest of Elvis's tour—he at first regarded it as a slight put-down.

The sergeant told him it wasn't that way at all. The scouts had the really "hard duty" to position tanks without alerting the enemy. "Working as a scout is a dangerous, essential occupation," Jones stressed. "Uh-huh," Presley replied. "But I still don't get to shoot a tank."

He soon adapted. Working as a scout, Presley was on his own most of the time. He became an expert in terrain, a dynamo with a map, precise to the millisecond with a watch, and a master of stealth. He also had control of Sergeant Jones's jeep, and he maintained it with the fervor he showed toward all his other duties. Once, around midnight, some members of Presley's battalion returned from a bar and discovered Elvis on his back, under the rear fender of the jeep. He was slowly sanding the metal to remove tiny dots of rust that had formed on the exhaust pipe. The carousing soldiers doubled over in laughter. From under the jeep, Elvis growled, "When this thing gets inspected—against yours—you won't think it's so goddamned funny."

Although he could get under a car, he had no hopes of hiding from the constant barrage of fans. Despite all the precautions the military developed to keep the teenage hordes away from "the best jeep scout on the base," despite a special corps of military police to keep them away, they still breached the base, waving their autograph books. On one of these occasions, when Elvis was driving Captain Taylor, their jeep was surrounded by some twenty persistent females. "I was amazed to see how Elvis reacted to the fans—even though I discovered that Presley secretly reveled in their presence," said Taylor.

As the amused captain watched, Elvis carefully took off his cap—as if slowly initiating a celebrity striptease. Then he used his sultry eyes and his mouth to flirt with the girls as he signed their books. What Taylor saw was the emergence of his carefully created persona—Elvis's total creation.

Finally, Taylor protested over the "show." "Private Presley, can you bring this to a reasonable conclusion?"

"Yes, sir," said Elvis, immediately turning off the sensuality and charm. "Why'd we stop here anyway?" he added, giving the girls a broad wink.

Off the base, usually dressed in one of his specially cut khaki uniforms—hand-tailored in Munich—he went on the prowl himself. Young, beautiful German girls couldn't wait to get their hands on this rocker with the bedroom reputation.

The most constant of his companions, though, would be an American sergeant's daughter, Elisabeth Stefaniak. Having learned that Presley frequented a cinema not far from her house, she dressed up, took along a girlfriend for safety, and went night after night until finally they stumbled into the star at the snack bar.

At first Elisabeth's parents refused to let her date the controversial singer, especially after her mother noticed that "some clever seamstress had turned the private's khakis into the sexiest uniform in the Fifth Army." But eventually, after having a reverential Thanksgiving dinner with the family, Elvis and Elisabeth were allowed to attend the movies. They were soon enmeshed in what one Elvis buddy called "a passionate romance . . . maybe so hot it burned itself out too quickly." Elvis convinced Elisabeth's parents to let her work for him as a secretary. Supposedly, there was no danger. As Elvis sincerely explained to the girl's mother, "We're surrounded by twenty-five people all day."

So the eighteen-year-old Elisabeth moved into 14 Goethestrasse, becoming another inhabitant of the crazy world of Presley Haus: a world turned upside down, where dinner was often served in the morning; where fans gathered night and day outside the gate; where autograph hours were posted (7:30 to 8:30 P.M.); where sex took place in the master bedroom after the house was dark and quiet—usually 2:00 A.M. or later.

Although Elisabeth has never divulged intimate details of her romance with Elvis, according to Joe Esposito, who met Elvis while in the Army, she became more than an employee. She was, he said, "always in the shadows, available and waiting" for Elvis. "He would spend an evening with a girl in his bedroom, the girl would leave, and he'd call in Elisabeth to sleep with him," recalled Esposito.

This didn't necessarily include sex. Ever since his childhood—when he was tormented by vivid nightmares—he had been monitored in the night, by his mother or a friend, who sometimes had to interrupt sleep-walking episodes. During her son's concert tours, Gladys used to plead with Red or Gene Smith to keep a nightly watch on Elvis. It wasn't uncommon for one of Elvis's friends to share his room. But as Elvis's fame grew, female bedmates became the norm—a habit he would keep right up to the end.

During her tenure, Elisabeth saw a surprisingly ugly side to Elvis— fostered by his growing problems with his father. She and Vernon were on the autobahn trying to pass a car, which suddenly swerved right in front of them. Vernon braked so hard that his car skidded into the median, flipped, and rolled three times.

After pulling himself from the overturned car, Vernon poked his head back inside. "Elisabeth! Honey, are you okay?" With the help of some passersby, Vernon pulled out the terrified girl, who was rushed to the hospital. Miraculously, there were no permanent injuries, but Elisabeth was told to stay in bed for almost a week.

Back at the house, she was given the royal treatment by Vernon and Minnie Mae. Red West and Lamar Fike were at her beck and call.

But Elvis was initially surly. As soon as he was alone with her, he snarled, "What the hell were you and my daddy doin' that caused that wreck?"

Elisabeth was unnerved by the intimation: he suspected her of being involved with his father! Moreover, he hadn't even inquired about her condition. As he ranted and raved, she fought back the tears and assured him, "I am not involved with your father!" Elvis at last cooled off and even cooed, "Honey, ahm so glad you're okay."

In the meantime, Elvis was constantly on the prowl for new conquests. His tight circle of friends allowed him to burn the candle at both ends. With Esposito, a tough kid from Chicago who liked to joke about having Mafia connections, Lamar Fike, easygoing Charlie Hodge, and hulking Red West, they made a rough, randy band. Eventually, this group would go on to acquire the famous sobriquet the Memphis Mafia.

Not a few of Presley's fellow soldiers were amazed at his ability to work and march all day and then reinvent himself as the "Playboy of Bad Nauheim," staying up until three o'clock in the morning or later. How did Elvis do it? Rex Mansfield, a young recruit from Tennessee, discovered the secret one afternoon when Elvis sped up to the back door of the pharmacy near the entrance to the Friedberg gates. Presley was in and out in about five minutes with a jar of amphetamines, "containing hundreds of them," according to Mansfield.

"Who gave 'em to you?" he asked.

"A medical technician," Elvis said, smiling. "You just have to know the right place to go."

"He used them to keep himself awake during battle tests and to heighten his sexual stamina on the forays to the fleshpots of Paris and Frankfurt," said Mansfield. "It wasn't long before the other guys started taking them."

"You should take 'em, Rex," said Elvis. "They are totally harmless, prescribed by physicians and used all over the world. Doctors even give them to children if they're a little bit overweight."

Presley so fervently believed in the harmlessness of prescription drugs that he convinced many of his friends to use amphetamines regularly. Others, such as Elisabeth Stefaniak, avoided them. Indeed, she once angrily flushed fistfuls of pills down the toilet.

Not even speed could help him sometimes, though.

As soon as Elvis was settled into his unit, the Pentagon—prodded by Colonel Parker—began badgering Army publicity officers for a splashy press conference to showcase Elvis's success as a field soldier. "I've got some pretty major reporters to send over there myself," Parker hinted. "And *Life* magazine's very, very interested."

Hurricane force winds buffeted the Army post the day of the event at the post exchange, where a ravenous media was provided with a buffet, coffee, press kits, and what they really wanted, a selection of photographs of Elvis (sometimes obviously posed) at various duties. At the last minute, the decision was made not to hand out a shot of the bare-chested Private Presley as he shaved.

Just ten minutes before the conference, Private *First Class* Presley—whose promotion was to be grandly announced at the gathering—was missing. Where was the man of the hour? The company's executive officer said Elvis was at the post exchange. A first sergeant speculated "he was tied up in traffic because of the fans."

Der Elvis, as the Germans called him, was nowhere in sight, prompting a young lieutenant from the Public Information Office to corner Sergeant Ira Jones. "Where is he?" the young officer demanded. "We have worked around the clock at division headquarters to get this set up, and now what are we going to do if he doesn't come?"

Jones sat alone in the dressing room awaiting the young truant. He waited ten minutes, then twenty. At 10:14 the door flew open and Presley tumbled in, a good deal less than presentable. His shirttail was out and lipstick was smeared across his lips and face.

"You look like you've slept in that uniform," said Jones.

Presley didn't deny the statement. He merely looked down. "Sorry, sir."

"Well, what in God's name happened?"

Presley tried to sound sheepish, but he couldn't stop a smile from forming. "Elisabeth happened, sir!"

Jones had to stifle a laugh.

With the help of additional platoon members, Presley was spiffed up with a shower and a complete change of clothing and walked jauntily into the mess hall shortly before eleven. Jones was both shocked and proud: "Damn if he didn't stand up there and dazzle the daylights out of them all."

Proud of his stripe, Private First Class Presley—who used to take a taxi to the base—celebrated by leasing a white BMW sports car, with white leather interior. Now he would screech onto the base in the BMW, park it, and climb into a jeep like an ordinary Army grunt.

New soldiers on the base looked forward to seeing his entrance. It was a reminder that not everything in the Army was gray and utilitarian.

Elvis on Ice

No sooner had winter descended upon Friedberg than the Hell on Wheels brass scheduled the war games. Elvis laughingly called them Operation Snowmen because, he said, "you froze your ass off twenty four hours a day." Yet the exercises were deadly serious simulations of winter warfare. Replicating real battles, they featured "hunt and capture" maneuvers between competing teams of American soldiers.

Elvis thrived on these missions, glorying in the frigid weather and the chance to later deliver dramatic soliloquies to his buddies about them. He loved portraying GI Joe for a couple of weeks to a captive audience, approaching it in the same way he had approached his early film roles—with unbounded enthusiasm. "He turned in Oscar-caliber performances," agreed buddy Joe Esposito. "It was a great acting gig."

He wasn't just acting. The first time out, he showed what a Tennessee boy could do. In the chilly hours near dawn, Elvis and two other scouts trapped the mock enemy tank corps by luring them into a pit of quicksand that was indistinguishable from normal forest terrain. But Presley and company underestimated the opposition. They kept advancing, avoiding the worst quicksand pools and the slickest mud hills. Elvis realized that some young soldier on the other side had memorized the terrain as expertly as he had.

"We can only do one thing," Presley whispered. "We'll fire over their heads."

With Sergeant Jones's okay, his troop—one-third the size of the mock enemy—fired a burst of machine gun blanks at the advancing regiment. "Not knowing they were stronger than us, and in a better tactical position, they surrendered without a fight," recalled Jones.

Jones's tank team was cited for "battle-ready excellence" by *Stars and Stripes*. Of course, the most coverage was lavished on the resident rock-'n'-roll tanker. The spate of articles angered Presley. "This is a team," he told one Army reporter. "I play a fairly small part in all of this. I'm just another private, and my fame doesn't make me more important." Sergeant Jones agreed with Elvis, admitting that the renewed rumors about Presley's special treatment "hurt the hell out of him."

As if this wasn't enough, tabloids in Berlin, Munich, Paris, and Rome printed stories that claimed Colonel Parker had arranged for an early discharge in order to spring the "gold-plated private" for a series of expensive concerts. The tabloids quoted the price tag as being in the millions.

In America, by contrast, decidedly pro-Presley articles filled Sunday supplements and the fan magazines. Behind the blitz was the ever-industrious Colonel, who had fired the first shots during the production of *King Creole* with the publication of Elvis's "farewell letters" to his fans. Then came Elvis's "last words" to the readers of *Photoplay:* "Please don't forget me while I'm gone!" That would have been impossible, considering the Colonel's publicity bombardment—everything from announcements about potential film and TV projects upon Elvis's return to Army "day in the life" features, with photos supplied by *Stars and Stripes*. And then there was the merchandising—Elvis Presley dog tags (in gold or silver plate), stamped with his name, rank, and serial number, khaki-green Elvis T-shirts, calendars, and more. To the Colonel's delight, a flurry of novelty records were also cut, ranging from the Three Teens warbling "Dear 53310761," to Anita Wood's plaintive promise "I'll Wait Forever" (for Sun Records, naturally).

"Whatever it takes to keep my boy's name in the news!" Parker would exclaim.

According to Sergeant Jones, it wasn't easy for Elvis to be "the most famous private in the Army," especially since "he didn't resemble the man depicted in the fan magazines." Said Jones, "He became one of us. We had the real guy."

He could sometimes be surprisingly stubborn about the exploitation of his celebrity. Despite being coaxed to perform for the Army in Europe, Elvis stood his ground: "I didn't spend all this time learning to be a field soldier so I could sing at anyone's pleasure." When the corps threw a benefit show, Presley wouldn't sing his hits—though he did help to organize it and performed a piano duet with buddy Charlie Hodge. On the other hand, when he learned that Lieutenant William Taylor was being reassigned and promoted to captain, Elvis hopped up on the stage of the "good-bye gala" and performed for more than an hour—doing not only his rock-'n'-roll hits but some of Taylor's favorites as well. "It was the highest tribute he could have paid," Colonel Taylor recalled. "And it was typical of Presley to do it without fanfare."

Other times he acted the part of the star. When Elvis learned that the battalion's day room, which served as a den for the barracks, had a faulty television, he arranged for a new one to be installed—not only there but in several other battalions as well. When one worried officer approached the base commander, complaining that the gift was a "conflict of interest," the top guy just smiled: "One, it's Elvis Presley. Two, it's already done."

Elvis traded on his celebrity in other ways, too. Once, near the Communist border, when the squad was eating on the run, Presley, his fur hat tilted jauntily to one side, yelled, "Sir, I gotta complain about the chow."

Captain Jack Cochran decided to play along. "Well, what the hell's wrong with the chow? It's the world's best chow for the world's best soldiers."

"Well, there isn't enough peanut butter in it." Presley grinned and held up a finger dripping with soupy peanut butter.

Cochran laughed. "Well, Elvis, I'm the one in charge of chow." Presley grinned good-naturedly.

The next morning, a half-ton supply truck arrived at headquarters. A transportation sergeant climbed down. "Captain Cochran, I gotta admit this is the strangest thing I've ever had to deliver to the war games."

"Whatcha got?" asked Cochran.

"A goddamned case of peanut butter—all of the jars oversize."

Elvis doubled over in laughter.

Despite his fame, Presley appeared "totally free of pretense," recalled Jones, who recounted an episode involving the star and a soldier who was so painfully shy he could not speak other than to answer his officers with a yes or no. A young crackerjack engine specialist, the black Southerner would sit alone eating in the corner of the mess hall, his eyes downcast. "No one could get him to speak, not on the job nor in the barracks," said Jones. Elvis made a point of helping to draw him out of his shell. One afternoon, when Jones dropped by the motor pool, he heard Elvis's voice from behind a large transport truck. He was in conversation with someone whose voice Jones didn't at first recognize. "Rounding the corner out of curiosity, I saw that Elvis was seated, talking and joking with the young black soldier," said Jones, who remembered that Elvis stayed friendly with the mechanic throughout his German stay. "Elvis was a very surprising young man," said Jones. Of course, Elvis had also been a painfully shy outsider who craved acceptance during his teenage years at Humes High.

His willingness to help fellow soldiers was revealed on another occasion. One night, when Taylor was on "courtesy patrol" duty—on the lookout for drunken or troublesome soldiers in areas that were off-limits, including the clubs on whorehouse row—he was startled to see Elvis and another GI climbing into a familiar BMW sports car.

"Presley . . . wait a minute!" ordered Taylor. Elvis climbed out of the driver's seat, saluted, and sheepishly began to make excuses for his passenger—one of his platoon members—who opened his door and leaned out to vomit.

"Don't mind him, lieutenant. Must have a virus or sumthin', " said Elvis.

"Presley, what's going on here? This place is off-limits."

It turned out that the soldier had put in a call to Elvis, concerned that he was going to be caught by the military police. Elvis had driven over to get him back to the barracks. Taylor was impressed by Elvis's concern for one of his buddies, despite the possibility of an Article 15—nonjudicial punishment by a company commander. "It was risky, but I admired Elvis for it," said Taylor.

Because Vernon Presley had long ceased to give his son fatherly advice, Elvis seized upon Sergeant Jones and, to a lesser extent, Lieutenant Taylor, as substitute father figures. When Elvis and Jones talked, Jones emphasized the rigors of an Army career and responsibility toward family. Then he "sat back and listened" as Elvis recounted the price of fame.

"You know, Sarge, nobody left Mama, Daddy, or myself alone after I became a star. It's like they wanted a piece of us. Wanted to make us seem lower class, to make fun of us.

"When we moved to that nice neighborhood which my mama adored, which meant a lot to her, the neighbors ran us off over little tiny things. They didn't like her hangin' the clothes on a clothesline. A whole bunch of them knocked on our door to tell her to get a clothes dryer. Others got up a petition, asking us 'hillbillies' and the fans to leave for the good of the neighborhood."

Presley shook his head: "Sarge, it like to broke my mama's heart."

He talked about the move to Graceland: "We had to move out where we could be alone, someplace where my fans could come and not be treated like freaks. We needed a place out in the country where we wouldn't bother nobody. That's when I bought Graceland.

"But you know, Sarge," Presley continued, "I don't think Mama was ever happy with that big house and all those things that went with it. Lookin' back, I see now that she wanted it more simple. And that, more than anything else, she wanted to spend more time with me.

"If I could do it again, I'd-a eased back on my singin' dates. Because all the money in the world can't buy my mama back."

The words came more easily out in the rolling backwoods of Germany, as if he had locked these thoughts inside for a long time. Said Jones, "I learned that one woman meant more to this young man than life itself—and her death tormented him and left him guilty."

Elvis talked about other things that bothered him as well. One afternoon when he was with Lieutenant Taylor, he asked, "Why do people look down on other people?"

Said Taylor, "I realized that there must have been times when his status in life really bothered him. The 'poor years' tenaciously stayed with him." Taylor recalled that, as Elvis spoke that day, "his face metamorphosed into an expression of sadness."

The most alarming episode of his two-year stint, however, stemmed not from depression but was purely an accident. While scouting one day, a map snafu put them several miles inside Communist territory. It was Sergeant Jones who suddenly recognized the terrain: "Shi-i-it, Presley," he yelled. "We're in Red territory. Get us out of here as fast as you damn well can."

Presley spun the jeep on the icy roads and roared back to the West German border. Jones shook his head. "Think of the international incident they would have made out of this if the commies caught you in

Czechoslovakia." As darkness fell and chilly winter winds swept the region, Elvis told Jones he was "almost" certain he was back in the West, but he was completely certain of one thing: he couldn't get them back to the base in the dark.

He parked the jeep in a "nest of trees and rocks" and left the engine idling, since alpine winds were pushing the temperature down below twenty. Within an hour, the snow was up to the door, and Elvis had to repeatedly gun the engine to melt it off the exhaust pipe.

Elvis and the sergeant took their regulation ponchos, hunkered down, and due partly to the intense cold, fell asleep instantly. Since spit-and-polish Presley had secured the ponchos like tents, they retained the maximum amount of warmth. But the makeshift "domes" also captured the intense levels of carbon monoxide from the idling engine.

"I was asleep within seconds," Elvis told Charlie Hodge several days later. "I don't know how much time had passed, but the next thing I knew a blast of wind blew the poncho off of my face. Fresh air gusted as if someone had thrown ice water in my face. The air had a sort of sweet smell to it."

Elvis tried to raise his hands. They wouldn't move. He closed his eyes, and as he had seen in a hundred spy movies, he concentrated on raising his hands above his head. "It was like they were full of lead," he said later.

Finally, Elvis began rocking back and forth in the front seat until he tumbled out into the snow. "I rolled in it and forced air in and out of my lungs again and again and again. Finally, I could feel my legs and arms. More importantly, I could crawl."

Presley dragged himself back in the jeep, turned off the ignition, and shoved Sergeant Jones until he tumbled free and landed face first in the snow. By then Presley was vomiting repeatedly. After he had recovered, he crawled to Jones.

"The sergeant looked to me as if he were dead," Presley told Hodge. "He seemed stiff."

Elvis kneaded and shook and threw snow all over Jones, trying to bring him out of unconsciousness. Finally, Elvis booted him as hard as he could. Jones choked, reared up in the snow, and staggered.

Then Presley blacked out—a secondary reaction from a body starving for oxygen. This time Jones crawled through the snow, grabbing rocks and small bushes obscured by the snow and the slick layer of ice beneath it. Now Jones kicked Presley, causing him to cough and regain consciousness.

On the long drive back to the base, both vowed not to tell of the experience because of possible consequences. As Jones told Private Presley, "Because of your fame, the media will make a circus of this."

However, the media trumpeted another of his achievements, one that would make any soldier proud. In the cold, wet, windy German spring of 1959, he almost single-handedly captured an enemy listening post during a mock battle nicknamed Winter Shield, staged to impress the nearby Czechs.

Elvis and his superior, Lieutenant Taylor, had to snake their way through muck and rotten pine needles to reach the post. Heavy rain sloshed off their slickers and camouflage makeup. Sensing that the listening post was near, Lieutenant Taylor signaled Private Presley to lead on—giving him a trial by fire. Moving about with just the tips of his fingers and his toes to avoid making sounds in the mud, Elvis led his lieutenant to the top of a small ridge.

The skies suddenly exploded with lightning strikes, so many and paced so close together that Presley and Taylor were virtually bathed in light every ten seconds or so. Then Presley heard something—a raspy noise from nearby.

"Lieutenant," he whispered, "that was a tank hatch closing."

The next bolt of lightning illuminated the shadows of two forward tanks—just in front of the operational command post for the games.

"We can squeeze right around these mothers and take 'em all," Presley said softly.

Taylor wanted Presley to have the capture. "He deserved it. He was so damn good." The lieutenant was going to neutralize the lone guard by shoving the barrel of the empty gun into his abdomen.

"Private First Class Presley reared up out of the mud, threw open the flap leading to the captain's headquarters, pointed his gun, and growled at the surprised captain, 'Your ass is mine.'"

Recalled Taylor, "That was one pissed captain, since Presley also captured a first lieutenant and a master sergeant—the entire command team."

Presley showed his characteristic sensitivity. He told Taylor, "There's something I've got to do." Elvis walked over and looked the defeated captain in the eye: "Sorry, sir!"

The captain laughed. "Either you guys are good or our security needs a lot of beefing up!"

While Taylor was filling in the endless War Game Incident Reports, he noticed that Elvis had moved over to a group of trees and was nonchalantly leaning against one, while looking down at his feet. All the while the first lieutenant Presley had just captured kept shoving a slip of paper at him while yelling orders.

Sprinting up the hill, Taylor shouted, "Leave the private alone. He's just doing his job!"

The lieutenant moved until he was up close and personal with Taylor: "Go mind your own fucking business." Taylor let loose with a "hard straight blow to the chest cavity," sending the brash young lieutenant sliding into the mud.

"That guy was pushing for your autograph, wasn't he?" Taylor asked. Elvis nodded.

"Why not just sign it?"

Presley responded defiantly, "Well, Lieutenant, that's my choice."

"My respect for this great guy grew even greater because of that answer," recalled Taylor.

All Quiet on the Western Front

Private Presley might have been a good soldier, but he still knew how to use his money and his status. By mid-June of 1959 he had grown sick of the drab German countryside, so he and his hand-picked buddies hired a driver to take them by Mercedes sedan to Munich, 250 miles away. There, Elvis went on much-publicized dates with the beautiful brunette starlet Vera Tschechowa, daughter of one of the country's great actresses, Olga Tschechowa, said to be a favorite performer of Adolf Hitler's.

According to Lamar Fike, Elvis became intrigued with a female contortionist in Munich. During one "date," they spent more than five hours in her dressing room. When Elvis at last emerged, he was "wringing wet."

Elvis also became enamored with the girls of Munich's Moulin Rouge, sometimes spending the night with one of them. One morning when he showed for breakfast with Vera Tschechowa, she took note that he still had "bits of tinsel everywhere, in his hair and his eyebrows." Elvis and the boys even smuggled some of the Moulin Rouge girls into their rooms at the Hotel Edelweiss. Because the hotel nightly locked its doors at nine o'clock, Lamar and the others would help the girls climb through the windows. When the management discovered what was going on, Elvis and his friends were asked to leave.

It's amazing that Elvis never got anybody pregnant during his German stay. "I make sure I don't come [during sex]. I pull out in plenty of time," he once explained to an Army buddy. Also, Elvis's proclivity was for foreplay more than actual consummation.

Elvis also whisked his friends to Paris—though the first time he suggested the trip, he was met by blank faces. "No, no, no, guys," he said, laughing. "This one's on me . . . I'll fix it with the Army. Everything will be taken care of in advance. Just leave this to me. We're gonna tear up the streets of Paris!" Elvis Presley, poster boy for the peacetime Army, got the green light and along with his gang took the night train to the City of Lights. Presley checked the group into the largest suite of the Hotel Prince de Galles, featuring five round-the-clock chefs, servants in knee breeches, crystal and silver, and Louis XVI furniture filling every corner. During their first night they took a drive into the low hills outside of Paris, where they sat and waited for the sun to rise over the city. In years to come, Elvis would reminisce about that first Parisian sunrise—the skyline silhouetted against orange and rose. "What a way to see that city for the first time," he would murmur.

On one nighttime taxi ride, Elvis, Charlie Hodge, and Rex Mansfield cruised down the glittering Champs-Élysées, saw the Arc de Triomphe, dramatically illuminated like a jewel, and then, at Elvis's request, headed back to the Eiffel Tower, itself a blaze of lights. All the while they sang spirituals and nostalgic tunes such as "I'll Be Home Again" and "Amazing Grace." The driver wanted to know where they wanted to go. "One more time. Up to the Arch and back," requested Elvis. Round and round they went. "I don't think we ever did get to the Lido that night," said Hodge.

There were plenty of other nights at the Lido, and Café Paris, the 4 O'Clock Club, the Crazy Horse, the Folies-Bergère, the Moulin Rouge, and the Carousel. The boys charted a rake's progress through the clubs, usually returning to the Lido just before it closed. The attraction there was the most glamorous chorus line in Gay Paree, including a British ensemble known as the Bluebells.

Nightly after the curtain dropped, Elvis—looking particularly dashing in his dark green dress uniform—corralled the Bluebells, plus an armload of the chorines, and repaired to his suite for a night of revelry. Remembered Esposito, "It worked this way: Elvis picked the girl he wanted, then the rest were up for grabs. It was the fulfillment of every young man's dreams."

Well, almost. Because Lamar Fike wasn't having the same luck as the other guys, Elvis said, "We've got to get him a hooker!" A call was put in to the hotel concierge, and in less than an hour a prostitute was at the door. The instant she saw Elvis, she let out a delighted, "Ellllveees!" and raced to grab and kiss him. Amid uncontrollable laughter Elvis pointed at Lamar. "No, baby, for him! You're for him." He spun the girl around to face Lamar. She squeeled, "Noooooooo!" and bounded back into Elvis's arms.

The prostitute wound up being paid—for *no* services rendered—and escorted to the door. "Of course, Elvis didn't want anything to do with her because it would have killed Lamar," recalled Esposito.

One after-dawn revel ended with chocolates and champagne—and with Elvis tumbling into satin sheets with two of the Bluebells. That afternoon the phone began jingling and was allowed to do so repeatedly. Finally Lamar Fike took the call and wound up being berated by a Lido manager.

"God damn!" he said. "Will you get the Bluebells back here so we can start our show? You're holding up the entire review!"

Fike called for a flotilla of cabs and dispatched the Bluebells back to the Lido. Meanwhile, Elvis diplomatically saved the girls a lot of trouble by having a long conversation with the show's manager, and by sending a nice gift.

"Pure magic," recalled Mansfield. "Elvis made sure we went first-class, even using his clout with the French offices of William Morris, Paramount, and MGM."

Elvis liked Paris so much that he made return trips—each of them sexually exhausting. "There were wall-to-wall women everywhere," said Fike. As one Prince de Galles room-service waiter put it, the women were "going in and out of Monsieur Presley's suite, in and out, like a door revolving."

He also indulged in a wilder side. Through the girls at the Lido, Elvis and his buddies were introduced to a small club called Le Bantu—intimate, smoky, and filled with attractive women—many of whom, it turned out, were actually men. The inveterate girl watcher was awed and amused.

During one visit a "girl" took a seat alongside Elvis and Lamar. Elvis slowly took a sip of his Coke, then glanced over at Lamar. "What do you think?"

Lamar was frank: "I have no earthly idea."

Another night, as he scrutinized a "woman" making exaggerated sucking sounds at a nearby table, Elvis said, "What do you think? Is it a he or a she?"

"I'm too nervous to find out," admitted Lamar.

The French capital offered more than just hedonism, though; it restored Elvis's ego about his fame. In Friedberg, where he felt compelled to blend in and do his duty, he would "get into a funk and worry about whether he was still hot," recalled Lamar. He was appeased by his return trips to Paris—where he was no longer an anonymous GI.

In Paris, he was *Elvis Presley*. Once, while being chased down the Champs-Élysées, he reared back his head for a joyous look at the French girls who were giving chase.

By this time Elvis wasn't sure about his status back in the States. His last movie, *King Creole*, had come and gone at the theaters. This after some of his strongest reviews. As the *Los Angeles Times* put it, "Well, for heaven's sake. Elvis Presley is turning into an actor." The timing was, of course, ironic. Little wonder that Elvis anguished about what would happen when he finally returned home. Would he be a has-been?

Paris reassured Presley that he was still a star. As he walked the streets, window-shopping or gazing upward at "the hunchback's house"—as he dubbed the Cathedral of Notre Dame—the crowds became so huge that the gendarmes were called out. There were traffic snarls as drivers who spied him slowed to get a look and call, *"Bon jour, Elvis!"* There were even spats as chorines vied to sit on his lap, in their gossamer costumes of feathers and sequins—sometimes bare-breasted—to have their pictures taken.

Elvis was all nerves the night he was pulled on the stage of the Lido by singers George and Bert Bernard. Elvis, who hadn't performed for fifteen months, said it was a strange feeling to be back in a spotlight. But he was clearly glad to be back. Along with singing a single tune, he sat down at the piano and performed the lilting "Willow Weep for Me."

All the while, Elvis agonized over what he would do once he was mustered out. He now had plenty of cause for worry: the music world that he had known was in the midst of an artistic and economic shake-up. Even his contemporaries were in trouble.

Chuck Berry was facing a two-year prison term for taking a minor over the state line to have sex. Jerry Lee Lewis's career had screeched to a scandalous halt when he married his thirteen-year-old cousin. Little Richard had given up music for the ministry (a decision due, in part, to the 1957 launch of the *Sputnik* satellite, which Little Richard saw as a heavenly message that it was time to bow out). Buddy Holly had died in a February 1959 plane crash that also took the lives of singers Richie Valens and the Big Bopper. And, after being sidelined by a disastrous car crash, Carl Perkins discovered that the rockabilly sound he had pioneered was ebbing, along with his career.

Meanwhile a new crop of singers with all-American faces and spiffy wardrobes had pushed its way onto the scene. Not coincidentally they—and their sounds—were tamer, less threatening. They were the boys next door that the mothers of America could trust with their daughters. Many of them had been "manufactured," plucked from obscurity to help fill a void sensed by the music promoters. These singing stars would come to be known as the teen idols.

"Most of these guys can't even sing!" Elvis Presley would say, shaking his head as he flipped through the pages of the American fan magazines. "They can't even goddamn sing!"

In fairness, some of the new teenage heroes could sing quite well—Ricky Nelson among them. But they eschewed the frenetic, devilishly leering deliveries favored by the rock-'n'-roll pioneers—Elvis included—and kept the tempo in check. From Frankie Avalon to Bobby Rydell, from Bobby Vee to Paul Anka, from Tommy Sands to Pat Boone (yes, Elvis's former "nemesis" was still securely around), the idea was to give young girls someone "safe" to scream for. Whereas Elvis had taken to the stage in shirts opened to his waist, with body movements that pressed panic buttons among parents, educators, and the clergy, the new hitmakers seemed harmless. Many of them even favored wholesome-looking V-neck sweaters.

Fabian Forte—professionally known by just his first name, or the moniker the Fabulous One—typified the new trend. When just a teenager, Fabian had been discovered by a shrewd Philadelphia record-label chief named Bob Marcucci, who came upon the handsome boy, with the dark good looks, as he sat on his front porch. "I thought he looked like a cross between Elvis Presley and Ricky Nelson, but that he was better looking than either of them," remembered Marcucci. He went on to ask Fabian, "Say, kid, can you sing?"

In fact, Fabian had failed his high school chorus classes. Undaunted, Marcucci sent him to three different voice teachers until one accepted him. Fabian went on to record songs such as "Turn Me Loose" and "Tiger," causing *Time* magazine to dub him the "tuneless tiger." It didn't matter: teenagers had already fallen prey to a massive publicity campaign, concocted by Marcucci, which led to overflow concert crowds. "There is no denying that Fabian has an appeal to girls the likes of which has not been seen here since the early Presley era," declared the *Los Angeles Mirror News*, which claimed the sixteen-year-old (an avowed Presley fan) had "unseated Elvis."

It was enough to send the twenty-four-year-old Presley on a quest to "look younger," and to further improve his appearance. Especially self-conscious about some of his facial pores—which were enlarged because of the serious acne he had once suffered—he wound up becoming a client of so-called health and beauty experts. One of them, who ingratiated himself into the Bad Nauheim household, administered special skin treatments—applying an "elixir" made of yogurt, honey, and ground-up orange blossoms, carnations, and other ingredients.

Presley's friends were incredulous when he walked around the house with his face covered with the goo. "For Christ's sake!" exclaimed Lamar. "Give yourself a break!" When Elvis protested, Lamar argued, "Bring the bastard [the skin-care specialist] in when you're about forty!"

Elvis never did get the complete treatment; the association came to a dramatic end when the so-called specialist made a pass. Elvis went into such a rage that both Lamar and Red had to restrain him. "I grabbed Elvis by the waist and pinned him up against the wall to keep him from killing that guy," Lamar related. All the while Elvis yelled, "He was a queer! A fucking queer!"

Ironically, much of Elvis's anxiety over his career was unwarranted. In 1958, during his first year in the Army, his music and movie deals resulted in earnings of $2 million. Throughout 1959 he remained on the EP record charts with the two *King Creole* EPs. Also, "A Fool Such as I" (flip side: "I Need Your Love Tonight") was released in March 1959, climbing to number two on the record charts and marking his nineteenth consecutive million-selling single. Still, the well had run dry: the tunes Presley had cut during his only 1958 recording session had all been released.

Partly due to what was happening at home, he actively sought a new "look." He wanted to change his image, to banish the cool "cat" who had so affected teenagers during the midfifties. In Paris he had seen new fashions—the kind favored by hot young stars such as Alain Delon, Jean-Paul Belmondo, and Jean-Louis Trintignant, the hip members of the New Wave cinema. Tight, continental slacks, sweaters that stressed the breadth of the shoulders, and medium-length hair controlled by hairsprays would affect his sense of style. Presley came home with suitcases of continental clothes.

When RCA's Rod Lauren announced that Elvis was going to have a new look, thousands of protests poured into the Colonel's office. "But it was too late," said Presley associate Marty Lacker. "Elvis himself had already changed. All of a sudden he wanted to be a crooner."

Actually, Elvis had always loved crooning. Back in June 1954, when he had at last got the chance to sing for Sun Records' Sam Phillips, he had crooned such tunes as "That's Amore," causing Phillips to admonish, "God damn, son, we already have a Dean Martin!" While he was in Germany he acquired more than two thousand records—virtually every hit released during his two-year tour of duty, a library dominated by male crooners. He spent more than a year practicing new singing styles—sometimes for several hours at a time, usually after spinning platters by Martin, Vic Damone, Jackie Wilson, Sam Cooke, and Bing Crosby.

Incredible as it might seem, his favorite was Mario Lanza. Elvis played the sound-track album from MGM's *The Singing Prince* so often that he wore out the grooves. Lanza's delivery of such songs as "Golden Days," "I'll Walk with God," and "Serenade" had such an impact on Presley that he went on to mimic the style in his own impending songs, including the ballad "Can't Help Falling in Love" and the operatic "It's Now or Never." The latter, Elvis Presley's first post-Army hit, was an American redo of the Mario Lanza standard " 'O Sole Mio."

From outside the house at 14 Goethestrasse in Bad Nauheim, fans who had gathered got to listen to Presley's tentative first steps toward a new musical style. "He sang every night in the living room," recalled Lamar Fike. "Charlie Hodge had gone to the Stamps School of Music and worked with Presley every night, concentrating on how to improve range and how to sustain notes at the top of the register."

Billy Smith noted, "Elvis had a range of about two octaves and a half, making him a high baritone who could nail high G's and A's full-voiced. That was just his natural ability. But practicing with Charlie in Germany made his voice even stronger. He now sang more from the diaphragm—with twice the vocal power of his rockabilly days."

"It's the same music," Elvis insisted, "but with more balls."

The same could not be said for the songs Elvis would go on to record following "It's Now or Never." In the early 1960s he released dozens of forgettable tunes—among them, the syrupy "Judy" and

"Soldier Boy"—that were obvious reactions to the teen-idol jitters. (Oddly, Elvis blew several solid chances. His bland rendition of "Suspicion" didn't chart, though Elvis fan and soundalike Terry Stafford later turned it into an enormous hit.)

As he was moving away from rock 'n' roll, Elvis was also grappling with the direction his movie career would take once he got home. Hollywood was uneasy about his impending return. Executives saw the new teen idols as solid proof that interest in rock 'n' roll had abated. Why not for Presley, as well? When Paramount Pictures tried to cash in on Army publicity with a reissue of *Loving You* and *King Creole*, the double bill was pulled in just one week. "This was the most disastrous engagement in the history of this theater," a New York exhibitor told Hal Wallis.

In a memo from Twentieth Century-Fox debating Presley's future on the screen, one executive volunteered, "From my own personal point of view, Presley can stay in the Army." Still another studio insider stated that after having been converted into a soldier, Presley would no longer want to return to civilian life as "the great exponent" of the "barbarian" rock 'n' roll.

Just months before his hitch was up, Elvis remained idealistic. He told reporter Bob Battle of the *Nashville Banner* that he wanted to make straight dramatic movies, without singing. "It will be terribly hard work, I know. But it will be a challenge. I thrive on challenges. I like to keep proving myself." Added Presley, "The best example I can think of is Frank Sinatra."

By that time the Colonel was paving the way for Elvis's return. He had fostered relationships with the fan magazines, especially *Photoplay*, which invited its readers to send Elvis a welcome-back message and "win a day at the studio with Elvis." The magazine also delivered a letter from Elvis. Datelined Bad Nauheim, it stressed, "I don't mind whether girls are redheads, blondes or brunettes, as long as they are truly feminine." Elvis added, "I don't like sophisticated girls who pretend to be something they aren't. The girl I like looks up to me as a man."

Lest anyone had missed out on the performer's rags-to-riches climb, the Colonel made sure the magazines received Elvis's "life story," lavishly illustrated with pages of photos from the "family scrapbook." This publicity avalanche marked the real beginning of the Presley "myth." As rewritten by Parker, Elvis "often went hungry" as a small child in Tupelo, where he sometimes looked up "toward the huge, red Mississippi sun and shouted, 'Oh, God. Please . . . I don't want to stay here for-ever like this." Other inaccuracies of this period included the revelation that Elvis's twin, Aaron, died when he was several months old, and that Elvis was then given Aaron as his middle name.

With Elvis's discharge—E Day—looming, the country's major newspapers warned readers to brace themselves: "Elvis Re-Invading; Is Nation Ready?" asked the *Los Angeles Mirror News*, which quoted a German psychologist who found Presley to be a "throwback to the caveman," and a French columnist who called Presley "uninhibited, free, a true animal spirit . . . animal, all animal."

What the readers didn't know was that the old Elvis was no more. Already producer Hal Wallis had chosen to capitalize on Elvis's military status. "The new mature Elvis," announced Wallis, was going to be showcased "in a series of pictures set in exotic locales." First out the pipeline would be *G.I. Blues*, with Presley playing a soldier who hap-pens to sing.

In the months prior to Elvis's discharge, Paramount Pictures sent a camera crew to Frankfurt for location footage, including scenes of tanks and tank crews provided by the Third Armored Division. Wallis also flew over, with screenwriters Edmund Beloin and Henry Garson, to talk with the star—who did not go before the movie cameras (a double appeared in location scenes) but did pose for the obligatory Hollywood publicity pictures. Elvis was polite, but he was also growing skeptical about the movie's mix of silly romance and songs.

He had no idea that this would be his cinematic future.

Priscilla

Elvis Presley sat in the room's best chair with one leg hoisted over the side and his head tilted back. He was dressed up in tan gabardine pants, hot-red sweater, and gleaming loafers. The hi-fi was playing a tune by Brenda Lee, and his friends were milling about with a group of young women. Elvis was bored and unimpressed. "Nothin' there," he said, shaking his head.

Despite the many women who had come and gone through his bed, he had yet to find someone who would ease the crushing loneliness he still felt following his mother's death. "Sex—that's the easy thing," he told Joe Esposito. "I want a girl who'll listen. All the rest is just *noise*, man."

Then the door opened and in came genial, handsome Airman Currie Grant, with his wife, Carole, and a hesitant, trembling young girl. She wore a demure navy-and-white sailor dress and white shoes and socks, and her dark brown hair cascaded in a mass of ringlets.

"The plain, almost drab living room was filled with people, but I spotted Elvis immediately: handsomer than he appeared in films, younger and more vulnerable-looking," Priscilla Beaulieu remembered years later.

He also spotted her, and he stood up when Currie brought her forward. Surveying her from head to toe, Elvis asked, "Well, what have we here?"

Small talk followed, with Elvis quizzing the girl about her age. Was she in the eleventh or twelfth grade in high school? "Ninth," replied a barely audible Priscilla.

Elvis leaned forward to better hear. "Ninth what?" he asked.

When he realized she was in the ninth grade, he let loose a laugh and exclaimed, "Why, you're just a baby!"

"Thanks!" said Priscilla brusquely, and blushed in spite of herself. Even so, she was smiling.

Then the world's most famous GI stood and took the fourteen-year-old girl's hand. "Look, you stay right here. I'm going to sing to you." As he slid onto the piano seat, silence fell over the room—as it did every time the soldier turned into the singer. Presley staged his surprise act only when he was particularly anxious to impress someone. For this "performance" he eschewed hits like "That's All Right (Mama)" and "Heartbreak Hotel." Instead, he performed a slow, sensual rendition of the Tony Bennett standard "Rags to Riches," and then slid into "Are You Lonesome Tonight?"—all the while glancing at Priscilla. He wrapped up the show with "End of the Rainbow," and his friends joined in on harmony.

Through most of the serenade Priscilla avoided his eyes: "I couldn't believe that Elvis Presley was trying to impress me."

Sensing her timidity, Presley later took her by the arm and led her into the kitchen to meet Grandma Minnie Mae, who Priscilla soon learned ran the household. "My goodness, you're a pretty little thing," said Minnie Mae with a smile. "I'm fixin' my boy a sandwich. Can I fix something for you?"

The girl shook her head. "I'm much too nervous to eat." In fact, Priscilla was awestruck as she sat across the table from the rock-'n'-roll star.

"You're the first American girl I've met in a long time," said Elvis between bites of a bacon sandwich slathered in mustard. "Who're the girls listening to back there? I hear Rick Nelson and Fabian are taking my place . . . They're younger and they're slicker, aren't they?"

"Are you kidding?" Priscilla protested. "Everyone listens to you."

Elvis was unconvinced. "All I hear about are Ricky and Fabian, their looks, their big movie deals. They're on the cover of every magazine." Priscilla could sense that Elvis was uncertain where he stood in his career. It was no secret on the base that he was due home in six months.

She tried to reassure him. "I really think we're all just waiting for you to come back. These guys are stand-ins."

Elvis stared intently into her eyes. He was so clearly entranced that when Currie Grant opened the kitchen door and saw Presley's attention so rapt, he had mixed emotions as he tapped on his watch. It was time for him to escort the pretty Priscilla home. "I'm not breaking a promise to Captain Beaulieu," Grant said. "We've got to go."

Elvis was disappointed. "Currie, what about another hour? Can't you call her parents?"

Currie shook his head. "E, this is a fourteen-year-old, and I made a promise to the captain . . . no chance."

Taking Priscilla by the hand, Elvis walked her to the door and promised, "I'll make arrangements for you to come back in a couple of days. See you then."

Priscilla said she left thinking, "It will never happen." She was so sure that she would never again meet Presley that the next day at school she didn't even want to tell her classmates about the encounter. "After all," she later said, "who would believe it anyway?" But Currie did call, just days later, and Priscilla was once again escorted to Presley's continuous house party at 14 Goethestrasse, where she again stood out among the brassy German girls and young soldiers.

Because she was an "Army brat," who had grown up having to regularly trade in one set of friends for another in the cycle dictated by military life, Priscilla saw through the false gaiety surrounding Elvis. She recognized in him the same sort of loneliness that had made her own childhood so solitary.

For decades, Elvis scholars and enthusiasts have analyzed the instant attraction Elvis Presley felt for the schoolgirl Priscilla Beaulieu. How could one of the world's most desirable men suddenly fall for an unknown teenager? Yet Elvis and Priscilla were not only linked by the bond of painful shyness, he was also sorely in need of someone to talk to. In Priscilla he found an eager listener who also commiserated with him over the loss of his mother. Because of her tender age, he didn't have to assume the role of a Hollywood stud in her presence. With Priscilla, Elvis could be himself.

In a February 1997 interview with *Parade* magazine, Priscilla theorized that she and Presley bonded instantly because they had both suffered mutual loss. Her father, a Navy pilot, had died in a crash when she was just six months old. And of course, Elvis was still grieving for Gladys.

Moreover, each helped to fill the other's void. "I guess I brought out the father in Elvis, and he brought out the mother in me." As Elvis used to tell her repeatedly, "I wish my mama was alive."

She was also a lovely girl, bearing a striking resemblance to Debra Paget, the sophisticated young actress who had spurned Presley's attentions during the making of his first movie, *Love Me Tender*.

During her second visit to Presley's rented home, she was cornered by her host, who whispered, "Will you come upstairs to my room?" As her eyes widened, he reached out to run his fingers through her hair. "There's nothing to be frightened of, honey. I swear I'll never do anything to harm you. I'll treat you just as if you were my sister." Ironically, Priscilla looked more like Lolita than a little sister. Having learned of Presley's affinity for light blue, she had worn for this visit a light blue, tight skirt, with a matching form-fitting sweater and a blue ribbon in her hair. Still, she took Elvis at his word. And so the teenager tentatively climbed the stairs leading to the lair of one of the world's most famous bachelors.

Once inside the door, she stiffly took a seat and surveyed the surroundings. The room was surprisingly spartan—several Army hats, a leather jacket, brushes, combs. She scowled when she saw a pinup poster of a half-naked Brigitte Bardot. Then her eyes focused on a stack of freshly laundered T-shirts. Scattered on top were letters. By quickly scanning the envelopes Priscilla could see that they were from girls in the United States—including a number of perfumed messages from the same female sender. "I wanted to read the letters, but was afraid he'd catch me," Priscilla candidly admitted in her memoirs. But she did manage to make out the name of the avid writer: Anita.

Priscilla sat in Elvis's room for nearly twenty minutes before he came in, sauntered across the room, and began to slip off his shirt.

Priscilla leapt up and began to leave. "Look, I'm not that kind of—"

Elvis whirled around, cutting her off. "No, honey, no. I'm just putting on my pajama top . . . I'm just getting comfortable."

Buttoning his top, he plopped down on the bed and motioned for her to join him. She was "flattered, confused, and frightened all at the same time" by the attention as they at first sat and later "cuddled." For a while he talked freely about the confusion he had felt since his mother's death. And right then and there he told her he felt she was going to be significant in his life. "Of course, you realize that I've known lots of girls, and many have come to visit me here, but I have never felt such real closeness as with you." Then he added, "You know, I just wish Mama could have been here to meet you. She would have liked you as much as I do."

Presley talked with heartfelt passion for several hours, though to Priscilla it seemed that their meeting was "over in a second" when Currie knocked lightly on the door. It was time to take her home. Priscilla began to cry, which led Elvis to take her hand and insist, "Don't worry, we have plenty of time ahead of us."

"I was very young and impressionable," Priscilla admitted decades later. "No one else was important anymore. He doted on me, confided in me, told me things he told no one else." He came to so dominate her thoughts that she realized she was in love.

"It was like it was almost meant to be. . . . He gave me hope." Early on, in what would be a long, frustrating relationship, Elvis promised to bring her to Graceland.

But it would be three years before this pledge was fulfilled.

All the while they saw each other in Germany, until Elvis left for home, he conveniently downplayed his relationship with Anita Wood, who was still in Memphis and nominally his fiancée. Nor did he bring up Elisabeth Stefaniak, who still lingered in the house as Presley's secretary and sometime companion.

"That was the single thing about Elvis Presley that truly disappointed me," recalled Rex Mansfield, who had become a member of Elvis's elite but growing entourage. Moreover, according to Joe Esposito, Elvis nightly picked through the throng of girls who milled about the house as if they were part of a harem. If none of them were to his taste, he casually slept with Elisabeth.

Back in Memphis, Anita understandably fumed about fan stories linking Elvis with this or that fräulein. But she was a realist: she continued her career as a disc jockey, and singer, knowing full well that some of Elvis's "dates" were starlets who wanted to bask in publicity about their "romance" with the American star. Still, when Anita read about his dates with a beguiling, petite typist named Margrit Buergin, she fired off a blistering letter to Elvis. Another flurry of letters traveled across the Atlantic when she saw the news accounts of Elvis openly dating actress Vera Tschechowa. In his letters Elvis kept renewing his promise of marriage; Anita expected a big, splashy wedding at Christmas, following his discharge.

Elvis wrote and rewrote a reply to Anita. In the final version—which

Minnie Mae later looked over before her grandson sent it off, deeming it "barely believable"—Elvis tried to soothe Anita with the declaration, "I haven't dated a single girl." He called her by her pet name, Widdle Beadie, and promised, "You can believe that when I marry, it will be Miss Wittle Wood Presley." Added Elvis, "You can trust me to the utmost, and please keep yourself clean and wholesome." As he signed off, he asked her to "never, ever reveal this letter to anyone . . . Yours alone and forever, Elvis."

Of course, he was not Anita's "alone." Yet Joe Esposito, Lamar Fike, and other Elvis associates have recalled that Elvis was concerned about whether Anita was being faithful to him back in Memphis, despite his own rampant infidelities in West Germany. His thinking—impacted by his Southern roots and heightened by his celebrity status—was a common mind-set of the era: women were supposed to remain monogamous, men were not. When a rumor reached Elvis that Anita was seeing a young Memphis lawyer, he groused about it for hours.

When he cooled off, he returned to his chivalric romance with Priscilla. But that eccentric union was running into trouble. Though Priscilla's mother was somewhat giddy at her daughter's "little flirta-tion" with the singer—"my mother felt that it was a once-in-a-lifetime opportunity," Priscilla has recalled—her stepfather, Captain Joseph Paul Beaulieu, was less impressed. "This isn't decent!" exploded the captain, who was a powerful liaison between the U.S. Army and the Air Force in West Germany. The next time Currie called to collect Priscilla for a dinner date, the captain said, "No, this is it! Unless and until Mr. Presley comes in person for a talk with me, my daughter will not be free to go out."

If Captain Beaulieu was deliberately seeking a way to encourage Elvis Presley's pursuit of his daughter, he couldn't have done better than to ask the young man to call. Presley was up for the challenge. He had his father spiff up and come along—ostensibly to chaperone the young suitor. Elvis arrived on time in a tightly creased uniform, with gleaming brass and mirror-shine shoes. Vernon, in suit, tie, and brogans, looked more businessman than transplanted hillbilly.

Private Presley stepped briskly forward, shook the captain's hand, and said, "Glad to meet you, sir. I'm Elvis Presley, and this is my daddy, Vernon." Beaulieu was impressed by the young man's firm, opti-mistic handshake.

The captain wasted no time: he looked Elvis in the eye and asked, "What do you want from my daughter? Beautiful women everywhere are throwing themselves at you."

Elvis stared back at Priscilla's father, then cleared his throat and said, "Captain, I have been awfully lonely since my mama died just before I shipped out for Germany. And, as you know, your daughter is very mature for her age and is the first girl I've found who understands my loneliness. She is the only girl who has helped me in any way."

Shifting his gaze to Priscilla, Elvis added, "You may be sure that I will be the perfect gentleman. I would never do a thing to harm her. We just sit and talk."

Vernon enthusiastically volunteered, "I'm there at all times, Captain. We're like a family there. And I'll even pick her up and drive her home. That's how much she means to my son."

The tall, imposing Air Force captain at last gave his approval—along with a set of rules. One of them decreed that Elvis be the one who drove Priscilla home after their visits.

"I promise, sir," Elvis answered as he again shook hands. "I'll take good care of her, Captain."

By this time Elvis had begun to dominate Priscilla's every thought. She couldn't believe it: he liked *her*. He was increasingly attracted by her warmth—and her inquisitiveness. She used to sit and wait for him as he took his lessons in karate—to which he was introduced in Germany—and then listen as he discussed the martial art. She didn't even mind when he talked on and on about cars or football. Together, they debated the possibility of World War III, the dangers of communism, and the differences between mysticism and religion.

In his psychological study *The Inner Elvis,* Dr. Peter Whitmer linked this relationship—which would outlast all others for Elvis—with Gladys's death. Whitmer, who talked with many of the principals at the Presley house parties in Germany, said, "Elvis doted on Priscilla, but in an asexual way, confusing giving care with giving love, thereby building a replica of Gladys." He added, "The specter of Gladys was always present. To Elvis, Priscilla was an embodiment of his mother."

Esposito agreed. "Priscilla did remind Elvis of his mother. I was there, and the look on his face when she entered a room was a giveaway. The look. The dark hair, the deep-set eyes."

However, Priscilla soon learned that her Oedipal beau was also a sexual tomcat. Sometimes he slept with a girl both before and *after* her visits to his bedroom.

On her third date with Elvis, the two climbed the stairs at his house, hand in hand, heads pressed together like two high school lovers, and tumbled onto Presley's bed, where they talked and petted beyond her curfew. But Elvis would not go beyond foreplay. "Not now," he murmured in her ear, heightening the excitement she felt. "You're too special, Priscilla, and I want to keep you that way for later—after marriage."

Joe Esposito, who would later become a close friend of Priscilla's as well, said that the two spent hours in Elvis's bedroom. "They were so intense that we had to knock on the door to get Priscilla home on time." Some of Elvis's friends considered his interest in Priscilla reminiscent of the pajama party-type encounters he used to have with his teenage fans at the house on Audubon.

In Priscilla's memoirs, *Elvis and Me*, she claims to have pleaded with Elvis to consummate their relationship during their time together in Germany. She insists that Elvis steadfastly refused.

According to Priscilla's coauthor Sandra Harmon, "They did everything but actual intercourse." Harmon also notes that they played all sorts of masturbation games—a form of sex Presley preferred over consummation. Said Harmon, "Sexual game playing is what they were into—of all types." Indeed, at breakfast one morning Presley volunteered that, as beautiful as Priscilla was, "I wouldn't lay a hand on her." He added, "But, to have her sit on your face!"

To the schoolgirl who felt she had to compete against the worldly young women who lusted after Presley, his refusal to consummate their romance seemed deliberately cruel. She did not understand that he was, in effect, putting her on a pedestal—in the same class as Anita Wood and his mother.

Priscilla had seen magazine photos of the beautiful, blond, curvaceous Anita and could not believe that Elvis wasn't seriously involved with her. In the *Elvis and Me* television miniseries, one scene shows Priscilla and Elvis wrestling around on his bed. When he bends down to kiss her, she wonders aloud what "your beauty queen back home" would think of their nightly romps. Elvis responds by telling her that his relationship with Wood is an old one, and so he feels compelled to be "nice to her."

Priscilla had another worry: "Time had become my enemy." Elvis's discharge was scheduled for March 1960. She wanted to spend every minute with him that she could; she didn't even care when her grades dropped at school, the result of staying out so late at night with her famous beau. Elvis, meanwhile, was reeling under the pressure of returning home.

"How'll I be able to live in Graceland with Mama gone?" he asked one night as they clung together. He also wondered about his future in music and in the movies. Already his "past" was looking illustrious: on January 20 he became the first man in his class to be promoted to sergeant—thereby commanding a three-man reconnaissance team. (This was the position Sergeant Ira Jones had held.)

When news of Presley's making sergeant got out, there was initially grumbling in the ranks—and several negative items in newspaper columns suggesting that the singer had been promoted because of his celebrity. "Nonsense!" said Colonel William Taylor. Interviewed decades after his association with Presley, he stressed, "It was bound to happen to a man who performed so outstandingly during his tour of duty. When you can handle the responsibility, they give you the command."

For any other Army scout the promotion would have led to a fast track to the noncommissioned-officer ranks. But of course, there was to be no reenlistment. The Pentagon's most famous soldier would be processed out of the service on March 1. The impending discharge meant a return to the pressures of being *Elvis Presley*. "In a way, Elvis's stint in the Army was a breathing period," said Lamar Fike. "It freed him from the crushing demands of his career, and in some ways, from the needs of his family. Now he had to go home and start all over again."

During his last month in the service, a hysterically insistent Priscilla intensified her demands that they consummate their relationship before Elvis flew home. Again, he demurred. "You're too fine a girl, and our love is too strong to do this now." He reassured her, though. "This will all happen at the proper time."

The formidable Anita Wood was already generating considerable publicity as the "girl Elvis would return to." In an interview with *Movieland and TV Time* magazine she seemed to be sending a message to any other wanna-be-girlfriends when she flashed a beautiful cocktail ring he had given her and recounted the time he called her "his number one girl."

Elvis sent a message of his own—but it was aimed at Priscilla. Free-lance journalist Peter Hopkirk, who had been dogging Presley's steps for months trying to be anointed as the "guy who got the story from Elvis," was astounded when it finally happened. On February 27 he picked up a ringing phone and heard Elvis's voice. Would he meet Elvis at 14 Goethestrasse?

It was a cloak-and-dagger interview. Elvis closed the window shades the minute Hopkirk entered: "I'll be in trouble tomorrow for talking to you," he whispered, "but I've got something to get off my chest.

"Mr. Hopkirk, there's only one reason I'm truly sad about leaving Germany—and her name is Priscilla. Hardly anyone knows about her. She's . . . very mature. And intelligent. I think she's the most beautiful girl I've ever seen, both German and American. I've dated plenty of girls while I've been here, but Priscilla is definitely the sharpest of them."

"How serious is this?" Hopkirk pressed.

"Serious. I think I've said enough already."

The interview ricocheted around the world, sending Colonel Parker into a fury. The revived career he was orchestrating relied on Presley's returning home as a dashing, *single* rock-'n'-roll prince.

Elvis's interview would have stirred up even more trouble—with his fans as well as the Colonel—had he not lied to Hopkirk about Priscilla's age. When asked how old she was, Elvis looked him straight in the eye and said, "Sweet sixteen." The truth could have been a public relations fiasco: Jerry Lee Lewis was already paying the price for cradle robbing.

It is fair to say that confusion reigned in Elvis's heart. He knew Priscilla would remain waiting in Germany and Anita Wood would welcome him home with open arms. Yet he also remained attached to Elisabeth Stefaniak; she was going to accompany him to Memphis as his secretary.*

Elvis was also coming home with some new aides. Charlie Hodge and Joe Esposito would go on to join Lamar Fike and Red West in the so-called Memphis Mafia.

Elvis wasn't the only one coming back to Memphis with a surprise. Vernon Presley was returning with a brassy platinum blonde. A Tennessee native, Dee Stanley had been in the midst of dissolving her marriage to a master sergeant when she met Vernon. Elvis was not thrilled by his father's courtship of Dee, who at thirty-five was just ten years

---

*Elisabeth Stefaniak did, indeed, come to Memphis—along with Presley's military buddy Rex Mansfield, whom Elisabeth went on to marry. The Mansfields have since authored several books about their recollections of Presley.

older than he was. As his friends used to note with wry smiles, she also seemed awfully interested in the younger Presley.

The mother of three young sons, Dee was at Vernon's side the day he approached Elvis and said, "Son, I want your blessing to marry." Elvis gave it through clenched teeth, then pulled himself together and diplomatically added that he had always wanted brothers. But his friends knew he was upset: Vernon and Dee would share the opulent bedroom where his mother had once slept. "I don't like it," he confided to Joe Esposito. "I think she's only marrying him because he's my daddy." He petulantly added, "I'll never call her Mom."

On the day before Elvis was scheduled to leave Germany, he attended a massive press conference at the base. Nineteen public relations personnel were on hand to assure that the event went smoothly. A hundred reporters from London, Paris, Rome, Germany, and America were on hand.

Among the crowd Elvis spied an old friend. Marion Keisker, the woman who had worked for Sam Phillips at Sun Records—the woman who had tucked away Elvis's name and phone number when he came in to make his vanity recording—was there, for Armed Forces Television. "Marion! In Germany!" said Elvis. Looking over her uniform—she was a captain with the Women's Air Force—he said, "What do I do? Kiss you or salute you?"

"In that order," Keisker said, smiling, and then warmly embraced Elvis.

The officer in command was furious. Suspicious that the encounter was some kind of publicity stunt, he threatened to report Keisker. Jumping to her defense, Elvis said, "Captain, you don't understand. You wouldn't even be having this thing today if it wasn't for this lady." Marion Keisker would never forget those words.

When the press conference got under way, Elvis had her stand behind him. From time to time he reached back to feel for Keisker's hands and make sure she was still there.

As the press scribbled into notebooks and held out their microphones, Elvis answered two hours' worth of questions. Plans for marriage? "I have to wait until the bug bites me. I haven't been bitten yet." Plans for sideburns? "Well, maybe a little. But not as long as before." Plans for a final date—and with whom? Cleverly, Elvis pointed to the PR man seated nearby and said, "I guess it's him." Everyone laughed.

When it at last ended, Elvis quipped, "I felt like I was on trial for something."

Before dawn the following day, March 1, 1960, Elvis boarded a bus with other soldiers being discharged and headed for Frankfurt's Rhein-Main Airport for the trip back to the United States. Priscilla followed in a limousine that deposited her into a crowd of fans. Nonetheless, she elbowed her way to the front for a last glimpse. Elvis was able to do as he'd promised: he turned at the top of the ramp and waved at her. Five minutes later, his airplane was gone.

The twenty-five-year-old former soldier was off to face the ravenous American public once again.

He left behind in Europe a fourteen-year-old girl full of dreams and living on promises.

#

The plane was coming in for a snowy landing at the McGuire Field Air Base in New Jersey. Elvis had slept much of the way on the trip back from Germany. But the moment he stepped from the DC-7, with seventy-seven other GI's, he felt instantly revitalized. Elvis Presley arrived back in the States to a red, white, and blue welcome that was, said *Life* magazine, "possibly the most heavily reported Army homecoming since General MacArthur's," a comparison that amused Elvis's close friends. All the while he had been in Germany, he used to intone, in MacArthuresque speech, "I shall return!"

Like a conquering hero, he endured another celebratory press conference at nearby Fort Dix. Flashing his lopsided grin, Elvis acknowledged that the military had put him through some changes, but "if I say the Army made a man of me, it would give the impression that I was an idiot before I was drafted. I wasn't exactly that."

Along with fielding a barrage of familiar questions from two hundred reporters, Elvis accepted a gift of lacy dress shirts from an obviously enamored Nancy Sinatra. Frank's nineteen-year-old daughter was acting as an emissary for her father, who was going to officially welcome Elvis Presley back home in front of all America—Elvis was to be a guest on Frank Sinatra's TV show.

As Elvis received the accolades, Colonel Tom Parker sat at his feet—on the floor—with a cigar clenched between his teeth and a French beret atop his head. There were dollar signs in his sparkling eyes.

From Fort Dix, Elvis and the Colonel traveled by chauffeur-driven limousine to the Warwick Hotel in Manhattan, where Elvis obliged the waiting photographers by posing as he waved his separation papers. But he didn't look happy amid the popping of flashbulbs. What he really wanted was to go home to Graceland.

The Colonel wouldn't hear of it. "Why, son, the people want to get a good look at you! The American taxpayers want to see what kind of soldier was defending 'em."

The next morning Elvis had his final meal in the military: scrambled eggs, a plateful of crisp bacon, coffee with lots of cream. Then came the final hours of processing, including a farewell lecture for all Army separatees. When it was all over, Elvis Presley was once again a free man. That is, he was free of the military.

With the beaming Colonel at his side, he climbed aboard a specially arranged private train and began the forty-eight-hour trek to Memphis, a whistle-stop tour in which Elvis waved to the crowds who gathered at each station. The Colonel waded through the throngs of fans, passing out autographed photos of "my boy" and enlisting their promises that they would "remain true to him, no matter what."

When the train stopped at Grand Junction, Tennessee, Elvis spied familiar faces. *Memphis Press-Scimitar* reporter Bill Burk and photographer and former classmate William Leaptrout climbed aboard for an exclusive. "Man, there's been a lot of water gone under the bridge since we graduated from Humes, hasn't there?" Elvis said to Leaptrout. As the train moved on, the writer and photographer joined Elvis on the back of the train platform. Waving to one group of youngsters, Elvis grinned and said, "They will probably put me in jail for the kids staying out of school today."

He wore a nonissue Army dress blue uniform with an unauthorized white lace shirt and, it turned out, one more stripe than he should have been wearing. When Sergeant Presley caught Bill Burk scrutinizing his stripes, he blushed. A former military man himself, Burk recognized the bright yellow staff-sergeant stripes on the sleeves. Explaining the "accidental" fourth stripe, Elvis said, "It was the tailor's mistake in Germany. We had a rush job on it the last day there."

When the train at last rolled into Memphis's Union Station, crowds were so great that Elvis required a police escort. But first the Colonel had him hold yet another press conference—a brief one from his railroad car. Apologizing to reporters that "I can't take my hat off. My hair ain't combed," Elvis politely fielded questions. Only when asked about Dee Stanley, the mysterious blond woman who had been spotted with his father as they arrived by a previous train, did Presley clam up. "I don't know much about her," he lied.

Outside the train, a handful of friends had assembled with the fans. Elvis made a point of singling out Gary Pepper, a wheelchair-confined cerebral palsy victim who had formed the Elvis Presley Tankers fan club during his absence. When Gary weakly motioned to him, Elvis bent down for a whispered message. As he stood back up, he seemed to be fighting back tears. Clasping Gary on the shoulders, the singer said, "I'll see you later, pal."* Then he climbed into a waiting police car for the ride back to Graceland, where yet another press conference awaited. And questions about Priscilla.

Wearing civvies—black pants and a black knit shirt opened down his chest—and seated behind the desk of a small office out behind his home, Elvis did his best to look alert for the cameras the following morning. But it was a fight to keep his eyes open. As soon as he'd arrived at Graceland, the partying had begun—lasting through the night. Among the well-wishers was Anita Wood.

Elvis didn't mention Anita during the press conference, an omission that bore the crafty handiwork of the Colonel. As did the setting. A religious plaque was carefully positioned on one wall: *Let not your heart be troubled. Ye who believe in God believe also in Me.* In one corner of the room was a small lighted Christmas tree—supposedly there since 1957, Elvis's last Graceland Christmas before induction. Still another corner was piled with stuffed teddy bears.

Once viewed as the devil incarnate, Elvis Presley had been transformed into the all-American boy—one who spoke proudly of the military.

He had certainly mastered the art of maneuvers, kicking off the proceedings with a nod to President Dwight Eisenhower. Clearing his throat, Elvis intoned, "Now, gentlemen, I have called you here to dis-

---

*In awe of Pepper's inner strength and resilience, Elvis went on to make sure that Gary was a guest at his New Year's Eve and birthday parties, as well as at his movie sets and Las Vegas shows. He also hired Pepper's father to be a Graceland guard. Following the senior Pepper's death, Gary was put on Elvis's payroll as a "fan club coordinator." Still later, Elvis bought a house for Gary and his mother.

cuss a very important matter . . ." When the laughter subsided, he became serious and spoke of C rations and the mess hall and claimed that in the entire time he had been in Germany, he never once ate out. He failed to mention the nights of club hopping in Munich and Paris. Asked if he felt too old for rock 'n' roll, Presley quipped, "Man, I'm not that old yet. I'm not feeble. I can still move around."

As the inevitable questions about his love life came up, he deflected talk of a romance with Nancy Sinatra, reminding the press that he had only met her for the first time at Fort Dix. Besides, he added grinning, "I think she's engaged to Tommy Sands. I don't think he'd appreciate it very much."

Pressed about leaving any broken hearts behind in Germany, Elvis at first claimed that there hadn't been anyone special. Then, mindful of the bank of newsreel cameras, he did an about-face, admitting, "Well, there was this one little girl . . ." But he lied about the particulars, insisting that he'd seen her only the final two months he was there. "It was no big romance," he stated, never mentioning the name Priscilla Beaulieu, whose photograph had recently traveled the news wires. Captioned "the girl he left behind," it showed Priscilla wearing a heart locket and a determined look as she contemplated writing a letter to Elvis, whose own photograph was prominently featured on the desktop. No candid snapshot, Priscilla had arranged for her picture to be taken.

In Memphis, though, all eyes were on Elvis. He was issued a lifetime guest card to the clubhouse of Memphis's Post No. 1 of the American Legion. Tennessee senator Estes Kefauver read Elvis's name into the *Congressional Record*. The *Commercial Appeal* editorialized, "The place has been sort of dull without you . . . We may disagree about the merits of 'Hound Dog,' but we're sold on the guy who sang it." Once widely viewed by Memphians as a hillbilly embarrassment, Elvis was becoming the king of his hometown.

For a while the partying at Graceland was nonstop. Family and friends clamored to salute Elvis. When acquaintance Roy Orbison pulled up to the gates, asking to talk to Presley about a particular song he thought the artist should record, a messenger ran back from the house and handed Roy a scribbled note. "Everybody's all over the place. Everybody's sleeping everywhere there is a place," Elvis had written, explaining that they'd have to connect later.

Orbison left feeling slighted. He later recorded the song himself. "Only the Lonely" went on to become a signature song in an extraordinary career.

On March 20, Elvis went to Nashville for his first recording session in two years. Several weeks later there was a second. Both Colonel Parker and RCA recording chief Chet Atkins wouldn't divulge what Elvis was singing. But listeners would find out soon enough: along with watered-down "rock 'n' roll" tunes for his first post-Army movie, *G.I. Blues*, Elvis would display his octave-spanning vocal talents with "It's Now or Never," released in late summer.

In between sessions he appeared on Frank Sinatra's TV show. The man who had once lambasted Elvis, his fans, and rock 'n' roll now feted the music idol's homecoming with the Timex-sponsored TV special *Welcome Home, Elvis*. For Elvis, revenge wasn't just sweet; it was also lucrative. He earned a then unheard-of $125,000 for a single show.

Taping took place March 26 at the spectacular Fontainbleau Hotel in Miami. Along with Sinatra's daughter, Nancy, the program's guests included Sammy Davis Jr., Peter Lawford, and Joey Bishop, all members of the so-called Rat Pack, the hip Hollywood contingent headed by Frank. But the audience that filled the Grand Ballroom wasn't there to see them; Colonel Tom Parker had made sure that four hundred Elvis Presley fan club members were in the audience of seven hundred.

Prior to showtime, Elvis paced backstage, readjusting his massive bow tie, checking his cummerbund. Once again he was tuxedo-clad, but unlike the time he teamed with the little hound dog on Steve Allen's show, this was no joke. Sinatra was known for his spiffy elegance; so Elvis would be similarly attired, and coiffed. His once greasy, longish hair—which had been dyed black again—was tamed into a luxuriant pompadour lacquered into place.

"Man, I got butterflies," Elvis said in the moments before going onstage with Sinatra. "I've been waiting for this day for two long years." His fans had also been waiting; they shrieked the instant their idol nervously walked out onstage. But this time Elvis seemed embarrassed by their reaction. "Perhaps it suddenly dawned on him that he's twenty-five now, ten years older than most of the squealers," said one observer.

Indeed, the man who used to sweat, shimmy, and swagger across the stage, all the while taunting and teasing his fans into a frenzy, was no more. Just three years earlier Elvis Presley had riled Los Angeles with his audacious, blatantly sexual Pan Pacific show. Now, amid the gilded splendor of the Fontainbleau, he joined Frank for a duet on the Sinatra hit "Witchcraft." He also did the standard "Fame and Fortune" along with his newest hit, "Stuck on You." Frank, meanwhile, took a turn with Elvis's "Love Me Tender."

For many, Elvis's appearance on the Sinatra show symbolized the Army's taming effect on a onetime wild child. When the show aired a few weeks later, TV viewers saw just six minutes of Elvis. For most critics that was more than enough. Not content to take shots at Elvis's singing ("as tortured as ever") and his song selection ("as deplorable as ever"), Jack O'Brien of the *New York Journal-American* likened his hair to Mt. Vesuvius. Columnist Dorothy Kilgallen called the show "Colonel Parker's mistake" and said the best thing about it was the "charming talented doll," Nancy Sinatra.

Reporters in Hollywood couldn't get over how much he'd changed.

Shortly after the Miami taping, Elvis and nine of his friends, who'd been given job titles ranging from valet to bodyguard—and were now on modest salaries—traveled by private railway car to Los Angeles, where Elvis Presley got back into uniform. When Elvis showed up at the Paramount Pictures lot in April 1960 to begin work on *G.I. Blues,* the *Los Angeles Mirror News* took note of his newly "slim and elegant" physique—he was fifteen pounds lighter than his pre-Army days. He was also "more sophisticated."

Hollywood columnist James Bacon helped spread the word about the transformation. Back in 1956, at the taping of the Milton Berle show in San Diego Harbor, Elvis had tentatively approached the journalist. "You're from Hollywood, huh?" said the young performer, who nervously went on to inquire about producer Hal Wallis, with whom he had just signed his contract. But when Bacon met with Elvis on the set of *G.I. Blues,* he encountered a self-assured star who philosophized about everything from the possibility of World War III ("There won't be any. . . . I know the Bible says the end of the world will come by fire and brimstone, but I don't think anyone wants to push that button first") to Soviet leader Nikita Khrushchev ("He's a bully"). Taking drags off a Hav-a-Tampa Jewel, Elvis frequently looked over to his friends—now considered his "entourage" by Hollywood—who sat nearby, nodding in approval.

Elvis was in the midst of talking about television—and how it limited his performance—when clothing designer Sy Devore appeared, his arms laden with a pile of slacks. The performer who had once favored loud sports coats and pegged pants sifted through Devore's offerings. Fingering a pair in a wild paisley design—something he would once have favored—Elvis shook his head. "It looks like those camouflage fatigues that I wore in Germany. Take them back." Before Devore exited, he seemed pleased to tell Bacon that Elvis was "no longer the leader of the black leather jacket set." Said Devore, "He's now more Madison Avenue than Harley-Davidson."

Life also took note of the new Elvis, declaring, "The Elvis Presley everyone thinks he is—isn't." Alongside photos of Elvis at play with babies—for a scene in *G.I. Blues*—the magazine reported that the "sneering, hip-twitching symbol of the untamed beast" had come back from the Army "easygoing, unassuming, fatherly, in an adult movie sort of way."

Not everything had changed, though. As the press combed the film set, Colonel Tom Parker was omnipresent. He was impossible to miss— wearing khaki pants, sandals, and a bright pink satin shirt emblazoned on the back with ELVIS. From his own office at the studio—an unprecedented perk that he arranged through Hal Wallis and Paramount—the Colonel bragged, "It would take us five years to play all the dates we now have requests for."

Reporters who met him were both awed and perplexed. Though the Colonel needed no introduction in the world of country music, he was a singular presence in Hollywood, which had heretofore regarded Elvis and his adjutant as mere interlopers. Suddenly, writers found themselves scribbling quotes from a rotund "Southerner" who chomped on a fat cigar and wore an Elvis beanie lettered with the names of the singer's hit tunes. "Just call me Colonel," he would say, eyes twinkling. Unfamiliar with the Southern tradition of bestowing honorary titles, reporters wondered just what kind of colonel he was. As journalist Vernon Scott noted, "The rank is somewhat obscure."

Seated behind a desk cluttered with Elvis merchandise—tubes of lipstick, plastic purses and wallets, pairs of sneakers, and more—as Elvis's tunes played on a console, Parker gleefully claimed, "We got lots more planned where this came from." He added, "I tell ya, it's a snow job." This was a favorite expression of the Colonel's, who had a sign on his office door reading SNOW DIVISION. He proudly proclaimed to be the "imperial potentate" of American "snowmen." No one disputed him. This was, after all, a man who kept a huge photograph of Dean Martin displayed on his office wall, in full view of passersby. "People going by may mistake this for Dean's office," said the Colonel, "but when they come in, I sell 'em on Elvis!"

Among other promotions, the Colonel arranged for Judy Fowler, the winner of *Photoplay*'s "win a day at the studio with Elvis" contest, to be escorted to the set, where she shyly and tearfully met the performer. Elvis kidded to her mother, "What's the matter? I don't believe she knows how to smile." A high school sophomore when she met her idol, Fowler never did get up the nerve to ask Elvis for a kiss during her momentous visit. But she was presented with a special gift, a lovely china dog, to place alongside the rest of her china dog collection. "It was Elvis's," said Colonel Parker without a trace of the con artist in his eyes.

More shrewdly, during this period the Colonel wooed a select cadre of show business reporters—respected writers from both the fan magazines and the "mainstream" press. Over the years this group of journalists would have some degree of access to Elvis, and as a result, many of them would write largely sympathetic stories—some of them leaked by Presley associates who had been handpicked by Parker or his star.

Like Elvis, the Colonel was now a legend, no less than "one of the most colorful figures in show business." After all, explained the *New York Journal-American*, he had "built" Elvis Presley's career, turning him from a "hillbilly hoot 'n' holler huckster to a crooning Croesus."

Over Elvis's personal life, however, the Colonel no longer had as much control as he would have liked. Elvis's womanizing would soon reach Hollywood-size proportions. With *G.I. Blues* he would conduct his first of many blazing affairs with leading ladies. Fittingly, the fireworks started with the exotic redhead Juliet Prowse.

As physically striking as she was fiercely independent, Prowse had been born in Bombay, India, and raised in South Africa. She had been on her own since she was sixteen and was still a teenager when she moved to Europe to study ballet. She was dancing in a show in Rome when she was spotted by legendary Hollywood choreographer Hermes Pan, who had worked with Ginger Rogers and pinup queen Betty Grable.

Pan knew a great pair of legs when he saw them, and he immediately cast the five-foot-eight Prowse in a supporting role in *Can-Can*, the movie musical set in 1890s Paris. Audiences learned about her even before the movie opened. When Nikita Khrushchev visited the set during production, he was feted with a performance by the cancan dancers, including Prowse. The next day the Soviet chief denounced the movie as immoral. A photograph of Prowse, letting loose a kick, flashed around the world. Frank Sinatra starred opposite Shirley MacLaine, but many moviegoers ooh-la-laahed over Prowse, especially when she slid into view during the number "Tree of Life," wearing a sexy flesh-colored snakeskin outfit and carrying a big, tempting red apple.

By the time she was cast in *G.I. Blues*, Prowse was involved in a very public affair with Frank Sinatra, a liaison that raised eyebrows because of the difference in their ages: he was forty-five to her twenty-three. Enter Elvis Presley, twenty-five and sexually emboldened from his Army escapades.

In the movie, Presley portrays a singing GI in West Germany who takes on a bet that he can "break down the defenses" of a sexy night-club singer (Prowse) and spend the night at her place. Privately, Elvis griped to his friends that the script was silly. The musical numbers were worse: he "felt like an idiot breaking into songs while I'm talking to some chick on a train." But if he was turned off by the movie itself, he was turned on by his costar.

He couldn't help but be intrigued. Juliet Prowse was worldly and sophisticated. She was also refreshingly frank about her relationships, and proud of her body—of which she bragged, "I have the best-looking belly button anyone has ever seen. I need it in my dancing. You can't wear those skimpy costumes and have a navel that looks like a summer squash and get anywhere." She certainly liked flaunting her figure: in one scene in *G.I. Blues* she appears in a flesh-colored skirt cut in panels from hem to hips.

Whereas Elvis spoke with a Southern drawl that he increasingly sought to temper, Juliet had a clipped English accent. He thrived on greasy burgers and pounds of crisp bacon; she was a "food faddist"— years before it was the rage—as well as an inveterate exercise buff. She also had a chilly demeanor. Elvis was up to the challenge. As he told buddy Alan Fortas, "She has a body that would make a bishop stamp his foot through a stained-glass window." According to Red West, Presley started pouring on the "professional country-boy charm" to break through the actress's cool exterior. It worked. She soon affectionately took to calling him "Chickie Baby."

Of course, Elvis denied any interest in his costar to Priscilla, with whom he regularly talked by phone. "Oh, Cilla, just look at Juliet Prowse with those long legs and those big shoulders. You know I hate big women!" He sighed, adding, "Honey, you can just put those thoughts out of your head." Elvis Presley never did get the credit that he deserved for his acting.

On the set he turned up the heat during the movie's screen kiss, which lasted so long that director Norman Taurog kept yelling, "Cut! I said cut!" But Elvis would not, using his free arm to wave Taurog away.

Little wonder that the press began to call Elvis and Juliet "a torrid twosome." The era's popular "scandal" publications, such as *Top Secret* and *Untold Secrets*, had a field day with stories pitting Sinatra and his Rat Pack against Presley and his Memphis gang. As *Uncensored* breathlessly reported, "Right from under Sinatra's nose, the *gee-tar* twanging kid from Memphis moved in, and moseyed off with the Frankie's girl."

Drawn by Elvis's star power, visitors showed up all the time on the set of *G.I. Blues.* When Scandinavian royalty came visiting, Elvis dropped to his knees for a serenade—eliciting delighted giggles from princesses Margrethe of Denmark, Astrid of Norway, and Margaretha of Sweden. He was similarly charming to the king and queen of Nepal and the king and queen of Thailand.

So many people were coming and going that everyone used to kid Elvis that his nemesis, Sinatra, might show up next. Choreographer Charles O'Curran used to jokingly shout to Elvis, "Here comes Frank!" In the beginning Elvis would warily peek out the door of his dressing trailer—where he and Prowse were ensconced—just in case.

Then one day Sinatra really did arrive. "Here comes Frank!" yelled O'Curran, whose voice had an anxious edge. Elvis's Memphis pals, who were stunned as Sinatra swaggered by—wearing a dapper three-piece suit and a jaunty Panama hat—also tried to sound the alarm. Red West even broke into a run and pounded on the door of Elvis's dressing room. "Aw, Red, fuck you," was Elvis's reply.

When Sinatra breezed up, West stepped aside.

Sinatra knocked lightly. The door flew open, and Elvis angrily popped his head out. For an instant there was silence. Then Presley stuttered, "F-F-F-Frank. C'mon in." Elvis held the door as Sinatra entered, all the while shooting a daggered look at his buddies who lingered nearby. When the door closed, they burst into laughter.

To everybody's relief, there was laughter inside the trailer, too. According to Prowse, when Frank showed up, she and Elvis were in the midst of an innocuous card game. "Thank God!" she recalled, smiling.

Brazenly continuing their affair, Elvis and Juliet were spotted holding hands at the brightly lit Pacific Ocean Park in Santa Monica, where Elvis rode the wooden roller coaster and ate hot dogs along the midway. (Whenever she could, Prowse got Presley to eat yogurt.) They slipped away to Las Vegas, where Elvis was seen playing the slots at the Sands. They were also seen together at the Cloisters, a Sunset Strip nitery where Elvis uncharacteristically snapped at the house photographer for taking their picture. "No, sir! I was focusing on Tony Bennett, up on the stage," sniffed the cameraman.

The Colonel became concerned. Cornering Elvis on the soundstage one day, Parker clenched his teeth, swearing, "God dammit! You're supposed to be a clean-livin' Army hero!"

Elvis stood his ground, though, and the Colonel was forced to back off. Soon he would tell reporters, "Elvis can do what he wants after hours. I don't handle his social life. I gave up baby-sitting a long time ago."

But if the Colonel was losing control over Elvis's personal proclivities, he was now maintaining ironclad control over his star's professional ventures. Elvis didn't know it, but while he was in Germany, Parker and the executives at William Morris had mapped out a battle plan. Their goal: three movies a year—to be released in spring, summer, and Christmas of each year—and their accompanying sound tracks. The man who had shaken up the fifties was supposed to run like clockwork.

One thing Parker and his cronies didn't anticipate, however, was the changing audience for Presley's ventures. The mood was summed up by an irate fan who went to the trouble of copying Hal Wallis, William Morris, RCA, the Colonel, and Paramount with letters that decried the changes wrought by *G.I. Blues*. "It was great for people who *hate* Elvis Presley. It was everything that he isn't. Did you put a girdle on him? Did he have polio recently? There must be some explanation for all that lost motion." The fan went on to ask, "Just who do you think buys 99.9 percent of his records? It ain't my mother."

But in fact, as Presley's movies and music continued to change, it would be the matrons—not the teenagers—who would embrace him.

Heart of Glass

lvis Presley was noticeably absent from his father's wedding in July 1960. Claiming that his presence would have been disruptive, the performer instead telephoned his congratulations to Vernon and Dee in Huntsville, Alabama. "It was your day," he said unconvincingly.

Before the nuptials there had been considerable speculation over the identity of the "mystery blonde" who was frequently sighted at Graceland. Dee Stanley was even identified as Elvis's new girlfriend in several newspaper photographs. Finally, Vernon Presley himself sat down with reporters to set the record straight, earnestly stating "I wouldn't do nothin' to hurt my boy, or his career." Announcing plans for marriage, he stressed that no one could ever take the place of the late Gladys. Lest anyone think any hanky-panky had been going on between the elder Presley and his sweetheart, he added, "Everything's been proper between us. We were well chaperoned. My mother [Minnie Mae] lives with us, and Elvis always has his gang of friends around."

Dee's three sons were on hand as well. Billy, Ricky, and David were then eight, seven, and five, and though Elvis would never be truly fond of Dee, he made her boys feel welcome. The first morning the youngsters awoke at Graceland, they found their "big brother" had filled the downstairs with sleds, bicycles, toy soldiers, even puppies and kittens. "That was the first thing any of us remember about him," said Rick Stanley years later.

The Stanley boys, who grew up in the shadow of Graceland, would have other memories—ones that have varied over the years in tandem with various book deals and other ventures involving their late step-brother. Dee Stanley Presley has also recounted her experiences, but with such unfounded sensationalism that she has become anathema to Elvis fans.

At first Vernon and Dee planned to make Graceland their home. "I'll take care of the place while Elvis is off on trips, and makin' movies," Vernon declared. But his son had other plans: he bought the newlyweds the house that backed up onto the Graceland property and had a gate installed on the back fence for convenient coming and going. "That way she won't be sleeping in my mama's bedroom," Elvis explained.

Because he was increasingly on the West Coast, Elvis Presley looked upon Graceland as his special retreat. He got to go home for just two months when filming of *G.I. Blues* was completed. Then he was back in Hollywood—to make two movies back-to-back. Both were what he called "straight dramas." They would be the last such pictures of his career.

Originally written for Marlon Brando, *Flaming Star* was a moody western with a revisionist sensibility. Elvis played a young man trapped between two societies, with a Kiowa mother and a white father. The director, Don Siegel, was a talented up-and-comer who had already made his mark with such modestly budgeted movies as *Riot in Cell Block 11*, *Baby Face Nelson*, and *Invasion of the Body Snatchers*. In these, he had established a knack for telling the story of outsiders at odds with the world.

Hollywood insiders were surprised by the teaming of Presley and Siegel. Opined one columnist, "Elvis is making the switch from rock 'n' roll to Stanislavsky."

He definitely didn't want a replay of *G.I. Blues*, with its endless stream of VIPs across the soundstages, and what seemed like wall-to-wall interviews, all arranged by the Colonel. "I felt like I was some kind of zoo animal, like everyone was watching me every minute," he admitted to a costar on that picture. When a press agent wanted to bring visitors to the set of *Flaming Star*, Elvis briefly blew up: "What is this? Another Your Highness deal?"

For the movie, only a handful of journalists trekked to the set, at a Twentieth Century-Fox–owned ranch in Thousand Oaks, a rustic area thirty miles north of Los Angeles.

A small problem arose at the beginning. Fox felt Elvis's half-breed character should be brown-eyed. Special contact lenses were made, at a cost of $500. And another $2,500 was spent on a screen test. But Elvis felt uncomfortable with the lenses, and after talks between the producer and the director, it was decided he could be a blue-eyed Indian; after all, the character had a white father. Presley was relieved. "I got enough to worry about with my dialogue," he told the filmmakers.

This wasn't true. As with his earlier movies, Elvis was a quick study—able to easily memorize scripts (as well as song lyrics). He also stubbornly rejected the notion of acting or dialogue coaches—which is why he would always retain his Southern accent. "I just do the best I can," he said of his acting, which he considered naturalistic.

Although the press stayed away, the Memphis Mafia was ever present.

Between takes on *Flaming Star*, Elvis delighted in showing off his martial arts prowess—to the applause of his pals. "He would go around breaking wood with his bare hands," said Siegel, who one day tried to pull one over on his star. "I had the propman get me some balsa wood, and I smashed through it, just like Elvis did."

Elvis just grinned and declared, "Mr. Siegel, my last director did exactly the same thing."

Elvis wasn't smiling when he learned that executives at Fox were planning to repeat what they had done to *Love Me Tender*. They wanted to add songs to a picture that had previously been written as a straight western. By this time "It's Now or Never"—which became a personal favorite of Elvis's—was number one on *Billboard*'s Hot 100. It would stay in the top spot for twenty weeks and go on to become Elvis Presley's biggest-selling single. Mindful that a hit song could boost box office receipts for *Flaming Star*, Fox wanted Presley to sing four songs—one of them while on horseback.

Elvis's eyes flashed when the film's producer broke the news to him between takes at the studio's location ranch (where the TV series *Wagon Train* was filmed). He didn't protest then, but later that day he purposely flubbed some lines of dialogue while the cameras rolled. Don Siegel quickly stepped in. From the sidelines he bellowed to his star, "Stop it, son! Don't rack up any bad film on yourself."

Presley glared briefly at the filmmaker, then looked away. As cast and crew looked on, he took several deep breaths to calm down. Then he went back into character, for a scene opposite the Mexican actress Dolores Del Rio, who was playing his mother. He finished the scene in that take. "You see, son, you've got to maintain your cool," said Siegel. "You don't ever wanna go and hurt yourself in this business."

Later that day, director and star talked out the problem. "Mr. Siegel, I just can't sing a damn song while I'm riding a horse. I can't do that to this picture," Elvis declared.

The filmmaker was reassuring. "You stay calm. I'm going to get that song out of the movie."

Siegel was true to his word. *Flaming Star* eventually included only two songs, one heard over the opening credits, another briefly performed early in the story in the family cabin. The film also featured what many critics felt was Elvis's finest performance. "God, that boy had potential," Siegel reflected decades later. "You could see that he had a lot of layers, a lot going on."

Elvis was so upset about a scene in which he was to mourn the death of his mother that he begged Siegel to push back the production schedule. The specter of Gladys's death had risen to haunt him. Remembered Siegel, "He had just bought this new Rolls-Royce, and he told me, 'Mr. Siegel, if you'll let me do that scene last, you can drive the Rolls until the end of the picture.' " And so, for the duration of the shoot, Siegel arrived at the dusty locations in the gleaming black Rolls sedan.

Elvis delivered earnest, affecting performances in *Flaming Star* and the ensuing *Wild in the Country*. During the production of these movies, he also began to emerge as a man with dark complexities. His temper flare-ups intensified; it was becoming apparent to those closest to him that Elvis Presley harbored considerable rage.

By now Presley had a sturdy media image as a nondrinker. "My family never served liquor, and I daresay I'll never take it," said the man whose mother used to hide beer cans behind the sofa, and whose father was a regular at the bars in Germany. Though Elvis Presley never drank regularly, he would drink at times—and he did it as he did everything in his life: excessively.

But when he suffered from hangovers, he protectively attributed his condition to an "allergy" to alcohol. "He couldn't understand that if he would just limit himself to one glass of wine, he wouldn't have a hang-over," said Dr. George Nichopoulos, who became Elvis Presley's personal physician sometime around early 1967, and one of the most controversial figures associated with the performer.

According to Alan Fortas, Elvis's drinking sprees sometimes found him chugalugging screwdrivers. Another time, during a drive from Los Angeles to Palm Springs with Joe Esposito, Elvis drank so much blackberry brandy that by the time they got to their hotel, he needed to be helped to bed. Later that night he awakened Esposito, saying, "Call a doctor, because I'm really sick." But before Esposito could get to a phone, Elvis began vomiting—all over Joe.

When Elvis was drinking, he sometimes displayed frightening bursts of temper, but not just alcohol was altering his disposition: his pill-popping had intensified. He was taking amphetamines in the morning to rev himself up, and the mood calmers Librium and Valium—when he felt the need. At night he relied on the sleeping drug Seconal. At the time these were not considered too dangerous—or even habit-forming. Seconal in particular would go on to take its toll on stars ranging from Elizabeth Taylor to Marilyn Monroe.

In Elvis's case, they brought out a mean streak.

In a 1962 interview, he uncharacteristically admitted that he had an "extremely bad temper" that led to uncontrollable acts in which "I don't know what I'm doing." When those acts were over, confessed Elvis, "I don't like myself."

Such was the case when he lashed out at Red's cousin Sonny West in 1960. Both Elvis and Sonny had been drinking, and both were vying for the attention of a young woman. Angry words led to threats, and Elvis snatched up a bottle and held it as if to clobber Sonny.

"You're not going to hit me with no bottle," Sonny growled. "I've had enough of this shit." And so, he told Presley, "I quit!"

"You're not quitting, you're fired!" retorted Elvis. Never able to stop while he was ahead, Elvis then let loose a punch that connected with Sonny's jaw. Sonny actually teared up—not from pain, but from anguish. "I didn't think you could do that to me," he said, his voice breaking.

"It was the first time any of us ever saw Elvis hit one of his employees," recalled a shaken Alan Fortas. This is not entirely accurate. Two years earlier, poor Lamar Fike had taken a pummeling when Elvis erupted over a sexual advance made to him by the masseur who was giving him "youth" treatments. Elvis used Lamar as a human punching bag—a convenient target for his anger.

Another embarrassing incident brought his temper to public light.

By this time the Beverly Wilshire Hotel was the home away from home for Elvis and his boys, whom the press was now calling El's Angels. As in Germany, Elvis and his guys riled the hotel management—and more than a few guests, who wondered at the loud noise, the sounds of rambunctious horseplay, and the continual comings and goings of women. Then came a turning point, a prank that got out of hand.

Someone took a fall in the kitchen of Elvis's suite and was cut by a broken bottle. At the moment that Elvis leaned over to help, Joe Esposito, Red West, and Sonny West jumped him—pinning him to the floor. When Elvis at last struggled free, he was so incensed that the trio made a run for the door. But Elvis caught Esposito, whom he pulled to the ground and furiously kicked until Joe screamed. Elvis didn't stop there: he grabbed a guitar and whacked Esposito on the arm.

Joe let out a wail. Hearing Joe's cries, Red and Sonny returned, but after catching sight of the red-faced Elvis, they again went on the run. Grabbing up the guitar, Elvis went right after them—down the fire escape and onto another floor. Elvis realized the Wests had too much of a head start and he cried, "Fuck it, then!" He sailed the guitar in their direction. At that very moment one of the hotel's residents—an elderly woman—peered out her door. "The guitar missed her by inches," said Fortas in his 1992 memoirs.

Though Elvis immediately apologized, the woman issued a complaint. It was just what the hotel management had been praying for. The very next day, Elvis Presley and his rowdy camp followers were ordered to vacate. "And don't plan on coming back," hissed a hotel spokesman.

When Elvis meekly told the Colonel what had happened, Parker erupted, "You want to kill off your career? You want your fans to think you're some kinda wild man!" Elvis was contrite and readily agreed when the Colonel ordered him to pack up his boys and move somewhere "where you won't be bothering folks."

Elvis and his gang moved to a rented house in Bel-Air. Located on Perugia Way, the oriental-style house had a royal heritage. The shah of Iran had lived there; so had the jet-setting Prince Aly Khan and his stunning actress-wife Rita Hayworth. Circular, it had numerous soundproof bedrooms—which would come in handy for Presley and his cohorts.

He wanted only minimal redecorating. "Change the carpet. Get white shag," Elvis said. Pointing to a playroom, he added, "And bring in the jukebox." A two-way mirror would also be installed, to accommodate Elvis's growing attraction to voyeurism.

As the house on Perugia underwent its modifications, Elvis went to work on *Wild in the Country*, one of the oddest entries in his film career. It was directed by the respected Philip Dunne (*Prince of Players*); the screenwriter was Clifford Odets (a former playwright famous for *Golden Boy*). Based on a popular novel of the day, it was tailored for Elvis, who stars as a young would-be writer who has to overcome family problems, a tendency to get into trouble, and also come to terms with his feelings for a trio of women: the psychologist assigned to his case (Hope Lange), his patient girlfriend (Millie Perkins), and the town tramp, who has a baby and no apparent husband. Cast as the latter was Tuesday Weld, who had a field day enticing Elvis—offscreen as well as on.

In an era not known for free spirits (that would be several years down the road), Tuesday Weld was nothing less than a revelation to Elvis. She was gorgeous, with flyaway blond hair, a sensual pout, and teasing chameleon green eyes. Known for playing nymphets in such movies as *Sex Kittens Go to College* and *Because They're Young*, she segued into more adult roles with *Return to Peyton Place*. Just eighteen when she costarred in *Wild in the Country*, the former child model claimed to have had her first nervous breakdown at age nine. She smoked, she drank, she used shocking language, she discussed Freud, and she drove around town wearing nothing but her nightgown.

The press was bewildered. During one interview she poured her glass of water into a nearby vase, then refilled it with a reporter's alcoholic drink. Her answers to questions could be off-putting: "No, I don't bite my nails—I have someone come in and do it for me," she once quipped. When asked what she wore to bed, she once said slyly, "I sleep under a sheet of cologne."

To Elvis Presley, who had spent his career nodding "Yes, sir" to the Colonel, as well as film and recording executives, Tuesday Weld embodied nothing less than total freedom. He adored her, and Tuesday was likewise infatuated. As she said in a 1989 interview, "Sure, he was easy to get close to. I mean, he was just drop-dead! . . . He walked into a room and everything stopped." Added Weld, "I was totally, absolutely in love with him. I was gaga about him."

According to Joe Esposito and Alan Fortas, the romance between Elvis and Weld was brief but fiery. During the film's location filming in northern California's Napa Valley, they took fast drives along the roads that wound through the lush wine country. Tuesday would reportedly throw things out the window to see if she could hit passengers in oncoming cars.

At the house on Perugia Way she sometimes slept in Elvis's room, leaving Alan Fortas to baby-sit her white German shepherd, Wolf. Presley and Weld went to Pacific Ocean Park to ride the roller coaster; and they slipped into the darkly lit private balcony of the Cross Bow, a Van Nuys club where Elvis liked to listen to a rock 'n' roller named Lance Le Gault. As Elvis tapped his fingers, remarking on the "great beat," Weld downed drink after drink. As with *G.I. Blues* and the blatant romance with Juliet Prowse, the cavorting led to breathless accounts in the fan magazines.

There was, however, a quieter side to the romance between Presley and Weld. According to the actress's mother, Jo Weld, her daughter "fell totally under Elvis's romantic spell." He wrote poetry for her. He also impressed Jo Weld with his Southern courtesy as he waited for Tuesday to get ready for their dates. Said Mrs. Weld, "You could sense his loneliness and his vulnerability, which was certainly rare in the young stars I met during the early phase of Tuesday's career." Tuesday saw this as well: "You saw great needs [in Elvis]."

One of these was not the need to be faithful. Along with his dalliance with Weld, Presley also dated *Wild in the Country* wardrobe girl Nancy Sharp—whom he had first met on *Flaming Star*. He also flirted with Hope Lange.

Only slightly older than he, Lange was worlds ahead in terms of sophistication. One evening at Elvis's house when she was asked what she wanted to drink, she casually asked for vodka—not realizing that he usually served only Cokes or lemonade. Instead of telling her the "house rules," as he had done countless times before to female visitors, Elvis turned anxiously to one of his friends and stammered, "Do-do-do-do we have some vodka?" He knew full well that the guys sometimes hid booze in their rooms. In short order, Hope Lange had her drink, and the boys were instructed by their boss to "keep a little something at the bar."

Weld herself was not pining away by the phone for his call. She also carried on a fling with actor Gary Lockwood. A former UCLA football player and stuntman, the handsome Lockwood was a neophyte actor when he was signed to play a troublesome rich kid in *Wild in the Country*. One night during production Weld frantically summoned him to her house. After driving to her place in the hills, Lockwood discovered that she already had company. Elvis was there, "with what seemed like twenty of his guys." The atmosphere was instantly tense. Lockwood paced the room, and Elvis—flanked by his buddies—sat and methodically cracked his knuckles.

Lockwood finally turned and challenged Weld, asking, "Who do you want to stay? Him or me?" The room turned silent. Weld dramatically pursed her lips and looked from one man to the other. Finally she said, "You!" and pointed a painted fingernail at Lockwood.

Lockwood braced himself, thinking, "Man, I'm gonna have to fight *all* these guys." But to his surprise, Elvis slowly pulled himself from the chair and snapped his fingers, motioning to the door. "Let's go, guys," he said, leading his soldiers out.

Mused Lockwood, "You could look at that and think that Elvis was trying to get out of having to fight—that he didn't have nerve. But I always thought his reaction was very cool. And I always looked upon him as a gentleman for the way he handled the situation."

During the production of *Wild in the Country*, Elvis was presented with a platinum watch from RCA for having sold 75 million copies of his records. No one else in show business had ever achieved such a feat. It was just the impetus the filmakers needed: four songs were added to *Wild in the Country*. Though the songs were used in understated fashion, as in *Flaming Star*, Presley was embittered. It seemed that no matter what he wanted, he always wound up giving in to others.

19

Man Overboard!

Elvis Presley stood at the open window of his penthouse suite surveying the beach below. From the fourteenth floor he took in the glistening white sands of Waikiki and, farther beyond, the sea with its diamond sparkles. Shielding his eyes with his hand, he scanned the beach until he spotted some of his friends—and country artist Minnie Pearl, who waved up at him. He waved back but didn't go down on the beach to join her. She would remember him looking like a lonely man encapsulated by his fame.

In early 1961 he had signed a new five-year contract with Hal Wallis, who promptly announced that the star of *G.I. Blues* was now headed for the Hawaiian Islands, as the star of a movie that would eventually be called *Blue Hawaii.*

Since his arrival in the newly designated fiftieth state of the Union, Elvis had been as much a tourist attraction as hula dancers and luaus. When the commercial airliner carrying the performer touched down at Honolulu International Airport on March 25, 1961, three thousand spectators craned their necks and screamed in welcome. Many clutched tickets for that night's much publicized fund-raiser—Presley's first concert performance in three years.

Pearl, one of the stalwarts with the Grand Ole Opry, and a guest artist on the program, had chatted with Presley during the flight from Los Angeles. Along with Elvis, she and her husband had clambered into the safety of a waiting limousine, which slowly made its way through the fan-congested streets to the Hawaiian Village Hotel. Another five hundred fans were waiting there. "It was awful," recalled Pearl. "My husband was afraid that we'd be killed trying to get inside the hotel. I felt myself being lifted completely off my feet by all these people."

As the petite Pearl was fighting for her equilibrium, she caught sight of Elvis being escorted by dozens of policemen to the elevators that would carry him to the penthouse suite. All the while Pearl kept thinking that to avoid being trampled, it was best to keep a distance from the twenty-six-year-old performer. Like most people who encountered him, she was also struck by his compelling good looks. "He was beautiful—absolutely beautiful—at the time," marveled Pearl. "His skin was so pretty, and his eyes so pretty, and his hair. He was so healthy looking. So trim and lithe."

Presley certainly worked out when he went before a crowd of 5,500 in a show concocted by the indefatigable Colonel Tom Parker. Though Parker would later largely eschew charitable performances—refusing to let his boy perform "for free" even at the request of the White House—the crafty promoter had seized upon a particularly patriotic notion when he'd learned about efforts to recognize the battleship USS *Arizona*, the sunken ship on which 1,102 American men were entombed during the Japanese attack on Pearl Harbor on December 7, 1941.

Who better to help raise money for a military memorial than a famous former soldier in a benefit concert? "Hell, my boy will even buy the very first ticket—at one hundred dollars," Parker bragged. Elvis not only bought that initial ticket but also stressed that "every penny" of the proceeds ($52,000, as it turned out) would go toward the *Arizona* fund.

When the visibly nervous Elvis Presley strode onto the stage of the sold-out Bloch Arena, with his mother-of-pearl-inlaid guitar slung across his shoulder, the audience let loose with thunderous applause, foot stomping, screams, and whistles. Emboldened by their response, Elvis let loose as well. Wearing his gold-lamé jacket with dark blue slacks, white shirt, and electric blue tie, he delivered nineteen songs with such frenzied passion that even his musicians were caught off guard. In fact, when Elvis dropped to his knees in the midst of a number, Jordanaire Gordon Stoker thought that the singer had slipped and fallen. To Stoker's surprise, Elvis followed through with one of his

Gladys, Vernon, and two-year-old Elvis Presley. (MICHAEL OCHS ARCHIVES/ VENICE, CA)

Striking a pose at the annual fair in Tupelo, Mississippi, at age thirteen. Elvis would always love role playing—especially in costume. (GLOBE PHOTOS)

Elvis shows off his record collection and his nineteen-year-old physique after the release of "That's All Right (Mama)." (UPI/CORBIS-BETTMANN)

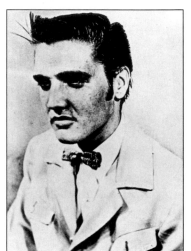

Elvis was so shy when interviewed by the *Memphis Press-Scimitar* in July 1954, he wasn't even quoted in the story that ran with this photograph. (ARCHIVE PHOTOS)

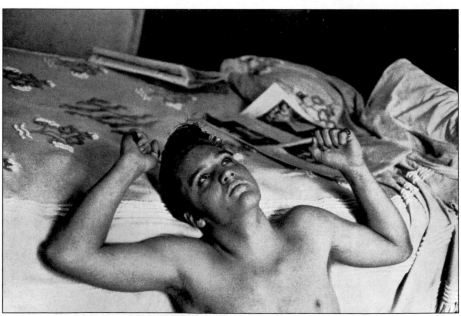

On the rise in 1955 and already savvy: "I know you can't be sexy if you smile," said Elvis. (MICHAEL OCHS ARCHIVES/VENICE, CA)

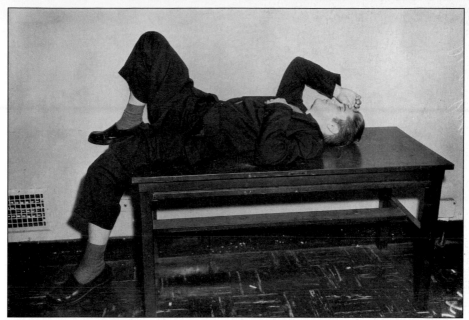

Twenty-one-year-old Elvis takes time out for a break at the Shrine Auditorium in Los Angeles. (HEARST COLLECTION/USC DEPARTMENT OF SPECIAL COLLECTIONS)

Elvis greets his fans at the Long Beach Municipal Auditorium, June 1956. (HEARST COLLECTION/USC DEPARTMENT OF SPECIAL COLLECTIONS)

Gladys and Vernon Presley in 1956—the year stardom erupted—with a single day's delivery of mail and gifts for their son. (UPI/BETTMANN)

Contemplating showtime in Tampa, Florida, August 1956. (PHOTO BY BOB MORELAND)

In a reflective moment at
the Shrine Auditorium.
(HEARST COLLECTION/USC
DEPARTMENT OF SPECIAL
COLLECTIONS)

As if in ecstasy...Elvis at the Old Florida
Theatre in St. Petersburg, August 1956.
(PHOTO BY BOB MORELAND)

Cutting loose in August 1956.
(PHOTO BY BOB MORELAND)

The rest of the country was at odds over him, but he received a
hero's welcome in his hometown of Tupelo in 1956. (GLOBE PHOTOS)

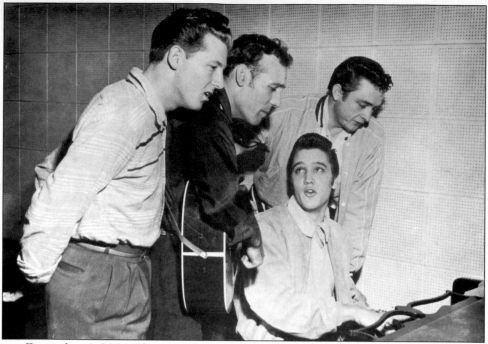

December 4, 1956: Elvis and three future music legends (from left), Jerry Lee Lewis, Carl Perkins, and Johnny Cash at an impromptu session at Memphis's Sun studios. The local paper heralded them as "The Million Dollar Quartet." (MICHAEL OCHS ARCHIVES/VENICE, CA)

Making his debut on *The Ed Sullivan Show*, September 9, 1956. (ARCHIVE PHOTOS)

Two singing sensations teamed up for the May 1960 Frank Sinatra–hosted special, *Welcome Home Elvis*. (MICHAEL OCHS ARCHIVES/VENICE, CA)

Elvis strikes a proud pose in front of his
beloved Graceland. (GLOBE PHOTOS)

Colonel Tom Parker was as much
an original as his famed client.
(MARC WANAMAKER/
BISON ARCHIVES)

At home with his parents in 1956. His mother couldn't comprehend the enormity
of her son's stardom, or the price it would bring. (GLOBE PHOTOS)

On the eve of his induction into the Army, Elvis bids farewell to his parents. Gladys was so devastated at the thought of losing her son that her health would suffer during his military service. (UPI/BETTMANN)

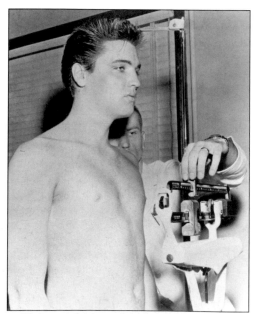

Elvis weighs in at his Army physical in March 1958. (MICHAEL OCHS ARCHIVES/VENICE, CA)

Sergeant Elvis Presley shows off his stripes. (AP/WIDE WORLD PHOTOS)

Vernon Presley and his son mourn the loss of Gladys Presley. Elvis would never fully recover from the death of his mother. (AP/WIDE WORLD PHOTOS)

Rockin' and rollin' Army style in Friedberg, West Germany. (AP/WIDE WORLD PHOTOS)

Nancy Sinatra, nineteen, acts as emissary for her famous father at a Fort Dix press conference welcoming Sergeant Presley home from Germany. (AP/WIDE WORLD PHOTOS)

During the making of *Follow That Dream*, Elvis catches the show at Florida's Weeki Wachi Springs with co-star Anne Helm, Vernon, and Dee. (PHOTO BY BOB MORELAND)

Elvis was smitten with co-star Debra Paget during the making of *Love Me Tender* (1956). He went on to fall for a Paget lookalike named Priscilla. (MICHAEL OCHS ARCHIVES/VENICE, CA)

Natalie Wood dated Elvis in 1956, and couldn't get over how religious he was. (MICHAEL OCHS ARCHIVES/VENICE, CA)

Elvis with sweetheart June Juanico in 1956. (UPI/BETTMANN)

Elvis and Anita Wood broke up shortly after his return from the Army. (UPI/BETTMANN)

With Ann-Margret in *Viva Las Vegas* (1964). (CULVER PICTURES)

Linda Thompson, who entered his life in 1972, was a girlfriend, confidante, and surrogate mother. (MICHAEL OCHS ARCHIVES/VENICE, CA)

During his final months, Presley talked hopefully of marriage to beauty queen Ginger Alden. (UPI/BETTMANN)

Starring opposite Lizbeth Scott in *Loving You* (1957). (CULVER PICTURES)

With Dolores Hart in *King Creole* (1958), arguably Presley's finest film—and performance. (CULVER PICTURES)

Jailhouse Rock. (1957) (CULVER PICTURES)

Elvis drew accolades for his role as a half-breed at odds with both the white and Indian worlds in *Flaming Star* (1960). (CULVER PICTURES)

With Juliet Prowse in *G.I. Blues* (1960).
(CULVER PICTURES)

Romancing Anne Helm in the musical
comedy *Follow That Dream* (1962).
(CULVER PICTURES)

MGM director George Sidney readies
Presley and Ann-Margret for a scene in
Viva Las Vegas (1964).
(MARC WANAMAKER/BISON ARCHIVES)

With Nancy Sinatra in *Speedway* (1968).
(MICHAEL OCHS ARCHIVES/VENICE, CA)

An estimated 1.5 billion people in forty countries tuned in to the 1973 satellite broadcast of *Elvis: Aloha from Hawaii.* (MICHAEL OCHS ARCHIVES/VENICE,CA)

President Richard Nixon meets the King and makes him an honorary narcotics agent (1970). (NATIONAL ARCHIVES)

Elvis at forty. The media took note of the physical changes, much to Presley's chagrin. (MICHAEL OCHS ARCHIVES/VENICE,CA)

old moves—a slide nearly twenty feet across the stage, all while clutching the mike in his hand.

The audience responded with celebratory whoops and cheers. Elvis may have been shorn of his sideburns, but he hadn't forgotten his moves. He performed "Heartbreak Hotel," "All Shook Up," "I Got a Woman," "Fever," and the teasing "Such a Night." Encore after encore followed: "Surrender," "Treat Me Nice," and finally, a climactic, hip-grinding "Hound Dog."

The moment Elvis hurried from the stage, fans rushed for the exit—the better to grab at their idol as he made his escape from the building. According to Minnie Pearl, who watched the goings-on with astonishment, "Operation Exit Elvis" was carried out "with split-second timing." Running from the building, Elvis leaped into a waiting car that was already moving. "It was," recalled Pearl, "like watching a getaway scene from one of those gangster movies."

The concert, as dynamic as it was, was only the prelude to the making of the movie *Blue Hawaii*. It was the first of three pictures Presley would film on the Hawaiian islands—a locale the young Southerner would come to embrace. As he told Joe Esposito, "When I get off the plane in Hawaii, it's like a big weight is lifted from my shoulders." In Hawaii he could escape the pressures of Graceland, where kinfolk seemed to materialize constantly with their hands outstretched. He could also conveniently ignore promises he'd made to women in other cities—and countries.

As an actor, he was riding a wave of success. *Flaming Star* opened to strong notices, as well as predictions that his acting career could go in new directions.* As for *G.I. Blues*, both the movie and the sound-track album were doing blockbuster business. Released just six weeks before the year ended, the film still ranked fourteenth in box office receipts for 1960.

Moreover, some of the same critics who had excoriated him for his infamous Los Angeles concerts had since done about-faces. Hedda Hopper, who had once pleaded with parents to "work harder" in their efforts "against the new alleged singer, Elvis Presley," now regularly heaped praise on the young man. "I am devoted to him. He's the best-mannered star in Hollywood," said Hopper. "I was no great admirer of his until the day his [Army] colonel told me, 'I wish I'd had ten thou-

---

*Elvis was inducted into the Los Angeles Indian Tribal Council for his "constructive portrayal of a man of Indian blood."

sand soldiers just like him.' " It certainly hadn't hurt that Elvis also poured on the charm during her visit to the *G.I. Blues* set, where he complimented her son, William Hopper, for his work on the *Perry Mason* TV series, a favorite show of Presley's. He mentioned as well her own recent appearance on TV's *Person to Person*. To top it all, he remarked on the staircase in her home, "When I got back to Graceland, I told my daddy to have one built in just like it."

He similarly wooed the fearsome Louella Parsons, who wrote about how the health-conscious young patriot sat through a luncheon interview without eating. "Makes me too sleepy when I return to work on the set," said Elvis (who undoubtedly went on to consume a half dozen bacon sandwiches in the privacy of his dressing room).

With Parsons, Elvis went so far as to poke fun at his old image. Wearing a subdued sports coat, dark trousers, solid-colored shirt, and black shoes, he took shots at the way he'd dressed during his first Parsons interview in 1956, when his hair was long and greasy. "And you wore four rings, and tennis shoes covered with your picture on them!" added Louella. As the two laughed, the Colonel—who hovered over coffee in an adjacent room—made his presence known. After loudly clearing his throat, Parker bellowed indignantly, "Those shoes made a lot of money. Lotsa folks bought 'em." Once again Presley and Parsons burst out laughing.

Elvis, who still spoke proudly about his work as Danny Fisher in *King Creole*, was matter-of-fact about *Blue Hawaii*. "My fans are growing older. The old wiggle is on the way out."

In years to come, *Blue Hawaii* would be regarded as a benchmark. Analyses of Presley's career would single out the picture as a symbol of what went wrong with a promising movie career. But at the time Elvis made it, *Blue Hawaii* wasn't considered an embarrassment; it was a formulaic star vehicle.

Cast as the heir to a pineapple-plantation fortune, Elvis "rebels" against the family business and instead joins his girlfriend in a travel agency venture. The movie culminates with their wedding—in colorful Hawaiian ceremonial dress—as Elvis sings "Hawaiian Wedding Song." In between are countless luaus and musical numbers, including "Rock-a-Hula-Baby," "Can't Help Falling in Love," and "Beach Boy Blues." Elvis performed the latter from behind jail bars, following a brawl at an island inn.

He had come a long way from 1957's *Jailhouse Rock*—and from Danny Fisher's Bourbon Street. But then, Hollywood had also come a long way from the era of the studio system—which had disintegrated by the early sixties. The studio executives who had originally shrewdly overseen careers were no longer running the show. Producers, agents, sometimes even performers, were making decisions. Great companies such as MGM and Paramount began to act primarily as distribution companies for producers they had under contract.

The era's most acclaimed movies were either foreign-made (*La Dolce Vita, Tom Jones*), filmmaker-driven (from artistes such as Elia Kazan or Stanley Kubrick), or major musicals and epics (*West Side Story,* * *The Sound of Music, Lawrence of Arabia*).

For many performers, it was a time to sink or swim. Marilyn Monroe's last (uncompleted) film was a six-character, low-budget comedy called *Something's Got to Give*. Dean Martin and Lana Turner bumbled through the so-called comedy *Who's Got the Action?* Shirley MacLaine went from being an Academy Award nominee to the star of ridiculous comedies such as *What a Way to Go!*—which was touted with publicity photos in which MacLaine and costar Dean Martin snuggled inside a five-story-high, mink-swathed champagne glass.

Promising young stars such as Richard Chamberlain and Yvette Mimieux never did find film roles worthy of their abilities. Robert Redford did—but only after having survived the silly *Situation Hopeless—But Not Serious*. Connie Francis starred in four successful MGM teen-oriented musical comedies between 1960 and 1965; she claimed none of her films were even watchable. Had her last name not been Fonda, Jane might not ever have been in a second movie. Her first was the innocuous comedy *Tall Story*, in which she played a too-tall baby-sitter in love with a too-tall basketball player.

The period altered Elvis's own attitudes about making movies. As he saw it, if he couldn't make the movies he wanted, at least he could have fun on the sets of those he had to make. The Presley films became known for the raucous between-takes gags involving the star and his buddies. "It was like being on a Marx Brothers set," said Will Hutchins, who costarred in two Presley movies, and watched as the star and his pals set off surprise firecrackers, had water-pistol fights, and sent water balloons flying. Not everyone was amused. "The cameraman didn't think it was so funny having to clean shaving cream off the camera lens," recalled director Norman Taurog.

*At one point, the *West Side Story* producers envisioned Elvis as the leader of one of the film's gangs, with teen idols Fabian, Frankie Avalon, and Paul Anka among the members.

For all the on-set silliness, his costars and crew members also remember myriad acts of kindness on Presley's part. The day that actress Merry Anders brought her mother and daughter to the set of *Tickle Me*, Elvis ambled over and sat in the director's chair alongside Merry's mother. "He spent about forty-five minutes talking with her," said Merry, "just about generalities . . . he wasn't trying to impress anybody." Presley later took Merry's eight-year-old daughter by the hand and gave her a tour of the set.

When Elvis learned that the mother of director Fred de Cordova had passed away during the filming of *Frankie and Johnny*, he sat down across from the filmmaker one day and said, "I know what you're going through. I lost my mother, too." Commented de Cordova, "We went on to have a brief, soul-searching talk. I will always remember him with fondness for thinking of me at that time in my life."

If Elvis learned that someone's niece or nephew was a fan, or that a relative was ailing, he took down their phone number and headed for his dressing trailer—to put in surprise phone calls. He also went to lengths to talk to fellow actors, crew members, and extras. Michael Ansara was surprised when Presley approached him on the set of *Harum Scarum* to profess his admiration for *Broken Arrow*, the 1950s TV series in which Ansara had played Cochise. The teenage Annette Day, Elvis's leading lady in *Double Trouble*, was presented with a brand-new white Mustang when Elvis learned she didn't have a car.

He was so respectful of the feelings of others that he was easily crushed when the favor wasn't returned. "You could offend Elvis, he was very sensitive to things. In the case of Barbara Stanwyck, well, I think she was just too strong a lady," said Sue Ane Langdon, referring to several uneasy exchanges between Presley and his legendary costar during the making of *Roustabout*. Presley was especially ruffled following a conversation in which Stanwyck referred to a Greek goddess. He wasn't familiar with the name. "You don't know who Athena is?" said an aghast Stanwyck. Elvis actually flushed red, then coolly walked away. The next day in his dressing room, he rifled through a stack of books about Greek mythology.

On most Presley pictures, Colonel Parker was an unmistakable presence. He certainly contributed to the carnival atmosphere on *Blue Hawaii*. In his massive Hawaiian print shirts and baggy khakis, he relished playing the role of the kooky Svengali. Crew members used to watch as Parker—who considered himself a better-than-amateur hypnotist—"hypnotized" Elvis's buddies into thinking they were assorted animals. Under the Colonel's trance, they would yap and bark, or oink and moo, and sometimes fight one another while on all fours.

Over the years there would be conjecture from well-respected industry figures that the Colonel performed more than parlor tricks where Elvis was concerned. Steve Binder, producer of a 1968 Presley television special, is among those who believe that Parker used hypnosis on Elvis—to elicit his stunning concert performances. "Elvis would be a bundle of nerves, so frightened, so unsure. Then the Colonel would go in for a private talk with him, and the next time you saw Elvis he would be this completely other person, so commanding, so magnetic."

The Colonel and Elvis did huddle before each major show, to deal with the singer's lifelong stage fright. But members of Presley's inner circle eschew theories that he was put in a hypnotic trance by Parker. They argue that the Colonel's persuasive powers simply knew no bounds. A student of Dale Carnegie—who promoted the theory that power could be attained by positive thinking—the Colonel was always hustling. Richard Davis, who joined the Presley camp in 1962, used to watch as top studio executives crossed the street when they caught sight of Parker heading in their direction: "They knew that he wanted something, and that if he got to them, he would get it."

He could be domineering down to the smallest detail. When he spied Elvis wearing his own wristwatch in a scene, the Colonel barged in front of the rolling cameras. "Do you remember the terms of Elvis's contract?" he yelled to Hal Wallis.

Wallis was perplexed. Motioning toward Elvis, the Colonel added, "That is out!" To Wallis's confused look, he added, "The wristwatch!"

Contractually, the producers were supposed to provide Presley's movie wardrobe. The Colonel demanded that Elvis receive an additional $25,000 for wearing his own watch. Hal Wallis instead instructed Elvis to remove his watch, and the scene was reshot.

Always wheeling and dealing, Parker talked several island disc jockeys into walking around the lobby of the Coco Palms resort hotel, which was home to cast and crew, in fluffy snowman suits. In exchange they received membership into his Snowmen's League, the fanciful "club" the king of "snow jobs" liked to tout. (Parker was fond of saying, "Admission is free, but it'll run you ten thousand dollars to resign. Haven't lost a Snowman yet.")

Once the Colonel himself roamed the lobby, carrying a fake microphone attached to a pineapple, interviewing guests for what he called the Pineapple Network.

The Presley pictures also became known for their casts of beautiful young women—many of whom were pursued offscreen by the star and his friends. There was so much partying in and around the private beach of the Coco Palms that Hal Wallis finally imposed a curfew on the film's actresses.

That didn't stop Elvis. He romanced his leading lady, Joan Blackman, who recalled, "We had rooms next to each other in the hotel, and for weeks we just about lived together." The green-eyed brunette had briefly dated Elvis in 1957, when she first came to Hollywood under contract to Hal Wallis. By the time they teamed in *Blue Hawaii* she was twenty-three—and as independent as she was outspoken. She was also career-minded: "If it came to a toss-up between meeting Elvis for dinner or getting my sleep because of having to be on the set the next day, my work always won." Another divisive factor was Elvis's growing entourage. "It's hard," Blackman said, "to talk with eight people at a time and really relate."

He also had a reputation. Though he was an attentive lover during his on-the-set romances, Elvis Presley tended to pack up his emotional ties, along with his clothes and toiletries, once production wrapped on his films. Anne Helm, who became Presley's lover during the making of *Follow That Dream* on the Florida Gulf Coast, said the change of heart was apparent when shooting wrapped and they returned to southern California. "Though I went on to see him for a while afterward, it was different. In Los Angeles he had his chauffeur come and pick me up to bring me to his house, where there were these parties with young girls all around. I mean, carpet-to-carpet women. No longer did he knock at my door and bring me flowers."

One of the few Presley vehicles in which he displayed his comedic talent, *Follow That Dream* followed the adventures of rural Southerners who try to homestead along a highway. In a sense, admitted Helm, she and Presley lived out their film roles. "As I fell in love with him during our scenes, I was really falling."

A former teenage model, the delicate brunette didn't meet Presley until she arrived at the Port Paradise Hotel, a bungalow resort situated on a lagoon in Crystal River, ninety miles northeast of St. Petersburg. "We were in the middle of nowhere—there certainly were no florist shops around. When he showed up at my front door with flowers, they looked as though he'd picked them himself."

It was hard to ignore his physical allure—the hair that was dark blond again, the deep olive tan. But, stressed Helm, his appeal was more than physical. "He was so very, very sweet. I think a lot of women reached out to him because they felt he was so lonely. I actually wrote some poetry about him when we were making the movie. It was that kind of romance." It was also very physical.

"He really liked sex. A lot of nights I didn't go back to my own bungalow. I felt a little ashamed about it the next morning, because I knew that the people on the set realized what was going on." But, Helm added, "I have to tell you, I had fun. And it was special."

They went for nighttime drives in his Cadillac, gazing at silhouetted palm trees and scrub oak as they wound along State Road 40. Presley persistently played with the radio dial. "It was so strange when 'Hound Dog' would come on, and there I was, sitting next to him," Helm recalled. They were photographed during a visit to a "mermaid show" at Weeki Wachee Springs, where Presley later walked along a wire fence a quarter-mile long to meet and talk with fans who'd gathered outside the nautical arena.

Back at the hotel, she kidded him about his eating habits. "He would fry up a whole pound of bacon just dripping in grease, and that would be his whole meal. It was just horrible." They sometimes played cards into the early-morning hours, when Presley would ask her to slip into a flouncy, yellow baby-doll nightie he had bought her. "I wasn't crazy about them, but he just loved them," Helm said, laughing.

After they made love, he would give her pills—"probably Valium"— and take some himself so that they could sleep. The next day on the set he would give her Dexedrine so she could stay awake and energetic. "Everybody used Dexedrine at the time," said Helm, who was first given the pills by a doctor when she was a teenage model "so that I could maintain a nineteen-inch waistline." Because Elvis was already battling a weight problem—evident in his shirtless scenes in the picture—he had been prescribed the medication. "You didn't use them to get high, but to sustain your energy," said Helm, adding, "At the time I didn't think anything about the pills." Unbeknownst to Helm, Presley was by then in the grip of a growing list of pharmaceuticals, including Dexamil, Placidyl, Percodan, Seconal, and the whole family of tranquilizers.

Nor did it ever dawn on her that Presley might have been involved with someone else during the film's production. Not until they were back in Los Angeles did Helm realize that actress Joanna Moore—with whom she fought over Elvis in the movie—had had designs on him in real life. One night at the house in Bel-Air, Helm was already tucked into Presley's bed when she heard the guards calling him about a commotion outside. Joanna Moore had been caught trying to break into the compound. "The guards were talking to Elvis, and he was pretty mad, and I got to thinking that she must have known him in Florida, too."

According to Joe Esposito, Presley and Moore had a fling of several days—after which she became fixated upon Elvis. The same night she tried to see Presley, she took an overdose of sleeping pills. Esposito and Charlie Hodge had to rush her to the UCLA emergency room, where doctors pumped her stomach. The next day, when told about what had happened, Presley matter-of-factly told his friends, "I knew that girl had problems. That's why I stopped seeing her."

Helm never asked Elvis about what happened that night, but she had no doubt that their romance was on the wane. "Once we got back to L.A., we never went anywhere. We just sat in his house, with all those people around. Sometimes he would play the piano and sing, and I know this sounds odd, but, it would be so boring. I would wonder why we couldn't go see a movie or go to a club. And with all those girls around, I got a feeling something wasn't right. That I didn't belong anymore."

One night they were sitting at the piano, "goofing off," when Helm did something she immediately regretted. "He said something to me— I can't even recall what—as he was playing the piano. I got upset and pulled the piano top down, and it hurt his finger. He was really mad, for the first time, at me."

She apologized but realized that he was still angry. So the next day she went into a gag-gift store and bought a giant rubber thumb, which she sent to him with a note of apology. "I never heard from him again."

Helm, who went on to work extensively in films and on television in the sixties and seventies, said she was never bitter about the experience. "I will always think of him as a gentleman. But honest to God, I think there were a lot of tears in Elvis. And a lot of anger. But at the same time there was this enormous heart. I'll always remember being with him that day he walked along that fence, talking with his fans. I got the sense that they brought out all the sweetness and cream in him."

By the time Gail Ganley became involved with Presley, he had largely withdrawn from the public eye. That was fine by Ganley. As she explained, "I had been indoctrinated into secrecy. I fit into Elvis's mode of wanting privacy."

The stunning brunette met Presley in October 1963 on an MGM

soundstage where they were filming *Kissin' Cousins,* a musical comedy set in the Smoky Mountains in which Elvis plays twins. Ganley was one of the film's dancing mountain girls, the "Kittyhawks." She was in the midst of rehearsing a dance number the day she felt a hand on her shoulder. She turned and found herself looking at a man in a blond wig. He said, "How do you do? My name's Elvis. What's yours?"

She was momentarily caught off guard. Not because she was being addressed by the film's star, but because in his blond wig he was a ringer for her former boyfriend. She told Presley that, catching him off guard in turn.

Over the next several days on the set, she often caught him looking at her. In the meantime, some curious things began to happen. Ganley, who was knitting a sweater during the breaks, once returned to her chair and found that her sweater had been unraveled. Another time her shoes turned up missing. A few days later, Elvis ambled over and confessed, "I couldn't stand it anymore. I have to tell you that I hid your shoes."

With a nod to the sweater that continued to mysteriously unravel, he added, "You are knitting that sweater for me, aren't you?" Ganley smiled. "At the rate I'm going, I don't know if this sweater is ever going to get done."

Later that day, one of Elvis's buddies approached her to say, "He wants to know if you'd like to come up to his house tonight."

Ganley was leery. "So I said I was going to a bridal shower that night." Elvis's friend was surprised: she had turned down the boss.

Worried that her refusal could get her fired off the picture, Ganley brought some See's Candies fudge to the set the following day. "Give this to Elvis," she told one of his aides. In response she was asked to come to Elvis's dressing trailer.

Once she was inside, he teased, "Did you think about me last night?" Then he personally asked her to come to his house that evening.

"Can't we get to know each other?" asked Gail. "Couldn't we first go out for coffee or something?"

Presley laughed, then explained that he was unable to go out on "regular dates" because of the crowds that gathered. "We couldn't have any privacy on a date. But we could get to know each other at my place."

Ganley agreed to the visit, but only if she could first stop by her parents' house. "I said I had to drop something off. Really, I just wanted to tell them where I'd be," she recalled decades later.

When his chauffeured Rolls-Royce pulled up in front of the modest Ganley home in Baldwin Hills, Gail ran up to the front door to alert her parents that she was going to spend the evening with Elvis, who was just climbing out of the car. Gail motioned for him to stay where he was. "I told him, 'It's okay, Elvis! My mom has her hair in rollers. She doesn't want you to see her with them.' "

Later, as they drove to his house in Bel-Air, he held her hand and told her how much he liked her figure and her dancing ability. "When the car pulled into the driveway, I saw all these girls clustered at the gates. I thought he was having a party," said Ganley, who was unaware that fans gathered, day and night, outside of Elvis's house.

They spent their first evening watching television. "I can tell you're nervous," Elvis said to the guarded Ganley. She confessed that she was. "I admire you for that," he responded.

Before she was driven home that night, he asked, "Is it okay if I kiss you?" She nodded, and he gently kissed her cheek. Then he kissed her forehead. When she didn't move away, he kissed her on the lips. "And I was so relieved, because his hands didn't wander," recounted Ganley, adding, "Up to that time I'd only had one boyfriend. So I was real innocent."

The next day on the set, no one unraveled her sweater.

But a few days later, there were several surprise visitors—including Hollywood columnist Harrison Carroll. Presley thought Carroll wanted to talk to him. "No. I'm looking for the Howard Hughes starlet," said Carroll.

"Who?" asked Elvis.

As he would find out, Gail Ganley was "the Hughes starlet"—the final beauty to have been put under contract by the enigmatic billionaire Howard Hughes. Moreover, she had recently made headlines— there was even a major *Life* magazine article—with her lawsuit against Hughes for failing to put her to work in a film she had signed to do. That lawsuit, which resulted in an out-of-court settlement, helped to tear away the secrecy of Hughes's mysterious empire.

Elvis Presley was fascinated when he heard this. But now it was his turn to be leery. For he was sure Ganley was going to capitalize on her newest relationship with a famous figure. To his surprise, Ganley told Harrison Carroll that she wanted to maintain a "low profile," and that she wouldn't talk to the media about either Hughes or Presley.

When Presley realized she had no intention of generating publicity with their dates, he returned to his pursuit of the five-foot-three, 110-pound beauty, who looked startlingly like Elizabeth Taylor. And now the attraction was mutual.

On their fourth date at the house, he spoke earnestly about his mother's death. She spoke candidly about her heartbreak over the recent breakup with her boyfriend, and having her career—which she had been working toward since childhood—go into limbo because of the Hughes situation. "Suddenly, the two of us were just sitting there, crying, tears streaming," Ganley said.

"Maybe we should go somewhere else to do this," said Elvis, rubbing his eyes. He motioned to an adjoining room. Ganley got up and discreetly went to the doorway she thought he'd singled out. "I found myself in the kitchen. And I wondered what we were going to do here." She took a seat and waited. And waited. "Eventually, I started wondering if I was supposed to cook something," she admitted. An hour passed. Then an hour and a half. Finally, Presley appeared in the doorway—shoulders shrugged. "So here you are! What are you doing in here?"

"I thought this is where you told me to go," said Gail.

He laughed, then motioned toward another door. "That's where my room is," he declared.

So began an on-again, off-again romance that spanned fifteen months and three movie productions.

But during her first trip to his bedroom, Ganley didn't make love with the star. "He told me we could just lie down together on the bed and enjoy touching and hugging one another. That we didn't have to take our clothes off," she said.

"His warm, passionate kisses held me captive all night. And, he never tried to undress me. He was just so terrific, because he was careful with his hands, and so loving. And he was so tender when he kissed me. The next day, I was just floating on the set," she smiled.

When they did finally consummate their relationship, Presley was not only gentle but determined to make the experience meaningful for Gail.

"Is that all right?" he would ask. "Is it okay if I do this?" he would say. And he kept asking, "Are you okay? Is this all right?"

Presley used to insist to Ganley that there were no other women in his life. "But I can't make any kind of plans for the future right now," he stressed. At the same time, he challenged her about her drive and determination to have a career. "How come you don't just want to get married and have kids?"

"He had a really tough time understanding women and careers," said Ganley, who further mystified Elvis when she turned down the chance to visit Graceland because of a recording contract that he himself had helped to set up.

When Ganley completed her recording, she wanted to take Elvis up on the offer. But suddenly it seemed he no longer wanted her to come. "I was suspicious," said Gail, who had heard rumors in Hollywood of a Memphis girlfriend. "But when I asked him about it, he said they'd broken up."

She and Presley went on to see each other during the making of *Roustabout*—in which she appeared as a harem dancer in his "Little Egypt" routine. In fact, they were together on the set so often that Colonel Parker used to waddle over to tell Gail she had a meeting, or Elvis that he had a phone call.

During the making of the film, Presley tried to tell Gail the kind of hair color she should have, and how she should wear her makeup. "And I got this sense of déjà vu. When I was under contract to Howard Hughes, he dictated my life. Suddenly, it was Elvis."

One day Elvis came to her to say that "an old friend" was going to visit the set. "And that I should be cool about what was going on between us," said Ganley. That old friend turned out to be Priscilla Beaulieu.

Though Ganley continued to be involved with Presley through the end of 1964, she realized that their relationship had no future. Then her old boyfriend reentered her life, ready to commit to marriage. Elvis clearly was not ready for any such commitments.

Something else was becoming apparent as Presley cut his romantic swath through Hollywood: he was not capable of compromise, in any sense. His *Blue Hawaii* costar Joan Blackman once predicted that any prospective bride would have to live up to certain standards. She said Presley would appreciate a sense of humor—as well as "a certain naïveté." After all, Blackman added astutely, she would have to "put up with an awful lot."

One girl in particular would soon be put to the ultimate test.

20

Foreplay

All the while Elvis Presley romanced his various Hollywood leading ladies, he kept Anita Wood and Priscilla Beaulieu in a romantic purgatory.

Because Wood made her home in Memphis and was regularly in and out of Graceland, she had an edge over Priscilla. In news stories about Elvis's comings and goings in Memphis, the name of Anita Wood was often prominently mentioned.

Priscilla, on the other hand, was languishing more than three thousand miles away in West Germany. The teenager was connected to Elvis only through the perfumed pink letters she sent faithfully, and the singer's transatlantic telephone calls, which were conducted in baby talk. Again and again the performer, who was now twenty-seven, repeated that he "wuved and wuved his li'l nungen [young 'un]."

Priscilla lived entirely for those infrequent calls and Elvis's equally infrequent letters. Otherwise she stayed locked in her room, dreaming of becoming Mrs. Elvis Aaron Presley and of being swept out of dingy military life to the glitter of Hollywood and the opulence of Graceland.

After the initial media hullabaloo over Presley's heroic departure, she didn't hear anything for twenty-one tearstained days. When Elvis finally did call, he failed to say, "I've missed you." Instead, he bitterly complained about making *G.I. Blues.*

"I thought you had forgotten me," Priscilla sobbed, "and that you had fallen in love with Nancy Sinatra, like the papers said."

"It's not true wittie nungen, it's you that I love."

"And Anita Wood?" Priscilla insisted bravely.

"My relationship with Anita is not what I expected it to be. I'm no longer sure I want to be with her."

Priscilla said later that she wanted to scream, "Where do I fit into your life?" But instead she mumbled a tearful "love you and good-bye."

In March 1962, when Anita was still occasionally residing at Graceland in a small suite of rooms, Elvis asked Joe Esposito to assist in a little charade so that he could bring Priscilla from Germany to Bel-Air, during her spring vacation from school in Wiesbaden.

Joe and his wife, Joanie, were to plan a fishing trip with Anita, allowing Presley the chance to romance the now sixteen-year-old Priscilla without fear of being discovered by "wittle beadie Wood."

Priscilla's stepfather, Captain Beaulieu, reluctantly allowed the visit. "I don't trust him, and I don't know what he wants from you," he commented frankly. In a vain hope he added, "Maybe this will end this infatuation." His conditions were that Presley fly Priscilla first-class and agree to have her back in time to resume school. Additionally, he wanted a copy of her itinerary and a promise that his pretty step-daughter would be chaperoned by Vernon and Dee Presley.

Priscilla was ecstatic, though before her very first day with Elvis in southern California was over, many of her schoolgirl illusions were shattered, as her stepfather had predicted.

She was glad to see Joe Esposito again—it was he who picked her up at the airport. Playing chauffeur, he drove her to Presley's rented Bel-Air home. Escorted into the enormous den, Priscilla found her would-be lover bending over the pool table, about to make a shot. "Cilla!" he cried out on seeing her. "I can't believe you're finally here!" He sprinted across the room, put his arms around her, and lifted her off the ground.

"Priscilla, I'm so glad to see you . . . I've missed you every day since I came back."

"I was crying when he held me in his arms," she recalled.

Holding the lovely girl by the hand, Presley led her around the room, introducing her to a crowd of mostly young women, several of whom would cue her in that Elvis held these get-togethers nightly.

Immediately, Priscilla understood that she had entered a world that was vastly different from Bad Nauheim. Elvis's uniform days were behind him. Instead, he sported expensive continental slacks, a white shirt, Italian leather boots, and a yachting cap.

Priscilla could see he had changed in other ways. "He'd been a sensitive, insecure boy when I had last seen him. Now he was self-confident to the point of cockiness."

The couple didn't slip away together until after midnight. Elvis sidled alongside Priscilla and said, "It's time for us." He gave her directions to the bedroom, saying he would follow in a few minutes—so that no one would suspect anything. But, as Priscilla candidly declared years later, she exited the den "hoping everyone would know exactly where I was going."

In the darkened bedroom, Elvis slowly undressed the teenager, whispering, "Cilla, you don't know how much I've missed you." Then they slid into bed for their most passionate encounter since they had met more than two years earlier. In her 1985 autobiography, Priscilla wrote that she expected Elvis to consummate their relationship during this reunion, and that she was "ready to submit entirely to him."

Instead Elvis pulled back. "Wait a minute, baby," he said softly. He went on to whisper that there would be "a right time and place." Priscilla was infuriated. She was even angrier when he had her escorted to a friend's house where she would spend her nights, as he had promised the captain. "We don't want him to change his mind about you staying here," he explained.

The next afternoon, Presley called his houseguest and announced, "Alan [Fortas] will pick you up in a few minutes." Before she could wonder why, he breathlessly added, "We're going to Las Vegas."

They traveled by night in Elvis's customized bus across the desert roads. To Priscilla it seemed that they would never reach their destination. In fact, the party didn't check into their rooms at the Sahara until seven o'clock the next morning. Priscilla couldn't believe what she saw: despite the early hour, the dice pits were filled, slots were being played, and even the cocktail lounges were open. Elvis was amused at her amazement at the twenty-four-hour city.

In Las Vegas, Elvis engineered a makeover for Priscilla—the first of many over the years—sweeping her off to a chic boutique, where she was outfitted in evening gowns of chiffon, brocade, and silk, accessorized by matching capes, glittering evening bags, and silk shoes dyed to match.

Elvis next arranged for the hotel's hairstylist to remake the overwhelmed girl. Her transformation—done to Elvis's specifications—took two hours, and when Elvis saw her, he let out a wolf whistle. Her hair had been styled high atop her head, with one long curl falling over her left shoulder. Her face was a mask of alabaster Pan-Cake makeup, eyes ringed with several thick shades of eye shadow—Cleopatra-style—and her lips were bloodred. She would be remade that way each day of her stay with Elvis.

That night Elvis swept Priscilla into the Sahara's midnight show, where they occupied the premier table. As Red Skelton performed, Elvis laughed heartily. Priscilla smiled, but she was mostly riveted on Elvis, studying his handsome face.

During their two weeks in Las Vegas, she discovered that Elvis became "another person by night": more romantic, more demonstrative, and definitely more gallant. She also learned to adapt to the singer's lifestyle, lounge-hopping until dawn, then rushing to their room where they drew the shades and tumbled into bed. After their first night in Las Vegas, Elvis popped two sleeping pills and snuggled alongside her. "I lay there blissfully happy," Priscilla recalled. As for Elvis, he talked for a while, slurring words of passion, then passed out.

To keep up with Presley's nighttime schedule, Priscilla joined the rest of his court in their drug rituals. Elvis's medicine chest was full of amphetamines, sleeping pills, and tranquilizers. "Otherwise," she recalled, "I would fall asleep on him."

She was also exposed to Elvis's incendiary temper. One day after he proudly played his new record for her, she innocently suggested that he also record some more "fast-paced" songs, like his early hits. "Goddamn it! I didn't ask for your opinion!" he said, eyes blazing. "I get enough amateur opinions as it is!"

He could be equally ugly if she chided him for flirting with other women while in her presence. "Nobody ever tells me who I can and cannot look at. *Nobody!*" he once snapped. "You got that straight?" She flushed and nodded.

This nastiness was balanced by a certain amount of sweetness, though. He dispensed promises with such sincerity she couldn't bear to think they might not be true. One night as they lay next to each other in bed, Elvis kissed her and said, "I can't believe we pulled this off; that we're here together where we belong." But he tumbled into a narcotic sleep after one final kiss. As their stay ended, Elvis promised to have her back for Christmas. "Christmas at Graceland," he said. "It will be beautiful, you'll see."

When the limousine dropped her off at the airport, Priscilla doubted she would return to America at Christmas or anytime soon. She couldn't imagine her parents agreeing to let her go away during what they considered a "family holiday." As it turned out, they were horrified by their daughter's metamorphosis. She had left Germany as Priscilla Beaulieu, high school student, and arrived back home a heavily coiffed, made-up, and overdressed parody of a chorus girl.

Captain Beaulieu was furious, and Mrs. Beaulieu reacted by pulling a mirror from her purse and holding it up to her daughter's face. "How could you get off a plane looking like this?" she demanded. As Priscilla looked at her reflection, she saw dried mascara on her cheeks—a residue of the tears she had wept at leaving Presley's side. "Totally dissolute," mumbled her stepfather.

Now the thought of going to Graceland for Christmas seemed even more unlikely.

Back in Memphis, meanwhile, Anita Wood was tired of waiting. Recently Elvis had told a reporter, "I want to get married and have children and all that, but, I'm still shopping around." Since the days before he went overseas, Presley had talked to her of marriage. That promise was growing hollow and she was increasingly suspicious. One afternoon in late summer, she stumbled across a memento from Priscilla's visit to the West Coast—a five-by-seven color photograph of the teenager. Pulling the snapshot from a drawer, Anita carefully tore it into eight pieces and then placed the photo, in pieces, back where she had found it. She meant, of course, for the jigsaw-puzzle photograph to be a message to Elvis. She also realized that her breakup with Presley wasn't far off.

When Presley discovered Anita's act of jealousy, he confessed to Joe Esposito that he "didn't know how to tell Anita that I'm in love with Priscilla."

Presley confided, "Joe, this is very, very hard. I've never broken anyone's heart before."

As the relationship continued to crumble, Anita found one of Priscilla's perfumed letters tossed carelessly atop a bureau in Graceland. Inside were minute instructions to Elvis on how to convince Captain Beaulieu to allow her to spend Christmas at Graceland. Anita phoned Hollywood and reached Elvis in his dressing room at MGM. She wasted no words: "I found the letter. And I'm leaving for good."

After a lengthy silence elapsed, Elvis said sternly, "I don't know if I should allow you to do this."

"What do you mean you won't allow me to do this? Who do you think you are? It's not your choice," Anita replied before decisively replacing the receiver.

When Presley was called back to the set, he was obviously shaken. "Nita dropped me," he told Nancy Anderson, a *Photoplay* reporter who happened to be doing an on-the-set interview. A Tennessee native with a frank demeanor, Anderson was not only a respected journalist but a Presley confidante and family friend. She suspected that Anita had grown tired of being the hometown girlfriend who was kept in the shadows. Elvis confirmed her suspicions: "After five years, I guess she got tired of waiting,"

In an interview with Bill Burk of the *Memphis Press-Scimitar*, Wood said she intended to concentrate on her career. She was scheduled to record the song "Love's Not Worth It" in Nashville. "There is no bitterness," she said. "Elvis isn't ready to settle down, and I sometimes doubt that he ever will."

Indeed, later in the year Elvis admitted, "The older I get, the more choosy I become." He said he was looking for a girl with a sense of humor, who was also understanding and loyal. He didn't mention that he also liked women who were young and malleable. Many women who dated him and then told all to the fan magazines mentioned his need to be totally in charge.

Presley certainly took charge when Priscilla came to visit for the Christmas holidays—a coup for the teenager, who had to plead with her parents for weeks before they allowed her to return. Once again they gave her a list of rules, and Elvis agreed to abide by them.

She flew first-class to New York, where she was met by Vernon and his wife, Dee. Then they all boarded a flight to Memphis.

During her stay in Elvis's hometown, Priscilla would come to see why Memphis—named for the ancient Egyptian city on the Nile—was so close to his heart. From the raucous sounds that spilled from the clubs on Beale Street to the quiet riverbanks of the Mississippi River to the lights of the brightly lit historic downtown, Memphis was a century away from the linoleum and stucco military housing where Priscilla had spent her childhood. She could see what Elvis had meant when he told her, "It's real down there and looks like it will last forever."

She had barely set down her small suitcases inside the front door of

Vernon and Dee's house when she felt someone grab her from behind. "Satnin!" Elvis cried—for the first time anointing her with the special name he had previously reserved for his mother. Swooping up her luggage, Elvis loaded it into the Rolls-Royce sedan, his fanciest car. As he backed out of Vernon's driveway, he commanded, "Close your eyes. I'll tell you when to open them." The Rolls rounded the residential neighborhood and continued on South Bellevue Boulevard. When the car reached the signature musical gates of Graceland, he softly said, "Look, Priscilla." Then he ceremoniously drove her up the winding, tree-lined drive.

Later she would remember her first look at Graceland as being a rush of color and unequaled luxury: the million tiny lights flickering through the trees; a life-size nativity scene bathed in golden hues; the towering porch columns reminiscent of *Gone With the Wind* grandeur. And velvet red poinsettias everywhere. "A fairyland, like a dream," she called it.

On arrival, Grandma Minnie Mae wrapped her arms protectively around the girl. "Remember, Priscilla, if anything bothers you—anything at all—you just come right upstairs to me, and we'll take care of it."

Priscilla nodded, tears running down her cheeks.

Elvis showed unusual sensitivity by temporarily banning some of the rowdy Memphis Mafia from the house. He wanted to ease his young lady into his private life, which had grown even more boisterous and crowded since his Army days. Priscilla was given a tour of the house, which culminated in the baronial bedroom suite with its two grand crystal and gold bathrooms, its his and hers dressing rooms, and a luxurious oversize bed. When the couple was snuggled in it, with snow flurries pelting the windows and wind off the Mississippi roaring through the trees, Elvis handed the teenager two large red pills. "Take these," he said. "They'll relax you."

Priscilla dutifully swallowed them with mineral water, but regretted it almost immediately. In the bathroom she began to feel heavy; her eyelids drooped; she was barely able to pull herself from the tub in which she was soaking. As she walked toward the bed to join the sleeping Elvis, she began to feel dizzy and then as if she were spinning down an endless tunnel. Then came absolute darkness.

After what seemed an endless amount of time, she emerged from the blackness to hear voices: Vernon's low growl, Minnie Mae's twang, and somewhere in the mix, Elvis's. All were beseeching her to wake up. For the time being, however, the stupor kept her in its grip.

Hours and hours later she finally opened her eyes and saw the worried face of Minnie Mae hovering above. "Priscilla, it's Grandma. Sweetheart, you're okay now. Sit up, hon."

As Priscilla tried to pull herself up, she was confused to discover she was no longer in bed—but on a chaise longue in Elvis's office. He had pulled her there in an effort to revive her. Now Minnie Mae whirled to face her recalcitrant grandson. "Young-un, what did you give this little girl? You take all the drugs you want. Stagger around all you want! But don't you ever give this little girl any of that god-awful stuff!"

The teenager had been given two 500-mg Placidyls, a hypnotic sleeping drug. Despite Vernon's plea to rush her to the hospital, Elvis had insisted, "No, Daddy, she'll come to."

Priscilla began crying. "How long have I been out? What day is it?"

Elvis sheepishly broke the news: "You've been unconscious for two days; it's December twenty-third."

"But I've lost two days of my trip," she sobbed.

Elvis dropped to his knees alongside the chair. "No, hon, I'll make it up to you. We're going to have the best Christmas ever . . . I'll make it up to you."

On Christmas morning three inches of snow formed a backdrop for a mountain of presents beneath Graceland's king-size tree. The night before, Elvis had donned a red velvet and white-fox-trimmed cap to play Santa. He delighted in watching David, Ricky, and Billy open their gaily decorated packages. He acted like a kid himself as he passed around their toys. He had a special surprise for Priscilla—a living gift. "Oh, Elvis!" she said, beaming, as he put a honey-colored puppy in her hands. Honey, as she would be named, proceeded to bound through the mountains of torn gift-wrap paper and pull at ribbons and bows. Then, Priscilla handed Elvis his gift. She was apprehensive as he opened the ornate cigarette case, which was also a music box. Priscilla had wound it before wrapping it, and the instant Elvis opened the lid, it began playing "Love Me Tender." He grinned: "I love it!"

Still, amid the gaiety Priscilla saw "a sadness in his eyes," and she guessed he still missed his mother's presence on Christmas.

In the days that followed, Elvis spared no expense as he introduced her to his nocturnal world in Memphis. He rented out the Rainbow roller rink, where Priscilla wobbled off the floor to get out of the way of Elvis's speed-happy buddies. The couple held hands at the movies—seated all by themselves in the empty auditoriums of the Malco and Memphian theaters. As Priscilla discovered, when Elvis wanted to see a movie, he rented out the entire theater; his cronies sat along the sides or above in the balcony.

On New Year's Eve, Memphis's Manhattan nightclub was taken over by Elvis and two hundred invited guests, including some of the fan club presidents. Though the rest of the crowd began assembling at ten o'clock, Elvis and Priscilla didn't sweep in until minutes before midnight. They had barely got a chance to order double screwdrivers when the countdown to 1963 began. At the stroke of midnight, as the crowd broke into celebratory cheers and "Auld Lang Syne," Elvis began to speak intently to Priscilla. She had to strain to hear him above all the noise. He was saying something about wanting her to stay. When she heard the words, "Baby, I don't want you to go back," she felt giddy.

She celebrated her newfound joy with another double screwdriver, then another. By the fourth, she was "reeling." Excusing herself, she managed to get to the ladies' room, where she hid in a stall "for what seemed like hours." When she at last returned to Elvis, he took one look at her and summoned George Klein. "Buddy, could you give this little girl a ride home?"

Priscilla had to concentrate to make it up the Graceland staircase. Once inside the master bedroom, she struggled out of her clothes before collapsing on the bed in her bra and panties. Hours later she awakened to find Elvis easing her out of the lingerie, kissing her lightly all over. She turned and wrapped her arms around him. This, she thought, was the moment.

But just as she believed that Elvis was about to enter her, at last, he held himself back, murmuring, "No, Priscilla. Not like this. The next time you come, I want you to stay forever. I'll fix it, you'll see."

Priscilla understood completely: she almost had him. Or so she thought.

21

Toys in the Attic

lvis Presley sat cross-legged on his bed at Graceland and ran through a scenario of what would be one of the most significant performances of his life—one that depended on the appearance of utter honesty and a sense of trustworthiness. That he had to make the pitch over transatlantic phone lines didn't make his job any easier. To convince Captain and Mrs. Beaulieu to allow Priscilla to come and live with his family in Memphis, Elvis declared his love for their daughter, but added seriously, "My intentions are strictly honorable." According to Priscilla, he told her parents he couldn't live without her and "intimated" that they would one day marry.

Presley earnestly promised that Priscilla would move in with Vernon and Dee Presley and attend classes at Immaculate Conception Cathedral Academy, an impeccable all-girls Memphis high school.

Captain Beaulieu angrily dismissed Presley's plan. "That's the most ridiculous thing I've ever heard of. What sort of parents would agree to such a scheme?"

"But, sir, I'm utterly serious," Presley answered. "What if I send you two first-class tickets to Los Angeles and we discuss this man to man?"

Although Captain Beaulieu was suspicious of Elvis's intentions, he was nonetheless determined to be fair. "Son, I'll come out and discuss it with you," he said.

Mrs. Beaulieu was less sanguine—and indignantly withdrew her support. "But we're in love, Mom," Priscilla pleaded through tears. "And I want to move to Graceland and eventually to be married there." The "eventually" bothered Mrs. Beaulieu. "Why you?" she asked. "He has some of the most beautiful movie stars in Hollywood chasing him." The captain was also infuriated by accounts of Elvis's romances in the gossip columns. "It all seems so tawdry," Mrs. Beaulieu said. "If I let you go and you come back with a broken heart, I'll never forgive myself. And I still don't understand why he picked you out of the hundreds of women he knows."

Even Priscilla was mystified by this question. Years later she surmised, "I think my stable childhood attracted him. Plus, he knew he could always depend upon me." In her autobiography, Priscilla frankly admitted that Elvis also wanted to groom her—to raise her to become his conception of the ideal woman. "I realized that I had the basic attributes he required, but that he wanted to shape me into his ideal bride. As for myself, I intended to do everything I could to hold on to him."

Priscilla admits that her parents were tormented by her pleas to move to Memphis. Earlier this year her mother said to her, "You don't know what this did to us as parents, because we didn't want to ruin your life if we were to say no to you and Elvis. We thought it was just temporary." As Mrs. Beaulieu explained, "We trusted him."

The rendezvous in Hollywood proved effective. Elvis won over the captain as he drove him up and down the streets of Hollywood and Beverly Hills, pointing out the sights. "Elvis could be so charming, such a good talker. He could talk anybody into anything," said Joe Esposito.

Next, the captain visited Graceland, where he was impressed by Vernon Presley's solid, dependable "down-home" character. Vernon said, "I promise you, Captain Beaulieu, that Priscilla will get her schooling. And that she will live off the Graceland grounds with my wife and I."

However, as Becky Yancey, Elvis's secretary, noted, the latter promise "wasn't the case at all." Said Yancey, "From the beginning, she slept in Elvis's room, though every now and then she might stay at Dee and Vernon's to look good."

Priscilla and Elvis maintained the charade until Captain Beaulieu said good-bye to his daughter at the door to Vernon's house. Two hours later, Priscilla filled a small suitcase with nightclothes and toiletries and entered the estate through a back gate. She spent that night in Elvis's bed. Though she would go on to become the mistress of the mansion on Whitehaven Hill, she would also become its prisoner.

There were few secrets among the Graceland staff. Sometimes, when Elvis slept late, Priscilla would slip out of his bedroom, with a light robe thrown over her pink shortie nightdress, and wander casually down the stairs. "It was obvious to everyone that Priscilla was not sleeping at the Vernon Presleys'," said Becky Yancey.

At Immaculate Conception, the perception was somewhat different.

The sisters at the school briefly raised their eyebrows over the arrangement, but then admitted her—a sign of Presley's growing civic significance. When the first notice concerning Priscilla arrived via mail, principal Sister Adrianne ran down the hall to class administrator Sister Loyola. "You'll never believe this, but Elvis has a protégée who wants to go to school here. She's about sixteen and living with his father, Mr. Presley.

"Do you think we can ethically enroll her?" Sister Adrianne asked.

Sister Loyola paused thoughtfully. "I guess it would be okay, since she's living with the father."

As for the students, Sherry Riggins remembers Priscilla as "standing out" because of her makeup and hair—she was the only student allowed to have dyed hair—and because of her status as Elvis's girlfriend. "It was a novelty: the girl that was living out at Elvis's was going to school with us." With a nod to an era that was more innocent than today's, Riggins added, "I was so naive that the thought never crossed my mind that they were sexually involved."

Classmate Dorothy Weems said that Priscilla was polite but remote. "She had a whole other life apart from school . . . she was living in a different world from us." Unlike the other girls, she didn't participate in school activities and seldom went out with them after school for Cokes or malts. "Most of the time she came to school in a limo, or in one of Elvis's cars," remembered Riggins. Added Johna Danovi Fenrick, "She kept a low profile, while the rest of us were wrapped up in our special cliques."

Astoundingly, word of Elvis Presley's teenage houseguest was not reported in the mainstream media for the first three years of her stay in Memphis. Everyone, including the press, preferred to look the other way. As Joe Esposito put it: "Elvis *owned* the city of Memphis. . . . He was great to people there. He donated huge amounts of money to charity. He was great to his fans. And so he got to do what he wanted."

Priscilla had no sooner hung her wardrobe in his closet than Elvis ordered, "Toss it out." Off they went on a shopping spree that lasted several days. Elvis critiqued every outfit she tried on as she shyly emerged from the shop's dressing room. He liked her in bright colors— the same ones he favored. "But no brown or green," he dictated. "Too much like my Army days." To match, he again orchestrated her hair and makeup, requesting that she dye her hair jet-black like his and heavily rim her eyes with black eyeliner. If the liner wasn't as thick as he liked, he would send her upstairs "so you can fix your eyes."

Yet he also loved her school uniform, consisting of a white blouse, plaid skirt, and a little waistcoat. "There goes my little schoolgirl," he would adoringly yell.

Priscilla readily admits that she became a living Barbie Doll, manipulated by Presley. "Elvis created me. He made me how he wanted me to be. I thought that's what men did with women. I thought he was supposed to pick out my clothes and tell me what to do. All I wanted was to please him."

She seldom balked at his instructions. "I did what he said to do."

In retrospect, some of those actions are embarassing. "I guess we were caricatures. I don't mean to be sacrilegious, but when we got motorcycles and rode around, I was Mary and the guys were the twelve disciples."

From 1963 to 1967, Priscilla Beaulieu haunted the Graceland mansion, living according to the pleasures of Elvis and bowing to the demands of his schedule. When he roared into town on his Hollywood bus, the great house came alive with parties and long nights at the amusement park. But when he was away filming, eight to nine weeks at a time, Priscilla wandered the grounds, sometimes going to the little office out back and visiting with Becky Yancey and Elvis's cousin Patsy Presley as they fielded bills and fan mail.

The secretaries also kept scrapbooks of news and fan magazine stories that were written about Elvis. Priscilla liked to flip through the articles, paying special attention to the ones that "told all" about Elvis's romances. Sometimes the articles were so upsetting that she would telephone Elvis out on the West Coast. "Little baby, don't you know those things are all made up? Don't you know that you're my only girl?" She desperately wanted "to believe everything he promised."

Back inside the big house, silence echoed off the walls. Priscilla often ate dinner alone at the formal black-marble dining-room table, set with gilded chairs. When Elvis was away, Priscilla seemed to live on tuna fish salads and sandwiches, but when he was home, she joined in passing around the meat loaf or hamburgers. As she told Becky Yancey, Elvis hated fish—so she didn't want to eat it around him. "He doesn't even like it on somebody's breath." Because she had to maintain secrecy about her relationship with Elvis, she had few friends over. The Avon lady, however, made frequent Graceland visits.

For a teenage girl virtually on her own, the nights were the worst. The wind whipped up the hill and rattled the roofs of the outbuildings. Frequently, Priscilla would slip out of Elvis's room and creep downstairs to Grandma's room, where she would snuggle under the covers. Often Minnie Mae would pull the scared teenager close to her and whisper, "Shhhh . . . honey, I'm here. Everything's okay."

Sandra Harmon, the author behind Priscilla's autobiography, says that the girl willingly suffered the loneliness, the neglect, and even the derision that Elvis sometimes directed at her. "She was in love with him . . . madly in love with him." Added Harmon, "She was a kid, and he was *Elvis*. That made her feel very special because he had hand-picked her. Plus he was hurt and vulnerable because of the loss of his mother. In fact, I think she tried to be the mother in the relationship. She tried to give him what he needed and to be what he needed."

During her first few years at Graceland, Priscilla was treated like a new and magical toy. The servants were instructed to give her whatever she wanted; and eventually she had her own car to drive back and forth to Immaculate Conception.

When Elvis's bus pulled up in front of Graceland, following the completion of a film, the performer would bound out, rush up the steps to Graceland, and push through the front doors, yelling Rhett Butler-style, "Where's my little Cilla?" Seconds later she would swoop down the stairs. Then the couple would walk arm in arm up the grand staircase and into the bedroom suite

They would shut the doors behind them for four or five days. It was, Priscilla recalled fondly, a "magical, romantic world of our own." She would change into one of the shortie nightgowns Elvis liked (she had them in every shade of pastel), while he slipped into silk pajamas. No calls were forwarded to the room, unless they were from Vernon or the Colonel. Elvis's favorite meals, including double-batter fried chicken, and deep-fried banana-and-peanut-butter sandwiches, were left outside the bedroom door.

The passion of their first reunion almost pushed them "over the edge," according to Priscilla's memoirs. "I was drunk with ecstasy," she confessed. But as so many times before, Elvis again pulled back. "Let's stop for a second," he whispered. "Let me decide when it happens."

"What about Anita?" argued the teenager. "You mean, you didn't make love to her in the four years you spent with her?"

By now Elvis was back in control and very patient: "No, Cilla, Anita and I went just to a point and no further. It was hard on her as well. This is the right thing to do. It will make our wedding a beautiful thing, a special thing."

Once Priscilla accepted his guidelines—it was important to him that she remain a virgin—they embarked on an imaginative erotic journey. As she has related, "He began teaching me other means of pleasing him." They indulged in sex games and fantasies that sometimes lasted for hours and involved costumes and fanciful scenarios. Though he forbade traditional consummation of their union, Elvis was up for everything else—including having his sweetheart "star" in revealing Polaroid photos and videos, all of them "directed" by Presley. These sexual trysts, said Priscilla, led to "some exciting and wild times."

They were clever and inventive. In a favorite game Priscilla would don the virginal-looking uniform she wore to Immaculate Conception. Elvis would pretend to be a stern schoolteacher; Priscilla was his naughty, tardy, or sassy student. In a twist, he sometimes played the student, and she was the seductive schoolteacher.

His favorite fetish was to take Polaroid photos of her in plain white cotton panties. He took shots from all angles as she tumbled and cavorted on the super-plush carpet of the bedroom suite. They shot so many Polaroids that Priscilla made near-nightly trips to the drugstore to buy more boxes of film. Since only one such store stayed open late, the young beauty in dark sunglasses became a familiar presence to the night clerks.

Of course, Elvis also enjoyed photographing women at his southern-California getaways. "He was a classic voyeur," explained Sandra Harmon. "He liked to see girls with a little pubic hair coming out of their white underpants. He took hundreds of stills of Priscilla alone and films of her prancing around with other girlfriends. And from what I can tell, she liked it. She used to tell him hot stories as well—he loved that."

Oddly, the "secret" play sessions were common knowledge around Graceland. On occasion the maids would find revealing Polaroids beneath the bed. And though the subscription was in Becky Yancey's name—at Priscilla's request—the teenager regularly scrutinized the pages of the Frederick's of Hollywood catalog, which offered a harem's wardrobe of adventurous lingerie.

Joe Esposito offers an explanation for Elvis's fascination with young girls—Priscilla included: "Early on, Elvis didn't know much about sex. He never had a bunch of guys to hang around with and talk about sex and women. So he learned it all on his own. And so he, in turn, liked young girls because he could be the older man teaching the young girl about sex. He remained in total control. That's the way he did it with Priscilla . . . no two ways about it. But he always said to us, and I believe to her, 'This is the girl I'm going to marry.' "

Psychologist Peter Whitmer offered this view of Priscilla: "Elvis could never relinquish his investment in Gladys sufficiently to invest himself wholly in another meaningful relationship. In Priscilla, Elvis had regained his old family-system role. As Priscilla's caretaker, Elvis's emotional satisfaction was immensely fulfilling. This was the role he knew best."

Whitmer also believes that the lovers played roles in real life as they did in their sexual adventures. He notes that Priscilla assumed Gladys's place "adoring Elvis unconditionally, fully accepting and fully needing his care." Elvis, in turn, "found in her youthful naïveté a representation of his own lost innocence."

In between all the sexual games and role-playing, Priscilla often found life at Graceland barren. To while away the lonely afternoons she combed Graceland—top to bottom. One lazy, warm Tennessee afternoon, Priscilla dressed up in a pink cotton sundress and took her little poodle, Honey, out beneath the grove of trees where a breeze was rustling. She leaned back against a massive tree trunk and allowed Honey to run free. It was a dreamy idyll before she collected the pooch and ran back up the hill.

By evening, reports of her "public" appearance had reached Colonel Tom Parker, who put in a stern call to Vernon. "This is a very dangerous situation," Parker said. "It's bad enough that Elvis has this girl there at all. We certainly don't want anyone even thinking that she's living in Graceland." Added the Colonel, "I would prefer it if Priscilla stayed with you and Dee, in the manner that was presented to the Beaulieus, but I know Elvis won't accept that."

Before he hung up, he stressed, "This could not only ruin his career but could land him in prison." Priscilla, of course, was underage.

In retrospect, it is nothing short of amazing that none of the major gossip columnists of the day stumbled onto the story of Elvis's teenage temptress. If such an arrangement took place today, the tabloids and tabloid TV shows would have a field day. Telephoto lenses would be used to capture grainy photos of Priscilla and Honey at play. Servants would be bribed to tell all. News of the underage paramour would cause a national scandal.

When Priscilla did venture beyond the high, protected walls of Graceland, she was instructed to use the back gate leading into Vernon's backyard. If Vernon and Dee couldn't drive her where she wanted to go, she'd ask to use Elvis's Lincoln Mark V.

To her discomfort, she also sometimes had to ask for money. Vernon once gave her $35, then was shocked when, two weeks later, she asked for more. Becky Yancey remembers times they went to lunch, "and the poor little thing, bless her heart, only had money for coffee." On another occasion, when Becky also happened to be broke, she and Priscilla had a lunch date with several acquaintances. All the way to the meal the two worried about who would pick up the bill. To their relief, the other diners did. "Here we were, the girlfriend and secretary of the most famous entertainer in the world . . . and we didn't even have enough money between us to tip the waitress," recalled Yancey.

When she was within the confines of Graceland, Priscilla did what any lonely, curious high school girl would do: she went snooping. Her favorite destination was the attic, with its dusty contents tracing the Presley family's life back to Tupelo. She came upon an Easter bonnet from the thirties, Elvis's beloved comic books, and toys piled together in a corner. There were boxes of water-damaged photographs, including many of Elvis as a child. His fans never saw those pictures—just a handful were doled out to the press by the Colonel, the better to stress the Presley family's poverty.

In an oak standing cabinet, which once held Elvis's clothes from the Lauderdale Court project days, she came upon a shoebox filled with correspondence dating from Presley's first day in Germany until just before he flew back to the United States. Two years earlier, Priscilla had quickly read over the return address of a stack of letters she spied in Elvis's room in Bad Nauheim. Now she took her time, reading each perfumed page sent by Anita Wood.

In her letters Anita spoke of her secret engagement to Elvis, and her love for him. Sometimes her words had a familiar ring. It took a while for Priscilla to realize that Elvis had written some of those very lovey-dovey phrases to her, as well. For the first time the girl realized how duplicitous her lover could be.

Rummaging through a cabinet that smelled of lilac and rose petals, Priscilla found a fading collection of Gladys's clothes. Fingering the dresses, Priscilla was surprised at how soft they were; she liked some of the floral prints, in pastel colors. Unable to resist, she actually tried on some of Elvis's mother's clothes. As she preened in the attic in Gladys's dresses, she wondered how closely she resembled the young Gladys.

She also wondered how well she really knew the man who held her fate in his hands. She was determined to find out more about him.

22

Viva Ann-Margret

riscilla was still luxuriating in her naively romantic idyll when Elvis returned to Hollywood to prepare for his splashiest production yet, the MGM musical *Viva Las Vegas*. His costar was to be Hollywood's hottest starlet in years, the fiery, multi-talented Ann-Margret.

"Wait just a week," Priscilla pleaded.

"Can't do it," said Presley. "I've got to be ready for this one. They say that this girl can do everything."

For days Priscilla had been overwhelmed with the fear that Elvis would fall in love with Ann-Margret, putting an end to their relationship. Ann-Margret wasn't just talented, she was also extraordinarily beautiful—and sexy: the media had been calling her "the female Elvis Presley."

Since the realization that Elvis had been writing to Anita Wood at the same time he had been seeing her in Germany, Priscilla had been skeptical of Elvis's fidelity. She imagined him romancing every single one of his beautiful leading ladies. Why not Ann-Margret, too?

If she accompanied him to Hollywood, Priscilla reasoned, her mere presence would act as a barrier to any lovemaking between Elvis and the "Swinger from Wilmette," as the fan magazines were calling the

Swedish native who had grown up in Illinois. She had taken dance lessons since the age of five, performed on *Ted Mack's Amateur Hour* at age sixteen.

At Northwestern University she became a sorority girl who sang with the school band, then moved on to perform with a combo. By late 1961 she had made a potent movie debut opposite Bette Davis, Hope Lange, Glenn Ford, and Peter Falk in *Pocketful of Miracles*. She also brought down the house by singing "Bachelor in Paradise" on that year's Academy Awards telecast.

When cast in *Viva Las Vegas* she was buoyed by strong headwinds from her latest film, *Bye Bye Birdie*, a clever musical parody about what happens in small-town America when rock-'n'-roll idol Conrad Birdie is drafted. Naturally, it was inspired by Presley's own Army stint; not coincidentally, he had been sought for the role of Birdie.

Priscilla had, of course, seen *Birdie*; she had also read about Ann-Margret in the fan magazines and gossip columns, which depicted the twenty-two-year-old as a blithe spirit who liked riding motorcycles and playing the field. But Priscilla also realized that Ann-Margret had worked her way toward stardom. She had recently bought herself a home in the Hollywood Hills. By comparison, Priscilla—who had recently graduated from Immaculate Conception and was now taking modeling classes—had concentrated solely on trying to become Mrs. Elvis Presley. The teenager was understandably jealous.

At dinner the night before Elvis was to leave, she timidly suggested that she accompany him to Hollywood. "Cilla, that's impossible, and you know it. The press is going to be all over this picture. Plus, a lot of it is to be filmed in Las Vegas."

So early the next morning, she followed him to the door of his bus and kissed him before he climbed aboard. "I wish we had more time," she said through her tears. "I do, too," he answered. "Give me just a couple of weeks to get into the film, and maybe you can come out for a while."

Before Priscilla could say anything else, the doors closed and she heard the familiar shout, "All right! Let's roll it!" She said later, "I cursed myself for not confiding my fears to him. But I realized if I told him my fears, he could have said nothing to put my mind at ease because one evening he'd made the mistake of telling me about the romances he'd had with many of his costars."

What she didn't know was that several years earlier, Elvis had had a friend approach Ann-Margret; the idea was for the go-between to bring the starlet to his house in Bel-Air for a date. Ann-Margret turned him down. With a toss of her hair she explained, "I don't date men who don't come to pick me up personally."

Priscilla wasn't the only one who anticipated that Elvis would have an affair with Ann-Margret. Hollywood's gossip columnists were also sharpening their pencils, preparing to chronicle what they considered the sultriest teaming since Elizabeth Taylor and Richard Burton wrought their havoc on the set of *Cleopatra* two years earlier.

On the surface, Ann-Margret, with her tumbling red hair, iridescent green eyes, go-go wardrobe, and torrid dancing style, was the jazziest thing to hit town in ages. Yet under the brass, Ann-*Margret* Olsson was quite shy and sensitive. The daughter of an Illinois electrician, she had grown up the poor girl in a wealthy community, and the outsider in a cliquish high school for society kids. Moreover, her image as a Hollywood sex kitten was just that: despite her penchant for careening through the hills on her motorcycle, she was no extrovert. So she tended to isolate herself from the showy social set. In that respect she shared a bond with Elvis Presley, whose self-assured bravado hid the uncertainties of a country boy.

The two stars met for the first time on the cavernous MGM musical soundstage where, among many other productions, Kathryn Grayson and Howard Keel had rehearsed *Show Boat*. Ready for sparks to fly, MGM had arranged for photographers to capture that first meeting. Elvis appeared in sartorial splendor, wearing a tight-fitting suit, Italian silk shirt and Italian boots. Every bit his match, Ann-Margret wore a dressy, expensive knit suit and an elaborate coiffure fashioned by the dean of hairdressers, Sydney Guilaroff.

Director George Sidney (*Show Boat, Annie Get Your Gun*, and *Kiss Me Kate*) did the honors of guiding his leading lady over, saying, "Elvis Presley, I'd like you to meet a wonderful young lady, Ann-Margret." As if on cue, they each simultaneously said, "I've heard a lot about you." As the shutters snapped, the two attractive people stood and shyly exchanged small talk.

Instinctively, they moved to the farthest reaches of the soundstage, speaking quietly. "Elvis told me he'd enjoyed *Bye Bye Birdie* and offered his sweet smile. I thanked him and wished I could return the compliment as I had never seen him perform. Alas, I didn't have much to say and just smiled back," Ann-Margret remembered.

For the MGM publicists who had expected the stars to part the heavens, their shyness must have been a serious disappointment. "I don't know why I was so calm about meeting 'the King.' After all, this was *Elvis*, a man who had captured the heart of almost every woman in America," Ann-Margret recalled. "Little did I know he would soon capture mine."

On July 15, 1963, more than 225 cast and crew members headed for Las Vegas, where Elvis and his Memphis Mafia contingent took over the Presidential Suite on the top floor of the Sahara Hotel. Shortly after arriving, Elvis and Ann-Margret began blocking out the film's dance numbers. One in particular was difficult to stage, because it started at the dressing room of the Flamingo Hotel—where Presley stood outside, serenading Ann-Margret—then moved poolside, finally climaxing with the two climbing a high dive, where Ann-Margret gives Elvis a playful push.

The performers lip-synched to loud "playbacks"—which they'd cut at MGM's state-of-the-art facility in Los Angeles, where all the great musicals (*Singin' in the Rain, Gigi*) had been recorded. As the song traveled across the hotel grounds, choreographer David Winters demonstrated the basic movements and then turned the two stars loose. From the first chorus, Elvis and Ann-Margret moved as if they'd been dancing together as long as Astaire and Rogers. With looks of playful passion on their faces, they replicated the electric pelvic moves Presley had used to ignite the fifties. "We looked at each other and saw virtual mirror images," Ann-Margret said. "When Elvis thrust his pelvis, mine slammed forward, too. When his shoulder dropped, I was down there with him. When he whirled, I was already on my heel." Over the music, Ann-Margret—her hair blowing wildly in the desert wind—yelled, "This in uncanny!" Presley grinned and, in a throwback to earlier times, delivered even lustier moves.

The members of his coterie, who were often bored stiff during shooting, gathered in a group to watch. As did crew members. When the playback ended, applause erupted from the sidelines—a rarity on any film set. "Whatever happened up there, Elvis liked it and so did I," the actress remembered. "It was like discovering a long-lost relative, a soul mate."

The two enjoyed the same comradeship when they performed "C'mon Everybody" with dozens of dancers in the gymnasium at the University of Nevada.

At long last, Elvis Presley had met his musical match.

Several days after they had teamed for their first number, Elvis looked at his leading lady and said, "Rusty [the name of her movie character], how about going out with me and the guys to see a show?" And so, just before midnight that evening, Ann-Margret found herself surrounded by his bizarre brigade—all of whom were attentive. It was a tribute that these jaded men, who'd been in the presence of some of Hollywood's most beautiful starlets, found themselves in awe of the vibrant young actress.

As production continued, Elvis and his band continued to escort Ann-Margret—to shows, dinners, and casinos. "They were a combination support system and buffer to keep outsiders at bay," she remembered. "I was used to having my parents accompany me on dates, so Elvis's entourage wasn't a problem for me. The guys all treated me wonderfully."

"Oh, she was a great lady," remembered Richard Davis. "Those of us who worked with Elvis called her Rusty Amo, because her name in the movie was Rusty, and her initials were A.M.O. for Ann-Margaret Olsson."

Then came an evening when Ann-Margret showed up at Presley's suite—and the guys were nowhere to be found. Finally, and unexpectedly, she was on her first date alone with Elvis. "Where'd everyone go?" she asked as Elvis opened the door. "They're busy," he said with a devilish smile. According to Joe Esposito, Presley had decided the time had come to get to know his leading lady better. As his adjutant, Esposito had passed along the message to the Mafia to "clear out!"

Elvis Presley never spoke publicly about the romance that followed, and Ann-Margret has discussed it only in careful, veiled terms. "We both found solace in the quiet of the night," she once revealed. "While the rest of the world slept, we talked until three or four in the morning, alone and not bothered by the pressures and demands of our occupations. Our talks were wide-ranging and earnest."

The two were also constantly on the move. "Like me, Elvis was happiest way out in the desert where there weren't other people to bother you. I suppose the film people would have gone white if they had seen some of the things we both did out there."

She never ceased to be amazed by the fans' reaction to Elvis. As she noted, girls "saw him as a love god when he rode out in his leather gear. They would offer all sorts of things to be signed, including parts of their bodies."

The Memphis Mafia were amazed when Elvis and Ann-Margret holed up in his suite for an entire weekend. Said Marty Lacker, "That drove Red West and Lamar absolutely crazy. Elvis wouldn't even answer the door for room service. They had to leave the tray outside. Then when Elvis made sure everybody was away, he would pull the trays in. To play a trick on the couple, Red and Lamar stuffed a newspaper under the door and lit it. Didn't work. They even shined butter knives until they looked like mirrors and slipped them under the door to see them. Didn't work. They tried everything, but Elvis and Ann would not come out.

"She was the first girl in a good while that he really connected with."

Added George Klein, "It was intense. Don't let anybody ever tell you it wasn't. Hey, we could hear them in the room next door."

Writing in her autobiography, Ann-Margret said that she and Elvis had "special, treasured, intimate moments." Admitted the actress, "There's just no getting around it, our relationship was too big a part of my life to ignore. He had touched something deep within my psyche." Of her nights with Presley in Las Vegas, Ann-Margret has said, "I shall never forget the love we shared."

Despite the suspicions Priscilla had felt from the very start, she was nonetheless shaken when a media furor finally erupted. She happened to be in northern California visiting her parents—now living at Travis Air Force Base, near Sacramento—when the first stories came over the wire. Written by Associated Press reporter Bob Thomas, they asked, "Elvis and Ann-Margret? Is It Romance or Publicity?" Beneath the headline was a photo showing the pair looking cozy—Elvis had his head in Ann-Margret's lap. "Seeing is believing," wrote Thomas. "And their behavior on the film set might make you believe that something is brewing between the two. They hold hands, they disappear into his dressing room between shots. They lunch in seclusion."

Priscilla was both embarrassed and angry—embarrassed that her parents were reading about it, and angry that she hadn't insisted upon accompanying Elvis. Ensuing gossip columns said Hollywood was buzzing about the attraction between the costars. Some stories even hinted at a "torrid affair."

Priscilla put in a call to Elvis on the set. "Is there any truth to this?"

"Hell, no."

"Well, then, why can't I merely join you out there right now—this week?"

"No, not now," Elvis yelled. "We're wrapping up the film, and I'll be home in a week or two." When she persisted, he said, "Look, she comes around here on weekends with her motorcycle. She hangs out with the boys. That's it."

As he had done when she suspected the affair with Juliet Prowse, he soothed her. "I'll be home soon, baby. Get everything ready."

She fell for it: "I began eagerly making plans for his return."

But so jealous was Priscilla that she, in an effort to look more like Elvis's costar, dyed her hair blond.

As for Ann-Margret, she had no idea that Elvis was being unfaithful to another woman. All she knew was that Elvis thought she was special. When he left his Bel-Air house to go see her, even the members of his entourage realized the relationship was "serious." After all, said Joe Esposito, "this violated his long-standing rule that women had to come to him." He added, "He was spending stolen hours at Ann-Margret's place up in the Hollywood Hills . . . they would disappear for hours on their Harleys. It was a heady romance."

The all-hours drives continued. Elvis's buddy Richard Davis and cousin Billy Smith would sometimes ride in the backseat as Elvis drove, with Ann-Margret snuggling alongside. "Elvis loved to drive, so we would pick her up at her place and just roam for hours through Bel-Air and in the mountains," remembered Davis. On those evenings when she visited at Elvis's, she did so in private. The usual cluster of female friends was not around. "We were given the word not to come up, because he wanted to be alone with Ann-Margret," recalled frequent visitor Joni Lyman, adding, "We knew it was special when we heard it was a one-on-one relationship."

For some time they saw each other nightly, and after a while, Elvis began to talk to her about his sorrows. "I knew I had crossed into a certain uncharted territory when he began trusting me with his secrets. He didn't reveal this vulnerable side until everyone had disappeared, until those private moments when we were alone," said Ann-Margret.

She formed her own view of Elvis. "People think of him as having everything, but that wasn't true at all. He had a great capacity to love, and he wanted to be loved in return. But he knew the world he lived in, as well as all the people who surrounded him, who hurt him, who wanted something from him . . . made it virtually impossible for him to ever feel that affection; and if he did, he didn't know whether to trust it.

"There was a void in Elvis's heart because of his mother's death. He talked of how he missed her and described her in the most heartfelt manner."

Although Elvis had probably never had an adult relationship as earnest and passionate as that with Ann-Margret, it eventually ended. Part of the reason was Elvis's usual refusal to settle down. Another part, though, appears to have been a misunderstanding. One day Elvis read in the papers that Ann-Margret claimed they were "engaged." He felt betrayed—and, as he had done with previous associates, he wanted no more of her.

In November 1963, Ann-Margret flew to London for the premiere of *Bye Bye Birdie*, where she found herself surrounded by dozens of reporters who shouted out questions about her relationship with Elvis Presley. Determined to be discreet, she said, "We're seeing each other. That's all!"

Ann-Margret made the U.S. TV newscasts a few nights later, and Elvis happened to be watching—with Gail Ganley, the striking brunette who was appearing as a dancer in his movie *Kissin' Cousins*. "Elvis ordered the TV to be turned off. He was furious," she recalled.

When Gail pressed him about the Ann-Margret relationship, Elvis said, "There was something there, but not anymore." He would go on to complain that Ann-Margret was "too competitive." Presley had also told Gail that he and Priscilla were no longer together, that they were "over."

"I was very naïve," said Ganley, who had no reason—at the time—not to believe Presley. He had, after all, charmingly pursued her on the film's MGM soundstages. Moreover, their ensuing relationship, which was as soulful as it was sexual, lasted fifteen months.

But Priscilla was still very much in his life. In fact, she happened to be at his house in Bel-Air when word that Presley and Ann-Margret were engaged made the papers. Upon reading the story, Elvis yelled, "I can't believe she did it! I can't believe she had the goddamn nerve to announce we were engaged."

"Who?" asked Priscilla, though she knew full well.

"Ann-Margret! Every major newspaper in America has picked it up. The rumor has spread like a goddamn disease."

He turned to Priscilla. "Honey, I'm going to have to send you home. The press will be hanging around the gate and following me all over. Colonel suggests you should go back to Memphis until this calms down." After all, his secret bedmate had to remain just that.

Priscilla erupted in anger: "What's going on here? I'm tired of these secrets. Telephone calls. Notes. Newspapers." She picked up a flower vase and hurled it at the wall.

As glass flew across the room, Elvis grabbed her. "I didn't know this was going to get out of hand," he insisted. Looking her squarely in the eye, he added, "I want a woman who's going to understand that things like this just might happen. Are you going to be her or not?"

Priscilla stared back angrily, but finally announced with resignation, "I'll leave tomorrow." The next day she returned to Memphis—once again to become the girl back home.

When Elvis's bus arrived home two weeks later, they greeted as if they were long-lost lovers. After the obligatory dinner with the Mafia, in the bedroom Elvis took Priscilla's face in his hands, looked into her eyes, and said, "It's over, Cilla. I swear to you. It's over." He explained that he'd been caught in a relationship "that was out of hand from the beginning." In other words, he had lied earlier: he had been deeply involved with Ann-Margret.

Priscilla recalls looking up at Elvis "half-listening to what he had been saying, asking myself how I could go on, knowing that the future would bring more temptations for him."

Then Presley smiled, and in his best imitation of TV comedian Flip Wilson, he quipped, "I guess the devil made me do it."

Priscilla later went into Elvis's bathroom, where she rummaged through his makeup kit. In it she found a rumpled telegram. It read, I JUST DON'T UNDERSTAND—SCOOBIE. Priscilla's face flushed red. She had heard that Scoobie was a name of endearment Ann-Margret bestowed upon those she liked. Priscilla tore up the telegram and flushed it out of her life. But getting rid of Ann-Margret would not be so easy.

The actress followed up with another message to Elvis—one she delivered through gossip columnist Sheilah Graham on February 26, 1964. Explaining to Graham that she was "a victim of circumstance," Ann-Margret declared, "Those news reports from London are simply not true. I never said we were engaged, but I did consider that we were going steady."

Then she discussed her feelings about love and marriage, and in an about-face to her image as a fiercely independent woman, she said, "I believe in love. And when I'm certain love has come, he [her husband] will dominate the household. If he doesn't want me to work, I won't. For a happy marriage, the man must be the boss."

Elvis Presley, of course, always had to be the boss.

Ironically, at about the same time that Ann-Margret was sending Elvis a desperate message, an enterprising journalist unearthed all the ingredients of what might have been Hollywood's biggest scandal in years—had the so-called mainstream press taken notice of a story that appeared in the February 1964 issue of *Photoplay*.

Nancy Anderson, the magazine's West Coast editor, wrote the article under a pseudonym—a common practice at the magazine, which wanted it to appear that a multitude of writers were contributing articles. In the piece, Anderson secured interviews with Elvis, Ann-Margret, Priscilla—whom few in Hollywood were even aware of—and even Ann Beaulieu, Priscilla's mother, in an article headlined "We Say Elvis Is Married!" In the center of the page was a photograph (which had been taken earlier, in Germany) of Priscilla plucking dandelions. Under that tableau the fan magazine breathlessly continued, "—and this is his wife."

The story that followed revealed details of the girl who had come from Germany to live behind Graceland's walls. "Even casual acquaintances knew the romance was serious, but until Priscilla herself answered a phone call from Los Angeles to Graceland, and admitted she was living in Elvis's luxurious home, nobody comprehended how serious," wrote Anderson.

She went on to relate the first of four interviews.

"Priscilla," asked Anderson, "are you married?"

Through a burst of giggles Priscilla answered, "You'll have to make up your own mind about that."

"You must be married," the journalist persisted.

"Ask Elvis. He'll tell you what he wants you to know."

Anderson thought Elvis would stonewall her, so she instead found Priscilla's mother, Ann Beaulieu. Implausibly, Mrs. Beaulieu told Anderson that she didn't know if her daughter was married to Elvis. If they were, she said, Elvis would tell her. "I don't think he'd keep it a secret from us, if he and Priscilla were married."

She sounded helpless as she sighed, "You have a teenager yourself and you know how hard it is to get information from them. I only know I have a daughter of marriageable age. But I can't tell her whom she should marry or when." Priscilla's mother did volunteer that she would be "charmed" to be Elvis's mother-in-law. "We like Elvis very much. You know, we met him in Germany and became very fond of him. I think he's a fine young man."

Beyond that, Mrs. Beaulieu would not comment, other than to say, "Priscilla likes it in Memphis, just as she likes it in most places. She feels at home everywhere."

Anderson got more straightforward answers when she talked with Ann-Margret, who allowed the magazine's photographers to shoot the enormous circular pink bed that Elvis had given her; he had had it specially manufactured for the actress. According to the photographer who snapped it, it had a canopy "and looks as though it would sleep four."

The writer shot across town to MGM, where she was admitted to the set of *Kissin' Cousins*. "I hear you're going steady," she said to Presley.

"Oh, no; not yet," he replied.

"But I heard you were going steady with Ann-Margret."

"We see each other but we're not going steady—although she's a very attractive girl. She is. Very, very, very attractive. I like her." As he spoke, said Anderson, his eyes "twinkled."

Then she ambushed him: "If you aren't going steady, why did you give her a round pink bed?"

Presley whirled toward her with a mock expression of shock on his face. "A what? Did you say a bed?" He briefly stammered, "Th-th-th-that I gave Ann-Margret a bed? I never heard of that before. Why would I want to give her a bed?"

He walked on, looking at the ground, his hand on his chin. "A bed . . ." he repeated to himself. "That sure would be an unusual gift, wouldn't it? Where did you get information like that, anyway?"

"Ann-Margret."

Presley just shook his head.

"I let him off the hook," Anderson noted in the article. "He was speechless."

Now residing back in her native Tennessee, Anderson laughed when she was asked why the story she uncovered remained virtually undiscovered by mainstream publications. "The regular press didn't pay all that much attention to the fan magazines. But the fan magazines knew what was going on." In retrospect, she offered a succinct commentary on her feelings about the teenage Priscilla's stay at Graceland. "If that had been my daughter, I'd have yanked her out of there in a second." Added Anderson, "I'm surprised Joe [Beaulieu] didn't go over there with a rifle."

Several months after the Presley–Ann-Margret relationship ended, a carload of the Memphis Mafia chanced to pull alongside Ann-Margret on Sunset Boulevard one evening. She was on a motorcycle, in full tight-fitting leather regalia. Spying them, she smiled and took off her helmet—letting her hair shake loose.

"What gives?" yelled one of the guys. "I thought you had a thing with the boss."

"I did," she replied, shaking her head and flashing a look of sadness. "What happened?"

Ann-Margret put her helmet back on and revved up her motorcyle. "Ask him," she said, flooring the Harley.

23

Animal House

To the public, it seemed that one of the most potent sex symbols of the day had been castrated, Hollywood-style. Once denounced from pulpits for destroying the moral fiber of young people, he had come to be seen as an extension of the characters he portrayed in his increasingly bland movies. Invariably he was cast as a down-on-his-luck good guy who eventually comes up a success. En route to winning a car or boat race or similarly vapid challenge, he opts for the wholesome girl over the temptress. Indeed, he was considered so "safe" that he sometimes played the *chaperon* to beautiful young women. His buddies snickered at scenes where he spurned the advances of teenage girls; they roared at his convincing delivery of the line "I don't rob cradles."

Elvis Presley had become so respectable that he was considered a fashion plate, à la those sleek dressers Frank Sinatra, William Holden, and Peter Lawford. Designer Sy Devore said Elvis was as fashionable as President John F. Kennedy, adding, "He could pass for a Wall Street banker." (There was one chief difference, Devore noted with a sigh: Presley refused to wear underwear.)

This image is the essence of the carefully executed lie Elvis was living. His image may have been tamed down, but his private life was anything but. In a town and a time renowned for skirt-chasing bad boys, Elvis and his friends were perhaps the *baddest* boys of all.

Because Elvis was never without his male companions, he and the guys generated thinly veiled suggestions of homosexuality. In 1957, the scandal magazine *On the QT* featured a story headlined, "Presley's Powder-puff Pals," about the singer's "male worshipers" and his coed "publicity romances." Accompanying the article was a photograph of the "two prominent bachelors" Presley and Liberace. The truth, however, was just the opposite. In his 1981 biography, *Elvis*, Albert Goldman called Elvis and his boys "the most intently partying group of bachelors in the history of Hollywood." As family audiences flocked to Elvis's films, he and his friends were partying nonstop. "You have to understand about that group of people. They ran a lot of babes," said Gary Lockwood, recalling his days of hanging out with Elvis and his hangers-on. Lockwood became acquainted with Presley during the making of *Wild in the Country*, but not until he costarred with him in *It Happened at the World's Fair* did Lockwood see firsthand the impact Elvis's stardom had on women.

Ensconced in the penthouse suite of Seattle's New Washington Hotel, Elvis and his friends held parties every weekend. The action got under way in the evening, when some of the boys would take the elevator down to the lobby and instruct the hotel management to open the doors—letting in the hundreds of young women who had gathered outside. "Then the guys would walk around and choose the beauties," said Lockwood. "It was as if the women were waiting to be touched by God." Some girls were more savvy than others. They entered the lobby carrying their panties in their hands, sometimes twirling them above their heads. "I'm not saying that every girl who went up there got laid. But there's no question that some of them might have to do some tall fucking at some point during the night," said Lockwood candidly.

The girl fests continued in Los Angeles behind the gates of Elvis's Bel-Air home on Perugia Way. With ankle-deep white carpeting and a central lighting system that kept the red lights low, Elvis held court nightly.

Inside the house, the central party spot was the den, with its round open-hearth fireplace with a cone-shaped steel dome that was suspended from the ceiling. There was a mahogany pool table—which Presley loved—as well as a jukebox, and a huge red, curving couch, where the host sat facing a large TV, surrounded by attentive women. The television was always on so that Elvis could watch favorite shows such as *Perry Mason* or *Combat*. Guests were usually offered Cokes and potato chips, though the more adventurous visitors learned where to find the jars filled with amyl nitrates.

Some nights at the compound were nearly surreal, with or without a drug buzz, if Scatter was among the party animals. A pet chimpanzee—who had been a costar of a children's TV show in Memphis—little Scatter was taught to drink bourbon and Scotch and to rush at the girls. The guys encouraged him to become sexually excited, and they applauded when frequent visitor Brandi Marlo rolled about the floor, pretending to have sex with the three-foot simian.

At times the partying was rampant. "We would have parties seven nights a week, with seldom less than one hundred girls in the house. It wasn't uncommon for some of us to sleep with five women in a night," said Richard Davis, who joined the Presley pack in 1962. He added, "We were all very young, and Hollywood was a bad influence on us. You gotta remember, we were country guys. And these women, well, they all looked like movie stars."

Women who were granted admission were occasionally selected from the crowds that gathered outside the estate's iron gates. But more often they were approached by Presley's associates. In Memphis, introductions were arranged by disc jockey George Klein. In Los Angeles, Joe Esposito made calls for Elvis.

Then Kitty Jones reentered Presley's life. She had met Elvis during his debut performance on the *Louisiana Hayride*, when she was fourteen to his nineteen. Their friendship continued through his Army days at Fort Hood. Then they lost touch.

In the fall of 1961 she was walking across the lot of the Samuel Goldwyn Studios when she heard a familiar voice yell, "Is that Kitty Jones?" She turned to find Presley "and about twelve of his guys, all of them walking in a line alongside each other." She hadn't realized he was there, starring as a singing prizefighter in *Kid Galahad*.

Jones, a struggling singer, was doing some casting work for a production company. She was in her office the day Joe Esposito called to ask about a pretty redhead he had seen going into her office. Could Jones see if she was available for a date with Elvis?

"That was the beginning," said Jones, who went on to set up dates for Presley until 1966. "Remember, it was hard for Elvis Presley to just pick up the phone and call women and say, 'This is Elvis, would you like to go out?' Half of them would say something like, 'Yeah, right!' and immediately hang up."

Jones herself became a regular at Elvis's houses—first on Perugia Way, then at a Mediterranean-style house he briefly rented on Bellagio Way, then back at Perugia. Elvis often sent one of his drivers to get the girls. Or Jones would pick them up, parking her 1955 Chevy alongside Presley's fleet of Cadillacs. "He used to always get on me because the car dripped oil all over the damned driveway," said Jones, laughing. She sometimes dozed on the living room couch until Elvis's date was ready for her ride home.

Not all the women who were summoned to Elvis's side slept with him. In fact, on many nights the action primarily took place around the TV set, with young women jockeying to sit alongside Elvis as he watched TV. In the midst of *Have Gun, Will Travel*, he used to jump up and mock the "pockfaced pervert" Richard Boone, who starred as the hired gun known as Paladin. "Everyone would laugh and urge him on," recalled Joni Lyman. A frequent visitor at Elvis's, Lyman stressed, "It was a place to hang out. There weren't always huge crowds. Sometimes there were just a handful of us."

Presley would sometimes expound on his favorite entertainers, such as Bobby Darin, and his least favorite, Andy Williams. He was no Robert Goulet fan, either. Lyman discovered that one night as she sat watching a variety show alongside Elvis. Overcome by "an eerie feeling," she turned to find Presley holding a .22 to her head. "I jumped—of course! And almost wet my pants. And was absolutely furious. And Elvis was saying, 'Oh, honey, c'mon back. I'm just kidding. It's only a joke.' With that, he pointed the gun at the TV screen—and the image of Goulet—and fired, blowing up the set.

"It's so obvious that the man was bored to death," said Lyman. "And of course, we empowered him. Which is probably why he did such wacky stuff."

He was certainly bored—some would say stunted—intellectually. As a result, he reached out whenever he encountered a new subject. "Oh, God, it was so apparent that he craved to learn," said Lyman. "If you started talking about something he didn't know about, he was right in your face." A singer, she once came to the house after having undergone surgery in which nodes were removed from her vocal cords. "Whatsa matter? She mad at me?" Elvis asked someone when he thought Joni was giving him the silent treatment. Once Elvis learned what she'd been through, he sat alongside her, earnestly quizzing her about the procedure. "I couldn't speak, so I wrote out my answers on this thick pad of paper," remembered Lyman.

Of course, many women did come to the house with romantic inclinations. The unwritten rule was that Elvis chose his woman first, and then the Mafia could move in. But Presley was careful not to include his fans in the wilder get-togethers. "He was pretty protective about the girls who he'd gotten to know as fans," recalled Davis. But he could also be amusingly possessive about them. When he chanced to hear some of the guys talking about putting moves on the fans, Presley once snapped, "Dammit, they're my fans! If anyone's going to fuck 'em, it's going to be me!"

Once he got a girl into his bedroom, his modus operandi for setting up the seduction was to go through his closet and pull out a pair of oversize pastel pajamas. "These should fit you," he would say. As the girl dressed, he would modestly slip into a robe.

Not just any beautiful young woman qualified to be a date for Elvis Presley. He had certain requirements—such as pretty feet. "Elvis couldn't stand ugly feet," related Jones, who often asked the young women she "screened" to wear sandals so that she could see if their feet would meet his demands. As a child, Elvis had lovingly rubbed his mother's feet—her "widdle sooties," as he called them—and even after her death, he had bewildered family members and friends by cradling the feet of her lifeless body. He was similarly drawn to the feet of some of his dates. "I would take off my nylons—these were the days before panty hose—and he would rub and cuddle my feet. Sometimes he would kiss or suck one of my toes," recalled Karen Conrad. A petite dishwater blonde who appeared in a string of small roles in movies, Conrad was recruited by Jones, who told her, "You're just his type."

Unfortunately, she ran up against another one of Elvis's oddities. Though just in her early twenties, Conrad had two small children as the result of a teenage marriage. "Whatever you do, don't tell him about them or sleep with him," cautioned Jones. For Elvis could not bear to be romantically involved with a woman who had borne children. "He used to talk about it. It had something to do with him thinking he would be having sex with his own mother," said Jones, shaking her head.

Surprisingly, Conrad managed to keep her motherhood a secret from Presley for more than three months, a period in which she saw him several nights a week. Their evenings began in the den—among the crowd of his buddies and dozens of women. Elvis usually watched TV, jumping up during commercials to interject funny lines, "like he had to be 'on' all the time," observed Conrad. After a while he would take her by the hand and softly say, "C'mon, let's get out of here." Then he would pull her into the bedroom—located just off the den.

His huge bed and low lighting accommodated their "heavy make-out sessions." But, said Conrad, "nothing more went on. We kept our clothes on." Though Presley pressured her for sex, she wouldn't relent. She was too worried about what might happen if he discovered she had kids.

When he at last learned the truth—via an anonymous letter—he flew into a rage. According to Jones, "he went nuclear" in her presence. Karen Conrad was cut off—without so much as a phone call or a letter. She got her retribution by telling about her dates with Presley in the pages of *Modern Screen,* but the story, headlined "Elvis Left Me in the Middle of the Night," diplomatically made no mention of his sexual phobia about women who had given birth.

Karen Conrad also failed to mention another Presley quirk. The phobia was inadvertently triggered one night as she boosted herself up on his bed, and he chanced to see a bit of her black lace slip beneath her black skirt. "He absolutely went crazy. He started lecturing," said Conrad. "He told me to never, *ever* wear black underclothes—he went on and on about how only 'a *bad* woman' would wear a black slip." Added Conrad, "He had definite ideas on what made a woman 'good' and 'bad.' He was so complex, so confused. I don't think he understood himself at all."

The model Southern gentleman was the side June Ellis saw during her impromptu date with Elvis Presley. Ellis, who had recently migrated from Wales, was staying at a friend's house when Kitty Jones called in hopes of lining up a date. The young woman she'd had in mind was already out, but would Ellis be interested? "I thought she was kidding," said Ellis, who was wearing curlers beneath a scarf when Jones drove up. "I told her she looked like she'd just gotten off the boat," joked Jones, who talked Ellis into doing some primping during the drive to Bel-Air.

Once Ellis saw the estate's iron fence—and milling fans—she thought the whole episode had been a gag. But the gates opened to allow them through, and in short order they were inside the front door. Elvis was in the den, looking staggeringly handsome in all black. "He was filming *Fun in Acapulco* that day and was still wearing his makeup," said Ellis. They spent the evening drinking Cokes and conversing. "And I will never forget how nice he was."

One point Elvis made clear to his dates was that they could not talk to reporters or the relationship was immediately ended. That's what had happened to Margrit Buergin, the little German typist who "told all" to the German press about her romance with GI Presley. Actress Sherry Jackson, who used to play the daughter on the Danny Thomas TV series, incurred Presley's wrath when she described her dates with him for a fan magazine.

Termination came just as swiftly for male associates who talked. In January 1964, Currie Grant, the airman who had introduced the performer to Priscilla Beaulieu, wrote an article for *Photoplay* that began with the tantalizing sentence "I am going to tell you a story about Elvis Presley that will shock you." He went on to detail how the performer had a nubile teenager stashed at his home in Memphis. "That was the end of Currie. Up to that time he used to be up at the house," said Presley's friend Lance Le Gault. "Grant said he did it because he needed the money, but it would have been easy for him to go to Elvis and tell him that he needed a few hundred. Elvis had this belief that friendship was a sacred trust. It's like, if you come in my house, don't put my business on the street."

Some of that business involved a sexual kink that didn't require a sex partner. Along with the Polaroids he snapped of Priscilla during trips back to Graceland, he was also amassing a collection of 8-mm movies. His favorites were the ones that showed two women wrestling. As with Priscilla, he preferred films in which women wore brassieres and white panties. There was also a two-way mirror inside his bedroom closet that provided a secret window on the goings-on in the room next door. The women didn't know it, but sometimes their trysts with members of the Mafia were being watched.

The moniker Memphis Mafia was established during a period in which the guys flanked their boss while dressed in matching black mohair suits and sunglasses. There were so many queries about them that Presley occasionally got defensive, stressing that the men on his payroll all had specific jobs. "One is a bookkeeper [Joe Esposito]. Another takes care of the cars [Gene Smith] . . . and so on." They helped him pack, made travel arrangements, kept him company.

He was so sensitive about his friends that one night when a date remarked that he shouldn't "make the mistake of surrounding yourself with people you can't learn from," Elvis immediately stood up and, without a word, walked away. He later related, "She never caught on, but, in so many ways I was telling her, 'I can't learn nothing from you.'" He seemed proud to point out that his friends weren't "intellectuals," explaining, "I'd rather be surrounded by people who give me a little happiness, because you only prance through this life once, Jack. You don't come back for an encore."

There was no question that they were entertaining—living proof of Elvis Presley's lifelong penchant for collecting colorful people.

Over the years the guys would come and go for various reasons. In the early sixties, the Mafia was made up of the athletic Red West (a footballer and Golden Gloves boxer), his cousin Sonny West, Elvis's cousins Billy Smith and Gene Smith, hefty Lamar Fike, Marty Lacker (a Humes football player who hooked up with Presley in 1960), good-natured Alan Fortas, handsome Richard Davis, and Army buddies Charlie Hodge and Joe Esposito.

Though they weren't "officially" Mafia, Memphis deejay George Klein, musician Lance Le Gault (Elvis's movie double and assistant choreographer), former Arkansas State University football player Jerry Schilling, and rockabilly singer Cliff Gleaves often rounded out the crowd. A virtual one-man show, Gleaves was loud, boisterous, fast-talking, and funny; Elvis used to summon him when he wanted some diversion.

The boys had all sorts of ways to have fun. In Bel-Air, mealtimes sometimes gave way to food fights. "They'd play this game. And Elvis would usually start it," recalled Gary Lockwood. "One guy would pick up a glob of mashed potatoes and smear it on the face of the guy next to him, who'd have to do the first instantaneous reaction, like throw a glass of water, on someone else. And this would continue around the table." Added Lockwood, "It was all very tribal, very male, a real pack mentality." It was, he added, "some life: mashed potatoes by day, pussy by night."

For several years Presley had his own football team. Lockwood was a quarterback in the touch football games in which blood flowed along with the profanities. Elvis was a fervent football fan who could tick off the stats of his favorite pro team, the Cleveland Browns. His own team had its origins in Germany, where he and Red West had put together games with other GIs. On Sundays at Bel-Air's De Neve Park, their games brought out celebrity players. One afternoon, Pat Boone put together a team that fell to Elvis's. Then came a team captained by Rick Nelson. Rick and his guys—who happened to be USC and UCLA players—wore T-shirts and blue jeans. Elvis's had numbered uniforms—and the name E.P. ENTP., for Elvis Presley Enterprises. Captains Nelson and Presley were both receivers in a game so rough, Nelson said, that "people were flying through the air." Nelson's team came out the victor.

Naturally, such a cluster of healthy male celebrities brought out women—in midriff blouses and tight capri pants and heavily sprayed bouffant hairdos—who formed cheerleading squads. Some girls wound up with invitations to the Presley party compound.

Not only was the public fooled about Elvis's incessant activities. The girl back home was as well. On those rare occasions that he permitted Priscilla to visit Bel-Air, he canceled the nighttime gatherings—in favor of afternoon Bible readings. Although he obviously skipped over certain parts, he was a serious student of the Bible. Kitty Jones sometimes sat through his readings, at Presley's request. "He used to try to get me to participate in the exchanges, because my father had been a preacher," she said.

Wearing tan or all white, Elvis would emotionally read to a cluster of rapt females. After sermonizing for hours, Elvis would have a follow-up question-and-answer session.

Priscilla could not help but notice that some of the women wore low-cut blouses and miniskirts. During one Bible study, a young woman, with her blouse unbuttoned almost to her waist, leaned over to Presley and asked if he felt the woman at the well who gave Christ water was a virgin. "Well, honey," Elvis said, "that's something you'll have to decide for yourself." But, he went on, "I personally think Jesus was attracted to her, but that's my opinion. I'm not sayin' it's fact." Priscilla was furious.

The man who had it all was sinking under the excess of his lifestyle. During these years he popped increasing numbers of pills. Sometimes he retreated into his room for three or four days at a time with prescription drugs. For all of these reasons he would be caught totally unaware when a revolution in popular music struck.

He was forewarned. For a time Lamar Fike left Elvis's employment to manage singer Brenda Lee. The job took him to England, where he happened to see a new group perform. Once back in America, Fike told Presley what he'd seen. "Jesus, I haven't seen anything like this since you got your start," he said. Try as he might, though, he couldn't get Elvis Presley to take him seriously about a British quartet called the Beatles.

Nowhere Man

By the time Elvis Presley turned thirty, he was the highest-paid star in Hollywood. *Daily Variety* estimated that he would earn nearly $5 million in 1965 for making three movies and their subsequent sound-track albums. Presley commanded what was then a staggering $750,000 to $1 million a movie, plus 50 percent of the profits. No one was complaining, for no Presley title had ever lost money. His eighteen movies had netted almost $150 million. As for his records, he had sold more than 100 million copies over the past decade.

"Outside of Walt Disney, Elvis is the only sure thing in this business," said Ben Schwalb, producer of Presley's eighteenth movie, *Tickle Me.*

Despite a ridiculous story line about a rodeo rider who works at a dude ranch–beauty spa, the movie would save its production company from financial ruin. It was Allied Artists' third-top-grossing film, following *55 Days at Peking* and *El Cid,* two period epics that starred Charlton Heston.

At MGM, Presley was such a major force that he occupied dressing room A, the former lair of legendary leading man Clark Gable. He even had a second dressing room, the adjoining B, so that his Mafia buddies could hover nearby. No other star, at the time, had two rooms. But no other star on the lot was like Presley. A roster of big names used to crash his sets just to take a look at him.

For all the success, there was a troubling undercurrent. Despite a cavalier claim by an MGM executive that Elvis's movies were infallible ("These are Presley pictures. They don't need titles. They could be numbered. They would still sell"), Elvis himself was nobody's fool. He realized the scripts were growing weaker, and the films' musical numbers were no better.

"I'm tired of playing a guy singing to the guy he's beating up," Elvis used to say of movies that were growing indistinguishable. Except for the settings, which ranged from Acapulco to fictional Middle Eastern countries to the racing circuit, the plots were the same, as a good-guy character got into fistfights, romanced beautiful women, and sang a series of songs before finally winning the big prize and falling in love. As their quality declined, the casts and crews went through the motions. As Sue Ane Langdon, his costar in the carnival romance *Roustabout* and the riverboat musical *Frankie and Johnny*, noted, "It wasn't a big thing to do an Elvis movie. In fact, for an actress, it was either a step down or a 'take the money and run' type thing."

Elvis's excesses began to show on-screen as well. He blanched when *Time* used his thirtieth birthday as an excuse to call him "the grand-daddy of big-time rock 'n' roll" and to note that "his second-skin jeans have been replaced by somewhat wider slacks." In its observance of Presley's watershed birthday, the *Los Angeles Times*' career appraisal was accompanied by an illustration in which he was decidedly chubby. The truth was painful. Presley had always been self-conscious about his physique. When he had costarred with the athletic-looking Ursula Andress in *Fun in Acapulco*, he confessed to his pals, "Her shoulders are broader than mine. I don't want to take my fuckin' shirt off next to her." The added pounds added to his uneasiness. "He refused to go without a shirt in some of Hal's films," remembered the producer's wife, Martha Hyer Wallis.* Whenever he went out to the beach—even on the Hawaiian islands—he was so shy about his body that he would sunbathe only in privacy, usually on the rooftop of his penthouse suite.

Being constantly reminded of his weight problems so depressed him that he ate even more. "Crumble some more bacon in that, will ya, guys?" he would say, thrusting a massive bowl of mashed potatoes toward his buddies. He also loved sauerkraut piled on mashed pota-

*In several films in which he's shown waterskiing, he does so while fully dressed!

toes and gravy, corn bread with sweet onions, a plate of hard-fried eggs, and anything else that packed on the pounds.

"If you balloon, the girls won't want to pin you up anymore. And they won't be buyin' tickets," the Colonel used to lecture, ignoring his own pendulous gut. During recording sessions Presley could sometimes overhear his aides fending off calls from Parker, who wanted to know what his boy had eaten for dinner the night before. When a friend of the Colonel's or Hal Wallis's would stop by the film set to exchange greetings and give him a friendly hug, Elvis was sure that they were attempting to get a feel of his midriff. "Those motherfuckers are checking for fat! They're gonna tell the Colonel," he exclaimed.

As so many other stars at MGM had done, he defensively reached for diet pills. The studio that once prided itself on having "more stars than there are in heaven" also had a history as an amphetamine heaven. The lives and careers of Mickey Rooney (who survived) and Judy Garland (who didn't), among others, were a testament to a studio that treated its talent like race horses.

Yet Elvis's age wasn't measured only in pounds. A younger generation, the sixties generation, was fomenting a cultural upheaval that would shake all that had come before. Kids too young to know Elvis were eagerly embracing rock 'n' roll's new wave of stars.

When the Beatles arrived on American soil on February 7, 1964, they had already sold 2 million copies of "I Want to Hold Your Hand." By August of that year, John, Paul, George, and Ringo had earned more than $10 million. The numbers kept growing; by early 1965 the British group had sold an estimated 19 million singles, and a similar number of albums, in the United States alone.

Not just the Fab Four were shaking up the musical status quo. Everywhere Elvis turned there were younger musicians: the Rolling Stones, the Animals, the Kinks, the Zombies. Presley was threatened by the British invasion. "Look at that motherfucker! Doesn't he look like a faggot?" he would rail as Mick Jagger pranced across the TV screen.

Colonel Tom Parker decided to meet the threat head-on. When the Beatles made their American television debut, Parker composed a congratulatory telegram and signed Presley's name to it. As Sullivan read Elvis's warm words on the air, the quartet proudly grinned. Parker also boosted Presley's status by revealing to the press something that had heretofore been private: the performer's generous charitable donations. From the earliest days of his fame, Presley had felt a duty to give to those who were without, whether they were kinfolk or charitable organizations.

Elvis did not feel charitable toward the upstarts, though. At some of his Sunday football games, cars would cruise by and girls would gloatingly chant, "We love you, Beatles, oh, yes, we do . . ."—a mimic of the chants for a teen idol in the movie *Bye Bye Birdie*. Presley acted as if he didn't hear them. But once behind his gated Bel-Air home, he would yell to his aides, "I don't want to hear any more about those guys!" as they sought to deliver the latest Beatles update.

Not since Elvis Presley himself had there been such a musical phenomenon. But unlike the early Elvis, with his opened-to-the-waist shirts and striptease style, the English group kept their shirts buttoned and their body motions in check. Mop tops aside, they were considered clean-cut. Whereas Elvis had taunted, they teased. They were flip, they were funny, and unlike Elvis—who'd always hid any habits he thought might offend—they flaunted theirs, openly smoking, drinking, and gleefully chasing "birds."

They also announced that they wanted to meet one of their idols.

"Hell, I don't want to meet those fucking sons of bitches," Elvis said when the Colonel first told him that the four Liverpudlians had requested to meet him.

Undaunted, the Colonel sent the Brits gifts from Presley—cowboy suits, complete with ten-gallon hats. Explaining that Presley was too busy to meet, Parker told their manager, Brian Epstein, "Let's try it another time."

The politicking between the Colonel and Epstein continued. Finally, Elvis conceded: "But I'll only do it if those guys come here. I'm not goin' to their place."

The meeting between the two pivotal forces of modern pop music took place on the night of August 27, 1965. As the Beatles entered the house on Perugia Way, the first thing they heard were their own voices; Presley was playing their records. Ushered into the den, the foursome— who ranged in age from twenty-two to twenty-five—were greeted by the thirty-year-old Presley. As the Colonel proudly made introductions, Elvis looked cool and remote in tight gray pants, a red shirt, and black windbreaker. The Beatles were literally at a loss for words.

The silence continued after they'd all taken seats on the sprawling couch, with John Lennon and Paul McCartney on Elvis's right and George Harrison and Ringo Starr on the left.

Clearing his throat, Elvis at last spoke. "If you damn guys are gonna sit here and stare at me all night, I'm gonna go to bed." As the Beatles began to protest, he added, "I just thought maybe we'd sit and talk . . . maybe play a little, jam a little." Their response, in unison, was "God! Yes!"

"We were all in such awe that when Elvis and the guys started to play, no one even thought of taping the session," moaned Richard Davis, one of the Mafia on hand for the encounter. Like the December 1956 Sun Records gathering of Elvis, Carl Perkins, Johnny Cash, and Jerry Lee Lewis, the impromptu session was lost to posterity. Those who were there said that Presley handed out guitars, and they played some of his songs, some of theirs, and some Chuck Berry. At one point, as Elvis played bass on the Beatles's "I Feel Fine," Paul—who usually did those honors—quipped, "You're coming along quite promising there."

They talked music, too. Elvis wanted to know about their song-writing. They wanted to know how he dealt with the frightening crowds. "If you can't take the crowds, you're in the wrong business," declared Presley.

Then John Lennon leaned over and asked, "Why don't you go back to your old style of record?"

Presley was silent for a few seconds, then talked of his busy film schedule. He was in the midst of making *Paradise, Hawaiian Style*. But, he stressed, "I really do plan to get back into the recording studio to do something interesting."

"The casino is open for business!" The declaration came from Colonel Parker. Presley's coffee table opened up to become a gaming table. "I'm the pit boss," said the Colonel, smiling through yellowed teeth. Brian Epstein was elated; he'd always wanted to meet the Colonel, and now he was playing roulette with him. The Colonel, an inveterate gambler, wound up taking Epstein for several thousand.

The Beatles left at two in the morning, but not before the Colonel gave each a souvenir—small, light-up covered wagons, the kind that adorned his letterhead. As they climbed into their waiting car, covered wagons in hand, Paul turned to Elvis: "We've got this house up on Mulholland Drive. We'd like to invite you all to come up tomorrow." Elvis said nothing. Turning to the Mafia, McCartney politely added, "If he can't come, you guys are still welcome."

Elvis had too much pride to join them, but some of his buddies went over to Mulholland, where John Lennon said, "Last night was the greatest night of my life."

* * *

Elvis was not to be as hidebound toward other developments of the sixties. As the Age of Aquarius dawned, with its use of psychedelics and spiritual awareness, Elvis found that the times suited him just fine. He was ready to join in on a journey to "self-realization."

From his childhood in Tupelo—sitting in the open-air meetings of the fundamentalist Assembly of God church—to his final soul-searching years, he was influenced by the Bible and its teachings. Becky Martin, a childhood friend who was in touch with him throughout the seventies, said he used to reiterate, "Becky, just think what I could have done if I had become a preacher! Just think of the good I could have done if I'd lived my life spreading the word of the Lord."

When he was a teenager in Memphis, he had aspired to be a gospel singer. A few years later, in the midfifties, he was invited to join the Songfellows, influenced by the popular Blackwood Brothers gospel group. But by this time he had a sense that his career was beginning to take off; with some reluctance he turned down the offer.

He continued to revere religious music and perform it without prompting or embarrassment. Following a party at Sam Phillips's house, Elvis once ushered in Easter Sunday when he casually picked up his guitar and, as the sun rose, sang "Take My Hand, Precious Lord." From their lawn chairs around the swimming pool, the partygoers listened, moved, as his voice resonated through the quiet morning. On Ed Sullivan's show, the banned-from-the-waist-down singer had delivered a soulful rendition of "Peace in the Valley."

He recorded religious music when no other rock-'n'-roll stars would have so dared. Even as the Beatles were dominating the charts, Presley's presence was felt with "Crying in the Chapel." In the seventies, he dared to take religious music into the showroom of Las Vegas' International Hotel—despite protests from the management.

A true believer, Presley was also a searcher—as Larry Geller would discover.

The twenty-four-year-old Geller was a hairstylist with the Jay Sebring Beverly Hills Salon when he was asked to call on Presley at his Bel-Air home. Another musician had recommended Geller, who leapt at the opportunity to cut the hair of his onetime teenage idol. Their initial exchange took place as Geller trimmed Presley's baby-fine hair. As the hair fell to the floor, Presley said, "Don't worry about it. The maid will get it."

No, Geller said, he would clean it up. "We all have responsibilities. We shouldn't shirk them."

Presley looked quizzical. "It's part of my belief," said Geller, who went on to explain, "In yoga, the great masters say the means and the ends are the same. It's the way you run your life that counts. Picking up after yourself is a way of life."

As Geller continued talking, he mentioned finding purpose in life. The unique bond between Elvis Presley and the man who would come to be known as his spiritual mentor was forged that very day. Through Geller, Elvis became a follower of the late Yogi Paramahansa Yogananda, founder of the Self-Realization Fellowship.

Elvis began to speak of "higher planes" and mysticism and spiritualism. He delved into books on palmistry, parapsychology, the occult, and more. He'd always been intrigued with the life of Jesus; now he also traced the lives and teachings of Buddha, Muhammad, and others. According to Larry Geller, Elvis also wondered if he himself hadn't somehow been sent to earth as a messenger of God.

In his memoirs, Alan Fortas said, "We never really knew whether he was kidding or not." Along with calling himself a "divine messenger," Presley would grin as he sang, "What a friend we have in Elvis . . ."

Deborah Walley found more than a friend when she costarred with Presley in the 1966 movie *Spinout*. "I tell people quite honestly that Elvis changed my life. He was a pivotal point in my life," said Walley. The petite redhead had played the title role in *Gidget Goes Hawaiian* and had appeared in *Beach Blanket Bingo* when she found herself on the MGM lot working with Presley (in yet another race-car picture). The two "connected" upon first meeting and went on to have a platonic relationship on what Walley called "a deep soul level." In Walley, Presley found an eager pupil; with her, he assumed the role of spiritual teacher.

"He gave me books on the masters of the Far East, books on ancient Egypt, things about the initiation of the priestesses," said Walley. Inseparable during filming—and for some time afterward—Presley used to pick her up in the morning in his Rolls, then take her to the Self-Realization Center in Santa Monica where she was introduced to the teachings of Yogi Paramahansa Yogananda.

"He saw me as being very open—and I was. I had been raised a Catholic and I had a lot of questions about the dogma of Catholicism. He said he wanted to teach me everything he knew, within a short period of time." The reason: "He told me he wasn't going to be able to stay on earth very long, but that he would always be with me on another plane."

Their metaphysical odyssey, Walley acknowledged, "had a kind of twilight-zone ring to it." At times, Presley would look up at the clouds and claim that he was making them move. "At the time, it seemed he did," said Walley, smiling.

Presley's attempts to understand the mysteries of life and death led to some odd adventures, including late-night visits to the Memphis morgue. Using his celebrity status to gain entry, he would wander the rooms, intently studying the bodies atop the stainless steel tables. If a body was that of a tiny child, he would openly weep.

Also in the spirit of the times Presley embarked on the ultimate sixties trip. Armed with a Timothy Leary–authored primer on LSD, he dropped acid. "It wasn't to get high, but to attain greater self-knowledge and enlightenment," stressed Joe Esposito.

The first trip took place in Elvis's upstairs office at Graceland. On hand were Elvis, Geller, Lamar Fike, Jerry Schilling, and Priscilla. She and Elvis split a tab. "At first nothing happened," said Priscilla. Then her senses became more acute. "I became engrossed in Elvis's multicolored shirt. It started to grow."

The group wound up oohing and aahing over the tropical fish in the aquarium, which metamorphosed into a sea of fish. Venturing outside, they wandered the yard, examining the vibrant colors and marveling over the shapes and sizes of the greenery. Lamar Fike tried to dive into the hood of a black '64 Cadillac limousine because "I thought it was a swimming pool." Priscilla wandered off and curled up in one of the closets. When Elvis found her, she began screaming, "You don't love me! You've never loved me!"

There would be further acid trips in Bel-Air and Palm Springs, and Elvis would go on to occasionally smoke marijuana and to snort cocaine. Yet the illegal drugs were only flirtations. Throughout this period his use of prescription medication would continue steadily.

The performer's drug use had begun during his early years on the road, when he dipped into his mother's supply of diet pills, but by the sixties he had educated himself to the powers, effects, and even the dangers of prescription drugs. "They are okay," he would say, "because they are prescribed by a doctor." But Elvis was lying—to his friends and to himself.

He was a connoisseur of opiates, of Dexedrine and Benzedrine, and of powerful sleeping pills such as Seconal, Demerol, and Dilaudid. As early as 1962, when he was filming *Girls! Girls! Girls!* in Hawaii, Presley had an attaché case that he shared with other cast and crew members. It was, recalled a costar, "a potpourri of drugs," filled with "old yellers, speed, and God knows what else."

Like a devotee of fine wine, Elvis had favorite blends—to create the perfect "high." The painkiller Percodan led the list. Inducing a pleasant fog, it was used during the bloody, bruising roller-rink games in Memphis and during the rugged football games in Bel-Air.

In the 1970s, a Drug Enforcement Administration report revealed that Elvis had "dozens" of sources for these dangerous painkillers and sleeping pills. When he couldn't get drugs through his sources, he poured on the charm in pharmacies, emergency rooms, and the like. He was, after all, Elvis Presley.

One night when he and his buddies were cruising in Memphis, he suddenly had a craving for Percodan—though he had plenty of other pill bottles in a small black leather case. The drugstores were closed, so they drove for more than an hour until they spotted a suburban pharmacy that still had some lights on. From outside the locked doors Presley and his friends could see a lone pharmacist in the back.

They knocked and yelled, and the pharmacist came to the front and spied Elvis Presley. Opening the door for Memphis's favorite son, he was told that the entertainer was about to go on tour and needed some items. Presley and the Mafia were admitted inside, where Elvis roamed the aisles, picking up ointments, gauze bandages, aspirin, and the like. Then, as the druggist began ringing them up, Elvis reached for the back of his neck. "Oh, God . . . my headache is coming back." The pharmacist nodded blankly.

Presley continued, "Sir, my doctor is out in California. Do you think you could give me a couple of pain pills so I can last until tomorrow?" The druggist frowned, but then produced four Tylenol with codeine, which he tucked into a small white envelope. Presley juggled it in his hands before saying, "Sir, the only thing that will help me is Percodan."

"Ummm. I don't know. This is illegal," said the druggist.

"No, sir!" exclaimed Elvis. "No, sir. I'll have a prescription out here first thing in the morning." Agreeing, the druggist counted out four tablets. "Could you make it twelve?" asked Elvis. "I have to start work in the morning on a new picture." Out came eight more tablets. And

Presley and his boys went out into the night, after a hearty "Thank you, sir!"

"He was just a master at it, even feigning illnesses," said Lamar Fike. "He usually got what he wanted."

He sometimes resorted to extreme measures. Marty Lacker recalled Presley mutilating himself to get drugs. He sometimes jabbed his foot, once creating a hole "the size of a quarter" in his big toe. Then he would head for medical treatment, complaining of an ingrown toenail. On one occasion when Elvis removed his sock, Lacker was so shocked by the oozing blood and pus that he yelled, "God Almighty!"

Elvis replied, "Bet I get some good stuff now."

His friends got a kick out of his claim, to reporters, that he collected medical books because "I always wanted to be a doctor." The *Saturday Evening Post* never questioned this quote from the former truck driver who barely got out of high school.

Further measure of both Presley's skill as an actor, and his caginess, is that many of his movie colleagues had no idea of the seriousness of his drug dependency. "I never saw any narcotics around him, or any indication," said Lance Le Gault.

Actress Mary Ann Mobley—Miss America of 1959—who worked with Presley in 1964 on *Girl Happy*, and again the following year, on *Harum Scarum*, was a former Miss Mississippi and shared Southern roots with the star. "I think that gave us a closeness," said Mobley, who remained in touch with Presley over the years. She had no idea about the drugs at the time, but she sensed a double life. He used to kid her about his parties, saying that someday he'd throw one that she could be invited to. In retrospect, she feels Elvis lacked the sophistication needed to handle the demands of show business. "You must understand that no one really cared about him, except to keep him working," she said. "And you have to understand that he knew he wasn't being taken seriously. That's too bad, because he sure had the magic."

Actor Tony Curtis, who was at Paramount making a comedy at the same time Presley was there doing *Paradise, Hawaiian Style*, theorized that "by downplaying his talents," Hollywood hurt Presley. "Elvis made it look too easy. He was so artful it was artless."

The two men met one day as Curtis was passing Elvis's dressing trailer. "As I walked by, the door opened and an arm reached out, grabbed me, and started pulling me." It was Presley, who intoned, "Come on in, sir!" Curtis had no choice.

Once inside the trailer, he was told, "Mr. Curtis, I've admired you for a long, long time." Elvis went on to recount how he had even styled his look after Tony's. "We kept talking, and he kept calling me Mr. Curtis," recalled the actor. "Finally, I said, 'Don't call me Mr. Curtis. Call me Tony.'"

"Okay, Tony."

"So what do I call you?" Curtis continued.

Elvis grinned and shot back, "You can call me Mr. Presley."

"Wasn't he funny? Wasn't he fast?" said Curtis, adding, "He was talented, but he was also bored. And so he let his fame overwhelm him. It made everything available to him. Sadly."

As the decade continued, Elvis's dissolute lifestyle off the screen began to make its presence felt on the set. When Elvis showed up on the set of *Easy Come, Easy Go* in September 1966, the filmmakers were so alarmed by his weight gain that heated discussions, and a flurry of memos, ensued between Hal Wallis, Colonel Parker, and Paramount Pictures executives.

John Rich, who had directed Elvis two years earlier, in *Roustabout*, was appalled by how fat he was. Pointing out that Presley was to portray a Navy frogman who moonlights as a singer at a go-go club, Rich said, "The clothes keep getting tighter and tighter, and our hero fatter and fatter."

Paramount executive Paul Nathan jumped into the fray, stressing, "Navy men aren't supposed to be fat."

Hal Wallis told the Colonel to talk to Elvis about his weight. Wallis also thought that Presley's hair was beginning to look ridiculous, especially the way he was wearing it, "fluffed up, in some kind of pompadour." Said Wallis, "It's beginning to look like a wig."

During the making of *Easy Come, Easy Go*, Presley had one of his few on-set tantrums. When John Rich got tired of all the joking around between Presley and some of the Mafia, he chided the star and attempted to throw some of his friends off the set. Presley erupted, saying, "Now, listen just a minute. We're doing these movies because it's supposed to be fun, nothing more. Now, when they cease to be fun, then we'll cease to do them." The Mafia members later gloated that they didn't get thrown off the set.

What they didn't know was that at this period Hal Wallis was taking a longer view of his star. The box office receipts for Elvis's last picture, *Frankie and Johnny*, were not encouraging. Said a production executive, "It's dying all over the country."

Easy Come, Easy Go was the final film Elvis would make with Wallis, who chose not to renew his contract. The former rock-'n'-roll firebrand didn't know it, but his movie career would soon come to an end.

25

Don't Fence Me In

Shortly after the middle sixties, Elvis began returning from the wild life of Bel-Air with an apparent, palpable yen for the girl back home. His Harley again sped through predawn Memphis; there were shopping trips to see jewelers, and Elvis and Priscilla sat apart from the crowd in their special midnight movie marathons. His acts led some of his Mafia pals to surmise that the boss "had finally come to his senses" about his girlfriend. Others crassly believed that the hard-edged starlets of Hollywood had worn thin, and he was at last giving his "stored goods"—as several of the guys called Priscilla—her chance, possibly even at marriage.

Actually, there were many reasons—economic, artistic, emotional, romantic—for Elvis's return to Graceland and Priscilla. For starters, he was no longer enamored with making movies; and except for bland movie sound tracks, there was nothing to entice him back into the recording studio. Memphis provided escape.

The Colonel's urgings to "settle your ass down," combined with the Colonel's deals—which had made Presley one of the highest-paid entertainers—also led to his return home, where he indulged his fantasy to play another of his ever-changing roles, land baron.

Playacting had always permeated his existence and had even

determined the course of his life—for instance, his determination to become Elvis Presley. Full trappings were usually procured, such as the football helmet, shoulder pads, and jersey he donned to watch football games on Monday nights and on weekends.

As a youngster he had proudly posed in full cowpoke regalia for a photographer at the Mississippi-Alabama Fair. At Humes High he had loved wearing his ROTC uniform. In Germany he became a model, immaculately dressed soldier.

Secretary Becky Yancey recalled that he even brought his outlandish costumes back from Hollywood. "He would walk around Graceland in whatever costumes he was wearing in his movies," she said. During the production of *Harum Scarum*, about a movie star caught up in Middle Eastern intrigue, he strutted around the house in flowing pants and shirt—and a turban, which he insisted on wearing during mealtime.

Late one night in the early sixties, reporter Neal Gregory chanced to be at Baptist Memorial Hospital when Presley brought in a young cousin with a minor injury. "And I'll never forget it, because Elvis was in tight black pants, a bright red shirt opened to the waist, and a yachting cap. You've got to remember, this was Memphis. You didn't walk around with your shirt opened, and you sure didn't wear yachting caps." On into the seventies, he would collect badges and guns and police uniforms, which he used infrequently to play "cop" on the highway—sometimes pulling over understandably startled speeders.

He once showed up at a karate studio wearing the traditional karate *gi*—with a turban, claiming the turban was a necessity since he hadn't washed his hair.

"He just done it all big," recalled his aunt Delta Nash.

It shouldn't have surprised Priscilla, then, when he introduced her to his brief era as the "gentleman rancher."

One morning at dawn—not his favorite hour to be up and about—he crept into Priscilla's bedroom, awakened her, and led her down the back stairs of Graceland. "There, waiting, I saw a beautiful black quarter horse with one white stocking," she said. "I ran up and grabbed him: 'And you must be Domino,' I said as he nuzzled me."

Several days later a beautiful palomino appeared for Elvis. "Now, let's ride," he said, mounting the quarter horse, which he named Rising Sun. "Let's ride out, where we are the only two people in the meadow."

The idyll was soon ended when Elvis's sheer, fun-loving irrepressibility led to his purchase of more than a dozen other horses for the

Mafia and their wives, whom he then herded down to Whitehaven's most versatile Western store, where they were outfitted in the latest in dude wear. Presley went wild in grabbing up outfits. He even bought several sets of real ranch clothes for the weekdays.

Each day, with Elvis and Priscilla at the head, the Graceland contingent would gallop around the grounds in their rodeo costumes, often to the delight of the fans who daily gathered at the gates. Always "on," Presley loved to stage races with his friends—in view of his appreciative audience.

Not surprisingly, said Priscilla, "it was a constant search to be alone. There was a group we traveled with, the guys he trusted. That was our security. We didn't go outside those boundaries. We didn't make friends outside. It was a bubble we lived in."

Within that bubble she was seldom able to have his undivided attention. "Elvis was very complicated, very moody. . . . I went along with his whims. I wasn't there to nag. I don't think I would have lasted otherwise."

One of those whims was triggered during a weekend afternoon drive. She and Elvis were with Alan Fortas, driving out past Horn Lake, Mississippi—just across the state line—when they caught sight of an antebellum plantation house surrounded by 160 acres of velvet green hills and a lake with a bridge. Oddly, there was also a twenty-foot-high concrete cross, which caught the thin afternoon light. A few head of cattle grazed in its shadow.

"Elvis, look at this, it's beautiful," said Priscilla.

Presley stopped the car and gazed out over the land. She was enchanted. "Elvis, look at the beautiful old house. It's my dream house."

Elvis shielded his eyes for a better view. His eyes lingered on the cross—to him, "a good omen." He turned and said decisively, "I'm buying it, Priscilla . . . for us. We have no peace left, and this will be ours. I don't care how much it costs."

She moved closer to him as they drove back to Graceland through the growing snowstorm. "A few more seconds and we wouldn't have even seen it," Elvis murmured.

The bad news came in the morning. Yes, the hundred-year-old ranch was for sale, along with its 150 rare Santa Gertrudis cattle. But the asking price was a half million dollars. "No," thundered Vernon from his office. "No. No. No. The well is drying up."

"Daddy, at least come look at it. Then say no," Elvis pleaded.

It took some convincing, but as was his habit, Elvis got what he wanted. The papers were signed within seventy-two hours, and Priscilla and Elvis moved enough stuff to get them through a few days. They christened the ranch the Circle G, for Graceland.

The first morning, Elvis put on his rancher's coat with the sheepskin lining, his high boots, and began pacing the boundary of the ranch. That took him until lunch. Then he sat in front of a roaring fire—with Priscilla's domesticity for company.

"My picture was of us alone, without the entourage," Priscilla recalled. She dreamed of caring for Elvis on her own—cooking his meals, washing his clothes, going off with him for early-morning rides. It was a sweet, naive, wifely fantasy—but hardly realistic, given Presley's complexities and his enormous stature.

As the sun started to slip, Elvis looked up at the clock. He'd been in his bucolic hideaway for nine hours, and he was already bored.

As Priscilla watched, he picked up the phone and dialed his favorite Ford and Chevy agencies, placing rush orders on six deluxe Ford Rancheros and eight Deluxe Chevy El Caminos, demanding twenty-four-hour delivery. "I need 'em by tomorrow," he said. "I don't care where you have to get them." Salesmen worked the phones into the night; some dealers drove the trucks in themselves from as far away as Little Rock.

Eventually Presley bought more than twenty-five trucks. "Everybody got one, whether they wanted one or not," recalled Alan Fortas. That included some of the carpenters and electricians Presley hired. He would say, "This is a ranch! You gotta have a pickup!"

A very concerned Vernon, who had to co-sign the Presley Enterprises checks, was rushed from one dealership to another.

At two o'clock one morning Marty Lacker, then chief of staff, and the others exchanged anxious glances as they watched Elvis riding atop a tractor, to clear mud and snow. Then Vernon came out of the ranch's small office and held up a long adding-machine tape, which he illuminated with a flashlight. "Look at this!" said Vernon. "My son has spent ninety-eight thousand dollars on trucks. Look at this!" Presley went on to purchase a road grader, tractors, and fencing equipment. Vernon helplessly added, "I can't stop him."

Priscilla's romantic dream was over.

Elvis and his friends roamed the ranch, checking every loose fence post. Lamar gingerly balanced on his horse while taking copious notes. When their boss at last freed them to go home, it was well after dark.

But Elvis wasn't happy to see his pals ride off. "This just won't do, Lamar. I can't have y'all leaving just when it's getting to be fun. We've gotta have the ranch meals, plan for the next day. Why don't we pour foundations and give you all houses right up here—our own little commune?" Lamar Fike rolled his eyes.

When Vernon learned of the plan, he added up the cost of building the houses and informed Elvis that the cost of the Mafia compound would run about $5 million. "Impossible!" said Vernon. Elvis was willing to compromise: "Okay, Daddy, we'll just get every one of them trailers instead—the best we can find. And Priscilla and I will live in the main house."

Vernon groaned, "But, Elvis, you'll have to install concrete foundations, plumbing, and utilities."

"I know that, Daddy. That's why I expect you to have the contractors out there tomorrow." And they were—with bulldozers, jackhammers, and all. Soon there was a village of trailers.

Alan Fortas—a dog lover who had also taken care of Scatter the chimp—was designated the Circle G foreman, though he knew nothing about livestock or ranching. For him, Elvis picked out the most deluxe two-bedroom trailer on the market: plush carpeting, Danish-modern couches, beds with down comforters, and a full Formica kitchen.

"I gotta have the trailers in twenty-four hours," Elvis told the dealer. "You'll have your check [for more than $150,000] today."

The salesman stammered, "But, Mr. Presley, that's impossible." He had to make arrangements for wheeling in mobile homes across the country roads.

"Well, truck them in," said Elvis. "Forty-eight hours, tops."

Two days later, Priscilla awakened to the roar of semis and mobile homes pulling up to the house. (In time, there would be more than a dozen trailers.)

Later on, she warmed a little as Elvis showed off Al Fortas's trailer, with its gleaming Formica, modish carpets, and earth-tone interior. "Hey, I love this," Priscilla said, testing the Danish couches, bounding on the beds, and thinking, "With Elvis and me in here—this is closeness." Elvis himself was fascinated with the seemingly indestructible, pearly-hued cabinets and Formica counter, which he tapped and approvingly said, "Say, this is pretty neat."

Almost in unison, Elvis and Priscilla—of Graceland Manor—decided, "Let's move in here." That day they collected their ranch wardrobes and moved into the trailer.

"I was just as content as I could be," Priscilla remembered with fondness years later. "I was proud as a peacock, cleaning the Formica and the carpeting, and preparing ranch-style meals, because we were together, and show business couldn't break through."

Joe Esposito believes that Presley's preference for the trailer illustrates one of his most charming traits: he liked what he liked regardless of cost. "It didn't matter if one thing cost a million dollars and another cost a dime. If he liked it, he would pick the one that cost a dime. If people hinted that his taste was tacky, he would say, 'What the hell do I care?' "

Elvis's enthusiasm for his new life was boundless. He would roust out his wranglers at dawn. "I'll never forget it," Lamar remembered. "At six A.M., when Mississippi was still freezing its ass off, Elvis hammered on the door. I opened it in my T-shirt and underwear to confront him fully decked out as Bobby Ewing out to take on the great spread of *Dallas*. Lots of times we would just ride around in the snow. It was cold as hell, boring as hell. And Elvis carried a large green garbage bag around with him hooked to the saddle horn."

The first time the Memphis Mafia were baffled by the trash bag. After an hour had elapsed, though, Elvis stopped Rising Sun, reached into the garbage bag, and pulled out a hot dog bun. He ate buns out of that vittles bag all morning.

His frenetic energy went in all directions. One time Elvis hopped on one of the road graders and began to carve a network of roads through the unspoiled hills. "Get out here," he screamed at the others. "We got a lot of work to do in a short time." The guys rushed out, partially clothed, to discover a fur-coated, feather-hatted Presley furiously plowing the snow, trying to reach the frozen earth. Soon every machine on the spread was humming as the city boys plowed up the soil.

At least part of his activity was fueled by the pills he was taking, and at this juncture a key newcomer entered his life. One afternoon, after Presley had done too much riding, he came in calling for a doctor. His regular physician was out of town, so George Klein arranged for Elvis to be seen by his own doctor, Memphis's highly regarded Dr. George Nichopoulos.

After driving the thirty miles out to the Circle G, Nichopoulos found the entertainer awaiting him on the steps of his trailer. Elvis Presley had saddle sores on his rear end. "I got injured something awful, Dr. Nichopoulos. Been ridin' too much."

"We went into his trailer home and we talked a few minutes," said

Dr. Nichopoulos. "Then I looked at his sores. He didn't want to start his latest picture, and he was supposed to leave soon for California. So I was just a means of telling the Colonel he couldn't start the movie, and getting him off the hook."

He wound up giving Elvis some salve for his blistered bottom. When the doctor was through, Presley asked if he'd stop off at Graceland during his drive back to the city to check on Minnie Mae. She'd had a cold and was having some difficulty breathing.

Nichopoulos was at Graceland, completing his examination of Minnie Mae, when he got a call from Presley: "Could you come back out here? There's something else I need you to look at."

Nichopoulos, with his easygoing manner, got back in his car and headed toward Mississippi—again. Back at the Circle G, he discovered that Elvis wanted to talk. "We chatted for about fifteen or twenty minutes, then I drove back to Memphis."

Back in Memphis, he got yet another call from Elvis. "Dr. Nick," he said plaintively, using a nickname that would last to this day, "I need you back here." So Dr. George Nichopoulos went back to Circle G for the third time in a single day. Once again, the lonely Elvis Presley just wanted to talk.

Dr. George Nichopoulos would go on to discover that Elvis Presley suffered from much more than loneliness.

Visitors to the ranch used to comment about how terrific Presley looked at this time. Tanned bronze, he allowed his hair to grow out to its dark blond color—now joined by striking silver streaks. In his Western getup he was the picture of contented masculinity.

Yet he had become so hooked on pills that his efforts to get medication were sometimes as comical as they were desperate. Marty Lacker was sent to Las Vegas three times in two days—to get prescriptions, written by Dr. Max Shapiro, filled at the local pharmacies. The third time he worried about airport security "because we had pockets full of pills, and a whole briefcaseful." After delivering the stash to Presley, Lacker said, "I'm going home. Don't call me again."

Several hours later Elvis was beating at Lacker's front door. "No! I'm not opening the door," hollered Lacker. When Presley threatened to break the door down, Lacker wearily gave in. He opened the door wearing only his underwear and a pair of bedroom slippers.

Dangling a set of keys in his hand, Elvis said, "Come on out. Got something to show you." Venturing out into the frosty morning, the near-naked Lacker was presented with a Ford Ranchero. It turned out to be the one Presley had originally bought Priscilla.

Sometimes, he got so loaded, he gave away other people's gifts.

Then there was the Sunday he discovered he was out of pills. So he and his pals drove over to the local Walgreens—which was closed for the day. Undaunted, Presley suggested they check the phone directory for the pharmacist's address. After all, said Elvis, "he's like a doctor. He's probably got all kinds of shit at his house." So they pulled over to a phone booth and found the address, then headed over.

When the pharmacist opened his door, he was taken aback to find Elvis Presley—in cowboy hat, sheepskin coat, and boots—on his front porch. "Could we talk to you for a few minutes?" asked Elvis, who walked right in, with his embarrassed friends, and sat down at the man's kitchen table. Elvis went on to relate a series of aches and pains, and to detail the drugs that would abate them: Tuinals, Desbutal, Placidyls, Escatrol, and more.

When the pharmacist got up to check his medicine cabinet, Elvis brazenly followed him—the better to pick and choose himself. Though the pharmacist protested as Elvis reached for bottle after bottle, the performer told him, "If you don't tell, we won't tell." As Presley and his pals exited, he promised the pharmacist he would be sure to get a prescription for all the drugs he'd been given that day.

Some days Presley was so zonked out that he would nearly topple from the tractor. If the pills took effect while he was riding, he would loosen up on the reins, allowing Rising Sun to dictate the trail. The guys used to find Elvis half-asleep, leaning from the saddle. To hear Billy Smith tell it, he outdid Lee Marvin's portrayal of the drunken gunfighter—who's always hanging from his horse—in *Cat Ballou*.

Sadly, as drugs were taking a greater hold of Elvis Presley's life, his father's primary concern involved money—specifically, the cash flow necessary to run Graceland and Elvis's mounting spending sprees. Vernon didn't understand the full extent of his son's drug involvement, or the toll it was taking. Only after Elvis's death would his father come to realize how much his son had needed help.

The short-term solution was as simple as it was hard on Elvis, and particularly Priscilla. Incited by Vernon, Parker jerked Elvis back to Hollywood for another punishing schedule of films and recording dates.

But Priscilla didn't pack her cowboy gear quietly. She made some firm decisions of her own.

The Groom
Wore Black

The official version of the May 1, 1967, wedding of Elvis Aaron Presley and Priscilla Beaulieu reads like a lovely fairy tale, involving a proposal on bended knee, Learjets taking off into the starry night, a lavish six-tier cake, and a beautiful bride who shyly clung to her handsome bridegroom before a roomful of teary-eyed guests.

In this account, the proposal was made on Christmas Eve, 1966, at Graceland mansion, a-glitter with a million lights and perfumed with pine boughs from the Ozarks. Priscilla was ready for bed in a new silk robe, her tower of hair tied with a velvet ribbon, when Elvis slipped in through their bedroom door. She was fighting back drowsiness as he said, "Cilla, it's Fire Eyes [her nickname for him], and I have something very special for you.

"Look at me," he commanded.

She sat up, pulling her satin comforter around her. Elvis was on his knees before her, a small black box in his hand. "Elvis, what have you done?" she asked as she reached for the box. Inside was a three-and-a-half-carat engagement ring, surrounded by a row of smaller diamonds, and a separate ring of Brussels-cut diamonds.

Gathering her in his arms, Elvis said sweetly, "Her is going to be his." Then he cleared his throat. "Will you marry me?"

As Priscilla recorded in her 1985 autobiography *Elvis and Me,* her lover of eight years had finally fulfilled his promise. "Suddenly I could see it all disappear. The heartaches and fears of losing him to one of the many girls auditioning for my role. I put my foot in the glass slipper, and it fit just fine."

In Priscilla's account—now part of Presley mythology—the weeks flew by until the spring wedding. Then came a frenzied convergence on Las Vegas before dawn on May 1. The giddy couple, along with George Klein and Joe Esposito and his wife, Joanie, were aboard Frank Sinatra's Learjet, *The Christina,* as it glided down the runway of McCarran Airport. A limousine fleet was waiting to carry the party to the Clark County clerk's office. Elvis didn't carry any cash, so he had to borrow the $15 license fee from Esposito.

Then a DC-3 arrived, bearing the Beaulieu family and Dee and Vernon Presley. As for the blustery Colonel Tom Parker, he had been in Las Vegas for the previous two days, setting up the wedding and the $100,000 breakfast to follow, both of which took place at the Aladdin Hotel.

At 9:41 A.M., before twenty-five towering chapel candles, Nevada Supreme Court judge David Zenoff concluded an eight-minute ceremony—in which Priscilla promised to "love, honor, cherish, and comfort" her husband—with the declaration, "You may kiss the bride."

In short order, a follow-up press conference and breakfast reception sped by, and then a Learjet carried Elvis and Priscilla into the setting sun, for a honeymoon evening at their rented Palm Springs mansion. And that is the happy ending of the official version.

What is the real story? In a 1974 interview, Priscilla admitted that talk of marriage came about because "here I was a girl in my teens *living* with a man, at a time when that really wasn't the social thing to do." Explaining that Elvis worried about the impact marriage would have on his career, she candidly added, "I wondered what it would do to our relationship."

Presley told Marty Lacker about his woes one day the preceding November. He'd been under enormous pressures, Elvis said. "I've no choice. I've got to marry Priscilla this spring. I'm going out to have a ring made."

Lacker thought his friend was joking, but Elvis looked serious. "Is this something you want to do?" Marty wondered.

Elvis shook his head. "No, not now. . . . Hell, no." Why, he added, Priscilla wasn't even ready.

Lacker threw an arm around his friend's shoulder. "E, you don't have to do anything you don't want to do. . . . Tell them no."

"Can't. Priscilla's father has contacted the Colonel demanding that I make good on my word to marry Cilla now that she's twenty-one."

"Goddammit! You're Elvis Presley. Say no!" Lacker raged.

"You're not listening, Marty. I got no choice. The Colonel says the Beaulieus can do to me the same thing that happened to Jerry Lee Lewis when he married his teenage cousin. My image would be destroyed. *Z-i-i-i-p*. Everything would be gone."

"Did Priscilla do this? Because if she did, go and talk to her."

"No, Priscilla and I have an understanding. She'd have talked to me first."

Years later, Lacker wondered, "What would have happened had Elvis just said no?" Would there have been a lawsuit? Could Elvis and Priscilla have merely continued to coexist as they had for five years already? Or would she have silently departed, as Anita Wood had done?

What Lacker didn't know was that there had already been talk of a wedding—at the insistence of the two colonels, Beaulieu and Parker. They had hoped to have Elvis and Priscilla married in January in a Memphis church wedding, followed by a huge reception with all the Deep South trimmings. Presley managed to stave them off when he went on his hunt for the getaway ranch in Mississippi. But once the ranch was purchased, he had no viable excuse not to get married.

Time had run out for the world's most eligible bachelor.

According to Billy Smith, "Elvis had been with Priscilla for five years. If anything, he wanted to get rid of her. But she complained to her parents, and then to Elvis. She told him she was going to make him fulfill his promise to her or tell her story to the world."

The rumors continued among the divergent circles at Graceland and Bel-Air. There was talk that Priscilla's father had threatened to press charges under the Mann Act—for transporting a minor across state lines for sexual purposes. He had been more than patient during the five years his stepdaughter had existed at the mercy of Elvis's whims. There was talk that Elvis had offered millions to Priscilla to keep from marrying her. And that he had again approached Ann-Margret—who was then engaged to actor Roger Smith.* There

---

*Ann-Margret and Roger Smith tied the knot in Las Vegas just one week after the Elvis-Priscilla nuptials.

was also talk about the Colonel using the marriage to gain more control over Elvis.

As Lamar Fike put it, "All of the markers were called in by both colonels. And I guess Elvis could have said no and seen his career go like Jerry Lee Lewis."

As 1967 dawned, the Presley contingent unpacked their bags at a rented ranch-style house in Bel-Air, so Elvis could begin work on his twenty-fifth film. *Clambake* was more lightweight fluff—a variation on *The Prince and the Pauper*, about the son of an oil baron who trades places with a working stiff. During the film's production, Priscilla finally emerged from her status as the mystery girlfriend from Memphis.

She made publicized visits to the set. So did Colonel and Mrs. Beaulieu. To some columnists, Priscilla seemed to have come from out of nowhere. Recalling Priscilla's emergence in the public eye, the Hearst Syndicate's Dorothy Treloar admitted, "When she showed up, we didn't even have a name to associate with the face." The former assistant to Louella Parsons, Treloar wrote a column that cautioned, "Honey, this man has been a successful bachelor in Hollywood for ten years . . . it's too latesville."

As Elvis's longtime girlfriend finally became news, the Colonel continued to pester Presley about walking down the aisle. "But Elvis kept stalling," recalled Marty Lacker. Finally, two factors allowed the Colonel to force the issue.

The first was money. Profits from Presley's MGM films had been slipping with each title. Moreover, the studio's marketing studies, which dated back forty years, showed that the only way to halt a downward spiral was a startling, news-making event. "You're losing half of your audience now because you're thirty-two years old and still single," the Colonel told Presley. A marriage, he stressed, could make all the difference. The Colonel added a subtle threat, implying that RCA had talked to him about the morals clause in their record contracts.

Then came a mishap—that Parker used to his advantage. In early March, just as Elvis was to begin filming *Clambake*, he took a fall in the Bel-Air house. According to Alan Fortas, Elvis was "stoked full of pills and woozy" when he tripped over the cord to a television in the bathroom. Falling headfirst, Elvis hit his head on the porcelain bathtub. He was knocked out cold and lay there for an indeterminate time.

"Goddamn motherfucking cord!"

Priscilla awakened to hear Elvis cursing. Jumping from bed, she found him slumped on the floor. "Help me out of here," Presley moaned. "I have to lie down."

Later, as Elvis cradled his head, Esposito and the boys surrounded him. "Jeez, El, what happened?" asked Esposito.

"My head feels like it was kicked by a mule."

A festering lump had formed. Charlie Hodge reached out to touch it, saying, "It's the size of a golf ball!" Summoning up macho swagger, Elvis let his buddies take turns feeling his wound. But he grimaced and confessed, "I think I really did hurt myself."

Calls were put in to a doctor and to the Colonel, both of whom immediately responded. The doctor rushed over with an oxygen machine. Parker came with several anxious-looking representatives from MGM.

By this time the studio was well aware that their star had problems. His eating disorders were apparent when he was fitted for his *Clambake* wardrobe; his weight had ballooned from 170 to more than 200 pounds. His handsome face had become as noticeably bloated as his waistline.

The Colonel was enraged with Presley's inner circle. "Goddamn! Why'd you guys let him get this way?" Didn't they realize, he ranted, that the studio would cancel Elvis's contract if they thought he couldn't carry out his work?

For the first time in his movie career, Elvis Presley was ordered to bed. Glaring at the Memphis Mafia, the Colonel said, "He needs peace and quiet. I don't want him to be disturbed." The Colonel didn't want him to do any reading, either. "Get those goddamn books out of here!" he said, motioning to a stack of Elvis's books on religion and spiritualism. Pointing toward Larry Geller, Parker added, "And don't you *dare* bring him another one."

About a week later, Colonel Parker called a summit meeting at the Bel-Air house. He first talked with Marty Lacker and Joe Esposito. Marty would no longer be Elvis's chief of staff. That distinction now went to Joe Esposito.

As for Lacker, he was now to handle "special projects." The first was to be the wedding of Elvis and Priscilla.

Then came a meeting in the living room with all the boys. Looking out over his friends, Elvis said, "Fellas, the Colonel has got some things to say. And what he's got to tell you is comin' straight from me."

Presley cast his eyes downward as the Colonel said, "Things are going to change around here." He went on to detail a new regimen for the Memphis Mafia. There were to be payroll cuts. And no more elaborate gifts from Elvis. Further, the boys were not to approach Elvis about their problems. "He's not Jesus Christ walking down the street in robes, saving people," snapped the Colonel. "If you have problems, tell Joe Esposito and he will get in touch with me."

As Presley continued to stare at the floor, Parker ordered, "And leave Elvis alone! He's not well. . . . He's going back to the studio to start a picture. There are a lot of people depending upon him to fulfill his obligations."

Marty Lacker would later say that Parker's voice had the cold ring of a cash register. Parker certainly had a lot at stake: he and the man he claimed to love "as much as a son" had recently struck up a new business arrangement. Under the new terms Parker was collecting an unprecedented fifty percent of every penny that Elvis earned—not counting expenses, which Presley also paid.

Before he left, the Colonel turned, leaned on his cane, and added, "You're all lucky to be here. If any of you don't like the way things are, you can leave. The door is open. I'd say we've been more than fair. Isn't that right, Elvis?" In a pathetic spectacle, Presley merely nodded, his eyes cast downward.

His despondent mood was apparent during the drive back home to Memphis for his recuperation. Presley was at the wheel as they passed through Forrest City, Arkansas, and chanced to pick up George Klein's radio show on Memphis's WHBQ. Klein was playing "Green, Green Grass of Home" by Tom Jones.

"Beautiful . . . beautiful . . ." said Presley. He pulled the bus over to a pay phone so that Marty Lacker could call Klein and request that he play the song again. The ritual continued through the night. Stopping at pay phones, he would call Klein, who would again play the song "for the big E, who's on his way back to Memphis." Elvis wept as he drove.

Once back at Graceland, he continued his bizarre behavior. When he arrived, he claimed he saw his mother standing in her old bedroom. "I walked in the door and I saw her standing here. I saw her, man," Elvis swore to his bewildered friends.

When he at last showed up on the *Clambake* set, Presley was initially more subdued than usual. To Larry Geller, who was aboard as hairstylist, he seemed dark and brooding. Costar Will Hutchins, who'd worked with Presley just a year earlier on *Spinout*, said, "He had a certain melancholy." One day Presley invited his costar into his dressing trailer "to hear a new album." Hutchins was sure he would listen to the newest tunes by Elvis. "And I thought, great, what a treat," said

Hutchins. His jaw dropped when Presley instead played for him a Charles Boyer album in which the French actor recited love poems. "It. was definitely not what I expected," Hutchins said.

Eventually, the atmosphere did evolve into that of the typical Presley picture—with lots of zany between-takes shenanigans involving the star and his entourage. "And I think I know why," said Hutchins. "Since Elvis got married so soon after filming, I realized that the movie was really his prolonged stag party."

The days leading up to the big event did not create the impression of an excited fiancé. Yet among Elvis's friends, there is no consensus about his marriage.

Joe Esposito vehemently maintains that Presley was not a reluctant bridegroom. "He was thrilled to finally marry Priscilla."

Alan Fortas theorized that the Colonel believed that marriage would help stabilize Elvis's increasingly troubled personal life—putting an end to eating binges and drugs and even Presley's reliance on the Memphis Mafia. Fortas went so far as to speculate that Elvis's longtime bachelorhood and all his male buddies might have given rise to Hollywood rumors about homosexuality—which marriage would put to rest.

Larry Geller believes Elvis was determined to carry out his promise to Priscilla, despite his fears that marriage would alienate some of his fans—as well as members of his entourage. Likening them to disciples, Presley told his spiritual guru, "After all, Jesus never married, and he had twelve guys around him, and they wandered all over the country together."

According to Marty Lacker, because of the looming marriage, Elvis increased his use of sleeping pills in November 1966: "He was too tormented to fall asleep." Still others insist that Elvis Presley never did anything he didn't want to do. "That includes marriage," said longtime secretary Becky Yancey.

Was he marrying out of love or a sense of honor? In an interview following his son's death, Vernon Presley said it wasn't until after the wedding that Elvis realized "that he didn't really want to be married."

A journalist who was close to both Elvis and Priscilla offered, "He might have been happier if she had just drifted out of his life."

Sandra Harmon, who helped with Priscilla's autobiography, said, "By the time they got married, it was about doing the right thing, since this girl had been whisked away from her house when she was sixteen and was known to be living with him. There was nowhere to go but marriage. Elvis couldn't kick her out. His image would have been horrible had he done that."

On April 29, 1967, the Colonel told Elvis, Priscilla, a handful of family members, and favored members of the Mafia to gather at a rented house in Palm Springs. They were to all leave for Las Vegas in the early hours of May 1.

As the evening ticked away, though, Elvis apparently balked yet again. "Elvis holed up in his bedroom and would not come down," revealed Marty Lacker, who said that it took both Esposito and his wife to coax Presley from his bedroom and into the waiting limousine.

Elvis's longtime maid and cook, Alberta—whom Elvis lovingly nicknamed VO5—once addressed an Elvis Presley fan club gathering with an equally sobering account. She told of finding Presley sitting on his bed, tears streaming down his face, as the car awaited out front. "Why, Mr. Elvis, what's wrong?"

"I don't want to get married."

"Why, Mr. Elvis, if you don't want to get married, then don't."

He looked at her intently. "You don't understand. I don't have a choice."

As the Learjet traveled from Palm Springs to Las Vegas, the suite at the Aladdin was being readied. Fresh flowers were being slipped into place by dozens of skilled hands; the suckling pig was roasted; the poached salmon was candied. And a six-tiered wedding cake was iced with roses, candy pearls, and sixteen hundred spun-sugar rosettes. Meanwhile, the press began arriving in the lobby of the Aladdin. Colonel Tom Parker had notified them that there would be a press conference.

Up to this time there had been no official announcement about a wedding. When MGM publicist Stanley Brossette got a call from the Colonel, he requested two studio photographers to shoot an upcoming event. "He just told us to keep our bags packed. We didn't even know where we were going until we got on the plane." Once on board, one of the photographers guessed that Elvis Presley was finally going to tie the knot. "I didn't believe it for a minute," said Brossette, who'd long heard Presley insist that when he married, it would be in a church in Memphis. "Because of his strong religious beliefs, I just couldn't imagine him getting married in Las Vegas." He changed his mind when he and the photographers entered the Aladdin and saw the mass of reporters from around the world. "I didn't know the Colonel had contacted them. It all seemed so crazy. I started to get a sense that something major was happening."

Hollywood reporter Rona Barrett helped to trigger the media frenzy. The day before, she had reported in her syndicated column that Presley was to be married, but she said the nuptials would take place in Palm Springs. "One of the first things the Colonel had me do, when I got to Nevada, was to call Rona Barrett and tell her I was at Elvis's wedding in Las Vegas," recalled Brossette.

Up in the wedding suite, Brossette also worked with the Colonel in positioning the two photographers who would shoot the ceremony. "You stand here," the Colonel said to one of them. With a nod to the other he added, "And you stand here." As the men took their positions, Parker said, "You are not to move through the whole ceremony. And I mean don't move!" Before Brossette left the room, he whispered to the cameramen, "Please, do what he says. Don't move from your places."

Only fourteen guests were invited to the wedding of one of the world's most famous entertainers. Joe Esposito and Marty Lacker served as "co–best men." The maid of honor was Priscilla's thirteen-year-old sister. Other guests included George Klein and cousins Patsy Presley and Billy Smith.

Brossette watched the ceremony through the doorway of an anteroom. "I could see the back of the bride and groom, and the face of the preacher, and I could see one photographer. Well, I could tell right off that, from where he was standing, he was getting pictures with a lot of bridal veil and no bride—he wasn't at the right angle. And I was thinking, 'Uh-oh, don't move.' But just then he took a little step in order to get a better shot. And though I couldn't see the Colonel from where I was, I did see his cane come down—right on the photographer's head, in the middle of the ceremony. If you know the Colonel, you know it was a classic Colonel move."

When the brief ceremony was over, Parker made his way downstairs, where he addressed the cluster of reporters. "If you ladies and gentlemen will please leave your cameras and notebooks, you are invited to be a guest at the reception of Elvis and Priscilla."

The reception was as bizarre as the wedding. A string ensemble performed for a crowd that seemed selected for publicity purposes. The guests included comedian Redd Foxx—though no one seemed to know why—along with executives from MGM, William Morris, and RCA. There was also a smattering of family members, but some of Elvis's closest friends either weren't invited or chose not to attend.

Lamar Fike was at home in Madison, Tennessee, when he picked up a newspaper and read that Elvis had gotten married. Red West was in a Las Vegas hotel room waiting for a wedding invitation that never came. When he and his wife, Pat—a former secretary to Elvis—learned they weren't being asked to the ceremony, they not only boycotted the reception, but West, who had been with Presley since 1955, quit his job.

The Colonel claimed there was not enough room for additional guests in the expansive two-room suite. The snub would divide the Memphis Mafia into warring factions—that exist to this day. As late as 1976, Presley tried to explain that he had nothing to do with the proceedings. "It was railroaded through," Elvis insisted.

As for Priscilla, when she lifted the tulle veil at the reception and looked about the room filled with strangers, she cried out, "Who are these people?" Looking back, she would wonder how things had gotten "so out of hand." And how she had become so powerless that her only prerogative in the wedding was getting to choose her wedding gown.

"I wish I'd had the strength to say, 'Wait a minute, this is our wedding, fans or no fans, press or no press. Let us invite whomever we want and have it wherever we want.' "

There is no question that she and Elvis made quite a pair that day. In her billowy, off-the-rack gown, Priscilla looked so pudgy that columnist Rona Barrett snidely said she appeared to be "pregnant in tulle." What was more mesmerizing was her bouffant hairdo—dyed jet-black to match Elvis's—and her Cleopatra-style eye makeup.

Elvis wore an ill-fitting, constrictive black paisley brocade tuxedo topped by an outlandish pompadour that had been built up over a wire pouf. He also wore cowboy boots and heavy makeup.

At the press conference, reporters quizzed Elvis about why he'd waited so long to get married. "I guess it was about time," was his uninspired response. The Colonel was more creative when he shouted out, "Remember, you can't end bachelorhood without getting married."

As the media pressed the entertainer to flash a smile for the cameras, one reporter was overheard saying, "He doesn't smile much lately." The words reached Elvis, who retorted, "How can you look happy when you're scared?"

During the press conference, he spoke briefly about having met his "mystery" bride in Germany. As Mrs. Beaulieu went on to explain, "They became very close friends at the time." She added coyly, "but I don't think any of us had a thought they'd get married."

When word later got out that the bride had been living at Graceland for five years, the media was stunned. Rona Barrett said Priscilla was Elvis's "dirty little secret." Still, Tom Parker had reason to be pleased. He had breathed new life into Presley's image, averting what could have been an avalanche of ruinous publicity about the superstar and his live-in Lolita.

Priscilla and Elvis spent their first night as newlyweds at the house in Palm Springs, where Elvis carried her across the threshold, singing a breathless "Hawaiian Wedding Song." The bride later recounted how nervous they were, as if "we had never been together under intimate circumstances," when they retreated to the bedroom. "They were incredibly happy," said Joe Esposito, who had his movie camera rolling when he caught Elvis picking a rose for Priscilla from the backyard.

Yet anyone who attended the wedding could see that it was not the stuff of which dreams are made. Indeed, after at last formally bedding his bride, Elvis went back to work—to do some dubbing on *Clambake* because some of his lines were inaudible in an outdoor sequence. A planned honeymoon to the Bahamas was briefly postponed.

Before embarking for the islands, Elvis and Priscilla went to the Circle G for a few days. Not even there was Priscilla alone with her new husband.

Though Elvis hadn't invited Lamar to the wedding, he called his faithful friend, saying, "Buddy, I'd appreciate it if you would join us out on the ranch. With this weather, all these high winds, Priscilla would feel better if you were there." So the newlyweds shared their second connubial bed in a luxury trailer on the Circle G Ranch, with Priscilla and Elvis in the back bedroom and Lamar in the front.

Renaissance Man

nder Priscilla Beaulieu Presley—now officially the lady of the house—Graceland underwent minor refurbishing. The kitchen was modernized with new cabinetry and carpeting. Her upstairs dressing room and bathroom were redone in varying shades of pink. She bought several new pieces of modestly priced furniture, including a comfortable chair, as well as Sears draperies for the living room and the dining room. Because she preferred a less cluttered look, she swept through rooms and gathered up knickknacks—many of which had been sent by fans. She also removed the crocheted doilies fans had sent (and in some cases had made) that were atop tables and the backs and the arms of chairs.

She and Elvis attempted to repair hurt feelings by squeezing back into their wedding clothes for a lavish party for the many friends and relatives who hadn't been invited to the Las Vegas ceremony. Looking vibrant and beautiful, Priscilla toasted her nuptial glory with several glasses of champagne. Like many a new husband, Elvis seemed ill at ease as he wandered from room to room. Becky Yancey thought he looked as though he couldn't wait for the party to end.

By now Elvis's aunt Delta Mae (Vernon's sister) was living at Graceland, along with Grandma Minnie Mae. The women shared a room, as

well as a passion for the television soap opera As the World Turns. Elvis
would sometimes pop his head into the room to inquire about the
latest travails of fictional Oakdale, USA. Minnie Mae would wave
him away.

Just months into his marriage, Elvis went to work on the movie
Speedway. As he dryly noted, he played "kinduva singin' millionaire-
playboy-race-driver," something he had already done "about twenty-
five times." His leading lady, Nancy Sinatra, was far more intriguing.
She had weathered a marriage to teen idol Tommy Sands and transformed herself into a blond, brassy, go-go-booted queen of the late sixties. She was then at the height of her star power—power that was
greater than Presley's on the international record charts. Whereas Elvis
hadn't had a number one hit since 1962's "Good Luck Charm," Nancy
had recently topped the charts with "These Boots Are Made for
Walkin' " as well as "Somethin' Stupid," the latter a duet with her
famous father, Frank.

She had a tawny beauty that tempted Presley during lazy afternoons on the set. They sometimes spent lunch hours in her dressing
trailer indulging in the white-panties and slumber-party fantasies
Presley had nurtured since he was a child. On one occasion he hid in
her wardrobe and jumped out at her when she was down to tight jeans
and a brassiere. Recalled Nancy, "He just held me . . . and then he lifted
up my face and he kissed me and I started to melt." Before she could
melt any further, he pulled away. "I'm sorry . . . I'm sorry," he said.
With a shake of his head, he was gone. Though they fooled around in
her trailer, they never had a full-blown affair. On the last day of
shooting, Sinatra gave Elvis what she called "a warm, sincere I-love-you
kiss." It would also be their last.

Presley's marital fidelity wasn't helped by the news that he and
Priscilla were going to be parents. The pregnancy wasn't planned. To
the contrary, Priscilla was initially upset because she'd wanted to take
birth control pills. Elvis forbade them. "They're not perfected yet.
There's all kinds of side effects," said her husband, who kept a copy of
the Physicians' Desk Reference at his bedside. So Priscilla used the
rhythm method, as detailed for her by Becky Yancey. When the obstetrician certified the pregnancy, Becky commented, "Honey, you must
not have followed it as prescribed."

Filled with a foreboding that the child would end her passionate
relationship with the man who had finally married her, Priscilla briefly

thought of abortion. So sensitive was Elvis to his wife's moods that he pressed her, "What's wrong? What do you want to do, little one?"

Priscilla began crying. "I don't know. What can I do?"

"What do you think? I'll back you up whatever you do."

"It's our baby," Priscilla answered firmly. "I could never live with myself and neither could you."

Still, Priscilla had misgivings. "I was still uncertain about how my unexpected pregnancy would affect our marriage. This was supposed to have been our time alone. I wanted to be beautiful for him. Instead, my debut as Elvis's bride was to be spoiled by a fat stomach, puffy face, and swollen feet."

The day Elvis escorted his shy bride to the set of *Speedway*, costar Bill Bixby was struck by the way she let her husband take the lead. Recalled Bixby, "She didn't speak until he did." Of course, she was also visually memorable with her teetering hair and eyes so heavily rimmed that she made Sinatra look fresh-faced. (And Sinatra would go on to be hailed by MTV as "the patron saint of eyeliner.")

When Sinatra asked her about her pregnancy, Priscilla admitted she was so obsessed with keeping her weight down that she was eating only one meal a day, then snacking on an apple or hard-boiled egg. As Nancy Sinatra would note, "She's got her hands full trying to hold on to this man."

At eight o'clock in the morning on February 1, 1968, Priscilla woke up in wet bedding. As Elvis and his friends rushed through the downstairs, making necessary phone calls and readying the cars, she went into the bathroom and teased her hair into a gravity-defying beehive. Then she calmly applied heavy black eye makeup, including double bat-wing false eyelashes.

As at their wedding, she and Elvis were quite a sight when they arrived at Baptist Memorial Hospital. "He was in a white suit with a blue turtleneck sweater and blue suede hat. She was in this pink miniskirt with this huge black hairdo," recalled administrator Maurice Elliott.

She created a further stir when she refused to take off her false eyelashes during the delivery. "And her eyes wouldn't shut with them on, so the staff had to put a washcloth over them to keep the operating-room lights from burning the retinas," said Elliott.

Lisa Marie Presley was born at 5:01 P.M. She weighed six pounds fifteen ounces and had a head of jet-black hair, to match her parents' dye jobs. From her private room on the fifth floor, Priscilla declared, "She's perfect!" A still shaky Elvis said, "Oh, man, she's too much!" As the proud father passed out the traditional cigars, Elliott pocketed his as a souvenir.

In the natal ward of Memphis's Baptist Hospital, the news of Lisa Marie's birth caused such a sensation that her parents asked that she be shielded from view. Flowers, cards, and packages flooded the hospital; chief telephone operator Mildred McLain said they averaged one hundred calls an hour. Most were from well-wishers, though one man from Henderson, Tennessee, wanted to sell Elvis life insurance.

But at this juncture it was his career that needed an insurance policy. For after having defined one era, he was now floundering in another.

It was a new era, and the counterculture was shaking up the status quo. *Hair* was on Broadway; Andy Warhol's underground movies were showing uptown; *The Graduate* poked fun at societal mores. It was a time of free-flowing sensibilities and free-flowing hair. Like Priscilla's heavily lacquered bouffants, Elvis Presley had gradually become an anachronism.

He *knew* he was out of touch. When he starred in the 1968 comedy *Stay Away, Joe*, playing a roguish modern-day Navajo, he talked hopefully of "growing up" on the screen, and of being the instigator of the action instead of always being chased by girls and bad guys. Noting that the character Joe Lightcloud was "a wheeler-dealer who's always promoting something," Presley likened him to famous antiheroes of the day: "He's part Hud, part Alfie. He's a man, not a boy, and he's out looking for women, not just waiting for them to stumble all over him." Presley was deluding himself about yet another thin star vehicle, one that relied more on a series of rowdy fistfights than plot.

Live a Little, Love a Little (1968) was no better despite a "psychedelic" dream sequence and dialogue that actually generated news stories—since Presley's character uttered a few "dammit" 's and a "what the hell." He also tumbled into bed with beautiful starlet Michele Carey, but they were wholesomely separated by a divider. As an MGM spokesman stressed, "They never go to bed in a Presley picture."

He was just as out of sync in the music world, which had roared past the man whose name was synonymous with rock 'n' roll. It was a mind-altering era in which musicians were leading the sixties radical movement—war protesters, draft dodgers, and the drug culture. Rock entrepreneur Bill Graham, who booked acts at the popular Winterland

and Fillmore arenas, said, "Whether right or wrong, those times were about blind hope. They were once-in-a-lifetime."

The Beatles were by now spouting the philosophies of the Maharishi Mahesh Yogi. They had also become the poster boys for psychedelics. In California, the "far-out" talent included Big Brother and the Holding Company (with lead singer Janis Joplin), the Jefferson Airplane, Cream, Country Joe and the Fish, the Jimi Hendrix Experience, and a cerebral hard-driving group known as the Doors. Their lead singer was the darkly handsome Jim Morrison, an inveterate Elvis Presley fan who used to ask his friends to please rise when an Elvis song came over the airwaves.

There was no denying his influence: by 1968 Elvis Presley had sold more than 200 million records and had earned thirty-two gold records. Yet at the same time he was being written off as a has-been. At Capitol Records, home to the Beatles (and their sixteen gold discs), Elvis was referred to as "the Bing Crosby of the sixties."

Presley desperately needed a comeback. It took a television producer steeped in sixties music to give it to him.

What became known as the '68 *Comeback Special* had its origins in a meeting between Colonel Tom Parker and NBC's Tom Sarnoff, vice president in charge of operations on the West Coast. The Colonel had the idea for a Christmas special to feature holiday songs Elvis had recorded over the years. It would mark his first time on TV since 1960's Frank Sinatra-hosted *Welcome Home, Elvis*.

Interested in the idea, Sarnoff contacted Bob Finkel, whose company was under contract to NBC. Finkel had done variety shows with Tennessee Ernie Ford, Dinah Shore, and Eddie Fisher and was then at work on programs for Jerry Lewis and Phyllis Diller. Finkel in turn hired Steve Binder to produce and direct.

One of television's breed of Young Turks, Binder had made waves as the director of the 1964 concert film *The T.A.M.I. Show* (Teenage Awards Music International), a rock extravaganza featuring Diana Ross and the Supremes, the Beach Boys, Jan and Dean, Gerry and the Pacemakers, and a finale that exploded into a battle of the bands between back-to-back artists James Brown and the Rolling Stones. Binder had also worked on *Hullabaloo*, the midsixties NBC variety show known for its frug-dancing girls in cages and rock acts ranging from the Ronettes to the Supremes. Then came major TV specials, including a 1967 show starring British pop queen Petula Clark. It generated controversy when Harry Belafonte touched Clark on the arm. "It's hard to imagine, but at the time no black man had touched a white woman during prime-time TV," recalled Binder, who stood his ground and fended off censorship efforts.

Binder believed that as a result of butting heads with terrified NBC executives and advertisers, he was up to the daunting challenge of dealing with Colonel Tom Parker. "Looking back, I think I was too young and naive to be frightened by him."

The first meeting between Binder and Presley took place in the spring of 1968 at Binder's Sunset Boulevard office. Presley showed up wearing blue pants and a blue shirt with scarf. He was also slim, tanned, and so good-looking Binder couldn't quite take his eyes off him. "He was awesome. It didn't matter if you were male or female, you couldn't help but stare."

Presley was surprisingly candid, confessing to Binder that he was "absolutely terrified" at the prospect of facing the public on television again. "For nearly ten years I've been kept away from the public, making all those movies. And I'm not sure they're going to like me now." Admitted Elvis, "I may have waited too long."

At thirty-three, Presley hadn't had a Top 10 hit or a million-selling album since 1965's "Crying in the Chapel." His movie-ticket sales had dropped, too. The recent *Clambake*, which cost $1.4 million to make, grossed only $1.6 million. His latest movie sound-track albums were so anemic that they lasted just twenty minutes on the turntable. He hadn't had a song from his movies crack the top *seventy* in three years.

Binder realized that what was at stake was not just a return to triumphant television but also artistic survival. He remembers feeling "a great sadness" as he sat across from Elvis, who nervously drummed his fingers on the arm of his chair. Curious about Presley's creative sensibility, Binder asked, "If you'd had the chance, would you have recorded 'MacArthur Park'?" He was referring to Jimmy Webb's lyrical seven-minute masterwork about love and rejection, then a monster hit for Richard Harris.

Presley's response—"Absolutely!"—cinched it for Binder. "I could tell this was a really frustrated soul who wanted to explore new ventures and open new doors."

After Elvis departed, for a brief vacation in Hawaii with Priscilla, Binder and his staff went to work. "I knew we didn't want to do a traditional Christmas show. I knew we wanted something different. And I remember thinking that what we came up with would either kick-start his career or end it."

In those days TV had a make-it-or-break-it power. There weren't so many channels then, and a single show could have a tremendous effect. Elvis was all too aware of that: the Ed Sullivan show had made all the difference for him.

By the time Elvis returned to Los Angeles, Binder and writers Chris Beard and Allan Blye had come up with a fresh concept. In what would be essentially a one-man show—there would be no guest stars—Elvis would portray a struggling artist on his road to fame, complete with hard knocks and glory. Based on his immediate past, Presley was the perfect headliner for the vehicle that Binder diplomatically called a "renaissance."

NBC was shaken; so was Colonel Tom Parker. "They had something else entirely in mind. Elvis singing Christmas songs, and this list of possible guests stars such as Milton Berle, Ray Bolger . . . I said, 'No way,' " declared Binder.

As for Presley, he told Binder, "No one makes decisions for me." In what would be one of the few artistic decisions he ever made on his own, Elvis consented to Binder's terms. He would return to his roots, to the blues and the hollering, to the sexual bump and grind. Most unnerving of all, he would appear before a live audience in a concert sequence.

To be anchored by the song "Guitar Man," the show's production numbers were an amalgam of Presley's best film and TV moments, and his own personal interests. They managed to work karate moves into one number. For his performance of "Little Egypt" (the highlight of his otherwise lackluster 1964 film *Roustabout*) he wore a gold-lamé jacket—not the original but an update designed by Bill Belew. To reflect his strong religious beliefs, the writers had him perform the rousing "Where Could I Go but to the Lord?" To display his sexiness, one setting was a garish bordello—where he performed "Let Yourself Go," amidst the bumping and grinding of female dancers. (The latter was eventually cut after being deemed too risqué by the network's censors.)

"Binder gave Elvis a challenge," recalled Charlie Hodge. "Something which had not been offered since he had been taught to drive a tank in the Army." He was asked to bring back the sort of Elvis that his manager, the Colonel, had kept in hiding for years.

"The idea," said the special's musical producer, Bones Howe, "was to let people really see Elvis Presley, not just what the Colonel wanted them to see."

As Binder came to realize, Elvis had been sheltered for far too long. "He had this idea that he couldn't go out in public, that there would be this mass hysteria, so he had to keep apart from the rest of the world," Binder related, shaking his head. During the protracted negotiations for the NBC special—which would tape in June and air in December, and for which Elvis was paid $250,000—Binder challenged the performer one day when he was in Binder's office, which overlooked the Sunset Strip. "Let's go down on the Strip, stand there for a while, and see what happens."

"Okay," Elvis answered confidently. "But you're going to be surprised."

The two went out onto busy Sunset Boulevard, just west of Tower Records and down from the famous Whiskey-a-Go-Go. They found themselves among Los Angeles's young sophisticates and free spirits. Men with shaggy hair, jeans, and sandals; women in micro-minis with knee boots. There were head shops featuring hashish pipes and psyche-delic candles and boutiques filled with tie-dye clothing and Nehru jackets.

Binder and Presley stood in front of the Classic Cat topless bar. "We looked east. We looked west. We looked out toward the traffic. It got to the point where I thought Elvis was trying to be recognized," Binder said, laughing. "He was waving. He was smiling. Yet nothing happened. No one noticed him. It was actually pretty boring."

Elvis's ego got a further bruising during his first visit to the NBC lot in Burbank. Binder wanted to assuage his star's concerns about tele-vision—"where there's an audience, and visitors coming and going, unlike movies, with their closed sets." The two were standing in front of the artists' entrance, waiting for a car and driver, when a woman broke away from a studio tour and approached Elvis. "Pardon me, sir," she said to the man who was wearing signature black pants, with a black modified flier's jacket and aviator sunglasses, "do you think there are going to be any stars here today?"

"I really don't know, ma'am. Could be," Elvis deadpanned. As she returned to her tour, Presley and Binder burst out laughing. Yet the point was loud and clear.

The first rehearsals took place at Binder's office. As Elvis worked with the staff, the Colonel and several of the Mafia would sit in a recep-tion area, goofing around. "Parker would be out there hypnotizing them—turning them into goats and pigs, that kind of thing," said Binder. To this day, the producer-director speculates that the Colonel also practiced hypnosis on Elvis. "He had such control over him," said Binder, relating how the performer stood like a recalcitrant schoolboy, head bowed, during meetings with Parker. Because the Colonel also knew everything that was going on, Binder believes that some of Elvis's buddies were on Parker's payroll as spies.

When the Colonel learned that Binder had replaced Presley's hand-picked musical director, he shook his cane and declared, "The special is over! Elvis won't do the show!" But after Binder explained to Elvis why he wanted Billy Goldenberg over Billy Strange, Elvis acquiesced: "If you're happy, I'm happy."

Once production moved to NBC, the Colonel lived up to his larger-than-life reputation. He posed for a photograph wearing full Civil War military regalia—as a Southern colonel, naturally—and had it sent to Bob Finkel. In an attempt at one-upmanship, Finkel posed in a seventeenth-century English admiral's costume and had that photo sent to Parker. But it was hard to top the Colonel, who ordered his two William Morris assistants to dress like royal guardsmen and stand at attention outside his small studio office.

At a press conference held at NBC, the Colonel was an outlandish sight in a bright blue shirt, khaki pants, and a Tyrolean hat with feather. A cigar in one hand, he held his cane in the other and would occasionally crack it against the floor to make his points. When he heard Elvis talking about singing songs he was known for, the Colonel whacked the cane and declared, "Hell, if he sang the songs he's known for, that would take a couple of hours!" Presley just smiled, slightly.

With outsize trappings of his own, Elvis actually moved into his NBC dressing room during the ten days of studio rehearsal and taping. He had personal as well as artistic reasons. Instead of going home to his wife and daughter at their new four-bedroom, ten-bath French-country house in Trousdale Estates, he reveled in temporary bachelorhood. "After one or two o'clock in the morning, Joe [Esposito] and I would run girls in and out of the NBC dressing rooms as if the place were equipped with conveyors," recalled Alan Fortas, who said that Presley bolstered his ego and calmed his nerves with the trysts.

Presley also tore loose during jam sessions with his buddies, including Lamar Fike and guitarists Charlie Hodge and Lance Le Gault; the guys got together in Elvis's dressing room immediately after rehearsals on the stage. Convinced that "all this gold was slipping through our fingers," Binder asked the Colonel about shooting a session in the dressing room. The answer: "God dammit! Absolutely not!" So

Binder decided to bring the jam session out of the dressing room and onto an intimate stage. Calls were put out to guitarist Scotty Moore and drummer D. J. Fontana for what would become a legendary reunion. (Bassist Bill Black had died of a heart attack in 1965.)

All the while, Parker still wanted control over the finale. The Colonel was holding out for a Christmas song or the sentimental "I Believe." Binder wanted an original song. "We've heard him, we've seen him, we've lived with him," Binder told songwriters Billy Goldenberg and Earl Brown. "Please, incorporate what we know about Elvis as a person into one special song."

The very next morning Earl Brown called Binder to report, "I think we've got it."

Binder rushed to NBC. As Goldenberg played the piano, Brown sang from music sheets entitled "If I Can Dream." Binder was elated. "The song made a strong, liberal statement about the need for peace, kindness, and brotherhood—things Elvis really reflected in his religious songs and humanitarian acts." Binder told the songwriters, "We've just got to sell Elvis on it."

But he also had to sell the Colonel on it. Upon learning that they wanted Presley to sing a brand-new song rather than a holiday chestnut, he roared, "Over my dead body will this song get in the show!"

When Elvis arrived in the midst of the showdown, Binder urged, "Listen to the words. This is what you should do."

As the Colonel and RCA and NBC executives argued in the rooms beyond, Elvis sat and listened as Goldenberg and Brown performed "If I Can Dream." When they had finished, they looked to him for approval. He was expressionless as he said, "Play it again." They did, and he requested to hear it again. After a third run-through, Presley looked at Binder and said simply, "I'll do it."

To Binder's bemusement, when the Colonel and the various executives learned the song was a definite go, their battle suddenly became a tussle involving publishing rights. "They didn't skip a beat."

On the show, Presley performed the heavily orchestrated number wearing a white suit, his hair slicked back in place. He looked very much like the Southern preacher he sometimes thought he should have become. His emotional attachment to the song, with its message of hope, was apparent when he recorded it for the sound track. "He asked to have the studio cleared, except for the people in the control room," recalled Binder. "He wanted the lights turned down, and for us to give him a hand mike." Then, Presley dropped to the floor. With the mike clutched in his hand, he assumed a fetal position. He performed "If I Can Dream" as he lay writhing and weeping on the floor.

Then came the evening he faced his first live audience in eight years, in the concert segment of the show. Ticket holders began lining up outside NBC at four o'clock on June 29, for the six-o'clock show (to be followed by a second at eight). Nearly four hundred people, many from Presley fan clubs, filled the bleachers that surrounded a small central stage.

Backstage, Presley was having a panic attack. "Elvis sweated so much he had to reapply his makeup," recalled Fortas. "His hands were shaking, and he was staring blankly into the mirror."

Minutes before the show was to go on, Binder learned his star wanted to see him in the dressing room. "I literally ran through the soundstage to get there," Binder said.

Presley was seated in the makeup chair. He wore a tight-fitting black leather outfit—it would be enshrined as one of the most famous of his career—which Belew had patterned after Levi's jeans and a Levi jacket. Elvis's eyes were directed toward the floor.

"Steve, I've changed my mind," he said. "I'm not going on. It won't work. It's just too late."

Binder was floored. "What do you mean? The audience is out there; the set is lit; the orchestra has already started playing." Binder was panicked, and his throat went dry. At last he said, "Elvis, you have to go out there."

"I don't know what to say. I don't know what to do."

"Well, I can tell you, Elvis. You go out there and save your career."

Binder, who had spent months on the production, added plaintively, "If you won't do it for yourself, please, do it for me."

Throughout his career Elvis had always honored his contracts. Finally he nodded his head. Binder watched in relief as Elvis headed down the long, dark hallway, where his future waited.

When he reached the open entrance to the studio, he was a dark silhouette almost lost in the orange and blazing white spotlights. Then Elvis Presley stepped forward to face the crowd.

What happened that evening was yet another extraordinary benchmark of an already legendary career. He began with the lament "Heartbreak Hotel," then proceeded through hits ranging from "Blue Suede Shoes" to "Can't Help Falling in Love" and "Love Me Tender," the latter which he performed while looking straight at Priscilla, seated among the crowd in the bleachers. (He briefly toyed with the lyrics, saying,

"You have made my life a *wreck*," then grinned.) As the performance progressed, the self-confidence returned. Recalled Binder, "You can see it when he realizes that he's back, and they love him."

In between numbers he kidded with the audience ("Phew! Been a long time, baby . . .") At one juncture he borrowed a Kleenex from a fan—who then gratefully accepted the sopping tissue from him. When sound difficulties caused a delay in the show, he answered a few questions from the crowd, including a query about little Lisa. "Oh, she's fine. She's tiny, though." To illustrate, he held his hands about two feet apart; the audience collectively sighed.

At one point, to quell his between-takes nervousness, he did a falsetto "Tiptoe Through the Tulips," à la Tiny Tim. "It brought down the house," remembered Virginia Coons, an audience member.

When the concert segment was over, the media was as excited as the fans. Skeptical writers who were present found themselves rethinking Presley's career. Said one amazed *TV Guide* reporter, "This is the language—the only language—he speaks. . . . This man is a *performer*."

A much more assured Presley took the stage several nights later for an improvisational session with Scotty and D.J., as well as Charlie Hodge, Alan Fortas, and Lance Le Gault.

This time Binder was a nervous wreck, due to a mix-up involving the show's tickets. Though he hadn't liked the idea of the jam session, the Colonel told Binder he would pass out tickets for the show—to the same kind of handpicked crowd who had attended the concert. But just hours before the taping, a frantic call came from the head of NBC's guest relations: "Steve, we're in big trouble." Only twenty-five people were in line outside the studio gate; NBC had expected four hundred— two hundred each for the six- and eight-o'clock tapings.

(Binder still wonders if the slipup was deliberate—due to Parker's fears that the comeback would somehow lessen his hold over Presley.)

Binder couldn't believe it. "Elvis Presley was about to go onstage, and no one was there to see him! People would have paid a thousand dollars to see this thing!" He and his staff rushed to the phones. "We called everyone we knew on the lot and said, 'Can you get your wives and daughters over here?' " They also called several Los Angeles radio stations—which touted the availability of tickets. Studio gofers even ran over to the nearby Bob's Big Boy to talk diners into coming to see Elvis.

NBC eventually rounded up some two hundred people to watch Elvis Presley jam with his friends. The same audience also saw the second taping, "but we moved them around for the next show, to make it look as though we had a different crowd," remembered Binder. Many people considered the jam sessions the highlight of a show that ranks as one of Elvis Presley's finest projects.

Elvis himself sensed the significance of the occasion when he watched the show in a ninety-minute version (later edited to an hour for its initial airing) in a darkened room at NBC. When it was over, he asked that his buddies leave the room. Then he and Binder watched it again, and again. Finally, a deadly serious Elvis turned to Binder and said, "I will never sing a song I don't believe in again. I will never make another movie I don't believe in again."

Binder shook his head. "I hear you, Elvis. I just don't know if you're strong enough to follow through with that."

Ironically, when production on the special ended, Colonel Parker congratulated Binder and told him, "You're going to direct Elvis's next movie." Elvis slipped his personal phone number to Binder, telling him, "Stay in touch, man." But the Colonel never followed through on his talk of reuniting Binder and Elvis. And when Binder later tried calling Presley, he could never get past the Mafia members who fielded the calls.

The Elvis special, which aired December 3, 1968, was the week's top-rated program. It also earned a Peabody Award, the most prestigious honor in television, for executive producer Bob Finkel. As recently as 1996, when *TV Guide* spotlighted the one hundred most memorable moments in television history, Elvis's special was ranked in the top ten.

In the months between the end of production and the show's airdate, Elvis returned to his old life: making forgettable movies. His twenty-ninth movie was *Charro!*—an obvious attempt to cash in on the spaghetti-western craze that had made a superstar of Clint Eastwood. Presley looked unshaven and grimy as a former outlaw out to even the score with his old gang. As the ads touted, "On his neck he wore the brand of a killer. On his hip he wore vengeance." Actually, during filming in and around the Superstition Mountains of Arizona, Presley was frequently seen toting books on astrology and yoga.

The Trouble With Girls (and How to Get Into It) was filmed completely on the MGM soundstages, where Presley and his pals were up to old tricks. They'd suck up the helium from balloons on the set and then talk like Munchkins. "He loved to set off firecrackers," recalled leading lady Marlyn Mason. "I'd be doing a take with somebody and you'd hear,

'Boom! Pop!' somewhere in the distance." A Broadway-musical star, Mason kiddingly threatened Presley, "If you set off one of those things around me, I'm gonna sue you for every penny you have!" He got her the final day on the set, when he invited her into his trailer and offered her a seat. She noticed he and his pals had funny expressions. "Oh, my God—" began Mason, as a firecracker went off beneath her chair. "I've been waiting ten weeks to do that!" said Presley, laughing.

The upbeat mood was infectious during production. Elvis loved it when Mason's friend carved a huge pumpkin in his likeness for Halloween. Mason had it filled with little pumpkin cookies and wheeled out on the set on a red wagon. As cast and crew members clustered around it, Mason saw Parker and yelled, "Oh, Colonel, come over and look!" Elvis leaned over to Mason and in a low voice advised, "Don't *ever* ask the Colonel to come over. You have to go to *him*."

As the year came to an end, Presley's career was being revived—by the TV special as well as a trio of hit singles, including "If I Can Dream," which was released in November and climbed to number twelve. Then, shortly after Lisa Marie's first birthday, it was announced that Presley was going to return to Las Vegas—the city that had rejected him in 1956 when he was a rock 'n' roller.

This time his reception would be different. This time Elvis Presley would own the town.

A Place in the Sun

The resurrection that began in the NBC studios was completed in the neon capital of the Western World. The outside temperatures of Las Vegas neared 110 degrees the night of July 31, 1969. Another kind of heat permeated the showroom of the International Hotel as a VIP audience awaited Elvis Presley's return to the stage. It was his first major performance in nine years.

Presley was back doing what he liked best. Emboldened by his recording of "If I Can Dream," he'd started off the New Year with yet another momentous session in a studio. At the urging of Marty Lacker, Presley decided to work with producer Chips Moman, who ran American Sound Studios, located in a largely black area of Memphis. The tiny studio was known for its "Memphis sound."

Dusty Springfield so wanted that sound that she traveled from England to record there; it was where Neil Diamond recorded "Brother Love's Traveling Salvation Show"; it was at American that the Box Tops, five white Memphians who sounded black, recorded their recent number one hit "The Letter."

Moman was understandably interested in working with Elvis and used to ask Lacker to put in a good word for him. In January 1969, Lacker did just that when he chanced to overhear a conversation between Elvis and his RCA producer, Felton Jarvis. They were in Presley's den discussing an upcoming session in Nashville. Lacker sighed and shook his head. "What do you mean? What the hell's wrong?" Presley asked.

"Dammit, Elvis, I just wish that for once you'd record here in Memphis. And I wish you'd try Chips and American."

Lacker thought Presley would put him off, the way he'd done before. But later that night Jarvis said, "Elvis wants to talk to you about cutting in Memphis."

There were only four days to make the arrangements, and it turned out Neil Diamond was due in the studio when Elvis needed it. Lacker was sure the opportunity was lost. But Moman waved off the problem. Matter-of-factly he said, "Fuck Neil Diamond. Neil Diamond will just have to be postponed." Without skipping a beat, the producer added, "Tell Elvis he's on."

Elvis spent nearly two weeks recording at American—marking his first time in a Memphis studio since his Sun days. Afterward he asked, "We have some hits, don't we, Chips?"

Moman replied, "Maybe some of your biggest."

At American Sound, Presley recorded the most significant works of his later career, including "Kentucky Rain" (a song brought to his attention by Lamar Fike) and the "message" songs "In the Ghetto" and "Don't Cry Daddy," both of which were written by Mac Davis. In all, Presley cut enough material for two albums—both of which went gold, as did their four singles, which included "Suspicious Minds," which would be his final number one hit.

When interviewed at American, Presley was heartfelt when he told *Commercial Appeal* reporter Jim Kingsley, "It all started right here in Memphis for me, man, and it feels so good working in this studio." The singer was perched atop a tall stool, eating bites of fried chicken and drinking Nesbitt's orange soda. "It's the most relaxed I've ever seen him," Lamar Fike said.

For his month-long Las Vegas stint, Elvis spent weeks interviewing musicians in Los Angeles before selecting his backup band: guitarist James Burton, bass player Jerry Scheff, drummer Ronnie Tutt, pianist Larry Muhoberac (who would later be replaced by Glenn D. Hardin), and rhythm guitarists John Wilkinson and Charlie Hodge; during the show, Hodge would also fetch the boss's water and Gatorade.

The Jordanaires were tied up in Nashville, so Elvis selected the male gospel group the Imperials—as well as the Sweet Inspirations, a quartet of soul sisters who'd recorded with Aretha Franklin and Dionne Warwick. In Las Vegas, the International Hotel's orchestra would round out the act.

Presley would prove to be the perfect headliner for a brand-new hotel-casino that was being lavished with superlatives. Built for $60 million by Kirk Kerkorian—the town's second most famous tycoon, following Howard Hughes—it was Las Vegas's biggest hotel, with 1,519 rooms and suites. Next to Lake Mead, the 350,000-gallon swimming pool was the state's largest man-made body of water. The hotel's thirty-story main tower was the tallest structure in Nevada. At two thousand seats, the showroom was the largest of its kind.

His name—ELVIS—was displayed in twenty-foot electric letters on the International marquee. On opening night the luminaries who turned out to witness his career revival included Fats Domino, Petula Clark, Ed Ames, Carol Channing, Dick Clark, Paul Anka, George Hamilton, Henry Mancini, Shirley Bassey, Wayne Newton, Angie Dickinson and her songwriter husband Burt Bacharach, as well as Howard Hughes's leading executives. Old friends (Pat Boone) and sweethearts (Ann-Margret) turned out, too. Even protest troubadour Phil Ochs showed—to survey the man he considered a mythical figure.

With its relief carvings of winged gods and goddesses, Roman and Greek columns, and austere statues of George and Martha Washington standing guard at either end of the stage, the Showroom Internationale was a kitsch setting, but there was no denying the power of the act.

As the gold-lamé curtains rose, Elvis sauntered out, toting a guitar. He assumed a wide stance, tossed back his hair, and closed his eyes. Then he lit into "Blue Suede Shoes." From the get-go his electric charisma was apparent. Even from the distant balcony, adorned with plaster cherubs, it was obvious: thirty-four-year-old Elvis Presley still had *it*. He was but seconds into the opening number when the auditorium began to roar with applause, foot-stomping, and cries of "Bravo!" It was impossible for anyone to hear the rest of the song.

Presley went on to perform a songbook of his standards as well as newer material—including the recent Top 10 hit "In the Ghetto." Sometimes he did have to pause to kick-start the old pelvis, but he did it with likable candor—at one point musing, "You just look at me a couple of minutes, while I get my breath back." He *was* a sight to see: clad in a Bill Belew-designed black tunic shirt with opened neckline, black bell-bottoms, and black boots, he was slim and startlingly sideburned. At times the spotlight caught the glint of his chunky rings—

which flashed emeralds, sapphires, and diamonds—and his hefty gold identification bracelet, on which ELVIS was spelled in diamonds.

The next day, he said it was "one of the most exciting nights of my life." The reviewer for the *Los Angeles Herald-Examiner* put it another way: "Elvis Presley is back. He had been away."

His fans had never doubted him. Their devotion to Presley—who had for years graciously dealt with their affection, by corresponding with fan clubs or spending hours talking with those who gathered at the gates of Graceland and Bel-Air—played a large part in his resurgence on the concert circuit.

For his Las Vegas show, they came not just from across the country but from across the sea. Officials at the newly opened International received three hundred reservation requests from as far away as Great Britain and France—a rarity in Las Vegas. One Parisian secretary even sent a hundred-franc note to cover ten shows, dinner, and the late-night show, for five days in a row.

Members of the many Elvis fan clubs across the country, which the Colonel had championed since the 1950s and which Elvis had long supported, were out in force. At the end of the record-breaking run it was estimated that more than ten percent of the 101,500 paying customers were fan club members. To the uninitiated, their devotion bordered on the weird: some fans milling outside the showroom were literally covered in Elvis buttons. Still others climbed into their cars and followed the Elvis tour as it traveled the country. This emotional devotion grew as Elvis continued to tour. Indeed, in his final, troubled years Presley seemed to reach out most to his fans—who loved him unconditionally.

So popular was the Vegas run that even on the so-called "slow days," the lines for tickets formed in the early-morning hours at the reservation counter. By ten o'clock one Saturday morning five hundred people had showed up—most of whom had to be turned away. When the engagement ended, the hotel reported that there had never been an empty seat in the house. Over twenty-nine days Elvis had grossed $1.5 million.

The town had never seen anything like it.

Surprisingly, Parker came up short when the International offered a five-year deal for Elvis. Under the terms of the contract, Presley would earn $125,000 a week for eight weeks a year—during two semiannual engagements—for the next five years. The $5-million deal was impressive when it was first made, but when it became obvious that Presley was going to reign as the town's hottest ticket, Parker failed to renegotiate. Nor did the manager take advantage of a stock option of twenty thousand shares of hotel stock at five dollars each. The International stock would quickly climb to seventy dollars a share.

The Colonel preferred the casino floor to the stock market. An inveterate gambler, he became a familiar presence to the dealers, floor men, and cashiers at the International. At the roulette wheel, where nonvalue chips are used (only the dealer and the player know the denomination of the different colors), he had a "system" of betting on every number on the table. Parker also liked to roll the dice. At the craps table he'd place bets using stacks of hundred-dollar chips.

But the Colonel remained a promotional wizard. He paced the casino and lobby floors, passing out vintage color photos of his star and directing fans to the gift store, where they could purchase their souvenir hats, buttons, teddy bears, and more. The Colonel took out advertisements on two hundred or more Las Vegas billboards, and a hundred or more radio spots aired daily. Throughout the casino every employee seemed to sport a hat, scarf, or button touting the show. Elvismania was again under way.

For the first of his shows under the new five-year commitment, Elvis had once again reinvented himself. When he emerged before the glittery curtains in January 1970, he was a breathtaking figure in a white jumpsuit, with a five-inch standing collar and a neckline plunging nearly to the waist. Around his slim waist he wore a karate belt and ropes of pearls. On his fingers he had massive diamond rings. "If the songs don't go over, we can always do a medley of costumes," he quipped to a delighted audience.

"Not since Marlene Dietrich stunned the ringsiders with the sight of those legs encased from hip to ankle in a transparent gown has any performer so electrified this jaded town with a personal appearance," opined Albert Goldman, in his review for *Life*. To Goldman, Elvis "looked like a heaping portion of male cheesecake ripe for the eyeteeth of the hundreds of women ogling him through opera glasses." The writer went on to deride Presley as "the King of the Oldy-Moldy-Goldys."

Just as his television special had been a springboard to his reincarnation in Las Vegas, the Vegas show led to a revival on the road. It started with a February 1970 booking at the Houston Astrodome, as part of the Houston Livestock Show and Rodeo. The show's organizers touted Elvis as the biggest star in the thirty-eight-year-old history of the rodeo. He was certainly a different kind of drawing card. A year earlier the featured performers had been Roy Rogers and Dale Evans, with their matching Western outfits and wholesome repertoire that wrapped with wishes for "happy trails."

At a press conference prior to his opening, Presley stressed that he was no stranger to the Lone Star State. "I kind of started out in Texas," he said, referring to the countless small Texas towns he had toured in the midfifties. "You name 'em, I've played 'em." But, he readily admitted, he'd never played an arena with the 44,000-plus capacity of the Dome.

The first Dome show, a matinee, pulled in just seventeen thousand people—four thousand of them handicapped youngsters who were given complimentary tickets by the Colonel and Presley. The performer was unnerved. He paced the floor of his room at the Astroworld Hotel, lamenting, "I guess I just don't have it anymore." Later that evening, though, he looked out the window of the suite and was staggered by the sight of cars backed up for miles, making their way to the arena for the night's performance. "Damn! I guess I've still got it, after all," he muttered.

He had to keep his sense of humor in following *cattle* on the daily playbill. During one performance Elvis excitedly jumped from the stage and performed as he walked through the arena—stepping right into a pile of fresh manure. Try as he might, he couldn't shake the stuff from his customized boots—though he kept trying as he more or less limped his way back to the stage. Later that night, among his friends, he laughed until tears rolled down his face. "Did you see me step in that shit? I think it got more applause than I did!"

A logistical challenge was involved as well. The Dome had a farm tractor haul a small stage out to the arena center; the band members were atop the traveling stage. Following them, standing in the front seat of a red Jeep convertible, Elvis clung to the windshield for support. Before heading for the stage, the Jeep circled the arena, and Presley reached out his hands to touch the fans who were grabbing for him. Increasingly, he took on the aura of a king greeting his subjects.

More than 207,000 people saw Presley perform in six shows at the Dome—a record for the rodeo. At his last performance Priscilla showed up, sporting a black cowboy hat and a cheeky demeanor. To the head of security she joked, "Say, that guy who sings, he isn't too bad. I wouldn't mind meeting him."

By the time Elvis returned to Las Vegas for his second engagement of the year, he was basking in renewed glory. This time the town was touting the "Elvis Summer Festival." MGM was there to capture rehearsals and opening night with five Panavision cameras—two on cranelike booms—for a documentary that would be called *Elvis—That's the Way It Is*.

The International had to turn hundreds of people away nightly. In honor of the attendance records set by their headliner, the International presented Elvis with a massive gold belt—one that resembled a heavyweight champion's belt. Presley wore it proudly for several years thereafter.

During the Vegas run it was announced that Presley was going on his first extended tour since 1958. "It will put Elvis back in front of his demanding millions of fans," declared Parker.

This tour wasn't like the old days of barnstorming with Scotty and Bill. No bass was strapped to the top of a battered car; no honky-tonks or armory buildings to play. Elvis traveled by customized bus or plane—with what seemed a multitudinous crew. Heralding one Minneapolis-area play date, columnist Jim Klobuchar noted, "Elvis Presley arrived unpretentiously aboard [his personal jet] with his personal physician, security chief, twelve bodyguards, guitar tuner, and the balance of the city of Nashville."

The first tour, in September 1970, encompassed just six cities. But the fans in Phoenix, St. Louis, Detroit, Miami, Tampa, and Mobile spread the word: there was no other concert experience to equal the one generated by Elvis. A second tour immediately followed.

From the moment he entered an arena in all his jumpsuited glory, bathed in blinding white lights, his concerts took on an otherworldly aura. His staid movie depictions of the past decade had vanished. He sauntered; he pranced; he belted out. He dropped to one knee and crooned to women who sat ringside. He also sometimes got sexual, but did it playfully, not crudely. During one concert when his macramé belt happened to dangle suggestively between his legs, he sneered, pointed down, then reached between his legs. "Gotcha!" he yelled as he pulled something upward. The audience was breathless—until Presley held the belt out, with an innocent schoolboy expression on his face.

It wasn't just his image he had fun with. "Hi, folks, I'm Johnny Cash," he sometimes drawled into the mike, before breaking into a deft imitation of Cash doing "I Walk the Line." During his performance of "Polk Salad Annie" he sometimes showed how the competition did it. "Tom Jones!" he shouted, accentuating the striptease moves. "Engelbert!" With that, like Humperdinck, he hugged the microphone, softened his voice, and segued into "Please Release Me." To do Glen Campbell he teasingly lifted his voice. Lest anyone forget who was center stage, he'd wrap the routine by hotly yelling, "Me!" He'd complete the song in what one fan deemed "a low-down, evil stance," swaggering and sneering and sweating as if his very life depended on it.

Elvis could still twist an audience around his finger. In Phoenix, after more than an hour of performing, he dropped to the stage in the midst of "Suspicious Minds" and just lay there, practically motionless and silent. The musicians likewise torqued down the sound. The crowd became eerily quiet. Then, as the band members cranked up, so did Presley, slowly rising for the rest of the song—to deafening applause.

During "Funny How Time Slips Away" he once silenced an arena when he walked to the edge of the stage where a mother held up her crippled daughter. As the hushed crowd watched, the rock star bent down and gently kissed the child.

When he performed at the Los Angeles Forum in the fall of 1970, in a jumpsuit dripping with floor-length fringe, he thoroughly confused his audience—and the reviewers—with off-the-cuff banter that began, "A lot of things have been written about me, and most of it has been untrue." He went on to brag about his achievements, his fifty-six gold singles and fourteen gold albums—"and if there's anyone out there who doubts it, you can come to Memphis and argue about it, 'cause I've got every one of them hanging on the wall. I'm really proud of them . . ." He babbled on about having outsold the Beatles and Tom Jones, "all of 'em put together."

What the audience didn't know was that Presley was reacting to having just been served with legal papers for a paternity suit. He would go on to vehemently fight the suit (there were blood and lie-detector tests), and to win it, but the action pointed up a sad fact. Though he had returned to the music he loved, his private life was continuing to roll off the rails.

Crazy from
the Heat

t the Los Angeles Forum show Priscilla was luminous—looking every bit like royalty—in a simple white, floor-length dress with a hood. She stood by her man throughout the ordeal of the paternity suit. But she knew about the rampant infidelity.

Starting back in Las Vegas, he had cashed in on his status as a sex symbol. As in the 1950s, he was once again eliciting hungry eyes from his female fans. His thirtieth-floor suite at the International became a welcome wagon for the willing.

The modus operandi for lining up "dates" went this way: If a particular woman caught his eye as he performed, he would tell his pals during breaks between songs and they would approach the woman in question to arrange an introduction. Other times the Mafia members would spot beauties they thought he might like. Invited to the penthouse suite, the women were usually advised not to speak to Elvis unless he spoke to them first, and not to discuss the goings-on with any reporters.

According to Joe Esposito, some nights the guys would be relieved when Presley opted to bypass courtship. Instead he'd say, "Let's have a party tonight. Call down for a bunch of hookers." But Elvis didn't join the guys in taking turns with the girls. "I'd rather watch," he would say.

Only occasionally would he take a prostitute by the hand and guide her into his bedroom. As Esposito noted, "They weren't pure enough for him. Elvis romanticized sex."

Sadly for his marriage, the romance was gone.

No one defining incident led Priscilla to eventually turn loose of her desperate grip on Elvis Presley and their marriage. Rather, the problems that existed before they exchanged their vows never went away.

Initially, she was diverted. She attended to their tiny daughter and oversaw the family's move to a $335,000 two-story estate in Holmby Hills. "Decorating became my passion," recalled Priscilla, who decorated with her husband's tastes in mind. She also plunged into the dance-exercise crazes sweeping rich Los Angeles. "He was king of rock and roll, and I had to be his queen," she explained later.

Yet she still had to fight her way through the Memphis Mafia. Though their ranks were briefly thinned after the wedding, Elvis always thought of ways to bring the boys back in. "A bunch of guys and their wives are always around," Priscilla complained. "We never have any privacy."

In the royal bedchambers, though, privacy only led to embarrassment. The Elvis who had played sex games with Priscilla since she was a teenager, recording their romps on ten thousand Polaroids, now seldom touched her in bed.

For a while she shrugged off his disinterest, attributing it to the mild uppers and downers he was using to get through the Las Vegas appearances and recording sessions. But after finding another woman's toiletries in his limousine, she could shrug it off no longer. "I'd like to know what you're doing for sex these days, because you certainly aren't interested in me," she daringly said one night.

Elvis responded by gulping a handful of pills and throwing himself on the bed and reaching for one of his spiritual books. He began reading aloud about the "blending of the body and the soul."

Priscilla sat up in bed, declaring, "You know, Elvis, you ought to be reading a sex manual!"

He looked over angrily. "Don't start!"

Priscilla drifted in wifely purgatory, hearing rumors about other women—including those who nestled in "her" special booth at the International during the many nights she was at home with their daughter in Los Angeles.

For the first three years of her marriage, while Elvis reclaimed his career, she stayed in the background. Sometimes she spent entire days in bed. Still, she grew tired of being a wife of convenience. "You haven't really wanted me sexually since Lisa Marie was born," she told Presley.

He tried to change the subject. "You have all the money you want, two beautiful homes, all the help you need. What do you want from me?"

"I want you," she wailed.

She wanted him to make love to her, but, she pleaded, "Don't make me beg." Finally, Presley explained to Priscilla that his personal belief system prevented him from sleeping with the mother of his child. "It just isn't right," he said.

"Ever?" she asked.

"Ever," Presley said with finality.

He could be petulant; he was certainly childish. In many ways he never grew up. Stardom allowed him to indulge his boyish interests. In the fifties he rented out the roller rink. In the sixties he and his pals unleashed madcap pandemonium on his movie sets. In the seventies he played with guns and badges.

His gun fixation stemmed, in part, from threats on his life. They had started in the 1950s, with anonymous letters (which were duly reported to law enforcement agencies, including the FBI). In the sixties the grisly slaughter of actress Sharon Tate and her friends, at the hands of the Manson family, terrified all of Hollywood—Presley included. "That was when he started going crazy with security systems," recalled Richard Davis. It was also when he and the Mafia began stocking up on weaponry.

That weaponry was put to use in the seventies, when his public appearances led to more threats on his life. At one point, an unidentified male caller told Sonny West that an attempt was to be made on Presley's life in the International showroom. For fifty thousand dollars, the caller would reveal the would-be assassin's name. The FBI took the warning seriously—especially when a menu from the showroom appeared in Presley's mail, showing a drawing of a gun pointed toward the performer's heart.

It was at this time that Presley beefed up his personnel—even putting in a call to Red West, who returned to the fold. He also began to pack his pistols. On the night he thought he was to be targeted, Elvis performed with a derringer in his boot and a .45 tucked into his waistband. He also implored his buddies to exact revenge, should he be killed, declaring, "I don't want any son of a bitch running around saying, 'I killed Elvis Presley.' If some guy shoots me, I want you to rip his fucking eyes out!"

No one ever made good on those threats to "take Presley out" during concert. But fueled by drugs, Elvis's paranoia led to some wild escapades involving guns and gunplay. When the wife of one of his backup singers found her motel room had been burglarized, Elvis made his guys load up their weapons so they could form a "posse" and race to her rescue. She was wearing a flimsy nightgown and had her hair in curlers when Elvis Presley and company burst into her room.

Some of the Mafia have recounted how Presley liked to attach a "police light" to his car, so that he could pull over speeders—who were surprised to get a lecture from the superstar, who invariably flashed one of his honorary law-enforcement badges.

Like most boys, Presley was in awe of men who risked their lives in their daily jobs to protect and serve. The policemen and firemen he befriended, during his touring, were equally enamored of him, and more than happy to present him with guns, badges, and even uniforms for his collection. That passion led to one of the oddest incidents of Presley's life.

It happened in December 1970, when Vernon and Priscilla—who had formed an alliance—confronted Elvis about a flurry of bills that had come into Graceland. Ten Mercedes cars (which Presley presented as gifts to friends) had cost $85,000. And he had spent an additional $20,000 on guns.

"Son, this has got to stop!" said an exasperated Vernon.

Like a pouting child, Elvis would not be reasoned with. Instead, he stormed off into the night. For the first time, he had no bodyguards with him, and neither his wife nor his father knew where he could be going. "We were mystified," Priscilla recalled. After all, "Elvis didn't even know his own phone number."

Presley did have a phone number, though, for buddy Jerry Schilling, who was out in Los Angeles training to be a film editor. What happened next, Schilling said, was like "one of those Howard Hughes stories."

Schilling was asleep at 3:00 A.M. when the call came. "What are you doing?" asked Presley. "Meet me in the morning at the American Airlines counter in L.A." The mystified Schilling did just that, watching as passengers disembarked one by one. Finally, Elvis exited—looking somewhat sheepish. His face was also blotchy and swollen. "I had this penicillin reaction. And then I ate chocolate on the plane. I guess it brought the reaction back," explained Elvis. He needed to see a doctor, but first, he told Schilling, they had to give the plane's stewardesses rides home.

Schilling later accompanied Presley back to the airport—because Elvis said he "needed" to go to Washington, D.C. Schilling had no idea why, but he knew he couldn't go along due to his schedule in the editing room. But back at the airport Elvis ran into problems: he tried to board the plane with two guns, one tucked into his waistband, the other in his boot. "I'm sorry, sir," said the steward. "We'll have to take charge of those."

Elvis was infuriated and refused to climb aboard. Shortly afterward, the plane's pilot interceded—and personally asked Elvis to take a seat, with his weaponry! That's when Schilling decided it would be best to accompany his friend, though he still had no idea why they were journeying to the nation's capital.

Once on board, Presley generated some double takes: he was an ostentatious sight in his purple crushed-velvet suit with cape and his enormous gold "championship" belt. He also wore large sunglasses, which were by now becoming a Presley trademark. They were more than an exercise in vanity; the glare really did hurt his eyes. Elvis had been diagnosed as being in the early stages of glaucoma.

During the flight Elvis struck up a conversation with a young serviceman who had just returned home for Christmas from Vietnam. In a burst of patriotic pride Presley gave him five hundred dollars—despite protests from Schilling, who pointed out that was all the money they had for their impromptu trip. Elvis waved him off. He had more serious concerns.

As Schilling discovered, Elvis Presley was on a mission to meet President Richard Nixon. He wanted to participate in the country's war on drugs. What he really wanted, though, was his own federal narcotics badge.

The mania to acquire the badge had its genesis in a chance meeting with Paul Frees, the man who supplied the voices for some of the most famous characters in animation and television commercials. Frees was Ludwig Von Drake and the Pillsbury Doughboy and scores of others. He was also a police buff who had bragged to Elvis about his federal badge.

Elvis was determined to get one, too. After requesting a half dozen sheets of American Airlines stationery from a stewardess, Elvis went to work drafting a handwritten letter to Nixon—stressing his desire to "be of any service that I can to help The Country out." As Presley pointed out, "The drug culture, the hippie elements, the SDS,* Black Panthers, etc., do not consider me as their enemy or as they call it The Establishment." Of course, wrote Presley, to truly have an effect he would need to be named a "Federal Agent at Large" and to be presented with federal credentials.

P.S. He also had a personal gift he wanted to give the president.

On the morning of December 21, White House aide Egil "Bud" Krogh got a call from fellow aide Dwight Chapin, who asked, "Are you sitting down? You won't believe it, but the King is here."

"King who?" asked Krogh. "There are no kings on the president's schedule today."

"*The* King. Elvis. King of Rock."

Chapin went on to explain that Presley had personally handed over a six-page letter, for the president, to the guards at the Northwest Gate. He was requesting a meeting to discuss his participation in the drug war.

Krogh went to work on a memo to White House chief of staff H. R. Haldeman, stressing the positives of using the high-profile Presley in the antidrug campaign. As Krogh noted, the recent drug deaths of Janis Joplin and Jimi Hendrix underscored the seriousness of the issue. Heretofore, celebrities who had lent their names to the battle had been conservatives the likes of Jack Webb, the Reverend Billy Graham, and Art Linkletter.

After dispatching his memo, Krogh had a brief meeting with Presley, accompanied by Schilling as well as Sonny West, who had by then joined them in D.C.

The first thing Krogh thought, after taking in Presley in all his sartorial splendor, was, "Uh-oh, this could get a little dicey." At the Nixon White House, staid business suits were the order of the day. "He doesn't have a tie," Krogh kept thinking. Neither did Jerry Schilling, who was in a leather jacket. Sonny West was wearing a suit, but it was worn with an open-necked shirt and a chunky gold medallion.

"Gold chains hadn't quite made their way onto the necks of male staff members in the White House, at least during business hours," Krogh has recalled.

Yet if Presley and his pals were not White House fashion plates, they were sincere. Krogh told them he would try to arrange a meeting with Nixon. The minute the trio left, he put together another memo,

*SDS was the radical campus group Students for a Democratic Society.

this time to the president. Before lunch, Krogh got the okay for the meeting.

A call was put through to a D.C. hotel where Presley was registered as "Jon Burrows." He was asked to be back at the Northeast Gate at 11:45 for the 12:30 meeting. But when the trio returned, the guards called Krogh to report a problem: Elvis wanted to bring a gun into the Oval Office to present it as a gift to Nixon. What could have been a diplomatic nightmare was smoothed over by Krogh, who rushed to greet the singer and his bodyguards, and to explain that due to "standard policy" the gun (which turned out to be a World War II–era chrome-plated Colt .45 with a wood handle) couldn't be taken into the president's office. Presley could leave it with the guards, though, and it would later be presented to Nixon. Presley was appeased.

His meeting with Nixon was one of the more surreal encounters in the annals of American politics. Elvis showed Nixon family photographs, including one of tiny Lisa Marie. He also pulled from his pockets a cluster of his honorary badges, received from law enforcement agencies across the country. "I really support what our police have to do," said Presley. Describing himself as "just a poor boy from Tennessee," he said, "I've gotten a lot from my country. And I'd like to do something to repay for what I've gotten."

"That would be very helpful," said Nixon, who kept staring at Presley's enormous commemorative gold belt. Nixon looked up quizzically, though, when Elvis started in about a link between Communist brainwashing and the drug culture. Krogh was equally dumbfounded, but Elvis himself changed the subject when he eagerly asked, "Mr. President, can you get me a badge from the Narcotics Bureau? I've been trying to get one for my collection."

Nixon was uncertain. "Uh, Bud, can we get him a badge?" Krogh felt certain they could if the president would approve it. Nixon smiled. "I'd like to do that."

Presley would be designated a "special assistant" in the Bureau of Narcotics and Dangerous Drugs. Along with a badge, he received a photo identification card from the U.S. Department of Justice.

Elvis was so elated that he did something not at all typical of the usual White House VIP: he walked over to Nixon and gave him a hearty bear hug. He also charmingly requested that his friends, in the adjoining room, also get to meet the president. And so it was that Jerry Schilling and Sonny West also shook hands with Nixon, who presented all three men with tie clasps emblazoned with the presidential seal.

Krogh was to later muse, "While the tie clasps were probably great gifts for most men, I wasn't sure Elvis, Sonny, or Jerry even owned any ties." The trio were also presented with ballpoint pens, cuff links, and more.

After again shaking hands with the president, Presley and his friends left—their hands filled with the mementos of their day at the White House. Krogh escorted the trio through the halls of the West Wing and the Old Executive Office Building, and on to the White House mess hall—where they had lunch amid a roomful of startled staff members.

Ironically, it took thirteen months for the media to get wind of the meeting. On January 27, 1972, *Washington Post* columnist Jack Anderson detailed Presley's acquisition of a federal narcotics badge. By that time the honor brought guffaws from Presley associates, who knew that if ever there was a narcotics authority, it was Elvis Presley.

To Elvis, if the badge represented his decidedly misguided notions about what constitutes drug abuse, it was also indicative of his sincere patriotic beliefs. To him, it was also a triumph—one of a series of honors bestowed upon the performer in this period.

Less than a month after shaking Nixon's hand, Presley found himself in illustrious company when he was selected one of the Ten Outstanding Young Men of America for 1970 by the national Junior Chamber of Commerce—better known as the Jaycees. Over the years, honorees have included John F. Kennedy, Robert F. Kennedy, Orson Welles, Howard Hughes, and Henry Kissinger.

The night he accepted the honor, at an awards banquet held at the Memphis Municipal Auditorium, Presley was reflective, misty-eyed, and clearly humbled to be in the company of the nine others, who included Thomas Atkins, Boston's first black councilman; biophysicist Dr. Mario Capecchi of Harvard Medical School; and Dr. George Todaro, of the National Cancer Institute. During Presley's acceptance speech—the first such public address of his life—he was every bit the rock star in a customized black "tuxedo" worn with yellow *Easy Rider* sunglasses and massive diamond rings on his fingers. But he didn't think he outshone the other recipients, whom he acknowledged in his acceptance speech. "These men," said Presley, "they care. You stop to think, and they're building the kingdom of heaven."

As for himself, Presley told the crowd of two thousand, "I've always been a dreamer." Explaining that as a boy he had gone to movies and read comics "and I was the hero," he added, "My dreams have come true one hundred times over." Appropriately, he reached for the lyrics of a song when he said, "Without a song a man ain't got a friend. Without a song the day won't ever end. So, I'll just keep singing my song." He looked as if he was about to cry as he left the podium. In years to come, Presley would remember the night as one of the proudest in his life.

By this time RCA had announced that his record sales were the second largest in history after Bing Crosby's. Presley's incredible stats included more than eighty singles, forty albums, and nearly 300 million records sold. And though he didn't crack 1971's Top 10 hits, he received another kind of recognition: he was the subject of a biography written by respected rock journalist Jerry Hopkins, who called Presley one of America's three best-known contributions to the world—along with Coca-Cola and Mickey Mouse.

As befits a man who had been deemed an American institution, Presley's birthplace in Tupelo became a tourist attraction. The shotgun shack was restored—complete with Works Progress Administration mattress and a pie safe in the back room. Elvis's fifth-grade teacher, Mrs. Oleta Grimes, was a special guest at the ribbon cutting. In Memphis, twelve miles of Highway 51, including the strip in front of Graceland, was renamed Elvis Presley Boulevard.

Responding to the public's embrace, and his own heightened sense of power, he came up with a symbol for his most steadfast followers with the creation of the TCB emblem, which he had fashioned onto jewelry. It stood for "taking care of business," and because the TCB was accompanied by a lightning bolt, that business was taken care of "in a flash."

During one of his spiritual periods, Presley wrote down the philosophy behind the TCB: "More self-respect, more respect for fellow man, respect for fellow students & instructions. . . . Body conditioning, meditation for calming and stilling of the mind and body . . . a new outlook and personal philosophy." He wasn't entirely straight-faced, for the philosophy also stressed "freedom from constipation."

All the public acclaim did not mask his erratic private behavior. "I learned that Elvis couldn't serve two masters. He had a family and he had what he loved most, singing and being on stage. That's where he got his fulfillment from," Priscilla theorized in 1997. "After all the adoration from his fans, it was very difficult for Elvis to come home to quietness."

The fantasy that had begun when she was a schoolgirl had become nothing but a facade. She was married to Elvis Presley in name only. She had earned the name and she would keep it—until this day.

As for romance, she found it with a sensitive, handsome karate instructor hired by Presley for lessons. The instructor had performed at karate tournaments attended by Elvis and Priscilla, and several years later, he came backstage at a Presley show when he was working as a bodyguard for Phil Spector. That's when Elvis got the idea that his wife should study karate.

Mike Stone, who was part Hawaiian, was as strong as he was gentle. Priscilla used to say that, in some ways, he resembled Elvis. "He's very masculine. He treats me like a woman, and he never lets me forget that he is a man." Like Elvis, he was also charming. Before six months elapsed, Stone had captured Priscilla's heart—mainly because he focused on her needs rather than his own. She was soon regularly cheating on the most famous husband in the world. She was also crushed by guilt.

"In the end, I don't think either of them tried very hard," said Becky Yancey, who watched the marriage dissolve. "They just drifted slowly apart, even when they were both at Graceland."

There had been rumblings for a year or so when Priscilla finally decided to leave Elvis for good in February 1972. She plotted her move carefully, deciding there would be less chance of a confrontation if she broke the news just prior to one of his big shows and then caught a plane back to Los Angeles.

Mike Stone was surprised and worried that Priscilla was making a decision she would come to regret. She was leaving one of the richest and most powerful men in the entertainment world for a semi-employed karate instructor and bodyguard.

"I know what I'm doing," Priscilla told Stone. "Exactly what I'm doing. I'm going to tell him the truth. It's time we stopped hiding like this. I want everyone to know how much I love you and that I'm going to live with you."

Stone was so in love with Priscilla at that point that he was inclined to let her have her way. It was only fair that Elvis knew the marriage was over.

When Priscilla at last approached her husband—and father figure—she almost lost her nerve. Elvis, who was aglitter in spangled glory, stood before his dressing-room mirror with a commanding presence she hadn't seen since before his movie years.

"I'm leaving you," she said with as much decisiveness as she could muster.

Elvis leapt and pinned her roughly against the wall—as if they were about to make love.

"Elvis, please," she said.

"I thought this is what you wanted," he muttered.

"Not now, not anymore. Not this way," she answered, and slid out from under his bulk.

"Go on!" he yelled. "Leave."

In the next moment, however, the passive, dependent Elvis—who had subconsciously substituted Priscilla for his mother—took control. In a mixture of their private baby talk and the contrite-lover pose he'd portrayed in his movies, he made all the usual promises: he'd cancel the tours, they'd start all over again.

"Too late," Priscilla said with amazing resolve. "You've said all these things before. You never keep a single vow." She added more coldly, "Elvis, you can't change. But I have already changed. I'm leaving. You have no say in this matter."

In a candid interview with *Parade* contributing editor Dotson Rader, Priscilla recently revealed why she "had to leave" Elvis: "In a sense, he was lost. It was insanity. . . . It was bringing me down. That wasn't happiness to me.

"I realized that this was not the kind of life I wanted for myself and Lisa Marie, having my husband involved with pills—drugs for sleeping, then to get awake, drugs for diet. My husband was on the verge of self-destruction. . . . It broke my heart. I had to save my daughter and myself. I had to make a life of my own."

So she left, slipping out of his Las Vegas dressing room, closing the door on her life with Presley.

Amazingly, Elvis had regained his composure when he strutted out to where his Mafia buddies were waiting. "Priscilla's left me," he said in midstride—to no one in particular. "It's rock and roll. It won't let you have a wife."

Then he was onstage.

His Latest Flames

For months after Priscilla left, Elvis cursed her as a Judas. He told whoever would listen that she was an ingrate, "after all I've done for her." Furious that she had found another man, he also spoke of "betrayal!" Those around him took these statements with a grain of salt. As Joe Esposito put it, "Elvis simply could not be a one-woman man." Marriage and fatherhood, he added, "hadn't altered his behavior with other women in the slightest."

When Presley met raven-haired Joyce Bova, who was then beginning a career on Capitol Hill working for Congress, he told her how beautiful she was. "That work you do, it sure sounds interesting. Will you come back after the show?" Still later, he asked Bova to have dinner with him. When she expressed concern about his marital status, he was affronted. "What does 'married' have to do with this? I just want to be with someone I can talk to." Besides, he promised, "You should realize that with you I would have to be a perfect gentleman."

Bova, who recounted her affair with Presley in her book, *Don't Ask Forever*, was one of many stunning women who found themselves unable to resist the married Presley's seductive charms.

Another was the exotic actress Barbara Leigh, who met Elvis backstage in 1971. She was with her boyfriend, Jim Aubrey, the president of

MGM, which had produced the recent documentary *Elvis—That's the Way It Is*. Leigh, who appeared in a string of hip, early-seventies films, including *The Christian Licorice Store* and *Pretty Maids All in a Row*, was involved with Presley for six months. Presley even brought her to Graceland when his wife went off to see her family.

Savvy beyond her twenty-three years, Leigh didn't fall in love with Presley. In the first place she didn't anticipate his leaving his wife, so she didn't allow herself to fall in love. Besides, "I was traveling around, too, doing films and juggling men the way Elvis juggled women." She eventually broke with Presley when she became involved with her leading man in *Junior Bonner*. Steve McQueen, a leading box-office draw famed for playing antiheroes, used to jokingly dub Presley "that guitar guy," while Presley called him "that hick with the motorcycle." In the end, the guy with the bike triumphed in winning Leigh's affections.

In any case, Presley never wanted for company. He seldom had to do more than look at a woman in order to get her. Questions about Priscilla he dismissed. "Look, I am married. But my wife and I aren't committed to each other. We have an understanding. She lives her own life, and I live mine," he would say sincerely, sometimes hastening to add, "But if Priscilla should show up, be discreet, okay?"

One of Elvis's backup singers, Kathy Westmoreland, wasn't even involved with him when he popped into her dressing room one day to say that his wife was visiting, along with Joanie Esposito. "I've told them that you're engaged. So play along, please." When Westmoreland looked at him quizzically, Presley explained, "It's better if the wives don't think that other women are available."

Though Westmoreland felt uneasy about it, she eventually became a lover to the married Presley. But she also remained a friend and "kindred spirit" as they performed together from August 1970 through his final 1977 tour. A diminutive brunette, Westmoreland was only eighteen when she began singing with the Metropolitan Opera. She was performing on a string of television variety shows, including *The Red Skelton Show* and *The Tim Conway Show*, and with the Ray Coniff Singers, when she was asked to join the Presley revue.

When she showed up at the International Hotel, she had a brief meeting with Colonel Parker—whom she found to be "blunt, funny, and wearing a carnival hat that said ELVIS." She was handed a songbook filled with more than five hundred titles, plus a stack of records, to take with her to her hotel room. "Can you ad-lib?" asked producer Felton Jarvis, explaining it was a prerequisite for the job, since Elvis's musical selections—with the exception of opening and closing numbers—were not predetermined. "Anything could happen, and sometimes did," Westmoreland remembered.

She met Presley for the first time backstage. An elevator door opened and he came out, wearing caramel-colored slacks with a black leather jacket. She thought he looked "like a biker." But he wasn't surly like one. "Welcome to the show," he said warmly before disappearing into his dressing room. Later, before they went on, he said, "We're happy you're here. Just go out and have a good time. We're here to make people happy. We're here to have fun, otherwise it's work." Then with a wink he turned on his heel.

The soprano had been with the show a few weeks when Sonny West approached her and said, "Elvis would like you to come up and visit. He'd like to get to know you as a friend." When she went to the penthouse suite, she found about three dozen people milling about, including Mafia members. Soon, Presley swept into the room, looking theatrical in a deep blue velvet suit. "These voluptuous-looking blondes made a rush for him," recalled Kathy, who was surprised when Presley waded through the bosomy beauties and took a seat beside her, casually putting his arm around her tiny frame.

Westmoreland, who knew he was married, found herself thinking, "Uh-oh." When he escorted her into his bedroom, to show her a book they'd been talking about, she wondered, "How am I going to get out of this?" She wound up telling him she felt she needed to return to her room. He gallantly escorted her, but not before he also kissed her. "I remember thinking that he felt so soft. And that was somehow very surprising to me."

As time passed, they discovered they shared interests in reading, religion, music, and philosophy. "So why not sleep with me?" Presley asked.

When Westmoreland explained she was still a virgin, he was impressed. "I respect you for that," he said. He went on to stress that if she'd just share his bed, he wouldn't make any moves. "Just keep me company in the night."

So for five weeks she did. "I slept in one of his pajama tops, and he had a toothbrush for me." He let her know, however, that when she was ready, so was he. He occasionally embarrassed her in front of his friends, to whom he'd say, "This is one strong woman." She didn't like her virginity to be the topic of discussion.

When they at last became lovers, she found him to be gentle, caressing, and sweet. "There was never anything kinky, nothing abnormal." She wasn't asked to pose for any Polaroids. He never showed her any sex movies. He didn't ask her to play dress-up. "I'm always puzzled when I hear those stories, because it was nothing like that."

He bought her several gifts, which she felt "funny" about accepting. One was an Egyptian-style ring with a cat on it. Westmoreland was "a cat person," and Presley was fascinated with Egyptology.

Still, he could be callous. He used to say, "It's time," meaning she should go to her own room because another woman was on the way. "And sometimes he told me about whoever else he was seeing," said Westmoreland.

The two often talked about the Bible, Jesus, religions other than Christianity—"because Elvis was fascinated with all facets of religion"—as well as his fears about his mortality. "He was sure he wouldn't live past forty-two. He used to tell me that his mother died when she was that age [actually, Gladys Presley died at forty-six]. He was sure he would, too."

She saw his moods grow darker with time. Meanwhile, life on the road took a toll. The troupe numbered anywhere from eighty to a hundred people—including the musicians, all the singers, the Mafia, the roadies, and more. It was a tough way to live. "Oh, God, the rigors of the road," Westmoreland groaned. "Day after day, you're sometimes in two or even three cities daily. You get three hours of sleep. You get up, you eat hotel food, you travel, you perform, you eat hotel food, you go back on the road. And your body feels it. It's impossible physically. For a while, Elvis actually maintained his psychological health better than any of us."

He had reason to be upbeat in 1972, the year he made history by becoming the first performer to sell out four consecutive June concerts at Madison Square Garden. As with his Las Vegas debut, the shows brought out the VIPs, among them John Lennon, George Harrison, Art Garfunkel, and Bob Dylan.

The performances marked his first return to the Big Apple since his 1950s television appearances. A preconcert press conference was his first since returning to the road in 1969. Held in the Mercury Ballroom of the New York Hilton, the event drew more than two hundred reporters.

Seated alongside his father at a long table, he wore a pale blue Regency-style suit with a high collar and a flowing dark blue cape. The eye-catching championship gold belt was around his waist. His hair, now worn longer than ever, was sprayed in place. "No more greasy kid stuff," said Elvis with a grin.

Why was he back making public appearances? "I missed it." Why had he managed to last so long? "Vitamin E."

What did he think of war protesters? If he were drafted today, would he go? Presley hesitated ever so slightly, then looked at the female reporter. "Honey, I'd just as soon keep my own personal opinions to myself. I'm just an entertainer."

What about those entertainers who did speak up? "Do you think they should keep their opinions to themselves?" he was asked.

Presley, who privately cursed performers he viewed as anti-American (such as Jane Fonda) and rock stars he felt were offensive (such as David Bowie), shook his head and simply answered, "No."

The thirty-seven-year-old entertainer was less evasive when asked if he was "satisfied" with his image: "The image is one thing—the human being is another. It's hard to live up to the image."

During his Garden stint the image was glittering. The shows were all that Presley shows were reputed to be.

During opening night, Las Vegas comedian Jackie Kahane was booed off the stage by a hip crowd that had no patience for worn-out one-liners about teenage daughters, long hair, and college kids. Besides, they didn't want an opening act. They wanted Elvis. As a detachment of mounted police and a line of squad cars maintained control outside, and more than two hundred private security guards manned the aisles inside, the lights dimmed and the strains of "That's All Right" began.

That was the signal the crowd of 22,500 needed to hear. They rose from their seats to welcome the man who appeared in a gleaming white jumpsuit with flowing Apache ties and swirling cape. *Time* said he looked like "Mr. Tomorrow." The magazine that used to rail against his music and movies also hailed his comeback as "perhaps the most impressive in the history of pop music."

Though he was not up to par vocally during any of his Garden shows, Presley knew what the crowd wanted. He gave of himself until he was drenched through his clothes and slack with exhaustion. It was a tour de force that gave credence to Elvis's words: "I put my whole heart into what I do. Maybe people can see that."

Actually, his audiences were reacting to more than the heartfelt performance. At concerts in Las Vegas, and at Stateline, Nevada—where Elvis now regularly performed at the Sierra Tahoe Hotel—the showrooms became love fests for ardent females who sent their panties and room keys flying toward the stage. The strutting star responded by gifting his admirers with scarves as well as kisses—eliciting shrieks from the arena.

The fever was catching. It wasn't uncommon for women to rush the stage—sometimes bounding over tabletops, knocking over champagne buckets, glasses, ashtrays, and more—in order to reach their idol. Six-foot-four, 240-pound Jere Walker, who worked as an escort bodyguard at the Sahara Tahoe, sometimes found himself physically carting near-hysterical women off the stage and depositing them outside the show-room's doors. Some nights Walker and the other bodyguards would exchange smiles as they watched frenzied women squeal and bounce uncontrollably atop the laps of their clearly delighted dates. "You could see that there was a lotta love going on during those concerts," said Walker.

On a roll, professionally, Presley's private life also took an upturn. In July 1972, six months after Priscilla had walked out, George Klein invited languorous beauty Linda Diane Thompson to the Memphian Theater, which Elvis rented out for private all-night screenings. A stu-dent at Memphis State University, she was the current Miss Tennessee and third runner-up to Miss U.S.A. Thompson was too nervous to go on her own, so she brought along a girlfriend, Miss Rhode Island.

As the movie flickered on the screen, Presley zeroed in on Thompson. As she recalled, "He came and sat next to me and started getting a little friendly—you know, the old yawn and stretch of the arm behind the seat." Within a few weeks he had whisked her away to Las Vegas. She returned home proudly displaying an emerald ring with dia-mond clusters.

A virgin when she met Presley, theirs was a four-and-a-half-year romance that began in passion, turned to friendship, and eroded into what Linda would call a "mommy-and-baby relationship," intensified by Elvis's drug use. "He needed and wanted more love than anyone I've ever met," said Thompson. Along with the musicians and the Mafia, she packed her bags and went on the road with Presley, ultimately becoming "an appendage."

Unlike petite Priscilla, who had primarily kept in the shadows, the fresh-faced five-foot-nine Thompson accepted the spotlight with aplomb. Whereas Priscilla's shyness made her seem standoffish, Thompson was effervescent. She basked in the role of playing goddess to a rock god, happily giving autographs, and looking every bit as glamorous as Cher, Diana Ross, and the other divas of the day. She had been named the best-dressed coed at Memphis State University, and her relationship with Elvis allowed her to stock her closet with creations from Las Vegas' Suzy Creamcheese and Giorgio's in Beverly Hills. In her midriff-baring fringed outfits, peekaboo dresses, gossamer gowns, full-length furs, lace-up knee boots, and with all that tumbling blond hair, she looked fabulous on Elvis's arm.

Yet she was no mere trophy. A former English major, she was smart, witty, funny, and very much her own woman. When Elvis asked her to don her Miss Tennessee banner and tiara for a Graceland party, she raised her eyebrows, but said okay. That night as she descended the staircase, she asked, "Is this what you had in mind, darling?" Then she flashed a smile, sending Elvis doubling over in laughter. For Thompson had blacked out her two front teeth

Bolstered by the new relationship, Presley also embarked on what would be yet another career benchmark—a concert that would utilize the latest technology for broadcast around the world. "I'm going to be the first to do a live show telecast by satellite!" Presley excitedly told Joe Esposito. The prospect of playing to audiences overseas galvanized the singer. So did producer Marty Pasetta, who dropped in on one of Presley's shows a few months before the concert was to be shot. As he watched the show under way at the Long Beach Arena, Pasetta kept thinking to himself, "He's got to lose some weight." He actually told that to Presley when they met in Las Vegas. Initially taken aback, the singer's vanity kicked in. He spent the next three months dieting, taking vitamin injections, and rigorously working out with his Memphis karate instructor, Kang Rhee.

Presley also put Bill Belew to work on a special jumpsuit. Belew, who had designed the black leather suit for the 1968 TV special, had been doing Presley's jumpsuits since his return to Las Vegas. Elvis's seventies-era signature apparel (with the period's de rigueur flared legs) was made of one hundred percent wool gabardine—the same fabric used on ice skaters' costumes. Because of the body-hugging nature of the material, Presley usually wore long white underwear—resembling tights—underneath. While the suits were always attention-getting, with their studs and jewels and Napoleonic-inspired stand-up collars, it was imperative, said Elvis, that the Hawaiian suit be something "spectacular."

And it was. The so-called American Eagle outfit was all-white, with a huge bejeweled eagle on the front, as well as on the back of the matching cape. Along with the black leather suit, it is today considered one of the most famous costumes of his concert career.

Presley filled it out nicely. When he was helicoptered to his Hilton Hotel—where a thousand screaming fans awaited—he was a lithe and tan 165 pounds. During the rehearsals and through the concert, he was also drug-free—and creatively energized.

He was concerned about the stage set up in the massive Honolulu International Center. "Isn't there some way we can keep everybody together?" he asked Pasetta, who had originally planned to put the musicians on various risers and platforms. After surveying videotaped footage of one of the rehearsals, Presley also decided to get a haircut. Because the concert was a benefit for the Kui Lee Cancer Fund, he also made sure that one of the songs written by the late, beloved Hawaiian songwriter was included in his repertoire. In fact, he performed "I'll Remember You" at the dress rehearsal—before a packed house of ten thousand—and in the satellite-broadcast show two days later on January 14, 1973.

In all, Presley delivered twenty-three songs, ranging from his golden oldies to his "American Trilogy" (the moving show-stopper medley comprised of "Dixie," "The Battle Hymn of the Republic" and "All My Trials") to his contemporary hits such as "Suspicious Minds."

He closed, as ever, with "Can't Help Falling in Love." But the show didn't end there. As the arena thundered with applause, Presley stood—head bowed—and then suddenly, and expectedly, took his eagle-emblazoned cape and threw it into the audience.

Then, in a flash of Instamatics, the icon in white rushed from the stage.

The most costly entertainment special of the day, *Elvis: Aloha from Hawaii* was budgeted at $2.5 million and was watched by an estimated 1.5 billion people in forty countries. It also raised $85,000 for the Cancer Fund—$60,000 more than was anticipated. Presley, who bought his own ticket to the show, was ebullient over the statistics.

Contained within the triumph, however, were signs of trouble. During a press conference in anticipation of the event, Presley was dull-eyed and sometimes slurred his words. And the very day after the show, his friends arrived at his hotel suite and found him sitting out on the balcony, "stoned out of his gourd."

No one knew it, but the glory days of '72 were fading into the horror of '73.

Addiction

On the late afternoon of January 25, 1973, a long black limousine deposited Elvis Presley and Linda Thompson at the private entrance to the Las Vegas Hilton. They looked striking together, seemingly the perfect couple. He was rakishly thin, dressed in all black. She was sunlight blond in a clinging jersey, her diamond-encrusted fingers glimmering in the desert light.

As a mirrored elevator carried them up to their thirtieth-floor suite, Elvis preened in the mirror at his classic profile and ran his hands through the thick tousles of black hair, relishing the image that five hundred Dexedrines and a ruinous diet had wrought. Linda glanced wearily ahead, already mentally lost in the punishing task she faced, nursing her lover through a month-long engagement—two shows a night that would sharpen tempers and emotions to a razor edge and transform Elvis Presley into a stage-frightened paranoiac.

As they entered the room, a cluster of bellboys were closing and securing the blackout curtains to shut out all traces of sun. Over at the bar, a young hotel adjutant was stocking the room with Mountain Valley Spring Water. As soon as they bustled out and Linda began unpacking two elaborate wardrobes, Elvis disappeared into the master bath, nearly a suite in itself, and phoned the Hilton's doctor on call.

Dr. Thomas Newman was nicknamed Flash because of his ability to appear almost instantly with a cornucopia of the rarest drugs. True to his name, Dr. Newman arrived in minutes, conferring with his "patient' in whispered tones, then disappearing with a fistful of prescriptions clutched in his hands. They would be filled across the street at the Landmark Hotel Pharmacy, which had served Howard Hughes so well when the drugged-up billionaire resided in the Desert Inn penthouse. Flash was soon back, his sack of vials crammed with Dexedrines, Valium, Valmid (another tranquilizer), and the strongest painkiller on the market, Dilaudid. Presley had always been served drugs on arrival at the Hilton, but the size and scope of this batch heralded a slide into a dangerous new era.

Elvis had become a connoisseur of recreational drugs and of the fine nuances of their euphoric effects upon the brain. However, he wasn't a constant user and, because of a physiological condition, could stop any morning of his choice without a tinge of withdrawal. He would also take only drugs that had been prescribed by a physician. Yet relying on their ethical judgment was foolhardy. Slowly and subtly he was eased into a circle of physicians with big bills, big cars, and big prescriptions, who were used to servicing entertainment druggies.

To them, needles were a natural supplement to pills. Part of the inventory furnished by Flash Newman was an actual doctor's portable box of injectable Valium in various strengths and liquid Dilaudid— known on the street as the "poor man's heroin" because it was almost as deadly and addicting as the real thing.

For the moment, Elvis left the magic box in his small refrigerator and settled down on the bed, where he gulped down pills from three vials. Linda was able to read the names Dilaudid on one label and Demerol on another before he secreted the hoard beneath his mattress. She had learned to differentiate between "light, moderate, and heavy" doses of the chemicals. This was a light one. She could sleep rather than lie awake wondering if she'd hear the strangled breathing that signals an overdose.

The first three nights of the Hilton engagement proceeded smoothly—with only one major difference. Now Dr. Newman hovered about, administering a stimulant before each show and a sedative after—four injections in all. Elvis would panic if he failed to see the physician among the colorful backstage crowd. "Where's Flash?" he would ask, grabbing the arm of one of his aides. "Get him out here quick." These drugs, administered with syringes right through the fabric of his pants into the buttocks, left telltale signs. The inside of Elvis Presley's trousers were often dotted with tiny circular bloodstains.

Weakened by the drugs, Elvis collapsed with the flu on the fourth night of the run, spent the day in the city's Sunrise Hospital, performed a mediocre early show the fifth night, and then returned to his hospital bed.

Unable to procure the "magic box" left for him, Presley soon depleted the medicines in his pocket vials and was forced to visit a doctor selected from the phone book—Dr. Sidney Boyer, who, even though he was confronted by Elvis Presley, required forty-five minutes of salesmanship before he handed over the prescriptions.

Elvis was back on February 13, seeking premature refills. Boyer was blunt. "Mr. Presley, you are in danger of becoming a hard-core addict. This is very destructive medicine. I would seek treatment if I were you."

Though Elvis had already presented him with a white Lincoln Continental, Boyer refused to write additional orders for the chemists at the Landmark. Elvis stalked off, furious, shaking his fist.

On February 18, when four hulking South American men rushed the stage during the midnight show, a hyped Elvis, convinced that Priscilla's lover Mike Stone had sent them, began beating the first of the men, screaming for the Mafia to grab the others. In the end, Presley's hands had to be wrenched from around the throat of a man who, unbeknownst to the star, was merely trying to deliver a rare Peruvian wool coat as a gift. "I'm sorry, ladies and gentlemen," said Presley. "I'm sorry I didn't break his goddamned neck." The audience rose in a standing ovation. (The Peruvians were later arrested for drunkenness and released.)

Despite a pair of sedative injections from Flash, Presley prowled the suite until noon, dispatching aides to identify the "hired killers." When it was determined that there had been a gross misunderstanding, Elvis refused to believe it, requiring a handful of pills for sleep. Linda arose and assumed her lonely vigil.

In an unfortunate coincidence, Priscilla telephoned the next afternoon, informing Elvis that Lisa Marie would not be allowed to visit during the Vegas run. Drug usage was cited.

Elvis apparently dipped heavily into the elixirs in the magic box, returning to the suite at three o'clock in the morning in a towering rage. He stripped naked, yanked his M16 rifle from its case, and began twirling it around the room. "Mike Stone must die!" he screamed again and again.

Linda, huddled in the corner in a silk negligee, screamed so loudly that everyone in the suite froze, including Presley.

Presley's tirades—punctuated by roars of self-pity—against Mike Stone and the devious way he had "stolen my woman" led to the star's delirious threat to have Stone killed. "Never fucking mind, I'll do it myself!" screamed Presley. Then he recanted, deciding instead that what he needed was "a hit man."

After a series of late-night calls to her apartment, Priscilla was thoroughly terrified. Despite decades of overreporting of this Presley rage, he was all talk. When Red West grew fed up with Presley's "Mafia don" ravings, he told the boss he had located the perfect guy for the job. "But he wants ten thousand dollars in cash. If you get it for me tonight, I'll set it up."

Elvis blanched. "Uh, maybe it's not such a good idea. I'll get back to you on that."

During his Mike Stone obsession, another of the hotel physicians was summoned to administer a powerful sedative to the out-of-control superstar. This began a long personal and medical friendship between Elvis and Elias Ghanem.

But that evening, to boost himself up, he was once more refueled by Dexedrine, and his fury was renewed. During his shows that night he interspersed the songs with angry, rambling monologues.

At four the next morning, Linda Thompson, lying awake with her hand near Presley's mouth, sensed that his breathing had become lighter and lighter. Then he began struggling for breath, gasping and rattling as he twisted on the bed. She phoned Joe Esposito and Dr. Newman immediately. "He's dying!" she screamed.

Newman was there in less than five minutes with a full medical kit. After finding the Dilaudid injectable vials empty, the physician knew his patient had heavily overdosed and was in danger of slipping into a coma.

If the man on the bed were anyone but Elvis Presley, an ambulance would already have been en route to the Hilton. But Newman and Esposito were charged by Colonel Tom Parker with preventing just such a scandal. So they did the next best thing: they transported medical and oxygen equipment into the suite and built an intensive care unit around the silk-sheeted bed.

Dr. Newman forced an airway with a rubber hose to revive the lungs. An IV drip was inserted, and Newman flooded Presley's stomach with a corrosive antidote to Dilaudid—a pain medication so strong that it is usually reserved for terminal cancer patients.

With breathing restored, Newman initiated a regimen of shots and IV drips to repair the damage to Presley's system. A gallon of liquid was drained from his body. With Vernon Presley and Colonel Parker notified, Linda, Joe, and Newman could only wait until Presley roused from his drugged slumber. Finally on the afternoon of the twenty-fourth, Elvis awakened—sheepish and deathly pale.

"You almost killed yourself, Mr. Presley," warned Newman. "I would seek another pain remedy."

The life-and-death battle waged behind the closed and guarded doors of Hilton Suite 361 has existed only as rumor and innuendo until now, with the first release of the "sealed depositions" of Joe Esposito, Linda Thompson, and James K. Caughly Jr., Elvis's former valet and wardrobe keeper. Backed by the first interview on the subject by Joe Esposito, it's now clear that Presley's first near-death overdose was self-administered, following a three-day binge in which he took more than a hundred full-strength amphetamines.

Dr. Nichopoulos, who later looked back at those early "brushes with death" as part of his clinical treatment, believed that the Dilaudid and Valium "injectable kit" left with Elvis automatically led to the overdose since Presley had no knowledge of how much liquid to draw into a syringe. It was a skill he soon learned.

"He just did not understand," said Nichopoulos later. "He'd been taking uppers since he was a teenager, and he thought the drugs deposited with him were safe to use."

Dr. Newman never discussed how deeply Presley slipped into a coma, but Esposito noted that they "set up the best drug clinic possible in a hotel room and prayed for the best."

Presley had cheated death for the first of four times in 1973—a year that would later be called "the year of the drugs" by the medical experts who treated Elvis.

When Esposito and other members of the Mafia informed Vernon and Parker of the drastic measures—catheter drainage and injections of the risky antidote, noxozane hydrochloride—Elvis's father empowered fabled Hollywood private detective John O'Grady and his associate Jack Riley to seek out and stop the physicians who were supplying the drugs.

Elvis had hired O'Grady previously to investigate the bogus paternity suit that was filed against him. This time, unbeknownst to the singer, the private eye began to investigate him. What O'Grady discovered, in a six-week study that cost Vernon Presley $150,000, was a river of drugs flowing toward Presley.

Another startling discovery was that he had been spending $500,000 per year to procure prescriptions, have the Landmark fill them, and then have them ferried wherever Elvis was appearing. The gusher of drugs included more than twenty-five different types of barbiturates, amphetamines, and even steroids. Several Presley associates claim to have been deputized several times to rush to Vegas and back to Presley at Graceland with "briefcases full of drugs."

For his part, Elias Ghanem has always denied that he prescribed any "dangerous" chemicals for Presley, and no complaints have ever been filed against him. O'Grady and Riley reported that they "suspected at least six other Vegas physicians" serviced Elvis but were unable to identify any of them.

Exhaustive attorneys' reports and a massive Drug Enforcement Administration report indicate a hundred or more physicians and pharmacists may have been involved in supplying Elvis's increasing hunger, many of them temporarily such as Dr. Sidney Boyer. Nonetheless, according to the friends, police officers, and attorneys involved, Presley wasn't in the true meaning of the term a druggie. "Because of his mother, because of the Army, because physicians willingly gave him these prescriptions, he considered them 'medicine,' " said Dr. George Nichopoulos. A native of Alabama, the silver-haired, soft-spoken Nichopoulos would become a dominant figure in Presley's declining years. He would go on to make headlines—and to find himself the subject of notoriety—following Elvis's death, and revelations about the singer's drug use. "He first came to me seeking drugs because of insomnia, a debilitating condition he had suffered since the day his father was trucked off to prison and which worsened dramatically after his mother died in 1958. He could lick everyone and everything else," says Dr. Nichopoulos today, "but he could not go to sleep without some sort of medication; it had been that way since he entered the Army.

"Because he was only in Memphis for very short periods of time, I didn't take the extent of his insomnia seriously when he saw me off and on," the physician continued. "But when he was in town, I gave him Placydil, Valmid, and Valium—all sedatives capable of putting him to sleep."

The mildness of Dr. Nichopoulos's approach impressed both

Vernon Presley and Colonel Parker, who, in the early seventies, were seeking a stable, controlled source of drugs.

Because Elvis was sleeping better, he "was calmer and required less drugs," Dr. Nichopoulos recalled. "He didn't have the pressure of getting up for two Vegas shows a night or to make a six A.M. makeup call at the studio. These factors magnified his insomnia tenfold."

Presley's insomnia was so severe that, at one point, Dr. Nichopoulos tried a sleep-deprivation program at Graceland. "There wasn't that much known then about sleeping disorders," recalled the physician, who attempted to keep the singer awake, with books, videos and conversation. "The longest period of time we tried was three days and three nights. And we didn't accomplish anything."

By late spring, Elvis was back on the touring circuit. With the renewal of stress, Linda Thompson noticed he was gulping fifteen to twenty pills at a time periodically during the day. In Vegas, Flash Newman, with his rattling pill cases, deposited ever-heavier supplies in Elvis's suite.

Linda was reduced to baby-sitting Presley when he was awake and guarding him through the long days, which he slept away. To coax him to eat, she curled up beside him, indulging him with baby talk and playing with his hair as she fed him small bites of food, a laborious task since it often took him forty-five minutes to eat a hamburger.

He relished the caramel popcorn balls that Miss Tennessee whipped up in the kitchen of the gilded, glittering suite. Dressed in her little baby-doll nightie, she would break the gooey ball into small bites as she purred, "Bye, Baby Bunting, Mommy gonna feed baby some yum-yums. Baby like yum-yums . . . eat 'em all up."

Lulled by Valium and occasionally clothed in diapers—because the Dilaudid rendered him incontinent—he would lean back, burbling "goo-goo, ga-ga, ma-ma" until he'd had enough and was ready to disappear into chemical-induced darkness.

Gone were the days of foreplay fests. Her efforts almost never led to sexual relations, for the drugs dissipated Elvis's sexual urges. "Little Elvis"—the singer's pet name for his penis—was often rendered impotent by medication. Like an infant, Elvis often slipped off to sleep with the hem of Linda's nightie curled in his hand. Unfortunately, his pills sometimes put him to sleep while he was still chewing. During the Vegas appearances alone in 1973, Linda clawed impacted food from Presley's windpipe eight different times after he had virtually stopped breathing. "We'll never know how many times she saved his life," says Joe Esposito, "but dozens anyway."

Thompson later attributed Presley's dependence on drugs, in part, to the fact that "he was acutely sensitive to life." It was not uncommon for Elvis to cry as he read the morning papers and learned of the plight of strangers. Explained Thompson, "When he wanted to go to sleep, he couldn't shut his thoughts off. I think what he tried to do with the sleeping pills was just dull his mind."

During his trips to Los Angeles and Las Vegas before his June and July tour of the Midwest, Presley restocked his suitcase of chemical provisions to get him through the summer, including a prime stash of Dilaudid—which he saved for what he called "the mean blue days" when he was particularly depressed.

One memorable blue day struck on June 28, when Elvis was playing the enormous Kiel Auditorium in St. Louis, considered the crown jewel of the summer tour. When Presley failed to appear in the hotel lobby to catch the limousine, Joe Esposito rushed up to his room, opened it with the spare key, and found him sprawled atop the bed in his blue silk pajamas. His breath was heaving in and out, in almost undetectable whispers.

Fortunately, Vernon had insisted that Dr. Nichopoulos come along on a trial basis. "If he can regulate this stuff in Memphis, he can regulate it here." Parker authorized the fee, sucking the physician into four years of hell from which he would never recover.

Since Nichopoulos was right next door, he administered a powerful stimulant. Then they ripped off Elvis's pajamas and shoved him under an icy shower to revive him. A few Dexedrines allowed him to present a low-key, thoroughly mediocre show. "He didn't really come to until he was halfway through the repertoire," remembered Nichopoulos.

For once Elvis was embarrassed. "Man, we nearly lost you, you son of a bitch," Esposito yelled. "We would have had a DOA in the Holiday Inn. Don't you even care?" Presley hung his head.

Decades later, Esposito looked back on those years sadly. "I don't know if anyone could have stopped him." Whenever Elvis looked at himself and realized what he was doing, he became so depressed that he had to take more pills to feel better. Yet if his drug abuse was pointed out, however circumspectly, Elvis refused to listen. "I can stop at any time," he always said. Explained Esposito, "He was not aware that drugs regulated his life."

Ironically, as Presley's life was disintegrating, Priscilla was putting hers together.

After leaving her husband, she had shown up at Mike Stone's apartment in Belmont Shores, a coastal community south of Los Angeles, in an old station wagon loaded with what Mike saw "were just the basic essentials."

"She had abandoned all the rest," Stone said later. "I could hardly believe that Priscilla, who had everything, had given it up for me—a part-time karate instructor still burdened down with a wife and child." Stone was in the midst of a divorce.

Priscilla didn't slum it for long. She, Stone, and Lisa Marie soon moved into a plush penthouse apartment in Pacific Palisades. A reporter for *Ladies' Home Journal*, visiting Priscilla for an interview about her marriage and divorce, noticed that the name on the apartment door read Beaulieu. No longer wearing Cleopatra makeup ("Oh, how blind I was!"), Priscilla spoke of her new career. She and clothing designer Olivia Bis had recently opened Bis & Beau, a clothing boutique on Robertson Avenue in Hollywood. It was a tentative move toward independence for Priscilla, who used to help Presley put together his concert concoctions and even helped to design some of the clothes.

Refuting talk of any possible reconciliation, Priscilla stressed that she had no plans to marry Stone. "I think that there can be a very good relationship between people that marriage can ruin." She added, "Whatever it is that marriage does, it changes you. . . . People become less sensitive to each other's needs. . . . So I would rather be the girlfriend than the wife."

Priscilla had been so desperate to end her marriage that she initially agreed to an unrealistic settlement: $100,000 plus a paltry $500 per month in child support for Lisa Marie and an additional $1,000 monthly for the next five years. Presley's income was $7 million a year.

Los Angeles attorney Ed Hookstratten told her, "This is inadequate."

"I just want *out!*" she answered.

As she and Presley waited for their divorce to become final, he was involved in a drug-related disaster at his Palm Springs house. What happened was later reported by his bodyguards—including Sonny West, who was there—in a paperback exposé. But their version differs from that of another eyewitness.

In the book *Elvis: What Happened?*, the bodyguards claimed that it was Presley who enticed an eighteen-year-old girl to drink codeine-laced Hycodan cough syrup. But according to Sandi Miller, a Presley fan-turned-friend who often visited him in Palm Springs, the young woman was taking swigs of the syrup from a bottle she pulled from her own saddlebag-type leather purse. Moreover, when Presley scrutinized the label, he protested. "Oh, honey, this stuff's too strong." But the girl, who was feeling ill, continued taking sips.

She later excused herself, to take a shower, and then announced she was going to go to bed. A short while later, Presley followed her into the bedroom. It was about four o'clock in the morning.

It wasn't until one o'clock in the afternoon that Elvis's buddies began pleading with the boss to shake himself awake.

Finally, Sonny shoved open the door, unleashing a blast of sixty-degree air, the product of the warehouse-sized air-conditioning unit Presley had installed in the bedroom suite. Elvis lay unconscious. Next to him lay the fragile young girl, her eyes glassy and staring ahead. As Sonny moved closer, he could see blue streaks spreading up her chest and neck toward her cheeks, a portent of death.

Sonny slapped Elvis awake. The guys in the living room heard the smacks as Sonny's hands slapped the boss again and again.

Finally Presley struggled up. "Wha's wrong?" he mumbled.

Elvis, with his amazing chemical tolerance, began to come around. For the girl Hodge called a prominent Palm Springs physician, a friend of the Colonel's. He was in the room ten minutes later.

"Call an ambulance," he yelled. "Get 'em here as fast as they can make it!"

Elvis sat up in bed, sweating through his pajamas despite the arctic blasts, and yelled at the physician, "Doctor! Doctor! There's no need to take her out of here. Just give her a big shot of Ritalin. That'll do it. Please, don't take her to the hospital."

The physician stiffened. "Listen, Mr. Presley, what you gave this girl has left her a half hour away from death. I'd make you go too if it were in my power to do so."

After the ambulance left, the Memphis Mafia, with others consulting by telephone, made a momentous decision. If the overdose proved fatal, Charlie Hodge would take the fall, claiming the girl as his date.

Luckily for everyone involved, it did not.

Just before dinnertime, the young woman opened her eyes, gripped Sonny's hand, and emitted wild hissing sounds. "What happened?" she later asked groggily. She went on to spend two weeks in intensive care.

The Presley camp had her mother flown in to be with her. They also offered money, which both mother and daughter—rabid Elvis fans—rejected.

In October 1977, Page Peterson told her account of the overdose to *The Star*. She said that Elvis gave her pills after she complained of a headache. "I think it was pills. . . . I don't remember taking more than one, but I guess I did take more. . . . I remember the doctor being very angry at all of the drugs that were in me."

Doubtless, it was the mix of pills and Hycodan that nearly proved fatal.

Though she never saw Presley after the accident, she spoke with him by phone several times. "He told me he had paid out ten thousand dollars to the people who took me to the hospital so the whole thing could be kept quiet." While she was hospitalized, he also sent her a Bible verse.

The episode is detailed in "addendum papers" to the Drug Enforcement Agency's investigation of Elvis's addictions.

The papers, though, make no mention of the fact that as Page was being revived, Elvis anxiously paced the floor of his home. Wearing a robe, he continually ran his fingers through his hair, and bit his nails, as he repeated, "I told her not to take that syrup. I told her . . ."

"He was extremely worried about her," recalled Sandi Miller.

He was also anguished over the possible impact the overdose could have on his career.

After the near-fatal overdose, Parker and Presley had a tense session, after which the star stopped taking drugs for several weeks. Somebody erected a temporary dam against the river of drugs flowing in from suppliers.

About this time, Colonel Parker confronted Presley about his chemical dependence.

Elvis was frank: "Hey, I do drugs. You do other things and I don't question you. This is my thing. You don't question me."

Presley was now using his medical arsenal with wild abandon. When Linda Thompson spoke under oath during the aftermath of Elvis's death, she suggested that the amphetamines themselves clouded his thinking about the other drugs and "set him up for abuse."

His monstrous chemical hunger soon grabbed him again. Elvis spent the next six weeks flying back and forth between Palm Springs and Los Angeles, where he would disappear on a mysterious mission in a towering medical building on Wilshire Boulevard. As the driver waited, Presley spent from forty-five minutes to an hour inside and then returned seemingly floating on air. Nobody in the entourage asked questions. No one dared broach the subject of drugs to Elvis.

The night of October 8, Presley didn't sleep at all. He merely lay on his bed in the Bel-Air house and brooded, ingesting Valium to dull the ache of the next day, when he would face the public finale of his twelve-year love affair with Priscilla. His petition for divorce was going to be finalized in Santa Monica Superior Court.

Priscilla, who hadn't seen Presley for several months, recalls being taken aback by his appearance. "His hands and face were swollen and puffy, and he was perspiring profusely."

The divorce agreement had by now been redesigned at the demand of her new attorneys. She got $750,000 outright and another commitment of $1.2 million in monthly payments of $6,000. Her alimony was also increased to $1,200 a month, and the child support was raised from $500 a month to $4,000. Priscilla also received half the proceeds from the sale of the Holmby Hills house.

She and Elvis emerged from the courthouse, hand in hand, with Hollywood smiles. The photo opportunity was not lost on the wire services. He tenderly kissed her good-bye and then climbed into his customized Rolls-Royce. He seemed lost in a sad reverie as he was driven down Sunset Boulevard toward his empty rented mansion. At one of the intersections, his car pulled up alongside a limousine belonging to singer Diana Ross. Unaware of what he'd just been through, she rolled down the window and yelled, "Hey, Elvis. Let's go have coffee . . . talk awhile. I'm all alone in town."

Presley smiled wanly. But the man who had nowhere in particular to go shook his head. "Sorry, I'm busy," he replied.

The last link to the lifeline Priscilla represented had been broken. Another brush with death came frighteningly soon afterward.

On October 12, he flew home to Graceland with a worried Linda Thompson at his side. Never had she seen him so distant and unreachable. Several nights later his aides discovered him lying half off his bed. He breaths were long, drawn out, and rasping; his stomach and abdomen was swollen three times its normal size. His face bore the wan mustard cast of toxic hepatitis.

Sirens muffled, the medics of Fire Engine House No. 29—just five minutes from Graceland—arrived and bounded up the stairs. Baptist Hospital had already been alerted that Elvis Presley was en route.

Maurice Elliott, the communications director of Baptist Hospital, was notified as the ambulance sped from the outskirts of the city. It gave him just enough time to post extra security guards and medics at the hospital entrance. When the van squealed into the hospital entrance, a cordon of uniformed men shielded the famous patient from crowds that had already begun to gather.

Dr. Nichopoulos, riding next to Presley in the ambulance, was certain his patient would die of heart failure before they reached Baptist. "He was that sick!" the doctor remembers. "I thought his heart was failing."

The doctor had no chance to pinpoint which drugs Elvis had taken before he had flown home from Los Angeles. The singer writhed on the stretcher, mumbling incoherently. "Later I learned that he had initially collapsed on the West Coast, but insisted on returning to Memphis anyway," said Nichopoulos.

He assembled a distinguished team to treat the city's most famous patient. There was internist Dr. Larry Wruble; Tennessee's leading eye specialist, Dr. David Meyer; the mid-South's leading drug toxicologists, Dr. David H. Knott and Dr. Robert D. Fink; and cardiologist Dr. Daniel Brady.

As this team treated Elvis's chemically crippled body, Elliott authorized the Memphis Mafia's conversion of their boss's hospital room. The guys pasted aluminum foil on the large windows and installed a stereo, special comforters, and within six hours, a private line connected directly to Graceland.

Five floors below, the medical news was grim. Elvis's stomach, colon, and chest cavity appeared to be painfully bloated with edema—much as it had been during the February overdose. He had hepatitis, caused by massive overdoses of cortisone and steroids, plus a gastric ulcer. During the preceding five days he had somehow suffered a major concussion. Medical reports also listed eyesight-threatening glaucoma, further aggravated by drug abuse. Worse, liver specialist Larry Wruble was astonished at the size of Presley's enlarged organ, laden with fat and in danger of failing.

First the team frantically tried to drain the edema from his body. Inexplicably, the first catheterization produced less than a cup of liquid. So they tried again, freeing a couple of drops. This was even grimmer news; the bloating was due to something else entirely. Laboratory tests and X rays were rushed so doctors could determine the extent of the damage.

Detailed lab reports revealed that Presley's swollen face, back, and abdomen were due to Cushing's syndrome, a constellation of clinical abnormalities from chronic exposure to excesses of cortisol, an essential hormone. Although tumors can cause this flooding of the body by cortisol, by far the most common cause is the administration of "massive amounts" of cortico steroids by physicians. They have another, lesser-known side effect. In patients taking opiates such as Demerol, codeine or Percodan, it strengthens the addictive power of the drugs.

When the physicians gathered around the lab analyses, one of the doctors—Nichopoulos doesn't remember who—said disgustedly, "What kind of doctors did this to the boy? He didn't know what hit him."

By this time Memphis television stations had interrupted their broadcasts with news that an "unconscious Elvis Aaron Presley has been rushed to Baptist Hospital, suffering severe exhaustion due to his recent tours." A radio bulletin issued by United Press International noted that "pneumonia is a possibility."

Officially, the hospital said he was recuperating from pneumonia. "We could only pass the word we were given by the patient and his family," recalls Maurice Elliott. "It was a subtle veneer to obscure the truth, which, in the first hospitalization, remained controlled for decades."

Most of the story of Presley's closest call has been obscured for more than two decades. Only now, due to revelations contained in the nurses' notes, physicians' orders, and partial medical charts—from files ordered expunged by the Memphis Superior Court Authority—has the story been deciphered. Also helpful was the "confidential" report compiled by former Watergate prosecutor James Neal, who represented Nichopoulos in legal proceedings following Elvis's death.

The next morning, when Nichopoulos showed up with the test results, Elvis's face flushed red. He turned away, as if he knew what was coming.

"Dr. Nick," as Elvis fondly called him, made his patient look him directly in the eye as he said, "Elvis, you are badly addicted to morphine—one of the strongest drugs in the world. You've been receiving it in the form of Demerol, a powerful painkiller. Worse, your system has been poisoned by cortisone injections, masked by painkillers—novocaine, I suspect."

Elvis looked up innocently, then looked down, fiddling with the bedcovers. "Dr. Nick, I have no idea how this happened. It isn't possible. You know what I'm taking—a little Valium, some of those sleeping pills you give me, some amphetamines when I have to do a show."

Joe Esposito shifted uncomfortably in his chair, thinking back on his friend's disastrous year.

"Elvis, do you have any idea how this happened?" asked Dr. Nick.

"Honest, sir, I don't." Elvis glanced at Joe before saying, "The only thing I've had is some acupuncture treatments for my back, but he wasn't using any drugs, just needles."

Nichopoulos shook his head. "I don't think so, buddy."

Presley stuck to his story, which led to another myth in the singer's life—a tale of how he was addicted by a mysterious Japanese acupuncturist, procured by the Memphis Mafia and flown from city to city whenever the boss was in pain. Yet to this day, no one has produced a name to go with the tales of the mysterious, rambling drug merchant.

Dr. Nichopoulos was skeptical. "But why did an acupuncturist inject you with all the cortisone?"

In the expunged court records on the singer's death, one entry by the night nurse noted that the patient had insisted on telling her that his buttocks were rock hard, knotted, and scarred from what he insisted were the acupuncture treatments. But acupuncture needles leave no scar marks or wounds of any kind. It was obvious to the nurse that Presley's rear had received hundreds of hypodermic injections.

Confronted by the team of physicians, particularly the toxic-knowledgeable Fink and Knott, Presley admitted that he had gone to a Los Angeles physician, Dr. Leon Cole, complaining of constant back and neck pain that was "ruining his ability to perform." Dr. Cole, the mysterious man on Wilshire Boulevard whom Presley had seen through the early fall, had initiated a six-week course of Demerol shots— bolstered by massive amounts of cortisone to ease the "unbearable pain."

During a phone call with Dr. Nichopoulos and several of the consulting physicians, Dr. Cole allegedly admitted injecting Presley with a mixture of Demerol, cortisone, mild steroids, and novocaine—the latter to overcome the pain of the patient's injection-traumatized rear. But he was unaware that Elvis was obtaining other types of opiates— codeine, Dilaudid, and Hycodan cough syrup—which added to the load of narcotic-related drugs dumped into Presley's system during the previous six weeks.

Dr. Nichopoulos decided to confront Presley with the hard facts of his drug use, but he knew he would have to act quickly. His patient was already calling for his court—the Mafia and Linda Thompson, who was to move into the room with him for the duration of his treatment.

So a consultation took place between Elvis—who sat propped up in bed—Dr. Nichopoulos, and Dr. David H. Knott and Dr. Robert D. Fink, specialists in both addictive psychiatry and toxicology. Presley was wary and particularly frightened of the psychiatrists, whom he viewed as a threat to his machismo. As he'd told Priscilla many times, real men didn't need "the help of shrinks." If possible, Elvis would have shunned the consultation. But Nichopoulos forced his hand by denying the drugs his body craved.

Dr. Knott sternly took the lead, explaining to Elvis that he was so addicted that they planned to use methadone, part of a hard-core heroin cure, to bring him back down.

Presley's face registered shock. He felt complete contempt for what he called "street drugs," heroin and cocaine, and the "dirty street junkies" they created. The time a Las Vegas contact had brazenly offered to get him some heroin, "a new high"—right in front of several Mafia members, including Esposito—Presley had turned him down flat.

"I think we can get you free of drugs, including your own recreational use," said Knott, whose Memphis Psychiatric Center had already chalked up an impressive cure rate. "It will just take a six-week course of intensive therapy."

Elvis gripped his blanket tightly, gritting his teeth. Nichopoulos realized that there was no chance. They could only accomplish as much as they could in Baptist and then try to extend the program to Graceland and, impossible as it sounded, on the road with the rock star.

Knott told Elvis that he was the most dangerous sort of chemical experimenter, a "polypharmacy *junkie*." That word doubtless crushed Presley, who was further told that such a junkie experiments with all sorts of drugs: uppers, downers, diuretics, painkillers, antihistamines, and even deadly new antidepressants such as Elavil. "You can mix a deadly brew without even taking high levels," Knott explained.

Chastened, Presley nonetheless refused to be admitted to the toxicological center. He did agree to follow Knott's directions as long as he was in Baptist, but privately he told the guys he wanted those "headshrinkers out of my life. They give me the creeps . . . nothin' wrong with me anyway."

While Linda Thompson moved into Presley's room, Dr. Nichopoulos and Joe Esposito staged a raid in Elvis's master bedroom at

Graceland. They probed through the closets, fished through all the drawers, and even checked the seams of the blackout curtains, where small vials of drugs were discovered. In all, they came up with three thousand pills of various strengths, most of them addictive. Their major finds were three pharmacist-sized jars containing one thousand capsules of high-dose Seconal, Dexedrine Spansules (a time capsule), and Placydil, all of which were sent down the toilet.

The remainder of Elvis's stay in the hospital consisted of daily squabbles between the pampered patient and the doctors trying to get him off the dangerous combination of Demerol and cortisone. Nurses' bells rang incessantly night and day, and telephone arguments escalated as Presley fought for access to more opiates.

Linda slept beside him on a cot she had imported for the occasion. "Elvis would lower the hospital bed down beside me so that we could cuddle and giggle half the night," she recalls. One afternoon she exchanged her "sick garb" and headed for the gift shops downstairs. "Oh, no, you don't," Presley said. "Get back into that nightgown and into your bed. If I don't dress, nobody dresses." Laughing, Linda dutifully climbed back into bed. "They called us their 'little patients,' " she remembered, "as if both of us were ill."

By October 28, Presley's medical team was seeing good results. According to that night's report, Elvis had been reduced to a single 50-mg Vistaril (a mild sedative) tablet for sleep, at 12:45 A.M. He awakened at 2:30 A.M. and asked for another, but was already back asleep before the nurse returned.

"A line had definitely been crossed," Dr. Nichopoulos said, "but real success depended upon halting the drug caravans from the West." Only Dr. Nichopoulos would go the distance with Presley, however. Frustrated with the difficult patient and angered by the cordon of guardians who surrounded him, the other physicians drifted away.

"The most important thing to understand about this entire tragedy, or what became a tragedy, is that Elvis didn't take this dangerous combination of drugs on his own. A physician [Dr. Cole] actually combined huge amounts of Demerol and cortisone, which, in time, made him 'biologically dependent' on opiates," said Dr. Forest Tennant, one of UCLA's top toxicologists and a leading expert on opiates.

"The damage had been done," stressed Dr. Tennant. "The physician who used cortisone and Demerol over that unusually long period of time [six weeks] wrought major biological changes in Elvis Presley's body.

"Working together, cortisone and narcotics create these biological transformations much quicker when they are used together.

"Now, from a malpractice point of view, physicians have to inform patients of the danger of using these two drugs together for more than ten days."

Nichopoulos didn't know any of this in the winter of 1973. He only knew he was delivering a relatively drug-free Elvis back to Graceland.

But all was not well. When Christmas came, Elvis was so depressed that he didn't even bother to open some of his gifts. For weeks after the holiday, they sat unopened, beneath a drying, drooping tree.

It wasn't just the man who was in flux but also the career. Though he briefly had some success with the song "I've Got a Thing about You, Baby," which was recorded in the summer of 1973 at Memphis's Stax Records, it was now the *repackaged* Elvis who was selling. "Elvis—A Legendary Performer, Volume I," issued by RCA in January 1974, and containing golden oldies such as "That's All Right (Mama)" and "Heartbreak Hotel," actually went gold.

Meanwhile, though his costumes still glittered, his live performances became increasingly lackluster. It was growing more apparent to the bookers as well as the executives at the Las Vegas Hilton (formerly the International), that Elvis was tired—and in trouble. In order to curb the drug usage that invariably intensified during concert tours, Dr. Nichopoulos succeeded in getting Colonel Parker and the hotel management to pare down Elvis's Vegas schedule. And so, during his January engagement, Presley appeared for two weeks as opposed to the usual four and, except for weekends when there was a dinner and midnight show, he now performed only once nightly.

There were problems all the same. One night in February, a druggy Elvis decided to shoot out the hotel suite's light switch. The bullet went through the wall, nearly hitting Linda Thompson as she was getting ready for bed. She was understandably infuriated. Elvis feigned surprise. What was she getting so excited about? "Gonna be all right, hon."

Floundering creatively, he briefly considered jump-starting his movie career. He hadn't done any acting since 1969's well-intentioned but implausible *Change of Habit*, in which he'd played a singing ghetto doctor who falls in love with his assistant (Mary Tyler Moore), not knowing she's really a nun. Now he talked of producing his own movie—an action picture that would showcase his karate prowess. "I wanna play the baddest motherfucker there is," Presley explained to the project's screenwriter. He emphatically added, "And I'm not gonna fuckin' sing."

He would have sung had he accepted the intriguing offer to co-star with Barbra Streisand in the remake of A *Star Is Born*, the oft-filmed saga of a star on the rise whose fame ultimately eclipses that of her troubled, once great husband.

The frizzy-haired diva and her hairdresser boyfriend, Jon Peters, who was producing the film, met with Presley about the project in August between shows at the Hilton. As Presley's friends hovered nearby, Elvis, Streisand, and Peters sat "Indian-style" on the floor of his dressing room, passing around and discussing the script. "Elvis really liked the script, and he was so flattered to be asked to be in a Barbra Streisand movie," recalled Mafia member Richard Davis.

After Streisand and Peters exited, Presley kept telling his friends, "She's an Academy award winner! And she wants me!"

There are varying accounts as to why Presley did not accept the offer. Some say the Colonel nixed the deal because Streisand—renowned as a control freak—would have dominated the project, and would have received bigger billing and a bigger salary. But some of Presley's associates admit that Elvis himself had worries. "He kept saying, 'I can't play a loser. I just can't,' " recounted Joe Esposito.

The irony, of course, is that by then Presley was well equipped to play such a role.

Chemical Warfare

One afternoon in the spring of 1975, the Reverend Nicholas Vieron, of Memphis's Greek Orthodox Church, appeared in Dr. George Nichopoulos's office. The doctor knew why the priest was there, as did the physician's family and most of the congregation. George's devotion to Elvis and his obsession with keeping him alive and performing was destroying his own life.

"You know, George," said Vieron, "Elvis Presley can have any doctor he wants and doesn't really need you all of the time. I think you're doing your practice an injustice, your family an injustice, and your patients an injustice.

"Give it up. Stay home."

There were many things Dr. Nichopoulos could have said to the priest. He could have talked about the years he'd helped the troubled singer find sleep without morphine, of stemming the flow of drugs from less scrupulous physicians throughout America, of the awesome responsibility of keeping Elvis Presley functioning. He knew that they were talking about him in the medical establishment for having $200,000 in loans from his own patient, and because Presley was paying the exorbitant cost of substitute doctors to handle Nichopoulos's regular practice while he became a one-man doctor.

Yet drug disasters seemed to occur whenever Nichopoulos wasn't around. "It got down to the fact that if I didn't go, they weren't going to have any more tours." Added Nichopoulos, "I was caught up in a multimillion-dollar business decision."

Using a form of treatment advanced for its time, the physician had weaned Elvis Presley off of the most damaging drugs he had been abusing—Dilaudid, Demerol, and quaaludes, the triple threat that had laid waste to his body in 1973. By stationing a full-time nurse at Graceland and by rationing Presley's drugs and injections, Nichopoulos reduced him to one or two mild sleeping pills and several amphetamine tablets per week. They were all administered through two packets given to Elvis twice daily, one by Nichopoulos on his way home from the office and a second by Tish Henley, now Graceland's resident nurse. Any other medication required a phone call to Nichopoulos.

On the road, the drugs were personally administered by Dr. Nichopoulos before each show. The experiment was surprisingly successful. As bodyguard Al Strada noted, when the physician was along, "the medication was given in certain quantities and not at his [Presley's] own will."

Nichopoulos was so proud of the outcome that he couldn't resist telling Elvis, as the singer came offstage one time, that he'd triumphed without chemical assistance.

In that case honesty was not the best policy. Presley felt as though he'd been tricked. "I knew it! I knew it!" He glared at Nichopoulos, then taunted, "That's why I've been popping a handful of Dexedrine hidden in my pocket."

The pointed form of drug intervention was accompanied by at-home counseling as well. At Graceland, as the hour grew later and Presley increased his petulant commands, the physician would throw himself across the foot of Elvis's bed and talk until sleep engulfed them both. "His loneliness was almost frightening to comprehend," Nichopoulos remembered three decades later. "After his mother died, he felt himself alone in the world, and this ache kept him up night after night."

During much of 1974, a brief honeymoon from chemicals allowed Nichopoulos and a team of specialists to work on Elvis's most basic illnesses—his gluttony for fat-laden pork chops, chicken fried steaks, plates of biscuits, cakes, and puddings so rich a spoon couldn't sink into them.

"Death by heart attack, aggravated by drugs, if you will, seemed a likely and early possibility," said Nichopoulos. "His mother had died at forty-six, and most of the relatives on her side of the family expired before age fifty from sudden and massive heart attacks."

With the aid of a nutritionist and with Vernon's blessing, Nichopoulos once naively posted a dietary prescription on the front of the Graceland refrigerator. The morning's suggested menu consisted of two poached eggs on lightly "marjorined" toast, orange juice, and coffee, all of which Elvis despised. The actual meal served in Graceland's sunny kitchen nook featured three double cheeseburgers, half a pound of cottage fries, and a pound of bacon, burned to a crisp, on the side. When Dr. Nichopoulos surveyed the five-thousand-calorie meal, the cook on duty, Nancy Rooks, just laughed. "You ain't gonna get Mr. Elvis on a diet, Doctor. No force on earth can change his eating habits." As Elvis liked to say, "Eating is the only thing that gives me any pleasure."

The physician soon learned that Elvis's appetite had no limit whatsoever. During one of his hospitalizations, Elvis talked a nurse into making him a banana pudding—made with vanilla wafers. The pudding she made could feed a dozen people, but Elvis consumed it in a single sitting. "He ate every bite. I didn't even get a lick of it," remembered Marian J. Cocke, who made a second pudding the following day. Once again Elvis wolfed it down, without leaving so much as a crumb of a vanilla wafer.

Still other Elvis eating episodes have become a part of his lore. It is well known that at Graceland, he enjoyed fried peanut-butter-and-banana-sandwiches, especially as prepared by his beloved cook Mary Jenkins. She also prepared a nifty kraut dog, which Elvis had her smuggle into the hospital.

Perhaps most famous of all was the peanut-butter-sandwich odyssey.

A concoction of the Colorado Gold Mine Company, the 42,000-calorie sandwich is a $49.95 meal in itself—or rather, several meals. Made of creamy peanut butter, grape jelly, and lean bacon fried to a crisp, piled inside an entire loaf of bread that has been hollowed out and sliced lengthwise, it first came to Elvis's attention following a Denver concert. He loved that sandwich so much that he told two visiting Colorado law enforcement buddies about it. "Boy, I wish I had one of 'em right now," said one of the lawmen.

That was all Presley needed. Calls were made, and Elvis and his visitors and several of the Mafia climbed inside his private plane and took off for the Rockies. Meanwhile, out at the Colorado Gold Mine Company, the kitchen was at work on the most legendary order it had ever received. Restaurant owner Buck Scott and his wife, Cindy, along with a waiter, personally delivered twenty-two Fool's Gold sandwiches, along with a case of Perrier and a case of champagne, to Presley's plane when it landed at Stapleton Airport at 1:40 A.M.

Little wonder that when it came to Elvis's eating habits, Nichopoulos groaned, "It was like trying to diet a fifteen-hundred-pound elephant."

Before one tour, the singer traveled to a special diet clinic in Las Vegas for the latest fad, the "papaya juice–sleep cure." Enthused Presley, "It'll take off twenty-five pounds before the tour. And I don't have to do anything." But from the start things went wrong. The sleeping pills had little effect, which meant Elvis was up for hours drinking glass after glass of rich papaya juice. "Don't worry. Drink as much as you like," said the physician in charge. "You cannot gain weight on that."

When the singer emerged from the institution, he was fifteen pounds heavier.

Still, food would not kill him as surely as his ongoing addiction. Nichopoulos was confident enough to send Elvis to Vegas alone in early 1975, but the results were disastrous. The desert drug suppliers moved in, the engagement was cut short, and Presley headed home in order to enter Baptist Hospital a third time, for "exhaustion."

Again, the drugs were cut, but a suspicious Nichopoulos ordered a surprise blood screen just before discharge and discovered high levels "of various barbiturates in his blood." With Linda Thompson sleeping protectively in a hospital bed alongside Elvis, the doctor thought he had dammed up the contraband supplies. But some drugs came through, possibly via some of the Memphis Mafia. One evening Dr. Nichopoulos intercepted a postal package from Las Vegas containing one hundred capsules of Empirin with codeine.

Nichopoulos marched into the room and faced his patient. "Elvis, would you have any idea where these came from?"

"Well, sir, my daddy's been having an awful time with his back. And I thought, rather than bother you, I'd have some of those little pain pills sent out."

"Funny, Vernon hasn't mentioned anything to me. So I'll just take charge of them myself."

"No, sir. Please, sir. Let me keep the bottle. Just trust me with it, and I won't take any of the pills."

Urine screens eventually proved that Presley kept his word on this matter, but four times during the two-week stay, blood screens turned up contraband Demerol in Elvis's bloodstream. The nurses' chart entries for this stay, available for the first time from documents previously thought expunged, show what the detoxification team faced.

Some nights Elvis would get by on almost nothing; on others he would ask for the max. On January 30, for instance, he received 1 cc of saline solution and slept like a baby. But on February 6 he required a quaalude at midnight, called the nurse back in fifteen minutes, smiled weakly, and claimed to have "thrown it up." He had not. He was rewarded with another full-strength capsule. With a quavering voice, Elvis muttered, "I don't know if that will do it, ma'am."

The starched-uniformed nurse whirled about. "What? It's your regular dose."

"But not when I've vomited. When I've thrown up they also give me a Valmid."

"Oh, all right, Mr. Presley, go ahead and mix drugs that you shouldn't. After all, I'm not your doctor."

At 2:30 A.M., Elvis frantically rang his bell again. The night nurse found Elvis with covers pulled up around his neck. "I'm cold. I'm freezing. But just one more quaalude will fix it." She complied.

Thrilled with his drug bonanza, Elvis went on to drift in and out of sleep. In the morning he ran his fingers through his hair, smiled wanly, and talked the morning-shift nurses out of two more of his favorite mood elevators, which he quaffed down with milk, and a Valium dessert, which had been smuggled in among an armload of teddy bears.

On another evening, he made do with a half quaalude and two placebo pills. "Whew, that was a strong one," he said of a hefty injection in the rear. But in reality it was only one-fourth of a quaalude in salt water.

These easy rebounds made it hard to classify Elvis as a true addict. According to the physicians who treated him, Elvis's addiction was largely psychological. Baptist Hospital administrator Maurice Elliott, who made it a point to review the history of Presley's involvement with drugs, isn't at all "sure that Elvis was really addicted as we define the term. He was a big man with a gargantuan appetite, and I think he was a Goliath of chemical tolerance."

No sooner was Presley up from the massive detoxification effort—

which required ten days of recuperation—than he telephoned Dr. Nichopoulos to request plastic surgery. "I need my eyes done, Dr. Nick. I'm starting to look too old."

Patiently, the physician reminded Presley that much of his puffiness would recede if he could just take off some weight. "You don't need a surgeon's knife, you need a good long walk."

"Nope, I'm having my eyes done. You set it up."

Presley was reacting to the cruel press coverage that had accompanied his fortieth birthday on January 8. "Forty and fat" was the most-reported line. The *National Enquirer's* headline screamed, "Elvis at 40—Paunchy, Depressed & Living in Fear." The *Tupelo Daily Journal* was kinder with "Elvis Battles Bulge on 40th Birthday." What no one took into account was an enlarged colon, which prohibited Presley from eliminating fluids from his system. Like many singers, he went through gallons of water—especially while performing onstage. So he wasn't merely fat, he was also bloated.

He desperately wanted to be the way he once was.

The surgery was performed in mid-June by Memphis's Dr. Asghan Koleyni, who himself warned that the procedure was premature.

"Nope, go ahead with it," said Presley. "And while you're at it, I want a face-lift as well."

"No!" answered Dr. Koleyni. "Too early. Much too early."

"Nope, I'm gonna look twenty."

When the clandestine surgery was complete and Elvis returned proudly home to Graceland, nobody noticed—not even when he pointed it out. But everyone noticed that the sexy droop of his eyelids, the gorgeous legacy from the Smith family, had disappeared.

Dr. Nichopoulos's advice about his weight would have been a better solution. It wasn't easy for one of the leading sex symbols of all time to face a Las Vegas audience and confess, "You should have seen me a month ago when I got out of the hospital—I looked like Mama Cass." But that's what Presley did when he performed in Las Vegas in March to make up for the postponed engagement. This time there was no clinging jumpsuit. Instead he wore cream-colored pants with a loosely cut shirt. The better to hide the bulge, though he wasn't fooling anyone. In its review of the show, United Press International said Presley had "returned to this entertainment capital with all his old panache—and a little more paunch."

So many shots were taken at Presley's weight that a Hilton representative publicly admitted that its star suffered from "a little bit of a weight problem." For a change, there was a "no photographs" policy in the showroom.

Even in his hometown the media harped on the issue. Following a June performance at Memphis's Mid-South Coliseum, where he split his pants as he bent down to kiss a fan, the *Press-Scimitar* declared, "He Rocks 'n' Rolls 'n' Puffs Along While Fans Still Love Elvis Tenderly."

Shamed into dropping some weight, Elvis was twenty pounds lighter when he returned for an August show at the Las Vegas Hilton. "He looks healthy and sounds good," enthused *Las Vegas Review-Journal* columnist Forrest Duke.

The weight problem was more easily addressed than his drug usage. During that same Vegas stint Presley and crew indulged in an opiate orgy. On August 20 at just after midnight, only the third night of his two-week engagement—which the Colonel was promoting with eleven solid hours of radio spots, as well as hundreds of billboards, posters, and bus benches throughout the city—Elvis began slurring his words and singing choruses over again. At one point he leaned against the orchestra stand and cited passages from his collection of spiritual books. Finally, he crumpled onto the edge of the stage, his legs dangling over the side, tears, mascara, and rivulets of Cover Girl makeup running down his face.

"Folks, I'm sorry. . ," he mumbled before collapsing entirely.

Once again the Hilton canceled a Presley show "due to illness."

"Not everybody realized that, by this time, the drugs themselves had taken over, creating their own gargantuan hunger within Elvis's body," says Dr. Stanley Terman, founder and director of the Institute for Strategic Change and a major scholar on the subject of long-term drug addiction. "Minus the opiates, an addict's brain is starving for that chemical rush it needs to function properly," said Terman. "Those drugs hadn't given Presley a 'euphoric' feeling or any other sort of pleasant payoff for many, many years."

Presley had become a virtuoso in the fine art of obtaining pharmaceuticals. In the middle of some of his endless nights, Elvis resorted to gutter tactics that might have shocked the most hapless junkie. When Demerol was not enough and he craved the fireworks of Dilaudid, Presley would gulp down the painkiller to dull the pain, pull out a small pair of dental pliers, then methodically yank off his tooth caps. "That got to be an old trick," sighed Dr. Nichopoulos. Another surefire plan was to gouge bloody wounds in his hand. Pleasantly dulled by Demerol,

Elvis would slice into the palm of his hand, occasionally so deeply that he cut and splintered the bone.

Following the August collapse in Las Vegas, Elvis's private nurse, Tish Henley, wanted to rush Presley to the nearest hospital. But Elvis said no. He was worried about his reputation. So his plane was fueled for a trip to Memphis. Some associates felt he was too ill to fly across the country. Elvis was so sick he had to be carried onto the plane, where he laboriously pried open a vial and tossed back a few Dilaudid capsules before being eased into his armchair.

The plane was traveling over west Texas, headed toward Dallas, when Elvis's head jerked backward and his shoulders trembled uncontrollably as if he'd experienced a seizure.

Then, in all his bulk, he pitched forward into the aisle, using his hands to crawl along the carpet to the air-conditioning vent near the rear of the Commander. Shivering and rasping, he grabbed the emergency oxygen mask, pressing his mouth and nose to the vent. He made great sucking noises as he gulped the oxygen.

The pilot descended toward Dallas's Love Field.

"Hurry! Hurry! Get on the ground," Presley cried. "I'm not going to make it."

An hour later, they slipped Presley into a motel room next to the airport and were seeking a trustworthy physician—one who would keep his patient's identity confidential—just as Elvis began breathing naturally again.

After five hours of rest, the party reboarded and once again headed toward Memphis.

To this day, no one knows what caused Presley's airborne attack. Dr. Nichopoulos believes that the profound embarrassment of canceling the Las Vegas engagement after only two shows, along with the mortification of being bodily carried from the stage, drove his patient to a binge.

For the fourth time in three years Elvis Presley was checked back in to Baptist Hospital.

But unlike the other times, the hospital forms minced no words. Reason for entry was tersely listed as "Drug Detoxification." A medical analysis attached to the room assignment stated that Presley's abuse had resulted in "a dangerously fatty liver; high cholesterol; hypertension; early chronic obstructive pulmonary disease and a megacolon from overuse of laxatives [to counteract the constipation of codeine]."

The nurses, once so accommodating, were now cooler toward the

King. He had become another tiresome, complaining addict whose recidivism had become a waste of everyone's time. Even the usually unflappable Maurice Elliott was perturbed when he faced the press yet again with his press release delineating "Mr. Presley's exhaustion." Recalls Elliott, "We were stuck. Despite the international attention and the very acute suspicions that Elvis was on drugs, we were bound, as always, by the client-patient relationship."

This time Dr. Nichopoulos was disturbed when he was unable to lure his patient off Dilaudid and Demerol with his usual regime. With Presley's body crying out for the drugs, and a seizure possible without them, Dr. Nichopoulos had no choice but to reintroduce Demerol, sometimes in doses as high as 100 mg. Presley was also administered codeine, Amytal, Seconal, Placidyl, and occasionally Dilaudid.

Sometimes fortified with a Valium, Linda would cuddle against Elvis in the dark, watching the television until the national anthem gave way to test patterns. Just as he did on tour, Elvis would read deep, spiritual, and sometimes frightening meanings into the variations in the electronic snow.

Presley also had a special closed-circuit TV link established between his suite and the nursery, where the security camera would pan across Baptist's crop of newborns. Both Elvis and Linda would give names to the infants and wave to them when their favorites came into view. "Goo-goo," "kootchy-kootchy-koo," "ooh widdle cutie pie," and other babbled endearments could be heard down the hall from their room.

The lovebirds got a special kick out of compliant nurses who would carry the babies right up to the cameras and wave their tiny hands. "We'd just pick out little critters," Thompson said. "We both loved babies, and we fantasized about having a child. As Elvis watched, he would become very tender, like a baby himself, and regress back into the little, infantile state. I'd speak baby talk with him. I'd be the mommy and he would be the baby. He wanted to have a little boy, so we would search through the nursery for one. It was like our living test pattern."

Having a baby of their own was another matter. As Linda wryly commented to one nurse, "A baby for us is pretty damned unlikely. Sex once a year isn't so great, and it sure won't do the trick." By now Presley was often impotent due to the drugs.

In all probability, it was the drugs that also led to Elvis's refusal, in his latter years, to bathe. Simply put, though he drank a lot of water, he didn't like to be in it. So he took special pills, which came from

Sweden, that supposedly cleansed from within. In fact, his lack of bathing did not result in body odor—though it did sometimes bring about sores on his body. "Despite this, nothing anyone said could make him change his mind," said Nichopoulos.

During his two weeks in the hospital, which ended on September 5, Elvis complained of twenty-six headaches, fourteen bouts of insomnia, and moaned about "general pain—hurting all over" four or five times per shift. He alleviated much of his pain during the afternoon visits he was allowed to make to Graceland, where he dug into his stashes of drugs tucked throughout the mansion.

"By this time, Nichopoulos's only choice was to take charge of Elvis himself and maintain him on the smallest dose of opiates possible, perhaps for the rest of his life," said Dr. Forest Tennant. Nichopoulos could bring him down to "very low" levels when he was at Graceland. He could even retain control on several short road shows a year. But he could keep control in Vegas only if the runs were limited to one show per night, preferably an early show. In 1974, Elvis played 152 shows not including the two months in Vegas.

Nichopoulos approached Vernon Presley about his plan to save Elvis. "Cut back the shows and we can save him," said the doctor.

Vernon referred Nichopoulos to Colonel Parker.

"No!" boomed Parker. "Absolutely not. We have to keep him current, keep him before the public."

Despite having earned $7 million that year, Elvis didn't break even. At year's end, he was forced to take $700,000 from his bank account to pay the cost of running Graceland. Financially, Elvis had to stay on the road. So the only option Nichopoulos had was to accompany him.

"We couldn't see what was ahead, but we did follow orders," recalled road manager Joe Esposito. "Hell, we thought we would go on forever."

The game of Russian roulette with drugs would continue. On one harrowing night in Houston, Presley dangled a bag of drugs before his court and, eyes twinkling, asked jauntily, "Wonder which of these can kill a man?" He left no doubt in anyone's mind that the ultimate overdose could occur with the next flip of a bottle cap.

Not surprisingly, the drug-fueled shows were sometimes dominated by an eerie, anything-goes cadence. "I could see the end coming," said drummer Ronnie Tutt. "There were certain nights when you'd get ready to go onstage and you'd go to talk to him and he'd hardly be coherent. His eyes would be partly closed." Other nights Tutt pounded the drums as hard as possible "just to, like, kick Elvis in the rear, to say, 'Wake up! We're onstage!' "

During this period Elvis's ugly side was often revealed in public. Kathy Westmoreland, the soprano backup singer who Presley affectionately dubbed "Minnie Mouse," encountered that cruelty when she turned down Elvis's request that she sleep with him one night. "He told me he didn't want to be alone. But I had a new boyfriend who wouldn't have understood. I told Elvis that," Westmoreland recalled. Furious and hurt, Presley retaliated by making crude comments about her on stage in the segment when he introduced his backup singers and musicians. "This is Kathy Westmoreland. She'll take affection from anybody, anyplace, anytime," he said. As she fought back tears, he added, "In fact, she gets it from the whole band."

He delivered the line in Cleveland and later in Nassau, New York. When he did it again in Norfolk, Virginia, she pointed her finger at him. Curious, he walked over to where she stood. "You had better stop this!" she demanded. He cut short his routine—he left out the line about her getting affection from the entire band—and bent over to kiss her.

During that same show he made a rude comment about the Sweet Inspirations, claiming that he could smell garlic and onions on their breath. "They've been eating catfish," taunted Presley. The comment brought tears to the eyes of the group's Estelle Brown, who walked off the stage. When Presley went on to make a crude comment to Westmoreland, she also walked, along with the Sweet Inspiration's Sylvia Shemwell. Only Myrna Smith stayed to perform.

Presley later tried to give her a lavish ring in appreciation. Smith wouldn't take it. "You apologize!" she commanded. He did, the following night, on the stage of the Greensboro, North Carolina, Coliseum, before a bewildered audience that had no idea what had happened.

His singers forgave him, and Westmoreland would stick by him to the end. "He was so special," said Kathy. "I used to try to talk to him about going to a hospital. I knew he needed to be watched over, or there would be trouble. But he said he wouldn't go to a hospital and wait to die. He used to tell me, 'I hope I die onstage.' "

"He had created Elvis Presley as a young man with all the confidence and swagger that he could muster. He was the coolest," recalls Sam Thompson, Linda's brother and a Presley bodyguard during the seventies. "And when he was young, taking the world by storm, it was fun. He was on top of the world. But then came all of the bad movies, his transformation from a rebel to a teen idol, and the crushingly demanding concert tours. Now he was forty, and the papers were even calling him 'fat and forty.' Being Elvis had become an almost impossible job." Thompson saw Presley "losing some of his humanity. To keep going, Elvis turned to drugs, which helped him get up every morning as that magical minstrel everyone loved."

Charlie Hodge, who had watched his friend's transformation since 1960, believes Presley took the drugs to "make him feel onstage the way he had at twenty—something he missed very badly. Maybe the drugs eroded the years, and he was back up there singing 'All Shook Up' and really feeling it."

The two people who cared the most about the fabulous career, if not the man, wanted the self-destruction to end. Both Parker and Vernon Presley requested that Dr. George Nichopoulos be brought in full-time, for both the Vegas and the tour dates. This was not an assignment that Nichopoulos wanted. He did receive a hefty salary, plus more than $300,000 in annual payments to his medical corporation to pay someone else to treat his patients. He also formed a joint racquetball franchise—dealings that would be heavily censured later on. Yet the physician was reluctant to shoulder the task. As he told the Reverend Nicholas Vieron, he didn't want that life-and-death responsibility.

During his tenure on tour, Nichopoulos invented an intricate drug-management system, involving placebos, saline injections, and even hour-by-hour monitoring of Presley. Known only to Dr. Nichopoulos, nurse Tish Henley, and Elvis, the formula was largely a secret until this year, when a copy of it was discovered in a privileged and confidential "Attorney Work Product" developed when the State of Tennessee was trying to charge Nichopoulos with criminally overprescribing drugs to Elvis Presley.

The doctor's plan was to weed out the drugs of the opiate-morphine family, the most dangerous. For Elvis, treatments were given five times a day, beginning when he awakened at around four o'clock in the afternoon. The diet of drugs depended on Presley's condition for the day. As his valet, James Caughly, noted, "The boss would come up with the most intricately convincing symptoms to obtain as much of the drug rainbow as possible."

A typical rundown was as follows:

Elvis awakened around 3:00 P.M. before his show and was offered various diet aids: Ionamin, Dexedrine (the "E Special"), Biphetamine, or Sanorex, all members of the amphetamine family. He was allowed to select one—or one and a half. Between 3:30 and 4:30 he was administered a shot of Halotestin, a hormone to boost his potency; a capsule of Ruvert to combat the dizziness caused by Halotestin; a vitamin B12 injection; another Dexedrine Spansule to see him through the show; the diuretic Lasix to boost his chemically damaged kidneys; and the laxative Senekot. "I kept all of these initial pills at their lowest doses," says Dr. George Nichopoulos in his first-ever interviews on this drug regimen.

Elvis used to appear before Dr. Nichopoulos an hour before the show, dressed in his splendor and clutching the cape with its fifteen pounds of simulated jewels. Then he was administered Verinate for breathing problems (but which induced hyperactivity); Antivert (another mild tranquilizer); and Breathane, which cleared out his bronchial tubes.

Invariably, Elvis would demand Dilaudid, the one drug that infused him with a truly satisfying high and the necessary feeling of euphoria. Unless Presley was especially on edge, Nichopoulos handed him a placebo, one of a thousand he obtained from a medical company at $5.98 apiece. Other evenings Presley had to make do with a mild dosage of Mebroin, a compound effective in controlling brain or heart seizures.

Once the show ended—following the obligatory "Can't Help Falling in Love" and the announcement that "Elvis has left the building!"—the perspiring singer was given capsules of Inderal (to control his blood pressure); Periactin (for itching caused by his costume); Sinequaan, a long-lasting antidepressant; and if he was "very, very depressed," a prized quaalude. If he had sustained an injury during the show (and he invariably complained that he had), Dr. Nichopoulos gave him a shot of "watered-down Dilaudid, enough to dull the pain, but remarkably mild."

According to Nichopoulos, "If he didn't obtain some relief, the placebo experiments would have failed."

Up in his suite, Presley was handed his first sealed "bedtime packet No. 1." He was allowed one or two sedatives to prevent his insomnia: Carbital, a mild phenobarbital compound; Noludar, a hypnotic sleeping pill; or a quaalude, the chemical he craved most of all. All of the drugs combined should have been strong enough to put him to sleep, but most nights one packet wouldn't do it. So "bedtime packet

No. 2" was delivered, usually by Tish Henley. This offered Presley the choice of an Amytal sleeping pill or two quaaludes.

"This was a terribly time-consuming, often confusing juggling of medications to combine the least potent combination which would allow Elvis to do the show and then sleep afterward," noted Nichopoulos.

Making the placebos wasn't easy. Such diverse members of the troupe as Sam Thompson, Billy Smith, and Marty Lacker spent hours locked in their rooms, taking pills apart and putting them back together. Thompson remembers the nerve-racking hours of draining liquid from Placidyl and then blowing it back up with air or filling other celluloid capsules with powdered sugar or Sweet 'n Low. "Still, Elvis had a strong nose for placebos," recalled Billy Smith. "He was too attuned to the minute feelings produced by each of his favorite chemical combinations."

Basically, what other physicians called "Nichopoulos's impossible cure" worked for two years. Presley never experienced another major overdose while on the road.

Yet the toll was steadily wearing him down. His uncle Vester Presley, who had been a caretaker at Graceland since 1957, said, "It was fine from 1957 to 1974. But from 1974 he didn't really feel good. You couldn't talk to him even if you wanted to. We didn't push it." The sun was setting on the King.

Strange Days

The monumental strains of "Thus Spake Zarathustra" echoed through the massive new Silverdome of Pontiac, Michigan, on New Year's Eve, 1975. At the country's largest domed stadium, before a crowd of 62,500, out bounded the overweight Elvis Presley. For the first time in his career he was performing during the winter. Inconceivably, he was appearing due to sheer financial necessity.

During the concert Presley had to excuse himself and briefly leave the stage. When he returned to sing "Auld Lang Syne," he confessed that he had earlier split his pants.

When *Newsweek* wrote about the Pontiac show, there was no mention of how he sounded, or even the songs he sang, only the news that his clothes "have been under almost as much a strain as the singer himself." The magazine went on to call him "the roly-poly rock 'n' roller."

His weight had become such a topic of discussion that concert reviewers sometimes spent more time on his personal "stats" than they did discussing his music. Following a Long Beach, California, show, the *Los Angeles Times* ran a review headlined, "A Less Weighty Elvis Spectacle." In three out of the seven paragraphs, music critic Robert

Hilburn mentioned Presley's weight.* *Playboy* bestowed upon him its First Annual Golden Ice Cream Bar Award—claiming he had a "burning love for ten Eskimo Pies" a day, and suggesting a month at a "fat farm."

On his forty-first birthday he suffered the humiliation of newspaper reports that decreed "there was more of him to love." As Presley was to lament, "I keep hearing that shit about being fat and middle-aged."

Because of all the medication he was taking, he joked to his friend Larry Geller that he was going "on one cylinder." Geller noticed how labored Presley's breathing had become. "He rarely spoke more than a couple of sentences without stopping to draw a long, deep, noisy breath," recalled Geller in his memoirs, *If I Can Dream.*

Meanwhile, Elvis suffered aches and pains onstage and off. "Oh, God, I hurt," he used to say between clipped breaths. During one show, he looked over at Charlie Hodge and confessed, "Buddy, I'm just totally exhausted."

He was so despondent that when RCA wanted him to travel to Nashville or Hollywood for a recording session to fulfill a contract for an album, he refused. And so, in February 1976, the session had to come to Graceland. The musicians' equipment had to be moved in through the windows of the "jungle room" den, where the thick shag carpet proved to be good acoustical material. But after everyone had assembled, Elvis refused to come downstairs. He said he was sick.

Over the week that followed, Presley eventually recorded a dozen songs. Of the ten songs that are included in the album *From Elvis Presley Boulevard*, one has become a particularly haunting anthem of the latter-day Elvis. "Hurt," with Presley's voice not as strong as it once was, is undoubtedly a message from a man in pain. As rock critic Dave Marsh put it, "If he felt the way he sounded, the wonder isn't that he had only a year left to live but that he managed to survive that long."

As Elvis put it, that night, to producer Felton Jarvis, "I'm so tired."

"You need a rest," replied Jarvis.

"That's not what I mean," said Elvis wearily. "I mean, I'm just so tired of being Elvis Presley."

After years of excess, his world had become splintered, leading to increasingly erratic behavior. During these recording sessions, Elvis was so confused and so confounding that at one point he threatened to take a gun and shoot out the recording equipment.

---

*Then one of the country's leading rock music critics, Hilburn had previously authored an essay that declared, "Maybe it's time for Elvis to retire."

He was now known for his car-buying sprees, during which perfect strangers who happened to be passing certain car dealerships would drive away in a gift from Presley.

His jeweler, Lowell Hays, was always at his disposal, should Elvis get the urge to bestow jewelry on some lucky stranger—sometimes from the concert stage.

During a trip to Colorado, he reportedly went house-hunting wearing a ski mask with a jumpsuit. Another report claimed he was seeing a hypnotist about mind control. He made headlines when he sent his ailing pet chow, Getlo, by private Lear jet, to be treated at the New England Institute of Comparative Medicine for two months. (The canine suffered from a kidney ailment that ultimately proved fatal.)

At Memphis radio station WHBQ, where George Klein was the program director, disc jockey Bob McLain used to get morning calls on the station's unlisted hot line from an unnamed man who always requested Presley's songs. "I used to call him 'the vampire,'" recalled McLain, "but it was so obvious who it was. Like, I couldn't tell Elvis's voice!"

Though Elvis continued to pack concert arenas, his performances were wildly unpredictable. Some nights he was lucid, on key, and charismatic. Other nights he forgot lyrics, slurred his between-songs banter, and even messed up when he named his backup performers. "Oh, God, the boss is fucked up again" became a standard remark among his backup band.

At an August matinee performance in Houston, audiences saw a dramatically different man from the one who had victoriously played the Dome in 1970. A disoriented Presley rambled on incoherently between songs; when he did sing he had trouble remembering the lyrics. The reviewer for the *Houston Chronicle* wrote, "Attending an Elvis Presley concert these days is like making a disappointing visit to a national shrine." The *Houston Post* said Presley "looked, talked, walked and sang like a very ill man."

That summer, Priscilla was approached by several of Presley's colleagues about his condition. She immediately flew to Memphis and tried to talk him into entering the Scripps Clinic in San Diego, where alcohol and drug problems were being treated. At the time, rehab programs were not at all commonplace. The famed Betty Ford center was years down the road. Elvis, who could never acknowledge his drug problems, vehemently denied that he needed treatment.

His decline was exacerbated in July when Vernon Presley summoned Red West, Sonny West, and relative newcomer Dave Hebler—who had been on staff for two years—and unceremoniously fired them. They received just three days' notice and a week's severance pay. Vernon cited finances, but in fact the firings had been brewing over several years, the result of several fights involving the bodyguards that had led to lawsuits.

The trio was furious, more so since Elvis didn't even bother to personally speak with them. Red West, who had been on the road with Presley since 1955, was especially enraged. In revenge, they went in search of a writer for what would be a legendary "tell-all."

When Elvis got wind of their plans, he became frantic. Up to this time, what had gone on among his inner circle had been closely guarded. He was devastated the day he asked Jerry Schilling, "What am I going to do? What will Lisa Marie think of her daddy when all this comes out?" He worried, too, about his fans.

The Wests' departure was followed by that of Linda Thompson. She had been with Elvis since 1972 and wanted a new life. In an interview in *McCall's*, Thompson once explained, "I finally decided that this was not the way I wanted to spend the rest of my life. It was such a bizarre existence to be . . . totally removed from the rest of the world." She added, "One of the main reasons I decided to leave was that whole lifestyle, a part of which was the sleeping medication . . . I thought it was not fair for a young woman who's Suzie Straight to have to deal with this the rest of her life. To try to keep someone else alive."

Time and again Presley had disappointed her, often rebounding with the line, "You always hurt the one you love, the one closest to you." After saying that, he used to plaintively add, "But I know you'll love me and understand."

When she tried to talk to him about all the pills, he would declare, "Mommy, just relax. I want to see Lisa grow up and to watch her little kids. I'm going to live to be an old, old man."

The Presley-Thompson relationship had an explosive ending when Presley had her booted out of his Bel-Air house one night. Like the bodyguards, she got revenge. Not with a tell-all, but a $25,000 shopping spree—which she charged to Elvis. When the bills later came in to Graceland, a weary Vernon acknowledged, "She earned it."

Elvis once gave a friend a piece of paper on which he'd written down his philosophy for a happy life: *Someone to love, something to look forward to, and something to do.* The steadily narrowing world he had created—within his self-imposed exile—was devoid of such possibilities.

When he wasn't on the road, he now stayed at Graceland, often holed up in his bedroom, with its black walls and ceiling, and black curtains pulled tight across windows covered with aluminum foil. Sitting with the lights out, he would stare glassy-eyed at one of the televisions, which seemed to constantly be on. His buddies used to flash each other smiles when he sat watching *The Lawrence Welk Show*.

He also watched the closed-circuit monitor at the gate. Though Presley seldom wanted to see old friends, he could at least glimpse who was trying to visit.

Presley missed out on one of the odder episodes at the gate. At three o'clock one morning in November 1976, Jerry Lee Lewis showed up and belligerently demanded to see Elvis. Brandishing a .38 pistol, he proclaimed, "Just tell him the Killer's here." Lewis—nicknamed the Killer—was arrested for the disturbance.

A few months later, Elvis had another would-be visitor—a young man with a goatee who literally jumped the wall and began running toward the door. When guards intercepted him, the interloper gasped, "Uh, is Elvis home?" He was told that Presley was in Tahoe, and was then promptly escorted back out the gate. Years later, Bruce Springsteen confessed, "I had to try." Then riding a wave of popularity—he was the cover boy on both *Time* and *Newsweek*—Springsteen later explained, "Elvis had been my inspiration."

Despite his growing reclusiveness, Presley continued to maintain his alliance with his fans. He still went out to the gate to sign autograph books and talk through the fence. After all, these were the people who bought the tickets for the concerts, which had become his sole link to humanity. They still reached for scarves. If he had difficulty reaching down to them, they reached higher.

He would also phone Priscilla, sometimes talking for hours, and there were visits from eight-year-old Lisa Marie. Yet with the exception of his shrinking cluster of aides, including bodyguards Sam Thompson and Dick Grob, Presley was finally alone, as Priscilla had predicted, in his sprawling wing of the mansion he had purchased for his mother two decades earlier.

"It is fair to say that Elvis literally cut himself off from the outside world for a while in late 1976," recalls Joe Esposito.

Elvis hibernated in the perpetual twilight of his bedroom, and between eating platters of cheeseburgers and accepting his regulated pill packets—now five per day—he watched three television sets simultaneously while, concurrently, one radio played gospel and another country music for background.

Some days not even television was safe. One afternoon Sonny

West, whom he'd once called his "soul brother," appeared on an afternoon talk show. Sporting black sunglasses and a gut that protruded over his pants, he entertained 20 million Americans with tales of Elvis and drugs, disgusting sex, and thuggish violence.

Elvis moaned to Dr. Nichopoulos, "Why do they want to see me that way? Why?"

Dr. Nichopoulos and others sometimes lured Elvis out onto the colonnaded front porch of Graceland to reintroduce him to the outdoors. Wearing a huge white robe, Elvis would tote out a large wicker chair that he would position behind one of the columns. Sometimes kids on their way home from school would catch sight of him, stop their bikes, and yell out, "Hey, it's fat Elvis!"

"That was a rough period," said his longtime friend George Klein. "He really only cared about two things now, performing live and meeting really beautiful girls. And the girls did wonders for him. They could always see the sweetness buried inside him. The problem was finding the right lady."

Klein cast about with little luck until the fall of 1976, when he met the current Miss Tennessee, Terri Alden. She was a striking blonde with a bubbly nature—and two sisters. Rosemary was more outgoing that either Terri or her younger sister Ginger, who had just been named runner-up Miss U.S.A. Rosemary said, "George, Terri will go if you take all three of us." After all, she added, "I'm mighty interested in Graceland."*

For Rosemary, the instant she made her way through the front door, "it was like Alice going into the mirror and coming out on the other side again."

With Terri arranged as a centerpiece, the three sisters sat decorously on a bed in an upstairs room. "Suddenly, Elvis came in, in his karate outfit, and began talking to us," Rosemary recalls. His eyes darted back and forth between the three young women, but mostly he looked at the regal, silent Ginger. A dark-haired beauty with the grace and bearing of a young ballet dancer, Ginger also remarkably resembles Priscilla as well as the young Gladys Presley. While Rosemary asked nonstop questions about Graceland, she caught Presley shyly sneaking a look at Ginger while trying to politely answer. "I knew!" Rosemary says.

Finally, Elvis leaped up in his karate outfit and twirled to face

---

*Coincidentally, Walter Alden—the father of the Alden sisters—had been the U.S. Army officer who inducted Elvis into the Army on March 24, 1958.

Ginger. "Darlin', you're burning a hole right in the back of my neck. I can feel it. I don't even need to see you."

When the girls got up to leave, Elvis signaled to Rosemary to walk with Terri so he could quietly walk Ginger out to the car. "I'd like to call for you tomorrow and take you out to see my airplane tomorrow night," he told the young woman. Stunned by his attention, Ginger could only nod.

Vernon Presley said later that when Elvis met Ginger, "a great weight seemed to have been lifted from his shoulders. I saw him smiling again."

Though Ginger agreed, her mother, Jo Alden, wasn't so sure about her twenty-year-old daughter's going up for "a little spin" with the forty-one-year-old singer. But Elvis winked at Jo. "Just a wittle spin, ma'am," he said in baby talk. "We'll be home tomorrow afternoon."

At the airport, Ginger's eyes widened when she noticed that Presley's custom Convair 880 jet—the *Lisa Marie*—was fueled and ready for takeoff. Inside they met Elvis's cousin Patsy, and two other guests. When he buckled Ginger in her seat, located at the prime first window, Elvis called to the pilot, "Take 'er up and head for Vegas."

As the plane took off, Elvis leaned over to whisper, "You can call your mother as soon as we land."

Esposito recalls that the boss "was gone on Ginger." During the Las Vegas trip Presley gave her a massive gold and diamond bracelet—a preview of a hurried, passionate courtship the likes of which hadn't been seen since he met Priscilla in Germany. Dinners, long afternoons at Graceland, and gifts for her entire family followed.

One night during the second week in December, Elvis slept fitfully. Finally, shortly after dawn, he had a dream in which his mother appeared to him, but with Ginger's face. It was as if Gladys were giving her blessing.

He excitedly told Dr. Nichopoulos about the dream. "I have never seen someone fall in love so fast and so sure," recalled Dr. Nichopoulos, who saw the couple every afternoon as he tended to Elvis's declining drug needs. "The members of the Mafia make it sound like Jo arranged the whole thing, that she was a stage mother, and that Elvis was just pushed into the affair. That was not true. He dove into that relationship."

In nine months the four Alden women accomplished what a team of physicians, nearly a dozen blood relatives, and the Memphis Mafia had failed to do over years—to pull Presley back into the real world.

For instance, Jo, despised by what was left of the Mafia, who nicknamed her The Black Witch of Alden, once pulled her car into the Graceland entry and then talked Presley into getting out of bed and joining a crowd at a carnival midway. As he pulled on his jacket, he told Jo, "Nobody else would have dared do that."

In early December 1976 and again in spring 1977, Ginger, Rosemary, and Jo were the inspiration for the first true vacations Elvis had had for several years. They first flew into Las Vegas and occupied a series of suites in the Hilton, for which Elvis himself made the reservations. While Ginger and her mother were marveling at the view from the penthouse, Elvis's private phone rang. The number was available to only ten or twelve people, including Linda Thompson. "Elvis honey," she purred, "I heard you were in Vegas, so I rang up to see if we are going to be spending Christmas together as usual."

Elvis grinned and held the phone slightly to the side of his head. "Gee, I don't know, Linda honey, I gotta ask Ginger. Hey, Gingerbread," he yelled, "y'all mind if Linda spends Christmas with us?"

"You should have heard Linda screaming on the phone," said Jo.

As Elvis held out the phone, the call ended with a loud click.

Just before Christmas, Elvis took Ginger into his swank bathroom and study, got on his knees, handed her a $7,000 eleven-and-a-half-carat diamond engagement ring, and asked her to marry him. Ginger accepted the proposal.

Presley's circle derided Ginger, the engagement ring, and Elvis's attachment to the young beauty. They had a spate of nicknames for her, including One-Year Ginger (meaning she would be gone by the following Christmas). They also called her Jezebel, because they thought she was cheating on Presley with her old boyfriend.

Singly and in groups, they claimed to have followed her and verified that she was still "legitimately engaged to her high school sweetheart." They passed along the word to Presley. Uncertain of the veracity of the reports, he was nonetheless confused. "Elvis was sick at heart and grabbed for drugs instantly," remembered Nichopoulos.

In fact, Ginger Alden had broken up with her previous boyfriend, Larry Anthony, the first day she returned from the initial Las Vegas outing. "Actually, we were never engaged. We'd just gone together for a long time," says Anthony. "The day after I read about her Vegas trip in the newspaper, she came over to my house and sat down with me on the couch." According to Anthony, Ginger had tears in her eyes as she told him, "I know you love me, and I'm so sorry, but Elvis needs me more than you. This is something I must do."

Anthony is defensive of talk of her being an opportunist, "because I know she was none of those things." She was, he believes, determined to help Presley through his troubled times.

Shy, and private about her relationship with Presley, Ginger says she didn't fall immediately in love with the star—it happened gradually. Moreover, she was caught off guard when he talked about marriage. But she knew he had an agenda. "He told my mother I was an angel sent from heaven, to help him.

"I was very young, a sheltered twenty [-year-old]," says Ginger. "But I came to feel that maybe that's why I was put on earth. If I could make Elvis happy, I would have served my purpose." Added Ginger, "He wanted me with him night and day."

As her romance with Presley continued, a second spate of rumors materialized. This time, the story went, Ginger was secretly in love with an unnamed professional wrestler. "We will have the proof soon, boss," claimed one of the Mafia.

"I laughed right out loud when I heard that one," says Jo. "You would have to know Ginger to understand how impossible that story would have been."

In a third story, the guys listed the number of times Ginger had escaped Graceland to go out and spend the evening dancing with handsome young men. But, counters Rosemary, when Ginger went out dancing, it was to accompany her. "I went to discos every once in a while and convinced Ginger to go. And she was a wallflower who sat there, sipping a Coke."

As 1977 progressed into the next heavy tour schedule, these and other fabricated stories caused considerable heartbreak at Graceland. "I can't emphasize enough the damage to Elvis's emotional and physical health caused by these stories," said Dr. Nichopoulos, who stressed he had no way of knowing if the stories were true.

There seems no question that Presley's cadre wanted the boss to dump his much younger girlfriend. After all, not since Priscilla had a woman so monopolized Presley's time. He had taken a liking to Alden's family as well, dropping by unannounced, planting a forest of trees in their yard, once even spending the night—during a snowstorm—sleeping on an Aldens' bed, wrapped in a large bath towel.

The next morning, Walter Alden, an Air Force sergeant, found Presley sitting at the kitchen table.

"What can I get for you, son?"

"Well, sir, if you don't mind, I'd like three or four hamburger buns, buttered and toasted. And a glass of milk."

Walter Alden didn't raise an eyebrow over the odd request. Like a good host, he excused himself and went off to the store. Later, when Jo had awakened, she found her famous houseguest eating slightly over-toasted buns, dripping in butter.

"Really, Walter," she said in exasperation.

"Oh, no, ma'am," said Elvis, "this is just what I wanted."

On January 3, 1977, a drug-free Elvis, dressed in a new black suit, stood at Ginger's side at the Harrison, Arkansas, funeral of her grand-father. As the coffin was lowered, Ginger grasped Elvis's hand so tightly that her nails indented his hand. Elvis leaned down to kiss her softly on the cheek.

"It's so hard," she whispered.

"Yes, honey," he replied. "And take it from me, it don't get any easier."

To cheer up his fiancée and her family, Presley flew ahead to Palm Springs and rented the top floor of the Sheraton Inn for a week's vaca-tion with Ginger and Jo and just two security guards—minus the Mafia. To impress Ginger and her mother, he had them flown to the roof of the penthouse in a helicopter.

The idyll was brief. Once he returned to Memphis, ten days later, he found Colonel Parker had booked a backbreaking schedule of seven concert tours for the rest of the year, with minimal time off.

Ginger was thrown into a panic when she learned that Presley expected her to accompany him on them all. "But I can't," she said. "I'm just not up to that much."

"Neither am I, honey. Neither am I," offered Elvis. "But we're together now."

Ironically, though the relationship with Ginger brought Presley some of his greatest comfort during this period, it also led to additional drug-induced woes. On the afternoon of March 31, after thirteen thousand fans in Baton Rouge, Louisiana, had endured Jackie Kahane's creaky jokes, and listened to selections by the Sweet Inspirations and J.D. Sumner and the Stamps, they were told that the star attraction—Elvis Presley—would not be able to perform. Presley reportedly had the flu.

In truth, he had sated himself with drugs—in anger and confu-sion—when he was unable to locate Ginger prior to the show. After-ward, as he paced his hotel suite, he had also pulled a hamstring muscle and strained his back.

By the time Ginger returned to the room, after browsing in a hotel gift shop, arrangements were made to take Presley by ambulance to the airport, and then, via the *Lisa Marie*, on to Memphis, where he was again hospitalized at Baptist.

Admitted on April 1, for treatment of "gastroenteritis and mild anemia," Presley's drug intake was again altered by Nichopoulos, who had learned that his patient had been taking Demerol every two hours.

In confidential instructions to the nurses, the physician now called for the "alternation of Leritine [a mild opiate pain killer] and Demerol every four hours."

According to the nurses' notes, Dr. Nick also initially authorized that Presley be given a pass—so that he could briefly leave the hospital. But the pass was revoked when Nichopoulos feared that Elvis "would refuse to return to Baptist."

During his four-day stay—in which he missed four shows—Presley complained that he needed extra Demerol. Nichopoulos feigned treatment; unbeknownst to Presley, he was actually being administered placebos, which he accepted without any dissatisfaction.

But once out of hospital, Presley returned to his druggy ways. It didn't help his performances. After witnessing a show by the stumbling, slurry-speeched star, one leading concert promoter was so shaken that he called rock journalist Jerry Hopkins, who had written the first biography of Presley. Hopkins said, "I had taken my book and turned it into this twelve-part radio series, and the promoter told me, 'You should get ready to do a chapter thirteen.'" The promoter went on to tell Hopkins that word in the concert world was that Presley was "a walking dead man." Producer Felton Jarvis was also worried. "The man's dying, and nobody will do anything about it," he kept saying to anyone who would listen.

According to Larry Geller, who was Presley's hairstylist during the troubled tour, Presley was passed out cold, prior to a Louisville, Kentucky, show. "Eyes closed, jaw slack, Elvis looked helpless, as if he were in a coma," Geller wrote in his memoirs. Dr. Nick was attempting to revive Elvis with ice water when the Colonel barged into the suite.

The Colonel went on to have private words with Nichopoulos. Then he exited, but not before he turned to Geller, shook his cane, and said, "The only thing that's important is that he's on that stage tonight. Nothing else matters!"

A few nights—and uninspired shows—later, Presley was so despondent over troubles with Ginger that he sent her back home to Memphis. Then he lamented that he didn't want to be alone in the night.

At the urging of both Geller and Dr. Nick, Kathy Westmoreland came to the rescue, spending several nights sitting and talking and cradling the star. "He was bloated, he was weak, he was tired," said Westmoreland, adding, "I could see that he didn't have that much time."

She and Presley meditated. They talked about his career. Sitting in his pajamas, on the side of the bed, his hair a tousled mess, he asked, "What's it all about, Kathy?" To her quizzical look, he continued, "I'm talking about life . . . and what follows. How are people going to remember me? I've never done a classic film. I've never sung a lasting song."

He went on to weep, and to talk of his hopes that God would help to heal him of his health problems. "We prayed for that," said Kathy, who somberly added, "But when he fell asleep, I could hear the death rattle."

Elvis heard it, too. As he told Westmoreland, "I know I look fat, now. . . . But I'll tell you this, I'm going to look good in my casket."

Elvis's spiraling decline was increasingly apparent to ticket buyers.

When he performed at the Philadelphia Spectrum on May 28, before nearly twenty thousand people, he couldn't remember the lyrics, and he appeared to stagger. There were actually boos from the crowd, and when Elvis began singing "I Can Help," someone in the arena hollered out, "You need help!"

That was never more apparent than the following night in Baltimore.

Once again Presley used his relationship with Ginger to trigger his hunger for drugs. Only this time the drugs themselves were what led to their initial disagreement.

Ginger, who had rejoined Presley—only to find him taking double doses of his "medication"—pressed him about his need for pills and the toll they were taking.

"You don't know what I need!" Presley retorted. "So don't go talkin' about that again."

But as Ginger pointed out, because of the drugs he spent his days sleeping while she spent hers alone. "I'm tired of all this," she protested.

Glowering at the young beauty he had deemed his "soul mate," Presley threw the covers off his bed and rose, saying, "Okay, then, go back on home if you want to. Get your things and leave."

By concert time, Elvis was so shaky he was unable to hold the microphone. After he dropped it, during a stumble, an assistant had to hold it for him. Even worse, Presley's famed voice was so anemic that audiences could barely hear the songs. He finally left the stage— thirteen thousand ticket buyers wondering if he'd return. He did, thirty minutes later, following treatment by Dr. Nichopoulos.

For the rest of the show Presley sang without bursting into his trademark gyrations. Sometimes wincing—as if in pain—as he turned slightly, he was heard to mutter under his breath, "Sometimes it hurts me so fuckin' bad."

By this time the crew was toting oxygen tanks in case the boss had difficulty breathing. And Presley, who would no longer allow anyone to take his measurements, could fit into only two identical jumpsuits.

Inconceivably, during this period the Colonel struck a deal with CBS, which filmed two of Presley's concerts—in June 1977 in Omaha, Nebraska, and Rapid City, South Dakota—for a television special. The out-of-shape Presley was literally panting between numbers. When some of Presley's associates at last saw the footage, they were shaken.

"I was inconsolable," admitted Linda Thompson. "I could not believe he had deteriorated that much," said Jerry Schilling.

Late that month, when Presley returned to Memphis, and to Ginger, he was severely bloated and was coming down from 128 doses of drugs consumed during his most grueling tour in years. He murmured to Ginger that he wanted to be, "for the rest of the year, with you." But he had only $1.1 million in his ready checking account, a pittance to a man whose home and tours cost him $500,000 a month.

The burden could no longer be borne. Although no one knew it then, Elvis Presley had played his last set.

By the time the next tour beckoned, Ginger wasn't ready to go. She and Presley began a tug-of-war.

"You have to go," he said.

"Not right at first."

"But you're my inspiration," he insisted.

"Not when I'm menstruating," she groaned.

Finally, following intervention by Rosemary, Ginger agreed to pack her bags. Rosemary would also come along.

The plane was scheduled to leave the evening of August 16 for Portland, Maine, for Elvis's first concert in more than two months. One week prior to departure, Elvis went on a near-starvation diet. (In past years, he used to exercise and diet for months in order to get his weight down for his tours.) "He ate mostly Jell-O, made with artificial sweetener," recalled Dr. Nichopoulos. When there was no weight loss after five days, he tried a total fast.

Uncharacteristically, and to the concern of the Graceland cooks, he didn't try to "cheat." "Aren't you gonna eat something for me?" Mary Jenkins asked him in the wee hours of August 16. He just shook his head wearily at "May-wee," explaining, "I'm just not hungry." Later, after Pauline Nicholson had come on duty, he at last called down to request some ice cream and cookies. "But not as much as usual," said Presley. Curiously, along with his lack of appetite, his final days were marked by his reluctance to go out to the gates to talk with his fans.

At 5:00 A.M. on August 16, Elvis went out to the racquetball court behind the house. Ginger was with him. So was Billy Smith and his wife, Jo. They played for about two hours. Or rather, Elvis swatted at the balls that came his way.

Elvis and Ginger later climbed the stairs leading to his bedroom. But as ever, Elvis couldn't sleep. Plagued by insomnia, he began calling out for Nichopoulos's rationed packets to coax him to sleep. He didn't bother to tell anyone that his dentist had prescribed an additional fifty codeine capsules the evening before, or that he had a stash of syringes and morphine elixirs hidden in the bathroom.

When the first and the second packets didn't send him crashing by 8:00 A.M., in his day-for-night world, he called for a third packet.

When he still couldn't sleep at about nine, he rolled over and kissed Ginger and then retired to his bathroom, to read and fulfill bodily functions—since he suffered from constant constipation.

As Ginger drifted off to sleep, she heard him stirring and saw his shadow through a crack in the door. "Oh, Lord," she remembered, "the Elvis Presley show goes to Portland tomorrow."

When Ginger Alden awakened, she ran her hand over satin sheets, searching for her lover's arm. But his side of the bed was cold.

"Elvis?" she called out softly. "Darlin', are you up?" There was no answer.

She noticed a wedge of light emanating from the partially open door of Elvis's bathroom suite, a certain sign that his chronic insomnia had driven him to the library of books in his dressing chamber. Believing him to be engrossed in his new book, *The Scientific Search for the Face of Jesus*, about the Shroud of Turin, Ginger pulled her quilted robe around her, sank back in the pillows, and reached for the telephone to make her obligatory morning call to her mother.

"Hi, Mom," she began.

Jo Alden was angry. "Ginger, where are you? You're supposed to be home packing for Elvis's tour. Do you realize it's almost two-fifteen?"

"I'm still at Graceland, Mama. Elvis was even more depressed than usual. He wanted for me to stay."

"Where is Elvis?"

When her daughter said he was in the bathroom reading, Jo said, "Well, you go look for him and tell him you've got to get ready for that tour. He can have one of the guys drive you home."

So Ginger walked to the door of Elvis's inner sanctum, which included an office, a library, and an oversize bathroom, and called out his name again. But there was still no answer. Not bold enough to fling open the bathroom door, Ginger instead crept up and looked through the opening.

She instantly put her hand to her mouth and reached out to steady herself against the door.

In the reflection of the smoked-glass mirror she could see Elvis, his body contorted on the floor, his buttocks upward in the air, both feet splayed behind him. She saw his face, too. It was bloated, turned to one side, and pressed into the thick nap of the vermilion carpet. Blue streaks were spreading up through his face, and his hands, which were frozen into fists, were grasping the carpet fibers.

Shoving the door open, Ginger confronted the full horror of the scene. Elvis had been sitting on the toilet and had fallen face forward onto his knees. He was stiff and frozen in that position. The bottoms of his blue silk pajamas were bundled around his feet.

She caught her breath, as she found herself thinking, "Oh my God, he's dead." Trembling violently, she dropped to her knees and reached out for him. But when she tried to turn his head toward her, it seemed as if his neck had stiffened. She could only wrench his face a few inches, so she could see him in profile. Then, to her joy, he "exhaled." "And I was thinking, 'he's alive! Thank you, God, he's alive!' " recalled Ginger.*

She slapped him lightly on the face. No response. She tried again, harder. Scrambling to her feet, Ginger grasped the intercom connecting Elvis's suite with the rest of the mansion.

Below, in the kitchen, Nancy Rooks answered.

"Who's on duty?" Ginger asked.

"Al's right here next to me," answered Rooks, who handed the phone to one of the Graceland bodyguards, Al Strada.

"Get up here quick, Al," said Ginger. "Elvis has fainted and he looks real, real sick."

Strada bounded up Graceland's back staircase, followed shortly by the rock star's road manager, Joe Esposito, and another aide, Charlie Hodge.

*In fact, the "exhale" was actually air movement in the body.

They found Ginger Alden slumped against the wall, motionless. "Everything horrible was running through my mind," she said. "At first I thought he just hit his head. Then I suspected the worst but brushed it from my mind. Still, I couldn't move."

Strada dropped to his hands and knees. He grabbed Elvis's arms in a vain attempt to turn him over. They were ice-cold. "Joe!" he yelled. "You've got to help me turn him over!"

The "hollow ring of fear in Al's voice" startled Esposito as he knelt down to roll the boss over onto his back. Again Elvis exhaled. Though he wanted to believe Presley was still alive, Esposito knew the truth as soon as he felt Elvis's stiff, ice-cold arms: rigor mortis was obvious. At the time, however, Esposito was in deep denial. "You cling to any kind of hope," he said in retrospect. That hope intensified when Elvis again "exhaled."

"Everybody move away!" Joe ordered as he straddled Elvis's chest, administering cardiopulmonary resuscitation, as if force alone could yank the singer back to consciousness.

Vernon Presley, ill and partially infirm, entered the room on the arm of his niece Patsy Presley. Seeing his son, he began to cry. As the room descended into chaos, Patsy began to pray aloud and Vernon joined in. Charlie Hodge sobbed and Al Strada barked into the phone, summoning paramedics and dialing Dr. George Nichopoulos.

Strada glanced at his watch. It was 2:33 P.M.

The next fifteen minutes seemed like an eternity. "God, if he ain't dead already, they'll finish him," Patsy Presley whispered, shaking Vernon from his grief-stricken daze.

"Where's the ambulance?" he cried helplessly. "And where the hell is Dr. Nick? Call down to the gatehouse!"

Finally, the Memphis Fire Department's Unit Six careened around the corner at Graceland's entrance, crashing into a corner of the entrance gates. The driver, Ulysses Jones, braked for a second at the guardhouse and cried out, "What's up?"

The gatekeeper was nonchalant. "I think it's an OD. Just go through the front door and up the big staircase."

Upstairs, Elvis's nine-year old daughter, Lisa Marie, appeared at the bathroom door and clung pitifully to Ginger's satin robe. "What's wrong with my daddy?" she demanded.

Ginger took her hand and whispered, "Nothing much, honey. It's going to be all right."

Strada, though preoccupied and dazed, yelled, "Ginger, get her out of here. Now!"

"But I want to know what's wrong with my daddy," pleaded the child.

"Nothing, sweetheart," Ginger soothed.

But Lisa Marie had already seen too much. "Yes, there is something wrong with my daddy, and I'm going to find out." Barefoot and clutching a rag doll, she broke away from Ginger and ran out onto the landing, heading toward the dressing room's back entrance. Ginger followed her. Strada sprang up and locked it, leaving Lisa Marie sobbing in Ginger Alden's arms.

Ulysses Jones and his partner Charles Crosby thundered past Lisa Marie and Ginger as they headed for the bedroom. When he burst into the room, Crosby was surprised at the crowd, "about a dozen," many of them sobbing. Before he could ask what happened, a young man volunteered, "He OD'd."

Jones was hurriedly scrawling the amateur diagnosis onto his medic's report when another of Elvis's bodyguards, "an older man," blurted out, "Naw, it wasn't that at all. He swallowed something. He can't breathe."

Ulysses motioned the mourners aside and began working on Elvis. "I was stunned by the size of him," Jones recalls. "He must have weighed two hundred and fifty pounds, totally unrecognizable as Elvis Presley."

(In fact, Presley's family and closest aides went on to admit that he had weighed in at around two hundred and fifty pounds at the time of his death. They were being kind. A secret addendum to the private autopsy proves that he was even heavier.*)

The medic shined a penlight in the stilled eyes. There was no flicker of the pupil, the telltale contraction that separates life from death. The face was bluish purple, a mask of death.

With the anxious audience searching for any sign of hope, Jones looked up authoritatively and said, "Let's get this man to the hospital where they can take care of him." It was a gargantuan task to get Elvis

*Curiously, the coroner's death certificate failed to list Elvis's weight in the space provided for it. But Presley's weight was revealed in clandestine documents from the Presley autopsy, and was confirmed by Dr. Joseph Davis, former medical examiner of Florida's Dade County, who went on to conduct the second Presley autopsy. "Elvis was grotesquely overweight," said Davis, who said that during the initial autopsy, pathologists "shaved about one hundred pounds when they listed his weight as two hundred and fifty pounds."

onto the stretcher, requiring the five strongest men in the room. During the struggle the remaining aides groped through the bathroom gathering up used syringes and the scattered pills in the carpet.

In less than three minutes, the medics charged down the stairs followed by the frightened aides and Ginger Alden, now in pants and a simple blouse. "I've got to go with him," she said. "You've got to let me. He needs me."

"I arrived just as they were putting him in the ambulance," recalled Dr. Nichopoulos, who leaped into the ambulance first, positioning himself near the resuscitation devices. The stretcher carrying Elvis's body was shoved in after him. Then the tight group of aides jostled among themselves for space in the ambulance. Esposito jumped in, followed by Charlie Hodge. When Ginger, tears running down her face, tried to mount the tiny aluminum steps, one of the aides "rudely shoved" her aside, coldly saying, "You just stay here and keep out of the way."

Vernon came over to Jones. "He's dead, isn't he?"

The medic looked Elvis's father in the eye. "We will do the very best we can, sir!"

Chilled by the look on Jones's face, Vernon took Patsy Presley's arm and then gathered up Ginger. "Come on in the house, honey. All we can do is pray."

Unit Six sped off toward Highway 55 and Baptist Hospital, careening through the afternoon traffic at eighty miles an hour.

Inside, Nichopoulos and Crosby were trying to get oxygen into Elvis's lungs, but his neck had stiffened, a sign of rigor mortis. "We couldn't get the intubation tube into his neck," Nichopoulos said, "so I grabbed an oxygen mask and forced it over his face while Crosby began running an IV."

Since Elvis was stone-cold dead, all the miracle workers at Baptist Hospital could do nothing for him. Because the medics listed Presley as having been "found dead" on their official forms, the ambulance's destination should have been the Shelby County Morgue for an official autopsy.

"But we didn't have the power to make an official ruling," said Ulysses Jones, now a Tennessee state representative. "We could only follow the physician's orders." And Nichopoulos wanted Elvis taken to the hospital. Distraught and distracted, the physician—like Elvis's friends and family—refused to believe that his patient was gone.

He didn't know that, back at Graceland, a clean-up of Elvis's room—the death scene—was underway.

And so began the cover-up of the death of Elvis Presley.

In fact, the cover-up was made possible because of the decision to bring Presley to Baptist.

"Elvis Presley was absolutely dead at the scene," said Dave McGriff, a deputy attorney general who spent three years investigating the circumstances surrounding the death. But as McGriff notes, "Taking him to Baptist for emergency treatment gave the family total control over what happened to the body, and over what information was released to the press.

"It also allowed them to arrange for a private autopsy," the results of which were released only to the family.

Of course, the medical team awaiting the arrival of Memphis's most famous citizen was initially unaware of Presley's condition.

At 2:48, the ambulance reached the double door of the Baptist Hospital emergency room. The aides and medics formed a human curtain around the stretcher so that no one caught a glimpse of the famous patient as he was carried into the operating room.

At the admittance desk, a registrar hurriedly logged Elvis in: "John Doe. Profession: Entertainer." On a lower line she noted that he was "a white male, approximately 40; under intense CPR for more than a half hour. No response."

"Code Blue" had been sounded throughout the Baptist Hospital five minutes earlier. Two physicians—one of them a surgeon—a respiratory therapist, an anesthetist, and an operating-room nurse had dropped what they were doing and had rushed to the ER, where they ringed the steel operating table, preparing to pull Elvis back from death.

As soon as the patient was laid out on the table, the nurse removed his pajamas and two gold chains, depositing them in an impersonal plastic bag.

Elvis was so stiff and contorted that it took all three physicians to straighten his body so they could tend to him. The bluish fingers of death had spread down his legs and arms. His cheeks were discolored and swollen by pools of blood.

As an IV drip was inserted into his right arm, the most senior of the physicians injected epinepherine and Isuprel, powerful muscle stimulants, directly into Elvis's heart and gazed over at the cardiomonitor, hoping for those little electronic beeps that herald the return of life. But the monitor kept its silence. "This doesn't look good. They're using powerful stuff," the supervising nurse, Carole Bingham, whispered to an associate.

"We gotta defibrillate," the physician announced dejectedly as the

ER nurse pulled out the oddly shaped paddles. They violently shocked Elvis's chest once, then waited a few minutes, then zapped him again. Four weak beeps registered on the monitor, and the team stirred with excitement. Tears filled Dr. Nichopoulos's eyes. "Though my scientific training convinced me that Elvis was dead—the rigor mortis was too advanced, for one thing—the four small beeps caused me to hope against hope that he could be brought back."

Then the heart monitor went flat again.

In desperation the senior physician injected another strong dose of epinepherine into Elvis's heart, then injected a third drug, sodium bicarbonate.

Once again there were four faint beeps.

The electronic defibrillation paddles were applied again . . . and again.

The team worked on Elvis Presley's body for another thirty minutes, a futile effort since rigor mortis was speedily contracting and stiffening the body.

Finally Kim Davis, an emergency nurse, threw up her hands. "Why are we working on this corpse?"

The answer came from one of the physicians: "Because he's Elvis Presley."

They would not leave the side of one of the most famous men in the world, but Baptist Hospital's supervising nurse, Marian Cocke, who counted herself a good friend of the patient's, had overheard Davis's logical verdict.

"When I had walked in, Dr. Nick looked up at me, as did Dr. John Quartermous. I couldn't really see Elvis, but I read what was in their faces," she recalls. "So I intervened."

She gently moved two young interns aside and took Elvis's hand in hers.

"Please stop. Please let him go," she pleaded. "The soul of this wonderful boy has left his body. Please don't continue, I can't bear it."

Slowly, the team backed away.

Dr. George Nichopoulos looked at the face of his longtime patient and dear friend for a few seconds before he shuffled toward the waiting room.

It was time to break the news to Graceland, where hope was still alive.

Blue City

Bodyguard Sam Thompson showed up at Graceland around four o'clock in the afternoon of August 16. His father drove him over, and as they pulled into the gates, one of Elvis's stepbrothers, David Stanley, headed down the drive in a sports car. Pulling up alongside Sam, he called, "Have you heard, man? Elvis is dead!"

Thompson's immediate thought was that Stanley had been smoking some marijuana—as he was known to do—and had somehow gotten the story wrong. "My first thought was that it was poor Vernon." But when Thompson entered the doors of Graceland, he saw Vernon—seated in a chair in the kitchen—"and people were running around everywhere."

Dr. Nichopoulos was there, too, having just arrived from Baptist Hospital. He leaned over and whispered something to Vernon. Recalled Thompson, "I didn't hear what he said, but Vernon began to moan, groan, wail, and cry." A few minutes later, Vernon took Thompson by the hand and said, "My baby's gone."

As Vernon continued to lament, Thompson followed Nichopoulos, who had gone off to the den and had started to make a phone call. "Nick, what happened?" asked Thompson. Nichopoulos looked up, took a deep breath, and answered, "I'm sorry."

To Thompson, the scenario became "surreal" when nine-year-old Lisa Marie came running up to him, saying, "You know, my daddy's dead. They say my daddy's dead." She was crying, so Thompson put his arms around her.

"You know, I called Linda," said the child. "I called her from Grandma's room."

Thompson went into Minnie Mae's bedroom and found that his sister, who then lived in Los Angeles, was still on the line. "Sam, what's going on down there? Lisa Marie just called. She told me Elvis died."

He told Linda it was true, adding, "I think you might need to come home."

Though Presley's various associates had had their differences, they were reunited by a common cause—their love for Elvis. "We all just sort of assumed certain duties," recalled Charlie Hodge. "Nothing appointed or anything. We just knew we wanted everything to run smoothly." Sam Thompson immediately began setting up security at the house. Dick Grob called to say he would watch over the body at the funeral home. George Klein rushed over to help deal with the phone calls and inquiries from the gate.

Out of deference to the Presley family, Baptist Hospital at first refused to confirm Elvis Presley's death to the callers who tied up the switchboard. "We kept telling reporters that he was in respiratory distress, and we were working with him," said Maurice Elliott, the assistant administrator who oversaw what became a public relations nightmare. "But the press was on to us, because Elvis had come to the hospital in a fire department ambulance." Finally, Nichopoulos called from Graceland. "Go ahead and give the press its story," he told Joe Esposito.

By that time it had been decided that Esposito would tell the assembled reporters what had happened. But when Elliott and Esposito walked into the hospital's administrative library, which had been set aside for the press, Esposito choked up with tears. His eyes brimming, he looked at Elliott and said haltingly, "I can't do it." And so Maurice Elliott turned to the contingent and made an unprepared announcement confirming the death of Elvis Aaron Presley, at age forty-two.

What followed, said Elliott, was "sort of a mad-dash-to-the-phone type of thing."

Bob Kendall, the funeral director for Memphis Funeral Home, got his call from a hospital chaplain, who said, "You'll be hearing soon from an associate of Mr. Presley's. I just wanted to let you know, so that you'll be ready."

In the hours that followed, Kendall was asked to locate a copper casket similar to the one that had been used to bury Gladys Presley nineteen years earlier. "We didn't have anything like it in Memphis," said Kendall, who contacted coffin companies across the country before locating the requested model in Oklahoma City. Kendall also had to round up a fleet of seventeen white Cadillac limousines. There were only three in Memphis.

Some said that Elvis would have preferred to have been buried in one of his bejeweled Las Vegas jumpsuits. Instead, he was dressed in a cream-colored suit—his father's, actually—with a blue shirt and striped tie. He also wore a TCB pendant, which had to be donated by a family member. Elvis had given his own away.

At the time of his death Elvis had about an inch of silver gray at his temples. Charlie Hodge went to the funeral home and, using a mascara brush, meticulously colored it jet-black. Later, when Elvis's body had been placed at Graceland for viewing, Hodge occasionally wandered over to his old friend and "fluffed his hair back out," the way Elvis had liked it. Said Hodge, "Elvis would've kicked my rear end if I hadn't."

Elvis's cousin Donna Presley Nash worried that her uncle Vernon would faint at the sight of Elvis in his coffin. But Vernon, who needed to be supported as he stood opposite the casket, simply wept. He kept repeating the line, "Son, Daddy will be with you soon. Daddy will be with you soon."*

Meanwhile, the press was beginning to descend on Memphis. "It was *the* story, and everyone wanted it," recalled William Thomas, who covered the death for Memphis's *Commercial Appeal*. The only Elvis-related story Thomas had done before was about a determined fan who had mailed herself to Graceland in a large box. This time the subject was far grimmer.

He began by going down Elvis Presley Boulevard to Graceland. "I'll never forget it. I ran into this guy who worked in a drugstore in Detroit. He was just sitting there, outside the gates, with a day's worth of beard. It turned out he'd told his boss he'd see him in a few days. Then he just got in his car and headed for Memphis. So, of course, I asked him, 'Why?' And he looked at me and said, 'Well, man, it's the King.' Just like I should know."

*Vernon joined his son twenty-two months later, on June 26, 1979, at age sixty-three.

Suddenly, anyone who had known Presley was a would-be source. "Oh, honey, all hell broke loose," said Sun Records' Sam Phillips. He recalled that his phone rang off the hook, with calls coming from England, Australia, Japan, and points beyond. He was gratified that the majority of them were from writers "who wanted to eulogize Elvis." Said Phillips, "You know how you feel about a hero? Well, God Almighty, when it came to Elvis Presley . . ."

Added Phillips, "With those phone calls, I said to myself, 'What in the hell would Elvis like to have said about him?' "

Not surprisingly, the local newspapers got the biggest scoops. The *Memphis Press-Scimitar* got an interview with Ginger Alden. Columnist Bill E. Burk spoke with Linda Thompson—after she called him. Burk had taken his kids to the dentist when he heard that Thompson had tried to reach him. So he called her back from there, not realizing they would spend an hour and forty minutes tying up the dentist's phone. "I think I was a shoulder to cry on," Burk admitted.

Over at the *Commercial Appeal*, industrious reporter Beth J. Tamke began work on a piece that tabulated Presley's many hospital stays over recent years. It was a sign of investigative rumblings to come. After all, *Elvis: What Happened?* had just been published, leading to speculation about the cause of death.

The immediate reaction, though, was the sense of loss that was echoed across the country.

The *Memphis Press-Scimitar* adroitly summed up Elvis's forty-two years with a now famous headline: "A Lonely Life Ends on Elvis Presley Boulevard."

Texas's *San Antonio Light* was succinct: "The King Is Dead!" ran above the newspaper masthead, in red type.

The headline of the editorial in Colorado's *Denver Post* was reflective: "Suddenly We Feel Older."

New York's eclectic *Village Voice* had its readers reaching for the dictionary with "The World's Most Beloved Solipsist Is Dead."

The story in the *Washington Post*'s Style section was headlined, "All Shook Up on the Day the '50s Died."

The television networks rushed to their archives, pulling out newsreel footage, movies, and more. The night of his death, both NBC and ABC led off their newscasts with Elvis Presley's death. CBS didn't cover the death until seven and a half minutes into the newscast. NBC and ABC beat out CBS in the ratings.

The tabloids were active. Famous for getting "the untold story," the *Enquirer* was determined to get something no other publication would have. "That's why we immediately wanted the coffin shot," said one of the reporters on the team that covered the death. The ensuing issue, showing a black-and-white photograph of Elvis in his coffin, helped to sell more than 6.5 million copies—making it the top-selling issue of the country's leading tabloid.* To this day, the publication considers its Presley "death photo" to be one of its most hallowed achievements. But among Elvis's associates, it triggered finger-pointing that exists to this day. To get its photo the *Enquirer* armed a number of Presley insiders with "tiny spy cameras," in hopes that as they passed by the coffin they would have time to snap the shutter. Who took the photograph? Among some of the Mafia, Ginger Alden is considered suspect, an accusation that has long baffled and hurt the young woman who found Presley's body. "Absolutely not true," said an editor who helped to oversee the paper's death coverage. According to the woman who bought the little cameras and distributed them among the Presley associates, the distinction went to a distant relative.

Not only tabloid reporters resorted to surreptitious means to get their stories and photos. "If we'd known about Caroline Kennedy, we would have done that one different," admitted Charlie Hodge.

George Klein was inside Graceland when a call came from the gate: "Caroline Kennedy wants to come up." "We were all impressed. We'd always been such [John F.] Kennedy supporters," said Klein. "Vernon was especially touched."

What Kennedy didn't reveal was that she was on assignment for the *New York Daily News*. Because she missed her deadline, she instead sold her story to *Rolling Stone*. In it, Kennedy took note of Elvis's "swollen" face and of the potted plastic palms surrounding the coffin. Also, "on the wall was a painting of a skyline on black velveteen."

To those who had come to see Elvis as a symbol of the American dream, there was no such condescension. Flags were lowered to half-staff across much of the South. His native state of Mississippi declared August 18, the day of the burial, an official day of mourning. President Jimmy Carter issued a statement applauding Presley as a symbol of America's "vitality, rebelliousness, and good humor." Across the

---

*True to his words, Elvis looked great in his coffin. Because of the removal of major organs and fluids for the autopsy, his body was trim, his face devoid of puffiness. He was, once again, a mesmerizing and decidedly handsome icon.

country, radio stations put together tributes. Record stores sold out of Elvis's recordings. At airports, fans lined up to purchase tickets to Memphis.

On August 17, Vernon Presley allowed the fans to pay their respects. He could not have anticipated the crowds. Tens of thousands of mourners stood for hours, in the sweltering heat, outside the Graceland gates awaiting their chance to file past the singer's body.

On the day of the funeral, both sides of the three-mile route between Graceland and Forest Lawn Cemetery, where Presley was laid to rest alongside his mother, were lined with onlookers, many of whom dropped in prayer when the line of limousines slowly made their way through the streets. "It was as if the whole city of Memphis got together and worked to produce Elvis's final show," said Bob Kendall.

It was the largest funeral ever held in this country for a private citizen.

The private service held inside Graceland was packed with more than 250 friends and family members. Seated on folding chairs that had been arranged in the living room, they listened as the Reverend C.W. Bradley, a family friend, eulogized Elvis. "We are here to honor the memory of a man loved by millions," he began.

The reverend spoke of Presley's sense of humanity, his pride in his humble roots, his love of his family. He also added, "But Elvis was a frail human being . . . he was thrown into temptations that some never experience." The reverend asked those in attendance to remember that it is "more helpful to remember his good qualities."

In the most difficult performance of her life, Kathy Westmoreland sang "Heavenly Father" in her clear soprano. "I was trembling and felt faint most of the time," she said.

When the service ended, and the limousines readied to leave for the cemetery, there was jockeying for position—especially among the stricken women in his life. Already, Priscilla Presley, now brown-haired and newly slender—following a recent beauty spa visit—had denied Linda Thompson a seat on the *Lisa Marie*. Linda had had to take a commercial flight. "How would it look if I had allowed it?" Priscilla had said to her friend Joanie Esposito.

At the house, Priscilla summoned Ginger, who was wearing a black dress borrowed from her sister Terri. Briefly embracing the young woman, Priscilla said, "I know you loved him. I know you helped him. Thank you for that." She went on to tell Ginger that "limousine number five" had been reserved for her and her family.

Standing off to the side, in a lavender sundress—which she felt sure Elvis would have liked—was Linda, who was told by one of the Mafia that she was to ride in "limousine number sixteen," in the second wave of limos.

Ann-Margret was there, too, looking like a latter-day Lana Turner. Clinging to the arm of her husband, Roger Smith, she wore a sedate Edith Head–designed suit, scarf, and big sunglasses to hide her reddened eyes. "Thank you so much for coming. It means a lot to me. It means a lot to him," Priscilla said.

Joe Esposito remembers that the day was "quiet" as they all filed out of the house and began climbing into their respective limousines. Suddenly, there was a loud cracking sound. A huge limb fell from a tree, nearly hitting the Alden car. Was Elvis trying to speak to them? Just in case, Esposito and his girlfriend each pocketed a piece of the limb.

En route to the cemetery, Esposito stared out the window and marveled that so many people were on the streets to bid farewell to Presley. An estimated eighty thousand people turned out to observe the motorcade and burial. More than forty-five hundred separate floral displays were sent—many shaped like guitars, some adorned with small teddy bears.

At the conclusion of the graveside service the family decided that each fan should have a flower. In the frenzy that followed, some people pulled up chunks of grass from the ground near the mausoleum where Presley was buried. Family and friends took turns going inside. When Kathy Westmoreland entered, she came upon Priscilla—weeping hysterically.

When the tributes and eulogies had ended, some hard questions were fired in the direction of Dr. George Nichopoulos and the members of the Memphis Mafia. Those questions concerned Elvis's possible drug use. At the time, with the exception of *Elvis: What Happened?* the allegations had never surfaced in print.

Queried about something that had heretofore been secret, his friends did what they had always done. "We protected him," said Joe Esposito. "We'd always protected him, okay? We respected his privacy no matter what. I was with him for seventeen years, and for me protection was an automatic thing. That's the way it was." As Esposito noted, "Part of that protection was not talking about the drugs."

Esposito and Nichopoulos and Linda Thompson and the others

vehemently denied in print that Elvis had suffered from a drug problem. Though Nichopoulos did admit that Elvis had suffered from a medication problem "at times."

Sonny West and Dave Hebler continued to talk—in print and on television—about the excesses and the depression and, especially, about the drugs. Red West would not. In an interview in 1987 he said, "The whole point of the book was to embarrass [Elvis], to try to make him come to his senses. When we wrote it, he was here to defend it. Then suddenly he wasn't."

On October 21, 1977, Memphis medical examiner Dr. Jerry T. Francisco announced that Elvis Presley had died of "hypertensive heart disease." When pressed about the possibility of a drug-related death, Dr. Francisco acknowledged that while drugs had been found in the body, "had these drugs not been there, he would have still died."

By this time Elvis's drug use had become a media topic, fueled by story after story about his latter-year excesses. And so, from the beginning, there was rampant skepticism over the autopsy.

Adding to the talk of a "cover-up" was the decision of the Presley estate, now ruled by Vernon Presley and, at his request, Elvis's ex-wife, Priscilla, to keep the autopsy results private. Ironically, had they been less concerned about the image, the man himself could have been vindicated; though the autopsy materials detail drug use, they also detail the hows and whys of Presley's death by heart disease.

The secrecy added to speculation that persists to this day.

It would take nineteen years, twenty-two pathologists, a Drug Enforcement Administration investigation, dramatic breakthroughs in toxicological technology, a dozen mainstream books, and finally, desperate confessions by the members of the Memphis Mafia before the true cause of death could be revealed to a distrustful public.

In the intervening years, numerous theories emerged. There were claims that the rock idol had killed himself due to despondency over his fading career; that he had been felled by a karate chop; that he gulped a fatal dose of barbiturates because he was secretly dying of cancer; and even that he had faked his death to abandon fame for a safe place in the Witness Protection Program.

Obscuring all efforts was a "code of silence" ordered by the Presley family and followed to the letter by Priscilla and the Memphis Mafia—some of whom had themselves injected the drugs into the boss—to forever keep Elvis's name unsullied.

The puzzle was solved bit by bit, beginning with a watchful

coroner's investigator, Dr. Dan Warlick, who saw things at the death scene that no one else had noticed. After the body was removed and the others assembled for questioning, Warlick led medic Ulysses Jones back to the bathroom where Ginger had discovered her fiancé. Warlick found it had recently been cleaned: the fixtures scrubbed and three wastebaskets emptied and, suspiciously, scoured with caustic powder.

"Everything's gone," said Jones.

"What do you mean?" asked Warlick.

"Well, for one thing, two large syringes were lying beside the body," said Jones. "And that bag, that black bag over there, was full of packets and drawers containing some things that rattled when it was moved."

Warlick leaned over and picked up a slightly worn black kit, which was virtually identical to the one that Dr. Thomas "Flash" Newman had given Elvis years before. He noted that it was "built to simulate a man's fancy jewelry case, but all the small drawers inside were too small for cuff links and rings but perfect for small barbiturates, pills, and soft packets of Empirin with codeine."

The investigator also learned from the medics that a "considerable amount of cleaning, straightening, and rearrangement" had been completed after the medics rushed to the aid of the stricken Presley. The linens on the bed had been changed, the carpet vacuumed, and one section—the place where Elvis's chin had landed as he fell—had been scrubbed with antiseptic.

Back at the Shelby County coroner's office, Warlick stayed through the night, preparing the on-site evidence so that Francisco would have it at his fingertips during the autopsy. As the autopsy began, all of the scientists were aware of Presley's four nearly fatal overdoses and his extensive detoxifications on the hospital's sixteenth floor.

Dr. Eric Muirfield and his eight assistant pathologists found that Elvis had a grossly enlarged, "unhealthy gray-colored" heart, which weighed about 520 grams. (The average heart weighs approximately 375 grams.)

Presley's blood was put on ice and sent by air courier to the Bio-Science Laboratory in Van Nuys, California, to measure each drug in the singer's system. The results startled the Baptist team. At the time of his death, Presley had the following drugs (and levels) in his blood or urine: codeine at ten times the therapeutic dose (he took ten capsules); quaaludes at a toxic level (Presley had built up a tolerance over the years); Valium at a low therapeutic level; Valmid in the therapeutic range; Placidyl (four capsules); pentobarbital in the therapeutic range;

butabarbital in the therapeutic range; phenobarbital in the low therapeutic range.

All of that made for quite a concentration of downers—enough to make Muirhead and the other pathologists list Elvis Presley's cause of death as "polypharmacy."

This means a lethal combination of drugs, rather than a concentration of chemicals, killed him. This information was eventually printed, in one form, in the 1981 book *The Death of Elvis: What Really Happened* by Charles C. Thompson II and James P. Cole. The major part of their determination was based upon the ten codeine tablets Presley had obtained in the early-morning hours prior to his death, from Dr. Lester Hoffman. But Thompson and Cole based their "polypharmacy conclusion" on the fact that Elvis was allergic to codeine. Actually, Elvis's allergy to the drug was so minor that it merely induced itching.

But Dr. Francisco stood firm, insisting that Presley's death was a classic case of "fatal heart arrhythmia."

Still, the press overruled him.

Relying upon the Bio-Science determination and led by a sensational exposé by Geraldo Rivera on ABC's 20/20, journalists and authors barraged the public with details about Presley's life as a big-time druggie. It was the ultimate saga of sex, drugs, and rock 'n' roll.

The Cole and Thompson book, written in a somber and scholarly fashion, further ignited controversy as well as political wars in Memphis over the operation of the medical examiner's office.

All of this led to the decision, in 1994—seventeen years after Elvis's death—to reexamine the autopsy results. It was this study that revealed that the seemingly incendiary findings of the Bio-Science labs, regarding "polypharmacy," were actually built around a single paragraph in the laboratory report. It read: "A total of fourteen drugs were detected in the various tissues analyzed. While most were in the therapeutic range, codeine was present at ten times the therapeutic level. Methaqualone (Quaaludes) was on the borderline of toxicity."

The lab's entire thesis was based upon abnormalities in Presley's liver, which scientists later found to be mildly affected by the singer's sybaritic lifestyle.

"The 'polypharmacy ruling' was just an opinion, not a medical certainty . . . a well-educated guess," said Dr. Dwight Reed, who worked as a consultant on the Bio-Science study when he was a toxicologist in the Orange County (California) coroner's office. It was Reed who unlocked the chemical puzzle surrounding the death of John Belushi. Now chief toxicologist for San Diego County, he more recently handled the processing of the mass suicides of the "Heaven's Gate" cult.

During the 1994 reexamination, the Bio-Science report was scrutinized by a panel of toxicologists, among them Dr. Kevin S. Merigian, clinical pharmacologist at the Toxicology Center in the Elvis Presley Trauma Center in Memphis, who reexamined the codeine theory. "I strictly disagree with the Bio-Science Laboratory's ruling that the drug levels found in the body fluids and tissues exceeds some other known identifiable drug overdose cases where codeine has been implicated. This death is not the result of a multiple-drug ingestion. It's quite frankly silly, and is conjecture and totally without foundation."

Dr. Forest Tennant, the UCLA toxicologist, also points out that the Presley drug measurements were done twenty years ago "in the dark ages." "Now we could measure both the active drug [the substances Elvis had recently taken] and the metabolized drug (such as the Valium he had taken twelve hours earlier but which still showed up in his bloodstream]. Now we would subtract the traces of the 'metabolized' drugs, and the Bio-Science levels would have put Elvis's drug levels considerably lower. Because he had a really, really high level of metabolized chemicals. Taking out these chemicals would have probably dropped his total chemical load far below a combined poisonous level."

To end the controversy and close the official books on Presley's death, the state turned to a man some have called the dean of American pathology. Dr. Joseph Davis, former chief medical examiner of Dade County, Florida, was a coroner for forty years and is a veteran of more than twenty thousand autopsies. The past president of both the American Academy of Forensic Sciences and the National Association of Medical Examiners, and a professor of pathology at the University of Miami School of Medicine, it was Davis who examined all the Presley autopsy data: tissue samples, two thousand slides, a bulging book of autopsy photos and all the secret addendums to Baptist Hospital's original postmortem. Additional paperwork was provided by the Elvis Presley estate.

Davis found it relatively easy to discern that "Elvis Presley could not have died of a drug overdose, or of polypharmacy." Once his decision was publicly announced, the data was reclaimed, and his lengthy ruling was sealed by the state of Tennessee.

Dr. Davis broke his vow of silence only because the authors mailed him an identical set of the confidential paperwork which he received from the Shelby County medical examiner. (The authors' data was obtained from well-placed sources among the forensic scientists who worked on the case.)

Queried about the materials, Davis said, "There is nothing in any of the data which supports a death from drugs. In fact, everything points to a sudden, violent heart attack. Forget the Bio-Science lab results. The scene itself tells you what happened."

Explained Davis: "The position of Presley's body told me that he was about to sit down on the commode when the seizure occurred. He pitched forward onto the carpet, his rear in the air, and was dead by the time he hit the floor."

According to Davis, in a drug overdose Elvis would have slipped into an increasing state of slumber. He would have pulled up his pajama bottoms and crawled to the door to seek help.

"It takes hours to die from drugs," said Davis. The pathologist added, "The only way drugs could have killed Elvis Presley that fast was if he were sitting on the commode shooting up a lethal dose of heroin."

After combing through the mountainous autopsy data, Davis produced what he calls "the real scientific proof that Elvis Presley died of a heart attack":

• "He was grossly obese, with many of his three hundred and fifty pounds gained in less than two months, an enormous strain on the heart."

• The body had undergone "at least" two hours of rigor mortis before it was discovered. "A drug death would have taken much longer, and rigor probably wouldn't have been present at all."

• There was no drug residue in Elvis's system. "Not even a spot of the dye they use in most medicines. In fact, there was no internal sign that he had taken drugs several hours before he died." (Elvis had taken the contents of three of his drug packets before he had gone to sleep, some five or six hours earlier.)

• Finally, there was no pulmonary edema in his lungs, an almost certain trademark of a drug death. "It was the driest set of lungs I've ever seen," Davis recalled. "With this sort of death you would have seen a tremendous amount of pulmonary edema. Dry lungs are proof enough that he didn't die of respiratory failure due to chemicals."

Added Davis: "This was a textbook case of death by heart attack."

Why, then, have so many authors and readers wanted to believe that it was an overdose?

Above all, over the years, blame has been placed on Dr. Nichopoulos, who once prescribed as many as ten thousand drugs for Elvis during a nineteen-month period. But these drugs were for a series of tours, when Presley was accompanied by nearly 150 musicians and crew members. "Nichopoulos won't tell you this, but he had to prescribe in large amounts because Elvis only ended up getting two pills out of every ten pills prescribed," said Warlick. "The Mafia took them, the roadies took them, the girlfriends took them, and they poured thousands of them down the drain when they came back from the tour."

In interviews for this book the authors were able to verify that statement.

Dr. Nichopoulos went on to be charged by the State of Tennessee Medical Board for his violations with Elvis and ten other patients and was found guilty of overprescribing—but not of unethical conduct. His license was suspended for three months, and he received three years' probation. In May 1980 he was charged with fourteen counts of illegally prescribing drugs to Elvis and the other patients, but was acquitted.

Yet milliliters of blood and micrograms of morphine, arguments among pathologists, and pronouncements by the press are no more than footnotes to a life of international grandeur, and a death of great pathos.

Born with a genetically frail but innately generous heart, consumed body and soul by his music, Elvis Presley pursued his life and his career head-on, with a mix of determination and wild abandon. He was only in his early twenties when his star rose to heights never before experienced in popular culture. It was a time when fame was decreed by the people—not the media or the publicity machinery.

No mere celebrity, he was a bona fide phenomenon.

He was also a dichotomy—both innately shy as well as rebellious and resolute.

It is possible that his death at forty-two was decreed by his genetic code. There was a history of heart trouble on his mother's side; in fact, few males in her family had lived past forty-five.

Yet if his life was short, and his death untimely, his impact was and continues to be enormous. Like his music, he won't go away.

Long Live the King

He may be gone, but he is far from forgotten. Elvis Presley refuses to leave the building. He lives on in recordings, merchandising, books, films, and the collective conscience.

Some seven hundred thousand visitors annually make the trek to Graceland, which opened as a tourist attraction in 1982 and ranks as the second most-visited house in the country, following the White House. Though the audio tour delivers a sanitized depiction of Elvis's life and times, complete with girlish exclamations by Priscilla Presley about how much fun they used to have there, the house and grounds have retained the sense of sanctuary that was integral to Presley's pressured life.

For Elvis, Graceland is sanctuary still. He lies out beyond the swimming pool—alongside his mother, father, and Grandma Minnie Mae.

Though Elvis Presley Enterprises does not discuss monetary figures, in 1994 it was reported that the Presley estate was a $100-million-a-year industry of music, movies, and memorabilia. Much of that memorabilia was doubtless purchased at the sprawling shopping complex located directly across the street from Graceland, which operates the shops and maintains a close vigil over the licensing of merchandise.

It has been largely due to the wakefulness of Priscilla Presley—who reinvented herself as a tough and shrewd businesswoman—and her attorneys that her ex-husband's estate was turned into a monstrous moneymaker. Following Presley's death, and the scrutinizing of his financial status, Colonel Tom Parker was sued on behalf of Lisa Marie for fraud and mismanagement. A Memphis court went on to rule that Parker—who had taken between twenty-five and fifty percent of Presley's income, and who was then involved in his own Elvis licensing ventures—had no legal rights to the Presley estate.

Following additional lawsuits that accused him of having taken financial advantage of Presley, Parker sold his Presley master recordings to RCA for $2 million. It has been said that he also sold his silence. For Elvis Presley Enterprises acquired his paperwork about his extraordinary relationship with Presley.

In the meantime, Presley's sole heir has become a kitsch celebrity in her own right—the result of Lisa Marie's 1994 Dominican Republic wedding to pop superstar Michael Jackson.

But there are no photographs of Lisa Marie and Michael—whom she has since divorced—at Graceland, or in the adjoining shops. Nor are there any photographs of the troubled, bloated Elvis. Word is that the images on display are "holding" at 170 pounds.

Elsewhere beyond Graceland, there are plenty of celebrations of Elvis Presley the man, complete with flaws. As Sam Phillips, the man who discovered him, reminds, "Even when he was in horrible shape, emotionally and physically, Elvis always conveyed a real caring."

The tiny, restored Sun Records in Memphis offers a surprisingly affecting tour of the single room where a nineteen-year-old truck driver made his earliest recordings.

In Tupelo, Mississippi, a dollar buys a ticket into the shotgun shack where Elvis was born. It's just a short drive from the antiquated-looking Tupelo Hardware, "the store where Elvis bought his first guitar." That's what it used to say on a $1.50 key ring sold by the store, until lawyers from Elvis Presley Enterprises threatened legal action. The store's guitar-shaped key ring now reads, "Where Gladys bought her son his first guitar." For collectors of Presley memorabilia, it may be the best bargain of all.

And for a heartfelt tour, it would be hard to top Graceland Too—located in Holly Springs, Mississippi (between Tupelo and Memphis). The home of Paul MacLeod and his son, Elvis Aaron Presley MacLeod, is a virtual shrine to Elvis, open twenty-four hours. Repeat visitors get to be photographed in a special black leather jacket and have their picture showcased alongside those of thousands of other True Believers. Call it Roadside Elvis.

There have been tributes in song (including Paul Simon's "Graceland"), fiction (such as Alice Walker's short story "Nineteen Fifty-Five"), art (there are myriad Presley-inspired exhibitions), as well as in a twenty-nine-cent postage stamp. And if imitation is the sincerest form of flattery, there are always impersonators—of every nationality.

For serious students of Elvismania, there are now college courses and lectures dissecting his impact on society, on culture, on religion, and more. For several years, the prestigious University of Mississippi made headlines with its scholarly summer conference on the significance of Elvis Presley. Vernon Chadwick, founder and director of the conference, who also taught the country's first university courses on Elvis, hails Presley as "a rebellious, radicalizing force of democracy, equal opportunity, and free expression."

And lest anyone forget his generosities—to literally countless charities and causes—there are more than five hundred fan clubs worldwide whose members are known for their tireless efforts on behalf of various charities. As Elvis used to say, being generous "is like throwin' a stone in a pond. It ripples out."

Presley also reached out to fans in a way no star has done before, or since.

Has any star ever posed for more candid photographs? Signed more autograph books? To the consternation of his buddies, Elvis used to insist on climbing out of his limo—as they were about to leave one arena and head for the next gig—to race over for a Kodak moment. When his friends protested, Elvis said, "It's only because of them that we're here in the first place."

Of course, the music made it all happen in the first place. In that arena, Elvis truly is the King. In a feat unsurpassed in music history, he has sold more than 1 billion records worldwide.

In his lifetime, Elvis was constantly reinventing himself. The same holds true in death.

According to the *Los Angeles Times*, Nobel laureate Kary Mullis has obtained the rights to extract DNA from Presley's hair, for the manufacture of jewelry. The story was headlined: "A Hunk of Burnin' Love on a Chain."

And of course there are the sightings. The 1988 paperback curiosity *Is Elvis Alive?* by Gail Brewer-Giorgio contributed to the mania by raising questions about Presley's "death," and underlining assorted oddities regarding Presley. Example: *lives* is an anagram for *Elvis*.

Weekly World News, the supermarket tabloid known for its revelations about the "Bat Boy" and Bigfoot, regularly charts Presley's whereabouts, with some assistance from a Michigan housewife who has spotted Elvis twice—once at a Kalamazoo Burger King, another time at a Vicksburg convenience store. The tabloid somehow also listened in on "secret" White House tapes, proving that Presley telephoned President Clinton. He also reportedly continues to dispense advice to his daughter: "Elvis Tells Lisa Marie, 'Divorce Michael.' "

Ironically, *Weekly World News* is a sister publication of the *National Enquirer*—which took and owns the famed Presley coffin photo—whose editors steadfastly maintain that the star is dead.

Yet among those who maintain that Presley is dead and buried are those who insist that his spirit literally lives on. Examples abound in a recent book by a "psychic investigator," who revealed Presley's messages from beyond the grave. Among other things, the star's ghost helped a worried father locate his runaway son.

Still others—especially associates and fans—work through the fan clubs and various Elvis "conventions" to promote another kind of spirit: Elvis's own good nature. Mike McGregor, a lanky Mississippian who tended to Elvis's horses, and went on to make some of his jewelry, was in the Graceland guard gate the night a car bearing Louisiana plates pulled up. "They handed me a note that they wanted to get to Elvis," said McGregor. In it was a heartfelt thank-you from a boy's club which had been robbed of its kitchen supplies. Elvis had read a "teensy article" about the theft in the local paper, and had promptly sent off a check to cover the loss.

"When people talk to me about Elvis, I like to remind them that in addition to being the biggest star ever, he also had the biggest heart ever," says McGregor.

Don Wilson knows firsthand about that heart. He was just ten years old, and suffering the recent deaths of his parents and sister—as the result of a train crash—when his grandmother took him to see Elvis at the Houston Astrodome in 1971.

Wilson got to meet Elvis backstage. Later, unbeknownst to him, his grandmother sent a letter to Elvis, telling him about what had happened. To Don's surprise, Elvis later sent him a card expressing his condolences. It marked the beginning of a six-year "friendship" by correspondence, during which time Wilson received notes, albums, and even pieces of clothing. Wilson went on to visit Elvis at Graceland.

"What can I tell you? It literally changed my life to think that Elvis Presley cared about me," said Wilson, who is today a songwriter, disc jockey and also—and appropriately—an Elvis impersonator. He goes by the moniker "The Great Don El."

As to why it all happened to Elvis—out of everyone in the world— Carl Perkins, the rockabilly legend who wrote "Blue Suede Shoes," surmises that it was fated. "I've come to believe that when Elvis was born, God said, 'Here is the messenger, and I'm going to make him the best-looking guy, and I'm going to give him every piece of rhythm he needs to move that good-looking body on that stage.' " Mused Perkins, "I was fighting a battle working with him, knowing that I looked like Mr. Ed, that mule, and here was a guy that could go out and clear his throat and have ten thousand people scream."

Bob Dylan has called Presley "the deity supreme of rock-'n'-roll religion as it exists in today's form." For Dylan, "hearing him for the first time was like busting out of jail."

To Bruce Springsteen, "it's like he came along and whispered a dream in everybody's ear, and then we all dreamed it somehow."

Rolling Stone's Dave Marsh once surmised, "Elvis was the King of rock and roll because he was the embodiment of its sins and virtues: grand and vulgar, rude and eloquent, powerful and frustrated, absurdly simple and awesomely complex."

As Sam Phillips put it, "I think a little mystery will always remain."

Appendix I

CHRONOLOGY

FILMOGRAPHY

TELEVISION APPEARANCES

DISCOGRAPHY

Chronology

JANUARY 8, 1935: Elvis Aaron Presley is born in a two-room house in Tupelo, Mississippi. Twin brother Jesse Garon is stillborn.

JUNE 1, 1938: Little Elvis and his mother, Gladys, begin forming an impenetrable bond when Vernon Presley is sent to Parchman penitentiary for forging a check.

1945: Ten-year-old Elvis sings "Old Shep," about a boy and his dog, in the youth talent contest at the Mississippi-Alabama Fair and Dairy Show, held in Tupelo.

1946: His first guitar is purchased at the Tupelo Hardware Company.

1948: Moves with his family to Memphis.

1953: Is graduated from Memphis's Humes High School.

1953: Spends four dollars to make a demo acetate at Memphis Recording Service, home of the Sun label.

JANUARY 1954: Now working at Crown Electric—where he sometimes drives a delivery truck—Elvis makes a second demo acetate at Sun.

JUNE 1954: Sam Phillips needs a singer to record a demo called "Without You." Assistant Marion Keisker suggests the kid who's been hanging out at the studio, and a call is put in to Elvis's house. He's panting and out of breath when he arrives at the studio.

JULY 5, 1954: Teamed with guitarist Scotty Moore and bass player Bill Black, Elvis breaks into a sped-up version of Arthur "Big Boy" Crudup's "That's All Right (Mama)." It will be the first of five singles Elvis will release on the Sun label.

OCTOBER 2, 1954: Elvis performs for his first and only time at country music's great shrine, the Grand Ole Opry.

OCTOBER 16, 1954: Debuts on the *Louisiana Hayride*, a live Saturday-night country-music radio show originating in Shreveport, Louisiana. A one-year contract follows.

JANUARY 1955: Signs a contract with Memphis disc jockey Bob Neal, who becomes his manager. Presley, Scotty, and Bill are now on the road.

AUGUST 15, 1955: Signs a management contract with Hank Snow Attractions, owned by Snow and Colonel Tom Parker. But Snow will soon fade from the picture.

NOVEMBER 20, 1955: Elvis signs his first contract with RCA Records, after Parker negotiates the sale of Elvis's Sun contract to RCA. The price: an unprecedented $40,000, with a $5,000 bonus for Elvis.

JANUARY 10, 1956: Elvis, who has just turned twenty-one, makes his first RCA recordings at the label's Nashville studio. Among the titles he records: "Heartbreak Hotel."

JANUARY 27, 1956: "Heartbreak Hotel" is released by RCA and sells over three hundred thousand copies in its first three weeks on the market. It will become Elvis's very first gold record.

JANUARY 28, 1956: Elvis's first network television appearance, on the Jackie Gleason–produced *Stage Show*, starring Tommy and Jimmy Dorsey on CBS.

MARCH 13, 1956: His first album, *Elvis Presley*, is released by RCA. It earns more than $1 million in sales and becomes Elvis's first gold album.

APRIL 3, 1956: Elvis performs on NBC's *The Milton Berle Show*, broadcast from the deck of the USS *Hancock* aircraft carrier.

APRIL 6, 1956: Signs a seven-year movie contract with producer Hal Wallis and Paramount Pictures.

APRIL 23, 1956: Opens a two-week engagement at the New Frontier Hotel in Las Vegas. But he's too hip for the mostly gray-haired gamblers; the show is considered a bust.

JUNE 5, 1956: During a *Milton Berle Show* performance of "Hound Dog," Elvis performs with more bumps and grinds than a stripper. The next day he's under siege.

JULY 1, 1956: Steve Allen puts Elvis on his TV show and has him do a toned-down "Hound Dog," which he performs to a basset hound wearing a little top hat.

AUGUST 1956: Elvis begins filming his first movie, *Love Me Tender*.

SEPTEMBER 9, 1956: First of three legendary appearances on *The Ed Sullivan Show*.

SEPTEMBER 26, 1956: Elvis returns to Tupelo to perform two shows at the Mississippi-Alabama Fair and Dairy Show.

DECEMBER 4, 1956: Elvis drops in to the Sun records studio where Carl Perkins is doing some recording. Perkins's piano man is a newcomer named Jerry Lee Lewis. A while later, Johnny Cash ambles in. The (unrecorded) jam session that followed was heralded as "The Million Dollar Quartet." As Sun's legendary producer Sam Phillips put it, "It was a dilly."

JANUARY 6, 1957: For his third and final appearance on Ed Sullivan's show,

Elvis is shot only from the waist up. But Sullivan hails him as "a fine, decent boy."

MARCH 1957: Elvis purchases Graceland.

APRIL 1957: While on tour, Elvis performs for the first time outside the United States, with shows in Toronto and Ottawa. He returns to Canada for a Vancouver performance in August; it is the last time he performs outside the United States.

DECEMBER 1957: Uncle Sam wants him! Elvis officially receives his draft notice.

MARCH 24, 1958: A day of mourning for female fans across the country: Elvis Presley is inducted into the U.S. Army at the Memphis Draft Board.

MARCH 25, 1958: Hair today . . . then a GI cut, at Fort Chaffee, Arkansas.

MARCH 29, 1958: Private Presley and his parents move into a temporary home near the base at Fort Hood, Texas, where he is to undergo basic training and spend the next six months.

JULY 1958: *King Creole*, Elvis's fourth movie, opens—garnering his best reviews yet.

AUGUST 1958: Stricken ill, Gladys Presley returns to Memphis where she is hospitalized with acute hepatitis. Granted emergency leave, Elvis visits her on the twelfth and thirteenth.

AUGUST 14, 1958: Gladys Presley dies at age forty-six.

AUGUST 15, 1958: At the funeral for his mother, Elvis weeps openly and requires assistance walking and getting in and out of the car. His grief will never subside.

SEPTEMBER 19, 1958: Elvis boards a troop train to New York, and later the USS *Randall*, which sails to West Germany.

OCTOBER 1, 1958: Presleymania traverses the seas as the world's most famous GI sails into view. Stationed in Friedberg for eighteen months, he maintains an off-base residence in Bad Nauheim, which he shares with his father, grandmother, and Memphis friends. He also makes several new friends, who form the nucleus of the so-called Memphis Mafia.

JUNE 1959: Boys will be boys: during a two-week leave, Elvis and his friends cut a sexual swath through the clubs of Munich and Paris; they especially like the Lido dancers.

NOVEMBER 1959: At a party at his house in West Germany, Elvis meets Priscilla Beaulieu, the beautiful fourteen-year-old stepdaughter of an Air Force captain.

JANUARY 20, 1960: Elvis Presley is promoted to the rank of sergeant.

MARCH 2, 1960: He returns to the United States, where he is discharged from active duty.

MARCH 26, 1960: Frank Sinatra—who once cruelly criticized the rock-'n'-roll star—does an about-face, hosting the ABC variety show *Welcome Home, Elvis*.

APRIL 1960: Elvis returns to Hollywood to begin filming *G.I. Blues*.

JULY 3, 1960: Vernon Presley marries divorcée Davada "Dee" Stanley, whom he met in West Germany. Elvis does not go to the wedding.

MARCH 25, 1961: Elvis performs in Hawaii, in a benefit to help fund the building of the USS *Arizona* Memorial. It will be his final live performance until 1968.

LATE MARCH 1961: Filming begins on *Blue Hawaii*, the first of many formulaic Presley movies; their production will dominate his schedule throughout the sixties.

OCTOBER 1961: The *Blue Hawaii* sound-track album enters the *Billboard* chart where it stays for a year and a half.

DECEMBER 1962: Priscilla Beaulieu spends the Christmas holidays with Elvis at Graceland. In early 1963 she moves in with him and his family.

AUGUST 27, 1965: A legendary rock summit: the Beatles visit with Elvis at his Bel-Air home. Alas, no one bothers to record their jam session!

FEBRUARY 1967: Elvis purchases the Circle G, a 163-acre ranch in Mississippi, located just over the Tennessee state line, where he delights in playing cowboy.

MARCH 1967: Elvis falls in his Bel-Air home, pushing back the production of *Clambake*. The fall is drug-induced.

MAY 1, 1967: Just fourteen invited guests attend the wedding ceremony for Elvis and Priscilla at the Aladdin Hotel in Las Vegas; a press conference and breakfast reception follow.

FEBRUARY 1, 1968: He's a daddy; Lisa Marie Presley is born.

MID-TO-LATE JUNE, 1968: Elvis rehearses for the taping of his 1968 television special, *Elvis*. It will come to be known as the '68 *Comeback Special*.

NOVEMBER 1968: "If I Can Dream," a song of hope written expressly for Elvis for the 1968 special, hits number twelve on the pop singles chart; it is his biggest single since 1965.

DECEMBER 3, 1968: *Elvis* airs on NBC, marking the dawn of a career renaissance.

JANUARY–FEBRUARY 1969: For the first time since his Sun years, Elvis records in Memphis—this time at American Sound Studio with producer Chips Moman. The sessions produce arguably some of the finest work of his career, including "Kentucky Rain," "In the Ghetto," "Suspicious Minds," and "Long Black Limousine."

JULY 31–AUGUST 28, 1969: The resurgence continues with Elvis's four-week SRO engagement at the brand-new International Hotel in Las Vegas.

JANUARY–FEBRUARY 1970: Another triumphant Las Vegas engagement; Presley is now under a five-year contract with the International, where he will perform two months of each year.

FEBRUARY 27, 1970: Elvis performs the first of six shows at the Astrodome in connection with the Houston Livestock Show and Rodeo.

SEPTEMBER 1970: Elvis embarks on a six-city tour, his first since 1957.

DECEMBER 1970: Elvis pays a surprise visit to President Richard Nixon at the White House, where he is presented with an honorary federal narcotics badge.

JANUARY 16, 1971: The Jaycees (the United States Junior Chamber of Commerce) name Elvis one of the Ten Outstanding Young Men of America. The other recipients include scientists and civil rights activists. Presley is thrilled to be among such company.

JUNE 1971: The two-room shotgun shack where Elvis was born in Tupelo, Mississippi, is opened to the public for tours. And in Memphis, a stretch of Highway 51 South, part of which runs in front of Graceland, is officially renamed Elvis Presley Boulevard.

AUGUST 9–SEPTEMBER 6, 1971: He's back at the International Hotel, now renamed the Las Vegas Hilton International Hotel. During this engagement he is named the recipient of the Bing Crosby Award from the National Academy of Recording Arts and Sciences (the Grammy Awards), later called the Lifetime Achievement Award.

LATE 1971: Priscilla leaves Elvis, moving out on her own with Lisa Marie.

JUNE 1972: Elvis plays New York's Madison Square Garden in four sold-out shows.

JULY 1972: Elvis and Priscilla file for divorce; by now Elvis has started to see beauty queen Linda Thompson, who will be with him until late 1976.

JANUARY 1973: *Elvis: Aloha from Hawaii—Via Satellite* special, performed at the Honolulu International Center Arena is broadcast live at 12:30 A.M. Hawaiian time and beamed via satellite to countries around the world. A tape of the show airs in America on NBC on April 4. An estimated 1 billion to 1.5 billion people in forty countries see the show.

OCTOBER 9, 1973: Elvis and Priscilla appear in court together; their divorce is granted.

OCTOBER 15–NOVEMBER 1, 1973: Elvis is hospitalized in Memphis for recurring pneumonia and pleurisy, an enlarged colon, and hepatitis. But he is also dealing with an addiction to prescription drugs, and recurring weight problems.

JANUARY 29–FEBRUARY 14, 1975: Elvis is hospitalized again. During this period his recording of "How Great Thou Art" wins the Grammy for Best

Inspirational Performance. This is Elvis's third and final Grammy win out of fourteen nominations (one nomination posthumously). All were for gospel music rather than pop or rock.

AUGUST 18–SEPTEMBER 5, 1975: Elvis opens in Vegas but ends his engagement on the twentieth and is hospitalized in Memphis until September 5.

NOVEMBER 1975: A Convair 880 jet purchased earlier in the year has been renovated; Presley at last gets a ride on the *Lisa Marie.*

DECEMBER 2–15, 1975: Presley returns to the Las Vegas Hilton to make up for the shows that were canceled during his previous engagement.

DECEMBER 31, 1975: At a special New Year's Eve concert in Pontiac, Michigan, he sets a single-performance attendance record of 62,500.

JULY 1976: Fires bodyguards Red West, Sonny West, Dave Hebler. They retaliate by writing a "tell-all."

EARLY NOVEMBER 1976: Elvis's longtime steady girlfriend, Linda Thompson, departs.

LATE NOVEMBER 1976: Elvis meets beauty queen Ginger Alden. She will be with him until his death.

DECEMBER 2–12, 1976: Elvis plays the Las Vegas Hilton; it will be his final Vegas show.

DECEMBER 31, 1976: Elvis gives a special New Year's Eve concert in Pittsburgh, Pennsylvania.

APRIL 1–5, 1977: Elvis is hospitalized in Memphis; tour shows scheduled for March 31–April 3 are canceled.

APRIL 21, 1977: Elvis goes back on the road; is hospitalized for exhaustion and gastric problems.

JUNE 17–26, 1977: During Elvis's tour, some of the shows are recorded by RCA and videotaped by CBS-TV for an upcoming live album and television special.

JUNE 26, 1977: Presley performs at Market Square Arena in Indianapolis, Indiana; it will be his last concert.

JULY 1977: *Elvis: What Happened?* is published. The authors are the three former bodyguards.

AUGUST 16, 1977: Elvis Presley's lifeless body is discovered in the bathroom of Graceland.

AUGUST 18, 1977: Elvis is buried at Forest Hill Cemetery, Memphis.

OCTOBER 1977: His final TV special, *Elvis in Concert,* airs on CBS.

OCTOBER 1977 : The bodies of Elvis and his mother, Gladys Presley, are moved to Graceland.

Filmography

A note regarding the film career of Elvis Presley. Despite the obvious talent he was occasionally permitted to display, Elvis's range as an actor was never fully explored by Hollywood. With the exception of his earliest films, his body of work largely consists of lightweight musical comedies.

What primarily distinguishes them is Elvis's élan as a romantic lead, and his underrated comedic abilities. And the musical numbers.

Sadly, at the time Presley was making movies, the Academy of Motion Picture Arts and Sciences did not regard rock 'n' roll as a serious musical form. As a result, not a single one of the enduring songs from his movies was nominated for an Academy Award. Moreover, Presley was never asked to perform on the Oscar telecast—a telecast that over the years has subjected its audience to musical numbers performed by such non-singers as Ricardo Montalban, Teri Garr, Rob Lowe, Sally Kellerman, Telly Savalas, Dyan Cannon, and even Rock Hudson and Mae West.

According to members of Presley's inner circle, he was well aware of Hollywood's condescending attitude toward him and his films. He felt that he was looked on as "poor white trash." Yet he vehemently refused to shed his Southern trappings—retaining his accent as well as his Memphian buddies. Hollywood might have been embarrassed about where he came from, but Elvis Presley never was.

And movie-wise, he was nobody's fool. After making one of his sillier pictures, Presley once quipped, "Maybe one day we'll do one right."

LOVE ME TENDER (1956)—Anachronistic Civil War drama in which a side-burned Elvis marries the girlfriend (Debra Paget) of his eldest brother (Richard Egan), who has been presumed dead in battle. Then Egan rides back home, stirring up conflict—and guilt—in Presley's character. The much-publicized screen debut includes four songs—several of them performed in the young singer's contemporary bump-and-grind fashion—as well as the affecting title ballad.

LOVING YOU (1957)—Biographical parallels resonate—and it is no coincidence. Filmmaker Hal Kanter spent time "observing" Elvis before the screenplay was written. As country boy Deke Rivers, Elvis joins a hillbilly band on tour and finds himself pegged for rock-'n'-roll stardom by an aggressive press agent (Lizabeth Scott). With Wendell Corey as the wry bandleader in love with Scott, and Dolores Hart as the sweet singer who loves Elvis. (Elvis's mother, Gladys Presley, is among the audience in a performance sequence; following her death, Presley wouldn't watch this picture.)

JAILHOUSE ROCK (1957)—After a barroom brawl gets him thrown into prison, Vince Everett (Elvis) learns to sing and play the guitar, with an assist from a cellmate (Mickey Shaughnessy). Once out, Vince meets a pretty music promoter (Judy Tyler) who watches helplessly as he becomes a star—and a creep. Love eventually reforms the angry, surly misogynist. Includes Elvis's stunning "Jailhouse Rock" musical sequence. (As with *Loving You*, Elvis found it difficult to watch this movie, for costar Judy Tyler was killed in a car accident shortly before the film's release.)

KING CREOLE (1958)—The grittiest of his films casts Presley as Danny Fisher, a high school dropout at odds with his father (Dean Jagger), a hoodlum (Walter Matthau), and the women in his life (sultry Carolyn Jones and sweet Dolores Hart). Based on a best-seller by Harold Robbins, directed by the respected Michael Curtiz, enhanced by Bourbon Street locations and eleven songs, including "Trouble" and "Hard Headed Woman." Arguably Elvis's best performance.

G.I. BLUES (1960)—Producer Hal Wallis shrewdly capitalized on Elvis's military service by casting him in what was billed as "The Red, White and Blue Show of the Year." As a singing GI who takes on a bet that he can woo dancer Juliet Prowse and "break through her defenses," Elvis is clearly at ease in the innocuous picture, which includes the charming song "Wooden Heart," which he sings to a little puppet. Director Norman Taurog (who began making movies in the 1930s) went on to helm eight more Presley pictures.

FLAMING STAR (1960)—Allegorical western originally written for Marlon Brando, with Elvis as a half-breed torn between his Kiowa tribe and his white family. Directed by Don Siegel (who later became famous for his teamings with actor Clint Eastwood), the film costars Dolores Del Rio as Elvis's mother; her on-screen death scene so upset Presley, the actor asked Siegel to postpone its filming (Siegel did). Despite two tunes, this is largely a dramatic turn that Presley pulls off.

WILD IN THE COUNTRY (1961)—Based on a popular novel *(The Lost Country)* of the day, the story line was revamped with Elvis in mind and includes four songs. Presley portrays a troubled young man with an interest in writing who is tempted by three women—the town tramp (Tuesday Weld), his longtime girlfriend (Millie Perkins), and the psychologist (Hope Lange) who senses his potential. Directed by Philip Dunne and written by Clifford Odets—both well-respected artists—the movie is most notable for Presley's affecting performance. (Among other things, he ably quotes Mark 15:34, *"Eli, eli, lema sabachthani?"*—which means, "My God, my God, why hast thou forsaken me?") The last "serious" movie of his career.

BLUE HAWAII (1961)—Elvis Presley signed a five-year contract with Hal Wallis just before making this movie. The producer who had once convincingly spoken of Elvis's natural acting abilities, and sexually charged screen presence, decided to surround his star with songs, exotic locations, and plenty of girls. This is the first of the Elvis Presley "formula" pictures, and despite its thin plot—about the heir to a pineapple plantation who forgoes the family business to work as a tour guide—it was one of the year's top-grossing movies. With Joan Blackman as the girlfriend and Angela Lansbury as Elvis's obnoxious mother, as well as fourteen songs—including the ballad "Can't Help Falling in Love" and, in the final romantic scene, "Hawaiian Wedding Song."

FOLLOW THAT DREAM (1962)—All about a Southern family, headed by Arthur O'Connell, that homesteads on a Florida beach, only to have run-ins with gangsters and state welfare investigators, including Joanna Moore, who has eyes for Elvis. Presley then finds himself in a tug-of-war between Moore and his "adoptive sister" Anne Helm. Along with displaying a flair for deadpan comedy, and effectively emoting in a courtroom scene involving custody of adopted orphans, Elvis sings a half dozen pleasant songs including "What a Wonderful Life" and "I'm Not the Marrying Kind."

KID GALAHAD (1962)—Remake of a 1937 Humphrey Bogart movie puts Elvis in the boxing ring as a sparring partner who turns pro—but is exploited by the greedy manager (Gig Young), who schedules him for a rigged fight. With Joan Blackman (late of *Blue Hawaii*) as Elvis's love interest. Never a winner in the biceps department (Elvis hated to be seen bare-chested), the star proves a champ ballad-wise, with tunes including "Home Is Where the Heart Is" and "I Got Lucky."

GIRLS! GIRLS! GIRLS! (1962)—Story-line-slim scenario finds Elvis cast as a charter-boat pilot in Hawaii who's working the tuna fleet by day, and singing by night, in order to buy his own boat. The drama doesn't end there: he must choose between sultry, voluptuous nightclub songstress Stella Stevens and wealthy "good girl" Laurel Goodwin. With thirteen songs, including the hit "Return to Sender," and the title song, which Elvis performs while in the midst of bikinied wahines.

IT HAPPENED AT THE WORLD'S FAIR (1963)—Elvis is a bush pilot who has lost his plane because of his partner's gambling. So he and his sidekick (Gary Lockwood) hitch a ride to the fair, where Elvis winds up taking care of an adorable little Chinese girl (Vicky Tiu), as well as singing and romancing an attractive nurse (Joan O'Brien) at the fair dispensary. Costarring the 1963 Seattle World's Fair, and featuring ten songs, including "One Broken Heart for Sale."

FUN IN ACAPULCO (1963)—Elvis is a former trapeze artist who's lost his nerve—due to an accident that injured his partner. So he journeys to Acapulco where he becomes a singer and swimming-pool lifeguard at a hotel and winds up romantically involved with a both a lady bullfighter (!) (Elsa Cardenas) and the hotel social director (Ursula Andress). He also decides to confront his fear of heights by diving 136 feet off the famed cliffs of Acapulco. No less mind-boggling are the songs, which include "Bossa Nova Baby."

KISSIN' COUSINS (1964)—An Air Force lieutenant, sent to talk his mountain kinfolk into letting the military build a missile site on their property, discovers he has an identical cousin. In dual roles, Elvis was so embarrassed by the blond wig he had to wear as the hillbilly cousin that he didn't want to come out of the dressing room the first day of shooting. Produced by Sam Katzman—famed for quickie productions—this one lived up to his reputation: it was shot in just sixteen days, and looks it. Distinguished performers Arthur O'Connell and Glenda Farrell mug their way through the goofiness, and Yvonne Craig (TV's Batgirl) and Pam Austin prove adept at wearing short shorts.

VIVA LAS VEGAS (1964)—Finally, Presley is cast opposite a leading lady who is his match in terms of talent and charisma. Moreover, he and Ann-Margret (who was his romantic interest offscreen as well as on) display plenty of chemistry. This despite yet another formulaic plot about a down-on-his-luck race-car driver working as a busboy in Las Vegas, where he woos the hotel swimming instructor. Luckily, they're both competing in a big talent contest, leading to their teaming in the energetic musical number "C'mon Everybody," and the charming "The Lady Loves Me." His batteries clearly charged by his flame-haired costar, Elvis also performs a rousing "What'd I Say." Directed by MGM musical maestro George Sidney.

ROUSTABOUT (1964)—Elvis's nasty, grinding rendition of "Little Egypt," and the affecting ballad "Big Love, Big Heartache," are the highlights of this programmer set against the backdrop of the carnival world where he runs into tough carny owner Barbara Stanwyck and "good girl" Joan Freeman. Luckily the midway is populated by skilled character actors including sexy Sue Ane Langdon as a fortune-teller.

GIRL HAPPY (1965)—From the producer of *Where the Boys Are*—about college coeds during spring break in Fort Lauderdale—this clone is told from the boys' point of view. Elvis and his band members are dispatched to the

Florida resort community to watch over a businessman's vacationing daughter, played by Shelley Fabares. Initially taking her for a "loser," Elvis directs his attentions to curvaceous Mary Ann Mobley (aka Miss America of 1959). When Fabares turns out to be hotter to handle than anticipated, Presley redirects his attention—and discovers he's (yep) in love. Aside from its efforts to launch a new dance craze, via the number "Do the Clam," this one is more enjoyable than you'd think, with a stronger sound track than usual, including "Do Not Disturb" (which Elvis sings during his attempt to seduce Mobley), the romantic "Puppet on a String," and the title tune. Along with displaying adept comic timing, Elvis does his one and only cross-dressing scene.

TICKLE ME (1965)—As improbably plotted as it is ineptly produced, this one finds Elvis cast as a rodeo rider who's making ends meet while working at a dude ranch-beauty spa, where the subplots involve romance (natch), a ghost town, and a hidden cache of gold. Costarring Jocelyn Lane, who marries Elvis's character at film's end. Songs include the lilting ballad "(Such an) Easy Question."

HARUM SCARUM (1965)—Elvis was initially enthusiastic about doing this picture because he got to play a desert-sheikh type—à la silent-era heartthrob Rudolph Valentino. But the eighteen-day shooting schedule left little time for production values. As for the plot, Elvis is an American matinee idol involved in Middle Eastern derring-do along with a king, his daughter, pickpockets, and more. Costarring Mary Ann Mobley as a handmaiden who's really a princess, it was filmed on the temple set built for Cecil B. DeMille's silent epic *King of Kings*, with costumes recycled from the 1944 opus *Kismet*.

FRANKIE AND JOHNNY (1966)—Elvis looks great in the Victorian-era costumes, and against the period backdrop of this Mississippi riverboat tale based on the folk song, but altered for the formulaic Presley happy ending. With voluptuous Donna Douglas, then of TV's popular *Beverly Hillbillies*.

PARADISE, HAWAIIAN STYLE (1966)—Back in a Hawaiian setting—for the third time—Elvis looks bored, and puffy, as a helicopter pilot who's teamed with buddy James Shigeta in a charter service. When his license is temporarily revoked, Elvis risks his flying future by making a daring rescue; on the personal front, he romances a trio of women, including Suzanna Leigh.

SPINOUT (1966)—Once again, as in *Viva Las Vegas*, Elvis is a singer and race-car driver, but the most dangerous curves in his life are those of three marriage-minded women: Deborah Walley (as a drummer in his band), Shelley Fabares (daughter of an automobile executive), and Diane McBain (a self-help author). With nine songs, among them "Stop, Look and Listen."

EASY COME, EASY GO (1967)—Elvis is incomprehensibly cast as a Navy frogman who moonlights as a singer at the Easy-Go-Go nightclub. The plot, such as it is, involves a search for sunken treasure and efforts to save a community art center. Elvis was so overweight during this movie that a flurry of memos went back and forth between producer Hal Wallis and Paramount Pictures executives.

DOUBLE TROUBLE (1967)—Set amidst the British discotheque scene—but filmed on the soundstages at MGM—this spoof of spy movies involves jewel thieves, inept government agents (the Wiere Brothers), and finds Elvis's pop-singer character involved with two women, an exotic siren (Yvonne Romain) and a seventeen-year-old heiress (Annette Day), who winds up as Presley's true love, this despite his declaration early in the film that "seventeen will get me thirty."

CLAMBAKE (1967)—In a *Prince and the Pauper* scenario, Elvis plays the son of a wealthy Texas oilman who switches identities with a working-class stiff (Will Hutchins) at a posh Miami hotel. Masquerading as the water-ski instructor, Elvis falls for guest Shelley Fabares—who's tired of being poor and is in the market for a rich boyfriend. Along with waterskiing while fully dressed (?), Elvis warbles "Confidence" with a gaggle of kids, for the most embarrassing musical number of his career.

STAY AWAY, JOE (1968)—Elvis is again a Native American, but unlike the dramatic *Flaming Star,* he's now going for the laughs, playing rodeo rider Joe Lightcloud, a Navajo who schemes to get the government to help out his family in their plans to raise cattle. The emphasis, though, is on comedy—and Joe's roguish ways. With lots of fistfights and "groovy" party scenes and the (for an Elvis movie) anarchic touch of having him come on to both a mother (Joan Blondell) and her hormonally charged teenage daughter (Quentin Dean). Or, as the ads touted, "Elvis goes West . . . and the West goes wild (and that's no Sitting Bull!)."

SPEEDWAY (1968)—Once again, Elvis is in the driver's seat—as a stock-car champion whose gambling-crazy manager (Bill Bixby) has created problems with the IRS. Enter Nancy Sinatra, a platinum blond government agent, who gets up close and personal with the subject of her investigation and even joins with him in song (she's the one in white minidress and knee boots). On her own, and in her inimitable somewhat off-key style, she enthusiastically performs "Your Groovy Self." Elvis's (on-key) songs include "Let Yourself Go."

LIVE A LITTLE, LOVE A LITTLE (1968)—Attempt to be in sync with changing times and attitudes finds Elvis cast as a photographer who leads a double life—he shoots for a girlie magazine as well as a classy ad agency. On the personal front, he's being pursued by a kooky model (Michele Carey) who lives with her Great Dane named Albert. With just four songs, none of them memorable, this one also includes a psychedelic dream sequence involving Elvis and people in dog costumes (!); and Elvis and Michele are seen in bed—ah, but they're safely apart, thanks to a bed-divider.

CHARRO! (1969)—This one heralded Elvis's foray into "a different kind of role," actually an attempt to mimic Clint Eastwood's Man With No Name character from his spaghetti westerns. Cast as an unshaven reformed gunfighter, Elvis squares off against his old gang to save townsfolk, and the dance hall queen (Ina Balin) with whom he's been involved. For a change, Elvis really doesn't sing—save for the title song, which runs over the opening credits.

THE TROUBLE WITH GIRLS (AND HOW TO GET INTO IT) (1969)—Extremely odd Presley entry—he appears in less than half of the picture—about a Chautauqua, a traveling college for young performers in the 1920s. As the manager, Elvis must ponder whom to hire and fire and help solve a mystery. He also wins over his beautiful assistant, played by Broadway-musical star Marlyn Mason. (Not lost on Elvis fans: a line of dialogue in which Elvis tells his leading lady that they ought to continue a conversation while in bed.)

CHANGE OF HABIT (1969)—In yet another attempt at a change of pace, Elvis portrays a young ghetto doctor whose clinic gets a helping hand from three young women who are, unbeknownst to him, nuns (in street clothes). When Elvis falls for Mary Tyler Moore, she must ponder whether to forsake her vows. The film ends with Moore in church attempting to decide; God only knows what her decision was. Costarring Jane Elliot and Barbara McNair.

ELVIS—THAT'S THE WAY IT IS (1970)—Documentary in which the singer is depicted during the height of his white-fringed epoch, as he readies for his 1970 summer engagement at Las Vegas's International Hotel; from rehearsals at MGM, where Elvis is clearly at ease—and mugging for the camera—to the frenzied opening night in Las Vegas, the movie captures the rigors and rewards of his live performances, as well as Presley's considerable charm and sense of humor.

ELVIS ON TOUR (1972)—A young, up-and-coming filmmaker named Martin Scorsese helped to make this documentary a winner; Scorsese supervised the state-of-the-art montage sequences, along with the then-innovative split-screen technique (and Dolby). Winner of the Golden Globe Award for Best Documentary of 1972 (but completely ignored by the Academy Awards). Captures the flash and glitter of Elvis's fifteen-city tour of spring 1972, with the King performing songs ranging from "Memories" to "Never Been to Spain."

Television Appearances

It's appropriate that Elvis Presley made the bulk of his TV appearances in the fifties—an era that was defined by the emergence of both the "tube" and rock 'n' roll. Before going national, the young singer appeared on a handful of regional broadcasts, such as *Town and Country Jubilee,* hosted by country singer Jimmy Dean, out of Washington, D.C. But it wasn't until producer Jackie Gleason signed him for the CBS series *Stage Show* that Presley made his way into living rooms across America. Television helped to launch him; in turn, Presley delivered some of his most electric performances for the TV cameras. It was a mutual love fest, as evidenced by the following:

STAGE SHOW (January 28, 1956)—Big-band leaders Tommy and Jimmy Dorsey hosted this CBS series produced by Jackie Gleason, then a major TV force as the producer-star of *The Honeymooners.* Elvis performs "Shake, Rattle and Roll," then segues into "Flip, Flop and Fly," and later, "I Got a Woman."

STAGE SHOW (February 4, 1956)—Presley does "Baby, Let's Play House" and "Tutti-Frutti," sharing billing with guest emcee Joe E. Brown, and the performing chimps Tippy and Cobina.

STAGE SHOW (February 11, 1956)—For the first time, the country hears "Heartbreak Hotel," which Elvis sings while backed by the Dorsey Brothers Orchestra. He also does "Blue Suede Shoes."

STAGE SHOW (February 18, 1956)—Once again, Presley does a frantic "Tutti-Frutti," along with "I Was the One." This time, the guests include the acrobatic team the Tokayeers.

STAGE SHOW (March 17, 1956)—Guest emcee Henny Youngman introduces an eleven-year-old organist; Elvis does "Blue Suede Shoes" and "Heartbreak Hotel."

STAGE SHOW (March 24, 1956)—For his sixth and final Dorsey show, Presley performs "Heartbreak Hotel" for the third time. He also sings "Money Honey."

THE MILTON BERLE SHOW (April 3, 1956)—A household name, Uncle Miltie—aka Mr. Television—widened Presley's audience. Broadcast from the deck of the USS *Hancock* in San Diego, California, Presley clicks with the young military audience with his performances of "Shake, Rattle and Roll," "Heartbreak Hotel," and "Blue Suede Shoes." He also does a comedy skit with Berle, who appears as his twin brother, Melvin Presley.

THE MILTON BERLE SHOW (June 5, 1956)—Irish McCalla, star of the TV series *Sheena, Queen of the Jungle*, swings into view on a grapevine. And sultry starlet Debra Paget puts in an appearance, surprising Presley by screaming and jumping up and down, and planting a kiss on him. But it's Presley's act that provides the fireworks. His rendition of "Hound Dog" includes plenty of pelvic thrusts, bumps, and grinds—leading to a media assault the following day.

THE STEVE ALLEN SHOW (July 1, 1956)—Though the versatile and erudite Allen was telling associates that Presley "won't last," he knew a ratings bonanza when he saw one. Following the *Berle Show* controversy, he cleverly concocted a scenario that depicted "the new Elvis Presley." As Allen explains, "We want to do a show the whole family can enjoy." Enter Elvis, in a tuxedo, carrying white gloves, who sings "Hound Dog" to a scared-looking little hound dog in a top hat. Though Presley reportedly hated the routine, he's good-natured enough on camera to plant a kiss on the pooch at the number's climax. He is also a good sport as "Tumbleweed Presley" in the skit "Range Roundup," with Allen, Imogene Coca, and Andy Griffith. At end, all four sing "Yippee Yi Yo Yi Yay."

THE ED SULLIVAN SHOW (September 9, 1956)—From 1948 to 1971 it was a Sunday-night staple, and America's premier TV variety show. And Sullivan was *the* premier host. Because he initially declared he'd never book Presley—saying, "I'll not have him at any price. He's not my cup of tea"—it was a coup for the singer when Sullivan changed his mind. Presley got $50,000 for three appearances, the first of which was hosted by esteemed character actor Charles Laughton (because Sullivan was hospitalized following a car crash). Introduced as "Elvin Presley," he performed "Don't Be Cruel," "Love Me Tender," "Ready Teddy," and "Hound Dog."

THE ED SULLIVAN SHOW (October 28, 1956)—The eclectic bill included ventriloquist Señor Wences, the Little Gaelic Singers, and Presley, who cut loose with "Don't Be Cruel," "Love Me Tender," "Love Me," and "Hound Dog." He was also presented with a gold record for sales of "Love Me Tender."

THE ED SULLIVAN SHOW (January 6, 1957)—The famous censored broadcast. Because of criticisms leveled at Presley's first two performances on his show, Sullivan ordered that the singer be shown only from the waist up. Elvis's repertoire includes "Hound Dog," "Love Me Tender," "Heartbreak Hotel," "Don't Be Cruel," "Too Much," "When My Blue Moon Turns to Gold Again," and the spiritual song "Peace in the Valley." Despite Sullivan's initial prejudices and worries, the host goes on to deem Presley a "real decent, fine boy," adding "you're thoroughly all right."

AMERICAN BANDSTAND (January 8, 1959)—The rock-'n'-roll star proved to be thoroughly all-American by doing his duty for the U.S. Army. For his twenty-fourth birthday, he spoke by phone from West Germany, where he was stationed, with host Dick Clark.

WELCOME HOME, ELVIS (May 12, 1960)—Frank Sinatra, who knocked Presley in 1957, did an about-face when the famed GI returned home. The Timex-sponsored special, which was taped on March 26 in the Grand Ballroom of Miami's Fontainbleau Hotel, found the onetime wild child wearing a tux and a towering pompadour and dueting with Frank on "Witchcraft." He also performed "Fame and Fortune" and "Stuck on You," while Sinatra took a turn with "Love Me Tender." Presley earned a record $125,000 for the show, which opened to find all the guest stars, including Rat Packers Sammy Davis Jr., Peter Lawford, and Joey Bishop, and Frank's daughter, Nancy Sinatra, singing "It's Nice to Go Traveling."

ELVIS (December 3, 1968)—Sponsored by Singer, this famed special marked a phenomenal comeback for Presley, who had become an anachronism. Taped that June at NBC, the show featured several rousing production numbers—one of which was censored (the "bordello sequence" has since been restored on video issues of the show). But the highlights are the concert sequences—in which an initially nervous Presley faces his first audience in eight years. Encased from head to toe in black leather, looking slim and sexy, he gradually eases back into control, emerging as the King

ELVIS: ALOHA FROM HAWAII (January 14, 1973)—Presley, who had been reinvented with his concert performances in Las Vegas and arenas across the country, took his show on the biggest road trip of all: via the first satellite broadcast, an estimated 1.5 billion people in forty countries saw him in all his jewel-encrusted, jumpsuited glory. From the opening, monumental strains of "Thus Spake Zarathustra" to the final moment in which he tosses his American Eagle cape into the audience, Presley is in his glory, an icon bathed in a fusillade of lights.

ELVIS IN CONCERT (October 3, 1977)—CBS aired this special two months after Presley's death. Presley is shown performing that June in Omaha, Nebraska, and Rapid City, South Dakota, and he's clearly a man in trouble: overweight, exhausted-looking, glassy-eyed. When he forgets the lyrics to "My Way," he has to read them from a sheet of paper. Television, which chronicled his vitality and unsurpassed originality, also captured his death knell.

Discography

Because of the vast number of recordings by Elvis Presley—including numerous illegal bootlegs—we were forced to be selective for this listing. Our criteria included not only critical acclaim and longevity, but also sentimental interest and curiosity value.

Presley was so prolific that some of his records weren't released until years after they were recorded. Wherever possible, we have listed songs by their year of release.

1954

Blue Moon of Kentucky
Good Rockin' Tonight

I Don't Care If the Sun Don't Shine
That's All Right (Mama)

1955

Baby, Let's Play House
I Forgot to Remember to Forget
I'm Left, You're Right, She's Gone

Milkcow Blues Boogie
Mystery Train
You're a Heartbreaker

1956

Any Way You Want Me
 (That's How I Will Be)
Blue Moon
Blue Suede Shoes

Don't Be Cruel*
Heartbreak Hotel*
 (*Elvis's first number one hit*)
Hound Dog*

*Went to number one on *Billboard*'s weekly pop singles chart.

I Got a Woman
I Want You, I Need You,
   I Love You*
I Was the One
Just Because
Lawdy Miss Clawdy
Let Me
Love Me
Love Me Tender*
Money Honey

My Baby Left Me
Paralyzed
Reddy Teddy
Rip It Up
Shake, Rattle and Roll
Trying to Get to You
Tutti-Frutti
We're Gonna Move
When My Blue Moon Turns to
   Gold Again

1957

All Shook Up *
(You're So Square)
   Baby, I Don't Care
Blueberry Hill
Blue Christmas
Don't Leave Me Now
Got a Lot of Livin' to Do
Here Comes Santa Claus
   (Right Down Santa Claus Lane)
I Believe
I Want to Be Free
It's No Secret
   (What God Can Do)
Jailhouse Rock*

Lonesome Cowboy
Loving You
Mean Woman Blues
Oh Little Town of Bethlehem
Peace in the Valley
Santa Claus Is Back in Town
Take My Hand, My Precious Lord
(Let Me Be Your) Teddy Bear*
That's When Your Heartaches
   Begin
Too Much*
Treat Me Nice*
True Love
Young and Beautiful

1958

As Long As I Have You
Crawfish
Danny
Don't*
Hard Headed Woman*
I Beg of You*

King Creole
New Orleans
One Night
Trouble
Wear My Ring Around Your Neck
Young Dreams

1959

There were no recording sessions;
Presley was in the U.S. Army.

A Big Hunk o' Love*
A Fool Such as I
I Need Your Love Tonight

My Wish Came True
Silent Night

1960

Are You Lonesome Tonight?*
Fame and Fortune
Fever
GI Blues
The Girl Next Door
The Girl of My Best Friend
His Hand in Mine
If We Never Meet Again
It's Now or Never*
   (Elvis's biggest-selling single)

Jesus Knows What I Want
Joshua Fit the Battle
Reconsider Baby
Stuck on You*
Such a Night
Swing Down, Sweet Chariot
Wooden Heart
Working on the Building

1961

Blue Hawaii
Can't Help Falling in Love
Hawaiian Wedding Song
(Marie's the Name)
   His Latest Flame
I Feel So Bad
I Slipped, I Stumbled, I Fell

Judy
Little Sister
Moonlight Swim
Summer Kisses, Winter Tears
Surrender*
Wild in the Country

1962

(Such an) Easy Question
Follow That Dream
Good Luck Charm*
Home Is Where the Heart Is
I Got Lucky
I'm Not the Marrying Kind

King of the Whole Wide World
Return to Sender
She's Not You
Suspicion
What a Wonderful Life

1963

(You're the) Devil in Disguise
One Broken Heart for Sale

Please Don't Drag that String Around
They Remind Me Too Much of You

1964

Ain't That Loving You Baby
Big Love, Big Heartache
C'mon Everybody
  (performed with Ann-Margret)
Hard Knocks
It Hurts Me
The Lady Loves Me
  (performed with Ann-Margret)

Little Egypt
Roustabout
Viva Las Vegas
What'd I Say
When It Rains, It Really Pours

1965

Crying in the Chapel
Do Not Disturb
Girl Happy
Go East, Young Man

The Meanest Girl in Town
Memphis, Tennessee
Puppet on a String
Slowly but Surely

1966

Down in the Alley
If Every Day Was like Christmas
I'll Be Back

Spinout
Stop, Look and Listen
Tomorrow Is a Long Time

1967

Big Boss Man
How Great Thou Art
If the Lord Wasn't Walking
  by My Side
Long Legged Girl
  (with the Short Dress On)

Stand by Me
Where Could I Go but to
  the Lord?
You Don't Know Me

1968

Baby, What You Want Me to Do?
Blue Christmas
Can't Help Falling in Love
Guitar Man
High-Heel Sneakers
If I Can Dream
Lawdy Miss Clawdy
Let Yourself Go
One Night
Too Much Monkey Business
U.S. Male
You'll Never Walk Alone

1969

After Loving You
Any Day Now
Don't Cry Daddy
Gentle on My Mind
I Can't Stop Loving You
I'm Movin' On
Inherit the Wind
In the Ghetto
It Keeps Right on A-Hurtin'
Johnny B. Goode
Kentucky Rain
Long Black Limousine
Memories
Only the Strong Survive
Stranger in My Own Hometown
Suspicious Minds*
    (*Elvis's seventeenth and final
    number one single*)
Wearin' That Loved On Look
Without Love (There Is Nothing)

1970

Bridge over Troubled Water
I Just Can't Help Believing
I Really Don't Want to Know
The Next Stop Is Love
Polk Salad Annie
Proud Mary
Release Me (and Let Me Love Again)
See See Rider
You Don't Have to Say You Love Me
You've Lost That Lovin' Feelin'

1971

For Lovin' Me
Funny How Time Slips Away
Got My Mojo Workin'
Holly Leaves and Christmas Trees
If I Get Home on Christmas Day
I'll Be Home on Christmas Day
It's Your Baby, You Rock It
I Was Born About 10,000 Years Ago
I Washed My Hands in Muddy Water
Make the World Go Away
Merry Christmas Baby
Put Your Hand in the Hand
    (of the Man from Galilee)
Rags to Riches
Snowbird
Until It's Time for You to Go

1972

Always on My Mind
Amazing Grace
An American Trilogy
Bosom of Abraham
Burning Love
Early Morning Rain

For the Good Times
He Touched Me
Hey Jude
Miracle of the Rosary
Never Been to Spain

1973

Are You Sincere?
Don't Think Twice . . . It's Alright
I'm So Lonesome I Could Cry
It's Over
My Way

Promised Land
Raised on Rock
Spanish Eyes
Steamroller Blues
You Gave Me a Mountain

1974

Flip, Flop and Fly
Good Time Charlie's Got the Blues

I've Got a Thing About You Baby

1975

Green Green Grass of Home
I Can Help ‾
My Boy

Shake a Hand
Thinking About You

1976

Bitter They Are, Harder They
    Fall
Blue Eyes Crying in the Rain
Danny Boy
For the Heart

Harbor Lights
Hurt
Moody Blue
She Thinks I Still Care
Solitaire

1977

He'll Have to Go
Pledging My Love

Unchained Melody
Way Down

Appendix II

SOURCE NOTES

BIBLIOGRAPHY

ource Notes

1: Omens

THE BIRTH: Dundy, *Elvis and Gladys*; Goldman, *Elvis*; Guralnick, *Last Train to Memphis*; Hopkins, *Elvis: A Biography*; Nash, Smith, Lacker, and Fike, *Elvis Aaron Presley*; "Delivering Elvis Paid $15—From Welfare," *Memphis Commercial Appeal*, January 6, 1980; "Elvis by His Father Vernon Presley," *Good Housekeeping*, January 1978; "Elvis Presley Part 2: The Folks He Left Behind Him," *TV Guide*, September 22–28, 1956; authors' tour of the birthplace.

ABOUT MEDICAL AND BIRTH PRACTICES: personal interviews, Mitch Douglas, Dolly Parton; Lynn and Vecsy, *Coal Miner's Daughter*; "Born at Home: A Passing Southern Tradition," *Saturday Evening Post*, October 1946; "House Docs," *Mississippi* magazine, July 1978; "Medicine in the Hill Country," oral history compiled by Ruth Henson, Mississippi State College; "Midwives: Semi-Professionals of the '20s and '30s," oral history, East Tupelo Historical Collection, Tupelo Historical Society; Dolly Parton, "Crook and Chase," Nashville (TV) Network, September 7, 1992.

ON GLADYS AND VERNON: personal interviews, Becky Martin, Annie Presley, Corinne Richards Tate; Burk, *Early Elvis: The Tupelo Years*; De Witt, *Elvis*; Dundy, *Elvis and Gladys*; Goldman, *Elvis*; Johnson, *Elvis Presley Speaks!*; Whitmer, *The Inner Elvis*; "Elvis by His Father," *Good Housekeeping*; "Elvis Presley Part 2," *TV Guide*.

ABOUT TUPELO: personal interviews, Becky Martin, Annie Presley, Roy Turner; Elvis Presley Heights Garden Club (authors), *Elvis Presley Heights, Mississippi, Lee County, 1921–1984*; "Tupelo, Miss.," *Saturday Evening Post*, February 17, 1951; Burk, *Early Elvis: The Tupelo Years*; De Witt, *Elvis*; Dundy, *Elvis and Gladys*; Hopkins, *Elvis: A Biography*.

2: The Song in His Heart

VERNON'S IMPRISONMENT: personal interviews, Annie Presley, Corinne Richards Tate; De Witt, *Elvis*; Dundy, *Elvis and Gladys*; Goldman, *Elvis*; Nash, Smith, Lacker, and Fike, *Elvis Aaron Presley*; *Tupelo Daily Journal*, November 17, 1937, and May 26, 1938.

CLOSENESS OF MOTHER AND SON: personal interviews, Annie Presley,

Corinne Richards Tate, Roy Turner; Burk, *Early Elvis: The Tupelo Years*; Dundy, *Elvis and Gladys*; Goldman, *Elvis*; Nash, Smith, Lacker, and Fike, *Elvis Aaron Presley*; "Tupelo, Elvis' Home Town Shows Its Pride in Him," *Memphis Press-Scimitar*, October 18, 1965.

YOUNG ELVIS AND MUSIC: personal interviews, Becky Martin, Annie Presley; Burk, *Early Elvis: The Tupelo Years*; De Witt, *Elvis*; Dundy, *Elvis and Gladys*; Goldman, *Elvis*; Johnson, *Elvis Presley Speaks!*; Smith, *Elvis's Man Friday*; Whitmer, *The Inner Elvis*; "Amazing Grace," *Photoplay Presents: Elvis*; "Elvis by His Father," *Good Housekeeping*; "Elvis Presley Part 2," *TV Guide*; "Teacher Recalls Elvis' Favorite Tune While at Lawhon was 'Old Shep,' " *Tupelo Daily Journal*, July 28–29, 1956; also various other articles from the *Tupelo Daily Journal* in which Tupeloans who knew Elvis and his family reminisced.

3: In the Ghetto

LIFE AT LAUDERDALE COURTS: personal interviews, Margaret Cranfill, Jimmy Denson, Paul Dougher, Ruby Dougher, Evan "Buzzy" Forbess, Dr. Paul Grubb, Marty Lacker; Jerry Hopkins interview notes with Jane Richardson; Dundy, *Elvis and Gladys*; Goldman, *Elvis*; "She Has Helped Solve Problems for Hundreds of Families" (Jane Richardson), *Memphis Press-Scimitar*, February 12, 1970.

MEMPHIS MUSIC SCENE AND ELVIS'S MUSICAL INFLUENCES: personal interviews, Louis Cantor, Paul Dougher, Sam Phillips, Charles Raiteri; Booth, *Rhythm Oil*; De Witt, *Elvis*; Tosches, *Unsung Heroes of Rock 'n' Roll*.

AT HUMES HIGH: personal interviews, Gene Bradbury, Louis Cantor, Paul Dougher, Evan "Buzzy" Forbess, George Klein, Pat Lightell, Ronald Smith, Martha Wallace; West, West, Hebler, and Dunleavy, *Elvis: What Happened?*; *1953 Senior Herald* (Humes High School yearbook); Mildred Scrivener (history teacher), "My Boy Elvis," *TV Radio Mirror*, Southern edition, March 1957; "The High School Years," *Photoplay Presents: Elvis*; authors' tour of the "Elvis Presley Room" at Humes High.

4: The Memphis Flash

SAM PHILLIPS AND SUN RECORDS: personal interviews, Howard De Witt, George Klein, Sam Phillips; Jerry Hopkins interview notes with Marion Keisker; Keisker video interview, *Elvis: His Life and Times*; De Witt, *Elvis*; Guralnick, *Last Train to Memphis*; Marcus, *Mystery Train*; "Among the Believers," *New York Times Magazine*, September 24, 1995; "Lasting Legacy," *Memphis Commercial Appeal*, June 30, 1996; "One Day Into Our Office Came a Bashful, Nervous Young Man," *Memphis Press-Scimitar*, March 15, 1974; "Sam Phillips" (three-part series), *BlueSpeak*, June–August, 1996; "Sam Phillips: The Sun King," *Memphis*, December 1978; "Suddenly Singing Elvis

Presley Zooms Into Recording Stardom," *Memphis Press-Scimitar*, February 5, 1955; "The Sun Years," *Photoplay Presents Elvis*.

LIFE WITH ELVIS: personal interviews, Eddie Bond, George Klein, Marty Lacker, Ronald Smith, Walter "Buddy" Winsett; Booth, *Rhythm Oil*; Gordon, *It Came from Memphis*; Tosches, *Unsung Heroes of Rock 'n' Roll*.

ABOUT DEWEY PHILLIPS: personal interviews, Louis Cantor, George Klein, Dorothy Phillips, Sam Phillips, Charles Raiteri; Booth, *Rhythm Oil*; De Witt, *Elvis*; Gordon, *It Came from Memphis*; "A Hound Dog to the Manor Born," *Esquire*, 1968; "Daddy-O-Dewey," *Memphis Flyer*, January 4–10, 1996.

5: Road Trip

GRAND OLE OPRY: personal interviews, Bill Denny, Dolly Denny, Sam Phillips, Justin Tubb, Don Wilson; Byworth, *History of Country & Western Music*; Goldman, *Elvis*; Guralnick, *Last Train to Memphis*; Hagan, *Grand Ole Opry*; Jenkins, *Tennessee Sampler*; Nash, *Behind Closed Doors*; Tassin and Henderson, *Fifty Years at the Grand Ole Opry*.

LOUISIANA HAYRIDE: personal interview, Kitty Jones; Jerry Hopkins interview notes with Frank Page; "Elvis—seeing him before he was anybody," *Clarion Ledger–Jackson Daily News*, February 5, 1984; official souvenir album, circa 1970, *KWKH's Louisiana Hayride*.

EARLY TOURING: personal interviews, Lee Cotten, Sam Phillips, Justin Tubb; Jerry Hopkins interview notes with Bob Neal; Goldman, *Elvis*; Guralnick, *Last Train to Memphis*; West, West, Hebler, and Dunleavy, *Elvis: What Happened?*; Elvis Presley radio interviews of the fifties.

LOCAL BOY MAKES GOOD: *Official Elvis Presley Album*; "I Remember Elvis," *Parade*, January 29, 1978; "The Man Who Shot Elvis," *Memphis*, July/August 1996.

COLONEL TOM PARKER: personal interviews, Bill Denny, Sam Phillips, Hank Snow, Justin Tubb; "An Unrecorded Chapter of the Elvis Presley Story," *Billboard*, date unknown; Crumbaker and Tucker, *Up and Down With Elvis Presley*; Vellenga and Farren, *Elvis and the Colonel*.

SEXUAL AWAKENINGS: personal interview, June Juanico; Goldman, *Elvis*; Guralnick, *Last Train to Memphis*; West, West, Hebler, and Dunleavy, *Elvis: What Happened?*

GLADYS AND ELVIS: personal interview, Peter Whitmer; Dundy, *Elvis and Gladys*; Goldman, *Elvis*; Guralnick, *Last Train to Memphis*; West, West, Hebler, and Dunleavy, *Elvis: What Happened?*; Whitmer, *The Inner Elvis*.

ELVIS SIGNS WITH PARKER: personal interviews, Sam Phillips, Hank Snow; Snow, Ownbey, and Burris, *The Hank Snow Story*; Crumbaker and Tucker, *Up and Down With Elvis Presley*; Vellenga and Farren, *Elvis and the Colonel*.

6: Sing, Boy, Sing

FIRST RCA RECORDING SESSIONS: personal interviews, Joan Deary, Gordon Stoker; Goldman, *Elvis*; Guralnick, *Last Train to Memphis*; West, West, Hebler, and Dunleavy, *Elvis: What Happened?*; authors' tour of RCA Studios, Nashville.

PURCHASE OF SUN CONTRACT: personal interviews, Joan Deary, Bill Gallagher, Sam Phillips; De Witt, *Elvis*; Goldman, *Elvis*; Guralnick, *Last Train to Memphis*.

"HEARTBREAK HOTEL": personal interviews, Joan Deary, Sam Phillips, Howard De Witt; Bronson, *Billboard Book of Number One Hits*; Goldman, *Elvis*; Guralnick, *Last Train to Memphis*; *Elvis World* #40; *Life*, July 1956.

TOURING: personal interview, Justin Tubb; Cotten, *All Shook Up*; Cotten, *Did Elvis Sing in Your Hometown?*; Crumbaker and Tucker, *Up and Down with Elvis Presley*; Davis, *Bus Fare to Kentucky*; Goldman, *Elvis*; Prince, *The Day Elvis Came to Town*; Rijff, *Long Lonely Highway*; West, West, Hebler, and Dunleavy, *Elvis: What Happened?*; "These Are the Cats Who Make Music for Elvis," *Memphis Press-Scimitar*, December 15, 1956; Elvis Presley radio interviews of the fifties.

ELVIS AND HIS APPEARANCE: Goldman, *Elvis*; Nash, Smith, Lacker, and Fike, *Elvis Aaron Presley*; various articles regarding Elvis on the road; also, numerous photographs of Elvis during this era, in which his eye makeup is apparent.

SEXUALITY: personal interviews, Sandra Harmon, June Juanico; Fortas, *Elvis*; Goldman, *Elvis*; Halberstam, *The Fifties*; Prince, *The Day Elvis Came to Town*; West, West, Hebler, and Dunleavy, *Elvis: What Happened?*; "Jeanne Carmen Interview," *Blue Suede News* #33, winter 1996; *Time*, May 15, 1956.

EARLY TV APPEARANCES: personal interviews, Billy Harbach, Minabess Lewis, Andrew Solt, Gordon Stoker; Bacon, *How Sweet It Is*; Bowles, *A Thousand Sundays*; Harris, *Always on Sunday*; Henry, *The Great One*; Rijff and Minter, *60 million tv viewers can't be wrong!*; Shales, *Legends*; Weatherby, *Jackie Gleason*; "TV: New Phenomenon," *New York Times*, June 6, 1956; various articles including *Entertainment Weekly*, August 24, 1990; *Los Angeles Times*, July 3, 1956; *Newsweek*, July 16, 1956; *New York Daily News*, June 25, 1996; *New York Post*, August 14, 1996; *New York Times*, July 5, 1996; *Photoplay Presents: Elvis!* summer, 1987.

7: Wild in the Country

CONTROVERSY OVER ROCK 'N' ROLL: Guralnick, *Last Train to Memphis*; Halberstam, *The Fifties*; various articles, including *America*, June 23, 1956; *House & Garden*, October 1956; International News Service, June 17, 1956; *Newsweek*, June 18, 1956; *Time*, May 14, 1956.

CONTROVERSY OVER ELVIS: "America's Most Controversial Singer Answers His Critics," *Parade*, September 30, 1956; dozens of articles, including *Cosmopolitan*, December 1956; *Evening News* (United Kingdom); *Life*, April 30, 1956; *Memphis Commercial Appeal*, May 9, 1956; *Time*, July 23 and October 8, 1956; United Press, November 17, 1956; *Photoplay Presents: Elvis!* summer 1987.

PAT BOONE: Broeske, "Heartthrobs" (unpublished manuscript); Guralnick, *Last Train to Memphis*; "Rock 'n' Roll Battle: Boone vs. Presley," *Colliers*, October 26, 1956; Presley's own comments about Boone in various radio interviews of the fifties.

PRESLEYMANIA: personal interviews, Gregg Barrios, June Juanico; "I Was a Teen-Age Elvis Fanatic," *Los Angeles Times*, June 3, 1984; *Life*, August 27, 1956; *Memphis Press-Scimitar*, May 4, 1956; *Newsweek*, August 27, 1956; *New York Post*, April 29, 1956; *New York World-Telegram*, October 18, 1956; *Tupelo Daily Journal*, undated clipping, 1956; *TV Guide*, three-part series, September 8–October 5, 1956.

ON TOUR: Wertheimer, *Elvis '56*; *Memphis Commercial Appeal*, August 11, 1991; *Las Vegas Review-Journal*, February 13, 1996; *Memphis Press-Scimitar*, December 15, 1956; plus more than four dozen newspaper articles from various parts of the country where Elvis toured, including Jacksonville (Fla.), Houston (Tex.), San Diego (Calif.), Waco (Tex.); Elvis Presley radio interviews of the fifties.

PLAYS LAS VEGAS: personal interview, Shecky Greene; Hess, *Viva Las Vegas*; *Entertainment Weekly*, April 23, 1993; *Las Vegas Review-Journal*, various articles, April 20 May 1, 1956; *Los Angeles Herald & Express*, May 3, 1956; *Memphis Press-Scimitar*, May 1, 1956; *Newsweek*, May 14, 1956.

JUNE JUANICO: personal interview, June Juanico; Guralnick, *Last Train to Memphis*; *Memphis Commercial Appeal*, July 8 and 23, 1956; *Miami News*, August 4, 1956; interview, *Elvis in Hollywood* video; *Elvis's Summer of Innocence*, *Extra* TV series; Elvis Presley radio interviews, ca. 1956.

DOTTIE HARMONY: personal interview, Dottie Harmony, *Movieland Magazine*, April 1957.

ED SULLIVAN SHOWS: personal interviews, Minabess Lewis, Andrew Solt, Gordon Stoker; Bowles, *A Thousand Sundays*; Harris, *Always on Sunday*; Rijff and Minto, *60 million tv viewers can't be wrong!*; Shales, *Legends*; *Entertainment Weekly*, June 7, 1996; *Newsweek*, October 8, 1956.

TUPELO HOMECOMING: various articles, *Tupelo Daily Journal*, September 8–30, 1956.

"KID" PRESLEY (THE FISTFIGHTS): In Memphis: "I Collared Elvis," *Elvis World* #38; "Gas Station Fight Story Gets Updated, Amended," *Elvis World* #41; United Press articles, October 19–26, 1956. In Toledo: personal interview, Louis Balint Jr.; United Press articles, November 23–30, 1956.

AT HOME IN MEMPHIS: personal interviews, Peggy Jemison, June Juanico, Peter Whitmer; Guralnick, *Last Train to Memphis*; Whitmer, *The Inner Elvis*.

MILLION DOLLAR QUARTET: Carr and Farren, *Elvis Presley*; Lewis and Silver, *Great Balls of Fire!*; Perkins and McGee, *Go, Cat, Go*; authors' tour of Sun Records, 1996.

8: The Moving Image

LOVE ME TENDER: personal interviews, Valerie Allen, William Campbell, James Drury; Pond and Michael Ochs Archives, *Elvis in Hollywood*; "Presley Takes Hollywood," *Photoplay*, December 1956; various articles, *Hollywood Citizen-News, Los Angeles Times, Movietime, Nashville Tennessean, New Republic, New York Herald Tribune*; Twentieth Century–Fox production files; various interviews, *Elvis in Hollywood* video.

DEBRA PAGET: personal interviews, William Campbell, Joe Esposito; "Why Debra Paget's Mama Gave Elvis the Private Eye," *Uncensored*, September 1957.

NATALIE WOOD: Booth, *Rhythm Oil*; Goldman, *Elvis*; Hopper and Brough, *The Whole Truth and Nothing But*; Nash, Smith, Lacker, and Fike, *Elvis Aaron Presley*; Smith, *Elvis's Man Friday*; Wood, *Natalie*; various articles regarding Natalie's trip to Memphis, including "Is Natalie Going to Wed Elvis?" *Los Angeles Examiner*, November 3, 1956.

BACK ON THE ROAD: Cotten, *All Shook Up*; dozens of articles from the cities where Elvis left his mark, from publications including *Buffalo-Courier Express, Detroit Free Press, Ft. Wayne News Sentinel, Philadelphia Evening Bulletin, St. Louis Post-Dispatch*.

ELVIS, PRO AND CON: "Hate Elvis Campaign Launched in Iran," United Press, August 12, 1957; "Elvis the Indigenous," *Harper's*, April 1957.

9: The Cool and the Crazy

BUYS GRACELAND: Guralnick, *Last Train to Memphis*; Hopkins, *Elvis: A Biography*; United Press, March 27, 1957; rare one-hour video interview with Cliff Gleaves.

LOVING YOU: Whitmer, *The Inner Elvis*; various articles, *Los Angeles Herald-Examiner, Los Angeles Examiner, Time, Variety*; MPAA memos; documents, Hal Wallis Collection, Academy Library.

DOLORES HART: personal interviews, Valerie Allen, Joe Esposito, George Klein; "Mother Dolores: Bethlehem—postcard," *The New Republic*, October 4, 1993; Hart's autobiographical Twentieth Century–Fox press release, Hal Wallis Collection, Academy Library; authors' correspondence with Mother Dolores (1980).

JAILHOUSE ROCK: personal interviews, Frank Magrin in 1991, Gil Perkins,

Alex Romero; Minto, *Inside "Jailhouse Rock"*; various articles, *Daily Mirror* (London), *Hollywood Reporter, Los Angeles Examiner, Showmen's Trade, Time, Variety*; movie pressbook.

LIFE IN HOLLYWOOD: personal interviews, Valerie Allen, Dottie Harmony, June Juanico; Nash, Smith, Lacker, and Fike, *Elvis Aaron Presley*; Smith, *Elvis's Man Friday*; various articles, including "Our Love Song," *Photoplay*, June 1959.

ROMANCES: personal interviews, Valerie Allen, Dottie Harmony, June Juanico, Mamie Van Doren; Storm and Boyd, *The Lady Is a Vamp*; *Elvis: His Loves & Marriage*, 1957; "Elvis: Why Can't He Get Married?" *Photoplay*, November 1957; "My Weekend With Elvis" (Yvonne Lime), *Movieland*, August 1957; "Marry Elvis? He's Just a Friend, Says Starlet," *Los Angeles Times*, May 23, 1957; "Secret Loves of Hollywood's Love Idols," *Geraldo* TV show, October 23, 1989.

ON THE HOT SEAT: "Elvis Personally Answers His Critics," *Movieland*, May 1957; Elvis press conference of October 29, 1957; "I'm Not Doing Anything Wrong!" *TV Picture Life*, June 1957.

RETURNS TO THE ROAD: Burk, *Elvis in Canada*; Cotten, *All Shook Up*; Guralnick, *Last Train to Memphis*; various articles, including dozens of clippings from newspapers in Los Angeles, New York, and beyond regarding Elvis's notorious Pan Pacific Auditorium show, among them "6,000 Kids Cheer Elvis' Frantic Sex Show," *Los Angeles Mirror-News*, October 29, 1957 and "Elvis Tones Down Act When Police Move In," *Los Angeles Mirror-News*, October 30, 1957.

10: Soldier Boy

ELVIS IS DRAFTED: personal interview, Milton Bowers; Levy, *Operation Elvis*.

ARMY PRE-INDUCTION EXAMS: personal interview, Dottie Harmony; various articles, including *Tupelo Daily Journal*, January 5 6, 1957.

KING CREOLE: personal interviews, Leonard Hirshan, Carolyn Jones (in 1982), Walter Matthau, Harold Robbins; various articles, *Los Angeles Mirror-News, Los Angeles Times, Motion Picture Herald, New York Times, Photoplay, Variety*; *Elvis in Hollywood* video.

BACK HOME IN MEMPHIS: Fortas, *Elvis*; Mann, *Private Elvis*; West, West, Hebler, and Dunleavy, *Elvis: What Happened?*

ANITA WOOD ROMANCE: personal interview, Anita Wood; "You Are My No. 1 Girl," *Movieland*, December 1957; "The Day Elvis Made Me Cry," *Movieland & TV Time*, August 1959; "Elvis' Longtime Girlfriend Anita Wood Says It's All Over," *Memphis Press-Scimitar*, August 6, 1962; Anita Wood interview, *Elvis: His Life and Times*, BBC video.

MONEYMAKER: various articles, including *Memphis Press-Scimitar*,

November 5, 1965; *Newsweek*, February 18, 1957; *Tupelo Daily Journal*, September 26, 1957.

11: Private Presley

INDUCTION: personal interviews, Jo Alden, Mrs. Eddie Fadal, Jerry Hopkins, Michael Norwood, Mr. and Mrs. William Norwood, Anita Wood; Hopkins, *Elvis*; Nash, Smith, Lacker, and Fike, *Elvis Aaron Presley*; various articles, including "Army to Give Elvis Presley a GI Haircut," *Billboard*, October 27, 1957; "Elvis 'Least Bothered' by Army Draft; Jokes on Visit," *Nashville Banner*, December 21, 1957; "Farewell Squad for Elvis," *Life*, October 6, 1958; "Life All Shook Up for Elvis As He Leaves Home for Army," *New York Post*, March 24, 1958; "Presley Enjoys Last Few Hours as Civilian Before Army Inducts" and "Rock and Roll Idol Signs In," both United Press, March 24, 1958; "Private Presley's Debut," *Life*, April 4, 1958; *Elvis in the Army* magazine, 1959; three hours of unedited interviews (originally taped for TV's *Hard Copy*) with Mrs. Eddie Fadal and William Norwood; also, William Norwood's letters.

THE MOMENTOUS HAIRCUT: "Elvis Sheds Long Sideburns," United Press, February 13, 1958; "GI Jeers, 'Scalping' Greet Elvis—but He Just Yawns," *Nashville Tennessean*, March 26, 1958.

12: Broken Dreams

ELVIS IN KILLEEN: personal interviews, Jo Alden, Mrs. Eddie Fadal, Mr. and Mrs. William Norwood; Dundy, *Elvis and Gladys*; Fortas, *Elvis*; Nash, Smith, Lacker, and Fike, *Elvis Aaron Presley*.

GLADYS'S DEATH: See "Elvis in Killeen" above; also, personal interviews, Dr. Charles Clarke, Dr. Lester Hoffman, Dr. Forest Tennant; various articles about Elvis's mother's taking ill, the death and funeral, and Elvis's extended leave, including "Elvis's Homecoming Cheers Ailing Mother," *Nashville Tennessean*, August 14, 1958; " 'Goodby, Darling,' Says the Grief-Stricken Singer," *Memphis Press-Scimitar*, August 16, 1958.

13: The Solitary Private

FROM KILLEEN TO NEW YORK: Cotten, *All Shook Up*; Hodge, *Me 'n Elvis* (also, Hodge video of same title); Jones and Burk, *Soldier Boy Elvis*; Schröer, *Private Presley*; Taylor, *Elvis in the Army*.

ABOARD THE USS GENERAL RANDALL: Hodge, *Me 'n Elvis* (also Hodge video); Schröer, *Private Presley*; "The Joker and the King," *Graceland News*, 1987.

IN GERMANY: personal interviews, Joe Esposito, Ira Jones, William Taylor,

Diana Wentworth; Esposito and Oumano, *Good Rockin' Tonight*; Hodge, *Me 'n Elvis* (also, Hodge video); Jones and Burk, *Soldier Boy Elvis*; Levy, *Operation Elvis*; the Mansfields, *Elvis the Soldier*; Nash, Smith, Lacker, and Fike, *Elvis Aaron Presley*; Schröer, *Private Presley*; Taylor, *Elvis in the Army*; West, West, Hebler, and Dunleavy, *Elvis: What Happened?*; "An Ordinary GI," *Stars and Stripes*, July 11, 1958; "Elvis: Bigger Than the Generals Who Worked with Him," *Variety*, November 5, 1958; "Elvis and the Fräuleins," *Look*, December 23, 1958; "Elvis Presley in the Army," *Redbook*, February 1960; "Everybody's a Joke in a Jeep," *Variety*, March 25, 1957; "Has the Army Changed Elvis?" *Family Weekly*, October 12, 1959; "Look What Germany's Done to Elvis!" *Los Angeles Times*, July 19, 1959; "Presley Lives High off Base," *Los Angeles Mirror-News*, February 26, 1960; *Elvis in the Army* magazine, 1959; also various articles about life at Bad Nauheim.

14: Elvis on Ice

WAR GAMES AND SCOUTING: personal interviews, Joe Esposito, Ira Jones, William Taylor; Esposito and Oumano, *Good Rockin' Tonight*; Hodge, *Me 'n Elvis* (also, Hodge video); Jones and Burk, *Soldier Boy Elvis*; Levy, *Operation Elvis*; the Mansfields, *Elvis the Soldier*; Nash, Smith, Lacker, and Fike, *Elvis Aaron Presley*; Schröer, *Private Presley*; Taylor, *Elvis in the Army*; Elvis's recollections during his series of press conferences upon his return home.

KEEPING THE FIRES BURNING AT HOME: personal interview, Anita Wood; Goldman, *Elvis*; Hopkins, *Elvis: A Biography*.

IN MUNICH AND PARIS: Esposito and Oumano, *Good Rockin' Tonight*; Hodge, *Me 'n Elvis* (also, Hodge video), Levy, *Operation Elvis*; the Mansfields, *Elvis the Soldier*; Nash, Smith, Lacker, and Fike, *Elvis Aaron Presley*; Schröer, *Private Presley*.

FOREIGN AFFAIRS: Esposito and Oumano, *Good Rockin' Tonight*; Levy, *Operation Elvis*; the Mansfields, *Elvis the Soldier*; Nash, Smith, Lacker, and Fike, *Elvis Aaron Presley*; Schröer, *Private Presley*; "Elvis Kissed Me," *Photoplay*, March 1959; "Elvis Presley's New Girl," *TV Picture Life*, March 1959; "German Girl Becomes Elvis Fan After Dating," Associated Press, November 2, 1958.

BACK IN FRIEDBERG: See above sources for "War games and scouting."

15: All Quiet on the Western Front

CHANGING OF THE GUARD: Bane, *Who's Who in Rock*; Broeske, "Heartthrobs" (unpublished manuscript); Lewis and Silver, *Great Balls of Fire!*; Nite, *Rock On: The Solid Gold Years*; "Jerry and God," *Memphis Commercial Appeal*, April 21, 1996.

THE TEEN IDOLS: personal interview, Bob Marcucci (in 1984); Broeske,

"Heartthrobs" (unpublished manuscript); Nite, *Rock On*; "Chuck Berry," *Current Biography*, 1977; "Good Looks Started Fabian," *Los Angeles Mirror-News*, August 11,1959; "The Story of Frank and Fabe and Bob," *Los Angeles Times*, November 23, 1980; "Tiger Fabian Unseats Elvis," *Los Angeles Mirror-News*, August 10, 1959; "Tuneless Tiger," *Time*, July 27, 1959.

ELVIS'S PHYSICAL MAKEOVER: Esposito and Oumano, *Good Rockin' Tonight*; Nash, Smith, Lacker, and Fike, *Elvis Aaron Presley*; Presley and Harmon, *Elvis and Me*; also, the changes are obvious in post-Army photographs of Presley.

ELVIS'S MUSICAL MAKEOVER: Bronson, *Billboard Book of Number One Hits*; Hopkins, *Elvis*; Nash, Smith, Lacker, and Fike, *Elvis Aaron Presley*; again, the changes are obvious in post-Army recordings by Presley.

MEANWHILE, BACK IN HOLLYWOOD: various memos, Hal Wallis Collection, Academy Library; Presley interview, *Nashville Banner*, October 29, 1959; *Photoplay*, March 1960.

READYING FOR E DAY: "Elvis Dons Blue Suede Shoes and Polka Dots Today," Associated Press; March 1, 1960; "Sgt. Elvis to Return as Major Industry," three-part series, *Los Angeles Mirror-News*, February 24–26, 1960, "Hi, I'm Coming Home!" *Photoplay*, April 1960; "Win a day at the studio with Elvis" (homecoming contest), *Photoplay*, March 1960.

16: Priscilla

PRISCILLA BEAULIEU: personal interviews, Joe Esposito, Peter Hopkirk, Marty Lacker, Anita Wood; Esposito and Oumano, *Good Rockin' Tonight*; Goldman, *Elvis*; Nash, Smith, Lacker, and Fike, *Elvis Aaron Presley*; Presley and Harmon, *Elvis and Me*, also, mini-series of the same name, which was produced by Priscilla Beaulieu Presley, and over which she had script approval; also various articles about "the girl he left behind," including *Life*, March 14, 1960.

ANITA WOOD: personal interviews, Joe Esposito, George Klein, Anita Wood; Goldman, *Elvis*; Goldman, "The Day Elvis Made Me Cry," *Movieland & TV Time*, August 1959; "You Are My No. 1 Girl," *Movieland*, December 1957.

HOMEWARD BOUND: Jerry Hopkins interview notes, Marion Keisker; Burk, *Elvis Memories*; Hopkins, *Elvis: A Biography*; "Elvis to Swap His Army Rank for Civilian 'Mr.' Tomorrow," *Memphis Commercial Appeal*, March 3, 1960; "Elvis Dons Blue Suede Shoes and Polka Dots Today," Associated Press, March 1, 1960.

17: Déjà Vu

A RED, WHITE AND BLUE HOMECOMING: "Back to the Beat," *Photoplay Presents: Elvis*, Summer 1987; *Congressional Record*, March 1960; "Elvis

Comes Marching Home in Glory," *Elvis Presley: A Photoplay Tribute*, 1977; "Elvis's Final Army Hour a DeMille Production," *Variety*, March 9, 1960; "Elvis Signs Out, Draws Pay Today," Associated Press, March 5, 1960; "Elvis to Swap His Army Rank for Civilian 'Mr.' Tomorrow," *Memphis Commercial Appeal*, March 3, 1960; "Farewell to Priscilla; Hello to USA," *Life*, March 14, 1960.

RETURNS TO MEMPHIS: personal interviews, Bill Burk, George Klein; Burk, *Elvis Memories*; Hazen and Freeman, *Best of Elvis*; "Back to the Beat," *Photoplay Presents: Elvis*; "Crowds Greet Elvis at Memphis," United Press International, March 7, 1960; "Exhausted Elvis Plans to Stay Home, Visit 'Old Gang,' " United Press International, March 8, 1960; "Genuine Respect for Elvis Has Grown in Home Town," *Memphis Commercial Appeal*, March 8, 1960.

FRANK SINATRA SHOW: Jerry Hopkins interview notes, Gordon Stoker; "Fans Clamoring for Ex-GI," *Los Angeles Examiner*, June 1, 1960; "Idols Team Up on TV," *Life*, May 16, 1960; also, Associated Press, March 8, 1960; *New York Journal-American*, May 13, 1960.

BACK INTO RECORDING STUDIO: Amburn, *Dark Star*; Bronson, *Billboard Book of Number One Hits*; "Elvis Slips into Nashville for Platter-Cutting Session," *Nashville Tennessean*, March 31, 1960.

THE CANNY COLONEL: "Elvis Is Interviewed but Drops Few 'Poils,' " *Beverly Hills Citizen*, May 13, 1960; "He's a 'Man' Now—and an Industry," *New York Journal-American*, June 12, 1960; "The Man Who Sold Parsley," *Time*, May 16, 1960; "Money Blizzard Still Swirls Around Elvis," *Los Angeles Mirror-News*, May 11, 1960.

G.I. BLUES AND JULIET PROWSE: personal interviews, Joe Esposito, Norman Taurog (1979); Esposito and Oumano, *Good Rockin' Tonight*; Goldman, *Elvis*; "Beaming Nepal King Greets Elvis on Set," source unknown, May 11, 1960; "Elvis and Juliet," *Cosmopolitan*, October 1960; "Elvis' First Civilian Interview," *TV & Movie Screen*, May 1960; " 'New' Presley Back in States," *Nashville Tennessean*, June 19, 1960; "Is My Face Red" (Judy Fowler's account of her day on the set with Elvis), *Photoplay*, October 1960; "What You Don't Know About Elvis," *16*, January 1961; also, *Life*, October 10, 1960; *Los Angeles Mirror-News*, April 21, 1960; *Nashville Tennessean*, June 8, 1960; *Newsweek*, May 30, 1960; Hal Wallis Collection, Academy Library; Juliet Prowse interview, "Elvis Up Close," Turner Network Television.

18: Heart of Glass

VERNON PRESLEY'S WEDDING: Goldman, *Elvis*; Hopkins, *Elvis: A Biography*; Presley, the Stanley boys, and Torgoff, *Elvis*; "I wouldn't do nothing to hurt my boy, Elvis," *Photoplay*, July 1960.

DRINKING, DRUGS, AND TEMPER TANTRUMS: personal interviews,

Joe Esposito, Marty Lacker, Dr. George Nichopoulos; Esposito and Oumano, *Good Rockin' Tonight*; Fortas, *Elvis*; Nash, Smith, Lacker, and Fike, *Elvis Aaron Presley*; West, West, Hebler, and Dunleavy, *Elvis: What Happened?*; "Presley's Problem: If You Quit Rocking," *Chicago Sunday Tribune Magazine*, July 2, 1961; Elvis Presley recorded interview, on the set of *It Happened at the World's Fair*.

FLAMING STAR: personal interviews, Michael Ansara, Don Siegel (1982); "Author Revises Story So Presley Can Sing," *Los Angeles Times*, August 16, 1960; "Elvis Can Act, Says Director," *Los Angeles Mirror-News*, November 30, 1960; "Elvis' Secret Life in Hollywood," *Movie Mirror*, February 1961; press releases, Twentieth Century–Fox; also memos, Twentieth Century–Fox.

WILD IN THE COUNTRY: personal interviews, Joe Esposito, Gary Lockwood, Jo Weld; Esposito and Oumano, *Good Rockin' Tonight*; Fortas, *Elvis*; "Elvis One Jump Ahead of Fans," *Hollywood Citizen-News*, February 13, 1961; "Elvis as a Screen Lover Is 'Like a Teddy Bear,' " *Memphis Press-Scimitar*, January 7, 1961; "Elvis Presley: What the Army Did for Him," *Los Angeles Examiner*, January 3, 1961; Hedda Hopper column, various outlets, October 25, 1960; "Tuesday Weld Breaks 20-Year Silence," *Celebrity*, February 1989; "Tuesday Weld: New Girl in Hollywood," *American Weekly*, July 26, 1959; *Los Angeles Herald Tribune*, April 2, 1961; various fan-magazine accounts of the Presley-Weld romance, including "Can Tuesday Hold On to Elvis?" *Photoplay*, September 1960; various articles and reviews, including *Film Daily, Hollywood Reporter, Los Angeles Mirror-News, Variety*.

19: Man Overboard!

THE PEARL HARBOR BENEFIT: Jerry Hopkins interview notes with Gordon Stoker; Elvis Presley taped press conference in Memphis, February 25, 1961; Hopkins, *Elvis: A Biography*; Nash, *Behind Closed Doors*; "Elvis Barely Remembers but Will Aid *Arizona* Fund," *Nashville Banner*, February 27, 1961; "Elvis Raises $52,000 for Navy Memorial," Associated Press, March 27, 1961; Minnie Pearl's account of the concert in the *British Elvis Presley Fan Club Magazine*, date unknown.

BLUE HAWAII AND JOAN BLACKMAN: personal interviews, Norman Taurog (1979), George Weiss; Wallis and Higham, *Starmaker*; "The New Elvis: More Hip Than Hips," *Los Angeles Times*, July 2, 1961; "The Starlet Who Said 'No' to Elvis," *Midnight/Globe*, November 22, 1977; "Why Joan Would Say No to Elvis," *Movie Life*, October 1963; *Los Angeles Herald-Examiner*, October 28, 1963; Hal Wallis Collection, Academy Library.

WINNING OVER THE PRESS: "Elvis Presley: What the Army Did for Him," by Louella Parsons, *Los Angeles Examiner*, January 8, 1961; "Elvis: Ten Million Dollars Later," *McCall's*, February 1963; "Hedda Hopper's Hollywood," Chicago Tribune–New York News Syndicate, October 25, 1960; "If

You Keep Rockin, Can You Keep Rolling?" *Chicago Sunday Tribune* magazine, July 2, 1961.

FOLLOW THAT DREAM AND ANNE HELM: personal interviews, Richard Davis, Joe Esposito, Anne Helm; Esposito and Oumano, *Good Rockin' Tonight*; Fortas, *Elvis*; Nash, Smith, Lacker, and Fike, *Elvis Aaron Presley*; also, numerous articles regarding the making of *Follow That Dream*, including "Waiting for Elvis," *St. Petersburg* (Fla.) *Times*, July 23, 1961.

ROMANCE WITH GAIL GANLEY: personal interviews, Richard Davis, Gail Ganley.

ABOUT THE MEMPHIS MAFIA: personal interviews, Richard Davis, Joe Esposito, George Klein, Marty Lacker, Gary Lockwood, Dr. George Nichopoulos; Esposito and Oumano, *Good Rockin' Tonight*; Fortas, *Elvis*; Nash, Smith, Lacker, and Fike, *Elvis Aaron Presley*; Presley and Harmon, *Elvis and Me*; West, West, Hebler, and Dunleavy, *Elvis: What Happened?*; "At Home With Elvis," *Memphis Commercial Appeal*, March 7, 1965; "Elvis Sets Record Straight," *Los Angeles Herald-Examiner*, November 7, 1964; "Elvis Sparked a New Breed," Associated Press, August 13, 1965; "Elvis Wants Love, Marriage," *Nashville Banner*, February 26, 1965; "Forever Elvis," *Time*, May 7, 1965; "Millionaire Still Seeks Something," *Los Angeles Herald-Examiner*, November 17, 1965; "Peter Pan in Blue Suede Shoes," *Los Angeles Times*, January 31, 1965; "Presley's Powder-puff Pals," *On the QT*, June 1957; rare one-hour video interview with Cliff Gleaves; Elvis Presley recorded interview, on the set of *It Happened at the World's Fair*.

20: Foreplay

PRISCILLA: personal interviews, Nancy Anderson, Sandra Harmon; Fortas, *Elvis*; Presley and Harmon, *Elvis and Me*, also the miniseries of the same title; "My Cherished Memories of Elvis," *Elvis Presley: A Photoplay Tribute*, 1977.

ANITA WOOD: personal interviews, Nancy Anderson, Anita Wood; Presley and Harmon, *Elvis and Me*, also the miniseries of the same title; "My Cherished Memories of Elvis," *Elvis Presley: A Photoplay Tribute*, 1977.

ELVIS ON MARRIAGE: "Elvis Presley: How He Changed His Public Image," *Parade*, November 4, 1962; "Elvis Presley: Rich, Famous, Still Single," source unknown, June 14, 1962.

21: Toys in the Attic

PRISCILLA AT GRACELAND: personal interviews, Joe Esposito, Johna Danovi Fenrick, Sandra Harmon, Sherry Riggins, Becky Yancey, Dorothy Weems; Esposito and Oumano, *Good Rockin' Tonight*; Fortas, *Elvis*; Nash, Smith, Lacker, and Fike, *Elvis Aaron Presley*; Presley and Harmon, *Elvis and Me*, also the miniseries of the same title; Whitmer, *The Inner Elvis*; Yancey and Linedecker, *My Life With Elvis*; "Amazing Graceland," *Vista USA*, spring 1995; "My Cherished Memories of Elvis," *Elvis Presley: A Photoplay Tribute*, 1977.

22: Viva Ann-Margret

ROMANCE WITH ANN-MARGRET: personal interviews, Nancy Anderson, Richard Davis, Joe Esposito, Gail Ganley, Cathy Griffen, Sidney Guilaroff, George Klein, Joanne Lyman, Becky Yancey; correspondence to authors from Roger Smith (Ann-Margret's husband); Ann-Margret and Gold, *Ann-Margret*; Goldman, *Elvis*; "Ann-Margret to Be Presented to Queen," *Los Angeles Times*, August 30, 1963; "Ann-Margret's Success Story," Sheilah Graham column, source unknown, February 26, 1964; "Can Ann-Margret Make Elvis the Marrying Kind?" *Modern Screen*, November 1963; "It Looks Like Romance for Presley and Ann-Margret," Associated Press, August 6, 1963; Ann-Margret TV interview with Larry King, February 14, 1994.

23: Animal House

A CHANGED MAN: Nash, Smith, Lacker, and Fike, *Elvis Aaron Presley*; "Elvis Gets New $9,300 Wardrobe," Associated Press, September 19, 1962; "Elvis Presley: How he changed his public image," *Parade*, November 4, 1962; also, Elvis Presley's feature films produced between 1961 and 1967.

PARTY TIME: personal interviews, Karen Conrad (aka Bonnie Karlyle), Richard Davis, June Ellis, Joe Esposito, Anne Helm, Kitty Jones, Gary Lockwood, Joanne Lyman; Esposito and Oumano, *Good Rockin' Tonight*; Fortas, *Elvis*; Goldman, *Elvis*; Nash, Smith, Lacker, and Fike, *Elvis Aaron Presley*; West, West, Hebler, and Dunleavy, *Elvis: What Happened?*; "Elvis Left Me in the Middle of the Night," *Modern Screen*, August 1964; "Elvis Secretly Engaged to 18-Year-Old," *Photoplay*, January 1964; "Elvis Was a Dull Date," *Midnight Globe*, December 13, 1977; "How Elvis Stole Johnny Crawford's Girl," *Movie Stars*, August 1963; "I Got Dates for Elvis Presley," *Movie Life*, January 1978; "Is Elvis Afraid?" *On the QT*, September 1961; "The Truth About Those Presley Parties," *Photoplay*, October 1964.

FOOTBALL: personal interviews, Richard Davis, Joe Esposito, Gary Lockwood; Bashe, *Teenage Idol, Travelin' Man*; Fortas, *Elvis*; Goldman, *Elvis*; Hopkins, *Elvis: A Biography*.

24: Nowhere Man

ELVIS TURNS THIRTY: "At Home With Elvis," *Memphis Commercial Appeal*, March 7, 1965; "Elvis Sparked a New Breed," Associated Press, August 13, 1965; "Elvis Wants Love, Marriage," *Nashville Banner*, February 26,

1965; "Forever Elvis," *Time*, May 7, 1965; "Peter Pan in Blue Suede Shoes," *Los Angeles Times*, January 31, 1965.

MOVIE DAZE: personal interviews, Merry Anders, Michael Ansara, Edward Bernds, Tony Curtis, Richard Davis, Fred De Cordova, Richard Devon, Anthony Eisley, Anne Helm, Sue Ane Langdon, Lance Le Gault, Mary Ann Mobley, William Schallert, Jeremy Slate, Norman Taurog (in 1979); Jerry Hopkins interview notes with Michael Dante; Downing, *Charles Bronson*; Rijff and Van Gestel, *Elvis*; Smith, *Starring Miss Barbara Stanwyck*; Wallis, *Finding My Way*; "Day of the Kiss," *Los Angeles Herald-Examiner*, September 11, 1966; "Hollywood Women Talk About Elvis," *Midnight/Globe*, September 13, 1977; "How the King Changed My Life with a Song," *Midnight/Globe*, November 22, 1977; "Millionaire Still Seeks Something," *Los Angeles Herald-Examiner*, November 17, 1965; "Presley Sets Record Straight," *Los Angeles Herald-Examiner*, November 7, 1964; "Rugged Elvis Shows Muscle," *Los Angeles Herald-Examiner*, September 19, 1965; "Sue Ane Langdon," *Filmfax*, March/April 1996; *Elvis Presley: A Photoplay Tribute*, 1977; Hal Wallis Collection, Academy Library.

BEATLEMANIA: Goldman, *Lives of John Lennon*; Rayl, *Beatles '64*; "The Beatles: Music's Gold Bugs," *Saturday Evening Post*, March 21, 1964, plus scores of other articles regarding the British invasion, and single-issue magazines including *Beatles 'Round the World*, winter 1964; *Rolling Stone "Special Beatles Anniversary Issue*," February 16, 1984.

MEET THE BEATLES: personal interviews, Richard Davis, Joe Esposito; Fortas, *Elvis*; Goldman, *Elvis* and *Lives of John Lennon*; Nash, Smith, Lacker, and Fike, *Elvis Aaron Presley*.

RELIGION AND SELF-REALIZATION: personal interviews, Becky Martin, Dorothy Phillips, Sam Phillips, Dr. Peter Whitmer, Deborah Walley; Goldman, *Elvis*; Fortas, *Elvis*; Stearn, *Elvis*; Stearn and Geller, *Truth About Elvis*; "Daddy-O-Dewey," *Memphis Flyer*, January 4–10, 1996; plus literally hundreds of articles about Presley and his career that mention the significance of religion in his life.

RECLUSIVENESS: See articles cited above ("Elvis turns thirty"); also: "A Changed Man After the Army," *Los Angeles Herald-Examiner*, November 20, 1965; "Elvis: Ten Million Dollars Later," *McCall's*, February 1963.

25: Don't Fence Me In

THE HOME ON THE RANGE: personal interviews, Joe Esposito, Marty Lacker, Mike McGregor, Dr. George Nichopoulos; Clayton and Heard, *Elvis Up Close*; Esposito and Oumano, *Good Rockin' Tonight*; Fortas, *Elvis*; Goldman, *Elvis*; Nash, Smith, Lacker, and Fike, *Elvis Aaron Presley*; Presley and Harmon, *Elvis and Me*.

26: The Groom Wore Black

THE WEDDING: personal interviews, Nancy Anderson, Stanley Brossette, Richard Davis, Sandra Harmon, George Klein, Marty Lacker, Dorothy Treloar, Dr. Peter Whitmer, Becky Yancey; Esposito and Oumano, *Good Rockin' Tonight*; Fortas, *Elvis*; Goldman, *Elvis*; Nash, Smith, Lacker, and Fike, *Elvis Aaron Presley*; Presley and Harmon, *Elvis and Me*, also the miniseries of the same title; Stearn and Geller, *Truth About Elvis*; Tobler and Wooton, *Elvis*; "Elvis: By his father, Vernon Presley," *Good Housekeeping*, January 1978; "Elvis Trades Blue Suede Bachelor Shoes for Bride," Associated Press, May 2, 1967; "Presley, Brunette Beauty in Surprise Vegas Wedding," *Las Vegas Sun*, May 2, 1967, and various other articles about Elvis's hastily arranged wedding.

TROUBLES DURING CLAMBAKE: personal interviews, Joe Esposito, Arthur Gardner, Will Hutchins, Dr. George Nichopoulos; Fortas, *Elvis*; Goldman, *Elvis*; Nash, Smith, Lacker, and Fike, *Elvis Aaron Presley*; Presley and Harmon, *Elvis and Me*; Stearn and Geller, *Truth About Elvis*.

THE HONEYMOON: personal interview, Joe Esposito; also, Esposito's home movies; Presley and Harmon, *Elvis and Me*, also the miniseries of the same title.

27: Renaissance Man

LOVE AND MARRIAGE: personal interview, Becky Yancey; Goldman, *Elvis*; Presley and Harmon, *Elvis and Me*, also the miniseries of the same title; Yancey and Linedecker, *My Life With Elvis*; "Pelvis Out, Guns In for Elvis," *Los Angeles Herald-Examiner*, October 19, 1968.

BIRTH OF LISA MARIE: personal interviews, Maurice Elliott, Joe Esposito; Presley and Harmon, *Elvis and Me*, also the miniseries of the same title; various articles from Associated Press and United Press International, February 6–9, 1968.

THE COMEBACK SPECIAL: personal interviews, Steve Binder, Joe Esposito, Lance Le Gault; the Steve Binder Collection, UCLA; Clayton and Heard, *Elvis Up Close*; Fortas, *Elvis*; Goldman, *Elvis*; Hammontree, *Elvis Presley*; Hopkins, *Elvis: A Biography*; Marsh, *Elvis*; Whitmer, *The Inner Elvis*; "The Indomitable Snowman Who Built Himself—and Elvis Too," *TV Guide*, November 30, 1968; "Elvis to Sing, Swing Before TV Cameras Once More," *Los Angeles Times*, June 27, 1968; "RCA Rattle & Roll on Elvis," *Billboard*, November 30, 1968; also, dozens of reviews from around the country, and from various Elvis Presley fan clubs, including the Elvis Presley Fan Club of Southern California; also, the NBC-TV special itself and hours of outtakes from the production (authors' collection).

BACK BEFORE THE CAMERAS: personal interviews, Richard Davis, Lance Le Gault, Marlyn Mason; Goldman, *Elvis*; Moore, *After All*; "Elvis Presley . . . the Adult Comedian," *Los Angeles Herald-Examiner*, April 3, 1968;

"Elvis Lives!" *West* magazine, February 18, 1968; "Elvis Presley Lives," *Cosmopolitan*, November 1968.

28: A Place in the Sun

THE MEMPHIS SESSIONS: Bronson, *Billboard Book of Number One Hits*; Nash, Smith, Lacker, and Fike, *Elvis Aaron Presley*; "Elvis Returns to the Fount," *Billboard*, March 29, 1969; "Relaxed Elvis Disks 16 Songs in Hometown Stint," *Memphis Commercial Appeal*, January 23, 1969; "!64 Chart Records in 18 Months!" *Billboard*, March 29, 1969.

THE LAS VEGAS COMEBACK: Bova and Nowels, *My Love Affair With Elvis*; Hess, *Viva Las Vegas*; Hopkins, *Elvis: A Biography*; Nash, Smith, Lacker, and Fike, *Elvis Aaron Presley*; Riese, *Her Name Is Barbra*; "Elvis: An Artistic Renaissance," *Los Angeles Herald-Examiner*, August 12, 1969; "Return of the Big Beat," *Time*, August 15, 1969; "Return of the Pelvis," *Newsweek*, August 11, 1969; dozens of articles about the Las Vegas show from publications including *Billboard*, *Los Angeles Free Press*, *Los Angeles Times*, *New Musical Express*, *New Yorker*, United Press International, *Variety*; Las Vegas International Hotel press releases, July 1969; RCA Records press releases, July 1969; also, news footage regarding the Las Vegas opening, authors' collection.

THE CONCERTS: Shaver, *Elvis in Focus*; "A gross top-grosser," *Life*, March 20, 1970; "A King in a Velvet Jail," *Memphis Commercial Appeal, Mid-South Magazine*, May 24, 1970; "Elvis Is Back! Due at Rodeo Friday," February 26, 1970, and "Presley Headlines '70 Houston Rodeo," October 24, 1969, both *Houston Chronicle*; "Elvis Oozes in Denver," *Boulder*, December 2, 1970; "Promoter Swings Deal for Presley at the Forum," *Los Angeles Times*, October 25, 1970; "The Rediscovery of Elvis," *New York Times Magazine*, October 11, 1970; "Ringling Bros., Kings Never Traveled in Presley's Style," *Tupelo Daily Journal*, November 24, 1971.

29: Crazy from the Heat

THE CONCERTS: See "The concerts," chapter 28 notes.

LOCAL BOY MAKES GOOD: Elvis Presley Heights Garden Club (authors), *Elvis Presley Heights, Mississippi, Lee County, 1921–1984*; "Ribbon-Cutting Opens Presley Birthplace to Public Officially," *Tupelo Daily Journal*, June 2, 1971; numerous articles and photographs on the Jaycees' award, *Memphis Commercial Appeal* and *Memphis Press-Scimitar* during January 1971.

FIRST BIOGRAPHY: personal interview, Jerry Hopkins; Hopkins, *Elvis: A Biography*; "50,000,000 Elvis Fans Can't Be Wrong," *Coast*, September 1971; "The Making of the Presley Biography," *Rolling Stone*, September 30, 1971.

PATERNITY SUIT: *Los Angeles Times*, August 30, 1970; "Presley Paternity Suit!" *Rona Barrett's Hollywood*, November 1970;

ELVIS MEETS NIXON: personal interview, Jerry Schilling (1989); Krogh, *Day Elvis Met Nixon*; "Ex-Memphian tells about when the King met the President," *Memphis Commercial Appeal*, December 21, 1995; "Presley Gets Narcotics Bureau Badge," *Washington Post*, January 27, 1972; copy of letter from Richard Nixon to Elvis, December 31, 1970; authors' tour of the Richard Nixon Library & Birthplace (Yorba Linda, Calif.).

30: His Latest Flames

LOVE AND MARRIAGE: personal interviews, Joyce Bova, Joe Esposito, George Klein, George Nichopoulos, Sam Thompson, Jere Walker, Kathy Westmoreland; Bova and Nowels, *My Love Affair With Elvis*; Esposito and Oumano, *Good Rockin' Tonight*; Goldman, *Elvis*; Hopkins, *Elvis: The Final Years*; Westmoreland and Quinn, *Elvis and Kathy*; "Elvis," *McCall's*, July 1980; "Elvis and the Ladies He Left Behind," *Rona Barrett's Hollywood*, October 1979; "Linda Loved Elvis—But," *Midnight/Globe*, December 20, 1977; also, *Life*, February 10, 1995, and dozens of newspaper articles, circa 1972–75.

NEW YORK, NEW YORK: "Elvis! David!" *New Yorker*, June 24, 1972; "Elvis Says Madison Square Garden Finally Big Enough for His Show," *Memphis Commercial Appeal*, June 10, 1972; "Press Conference: Elvis & the Colonel," *Hit Parader*, December 1972; newsreel footage of New York press conference, authors' collection.

ALOHA FROM HAWAII: Esposito and Oumano, *Good Rockin' Tonight*; Goldman, *Elvis*; Hopkins, *Elvis: The Final Years*; Worth and Tamerius, *Elvis: His Life from A to Z*; the TV special *Elvis: Aloha from Hawaii*.

31: Addiction

DRUG PROBLEMS AND HOSPITALIZATIONS: personal interviews, Dr. Pierre Brissette (pharmacology consultant, Bois Physical Medicine Institute, Paris; specialist in cortisone), Maurice Elliott, Joe Esposito, Dick Grob, Tish Henley, Marty Lacker, Sandi Miller, Dr. George Nichopoulos, UCLA toxicologist Dr. Forest Tennant, Dr. Stanley A. Terman (medical director, Institute for Strategic Changes, San Diego, Calif.), Sam Thompson, Kathy Westmoreland, Dr. Ronald Wright (coroner, Broward County, Fla.); Goldman, *Elvis*; Hopkins, *Elvis: The Final Years*; "Elvis," *McCall's*, July 1980; "Elvis Sends Love, Flowers, to Woman, 84," *Memphis Press-Scimitar*, November 1, 1973; "Mystery drug girl in Presley book: I am the one who nearly died in Elvis's arms," *Star*, October 18, 1977; Memphis Board of Medical License Hearing—depositions of Dr. George Nichopoulos and Dr. Forest Tennant; the final copy of the "Attorney Confidential Work Project" of James Neal, Memphis Board of Medical License Hearing; complete set of confidential reports, logs, and lab tests of all of Elvis Presley's detoxification periods at Memphis Baptist Hospital; confidential statements given to physicians by Elvis Presley, Linda

Thompson, and Dr. George Nichopoulos; all test results from three different detox sessions; inventory of all drugs taken by Presley.

PRISCILLA AND THE DIVORCE: Goldman, *Elvis*; Presley and Harmon, *Elvis and Me*, also the miniseries of the same title; "My Life With and Without Elvis Presley," *Ladies' Home Journal*, August 1973; "Priscilla Presley: Bringing Up Elvis' Daughter," *Ladies' Home Journal*, February 1974; various newspaper clippings regarding the divorce, including "Priscilla Presley Gets a Kiss and a $1.5 Million Settlement," Associated Press, October 10, 1973; Priscilla's comments, BBC documentary *Elvis: His Life and Times*.

THE MIKE STONE "HIT": Esposito and Oumano, *Good Rockin' Tonight*; Parker, *Inside Elvis*; West, West, Hebler, and Dunleavy, *Elvis: What Happened?*

32: Chemical Warfare

DRUG PROBLEMS AND HOSPITALIZATIONS: See "Drug problems and hospitalizations," chapter 31 notes. Also, dozens of articles about Presley's hospital stays in Memphis, including "Elvis Suffering Enlarged Colon," *Tupelo Daily Journal*, August 30–31, 1975; "Elvis Suffering Intestinal Blockage," United Press International, February 3, 1975; and "Presley Feeling Well After Unknown Ailment," Associated Press, January 31, 1975.

DIETARY WOES: personal interviews, Joe Esposito, Marty Lacker, Dr. George Nichopoulos, Becky Yancey; Adler, *Life and Cuisine of Elvis Presley*; Cocke, *I Called Him Babe*; Goldman, *Elvis*; Jenkins and Pease, *Memories Beyond Graceland Gates*; countless newspaper clippings regarding Presley's eating habits; TV documentary, *The Burger and the King*.

THE CONCERTS: personal interviews, Joe Esposito, Dr. George Nichopoulos, Kathy Westmoreland; Esposito and Oumano, *Good Rockin' Tonight*; Goldman, *Elvis*; Hopkins, *Elvis: The Final Years*; Westmoreland and Quinn, *Elvis and Kathy*; "Hucksters, 49,100 Elvisites Whoop It Up," *Memphis Press-Scimitar*, March 18, 1974; "You Could Hear a Pin Drop," *Elvis International Forum*, spring 1996; also, various stories and reviews from newspapers including the *Los Angeles Herald-Examiner* and the *Los Angeles Times*; Ronnie Tutt comments, video, *Elvis: The Echo Will Never Die*.

"FORTY AND FAT": "Elvis the Pelvis Turns 40, but He Isn't All Shook Up," *People*, January 13, 1975; "He Rocks 'n' Rolls 'n' Puffs Along While Fans Love Elvis Tenderly," *Memphis Press-Scimitar*, June 11, 1975.

33: Strange Days

ON THE ROAD AGAIN: personal interviews, Ginger and Jo Alden, Joe Esposito, Dr. George Nichopoulos, Kathy Westmoreland; De Witt, *Auld Lang Syne*; Esposito and Oumano, *Good Rockin' Tonight*; Geller and Spector, *If I*

Can Dream; Goldman, *Elvis*; Hopkins, *Elvis: The Final Years*; Westmoreland and Quinn, *Elvis and Kathy*.

34: Blue City

GINGER ALDEN: personal interviews, Ginger, Jo, and Rosemary Alden, Larry Anthony, Joe Esposito, George Klein, Marty Lacker, Dr. George Nichopoulos, Sam Thompson; "Elvis Planned to Wed Ginger at Christmas," *Midnight/Globe*, November 15, 1977; "Ginger Alden Speaks: Elvis Was Gentle, Jealous & Passionate," *Midnight/Globe*, June 27, 1978; "World's at Standstill for Elvis' Fiancée," *Memphis Commercial Appeal*, August 18, 1977.

THE DEATH: personal interviews, Ginger and Jo Alden, Dr. Dan Brookoff (pathologist, director of medical education, Methodist Hospital, Memphis), Joe Esposito, Jerry Hopkins, Ulysses Jones, Dr. Kevin S. Merigian (Memphis pathologist), Dave McGriff, Donna Presley Nash, Dr. Thomas Noguchi (former coroner, Los Angeles County), Jim Orwood (Shelby County sheriff's deputy), Sam Thompson, Vernon Presley (1979); Esposito and Oumano, *Good Rockin' Tonight*; Goldman, *Elvis*; Hopkins, *Elvis: The Final Years*; Noguchi, *Coroner at Large*; Thompson and Cole, *Death of Elvis*; also, literally hundreds of articles, dated 1977–87, regarding the death of Elvis Presley, including "The Death of Elvis Presley," *Dixie*, August 12, 1987; "Dr. Nick: Did He Fuel Elvis' Pill Habit or Try to Help Him Kick It?" *People*, October 8, 1979; "Elvis Was a Pill Head," *Melody Maker*, February 2, 1980.

THE MEDIA COVERAGE: personal interviews, Bill E. Burk, Maurice Elliott, Joe Esposito, Bob Kendall (1987), Jim Kingsley (1987), George Klein, Sam Phillips, William Thomas (1987), Red West (1987); Gregory, *When Elvis Died*; "After Death It Was War," *Los Angeles Times*, August 16, 1987 (based on months of research/interviews by author Pat H. Broeske); also, literally hundreds of articles, dated 1977–1987, regarding the death of Elvis Presley.

Epilogue: Long Live the King

CONCLUSION: personal interview, Maurice Elliott, detailing the public relations disaster following Presley's death; Complete Autopsy: The Death of Elvis Presley (natural death: ordered sealed), addendum to the Autopsy; Dr. Forest Tennant's reports, studies and statistical tables (filling five file drawers); Orange County, Ca. Bioscience Toxological Report; Dr. Kevin S. Meridian, Analysis of the Toxological Reports; Complete statement, Memphis coroner Dr. Larry Francisco, from press conference.

Bibliography

Books

Adler, David. *The Life and Cuisine of Elvis Presley*. New York: Crown, 1993.

Adler, David, and Ernest Andrews. *Elvis My Dad: The Unauthorized Biography of Lisa Marie Presley*. New York: St. Martin's Paperbacks, 1990.

Amburn, Ellis. *Dark Star: The Roy Orbison Story*. New York: Lyle Stuart, 1991.

Ann-Margret, with Todd Gold. *Ann-Margret: My Story*. New York: Berkley Books, 1994.

Bacon, James. *How Sweet It Is: The Jackie Gleason Story*. New York: St. Martin's Press, 1985.

Bane, Michael. *White Boy Singin' the Blues: The Black Roots of White Rock*. New York: Da Capo, 1992.

————.*Who's Who in Rock: Over 1,200 Personalities That Made Rock Happen*. New York: Facts on File, 1981.

Bartell, Pauline. *Reel Elvis! The Ultimate Trivia Guide to the King's Movies*. Dallas: Taylor Publishing, 1994.

Barth, Jack. *Roadside Elvis: The Complete State-by-State Travel Guide for Elvis Presley Fans*. Chicago: Contemporary Books, 1991.

Bashe, Philip. *Teenage Idol, Travelin' Man: The Complete Biography of Rick Nelson*. New York: Hyperion, 1992.

Belz, Carl. *The Story of Rock*. New York: Harper Colophon Books, 1972.

Berkow, Robert, M.D., ed. *The Merck Manual: Diagnosis and Therapy*. New Jersey: Merck, Sharp and Dohme, 1995.

Booth, Stanley. *Rhythm Oil: A Journey Through the Music of the American South*. London: Jonathan Cape, 1991.

Bova, Joyce, As Told to William Conrad Nowels. *My Love Affair With Elvis: Don't Ask Forever*. New York: Pinnacle Books, 1994.

Bowles, Jerry. *A Thousand Sundays: The Story of the Ed Sullivan Show*. New York: G. P. Putnam's, 1980.

Bowman, Kathleen. *On Stage Elvis Presley*. Minnesota: Creative Education Society, 1977.

Bowser, James W., ed. *Starring Elvis: Elvis Presley's Greatest Movies, Stories and Photos*. New York: Dell, 1977.

Bronson, Fred. *The Billboard Book of Number One Hits*. New York: Billboard Books, 1992.

Brown, David. *Let Me Entertain You*. New York: William Morrow, 1990.

Brown, Gene. *Movie Time: A Chronology of Hollywood and the Movie Industry from Its Beginnings to the Present.* New York: Macmillan, 1995.

Brown, Les. *The New York Times Encyclopedia of Television.* New York: Times Books, 1977.

Burk, Bill E. *Early Elvis: The Humes Years.* Memphis: Red Oak Press, 1990.

———. *Early Elvis: The Tupelo Years.* Memphis: Propwash, 1994.

———. *Elvis in Canada.* Memphis: Propwash, 1996.

———. *Elvis Memories: Press Between the Pages.* Memphis: Propwash, 1993.

———. *Elvis Through My Eyes.* Memphis: Burk Enterprises, 1987.

Buskin, Richard. *Elvis: Memories and Memorabilia.* London: Salamander Books, 1995.

Byworth, Tony. *The History of Country & Western Music.* New York: Bison Books, 1984.

Carr, Roy, and Mick Farren. *Elvis Presley: The Illustrated Record.* New York: Harmony Books, 1982.

Choron, Sandra, and Bob Oskam. *Elvis: The Last Word: The 328 Best (and Worst) Things Anyone Ever Said About "The King."* New York: Citadel, 1991.

Clayton, Rose, and Dick Heard, eds. *Elvis Up Close: In the words of those who knew him best.* Atlanta: Turner, 1994.

Cocke, Marian J. *I Called Him Babe: Elvis Presley's Nurse Remembers.* Memphis: Memphis State University Press, 1979.

Cotten, Lee. *All Shook Up: Elvis Day-by-Day, 1954–1977.* Michigan: Popular Culture, Ink, 1985.

———. *Did Elvis Sing in Your Hometown?* Sacramento: High Sierra Books, 1995.

———. *The Elvis Catalog: Memorabilia, Icons, and Collectibles Celebrating the King of Rock 'n' Roll.* New York: Dolphin, 1987.

Crenshaw, Marshall. *Hollywood Rock: A Guide to Rock 'n' Roll in the Movies.* New York: HarperPerennial, 1994.

Crumbaker, Marge with Gabe Tucker. *Up and Down With Elvis Presley.* New York: G. P. Putnam's Sons, 1981.

Curtin, Jim. *Elvis and the Stars.* Pennsylvania: Morgin Press, 1993.

———. *Unseen Elvis: Candids of the King.* Boston: Bullfinch Press, 1992.

Davis, Skeeter. *Bus Fare to Kentucky: The Autobiography of Skeeter Davis.* New York: Birch Lane Press, 1993.

Dawson, Jim, and Steve Propes. *What Was the First Rock 'n' Roll Record?* Boston: Faber and Faber, 1992.

De Witt, Howard A. *Elvis: The Sun Years. The Story of Elvis Presley in the Fifties.* Michigan: Popular Culture, Ink, 1993.

De Witt, Simon. *Auld Lang Syne: Elvis' Legendary New Year's Eve Show in Pittsburgh, Pa., 1976.* Netherlands: Simon de Witt Prods., 1995.

Doll, Susan. *The Films of Elvis Presley.* Illinois: Publications International, 1991.

———. *Portrait of a Young Rebel: Elvis the Early Years.* Illinois: Publications International, 1990.

———. *Portrait of the King.* Illinois: Publications International, 1995.

Downing, David. *Charles Bronson*. New York: St. Martin's, 1983.

Dundy, Elaine. *Elvis and Gladys*. New York: Dell, 1985.

Edwards, Michael. *Priscilla, Elvis and Me*. New York: St. Martin's, 1988.

Ehrenstein, David and Bill Reed. *Rock on Film*. New York: G. P. Delilah Books, 1982.

Eisen, Jonathan, ed. *The Age of Rock: Sounds of the American Cultural Revolution*. New York: Vintage Books, 1969.

Esposito, Joe and Elena Oumano. *Good Rockin' Tonight: Twenty years on the road and on the town with Elvis*. New York: Simon & Schuster, 1994.

Farren, Mick and Pearce Marchbank. *Elvis in His Own Words*. London: Omnibus Press, 1994.

Fisher, Eddie. *Eddie: My Life, My Loves*. New York: Harper & Row, 1981.

Flippo, Chet. *Everybody Was Kung-Fu Dancing: Chronicles of the Lionized and the Notorious*. New York: St. Martin's, 1991.

———. *Graceland: The Living Legacy of Elvis Presley*. San Francisco: Collins Publishers, 1993.

Fortas, Alan. *Elvis: From Memphis to Hollywood*. Michigan: Popular Culture, Ink, 1992.

Frew, Timothy. *Elvis*. London: Grange Books, 1992.

Geller, Larry, and Joel Spector, with Patricia Romanowski. *If I Can Dream: Elvis' Own Story*. New York: Simon and Schuster, 1989.

Gentry, Tony. *Elvis Presley*. New York: Chelsea House, 1994.

Gibson, Robert, and Sid Shaw. *Elvis: A King Forever*. New York: McGraw-Hill, 1985.

Goldman, Albert. *Elvis*. New York: Avon, 1981.

———. *Elvis: The Last 24 Hours*. New York: St. Martin's, 1991.

———. *The Lives of John Lennon*. New York: Bantam, 1989.

Gordon, Robert. *Elvis: The King on the Road*. New York: St. Martin's Press, 1996.

———. *It Came from Memphis*. Boston: Faber and Faber, 1995.

Gray, Michael and Roger Osborne. *Elvis Atlas: A Journey Through Elvis Presley's America*. New York: Henry Holt, 1996.

Green, Margo Haven, Dorothy Nelson, and Darlene M. Levenger. *Graceland*. Michigan: Trio Publishing, 1994.

Gregory, James. *The Elvis Presley Story*. New York: Hillman Books, 1960.

Gregory, Neal, and Janice Neal. *When Elvis Died*. New York: Pharos, 1992.

Grissim, John. *Country Music: White Man's Blues*. New York: Paperback Library, 1970.

Grob, Richard H. *The Elvis Conspiracy?* Nevada: Fox Reflections, 1979.

Grove, Martin A. *Elvis: The Legend Lives*. New York: Manor Books, 1978.

Guralnick, Peter. *Last Train to Memphis: The Rise of Elvis Presley*. New York: Little, Brown, 1994.

Guterman, Jimmy. *Rockin' My Life Away: Listening to Jerry Lee Lewis*. Nashville: Rutledge Hill Press, 1991.

Hagan, Chet. *Grand Ole Opry*. New York: Henry Holt, 1989.

Haining, Peter, ed. *Elvis in Private*. New York: St. Martin's, 1987.

———. *The Elvis Presley Scrapbooks, 1955–1965*. London: Robert Hale, 1991.

Halberstam, David. *The Fifties*. New York: Villard Books, 1993.

Hammontree, Patsy Guy. *Elvis Presley: A Bio-Bibliography*. Connecticut: Greenwood Press, 1985.

Hanna, David. *Elvis: Lonely Star at the Top*. New York: Leisure Books, 1977.

Hannaford, Jim. *Elvis: Golden Ride on the Mystery Train, Volume II*. Oklahoma: Jim Hannaford Prods., 1991.

———. *Elvis: Golden Ride on the Mystery Train, Volume III*. Oklahoma: Jim Hannaford Prods., 1994.

———. *Inside "Jailhouse Rock."* Alva, Okla.: Jim Hannaford Prods., 1992.

Harbinson, W. A. *The Illustrated Elvis*. New York: Tempo Star Books, 1977.

Harbinson, W. A. with Kay Wheeler. *Growing Up with the Memphis Flash*. Amsterdam: Tutti Frutti Productions, 1994.

Harms, Valerie. *Tryin' to Get to You: The Story of Elvis Presley*. New York: Atheneum/SMI, 1979.

Harris, Michael David. *Always on Sunday: Ed Sullivan, an Inside View*. New York: Meredith Press, 1968.

Hazen, Cindy, and Mike Freeman. *The Best of Elvis: Recollections of a Great Humanitarian*. Memphis: Memphis Explorations, 1992.

Helfer, Ralph. *The Beauty of the Beasts: Tales of Hollywood's Wild Animal Stars*. Los Angeles: Jeremy P. Tarcher, 1990.

Hemfelt, Robert, Frank Minirth, and Paul Meier. *Love Is a Choice: Recovery for Co-Dependent Relationships*. Nashville: Thomas Nelson, Inc., 1989.

Hemphill, Paul. *The Nashville Sound: Bright Lights and Country Music*. New York: Simon and Schuster, 1970.

Henry, William A., III. *The Great One: The Life and Legend of Jackie Gleason*. New York: Doubleday, 1992.

Hess, Alan. *Viva Las Vegas: After-Hours Architecture*. San Francisco: Chronicle, 1993.

Higgins, Patrick. *Before Elvis, There Was Nothing*. New York: Carroll & Graf, 1994.

Hodge, Charlie, with Charles Goodman. *Me 'n Elvis*. Memphis: Castle Books, 1988.

Hopkins, Jerry. *Elvis: A Biography*. New York: Warner Books, 1971.

———. *Elvis: The Final Years*. New York: Berkley, 1983.

Hopkins, Jerry, and Danny Sugerman. *No One Here Gets Out Alive*. New York: Warner Books, 1980.

Hopper, Hedda, and James Brough. *The Whole Truth and Nothing But*. New York: Pyramid Books, 1963.

Hutchins, Chris, and Peter Thompson. *Elvis & Lennon: The Untold Story of Their Deadly Feud*. Great Britain: Smith Gryphon, 1996.

Jenkins, Mary, as Told to Beth Pease. *Memories Beyond Graceland Gates*. Buena Park, Calif.: West Coast, 1989.

Jenkins, Peter and Friends. *The Tennessee Sampler*. Nashville: Thomas Nelson, 1985.

Jones, Ira, as Told to Bill E. Burk. *Soldier Boy Elvis*. Memphis: Propwash Publishing, 1992.

Jørgensen, Ernst, Erik Rasmussen, and Johnny Mikkelsen. *Elvis Presley: Recording Sessions.* Denmark: JEE-production, 1977.

Kelley, Kitty. *His Way: The Unauthorized Biography of Frank Sinatra.* New York: Bantam, 1986.

Keylin, Arleen, ed. *The Fabulous Fifties: As Reported by the New York Times.* New York: Arno Press, 1978.

Kingsbury, Paul. *The Grand Ole Opry History of Country Music: 70 Years of the Songs, the Stars, and the Stories.* New York: Villard, 1995.

Krogh, Egil "Bud." *The Day Elvis Met Nixon.* Washington: Pejama Press, 1994.

Lacker, Marty, Patsy Lacker, and Leslie S. Smith. *Elvis: Portrait of a Friend.* New York: Bantam Books, 1980.

Latham, Caroline. *Priscilla and Elvis: The Priscilla Presley Story, an Unauthorized Biography.* New York: Signet, 1985.

Latham, Caroline, and Jeannie Sakol. *E Is for Elvis: An A-to-Z Illustrated Guide to the King of Rock and Roll.* New York: NAL Books, 1990.

Leviton, Jay B., and Ger J. Rijff. *Elvis Close-Up.* New York: Fireside, 1987.

Levy, Alan. *Operation Elvis.* New York: Henry Holt, 1960.

Lewis, Marlo, and Minabess Lewis. *Prime Time.* Los Angeles: J. P. Tarcher, Inc., 1979.

Lewis, Myrna, with Murray Silver. *Great Balls of Fire! The True Story of Jerry Lee Lewis.* London: Virgin Books, 1982.

Lichter, Paul. *The Boy Who Dared to Rock: The Definitive Elvis.* New York: Dolphin Books, 1978.

———. *Elvis in Hollywood.* New York: Simon and Schuster, 1975.

———. *Elvis Presley: Behind Closed Doors.* Huntington Valley, Pa.: Jesse Books, 1987.

———. *Elvis: Rebel Heart.* Huntington Valley, Pa.: Jesse Books, 1992.

Loyd, Harold. *Elvis Presley's Graceland Gates.* Franklin, Tenn.: Jimmy Velvet Publications, 1987.

Lynn, Loretta, and George Vecsy. *Loretta Lynn: Coal Miner's Daughter.* New York: DaCapo Press, 1996.

Mann, David. *Elvis.* Van Nuys, Calif.: Bible Voice, 1977.

Mann, May. *The Private Elvis.* New York: Pocket Books, 1977.

Mansfield, Rex, and Elisabeth Mansfield. *Elvis the Soldier.* West Germany: Collectors Service, 1983.

Marcus, Greil. *Dead Elvis: A Chronicle of a Cultural Obsession.* New York: Doubleday, 1991.

———. *Mystery Train: Images of America in Rock 'n' Roll Music.* New York: Dutton, 1975.

Margolis, Simeon, M.D., Ph.D., Medical ed. *Johns Hopkins Symptoms and Remedies.* New York: Rebus, 1995.

Marling, Karal Ann. *Graceland: Going Home With Elvis.* Cambridge: Harvard University Press, 1996.

Marsh, Dave. *Elvis.* New York: Thunder's Mouth Press, 1992.

———. *Fortunate Son: Criticism and Journalism by America's Best-Known Rock Writer.* New York: Random House, 1981.

————. *The Heart of Rock & Soul: The 1001 Greatest Singles Ever Made.* New York: Plume, 1989.

McKeon, Elizabeth. *Elvis in Hollywood: Recipes Fit for a King.* Nashville: Rutledge Hill Press, 1994.

Mellody, Pia, Andrea Miller, and J. Keith Miller. *Facing Co-Dependence.* San Francisco: Harper San Francisco, 1989.

Miller, Jim, ed. *The Rolling Stone Illustrated History of Rock & Roll.* New York: Random House, 1980.

Minto, Gordon. *Inside "Jailhouse Rock."* Loew's Incorporated and Avon Productions.

Moore, Mary Tyler. *After All.* New York: G. P. Putnam's Sons, 1995.

Morella, Joe, and Edward Z. Epstein. *Rebels: The Rebel Hero in Film.* New York: Citadel, 1971.

Nash, Alana. *Behind Closed Doors: Talking with the Legends of Country Music.* New York: Knopf, 1988.

Nash, Alana, with Billy Smith, Marty Lacker, and Lamar Fike. *Elvis Aaron Presley: Revelations from the Memphis Mafia.* New York: HarperCollins, 1995.

Nash, Bruce, and Allan Zullo, with John McGran. *Amazing but True Elvis Facts.* Kansas City, Mo.: Andrews and McMeel, 1995.

Nelson, Pete. *King! When Elvis Rocked the World.* New York: Proteus, 1985.

Nite, Norm M. *Rock On: The Illustrated Encyclopedia of Rock 'n' Roll—the Solid Gold Years.* New York: Thomas Y. Crowell, 1974.

————. *Rock On: The Illustrated Encyclopedia of Rock 'n'-Roll—the Modern Years, 1964–Present.* New York: Thomas Y. Crowell, 1974.

Noguchi, Thomas T., M.D., with Joseph DiMona. *Coroner at Large.* New York: Pocket Books, 1985.

Oliver, Paul, Max Harrison, and William Bolcom. *The New Grove: Gospel, Blues and Jazz.* New York: W. W. Norton, 1986.

Olmetti, Bob, and Sue McCasland, eds. *Elvis Now—Ours Forever.* San Jose: Olmetti and McCasland, 1984.

O'Neal, Sean. *Elvis Inc.: The Fall and Rise of the Presley Empire.* Rocklin, Calif.: Prima Publishing, 1996.

Parker, Ed. *Inside Elvis.* Orange, Calif.: Rampart House Ltd., 1978.

Parker, John. *Elvis: The Secret Files.* London: Anaya Publishers Ltd., 1993.

Peary, Danny, ed. *Close-Ups: Intimate Profiles of Movie Stars by Their Co-Stars, Directors, Screenwriters and Friends.* New York: Workman, 1978.

Perkins, Carl and David McGee. *Go, Cat, Go: The Life and Times of Carl Perkins, the King of Rockabilly.* New York: Hyperion, 1996.

Peters, Richard. *Elvis: The Music Lives On. The Recording Sessions, 1954–1976.* London: Pop Universal/Souvenir Press Ltd., 1992.

Petersen, Brian. *The Atomic Powered Singer.* Self-published.

Physicians' Desk Reference: 30th Edition, 1976. New Jersey: Litton Industries, 1976.

Pollock, Bruce. *When Rock Was Young: A Nostalgic Review of the Top 40 Era.* New York: Holt, Rinehart and Winston, 1981.

Pond, Steve, and the Michael Ochs Archives. *Elvis in Hollywood: Photographs from the Making of "Love Me Tender."* New York: Plume, 1990.

Presley, Dee, and Billy, Rick, and David Stanley, As Told to Martin Torgoff. *Elvis: We Love You Tender.* New York: Delacorte, 1980.

Presley, Priscilla Beaulieu, with Sandra Harmon. *Elvis and Me.* New York: Berkley Books, 1985.

Presley, Vester, as told to Deda Bonura. *A Presley Speaks.* Memphis: Wimmer Books, 1994.

Presley-Early, Donna, and Eddie Hand, with Lynn Edge. *Elvis: Precious Memories.* Birmingham, Ala.: The Best of Times, 1997.

Prince, James D. *The Day Elvis Came to Town.* Lexington, N.C.: Southern Heritage Publishing, 1995.

Pruett, Barbara A. *Marty Robbins: Fast Cars and Country Music.* New Jersey: Scarecrow Press, 1990.

Quain, Kevin, ed. *The Elvis Reader: Texts and Sources on the King of Rock 'n' Roll.* New York: St. Martin's Press, 1992.

Rayl, A. J. S. *Beatles '64: A Hard Day's Night in America.* New York: Doubleday, 1989.

Reid, James R. *Fond Memories of Elvis.* Memphis: James R. Reid, 1994.

Rheingold, Todd. *Dispelling the Myths: An Analysis of American Attitudes and Prejudices.* New York: Believe in the Dream Publications, 1992.

Riese, Randall. *Her Name Is Barbra: An Intimate Portrait of the Real Barbra Streisand.* New York: St. Martin's, 1994.

Rijff, Ger, ed. *Long Lonely Highway: A 1950's Elvis Scrapbook.* Michigan: Pierian Press, 1987.

Rijff, Ger, and Gordon Minto. *60 million tv viewers can't be wrong!* Amsterdam: Tutti Frutti Prods., 1994.

Rijff, Ger, and Jan Van Gestel. *Elvis: The Cool King.* Delaware: Atomium Books, 1990.

Rosaaen, Robin, collector, and others. *All the King's Things: The Ultimate Elvis Memorabilia Book.* San Francisco: Bluewood Books, 1993.

Rovin, Jeff. *The World According to Elvis: Quotes from the King.* New York: HarperPaperbacks, 1992.

Roy, Samuel. *Elvis: Prophet of Power.* Mass.: Branden Publishing, 1985.

Rubel, David. *Elvis Presley: The Rise of Rock and Roll.* Connecticut: New Directions, Millbrook Press, 1991.

Sandahl, Linda J. *Rock Films: A Viewer's Guide to Three Decades of Musicals, Concerts, Documentaries and Soundtracks, 1955–1986.* Oxford, England: Blanford Press, 1987.

Sauers, Wendy. *Elvis Presley: A Complete Reference.* North Carolina: McFarland, 1984.

Schröer, Andreas. *Private Presley: The Missing Years—Elvis in Germany.* New York: Merlin Group, 1993.

Shales, Tom. *Legends: Remembering America's Greatest Stars.* New York: Random House, 1989.

Shaver, Sean. *Elvis in Focus.* United States: Timur Publishing, 1992.

Shaw, Arnold. *The Rockin' '50s.* New York: Hawthorn Books, 1974.

Shaw, Sid. *Elvis: In Quotes*. London: Elvisly Yours Ltd., n.d.

Sheinwald, Patricia Fox. *Too Young to Die*. United States: Ottenheimer Publishers, 1979.

Smith, Ella. *Starring Miss Barbara Stanwyck*. New York: Crown, 1985.

Smith, Gene. *Elvis's Man Friday*. Nashville: Light of Day Publishing, 1994.

Smith, Wes. *The Pied Pipers of Rock 'n' Roll: Radio Deejays of the 50s and 60s*. Georgia: Longstreet Press, 1989.

Snow, Hank, with Jack Ownbey and Bob Burris. *The Hank Snow Story*. Chicago: University of Illinois Press, 1994.

Solt, Andrew, and Sam Egan, writers and editors. *Imagine: John Lennon*. New York: Macmillan, 1988.

Stanley, David, with Frank Coffey. *The Elvis Encyclopedia*. Santa Monica: General Publishing Group, 1994.

Stanley, David, with George Erikson. *Elvis, My Brother*. New York: St. Martin's Paperbacks, 1989.

Stanley, David, with David Wimbish. *Life With Elvis*. United Kingdom: MARC Europe, 1987.

Stanley, Rick, with Paul Harold. *Caught in a Trap: Elvis Presley's Tragic Lifelong Search for Love*. Dallas: Word Publishing, 1992.

Stanley, Rick, with Michael K. Haynes. *The Touch of Two Kings*. United States: T2K, Inc., 1986.

Staten, Vince. *The Real Elvis: Good Old Boy*. Ohio: Media Ventures, 1978.

Stearn, Jess. *Elvis: His Spiritual Journey*. Virginia Beach/Norfolk: Donning, 1982.

Stearn, Jess, with Larry Geller. *The Truth About Elvis*. New York: Jove, 1980.

Stern, Jane, and Michael Stern. *Elvis World*. New York: Alfred A. Knopf, 1987.

Storm, Tempest, with Bill Boyd. *The Lady Is a Vamp*. Atlanta: Peachtree, 1987.

Strausbaugh, John. *E: Reflections on the Birth of the Elvis Faith*. New York: Blast Books, 1995

Sumrall, Harry. *Pioneers of Rock and Roll: 100 Artists Who Changed the Face of Rock*. New York: Billboard Books, 1994.

Tassin, Myron, and Jerry Henderson. *Fifty Years at the Grand Ole Opry*. Louisiana: Pelican, 1975.

Taylor, William J., Jr. *Elvis in the Army: The King of Rock 'n' Roll as seen by an officer who served with him*. Novato, Calif.: Presidio Press, 1995.

Tharpe, Jac L., ed. *Elvis: Images and Fancies*. Jackson: University Press of Mississippi, 1979.

Thompson, Charles C., II, and James P. Cole. *The Death of Elvis: What Really Happened*. New York: Delacorte Press, 1981.

Thompson, Sam. *Elvis on Tour: The Last Year*. Memphis: Still Brook, 1984.

Tobler, John, and Richard Wooton. *Elvis: The Legend and the Music*. New York: Crescent Books, 1983.

Torgoff, Martin, ed. *The Complete Elvis*. New York: G. P. Putnam's Sons, 1982.

Tosches, Nick. *Country: Living Legends and Dying Metaphors in America's Biggest Music*. New York: Scribner's Son's, 1985.

―――. *Unsung Heroes of Rock 'n' Roll: The Birth of Rock in the Wild Years Before Elvis.* New York: Harmony Books, 1991.

Urquhart, Sharon Colette. *Placing Elvis: A Tour Guide to the Kingdom.* New Orleans: Paper Chase Press, 1994.

Uslan, Michael, and Bruce Solomon. *Dick Clark's the First 25 Years of Rock & Roll.* New York: Delacorte, 1981.

Vellenga, Dirk, with Mick Farren. *Elvis and the Colonel.* New York: Delacorte, 1988.

Wallis, Hal, and Charles Higham. *Starmaker: The Autobiography of Hal Wallis.* New York: Macmillan, 1980.

Wallis, Martha Hyer. *Finding My Way: A Hollywood Memoir.* New York: HarperSanFrancisco, 1990.

Ward, Ed, Geoffrey Stokes, and Ken Tucker. *Rock of Ages: The Rolling Stone History of Rock & Roll.* New York: Rolling Stone Press/Summit Books, 1986.

Weatherby, W. J. *Jackie Gleason: An Intimate Portrait of the Great One.* New York: Pharos Books, 1992.

Wecht, Cyril, M.D., J.D., with Mark Curriden and Benjamin Wecht. *Cause of Death.* New York: Dutton, 1993.

Wertheimer, Alfred. *Elvis '56: In the Beginning.* New York: Collier, 1979.

West, Red, Sonny West, and Dave Hebler, as Told to Steve Dunleavy. *Elvis: What Happened?* New York: Ballantine Books, 1977.

Westmoreland, Kathy, with William G. Quinn. *Elvis and Kathy.* Glendale, Calif.: Glendale House Publishing, 1987.

White, Timothy. *Rock Lives: Profiles and Interviews.* New York: Henry Holt, 1990.

Whitmer, Peter. *The Inner Elvis: A Psychological Biography of Elvis Aaron Presley.* New York: Hyperion, 1996.

Wilson, Brian, with Todd Gold. *Wouldn't It Be Nice: My Own Story.* New York: HarperCollins, 1991.

Wood, Lana. *Natalie: A Memoir by Her Sister.* New York: Dell, 1984.

Woog, Adam. *The Importance of Elvis Presley.* San Diego: Lucent Books, 1997.

Worth, Fred L., and Steve D. Tamerius. *All About Elvis: The King of Rock and Roll from A to Z.* New York: Bantam, 1981.

―――. *Elvis: His Life from A to Z.* New Jersey: Wings Books, 1990.

Yancey, Becky, and Cliff Linedecker. *My Life With Elvis.* New York: St. Martin's Press, 1977.

Zmijewsky, Steven, and Boris Zmijewsky. *Elvis: The Films and Career of Elvis Presley.* New Jersey: Citadel Press, 1976.

Major Magazine and Newspaper Articles

A note about these materials: In the days before the mainstream press became obsessed with entertainment and entertainers, the fan magazines were a major source on the lives and careers of celebrities. During his teenage years in Memphis, and throughout the rise of his career, Elvis Presley himself regularly read fan publications; through Colonel Tom Parker, he also frequently cooperated with them over the years. Many of Elvis's associates, including girlfriends and costars, also talked with these publications about their experiences with him. When we felt the subjects and the material were reliable, we utilized such materials for this biography.

We did the same in regard to the tabloid press. We realize that many Elvis fans and scholars negate the tabloids because of the way they reported Elvis's drug problems and death; because the *National Enquirer* audaciously (and secretly) photographed Elvis Presley in his coffin, it is especially anathema. Still, over the years, many notable Presley family members and friends have cooperated to some degree with the tabloids. Because the tabloids sometimes broke stories first, and because we were able to verify their reports, we sometimes utilized non-mainstream publications in our research.

ABRAMS, MALCOLM, AND HARRY MCCARTHY. "Ginger Alden Speaks: Elvis Was Gentle, Jealous & Passionate." *Midnight/Globe*, June 27, 1978.

ALLIGOOD, ARLENE. "Waiting for Elvis: Fans at Yankeetown are playing hide and seek with their hero." *St. Petersburg Times*, July 23, 1961.

"ALL SHOOK UP." *Newsweek*, August 29, 1977.

ANDERSON, JACK. "Presley Gets Narcotics Bureau Badge." *Washington Post*, January 27, 1972.

ANDERSON, NANCY. "My Cherished Memories of Elvis." *Elvis Presley: A Photoplay Tribute*, 1977

ANDERSON, NANCY, AS TOLD TO. "Elvis by His Father Vernon Presley." *Good Housekeeping*, January 1978.

ARONOWITZ, ALFRED G. "The Return of the Beatles." *Saturday Evening Post*, August 8–15, 1964.

———. "Yeah! Yeah! Yeah! Music's Gold Bugs: The Beatles." *Saturday Evening Post*, March 21, 1964.

BACON, JAMES. " 'New' Presley Back in States." Associated Press, June 19, 1960.

BATCHELOR, RUTH "How the King Changed My Life—With a Song." *Midnight/Globe*, November 22, 1977.

BECK, ROGER. "Elvis Tones Down Act When Police Move In." *Los Angeles Mirror-News*, October 30, 1957.

BEITIKS, EDVINS. "A quiet day at the first Elvis shrine: Tupelo misses the man from the humble shack." *San Francisco Examiner*, August 17, 1987.

BIANCULLI, AL. "Elvis: The Tupelo, Mississippi, Flash." *Zoo World*, September 13, 1973.

BLOUNT, ROY, JR. "Elvis! The King is dead but that thing still shakes" (from "50 Who Made the Difference: A Celebration of American Originals"). *Esquire*, December 1983.

BOCK, MITCHELL. "The Enigma That Is Elvis." *Fusion*, February 10, 1969.

BOOTH, STANLEY. "A Hound Dog to the Manor Born." *Esquire*, February 1968.

BOSQUET, JEAN. "He's a 'Man' Now—and an Industry" (four-part series) *New York Journal-American*, June 12–16, 1960.

BREO, DENNIS L. "Examiner is firm: heart disease fatal to Presley." *American Medical News*, October 12, 1979.

BROESKE, PAT H. "After Death, 'It Was War': Even Elvis' Coffin Made It to the Front Page." *Los Angeles Times*, August 16, 1987.

BROWN, PETER. "The Ghost of Elvis: Who Owns What?" *Los Angeles Times*, January 7, 1979.

BULL, BART. "By Presley Possessed: Doubts on the Critical Dogma About Elvis." *Washington Post*, August 16, 1987.

BURK, BILL E. "It Was Elvis, Elvis All the Way As Memphis Observed 10th Anni." *Variety*, August 19, 1987.

BUSER, LAWRENCE. "Death Captures Crown of Rock and Roll—Elvis Dies Apparently After Heart Attack." *Memphis Commercial Appeal*, August 17, 1977.

———. "Friendship Is Called 'Real' Story." *Memphis Commercial Appeal*, August 17–21, 1977.

———. "World's at Standstill for Elvis' Fiancée." *Memphis Commercial Appeal*, August 17–21, 1977.

CAMERON, GAIL. "Those Beatles Again." *Life*, August 28, 1964.

CANTOR, LOUIS, AND CHARLES RAITERI. "Daddy-O-Dewey: The Phillips family remembers the D.J. who introduced the world to Elvis—and rock and roll." *Memphis Flyer*, January 4-10, 1996.

CARPENTER, JOHN. "Vegas Pays the King's Ransom." *Los Angeles Free Press*, August 29, 1969.

CARTER, HODDING. "Tupelo, Miss." *Saturday Evening Post*, February 17, 1951.

CHAKO, LYNN. "Elvis Presley Kissed Me Four (Sigh) Times." *St. Petersburg Times*, July 31, 1961.

CHRIS, NICHOLAS C. "Presley Entombed As Fans Line 3-Mile Funeral Route." *Los Angeles Times*, August 19, 1977.

———. "Weeping Thousands View Presley Body." *Los Angeles Times*, August 18, 1977.

COCKS, JAY. "Last Stop on the Mystery Train." *Time*, August 29, 1977.

"Crowds Greet Elvis at Memphis." United Press International, March 7, 1960.

CRUMBAKER, MARGE. "A King in a Velvet Jail." *Memphis Commercial Appeal Mid-South Magazine*, May 24, 1970.

DALTON, DAVID. "Elvis." *Rolling Stone*, February 2, 1970.

DANGAARD, COLIN. "Priscilla Looks Back on Life With Elvis." *Memphis Commercial Appeal Mid-South Magazine*, November 24, 1974.

DAROFF, ELIZABETH. "Elvis" (Linda Thompson recollections). *McCall's*, July 1980.

DEAN, SHERRY. "The Truth About Those Presley Parties." *Photoplay*, October 1964.

DICKSON, KATE B. "Medic Describes 'Routine' Call to Graceland." *Memphis Press-Scimitar*, August 17, 1977.

"ELVIS AND THE FRÄULEINS." *Look*, December 23, 1958.

"ELVIS PRESLEY" (three-part series). *TV Guide*, September 8–14, September 22–28, September 29–October 5, 1956.

"ELVIS PRESLEY RETURNS WITH CHARISMA INTACT." United Press International, August 10, 1969.

"ELVIS'S WIFE TELLS OF 'EMPTY LUXURY.' " United Press International, July 19, 1973.

"ELVIS TRADES BLUE SUEDE BACHELOR SHOES FOR BRIDE." Associated Press, May 5, 1967.

ENGLISH, DANIEL. "Can Ann-Margret Make Elvis the Marrying Kind?" *Modern Screen*, November 1963.

FABER, CHARLES. "Setting the Record Straight: The Real Elvis, Told by May Mann." *Los Angeles Free Press*, November 18–24, 1977.

FARLEY, ELLEN. "The Story of Frank and Fabe and Bob." *Los Angeles Times*, November 23, 1980.

FARREN, MICK. "The Elvis Dossier." *Game*, May 1976.

FIORE, MARY. "Priscilla Presley: Bringing Up Elvis' Daughter." *Ladies' Home Journal*, February 1984.

FONG-TORRES, BEN. "Broken Heart for Sale." *Rolling Stone*, September 22, 1977.

"FOREVER ELVIS." *Time*, May 7, 1965.

"FORMER BODYGUARD SAYS ELVIS HAD DRUG PROBLEM." Associated Press, August 17, 1977.

"FORMER WIFE PRISCILLA TELLS OF . . . MY LIFE WITH ELVIS—14 Years of Happiness and Heartbreak." *National Enquirer*, August 22, 1978.

FREILICH, LEON. " 'Elvis Planned to Wed Ginger at Xmas.' " *Midnight/Globe*, November 15, 1977.

GEORGE, WALLY. "Elvis Wriggles, Fans Scream at Pan-Pacific." *Los Angeles Times*, October 29, 1957.

"G.I. Jeers, 'Scalping' Greet Elvis—but He Just Yawns." *Nashville Tennessean*, March 26, 1958.

"GLOBAL REPORT ON ROCK 'N' ROLL." *New York Times*, April 20, 1958.

GOODMAN, CHARLES. "Jordanaires Share Memories of Beautiful Years With Elvis." *Memphis Press-Scimitar*, August 15, 1978.

GORDON, GEORGE. "Mystery drug girl in Presley book: I am the one who nearly died in Elvis's arms." *Star*, October 18, 1977.

GORDON, ROSE. "Why Joan Would Say: No to Elvis, Yes to Dick!" *Movie Life*, October 1963.

GRANT, CURRIE. "Elvis Secretly Engaged to 18-Year-Old." *Photoplay*, January 1964.

GROSS, MIKE. "RCA Rattle & Roll on Elvis." *Billboard*, November 30, 1968.

"HEDDA HOPPER'S HOLLYWOOD." Chicago Tribune–New York News Syndicate, October 25, 1960.

HILBURN, ROBERT. "Elvis defined the attitude and style of rock 'n' roll." *Los Angeles Times*, August 9, 1987.

———. "Fan to Fan: What's Happened to Elvis." *Los Angeles Times*, February 6, 1972.

———. "Promoter Swings Deal for Presley at the Forum." *Los Angeles Times*, October 25, 1970.

HISCOCK, JOHN. "Exclusive: Priscilla and Lisa Presley at Home." *Star*, September 27, 1977.

HOEKSTRA, DAVE. "Elvis, how great thou art: Ten years later, the faithful still call him King." *Chicago Sun-Times*, August 9, 1987.

HOPPER, HEDDA. "Ann-Margret to Be Presented to Queen: Learns How to Curtsy, Then Parries Romantic Questions." *Los Angeles Times*, August 30, 1963.

———. "If You Quit Rocking, Can You Keep Rolling? Elvis Thinks So." *Chicago Sunday Tribune Magazine*, July 2, 1961.

———. "The New Elvis: More Hip Than Hips." *Los Angeles Times*, July 2, 1961.

———. "Peter Pan in Blue Suede Shoes." *Los Angeles Times*, January 31, 1965.

HOWARD, EDWIN. "Elvis Rocks to a $20-Million Roll." *Memphis Press-Scimitar*, January 14, 1964.

———. "One Day Into Our Office Came a Bashful, Nervous Young Man." *Memphis Press-Scimitar*, March 15, 1974.

HUTCHINS, CHRIS. "Elvis to Tom Jones, 'You Are Great!' " *Hit Parader*, November 1968.

"IS THIS A 'NEW' PRESLEY?" *Newsweek*, May 30, 1960.

JENNINGS, C. ROBERT. "Elvis Lives!" *West* magazine, February 18, 1968.

——— "There'll Always Be an Elvis." *Saturday Evening Post*, September 11, 1965.

JERONE, JIM. "My Daughter, Myself." *Ladies' Home Journal*, August 1996.

JOHNSON, ERSKINE. "Money Blizzard Still Swirls Around Elvis." *Los Angeles Mirror-News*, May 11, 1960.

JOHNSON, ROBERT. "Suddenly Singing Elvis Presley Zooms Into Recording Stardom." *Memphis Press-Scimitar*, February 5, 1955.

———. "These Are the Cats Who Make Music for Elvis." *Memphis Press-Scimitar*, December 15, 1956.

JONES, IRA. "Has the Army Changed Elvis?" *Family Weekly*, October 12, 1959.

JONES, KEN. "In 1955 Elvis Gave Ole Hank a Real Snow Job." *Memphis Press-Scimitar*, August 15, 1978.

JONES, KITTY. "I Got Dates for Elvis Presley." *Movie Life*, January 1978.

JOYCE, ALEX. "Elvis: Why Can't He Get Married?" *Photoplay*, November 1957.

KAISER, ROBERT BLAIR. "The Rediscovery of Elvis." *New York Times Magazine*, October 11, 1970.

KELLEY, MICHAEL. "Lasting Legacy: Phillips clan rocks on, hangs on, keeps going on." *Memphis Commercial Appeal*, June 30, 1996.

KESSLER, JUDY AND LAURA NELSON. " 'Elvis was the light that shined on everybody': A Year of Grief, Confusion, Riches." *People*, August 21, 1978.

"The King Is Dead, but Long Lives the King in a Showbiz Bonanza." *People*, October 10, 1977.

KINGLSEY, JIM. "At Home With Elvis Presley." *Memphis Commercial Appeal Mid-South Magazine*, March 7, 1965.

———. "The Colonel Speaks: Parker Denies Any Wrongdoing in Ties with Elvis." *Memphis Commercial Appeal*, August 16, 1981.

———. "Elvis Says Madison Square Garden Finally Big Enough for His Show." *Memphis Commercial Appeal*, June 10, 1972.

———. "Worldwide Tributes Serve to Lighten Father's Grief." *Memphis Commercial Appeal*, August 17–21, 1977.

KLEIN, DORIS. "Elvis Sparked a New Breed." Associated Press, August 13, 1965.

LEECH, MIKE. "Elvis Remembered: 'He Was Like One of the Guys.' " *US*, August 24, 1987.

LEFOLII, KEN. "The Last Days of Elvis Presley." *Dixie Flyer*, August 12, 1978.

LEWIS, JOSEPH. "Elvis Presley Lives." *Cosmopolitan*, November 1968.

LOLLAR, MICHAEL. "Ex-Memphian tells about when the King met the President." *Memphis Commercial Appeal*, December 21, 1995.

———. "Jerry and God: Wild man Lewis eyes his soul for final shakedown." *Memphis Commercial Appeal*, April 21, 1996.

"THE MAN WHO SOLD PARSLEY." *Time*, May 16, 1960.

MCCARTHY, GERRY. "Elvis Answers Frankie, Claims Rock 'n' Roll Music 'Greatest.' " *Los Angeles-Herald Examiner*, October 29, 1957.

MILLER, JIM. "Forever Elvis." *Newsweek*, August 3, 1987.

MITCHELL, HENRY. "The King: Remembering When It All Began." *Washington Post*, August 16, 1987.

———. "A Loving Army Pays Its Respects to Elvis." *Washington Post*, August 18, 1977.

MOSBY, ALINE. "Presley Sexy? He Denies It." *New York World-Telegram*, June 15, 1956.

MOSES, ANN. "Elvis Presley's Lead Guitarist, James Burton, Talks About Working With King." *New Musical Express*, January 3, 1970.

OCHS, MICHAEL. "50,000,000 Elvis Fans Can't Be Wrong . . ." *Coast*, September 1971.

O'DONNELL, RED. "Elvis 'Least Bothered' by Army Draft; Jokes on Visit." *Nashville Banner*, December 21, 1957.

O'DONNELL RED, AND BOB BATTLE. "Elvis Wants Love, Marriage." *Nashville Banner*, February 26, 1965.

O'HALLAREN, BILL. "We Love You Elvis (Still)." *West*, June 7, 1970.

PACKARD, VANCE. "Building the Beatle Image." *Saturday Evening Post*, March 21, 1964.

PALMER, ROBERT. "Sam Phillips the Sun King: A Revised History of the Roots of Rock and Roll." *Memphis* magazine, December 1978.

PARSONS, LOUELLA O. "Elvis Presley—What the Army Did for Him." *Los Angeles Examiner*, January 8, 1961.

PETT, SAUL. "Does His Mama Think He's Vulgar?" Associated Press, July 22, 1956.

POND, STEVE. "His Final Days." *US*, August 24, 1987.

"PRESLEY PATERNITY SUIT!" *Rona Barrett's Hollywood*, November 1970.

"Priscilla Presley Gets a Kiss and a $1.5 Million Settlement." Associated Press, October 10, 1973.

RADER, DOTSON. "There Had to be Something More Out There" (Priscilla Presley interview). *Parade*, February 9, 1997.

"RETURN OF THE BIG BEAT." *Time*, August 15, 1969.

"RETURN OF THE PELVIS." *Newsweek*, August 11, 1969.

RIEMER, GEORGE. "Look What Germany's Done to Elvis!" *This Week Magazine* (*Los Angeles Times*), July 19, 1959.

"ROCK 'N ROLL GETS HOOK FROM SINATRA." Associated Press, October 29, 1957.

ROSENBAUM, RON. "Among the Believers." *New York Times Magazine*, September 24, 1995.

SAMUELS, GERTRUDE. "Why They Rock 'n' Roll—and Should They?" *New York Times Magazine*, January 12, 1958.

SCHMICH, MARY T. "And the beat goes on: Memphis prepares for the high holy days of Elvis Presley." *Chicago Tribune*, August 9, 1987.

SCOPPA, BUD. "Elvis Is Back (or is he?)." *Senior Scholastic*, September 25, 1972.

SCOTT, VERNON. "Elvis: Ten Million Dollars Later." *McCall's*, February 1963.

———. "The Wild Twists in Elvis' Career" (three-part series). *Hollywood Citizen-News*, (three-part series), October 17–19, 1968

SHEARER, LLOYD. "America's Most Controversial Singer Answers His Critics." *Parade*, September 30, 1956.

———. "Elvis Presley: How he changed his public image." *Parade*, November 4, 1962.

———. "I Remember Elvis." *Parade*, January 29, 1978.

SHEELEY, SHARI. "Our Love Song." *Photoplay*, June 1959.

SHEVEY, SANDRA. "My Life With and Without Elvis Presley" (Priscilla Presley recollections). *Ladies' Home Journal*, August 1973.

SIMS, JUDITH. "At Last—the First Elvis Presley Movie." *Rolling Stone*, November 9, 1972.

SPARKS, FRED. "Sgt. Elvis to Return as Major Industry" (three-part series). *Los Angeles Mirror-News*, February 24–26, 1960.

TAMKE, BETH J. "Doctor Talks About Elvis' Problems, His Life and Death." *Memphis Commercial Appeal*, August 25, 1977.

———. "Presley Was No Stranger to Hospital," *Memphis Commercial Appeal*, August 18–21, 1977.

TERRY, POLLY. "Elvis' Boys: Why he hides behind them—even on dates." *Photoplay*, July 1964.

———. "We Say Elvis Is Married!" *Photoplay*, February 1964.

THOMAS, BOB. "It Looks Like Romance for Presley and Ann-Margret." Associated Press, August 6, 1963.

THOMAS, WILLIAM. "Delivering Elvis Paid $15—From Welfare." *Memphis Commercial Appeal*, January 6, 1980.

————. "Elvis is Dead, but the Colonel's Still Hustling." *Memphis Commercial Appeal*, August 16, 1978.

TREADWELL, DAVID. "King Elvis Still Reigns in Southern Lore." *Los Angeles Times*, August 10, 1987.

TRIPLETT, JOHN. "Partial List of Elvis' Assets, Graceland Inventory Filed." *Memphis Commercial Appeal*, November 23, 1977.

WANNENBURGH, A. J. "Presley Fans Will Hate His Wife, Says Biographer." *London Sunday Times*, July 30, 1972.

WARGA, WAYNE. "Elvis to Sing, Swing Before TV Cameras Once More." *Los Angeles Times*, June 27, 1968.

WELLER, HELEN. "Elvis Left Me in the Middle of the Night." *Modern Screen*, August 1964.

WELLER, SHEILA. "Priscilla Presley: Surviving Elvis." *McCall's*, May 1979.

WHITCOMB, JON. "Elvis and Juliet." *Cosmopolitan*, October 1960.

WHITE, JAMES, H. " 'Goodby, Darling,' Says the Grief-Stricken Singer." *Memphis Press-Scimitar*, August 16, 1958.

WHITNEY, DWIGHT. "The Indomitable Snowman Who Built Himself—and Elvis Too." *TV Guide*, November 30, 1968.

WILLIAMS, DICK. "6,000 Kids Cheer Elvis' Frantic Sex Show." *Los Angeles Mirror-News*, October 29, 1957.

WILLIS, ELLEN. "Musical Events, Etc." (Presley in Las Vegas). *New Yorker*, August 30, 1969.

WILSON, JOYCE. "Priscilla: Elvis Wanted to Reconcile." *Midnight/Globe*, September 6, 1977.

WOLMUTH, ROGER. "The King of Rock Keeps on Rollin'." *People*, August 17, 1987.

ZANE, J. PEDER. "Studying Elvis has some people all shook up, but others still love him tender." *Orange County Register*, August 8, 1995.

ZIMMERMAN, DAVID. "10 years later, we're still shook up." *USA Today*, August 10, 1987.

ZITO, TOM, AND LARRY ROHTER. "The Lives of Elvis: Presley Books Being Rushed Into Print Include a 'Torrid' Chronicle by Ex-Bodyguards." *Washington Post*, August 18, 1977.

Single-Issue Periodicals

The Amazing Elvis Presley (1956)
The Beatles (1964)
Beatles (U.S.A.) Ltd. (1964)
D.J. Fontana Remembers Elvis (1983)
Elvis (1987)
Elvis in Concert (1987)
Elvis' Graceland: The Official Photo Album of Elvis' Home (1982)
Elvis & Jimmy (1956)
Elvis: Portrait of a Legend (1976)
Elvis Presley (1956)

Elvis Presley (An Unauthorized Biography) (1976)
Elvis Presley in Hollywood (1956)
Elvis Presley: Memorial Edition (1977)
Elvis: Portrait of a Legend (1976)
Elvis: Precious Memories: Volume 2 (1989)
The Elvis Presley Museum Collection: Butterfield & Butterfield (1994)
Elvis Presley Speaks! (1956)
Elvis, 10th Anniversary Salute, Celebrity Spotlight Series (1987)
The Life and Death of Elvis Presley (1977)
The Love of Elvis (1979)
The Official Elvis Presley Album (1956)
Photoplay Presents: Elvis, 10th Anniversary Memorial Edition (1987)
Rolling Stone Special Beatles Anniversary Issue (February 16, 1984)
16 Magazine Presents Elvis: A Time to Remember (1977)
Souvenir Folio Concert Edition: Volume Six
Souvenir Folio Concert Edition: Volume Seven
A Tribute to the King: Elvis (1977)
The World of Elvis (1977)

Also: *Who's Who in Rock 'n Roll: Facts, Fotos and Fan Gossip About the Performers in the World of Rock 'n Roll* (1958)

———
———
———

The authors also utilized miscellaneous articles from the following publications, some of which are cited in the text and source notes.

America
American Statesman (Austin)
American Weekly
Behind the Scenes
Beverly Hills Citizen
Billboard
BlueSpeak
Boulder (Colorado)
British Elvis Presley Fan Club Magazine
Buffalo Courier-Express
Cashbox
Charlotte Observer
Chicago Sunday Tribune Magazine
Circus Weekly

City of Memphis
Clarion Ledger-Jackson Daily News (Michigan)
Cleveland News Dispatch
Cleveland Plain Dealer
Coast
Collector's Mart
Colliers
Commercial Appeal (Memphis)
Confidential
Cosmopolitan
Country Western Jamboree
Cowboy Songs
Crawdaddy
Creem

Current Biography
Daily Express (United Kingdom)
Daily Herald (United Kingdom)
Daily Mirror (United Kingdom)
Daily Sketch (United Kingdom)
Daily Telegraph (United Kingdom)
Dallas Morning News
Dallas Times
Details
Detroit Free Press
Disc
El News (London branch of the
    Official Elvis Presley Fan Club)
Elvis International Forum
Elvis: 1971 Presley Album
Elvis World
Entertainment Weekly
Evening News (United Kingdom)
Exposed
Film Bulletin
Filmfax
Films in Review
Film Stars
Ft. Wayne News Sentinel
Fusion
Gallery
Georgia Straight
Glasgow Sunday Mail
Globe
Graceland Express
Graceland News
Harper's
Hit Parade
Hit Parader
Hollywood Citizen-News
Hollywood Reporter
House & Garden
Houston Chronicle
Hush Hush
Inside Story
International News Service
Knoxville (Tenn.) News-Sentinel
Ladies' Home Journal
Las Vegas Review-Journal
Las Vegas Sun
Life
Los Angeles Daily News

Los Angeles Examiner
Los Angeles Herald
Los Angeles Herald-Examiner
Los Angeles Herald Express
Los Angeles Mirror-News
Los Angeles Times
The Lowdown
Mademoiselle
Melody Maker
Memphis Bar Association
Memphis Downtowner
Memphis Flash
Memphis Flyer
Memphis Magazine
Memphis Press-Scimitar
Midnight/Globe
Minneapolis Globe
Mirabelle
Mississippi
Movie Life
Movie Mirror
Movie Time
Music Scene
Nashville Banner
Nashville Tennessean
National Enquirer
New Musical Express (United
    Kingdom)
New Record Mirror (United Kingdom)
New Republic
Newsday
Newsweek
New Times
New York Daily News
New York Herald Tribune News Service
New York Post
New York Star
New York Times Magazine
New York World
On the QT
Oregon Journal
Ottawa Citizen
Ottawa Daily Journal
Ottawa Evening Journal
Parade
People
Philadelphia Evening Bulletin

Photoplay
Picturegoer
Picture Show
Playboy
Portland Journal
The Press-Enterprise (Riverside, Calif.)
Private Lives
Psychotronic
Publishers Weekly
Rave
Reader (Los Angeles)
Record Mirror (United Kingdom)
Record Whirl
Reveille
Rolling Stone
Rona Barrett's Hollywood
St. Louis Post-Dispatch
San Francisco News
Saturday Evening Post
Screen Stars
Senior Scholastic
Shake Rattle & Roll
Show
Shreveport Times
16
Smithsonian
Spokane Review
Sponsor
Star
Stars and Stripes
Sunday Dispatch (United Kingdom)
Sunday News (United Kingdom)

Sunday Pictorial (United Kingdom)
Sun Telegram (San Bernardino, Calif.)
Suppressed
Tacoma News Tribune
Teen
TeenSet
Tiger Beat
Time
Tip-Off
Top Secret
Toronto Daily Star
Tupelo (Miss.) *Daily Journal*
TV & Movie Screen
TV Guide
TV Radio-Mirror
TV Radio-Mirror (Southern edition)
TV Scandals
TV Stage
Uncensored
Untold Secrets
Variety
Village Voice
V.I.P.
Vista USA
Waco (Tex.) *News Tribune*
Weekend
West (Los Angeles Times)
Whisper
Wichita Beacon
Woman's Mirror (United Kingdom)
Woman's Own

Index